KT-584-571

Sixth Cole
Cay 3.92
Art Japan
"Japan

JAPAN

THE SHAPING OF
DAIMYO CULTURE
1185–1868

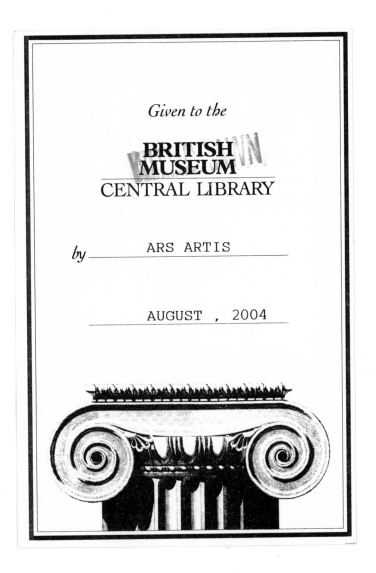

Given to the

**BRITISH
MUSEUM**

CENTRAL LIBRARY

by ___ARS ARTIS___

___AUGUST , 2004___

JAPAN

THE SHAPING OF DAIMYO CULTURE
1185–1868

edited by
YOSHIAKI SHIMIZU

NATIONAL GALLERY OF ART, WASHINGTON

The exhibition was organized by
the National Gallery of Art,
the Agency for Cultural Affairs, Tokyo,
and The Japan Foundation.

An indemnity for the exhibition has been
granted by the Federal Council on the
Arts and the Humanities

Exhibition dates:
National Gallery of Art, Washington
30 October 1988–23 January 1989

Photography courtesy of the Agency for
Cultural Affairs, except as noted

Copyright © 1988. Board of Trustees, National Gallery of Art. All rights reserved.
This book may not be reproduced, in
whole or in part, in any form (beyond that
copying permitted by Sections 107 and 108
of the U.S. Copyright Law and except by
reviewers for the public press), without
written permission from the publishers.

Library of Congress Cataloging-in-Publication Data

Japan : the shaping of Daimyo culture,
1185–1868 / edited by Yoshiaki Shimizu.
    p. cm.
  Bibliography: p.
  1. Daimyo—Exhibitions. 2. Japan—Civilization—1185–1600
—Exhibitions. 3. Japan—Civilization—1600–1868—Exhibitions.
4. Art, Japanese—Kamakura-Momoyama periods, 1185–1600—Exhibitions.
5. Art, Japanese—Edo period, 1600–1868—Exhibitions. 6. Material
culture—Japan—Exhibitions. I. Shimizu, Yoshiaki, 1936–
II. National Gallery of Art (U.S.)
DS827.D34J37   1988
952'.00740143—oc19   88-23604
                         CIP

ISBN 0-8076-1214-6 hardcover
ISBN 0-8946-8122-2 softcover

First printing.

Cover: Cat. 7, **Mounted Warrior,** Agency
   for Cultural Affairs, Tokyo, Important
   Cultural Property
Back cover: Cat. 265, **Jinbaori,** Sendai City
   Museum, Miyagi Prefecture
Frontispiece: Cat. 116, **Amusements at
   Higashiyama,** Kozū Kobunka Kaikan,
   Kyoto

The exhibition was made possible
by R. J. Reynolds Tobacco Company,
The Yomiuri Shimbun, and
The Nomura Securities Co., Ltd.,
with additional support from

The Tokyo Marine and Fire Insurance Company
Matsushita Electric Industrial Corporation
Nippon Life Insurance Company
The Japan Automobile Manufacturers Association, Inc.
The Federation of Bankers Associations of Japan
and its members:
    Bank of Tokyo, Ltd.
    Dai-ichi Kangyo Bank, Ltd.
    Daiwa Bank, Ltd.
    Fuji Bank, Ltd.
    Hokkaido Takushoku Bank, Ltd.
    Industrial Bank of Japan, Ltd.
    Kyowa Bank, Ltd.
    Long Term Credit Bank of Japan, Ltd.
    Mitsubishi Bank, Ltd.
    Mitsui Bank, Ltd.
    Nippon Credit Bank, Ltd.
    Saitama bank, Ltd.
    Sanwa Bank, Ltd.
    Sumitomo Bank, Ltd.
    Taiyo Kobe Bank, Ltd.
    Tokai Bank, Ltd.
Japan Air Lines provided transportation.

Additional support for the catalogue has
been provided by The Japan-United States
Friendship Commission and the Commemorative Association for the Japan
World Exposition.

All Nippon Airways assisted in transporting the catalogues from Japan to
Washington.

The Trustees of the National Gallery of
Art also wish to thank the donors to two
projects that greatly enriched the understanding of this exhibition.

For the Nō drama, The Yomiuri Shimbun.

For the Art of the Tea Ceremony, The Asahi Shimbun, the Yabunouchi School of Tea, The Nomura
Securities Co., Ltd., and All Nippon Airways.

BM8J (SHI)

11194

Contents

Lenders to the exhibition

Agency for Cultural Affairs, Tokyo
Akana Hachimangū, Shimane Prefecture
Chishōin, Kyoto
Chōmoji, Aichi Prefecture
Chōrakuji, Kyoto
Chōreiji, Ishikawa Prefecture
Chōshōin, Kyoto
Egawa Art Museum, Hyōgo Prefecture
Eisei Bunko, Tokyo
Engakuji, Kanagawa Prefecture
Enichiin, Shiga Prefecture
Fujii Akira Collection, Tokyo
Fukuoka Art Museum, Fukuoka
   Prefecture
Fukushi Shigeo Collection, Tokyo
Ganjōjuin, Shizuoka Prefecture
Gotō Museum, Tokyo
Gunma Prefectural Museum of Modern
   Art, Gunma Prefecture
Gyokuhōin, Kyoto
Hiroi Akihisa Collection, Tokyo
Hōfu Mōri Hōkōkai, Yamaguchi
   Prefecture
Hokkeji, Gifu Prefecture
Honda Takayuki Collection, Tokyo
Honzan Jionji, Yamagata Prefecture
Hōsenji, Kyoto
Idemitsu Museum of Arts, Tokyo
Ii Naoyoshi Collection, Shiga Prefecture
Imperial Household Collection
Ishikawa Prefectural Museum of Art
Jimyōin, Wakayama Prefecture
Jingoji, Kyoto
Jōdoji, Hyōgo Prefecture
Jōtokuji, Fukui Prefecture
Jōzanji (Shisendō), Kyoto
Jufukuji, Kanagawa Prefecture
Jukōin, Kyoto
Jushōin, Kyoto
Kagoshima Jingū, Kagoshima Prefecture
Kaihō Hiroshi Collection, Kyoto
Kawabata Terutaka Collection, Kanagawa
   Prefecture
Kenchōji, Kanagawa Prefecture
Kishida Eisaku Collection, Gunma
   Prefecture
Kitamura Bunka Zaidan, Kyoto
Kitano Tenmangū, Kyoto
Kobe City Museum of Nanban Art, Hyōgo
   Prefecture
Kōdenji, Saga Prefecture
Kosaka Zentarō Collection, Tokyo
Kōtokuji, Tochigi Prefecture
Kōzu Kobunka Kaikan, Kyoto
Kunōzan Tōshōgū, Shizuoka Prefecture
Kushibiki Hachimangū, Aomori
   Prefecture

Kyoto City, Kyoto
Kyōto Furitsu Sōgō Shiryōkan
Kyoto National Museum, Kyoto
Manshōji, Kanagawa Prefecture
Masaki Art Museum, Osaka
Miyazaki Kazue Collection, Kanagawa
   Prefecture
Myōchiin, Kyoto
Myōhōin, Kyoto
Myōkōji, Aichi Prefecture
Myōrenji, Kyoto
Nagoji, Chiba Prefecture
Nagoya City, Aichi Prefecture
Nanban Bunkakan, Osaka
Nanzen'in, Kyoto
Nanzenji, Kyoto
Nara National Museum, Nara Prefecture
National Museum of Japanese History,
   Chiba Prefecture
Nezu Institute of Fine Arts, Tokyo
Niutsuhime Jinja, Wakayama Prefecture
Okayama Prefectural Art Museum,
   Okayama Prefecture
Okayama Prefectural Museum, Okayama
   Prefecture
Osaka City, Osaka
Osaka Municipal Museum, Osaka
Private collections
Reiun'in, Kyoto
Rinkain, Kyoto
Rinnōji, Tochigi Prefecture
Rokuōin, Kyoto
Saikyōji, Shiga Prefecture
Seikadō Bunko, Tokyo
Seikeiin, Wakayama Prefecture
Sekai Kyūseikyō (MOA Art Museum),
   Shizuoka Prefecture
Sekkeiji, Kōchi Prefecture
Sen Sōsa Collection, Kyoto
Sendai City Museum, Miyagi Prefecture
Sennyūji, Kyoto
Shingetsuji, Fukui Prefecture
Shinjuan, Kyoto
Shōmyōji, Kanagawa Prefecture
Shūon'an, Kyoto
Sōjiji (Nishiarai Daishi), Tokyo
Sōunji, Kanagawa Prefecture
Suntory Museum of Art, Tokyo
Sword Museum, Tokyo
Taga Taisha, Shiga Prefecture
Takahashi Toshio Collection, Tokyo
Takamori Shigeru Collection, Kumamoto
   Prefecture
Tenjuan, Kyoto
Tokiwayama Bunko, Kanagawa Prefecture
Tokyo National Museum, Tokyo
Tokyo University of Arts, Tokyo

Toyosaka Jinja, Yamaguchi Prefecture
Ueda Municipal Museum, Nagano
   Prefecture
Ueyama Ikuichi Collection, Nara Prefecture
Umezawa Kinenkan, Tokyo
Unryūin, Kyoto
Watanabe Kunio Collection, Tokyo
Watanabe Yoshio Collection, Tokyo
Yamada Hitoshi Collection, Tokyo
Yamatane Art Museum, Tokyo

Foreword

Japan: The Shaping of Daimyo Culture, 1185–1868

I N 1875, SEVEN YEARS AFTER THE ABOLITION OF THE TOKUGAWA shogunate, a distinguished American student of Japanese culture named Professor William Elliot Griffis published in a popular magazine an article entitled "A Daimio's Life." His article dealt with the feudal lords who controlled the provinces of Japan for much of the medieval and early modern ages. The recent toppling of the Japanese warrior power hierarchy—shogun, daimyo, samurai—and the restoration to power of the Meiji emperor were being widely discussed by those who followed current world events, so Griffis did not have to bother to define his subject. Since that time, the word "daimyo" has fallen from currency.

In the late nineteenth and early twentieth centuries, as Japan increasingly looked to the West for models of government and education, the Western appreciation of daimyo culture also was eclipsed. As a result a romanticized, often fictitious view of Japan evolved, in which fierce samurai and shogun figured prominently, and the daimyo were neglected. Despite a proliferation of popular books and films about Japan, neither the term daimyo nor their extraordinary contributions as both patrons and practitioners of the arts have become familiar to Western audiences. Nor has any effort been made, until now, to present an exhibition that takes as its theme the art of the daimyo. Daimyo culture, as described by one of our distinguished catalogue authors, reflects "a synergy of warrior traditions (bu) and civilian arts (bun)." By bringing to Washington a resplendent array of daimyo-related art, we are breaking new ground and at the same time beginning to redress a longstanding oversight.

This exhibition is, we believe, the first attempt anywhere, including Japan, to explore the artistic legacy of the daimyo from the beginning of the Kamakura period in 1185 to the end of the Edo period in 1868. The scope of the project has been greatly expanded since 1983, when we had explored an exhibition examining the contribution of a single daimyo family to the history of collecting. For agreeing to a broader exhibition on the art of the daimyo, and for assisting us in every phase of the project, we are deeply indebted to our partners in this joint venture, the Agency for Cultural Affairs of the Japanese government and The Japan Foundation, especially to Nobuyoshi Yamamoto, Akiyoshi Watanabe, and Yūichi Hiroi at the former, and to Sadao Ikeya, Toshihisa Tanaka, Yōichi Shimizu, and Hayato Ogo at the latter.

The works of art exhibited here come from more than one hundred public and private collections, and we are immensely grateful to our lenders, who have allowed us to borrow works of unprecedented beauty and significance. Professor Yoshiaki Shimizu of Princeton University, curator of the exhibition and principal author and editor of the scholarly catalogue, deserves our deepest thanks for having worked tirelessly over the course of many years to help us realize this exhibition. Andrew M. Watsky ably assisted him over the past year, much of which they devoted to the catalogue, in which are published more than 330 works of art. Professor Martin Collcutt, also of Princeton University, contributed the incisive historical introduction to the catalogue and frequently served as advisor during the course of the project. Countless individuals at the Agency for Cultural Affairs, among them many of our catalogue authors, and at The Japan Foundation deserve our special thanks for carrying out myriad essential tasks, from securing loans to arranging photography. Their devotion to scholarship and to the cause of preserving Japan's cultural heritage has made possible this extraordinary achievement.

Thanks are also due to the staff of the National Gallery of Art, in particular the team who worked on this project. Gaillard Ravenel and Mark Leithauser designed the installation, with production management by Gordon Anson. D. Dodge Thompson, and his staff in the department of exhibition programs, including Cameran Castiel, Ellen Marks, and Deborah Shepherd, provided organizational expertise. Mary Suzor, registrar, supervised the shipping of the works of art, and Mervin Richard, exhibitions conservator, coordinated the packing and the conservation measures necessary to safeguard the objects. Susan Arensberg and her colleagues in the education department have implemented a number of programs for the interested visitor. The elaborate funding package that has made this exhibition possible has been the particular concern of the Gallery's corporate relations officer, Elizabeth A. C. Weil. Joseph Krakora was particularly helpful with the coordination of the Nō theater and the film on daimyo culture, while Genevra Higginson planned and guided all events related to the opening of the exhibition. Ruth Kaplan ably interpreted the content of the exhibition and its adjuncts to the media. Frances Smyth and Mary Yakush supervised the complex task of editing and producing the catalogue with skill and grace, with the essential collaboration of several people: Naomi Noble Richard, who served as an expert reader and editor; Virginia Wageman, who scrupulously edited a large portion of the manuscript; Kyoko Selden, who translated the Japanese authors' contributions; and Dana Levy, who designed the catalogue despite very pressing deadlines.

Many people associated with our numerous lenders shared their knowledge and time, allowing us to see their treasures and discuss the works of art in their collections. Special thanks are due to Hosokawa

Morisada, a descendant of one of the great daimyo families, and Ōkura Ryūji, curator of the Kumamoto Prefectural Museum of Art, for their enthusiastic support in the earliest stages of the project. Thomas Lawton, former director of the Freer Gallery, Smithsonian Institution, also offered encouragement and support. We would like to thank William Childs, former chairman of the department of Art and Archaeology at Princeton University, for his indulgence during the course of the preparations, and Professor Shimizu's students, both graduate and undergraduate.

In conjunction with this exhibition, our visitors are privileged to learn in greater depth about two aspects of daimyo culture that were, as this catalogue brings out, of great significance. One, the art of the tea ceremony, is exemplified by the reconstruction of the Ennan teahouse in its garden setting and the demonstrations of the ceremony, illustrated by precious objects associated with it. This part of the undertaking was supported by The Asahi Shimbun, the Yabunouchi School of Tea, The Nomura Securities Co., Ltd., and All Nippon Airways.

A second aspect of daimyo culture was its patronage of Nō drama. The construction of a traditional Nō stage and performances by the renowned Kanze troupe of Nō players have been supported by The Yomiuri Shimbun.

We would like to express our great appreciation to our American sponsor, R. J. Reynolds Tobacco Company, for its support. To the Japanese supporters of the exhibition goes our deepest gratitude for their generosity and leadership. We would like to thank especially The Yomiuri Shimbun for its help with the project since its inception, and in particular Yosoji Kobayashi, president, Akihiro Nanjo, and the Yomiuri's able staff. We are most appreciative of the support of The Nomura Securities Co., Ltd., along with The Tokyo Marine and Fire Insurance Company, Nippon Life Insurance Company, Matsushita Electric Industrial Corporation, The Japan Automobile Manufacturers Association, Inc., and the Federation of Bankers Associations of Japan and its members. Japan Air Lines provided transport for the works of art. In addition, we are grateful to The Japan-United States Friendship Commission and the Commemorative Association for the Japan World Exposition for their support of this exhibition catalogue. We thank All Nippon Airways for its assistance in transporting many of the catalogues from Japan to Washington. The exhibition was publicly announced in 1983 at the Tokyo Summit by Prime Minister Yasuhiro Nakasone and President Ronald Reagan. Since then the project has received the support of both governments at the highest level. We are particularly grateful to the National Gallery's former Trustee, Treasury Secretary James A. Baker III, for his timely assistance. The Federal Council on the Arts and the Humanities granted an indemnity for the exhibition. Special thanks are due to Kōichi Haraguchi, Toshiyuki Takano, and Makoto Hinei in the Embassy of Japan in Washington.

Finally to the former Ambassador Nobuo Matsunaga, as well as to the United States Ambassador in Japan, Mike Mansfield, go our special thanks for helping this complex but enormously rewarding effort in international understanding.

J. Carter Brown
Director

SINCE THE 1950S, THE AGENCY FOR CULTURAL AFFAIRS HAS endeavored to further the understanding of Japanese culture and history, through art exhibitions held at museums throughout the United States. The first such exhibition, in 1951, was held in San Francisco; in 1953 another exhibition traveled to several cities, including New York and Boston. Exhibitions of Japanese art organized by the Agency for Cultural Affairs have included painting, sculpture, applied arts, calligraphy, and archaeology.

Japan: The Shaping of Daimyo Culture 1185–1868, initiated at the 1983 summit meeting between our two countries and co-organized with the Japan Foundation, explores through art the culture created by the warriors of medieval and early modern Japan. From the end of the twelfth century, the warrior class, newly risen holders of political authority, developed cultural traditions inherited from the court, absorbing influences from China, including Zen Buddhism, resulting in the cultural legacy of the Kamakura and Muromachi periods. Later, the evolution of early modern culture in the Edo period resulted from the participation of both the daimyo and the merchant class.

The works of art gathered here reflect the active role of the warriors in the development of an important part of Japanese cultural history. The Agency for Cultural Affairs has planned and coordinated the realization of this complex project, and negotiated the loans that have made the exhibition possible. Although many exhibitions of Japanese art have traveled to the United States, none parallels *Japan: The Shaping of Daimyo Culture 1185–1868* in terms of quality and quantity, and in its distinctive theme.

We hope that American visitors to the exhibition will gain a better understanding of the cultural traditions of Japan, and of the physical and spiritual qualities that distinguish Japanese art. We believe that this exhibition will contribute to the future growth of cultural relations between our two countries.

In conclusion, I would like to express my appreciation to J. Carter Brown, director of the National Gallery, and the entire staff of the Gallery, as well as the many other people in the United States and Japan, for the great efforts made in realizing the exhibition. Special thanks are due to many generous lenders in Japan who agreed to part with their treasures for the duration of the exhibition, as well as to the Japanese Ministry for Foreign Affairs and the Japanese Embassy.

Hiroshi Ueki
Commissioner for Cultural Affairs, Government of Japan

SINCE ITS FOUNDING IN 1972, THE JAPAN FOUNDATION HAS fostered cultural exchange in diverse fields between Japan and many countries throughout the world. In recent years, art exhibitions that played a particularly important role in our activities have included *The Great Japan Exhibition* in London in 1981, *Japan des Avant-Gardes* in Paris in 1986, and *Paris in Japan, Japan in Paris*, which traveled to St. Louis, New York, and Los Angeles during 1987–1988.

Japan: The Shaping of Daimyo Culture 1185–1868 is an exhibition of the art related to the warrior class, important contributors to the cultural and political development of Japan from the medieval through the early modern eras. The daimyo-related art exhibited here will show, we believe, a side of Japanese culture not yet well known to the American public. We expect that this exhibition will be the first step in a new phase of Japanese-American cultural exchange.

We would like to express our gratitude to the many people who worked so hard and so long for this exhibition, and especially to J. Carter Brown who energetically traveled between the United States and Japan to make the exhibition possible. We would also like to thank all of the individuals and organizations who have kindly lent us their treasures. We are indebted to the Japanese Ministry for Foreign Affairs for its assistance since the 1983 summit meeting.

Yasue Katori
President
The Japan Foundation

Daimyo and daimyo culture

MARTIN COLLCUTT

DAIMYO WERE FEUDAL LORDS OR BAR-
ons who, as leaders of powerful
warrior bands, controlled the provinces of Japan for much of the medieval (*chūsei*), and early modern ages
(*kinsei*), from 1185 to 1868. The term daimyo combines the two characters
dai ("great") and *myō* ("name;" from *myōden*, "name fields," referring to
privately owned land). In the eleventh and twelfth centuries the term
was used to refer to absentee landholders such as nobles and temples
who held rights in privatized provincial estates within the public land
system administered by the central court government in the city of
Heian (Kyoto). By the fourteenth century the word daimyo was being
used to describe warrior leaders who had built up extensive military
power and landed wealth in the provinces. The daimyo thus emerged
from among warriors, known as samurai or *bushi*, who had come to
exercise increasing political and economic as well as military power with
the decline of the centralized imperial court government in the tenth
and eleventh centuries.

During the seventh and eighth centuries Japan saw the establishment of a centralized imperial government modeled on those of Sui and
Tang China. For several centuries the imperial court, headed by emperors (*tennō*), claiming direct descent from the Sun Goddess, Amaterasu,
held unchallenged sway. By the tenth century, however, the imperial
court was beginning to lose control over the provinces. Private estates
(*shōen*) held by temples and nobles living as absentee proprietors in the
capital proliferated, and local warrior bands sprang up as central military
influence waned. By the eleventh century the court was becoming reli-

Himeji Castle. Photograph by Mike Yamashita. Copyright © 1988, National Geographic Society.

ant on provincial warriors to enforce its authority and protect the capital. The leaders of powerful warrior bands, especially the chieftains of the Taira and Minamoto clans, were drawn into court politics. A watershed in the shifting balance of political power was reached in the later twelfth century when the Taira, led by Kiyomori (1118–1181), asserted control over the court, only to be ousted and crushed by the Minamoto, led by Yoritomo (1147–1199) and his half-brother Yoshitsune (1159–1189).

The establishment by Yoritomo of a separate warrior government, *bakufu*, in Kamakura in eastern Japan and his acceptance from the imperial court of the title of *Seiitaishōgun* (Great General Who Quells the Barbarians) following the destruction of the Taira at the Battle of Dannoura in 1185 marked a turning point in the shifting balance of courtly and warrior power. Hitherto the title of shogun had been held by imperial princes. The conferment of the title of shogun was a recognition by the imperial court that Yoritomo, as leader of the warrior order, exercised a legitimate delegated authority. Thus began a political arrangement that was to endure for the almost seven-hundred-year period covered by this exhibition, in which emperors heading the imperial court in Kyoto continued to embody a sacerdotal sovereignty while powerful warriors (as shoguns or military hegemons) were delegated with authority to rule. The emperors retained their legitimating function, and at times individual emperors sought to retrieve the powers granted to warriors, but until the mid-nineteenth century warriors controlled the movement of Japanese history, appropriating political, economic, and even cultural leadership. Within the warrior order those powerful feudal lords known as the daimyo were local rulers and leading contenders for power.

During the fourteenth and fifteenth centuries the Ashikaga shoguns gained the support of powerful provincial warrior houses by appointing them as constables, *shugo*, with military, administrative, and fiscal authority over one or more provinces. Historians have named them *shugo* daimyo. Strong shoguns like Ashikaga Yoshimitsu (1358–1408), the

third shogun, were able to assert shogunal authority over the *shugo*. Under weaker mid-fifteenth-century shoguns like Ashikaga Yoshimasa (1436–1490), however, these constables, or *shugo* daimyo, extended their local power at the expense of the shogunate, tightening their feudal control over their provinces of assignment and enrolling local warriors as their vassals.

A second stage of daimyo evolution was set in motion when, in the fierce provincial warfare following the outbreak of the Ōnin War (1467–1477) the shogun-*shugo* coalition disintegrated in civil war and many of the *shugo*-daimyo, who were militarily overextended or entangled in politics in the capital, were toppled by their own deputies and retainers, who emerged as the rulers of smaller but more tightly-knit domains. These 250 or so warrior families were known as the daimyo of the Warring Provinces, *sengoku* daimyo. Fiercely independent, they sought to ensure survival in an age of privincial warfare by extending their feudal control over all the warriors, merchants, and peasants within their territories, and by mobilizing all the human and economic resources of the domain for attack and defense. The Ashikaga shogunate and the imperial court both survived, but shogunal power did not extend far beyond Kyoto. The imperial court was too impoverished and politically impotent to assert any authority. This period of *sengoku* daimyo development, between the mid-fifteenth and mid-sixteenth centuries, marked the extreme of political decentralization in Japan. This decentralization was hastened by the weakness of the shogunal leadership and by the rivalry of warring daimyo. *Shugo-* and *sengoku* daimyo houses rose and fell with bewildering rapidity. Very few of the medieval daimyo families survived into the late sixteenth century, the beginning of the early modern age, *kinsei*, in Japan. Among the survivors were the Shimazu family of Satsuma (Kagoshima), the Mōri of Chōshū (Yamaguchi Prefecture), and the Hosokawa, whose fortunes were revived in the sixteenth century by members of a collateral line.

Himeji Castle, interior view. Photograph by Mike Yamashita. Copyright © 1988, National Geographic Society.

By the mid-sixteenth century the pendulum of feudal decentralization had swung about as far as it could go without total political fragmentation of the country. Among the contending daimyo were some who dreamed of crushing their rivals and conquering and reuniting the country. During the later sixteenth century a process of military unification was set in motion by the young daimyo Oda Nobunaga (1534–1582), carried forward by his leading general Toyotomi Hideyoshi (1537–1598), and brought to completion by their former ally Tokugawa Ieyasu (1543–1616), a powerful daimyo from eastern Japan, after his victory at the Battle of Sekigahara in 1600. All three unifiers relied on daimyo vassals to crush other daimyo who blocked the path to power. Thus the daimyo, who intrinsically represented decentralizing tendencies and frequently impeded unification, were used in the process of recentralization of power and were included in the political structure eventually hammered out by Toyotomi Hideyoshi and revised by Tokugawa Ieyasu. The daimyo who served Oda Nobunaga and Toyotomi Hideyoshi and were rewarded by them with generous fiefs are known as *shokuhō* daimyo (the word *shokuhō* is made up out alternative readings for the first characters of the names Oda and Toyotomi).

The full maturation, and fourth stage, of daimyo evolution occurred in the Edo period (1615–1868) when the daimyo, as heads of warrior houses (*buke*) and vassals of the Tokugawa shoguns, governed 250 or so provincial fiefs (*han*). The Edo period is also commonly referred to by Japanese historians as *kinsei*, which most western historians of Japan translate as "early modern." Thus these Edo-period daimyo are known as the "early modern" or *kinsei* daimyo. The political system established by Tokugawa Ieyasu (1543–1616) after his assumption of the title of shogun was one in which the Tokugawa shogunal government (*bakufu*) ruled the heartland of central Japan and controlled the great cities and mines, while vassal daimyo were appointed to administer some two hundred and fifty domains (*han*). This centralized feudal system of rule in which shoguns heading the *bakufu* shared power with daimyo as the administrators of domains has been called the *baku-han* system.

Tokugawa Ieyasu and his shogunal successors went furthest in regulating and institutionalizing the role of daimyo. By definition Edo period daimyo governed domains yielding at least the equivalent of 10,000 *koku* in rice (one *koku* equalled about five bushels). This was merely the minimum income for recognition as a daimyo. Some daimyo administered domains assessed at over 500,000 *koku* and headed bands (*kashindan*) of several hundred samurai retainers. The Tokugawa bakufu issued regulations for daimyo, spied on them, and interfered with marriage and succession in order to preempt the formation of threatening alliances. Under the Tokugawa control system, daimyo were ranked on the basis of the closeness of their relationship to the Tokugawa and required to divide their time between attendance upon the shoguns in Edo and the administration of their domains. The daimyo survived until 1871 when the Meiji (1868–1912) regime abolished the feudal fiefs in creating a modern prefectual system and pensioned the daimyo off as members of a new nobility resident in Tokyo.

The daimyo belonged not under the imperial court hierarchy but in the upper echelons of the hierarchy of warrior power. Tokugawa Ieyasu was a daimyo who rose to become shogun and establish a shogunal dynasty. Other daimyo had similar ambitions. Most daimyo, however, remained shogunal vassals, allies, or rivals for power. They in turn had their own vassals and rear vassals to whom they awarded fiefs in land or stipends in rice in return for military service. Like shoguns, daimyo were granted nominal rank in the imperial court hierarchy. They were not, however, vassals of the imperial court. Indeed, shoguns sought to prevent alliances between daimyo and the court, because through such ties daimyo might secure the political legitimation that would allow them to subvert or usurp the shogunal office. While many daimyo were hardly more than petty provincial upstarts with little to spare for cultural patronage, others commanded domains covering one or more provinces, lived luxuriously, and were contenders for power on a national scale.

Daimyo culture, then, is the culture of the upper echelon of the warrior order. But since daimyo were associated with shoguns, and in some cases rose to become shoguns, daimyo culture also embraced shogunal culture. At the same time, because many prominent daimyo houses began as lowly provincial samurai, daimyo culture absorbed and refined traditional samurai culture, and in its turn reshaped samurai cultural style. Moreover, elite warrior culture drew heavily on the classical Japanese traditions of the imperial court and on Chinese culture, especially through Zen Buddhist monks who derived their distinctive religious and cultural traditions from China and became cultural advisors for warrior chieftains. But in the final analysis daimyo culture was rooted in the Japanese samurai tradition.

The art and culture of the daimyo was created by and for a class whose existence depended on military power, but whose social function and self-image called increasingly for mastery of the arts of peace. The interests, artifacts, and activities that embody daimyo culture thus represent a synergy of warrior traditions (*bu*) and civilian arts (*bun*). Daimyo united in their persons military power, landholding, administrative and judicial functions, and social prestige. This meant that while military values were becoming prevalent and predominant in Japanese society, civilian arts were becoming indispensable to the military men. As warriors acceded to the *powers* of the civilian government, they required the civilian arts of governance; and as they acceded to the *prestige* of the courtly nobility, they required the cultural attributes and abilities that distinguished those civilian aristocrats.

Daimyo were warriors by training and vocation. War was their metier. To succeed they had to be ruthless, cunning, callous, and aggressive. Even when, in the early seventeenth century, conditions of peace and order replaced endemic warfare and the daimyo turned their attention from fighting to governing, they continued to think of their lineages as military houses (*buke*). But few daimyo could survive and prosper simply as illiterate, boorish ruffians. As early as the twelfth century, warrior leaders like Taira Kiyomori (1118–1181) or Minamoto Yoritomo were finding that their newfound political power and the territories they had acquired called for the exercise of administration, and that the social distinction and political power conferred by victory in war, attainment of office, and possession of territory had to be legitimated—not least in their own eyes—by the acquisition and exercise of the arts of peace (*bun*), which included administration, scholarship, poetry, painting, and the study of the Chinese and Japanese classics. And what may first have been assumed as a convenient veneer, or borrowed cultural credential, to dignify naked military power, soon became a consuming interest in its own right—so much so that in much of Japanese warrior culture we can detect both complementarity and tension between the demands of *bu* and the appeal of *bun*.

Among daimyo from medieval to early modern times, there is commonality as well as considerable diversity. Although most rose from rural samurai origins, a few, such as Saitō Dōsan (d. 1556), got their start as provision merchants for other daimyo. While many daimyo were hardly more than petty provincial chieftains with limited resources and little to spare for cultural patronage, others commanded domains covering one or more provinces, lived luxuriously, and were contenders for power on a national scale. Tokugawa Ieyasu emerged from the ranks of the daimyo to establish the Tokugawa shogunal dynasty. Oda Nobunaga, who began life as a small-scale daimyo, and Toyotomi Hideyoshi, the son of a peasant, imposed their wills on other daimyo and achieved a military hegemony that any shogun would have envied, though they did not take that title. In the century or more of warfare prior to the seventeenth century, instability was the norm, and daimyo families rose and fell with almost bewildering rapidity. Very few families—the Shimazu of Kyushu were among the rare exceptions—survived as daimyo from the twelfth through the sixteenth centuries and beyond.

Warriors and daimyo in the early medieval age

The four main types of daimyo, then, are: the *shugo* daimyo (constable daimyo) of the late fourteenth and fifteenth centuries; the smaller but more effectively organized daimyo of the Age of Wars (*Sengoku jidai*); the *Shokuhō* daimyo of the Momoyama period; and the *kinsei* (early modern) daimyo of the Edo period. (Though the *kinsei* period encompasses both the Momoyama and Edo periods, only the daimyo of the Edo period are customarily referred to as *kinsei* daimyo.) The closing decades of the twelfth century and the opening years of the thirteenth mark the emergence of local warrior power in the early medieval period, and one of the great shifts in Japanese history: from a society ruled exclusively by a court aristocracy (*kuge*) to a society increasingly dominated by warriors (*bushi*). By the eleventh century the hegemony of the centralized government of the imperial court that had been established in the eighth century was being undermined by provincial disturbances and warrior incursions. Warrior bands from the provinces were increasingly drawn into court politics in the Heian capital in the tenth and eleventh centuries. In the mid-twelfth century one such band, the Taira, led by Taira Kiyomori (1118–1181), seized control of the court. In the process they eliminated most of their principal warrior rivals, the Minamoto (also known as Genji) clan. After Kiyomori's death the Minamoto rallied under a young General Yoritomo (1147–1199). In 1185 Yoritomo's half brother Yoshitsune (1159–1189) and other Minamoto leaders drove the Taira from the capital and crushed them at a great battle at Dannoura in the inland sea. Later, Yoshitsune was hounded by his brother Yoritomo, who was suspicious of his intentions and jealous of his victories. He fled to northeastern Japan, where he was captured and forced to take his own life.

For his services to the court Yoritomo received the title of *Seiitaishōgun* (Great General Who Quells the Barbarians) and established a warrior government, known as a shogunate or *bakufu*, well away from the court at the small coastal town of Kamakura in eastern Japan. Although this catalogue and exhibition begin with Yoritomo's portrait, it is important to note that Yoritomo is never regarded as a daimyo, because the notion of the daimyo as feudal lord had not yet developed in the late twelfth century. Yoritomo was the chieftain (*tōryō*) of the Minamoto warrior band. He assumed the military title of shogun and the imperial court title *Utaishō*, Great Commander of the Right, by which he was remembered. Yoritomo's combination of warrior virtues (*bu*) and civilian skills (*bun*) established a pattern that later warrior chieftains, including the Ashikaga and Tokugawa shoguns, the unifiers Oda Nobunaga and Toyotomi Hideyoshi, and most daimyo, were to emulate.

The rout of the Taira by the Minamoto, Yoritomo's establishment of a separate warrior government in eastern Japan, his assumption of the title of shogun, and the crushing defeat by the Kamakura *bakufu* of an ill-planned attempt at a recovery of power by the imperial court in 1221 all signaled the effective acquisition of political as well as military leadership in Japan by warriors. The authority of the court was not completely undermined by the formation of Yoritomo's *bakufu* nor by the defeat in the ill-fated Jōkyū War of 1221. While the political functions of the court were dwindling, its cultural influence was more enduring. In fact, these years were the critical phase of a momentous shift from a society ruled by the imperial court and the court nobility (*kuge*) to a society increasingly dominated by warriors (*bushi*). The Taira had been warriors, too. Rather than establish new organs of government, however, they had tried to rule the court and the country much as the Fujiwara nobles had done, through offices of the civilian government and by the manipulation of the imperial office. The Kamakura *bakufu* was the first in a series of warrior regimes that until the nineteenth century governed Japan through institutions outside the structure of the ancient court bureaucracy. The imperial court government survived, *tennō* maintained their sovereignty, and nobles maintained their cultural influence, but the court steadily declined in wealth and political leadership as power steadily shifted into warrior hands.

Yoritomo had dreamed of establishing a Minamoto shogunal dynasty, but that ambition was thwarted by the assassination of his second son, the shogun Sanetomo, in 1219. Thereafter, until its overthrow in 1333, the Kamakura *bakufu* was dominated by the Hōjō warrior family of eastern Japan, who brought imperial princes and nobles from Kyoto to serve as figurehead shoguns while they actually ruled as shogunal regents. The early Hōjō were effective warrior administrators and earned a reputation for strong government. Hōjō Tokimune organized the defense of the country against the attempted Mongol invasions in 1274 and 1281.

Although the term daimyo was in use by this time to describe local powerholders and was taking on an increasingly martial connotation, it had not yet become part of the political nomenclature of the age. Yoritomo's vassals were called housemen (*gokenin*). To police the country he established the offices of provincial constable (*shugo*), and estate steward (*jitō*). *Shugo* were selected from among his principal vassals and appointed as military overseers of the various provinces. *Jitō* were vassals placed within the provincial estates of the nobility to ensure local order. Hōjō power rested heavily on the appointment and control of these warriors. As *shugo* and *jitō* built up their local control, extended their land holdings, and brought other warriors under their influence by oaths of allegiance, they can be described as the forerunners of the daimyo as territorial hegemons. By the early fourteenth century some of these *shugo* vassals of the Kamakura *bakufu* were becoming disaffected. In 1333 a coalition of forces led by Emperor Go-Daigo and the eastern warrior Ashikaga Takauji (1305–1358) toppled the Kamakura *bakufu*. After a brief resumption of imperial rule, known as the Kenmu Restoration, Go-Daigo was ousted from the capital by his former ally, who set up a rival emperor and established a shogunate in the Muromachi district of Kyoto under Ashikaga warrior control.

The origins of daimyo culture: the tradition of *bu* and *bun*
In terms of the later development of the Japanese warrior ideal in general and daimyo culture in particular, the twelfth and thirteenth centuries were crucial. These centuries saw the full emergence of warriors, their involvement in court politics with the Taira, and the formation and development of warrior government by Minamoto Yoritomo and the Hōjō. Moreover, it was in the early medieval centuries that the basic integration into warrior culture of *bu* and *bun* took place. This interplay of *bu* and *bun*

was not discovered by warriors, nor was it unique to Japan. The ideal of the ruler who combines civilian and military arts had been established in ancient China and enshrined in Confucian texts, which had shaped Japanese thinking from as early as the sixth century. The early political reformer Prince Shōtoku, author of the *Seventeen article constitution* in the early seventh century, might be regarded as one of its first conscious Japanese exemplars. An early emperor is known posthumously simply as "Bun and Bu," or "Monmu" *tennō* (683–707). Imperial princes and nobles serving the court in the Nara and Heian periods also sought to embody the ideal of *bu* and *bun*, although the court nobility in Heian times quickly lost their martial tradition and ceased to bear arms. Daimyo culture thus encompasses the absorption, transformation, and application of an ancient civilian ideal by a newly emergent warrior elite.

In the cultural arena, a sense of the emerging military ideal and the conflict between the old aristocratic order and the new military elite may be gleaned from the war tales of the medieval age. The *Heiji monogatari* (Tale of the Heiji Wars), for instance, a contemporary chronicle that tells of the struggles between the Taira and Minamoto warrior bands during Taira Kiyomori's rise to power, is one of the first war tales to recognize the impending conflict between the old aristocratic and the new military elite. It warns members of the imperial court that, in a troubled age, both learning (the *bun* of aristocratic bureaucrats) and military skill (the *bu* of warrior generals) are essential to survival:

> If we look at precedents followed in both China and Japan, we will find that when rewarding subjects and ministers, rulers have always assigned high priority to both learning and military might. Learning is helpful in various areas of administration; and military power enables rulers to suppress disturbances. So in his plans to preserve the empire and rule the land, a ruler seems to place learning at his left and military strength at his right—making them like a person's two hands. Neither can be dispensed with (Brown and Ishida 1979, 392).

Unfortunately, members of the imperial court proved unable to recover military skills that might have restored their power, while the warrior leaders were increasingly able to master, or hire, the civilian arts they needed to rule. Warrior chieftains proved best able to command the mix of military and civilian skills that were essential to survival and success in an unstable age.

Warriors (*bushi*) saw themselves as distinct from the courtiers, while courtiers were fascinated with the valor and martial tradition of *bushi*. The martial aspect (*bu*) of the emerging warrior ideal is shown very clearly in the many war tales of the early medieval age. The *Mutsu waki* (Tale of Mutsu) was written by a courtier in the eleventh century and chronicles the victories of Minamoto Yoriyoshi (999–1075) and his son Yoshiie (1039–1106), ancestors of Yoritomo, in the wars of pacification of the northern provinces. The long campaigns in the north provided many opportunities for the display of warrior courage. Yoriyoshi's victories established his reputation as a great chieftain and, through the granting of spoils, allowed him to forge strong vassal bonds with the eastern *bushi* who joined his armies. The *Mutsu waki* already contains many of the facets of the warrior ideal more fully developed in later war tales. Yoriyoshi is presented as the seasoned leader and master of the way of the bow and horse:

> At that juncture the court nobles met in council determined to appoint a general to punish [Abe] Yoritoki, and settled unanimously upon Minamoto-no-ason Yoriyoshi, a son of Yorinobu-no-ason, the governor of Kawachi province. Yoriyoshi was a cool, resourceful man, well suited to command. Numbers of eastern warriors had long ago joined their fortunes to his, won by his courage and enterprise as a soldier under his father during the Chōgen era [1028–1037], when Yorinobu-no-ason went on behalf of the court to subdue Taira Tadatsune and his sons—rebels who were perpetrating

shocking outrages in eastern Japan. For a time Yoriyoshi had served as a third-ranking official in Kōichijōin's household. Kōichijōin was a prince who delighted in the hunt. Whenever one of his parties came upon a deer, fox, or hare in the field, it was invariably Yoriyoshi who took the game, for although he carried a weak bow by preference, his aim was so deadly that every arrow buried itself to the feathers in his prey, and even the fiercest animal perished before his bowstring (McCullough 1964–1965, 187).

But Yoriyoshi is also the ideal type of warrior chieftain who wins the loyalty of his followers by his generous concern for them as well as by sheer force of arms:

> Yoriyoshi provided a filling meal for his men, saw that their weapons were put to rights, and personally visited the injured to care for their wounds. The warriors were deeply touched. 'Our bodies shall repay our debts; our lives shall count as nothing where honor is at stake. We are ready to die for our general now' (McCullough 1964–1965, 197).

Minamoto Yoshiie, who like Yoriyoshi played an important role in the consolidation of Minamoto power in the eastern provinces, is presented as being cut from the same heroic mold as his father. For his valor Yoshiie earned the title of Hachiman Tarō, eldest son of Hachiman, the god of war and patron divinity of the Minamoto warriors:

> Nevertheless, the great hero of the battle was Yoriyoshi's eldest son, Yoshiie. He shot arrows from horseback like a god; undeterred by gleaming blades, he lunged through the rebels' encirclements to emerge on their left and right. With his great arrow heads he transfixed one enemy chieftain after another, never shooting at random but always inflicting a mortal wound. He galloped like the wind and fought with a skill that was more than human. The barbarians fled rather than face him, calling him the firstborn son of Hachiman, the god of war (McCullough 1964–1965, 191).

The distinctive martial values of the *bushi*, so clearly delineated by the anonymous courtier who compiled the *Mutsu waki*, were vaunted and embellished in the war tales of succeeding centuries, culminating in the *Heike monogatari*, in the thirteenth century. Strength, courage, cunning, loyalty to one's lord, concern for personal and family honor were lauded; cowardice and treachery castigated. By the time of the diffusion of the *Heike monogatari* the ultimate test of courage, loyalty, and warrior virtue was the willingness to die for one's lord, or one's honor, to disembowel oneself if necessary to avoid the ignominy of capture and disgrace.

The martial character and lifestyle of the medieval *bushi* are richly illustrated in the art of the thirteenth century included in this exhibition. Attention was lavished on finely made swords, richly decorated armor and helmets, and on horses and their equipment. Paintings from the medieval period show bands of mounted warriors setting off on campaigns and honing their fighting skills in martial recreations. Befitting warrior society, the horses that carried warriors into battle were especially prized and pampered. Sometimes, as in scenes from the biographies of the monks Hōnen and Ippen, stables are shown close to the warrior residence, or *yakata*. In the *Seikōji engi emaki* (Illustrated handscroll of the founding of Seikōji), however, the horses are shown stabled in the retainers' quarters of the *yakata*. While one warrior sweeps the floor another brings a tub of mash to the waiting horses. Horses were so important that they were given magical protection. Monkeys were believed to provide that protection. In one scene in the Ippen biography a monkey is tethered near the stables.

Several Kamakura-period scroll paintings clearly illustrate and idealize the martial aspect of the warrior profession of arms. *Mōko shūrai ekotoba* (Illustrated scrolls of the Mongol invasions), for instance, depict the heroic exploits of the warrior Takezaki Suenaga of Higo in the defense of the country during the Mongol invasion attempts of 1274 and

1281. Suenaga had the scrolls painted to glorify himself and his exploits for posterity and to lay claim to spoils for his contribution to the salvation of the country. The two scrolls express Suenaga's leadership, his fearlessness, and his ferociousness in hand-to-hand combat with the invaders. They may exaggerate his individual contribution to the rout of the Mongols but they do give a vigorous impression of the martial ideal of the *bushi* as it existed in the late thirteenth century.

Another illustration of the life of the Kamakura warrior and his disdain for the ways of the courtier is provided by the *Obusuma Saburō ekotoba* (*Tale of Obusuma Saburō*, cat. 79). Painted around the year 1300, this scroll contrasts, we might almost say caricatures, the lives of two eastern warriors from Musashi Province, Obusuma Saburō and his elder brother Yoshimi Jirō. Yoshimi Jirō is presented as an aesthete who has admiration only for the ways of Kyoto and its courtiers. His residence, completely out of place in the frontier territory of the eastern provinces, is a copy of a nobleman's palace. He takes as his wife a noblewoman from the imperial court, who bears him a daughter. He shows no interest in the cultivation of martial skills but instead devotes his days and nights to composing poetry and playing the flute.

Obusuma Saburō, by contrast, is a dedicated warrior who thinks of nothing but the cultivation of martial arts. The text of the scroll sums up his attitude in this way:

> Because I was born in a warrior house, [*yumiya no ie*], what could be more natural for me than to practice the skills of the warrior. What is the use of filling one's heart with thoughts of the moon or flowers, or composing verse, or plucking a lute? The ability of strum a zither or blow a flute doesn't count for much on the battlefield. Everybody in my household—women and children included—will learn to ride wild horses and train daily with the longbow.

Saburō takes as his wife an ill-favored but stalwart woman from the eastern provinces. She gives him three sons and two daughters, all of whom are obliged by Saburō to devote their days to martial pursuits.

One autumn the two brothers are called to Kyoto to perform military service as guards at the imperial palace. Saburō sets out first, with his retinue. On the way he encounters a band of brigands in the mountains but the mere reputation of his martial ability frightens them off. Some days later Jirō and his men encounter the same bunch of brigands. The bandits are less intimidated by the courtly Jirō and his band. They kill him and rout his retinue. When Saburō returns from the capital, in spite of the fact that he has sworn to take care of his elder brother's interests, he steals Jirō's lands, makes his wife and daughter his servants, breaks off a marriage arrangement between Jirō's daughter and the local provincial governor, and tries to interest the governor in marrying his own ugly daughter. The last section of the handscroll has been lost, but stories like this were generally provided with happy endings, often through the intervention of a compassionate Buddhist deity.

Whatever the original intent of the scroll, it reveals a tension between *bu* and *bun* in thirteenth-century warrior society and an awareness that over-indulgence in courtly or literary arts could undermine the warrior spirit and bring disaster to warrior families. The behavior of Saburō, ready at every turn to advance his own, and his family's, interests was perhaps intended as a caricature of the martial spirit and realism of eastern warriors.

Warrior leaders like Yoritomo and the Hōjō regents frequently warned their vassals against excessive indulgence in scholarly and literary pursuits and preached the virtues of spartan living, battle readiness, and cultivation of the martial arts. Early medieval warriors, especially the warrior elite, those who would later be described as daimyo, also cultivated the civilian arts, due to necessity and personal interest. As they achieved political power they found, as many warriors rulers have found at other times, that while they might conquer territory on horseback they could not rule it from horseback. They needed literacy, legal training, governing skills, and skill in calligraphy, facility in the drafting of documents, and prestige conferred by participation in the courtly traditions of the *kuge*, the courtly elite they were displacing. These administrative and literary skills (*bun*) were acquired by associating with nobles and Buddhist monks, especially Zen Buddhist monks. With little of their own to contribute in the way of political philosophy, administrative expertise, and artistic and literary creativity, and lacking traditions of literacy and scholarship, the warrior elite in medieval Japan, eager to embellish their growing political power and social influence with trappings of cultural legitimacy, had to look to the Kyoto court, Buddhist monasteries, and Chinese culture to supply their cultural and intellectual deficiencies. Like contemporary European clerics, Japanese Buddhist monks were custodians of literary and high culture in a world of warriors. Zen teachings in particular proved congenial to the *bushi*, and the Zen Buddhist monks became favored educators, advisors, and companions to the warrior elite.

In many ways the warrior's pattern of acquisition of civilian arts was set by Yoritomo himself. In later periods daimyo, and shoguns like Ieyasu, read about Yoritomo, the founder of the first *bakufu*, in the pages of the *Azuma kagami* (*Mirror of the East*), a thirteenth-century account of the Minamoto rise to power and the Kamakura *bakufu*. They modeled themselves on those aspects of Yoritomo's life they particularly admired. Before his exile to a remote peninsula in eastern Japan, Yoritomo had been reared in the capital. Quite apart from his administrative and martial skills, one intangible but important asset in winning the adherence of eastern provincial warriors in his campaigns against the Taira was the aura of courtly lineage or pedigree (*kishu*) that surrounded him. Yoritomo had been brought up in Kyoto and traced his Minamoto ancestry back to emperor Seiwa. Despite his exile in Izu, his warrior training and family connections, his determination to base his government in eastern Japan, and his preference for the title of shogun over high court rank as a basis for his authority, Yoritomo was always respectful toward the court and receptive to its culture. He made several visits to the capital, cultivated a pro-*bakufu* faction within the court, and invited lower-ranking courtiers to serve as his political advisers and bureaucrats in Kamakura.

Yoritomo legitimated a warrior interest in poetry and the arts. He received instruction in the rules of Japanese verse (*waka*) and composition from the monk Jien, who was a member of the noble Fujiwara family and an accomplished poet and scholar. The *Shūgyokushū* (Collection of gathered jewels), compiled by Jien, contains more than thirty *waka* poems attributed to Yoritomo. Yoritomo's poetic talents and, of course, his political power were also accorded recognition by the inclusion of two of his poems in the prestigious anthology *Shinkokinshū*, commissioned by imperial order in 1201. Appropriately for a warrior, his verse tended to be straightforward and descriptive, technically proficient and sometimes witty, but not marked by deep emotion. This verse, number 975 in the *Shinkokinshū*, for example, describes his feelings on seeing Mt. Fuji during his first triumphal visit to the capital after the destruction of the Taira:

Michisugara	Along the road
Fuji no kemuri mo	Smoke from Mt. Fuji
Wakazariki	Could not be distinguished
Haruru mamonaki	In a sky
Sora no keshiki ni	Of unbroken cloud.

Among Yoritomo's generals at least one, Kajiwara Kagetoki (d. 1200), shared his interest in poetry. Yoritomo's second son, the third Minamoto shogun, Sanetomo (1190–1219), became so enthusiastic about the study of poetry and such other courtly pastimes as kickball (*kemari*) that he was criticized by warrior leaders in the *bakufu*, and used as an example *not* to be followed, for over-indulgence in frivolous activities. But Sanetomo was not alone among warriors in his interest in poetry and scholarship. An entry in the *Azuma kagami* for 1213 records that

> A gathering for the composition of Japanese verse [*waka*] was held in the bakufu. As a title 'Plum Blossoms, Myriad Springs' was set. The lords of Musashi, Iga, Wada and others were in attendance. Ladies were also present. After the *waka* composition linked verse [*renga*] was composed.

It is, of course, quite possible that the stimulus for such literary gatherings came from Sanetomo and that the Hōjō and other powerful vassals merely humored his passion for poetry. The important point here, however, is that such gatherings were being held in the residences of courtier-bureaucrats and warrior chieftains in Kamakura and that all the participants were expected to be able to compose creditable *waka* or join in a *renga* sequence. It was becoming accepted that warriors, or at least warrior leaders, should have some command of *bun* as well as *bu*. Sane-tomo was criticized by Oe no Hiromoto, Jien, Hōjō Yasutoki, and lesser retainers not because he was interested in literary activities, *kemari*, and court titles, but because he indulged those passions to the neglect of that other vital legacy of Yoritomo: attention to the arts of politics and war.

Intermittent warnings from the *bakufu*, urging warriors to spend more time on military training and less on courtly arts, seem to have done little to stifle warrior interest in literary and cultural activities or court culture. And during the thirteenth century this interest was extended to Chinese learning and culture as direct communication with China increased; the Hōjō and their vassals began to study Zen with Chinese and Japanese Zen masters and to acquire Chinese art objects (*karamono*). Through the latter part of the Kamakura period many members of the *bakufu* shared an interest in the composition of *waka*, the enjoyment of narrative tales (*monogatari*), diaries and histories, the study of Confucian ideas of good government and Chinese literary classics, and the discussion of Zen and other forms of Buddhism.

Whereas in Sanetomo's day the writing of *waka* and devotion to scholarship would have seemed an effete distraction to most warriors, by the close of the thirteenth century it was becoming quite common for Kamakura warriors to write poetry, and to copy and study Buddhist sutras and Chinese literary texts. An analysis of the *Sonpi bunmyaku*, a comprehensive genealogy compiled early in the fourteenth century, reveals that Yasutoki (1183–1242), third of the Hōjō regents, and more than one-third of the men of the Hōjō family are designated as "poets" (*kajin*) or recorded as contributors to the *Shinsen wakashū* (New collection of Japanese poetry) and other anthologies. The *Azuma kagami* and other documents of the period mention poetry gatherings and tea meetings (*cha yoriai*) at the residences of the Hōjō and their retainers. An entry in the *Azuma kagami* for 1263 records a poetry gathering attended by seventeen *bakufu* officials at which one thousand verses were composed. Such gatherings became common and brought together a variety of cultured participants. One such meeting at the Nikaidō residence late in the Kamakura period included not only warriors but the Kyoto nobles Fujiwara Tamesuke and Tamemori (members of a family of famous poets), and the Zen monk Musō Soseki (1275–1351). Although these warrior literary salons were most active in Kamakura, site of the *bakufu*, literary enthusiasm was also evident in some provincial warrior families. The

Utsunomiya and Katsumata warrior houses, for instance, both developed strong literary traditions and produced talented *waka* poets.

Minamoto Yoritomo and other warrior leaders urged their vassals to promote military arts and martial recreation—skill with a bow, swordsmanship, horsemanship, and hawking—and to be wary of excessive indulgence in courtly accomplishments. The Kamakura warrior legal code, the *Goseibai shikimoku,* and instructions by influential *bakufu* officials like Hōjō Shigetoki, all sought to impress on medieval warriors the need for a distinctively spartan, rigorous lifestyle appropriate to their calling as warriors. In a set of instructions left to guide his son, Hōjō Shigetoki, the *bakufu's* representative with the court in Kyoto, warned against the flaunting of literary and cultural abilities. At the same time, it is clear that he was less wary of the acquisition of cultural accomplishments than of their foolish display:

> [When asked to show your] skill in the polite arts, even if it is something you can do easily, it is best to say that you cannot because you lack such skill, and to comply only when they insist. Even then, never allow yourself to be puffed up with success, so that you come to angle for applause and expressions of personal popularity. You, a warrior, should [on the contrary] excel in the skillful handling of public affairs, in possessing sound judgment, and above all in specializing and excelling in the way of the bow and arrow. What lies beyond these fields is of secondary importance. Never immerse yourself unduly in the pursuit of polite accomplishments! Yet, when you are at a party with good friends and they are in the mood for having some relaxed fun together, you should not refuse too steadfastly [their pleas that you, too, contribute to the common pleasure by performing], or they will come to dislike you as a stand-offish person. Remember that you must on every occasion strive to be well thought of by others (Steenstrup 1979, 148).

In addition to the courtly traditions, other influences that were to shape warrior culture in general, and medieval daimyo culture in particular, were also evident by the close of the Kamakura period. These were religious influences derived from Buddhism and Shinto. Whenever medieval Japanese warrior culture, or the Way of the Warrior, is mentioned an association is usually made with Zen Buddhism. Certainly the association between Zen Buddhism and medieval warrior life was very close. Rinzai and Sōtō Zen teachings were introduced to Japan in the late twelfth and thirteenth centuries and spread rapidly and widely under the patronage of warriors in Kamakura and the provinces. Zen monks were not only instructors in meditation, but they were also bearers of culture and knowledge from China; and for the warrior elite that kind of knowledge was an enhancement of their power. Several of the Hōjō regents invited Zen monks to come from China, sponsored the building of Zen monasteries, practiced meditation, and became lay followers. Their example was followed by warrior chieftains throughout the provinces. Zen monasteries, especially those of the Rinzai tradition, proliferated. Zen monks and monasteries were not simply channels for the transmission of Zen meditation or Buddhist texts. Zen monks had associated with Chinese literati and frequently were accomplished ink painters, calligraphers, poets, garden designers, and architects. All of these interests were communicated to and eagerly adopted by their warrior patrons. The drinking of tea, the designing of dry landscape gardens, the vogue for ink painting, the study and printing of Confucian texts and Chinese poetry, the formal *shoin* style of architecture, the art of flower arrangement—all to become facets of daimyo culture—were all acquired by warriors through contact with Zen monks.

But Zen was not the only Buddhist spiritual practice to influence medieval warriors, or to help shape daimyo culture. Zen was simply one part of a wider religious transformation gathering force in the thirteenth century in which popular preachers and reformers were taking old and newer versions of Buddhism to the provinces and to the common people. Like Zen, and at about the same time, Pure Land Buddhism developed into an independent and enormously popular school: its simple teaching that faith in Amida (expressed by repetition of the formula "Praise to Amida Buddha") appealed to warriors as well as farmers. For warriors, who were constantly faced with the likelihood of sudden death, the compassionate promise of salvation by a simple expression of devotion to Amida had a profound attraction. Many warriors retained a devotion to such Esoteric Buddhist deities as the fierce Fudō Myōō. Warriors could, and did, patronize Zen and Pure Land, or Zen and esoteric Buddhism together. In addition, most warrior houses had ancestral founding deities they worshipped as *kami*. They set up shrines to ancestral or protective *kami*. The syncretic Shinto-Buddhist deity Hachiman, for instance, was venerated by many warriors, especially the Minamoto, acquiring over time the role of a god of war. The most important shrine in Kamakura, the center of Minamoto power and site of the *bakufu*, was dedicated to Hachiman and there were many local shrines in his honor patronized by warrior families.

In later centuries, the range of daimyo culture widened considerably. Even so, it is fair to suggest that by the close of the Kamakura period the basic paradigm had been established in terms of a tension between *bu* and *bun*. The ideal warrior was, by the close of the Kamakura period, neither the rough, ruthless Saburō nor the courtly Jirō of the *Obusuma Saburō* scroll. He was, rather, a composite of these and more. The ideal type would perhaps be closer to Minamoto Yorimasa as depicted in the *Tale of the Heike*, where Yorimasa urges Prince Mochihito to raise a revolt against the Taira in 1180. When the revolt is crushed he takes his own life with all the unflinching bravery expected of a warrior, after composing a verse that would have done credit to a courtier:

> Yorimasa summoned Watanabe Chōjitsu Tonau and ordered: Strike off my head. Tonau could not bring himself to do this while his master was still alive. He wept bitterly. How can I do that, my lord? he replied. I can do so only after you have committed suicide. I understand, said Yorimasa. He turned to the West, joined his palms, and chanted Hail Amida Buddha ten times in a loud voice. Then he composed this poem:
>
> > Like a fossil tree
> > Which has borne not one blossom
> > Sad has been my life
> > Sadder still to end my days
> > Leaving no fruit behind me.
>
> Having spoken these lines, he thrust the point of his sword into his belly, bowed his face to the ground as the blade pierced him through, and died. No ordinary man could compose a poem at such a moment. For Yorimasa, however, the writing of poems had been a constant pleasure since his youth. And so, even at the moment of death, he did not forget. Tonau took up his master's head and, weeping, fastened it to a stone. Then evading the enemy, he made his way to the river and sank it in a deep place (Kitagawa and Tsuchida 1975, vol. 1, 271).

Obviously, not all warriors could demonstrate such valor or such facility in verse. But there were many who by the close of the Kamakura period aspired to such standards, and others who added to them a growing familiarity with Zen and other forms of Buddhism and with the arts and culture of China. This blending of *bu* and *bun* in the warrior ideal of the thirteenth century did not end there. It provided a model for the samurai elite in later centuries: ruthless in warfare, ready to die for honor, adept in administration and practical affairs but able and eager, in times of peace, to enjoy literary and cultural pursuits.

Ashikaga shoguns and *shugo* daimyo In 1333 the Kamakura *bakufu* was toppled by a coalition of imperial princes, warriors, and monk-soldiers led by emperor Go-Daigo. Go-Daigo's attempts to restore direct imperial rule quickly alienated Ashikaga Takauji, his leading warrior supporter, who in 1336 forced Go-Daigo from Kyoto. The emperor with his supporters took refuge in the Yoshino Hills, south of Kyoto, where they set up the Southern Court and maintained the emperor's claim to the throne. Ashikaga Takauji installed a rival "Northern" emperor in Kyoto, took the title of shogun, and established a *bakufu* (shogunate) in the Muromachi district of Kyoto. Culturally, the return of the *bakufu* to Kyoto was significant, for it brought the Ashikaga shoguns, and later the daimyo on whose support they depended, back into close contact with members of the imperial court, the great Kyoto temples, and the burgeoning merchant and artistic communities of the capital.

The early decades of Ashikaga rule were marked by civil war. But even in the midst of war some daimyo, like Imagawa Ryōshun, found time for literary pursuits as well as conquest. Ryōshun, born into the Imagawa daimyo family in about 1326, served the Ashikaga *bakufu* and in 1371 was appointed governor general of Kyushu, charged with establishing the authority of the *bakufu* in western Japan. Ryōshun loved *waka* and *renga* and his skill was widely acclaimed. His writings were used as literary copy books by later generations of young warriors. One of these copy books begins with the line, "He who does not know the way of *bun* can never ultimately gain victory in the way of *bu*" (Dore 1965, 16).

Compared with the earlier Kamakura *bakufu*, the Muromachi *bakufu* did not have a strong political reach. The Ashikaga shoguns ruled as heads of an unstable warrior coalition of shogun and *shugo*, or provincial constables. The *shugo* included some of the earlier Kamakura-period *shugo*, members of Ashikaga cadet families or shogunal vassals. The shoguns treated *shugo* as vassals and gave them military and administrative responsibility for one or more provinces. The *shugo* took advantage of their administrative authority from the *bakufu* to build up their personal territorial control and to enfeoff local warriors (*kokujin*). They enjoyed the right to collect taxes on cultivated land (*tansen*) and to levy taxes on public and private lands to raise troops (*hanzei*). They were charged with keeping the peace, apprehending criminals, and settling local disputes. They also sequestered the private holdings of absentee proprietors, and divided spoils after war. As they added to their spheres of influence, increased their fief lands, and added local warriors to their vassal bands, they became territorial magnates on a grand scale; they have been given the name *shugo* daimyo, or constable daimyo, by modern historians. Some, like the Yamana and Hosokawa, came to exert nominal authority over half a dozen provinces. At the same time that the *shugo* controlled the provinces, they also held offices in the shogunal government. This simultaneously increased their influence, divided their attention, and brought them out of the provinces to live in Kyoto. Three influential *shugo* daimyo, the Shiba, Hatakeyama, and Hosokawa, held the powerful *bakufu* office of *Kanrei*, or shogunal deputy.

Strong shoguns like Ashikaga Yoshimitsu, the third shogun, and Yoshinori, the autocratic sixth shogun, were able to impose their authority on the shogun-*shugo* coalition by mobilizing alliances to crush unruly members, taking hostages, requiring *shugo* to live in Kyoto, and commanding expensive gifts and favors. The assassination of Yoshinori by a resentful *shugo* in 1441 and the protracted civil war (Ōnin War) of 1467–1477 seriously weakened shogunal finances and military power. The shogunate was reduced to bare control over Kyoto and the few nearby provinces. In the Ōnin War *shugo* daimyo banded together in rival military confederations led by Yamana Sōzen and Hosokawa Katsumoto. They laid waste to much of Kyoto and carried sporadic warfare into the provinces. Many *shugo* daimyo now found themselves in a very vulnerable position. Their large domains often exceeded the extent of their enforceable authority, and from the beginning of the Ōnin War their control was further diminished by frequent absences to fight in the field or play politics in Kyoto. Their deputies and other local warriors carved up the great *shugo* daimyo territories, building smaller but more tightly knit domains. In what has been called a process of "inferiors toppling superiors," *gekokujō*, these smaller warrior chieftains overthrew many *shugo* and claimed territorial control and daimyo status for themselves. These "upstarts" are known as the daimyo of the Age of Wars, the *sengoku* daimyo.

The cultural interests of the *shugo* daimyo

Leading *shugo* daimyo of the fourteenth and fifteenth centuries embodied a fusion of military and civilian interests and ideals. They were in effect, a new warrior aristocracy modeled in part on the old courtly aristocracy and formed in part under its tutelage. The *shugo* daimyo included the Hosokawa, Kyōgoku, Isshiki, Uesugi, Takeda, Toki, Shiba, Hatakeyama, Yamana, Ōuchi, Ōtomo, and Shimazu families. In an uncertain age much of their energy was inevitably given to preparation for warfare and the honing of martial skills. The general instability meant that daimyo, to survive, had to keep their swords sharp and their armor and horses in constant readiness. They had to maintain a tight rein on their vassals and look to their alliances and their defenses. Those daimyo who neglected these basic requirements of survival, or who preferred cultured life in Kyoto to the management of their domains, put their domains at risk and were easily overthrown.

On the other hand, daimyo were not constantly at war. The decision by Ashikaga Takauji to establish his *bakufu* in Kyoto close to the imperial court focused daimyo as well as shogunal interest on the court and the capital. The stronger Ashikaga shoguns required their *shugo* to maintain residences in Kyoto and to provide hostages and gifts. Yoshimitsu, the third Ashikaga shogun (1358–1408), set an example of cultural style and largesse. He exchanged envoys with the Ming Chinese court, representing himself to the court as King of Japan, or *Nihon kokuō*; consorted with emperors, sponsored lavish poetry gatherings, founded Zen monasteries, and built himself a magnificent retreat, the Golden Pavilion, in the northern hills of Kyoto. Cultural activities there and in the city itself brought *shugo* daimyo into contact with courtiers and with influential and highly cultivated Zen monks. Through mixing with shoguns, courtiers, monks, actors, and men of culture in Kyoto, many *shugo* daimyo were introduced to ink painting, the newly emerging Nō drama, Zen-inspired trends in domestic architecture and garden design, interior decoration and flower arrangement, *waka* (Japanese poems) and *renga* (linked verse) poetry, tea drinking, and the elaborate etiquette of the Ogasawara school, which trained warriors in the kinds of comportment needed in their social interaction with nobles, prelates, and shoguns.

Among educated warriors there was a passion for *renga*. Daimyo throughout the provinces were eager to keep abreast of the latest poetic styles in vogue in the capital. They sought the guidance of acknowledged masters. The courtier and poet Nijō Yoshimoto (1320–1388), for instance, who advised the shogun Ashikaga Yoshimitsu in matters of poetic composition, wrote a treatise on *renga* in 1376, the *Kyūshū mondō* (Dialogues with the governor of Kyushu) for Imagawa Ryōshun, the *tandai* of Kyushu and a noted poet himself. In 1383 Yoshimoto presented another treatise on *renga*, *Jūmon saihi shō* (Ten questions: A most secret selection) to the daimyo poet Ōuchi Yoshihiro. Yoshimoto's famous anthology of *renga*, the *Tsukubashū* (1356) contained sequences by shoguns and daimyo as well as courtiers. Among the daimyo represented was Sasaki Dōyo (1306–1373), a high-ranking military adviser to the Ashikaga shogunate, and an enthusiastic amateur poet. *Renga* was the preferred poetry of the Muromachi period, intricate in its form, intensely social in its setting. To compose *renga* a gathering of poets was necessary, each contributing verses in sequence, each carefully maintaining the overall mood of the sequence at the same time that he responded to the subtle nuance of the immediately preceding verse. It was an activity that required social as well as poetic finesse. The daimyo's passion for *renga* indicates the value that these ruthless warriors set in both kinds of skill.

Although the Ōnin War was destructive, and many daimyo and their warriors were killed, some provincial daimyo benefitted culturally as monks and nobles fled the burning capital and took refuge in the provinces. The court noble Ichijō Norifusa quit the capital and moved to his landholdings in Tosa where he lived as a daimyo. *Renga* poets were in demand in the provinces. The *renga* poet Iio Sōgi (1421–1502), a sometime Zen priest who had studied at Shōkokuji in Kyoto, spent the Ōnin years wandering from village to village and castle to castle composing linked verse sequences. During his lifetime Sōgi made many long journeys. He traveled seven times to the province of Echigo as a guest of the daimyo Uesugi Funasada. He went twice to Yamaguchi and compiled a major anthology of *renga*, the *Shinsen Tsukubashū*, under the sponsorship of Ōuchi Masahiro. This collection had many contributions by daimyo and commoners. Sōchō (1448–1532), a Shingon Buddhist priest and *renga* poet, traveled the provinces during the Ōnin War, perhaps as an intelligence agent and certainly as a negotiator for his patrons Imagawa Yoshitada and his son Ujichika. Sōchō's diaries contain many references to military fortifications and strategy. In 1517 he helped Ujichika negotiate for peace when his fortress was surrounded. He participated in *renga* sequences with Sōgi and Shōhaku, as well as with numerous daimyo. The Zen monk and poet Shōtetsu (1381–1459) is said to have maintained literary contacts with more than a score of daimyo between 1394 and 1455. All of these *renga* masters lived well, frequently on the generous stipends and gifts they received from provincial warrior lords.

Provincial military lords were also acquiring a taste for the developing dramatic art of Nō and Kyōgen. Kan'ami (1333–1384), and his son Zeami (c. 1364–c. 1143), synthesized, standardized, and elevated a number of ancient dancing and mimetic forms such as *sarugaku* and *dengaku* to create the masked dance dramas that we know as Nō. Zeami and his successors who headed the Kanze school of Nō were patronized by the Ashikaga shoguns. *Kyōgen*, literally "wild words," developed alongside Nō as an earthier, more active, humorous dramatic form, rooted not in some spiritual otherworld but firmly in the present. In sometimes farcical or ironical terms Kyōgen mocked contemporary conventions, including the authority of daimyo who appeared in some Kyōgen pieces. Both Nō and Kyōgen were further developed and formalized in later centuries. Their association with daimyo culture, however, was firmly established in the medieval period. From the shogunal court the enthusiasm for Nō spread into warrior society. Daimyo, too, became eager spectators and patrons of the numerous Nō troupes. Moreover, the Ashikaga shoguns frequently visited daimyo, either in their residences in Kyoto or in their domains. When they did so they demanded to be entertained by actors and poets in the proper setting and with the right costumes. This imposed upon daimyo a virtual obligation to provide the best possible *renga* parties and Nō and Kyōgen performances if they were to stay in favor— culture was very much an instrument of politics.

Many daimyo patronized Zen monks, practiced meditation, imported Chinese objects (*karamono*) and cultivated the arts associated with Zen. Back in their castle towns they built Zen temples, designed gardens, invited Zen monks and men of culture from the capital, and practiced the monastic, courtly, and literary arts to which they had been introduced in Kyoto. These years saw a proliferation of Rinzai and Sōtō Zen monasteries throughout the provinces. The monks Musō Soseki (1275–1351), Gidō Shūshin (1325–1388), and the eccentric Ikkyū Sōjun (1394–1481) were particularly influential in fourteenth- and fifteenth-century warrior society. Zen monks were constantly moving through the provinces. The Zen monk Keian Genju (1427–1508), for instance, who had studied in Ming China between 1467 and 1473, traveled westward from patron to patron, teaching Zen meditation and Confucianism to the Kikuchi, Shimazu, and other daimyo families in Kyushu. Genju revered Confucius and urged the Kikuchi to build a Confucian hall and revive the Confucian ceremony known as *sekiten* in the sage's honor. As a result of such activity by Zen monks Confucian moral and ethical teachings became increasingly prominent in the house codes of sixteenth-century daimyo. In the seventeen-article injunction of the daimyo Asakura Toshikage (1428–1481), we find the influence of the Confucian *Analects* blended with that of Buddhism in the training of warriors:

> A famous monk once said that a master of men must be like the two Buddhist deities Fudō and Aizen. Although Fudō carries a sword, and Aizen carries a bow and arrows, these weapons are not intended for slashing and shooting, but for the purpose of subjugating devils. In their hearts they are compassionate and circumspect. Like them, a master of samurai must first rectify his own way, and then reward his loyal subjects and soldiers and eliminate those who are disloyal and treacherous. If you can discern between reason and unreason and between good and evil and act accordingly, your system of rewards and punishments can be considered as compassionately administered. On the other hand, if your heart is prejudiced, no matter how much you know the words of the sages and study the texts they all come to naught. You may observe that the *Analects* [1.8] contains a passage saying that a gentleman who lacks steadfastness cannot command respect. Do not consider that the term steadfastness represents only heavy-handedness. It is essential that you conduct yourself in such a way that both heavy-handedness and leniency can be applied flexibly as the occasion demands (Lu 1974, vol. 1, 173).

One interest the medieval daimyo acquired from Zen monks was the custom of drinking tea. Like the practice of Zen meditation, the use of tea had been introduced to Japan in the eighth or ninth century. Neither had taken deep hold, however. From the late twelfth century tea drinking was reintroduced as one facet of Zen monastic life. Tea was used in monasteries as a medicament and stimulant to help keep monks awake during long sessions of meditation. It was also served ceremoniously to important visitors to the monastery. In this new tea style boiling water was poured over powdered green tea (*matcha*) in an open bowl, and a bamboo whisk used to whip the mixture.

Courtiers and warriors were quickly introduced to the custom through their contacts with Zen monks. Among the first daimyo to devote himself to tea was Sasaki Dōyo. Dōyo helped Ashikaga Takauji in establishing the Muromachi *bakufu* and served as an advisor to the second shogun Yoshiakira. A poet and patron of Nō, he loved tea competitions, or *tōcha*, and displayed the finest Chinese utensils and the taste for lavish gatherings that was known in the early Muromachi period as *basara*, or flamboyance. Tea-drinking gatherings quickly became social occasions at which shoguns, monks, and warriors mingled to recite poetry, compete in the identification of rare incense or tea, appreciate fine imported Chinese utensils and paintings, and enjoy refreshments and conversation. Tea gatherings were gradually taken out of the monastic setting and held in specially built large chambers (*kaisho*) of shogunal and daimyo residences. In order to display prized imported Chinese objects in a properly reverent manner, these *kaisho* gradually assumed features that we now think of as characteristic of traditional Japanese domestic architecture: staggered shelves (*chigai-dana*), the single alcove (*tokonoma*), and fitted desk (*tsukeshoin*), all probably derived from the Zen monastic style of *shoin* architecture. Thus the drinking of tea began to give rise to a kind of aesthetic revolution that was to reshape almost every area of Japanese cultural life and to transform daimyo taste, as well as that of shoguns, courtiers, townsmen, and villagers.

The Ōuchi and Hosokawa as medieval daimyo.

Typical of the medieval *shugo* daimyo were the medieval Ōuchi and Hosokawa families. The Ōuchi, as leading vassals of the Ashikaga shoguns, steadily extended control over Suō, Nagato and neighboring provinces along the Inland Sea and into northern Kyushu. Vassals of the Kamakura *bakufu* in the thirteenth century, they grew in influence during the fourteenth and fifteenth centuries under a succession of able daimyo including Ōuchi Yoshihiro (1356–1399), Morimi (1377–1431), Masahiro (1446–1495), Yoshioki (1477–1528), and Yoshitaka (1507–1551). Ōuchi Yoshihiro became *shugo* of the six provinces of Nagato, Iwami, Bingo, Chikuzen, and Buzen in western Honshu and northern Kyushu. Ōuchi Morimi earned a reputation as a powerful warrior but also as a poet and student of Zen Buddhism and Neo-Confucianism. He patronized Shinto and rebuilt the Usa Hachimangū, a shrine. Politically astute and militarily powerful, the Ōuchi made considerable profits from trade with China and Korea and imported cultural objects including ceramics, tea utensils, Confucian texts, and a Korean edition of the Buddhist canon. The Ōuchi made Yamaguchi into a miniature Kyoto. They patronized Zen monks and artists, including the painter Sesshū (1420–1506), who stayed in Yamaguchi on his journey to and from China. The *renga* poets Sōgi and Sōgin also stayed in Yamaguchi, and the monk Keian Genju and scholar Minamimura Baiken came from Yamaguchi. The Ōuchi issued a house code dealing with domain administration, a handbook for the proper entertainment of visiting courtiers and daimyo, and printed the Confucian *Analects* and other texts. The Ōuchi survived well into the sixteenth century as daimyo of the Age of Wars but they were eventually overthrown by the Mōri, a neighboring daimyo house. The Mōri were patrons of the Hagi pottery kilns. On the whole, however, they were less given to cultural interests than the Ōuchi and some historians have suggested that their victory over the Ōuchi was due not only to better military organization but also to less distraction in cultural pursuits.

The medieval Hosokawa, a branch of the Ashikaga family, traced their ancestry through the Minamoto leader Yoshiie to emperor Seiwa. They took their name from an ancestral village called Hosokawa in eastern Japan. When Ashikaga Takauji rose to power in the 1330s he was aided by Hosokawa Yoriharu (1299–1352). For his services to Takauji, Yoriharu was granted the title of *shugo* of the provinces of Awa and Bingo. Yoriyuki (1329–1392), his successor as daimyo, extended Hosokawa control over much of central Honshu and Shikoku. In 1367 he was granted the title of *Kanrei*, or shogunal deputy, and served as advisor for the young shogun Yoshimitsu. The Hosokawa were well on their way to achieving the prominence of daimyo.

The medieval Hosokawa reached their peak of political power under Hosokawa Masamoto (1466–1507) who as *Kanrei* treated the eleventh Ashikaga shogun as a nonentity and virtually ruled the country on his own. Like their rivals the Ōuchi, the Hosokawa were active in trade with China and Korea and sponsored merchants from the port of Sakai. Like many other *shugo* daimyo the Hosokawa were also patrons and practitioners of the arts. Yoriharu and Yoriyuki were both regarded as fine poets and had their verses included in a number of court anthologies. Yoriyuki studied Zen with one of the most influential Rinzai monks of the fourteenth century, Musō Soseki. Hosokawa Katsumoto, who led one of the warrior leagues in the Ōnin War, frequently held *renga* and tea gatherings. He too was an enthusiastic patron of Zen and established the Ryōanji, a Zen temple in Kyoto, with its magnificent dry landscape garden. Hosokawa Shigeyuki, *shugo* of Awa, had multifaceted cultural interests. In addition to *renga* and *waka* he was proficient in painting and kickball (*kemari*), and a patron of Nō. Divided by a bitter succession dispute after Katsumoto's death, the main branch of the medieval Hosokawa daimyo family declined after the Ōnin War. The family fortunes were revived in the sixteenth century by Hosokawa Yūsai (Fujitaka, 1534–1610) and Sansai (Tadaoki, 1563–1646), members of a branch family. Yūsai and Sansai were among the survivors in the cut and thrust of the military campaigns of the sixteenth century. They were also among the most cultured of the daimyo who showed an interest in the way of *bun*. We will look at them in a little more detail when we come to consider some of their peers as daimyo in the late sixteenth and early seventeenth centuries. Other daimyo who practiced the twofold path of literary and martial arts in this period were the Hatakeyama, Asakura, Takeda, Uesugi, and Hōjō. Hōjō Ujiyasu, for instance, was a vigorous patron of scholarship who supported the Ashikaga school for samurai, the nearest medieval Japan came to having a university. According to Francisco Xavier it was the largest school in Japan in the sixteenth century, with more than three thousand students.

The daimyo in an age of war and unification

Sporadic provincial warfare in the late fifteenth and early sixteenth centuries gave way after 1560 to large-scale campaigns by Oda Nobunaga, Toyotomi Hideyoshi, and Tokugawa Ieyasu. All aimed at reunifying the country. The escalating pace and scale of warfare brought greater unpredictability and change to daimyo. The process of unification demanded the reduction of daimyo autonomy. A weakening of the domain or a mistake in choosing an ally could lead to destruction in a single battle. A few families, including the Shimazu of Satsuma, survived all the warfare and continued as daimyo until the nineteenth century. Most of the medieval *shugo* daimyo, however, were overthrown. In some cases the smaller daimyo houses with more closely controlled domains who replaced them in the late fifteenth and sixteenth centuries were able to consolidate their positions and ally themselves with one of the unifiers to survive and flourish in the late sixteenth and early seventeenth centuries. In many cases, however, those daimyo who toppled *shugo* were crushed in their turn when they stood in the way of unification. In many parts of the country three or four daimyo families achieved local hegemony and lost it again in the course of the sixteenth century. This period of intense social upheaval is known as the age of *gekokujō*, "inferiors toppling superiors."

Underlying these almost bewildering surface phenomena of *gekokujō* were significant changes in the institutional character of daimyo. In the crucible of warfare and unification new types of daimyo were being forged. Over a century or so, from 1550 to 1650, the daimyo of the Age of Wars, *sengoku* daimyo, became the daimyo of the age of unification under Oda Nobunaga and Toyotomi Hideyoshi (*Shokuhō* daimyo) and then the daimyo of the early modern era (*kinsei* daimyo). Before turning to consider daimyo culture from the sixteenth century, let us look briefly at some of the political and institutional changes that were taking place in the character of the daimyo as Japan was brought back under centralized feudal control.

In the early sixteenth century more than 250 *sengoku* daimyo domains existed in Japan, several to a single province. The political map was constantly changing as these feudal lords enlarged their territories or were swallowed up by their neighbors. Most of these *sengoku* daimyo domains were created when one or more local warrior bands overthrew the regional *shugo*. Their domains were not only smaller than those of the *shugo*, but more tightly consolidated and rigidly controlled. Territory had been acquired in battle and the area of territorial control generally coincided with the daimyo's claim of political authority. The gap between legal and actual control was being reduced and it was becoming impossible to lay claim to local authority unsupported by military power. In the process the feudal lines of authority downward from the daimyo to his vassals and the peasantry were tightened. *Sengoku* daimyo were independent of central authority and had little respect for the Muromachi shogunate and little contact with Kyoto. They thought of their territories as "states" (*kokka*) and of themselves as the public authority (*kōgi*). Many of them issued codes of regulations for their domains. Some, borrowing an imperial prerogative, used their own private era names. Their principal justification for rule was that they brought law and order to their domains. They rejected external sources of authority and absentee proprietary rights in land, further impoverishing the *bakufu* as well as the imperial court and the nobles.

The *sengoku* daimyo devoted himself to the total mobilization of the domain for attack and defense. For most daimyo this meant fortifying garrisons and castles, strengthening armies by forcing local warrior families to accept vassalage and provide military service, moving vassals from place to place to weaken local ties that might conflict with the obedience of vassal to overlord, and taking hostages. To draw on the full agrarian and commercial resources of the domain, daimyo dammed rivers, built irrigation channels, surveyed land, established uniform weights and measures, licensed merchants, set village quotas for taxes and military services, and made villages responsible for self-administration. Land was held either as direct domain or granted as fiefs to vassals in return for service. *Sengoku* daimyo built castles and castle towns from which to control their vassals and the villages that made up their landed base.

For these *sengoku* daimyo martial concerns were uppermost. Many of them issued house codes or domain laws to remind themselves and their successors of how to survive in an age of war. These codes stressed constant readiness, the cultivation of a martial spirit, and attention to arms. Asakura Takakage (1428–1481) became *shugo* of Echizen in 1471. Like many other *sengoku* daimyo he devoted considerable attention to the government of his domain and drafted a code of injunctions for his son Ujikage to observe. In the seventeen articles of the code he stressed centralized control by the daimyo, constant preparedness for war, promotion of warriors on the basis of merit, frugality, impartial enforcement of laws, an emphasis on rationality, and the encouragement of indigenous domain culture:

> Do not give a command post or an administrative position to anyone who lacks ability, even if his family has served the Asakura family for generations. . . .

Do not excessively covet swords and daggers made by famous masters. Even if you own a sword or dagger worth 10,000 pieces [*hiki*] it can be overcome by 100 spears each worth one hundred pieces. Therefore use the 10,000 pieces to procure 100 spears, and arm 100 men with them. You can in this manner defend yourself in time of war. . . .

Refrain from frequently bringing from Kyoto actors of the four schools of Nō for performances. Instead use the money needed for that purpose to select talented local actors of *sarugaku*, and train them in the basic elements of Nō for the perpetual enjoyment of this province . . . (Lu 1974, vol. 1, 172).

These careful injunctions helped preserve the Asakura family for nearly a century. However, in 1573 they threw their weight against Oda Nobunaga, were defeated, and destroyed. Yoshikage, the last of the Asakura daimyo, committed suicide.

By the mid-sixteenth century political decentralization and warfare had reached an extreme. Among the *sengoku* daimyo were some who dreamed of marching on Kyoto and reuniting the country. The daimyo who actually started the process of reunification was Oda Nobunaga, a young daimyo from a small domain on the Pacific coast of Japan. In 1560 Nobunaga overcame the vastly superior forces of Imagawa Yoshimoto, the *shugo* of the three provinces of Suruga, Tōtōmi, and Mikawa, at the Battle of Okehazama and captured Yoshimoto. On the pretext of restoring the Ashikaga Yoshiaki to the shogunate, Nobunaga moved on Kyoto in 1568. By 1573 he had discarded Yoshiaki and claimed for himself control over the realm, the *tenka*, literally "all under heaven." To confirm his authority to rule the realm Nobunaga made alliances with some daimyo and crushed others who stood in his way. At the Battle of Nagashino in 1575, Nobunaga, in alliance with Tokugawa Ieyasu, another powerful daimyo from eastern Japan, defeated the forces of Takeda Katsuyori. Nobunaga's victory owed much to his readiness to adapt new technology to warfare. The major reason for his victory at Nagashino was his skillful use of the recently-imported muskets (*teppō*). Nobunaga organized his three thousand musketeers in three ranks, with one rank firing while the others reloaded. This allowed him to deliver a volley every ten seconds, devastating the mounted warriors of the Takeda. While he was bringing daimyo of central Japan to heel, Nobunaga also engaged in bitter campaigns against militant Buddhist groups, especially the monastic armies of Enryakuji on Mount Hiei, which he razed in 1571, and the supporters of the True Pure Land school of Buddhism organized around the Honganji who controlled the provinces of Echizen and Kaga and were as powerful as many daimyo.

Perhaps to spite Buddhist clerics, Nobunaga showed favor to the Christian missionaries who were beginning to make converts among the daimyo and commoners of western Japan. Luis Frois, a Jesuit missionary, was frequently entertained by Nobunaga and has left this vivid portrait of the ruthless daimyo who rose to be master of the realm of Japan. Frois, like other European visitors to Japan in the sixteenth century, referred to the various daimyo as kings or princes:

This king of Owari would be about thirty-seven years old, tall, thin, sparsely bearded, extremely warlike and much given to military exercises, inclined to works of justice and mercy, sensitive about his honor, reticent about his plans, an expert in military strategy, unwilling to receive advice from subordinates, highly esteemed and venerated by everyone, does not drink wine and rarely offers it to others, brusque in his manner, despises all the other Japanese kings and princes and speaks to them over his shoulder in a loud voice as if they were lowly servants, obeyed by all as the absolute lord, has good understanding and good judgment. He despises the *kami* and *hotoke* [Buddhas] and all other pagan superstitions. Nominally belonging to the Hokke [Lotus] sect, he openly denies the existence of a creator of the universe, the immortality of the soul, and life after death. He is upright and prudent in all his dealings and intensely dislikes any delays or long speeches. Not even a prince may appear before him with a sword. He is always accompanied by at least two thousand men on horseback, yet converses quite familiarly with the lowest and most miserable servant. His father was merely the lord of Owari, but by his immense energy over the past four years Nobunaga has seized control of seventeen to eighteen provinces, including the eight principal provinces of Gokinai [the region around the capital] and its neighbor fiefs, overcoming them in a very short time (Cooper 1965, 93).

Before Nobunaga could consolidate his conquest of the realm he was assassinated in the summer of 1582 by a disgruntled vassal, the daimyo Akechi Mitsuhide (d.1582). Mitsuhide was promptly hunted down by another of Nobunaga's generals, Toyotomi Hideyoshi. Like many self-made daimyo of the medieval period, Hideyoshi began life in lowly circumstances as the son of a peasant farmer in Owari. Taking service under Oda Nobunaga, he quickly won Nobunaga's respect as a precocious strategist and rose to become one of his favored lieutenants. In 1578, for example, Nobunaga granted Hideyoshi the rare privilege of holding formal tea ceremonies.

After seizing the succession, Hideyoshi continued to extend Nobunaga's conquests. At his death Nobunaga had conquered one-third of the country, twenty-nine of sixty-six provinces. But since this area included the major cities of Kyoto, Osaka, and Sakai, it would be more accurate to say that he controlled practically half the country, including its heartland. Hideyoshi proceeded to capture the western provinces of Japan and by 1587 had forced the Chōsokabe daimyo family of Shikoku and the Shimazu of Kyushu to yield to his vastly superior forces. According to one record Hideyoshi enlisted seventy-seven daimyo to lead a total of 250,000 samurai in the Kyushu campaign (Berry 1982, 89). Having subdued Kyushu, Hideyoshi announced a plan to invade the Korean peninsula, and turned to the conquest of eastern Japan. In 1590 Hideyoshi turned east, subdued the Hōjō of Odawara, and confiscated their domain. He then arranged a truce with the Date and other northern daimyo. As a reward for his help in the campaign against the Hōjō, Hideyoshi awarded Tokugawa Ieyasu, potentially his most dangerous opponent, lands yielding 2,500,000 *koku* of rice (a *koku* equals about five bushels) and ordered him to move his base farther east to Edo. All of Japan now belonged to Hideyoshi or to his sworn vassals.

With Japan now wholly pacified, Hideyoshi returned to his dreams of foreign conquest and imperial grandeur. In 1592 he declared war on China and launched an invading army into the Korean peninsula. Again the daimyo, especially the western daimyo, were ordered to raise huge troop levies. Thirty-two daimyo led more than 150,000 samurai in the main force. Under other daimyo 100,000 samurai brought up the reserves, and they were supported by a navy of 9,000 sailors raised by four daimyo. By the summer of 1593 it was clear that the invasion was failing and Hideyoshi was forced to find some way to extricate his armies without loss of face. In 1597, angered by the Chinese emperor's rejection of his peace terms, Hideyoshi launched a second invasion but with no greater success. The ill-fated and bloody campaigns cost thousands of Korean, Chinese, and Japanese lives and helped poison future relations between Japanese and Koreans. Out of the misery, however, came one cultural benefit for the Japanese. Daimyo fighting in Korea captured many Korean craftspeople and shipped them back to Japan. Among them were groups of Korean potters who built kilns in northern and southern Kyushu and raised the aesthetic and technical level of Japanese pottery.

While Hideyoshi was extending his military control he was also pushing through a social transformation that affected the daimyo and every other group in Japanese society. Enlarging on the example set by Nobunaga and some of the *sengoku* daimyo, Hideyoshi (beginning in 1584) ordered his officers to conduct land surveys of the provinces using standardized measures, so that the ruler, as well as the daimyo, would know the resources of the domains and the country. Land was assessed for tax purposes on the basis of its estimated annual yield measured in *koku*. This practice provided a basic module for grasping the worth of land, amounts due in taxation or levies, military obligations, and the stipends of daimyo and their samurai. Daimyo would in future be ranked in terms of the total anticipated yield (*kokudaka*) of the territory they held. Assignments of domain were made not in terms of specific villages or pieces of territory but in units of 10,000 *koku*, drawn from however many villages in the locality it took to provide that income. This made it easy for Hideyoshi to regulate daimyo income or move daimyo and provide them with an appropriate *koku* income elsewhere. After Hideyoshi's land surveys it was calculated that the total *kokudaka* for the country was approximately 18,000,000 *koku*. Hideyoshi and some 200 daimyo drew upon this tax base, with a small share going to the imperial court and Buddhist temples. Of this total *kokudaka*, Hideyoshi claimed 2,000,000 *koku*, 36 daimyo held domains assessed at 100,000 *koku* or more, and 68 daimyo were assessed at the minimum for a daimyo of 10,000 *koku*. The largest assessments among Hideyoshi's vassal daimyo included Tokugawa Ieyasu at 2,400,000 *koku*, Mōri Terumoto 1,205,000, Uesugi Kagekatsu 1,200,000, Maeda Toshiie 835,000, Date Masamune 589,000, and Ukita Hideie 574,000 *koku*. Hideyoshi also transformed society by disarming villagers and forcing samurai, who until then had lived in the villages, to choose between staying in the villages as farmers or keeping their swords and their hereditary profession of arms but moving into garrison towns as stipended vassals. Daimyo were ordered to collect swords, bows, spears, muskets, and other weapons from farmers and deliver them to Hideyoshi. The enforcement of this policy went a long way toward the implementation of the four-part status hierarchy of samurai, farmers, artisans, and merchants that was to characterize Japanese society in the seventeenth and eighteenth centuries.

Even before the last of his daimyo and their armies had returned from Korea to Japan, Hideyoshi was dying. In a final desperate attempt to establish a warrior dynasty he set up a council of five powerful daimyo to serve as regents for his five-year-old son Hideyori. In spite of their oaths of loyalty to Hideyoshi, they, and other daimyo throughout the country, immediately began to intrigue and vie for supremacy. Daimyo were again forced into fateful choices. While one faction continued to support the Toyotomi cause, others clustered around the patient and powerful eastern daimyo Tokugawa Ieyasu. The issue was decided on the Plain of Sekigahara in 1600 when supporters of the Toyotomi were routed in a great battle involving 160,000 samurai. Three years later Tokugawa Ieyasu received the title of *Seiitaishōgun* and consolidated his *bakufu*, and in 1614–1615 destroyed the remnant of the Toyotomi faction after the siege of Osaka Castle. After centuries of instability, war, and conquest, Japan settled into two centuries of peace, the *Pax Tokugawa*, under the carefully balanced system of shogunal and daimyo rule known as the *baku-han* system.

The century of transition from civil war through conquest and national reunification to peace wrought significant institutional changes in the character of the Japanese daimyo. This unification did not in any sense involve the eradication of the daimyo. Although individual daimyo houses were eliminated, the daimyo as a whole survived the process of political reunification and were entrenched by it. It was the daimyo Oda Nobunaga and Tokugawa Ieyasu who started and finished the sixteenth-century unification. All three unifiers relied on daimyo allies to marshall military forces, lead campaigns, and rule the provinces. Each of the unifiers, to one degree or another, shared power with daimyo in whatever political settlement they achieved. In this sense, the process of national unification in the sixteenth century ultimately remained incomplete. Two and a half centuries later, in the upheaval of the Meiji transformation, the daimyo were more harshly treated. They, too, were swept aside along with the shogunate they had sustained.

During the sixteenth century, while many older daimyo families were crushed, other daimyo were successful in building large and powerful domains as the scale of warfare and the opportunities for receipt of huge spoils and generous patronage increased. Responding to military necessity and the examples of Nobunaga and Hideyoshi, they consolidated their domains by centralizing their military organizations, controlling satellite castles, converting their samurai from landed vassals living on their own small fiefs to stipended officials attached to the lord's garrison, surveying land, disarming of the peasantry, and maximizing tax yield. Many daimyo maintained grandiose castles and mobilized thousands of samurai.

At the same time the independence of the daimyo was being steadily circumscribed as decentralized political authority was recentralized under three increasingly powerful hegemons. While daimyo were asserting their authority over their own domains they now had to seek their legitimacy from higher authority. They could only feel secure if they had been confirmed in their territories by Nobunaga or Hideyoshi. Moreover, heirs in their turn had to secure confirmation to the headship of the domain. Nobunaga and Hideyoshi exerted increasingly tighter control over daimyo, crushing some, and by such shows of power intimidating others into vassalage or alliances. After 1590 all the daimyo of Japan acknowledged Hideyoshi as their overlord. Vassal daimyo who resisted stood to lose all or part of their domains. The hegemons sought to regulate adoptions, marriage ties, and other alliances among daimyo.

> Item [1]: In marriage relationships, the daimyo should obtain the approval of the ruler [Hideyoshi] before settling the matter
> Item [2]: Greater and lesser lords [daimyo and shōmyō] are strictly prohibited from entering deliberately into contracts [with each other] and from signing oaths and the like
> (Berry 1982, 144).

The hegemons moved daimyo from one domain to another, either as punishment or to prevent the formation of local daimyo alliances and the tendency for lands held in grant to become hereditary property. And they constantly drew on them for military service, castle building, guard duty, and for gifts, hostages, concubines, wives, and entertainment.

Daimyo culture in the sixteenth century: the castle in war and peace

During the wars of the late fifteenth and early sixteenth centuries, as we have seen, men of culture had abandoned the devastated capital region for refuge in the provinces and the focus of daimyo culture had been the residences of those provincial daimyo whose cultural enthusiasm made them hospitable to such refugees. From the mid-sixteenth century, as Nobunaga and Hideyoshi secured control over the country, the Kyoto region (Kyoto, Sakai, and Osaka) again became the center of cultural leadership. This epoch is frequently known as the Azuchi-Momoyama era after Nobunaga's great castle at Azuchi and Hideyoshi's citadel at Momoyama. These towering castles were symbols of the power and ambition not only of the unifiers but of the daimyo who followed them in warfare and cultural style. Daimyo took their cue from Nobunaga and Hideyoshi who reveled in ostentatious self-glorification to exalt and legitimize their newly won political and military supremacy.

Moreover, the unifiers exploited the gold and silver mines of Japan and drew on the profits of foreign trade as well as the spoils of military conquest. Thus a second characteristic of Momoyama-period daimyo cultural style was its lavish and gilded grandiosity. The massive walls, vast audience chambers, and soaring donjons of great castles became one of the central cultural symbols of the age. Third, as Nobunaga, Hideyoshi, and the daimyo contributed, through their patronage of tea masters like Sen no Rikyū, to the articulation of an aesthetic of cultivated restraint, quasi-rusticity, and assumed poverty, *wabi*, the small, rustic-style tea room became another powerful cultural symbol. Fourth, daimyo culture in the late sixteenth century was open to the influence of Europe as many daimyo accepted Christianity or tolerated its acceptance by their vassals and villagers. At the same time, the sixteenth-century daimyo were the inheritors and promoters of medieval culture in that they continued to patronize Nō and Kyōgen, and to study *waka* and *renga*. In all of these aspects daimyo, like the unifiers, treated culture not merely as a personal vocation but as an expression and legitimation of their political and military power. Daimyo recognized that the complete ruler's cultural superiority was as important as military or political hegemony; that it was in fact an expression of that hegemony.

In 1576, a year after his victories over the Takeda in the Battle of Nagashino and the *ikkō* followers in Echizen and Kaga, Nobunaga set in motion the building of a magnificent new seven-story castle at Azuchi, overlooking Lake Biwa. Unlike most previous Japanese castles, which were spartan military fortifications, Azuchi Castle was designed to be at once a vast fortress resistant to gunfire, a princely residence, and an impressive stage for the public display of political power. In this Azuchi was among the predecessors of the many castles built for political purposes in the late sixteenth and seventeenth centuries. Befitting the residence of the lord of the realm, Azuchi was the physical symbol of Nobunaga's control over the realm, his *tenka*. Here he could hold lavish ceremonies and entertainments—the castle contained a Nō stage, tea ceremony rooms, and a Buddhist chapel—and display his power and majesty to courtiers, daimyo, Buddhist monks, and Christian missionaries who filled its audience chambers. Nobunaga commissioned Kano Eitoku to decorate walls, sliding partitions with large-scale paintings and folding screens. Some were in ink monochrome but many involved lavish use of gold pigment, gold leaf, lacquer, and vermilion, and other vivid colors. The huge scale of the paintings and their themes of giant pines, vast landscapes, birds and flowers, sages and immortals, were intended to overwhelm the viewer and to assert Nobunaga's political authority and domination of the *tenka*. Paintings on Confucian, Daoist, and Buddhist themes were related to the public or private functions of the rooms. A private study on the seventh floor, at the very pinnacle of the castle, was painted in gold pigment and vivid colors with Chinese founding emperors and Confucian sages symbolizing Nobunaga's claim to legitimate authority over the *tenka* (Wheelwright 1981a).

Hideyoshi, too, used his castles as political and cultural statements of power; as fortresses and princely residences. In Hideyoshi's great castle-residences of Jurakutei in Kyoto, Osaka Castle, and Momoyama in Fushimi, just south of Kyoto, he too had Kano Eitoku and other painters produce great screens and strongly colored wall paintings. The Jurakutei in particular was the nerve center for his patronage and control of emperors, courtiers, and daimyo. In 1588 Hideyoshi entertained Emperor Go-Yōzei, ex-Emperor Ogimachi, and their courtiers for five days at the Jurakutei. There they mingled with Hideyoshi and his vassals, were given precious gifts, and joined with daimyo in lively, and sometimes drunken, *renga* sessions. Hideyoshi also used the Jurakutei to entertain his vassals at tea ceremonies and Nō performances and granted land around the palace to favored vassals as sites for their own elaborate mansions.

Nobunaga and Hideyoshi were not the only builders of great castles. During the 1580s and 1590s there was a spate of castle destruction and reconstruction as daimyo fell and others rose to power and favor. In 1581 Toyotomi Hideyoshi, still a retainer of Nobunaga, was granted a castle at Himeji, which he fashioned into one of the most perfect examples of Japanese castle architecture. In 1600 Himeji Castle passed to the Ikeda daimyo family for their services to Tokugawa Ieyasu. The Hōjō castle at Odawara, until then the greatest in the Kanto, fell to Hideyoshi after a seven-month siege in 1590, but in the same year Tokugawa Ieyasu, still a daimyo, began the expansion of a castle at Edo that was to become the core of the most populous city in Japan. Katō Kiyomasa, one of Hideyoshi's leading daimyo, built the great castles of Nagoya and Kumamoto. Fine surviving castles were built at Matsumoto in 1597, and by the Ii family in Hikone in 1606. Each of these castles was at once a fortress, center of local rule, palatial residence, and node of cultural activity.

Hideyoshi and Nobunaga were both inveterate patrons of the arts and skillful exploiters of art as an assertion of power. With many daimyo, and a growing number of Sakai merchants, they shared a passion for the tea ceremony (chanoyu). Nobunaga studied tea with Sakai tea masters including Imai Sōkyū (1520–1593), Tsuda Sōgyū (d. 1591), and Sen no Rikyū. He gave tea utensils as rewards for meritorious service in battle and granted to certain few daimyo, as a mark of outstanding favor, the right to give formal tea ceremonies. Hideyoshi, a hard-bitten individual, professed himself moved to tears at the favor. Nobunaga also obliged his daimyo to surrender to him famous tea bowls or other utensils that he particularly liked. Not renowned for his literary accomplishments, Nobunaga exchanged congratulatory verses with Satomura Jōha (1524–1602), one of the leading renga poets of the age, when he marched into Kyoto in 1568.

Hideyoshi took chanoyu to unparalleled limits. He lavishly patronized Sen no Rikyū, and no doubt appreciated Rikyū's aesthetic of the small tea room, humble utensils, and spirit of cultivated poverty (wabi,) which Rikyū brought to the appreciation of tea. But Hideyoshi also provided himself with a golden tearoom and the most flamboyant utensils. And when Rikyū displeased him, he ordered his suicide. To his Grand Kitano Tea Ceremony of 1587 Hideyoshi invited the whole population of Kyoto to stroll in the glades, admire his finest tea vessels, and be served tea by himself and the leading tea masters of the day. Inaugurated as a ten-day festival of tea, Hideyoshi himself served tea to more than eight hundred people on the first day, then called the festivities off, feeling, perhaps, that his magnificence had been sufficiently demonstrated.

Although crude in some respects, Hideyoshi seems to have had more time and taste for cultural pursuits than Nobunaga. He realized that among the accoutrements of the ruler, especially a ruler who chose to assume the old court office of Imperial Regent (Kanpaku) to buttress his authority, should be the patronage of such courtly arts as tea, waka, renga, and Nō. As early as 1578 he joined with Jōha in a hundred-link renga sequence to pray for victory over the Mōri family—renga being credited with the capacity to move the gods.

The Nō had declined in Kyoto during the Age of Wars but had been kept alive in the residences of those provincial daimyo who saw themselves as patrons of culture. After Nobunaga's entry into Kyoto and the city's recovery, Nō again began to thrive. Hideyoshi became a passionate enthusiast. He patronized the four traditional schools of Yamato

Nō (Kanze, Hōshō, Konparu, and Kongō), sponsored plays, and gave gifts to actors. While the Korean campaigns were in progress he actually began to study and perform Nō, taking the lead in a dozen plays in the imperial palace. Obviously believing that practice of the dances, chants, and movements of Nō provided a valuable cultural discipline, he obliged his leading daimyo, including Tokugawa Ieyasu and Maeda Toshiie, to perform alongside the actors. Hideyoshi himself liked to play leading roles in plays especially written to record his conquests and other activities. In 1594, for example, Hideyoshi and a retinue that included Satomura Jōha journeyed to Yoshino to view cherry blossoms. The outing later was commemorated in a new Nō play.

Vassal daimyo learned from Nobunaga and Hideyoshi that the scale of their castle walls and chambers, the luxury of interior decoration, and the patronage of artists could contribute to a valuable ambience of power and prestige. They found it expedient and enjoyable to patronize the same men of culture, like Jōha, Kano Eitoku, and Sen no Rikyū, who were patronized by the hegemons. They also shared the hegemons' passion for the culture of tea. Among the great daimyo patrons of tea, known as *suki* daimyo, in the sixteenth and early seventeenth centuries, were Furuta Oribe (1544–1615), Oda Uraku, Nobunaga's younger brother, and Hosokawa Sansai. Oribe was a daimyo with an income of 35,000 *koku* who studied tea with Rikyū and after Rikyū's death came to be regarded as a tea master in his own right. Oribe helped shape a distinctive daimyo style of tea by commissioning large, irregular bowls to suit his own taste and by building tea pavilions—like the famous Ennan tea room—to accommodate daimyo and their attendants. Suspected by Tokugawa Ieyasu of plotting against him at the time of the siege of Osaka Castle, Oribe disemboweled himself. Oda Uraku served Hideyoshi at a stipend of 2,000 *koku*. At the Battle of Sekigahara he shifted his allegiance to Tokugawa Ieyasu and was awarded daimyo status and a domain of 30,000 *koku*. He had studied tea with Rikyū and after the Osaka campaign withdrew to Kyoto and devoted himself to tea. Hosokawa Sansai was the eldest son of Hosokawa Yūsai, a daimyo and one of the major literary figures of the age. With his father, Sansai served Nobunaga. He took as his wife the daughter of Akechi Mitsuhide, a young woman who was baptized and took the name Gracia. When Mitsuhide pressed Sansai to join him in assassinating Nobunaga, Sansai refused and instead gave his allegiance to Hideyoshi, temporarily repudiating his wife. He was rewarded with the headship of Miyatsu Castle. After Hideyoshi's death, Sansai went over to the Tokugawa at the Battle of Sekigahara and was granted Kokura Castle in Kyushu, reestablishing the fortunes of the Hosokawa family. Like his father Yūsai, he was a *waka* poet and painter and a devotee of *chanoyu*. He studied with Rikyū, built tearooms, and collected many famous utensils. Gracia's fate was less happy. Taken hostage by Ishida Mitsunari prior to the Battle of Sekigahara, she took her own life.

The composition of *renga* remained a fashion among sixteenth-century daimyo. Akechi Mitsuhide enjoyed a reputation as a tea man, poet, and man of culture. A few days before he assassinated Nobunaga, Mitsuhide is said to have participated in a *renga* session with Jōha in which he opened the sequence with a daring verse that could be read as an expression of his intention to seize the realm for himself:

toki wa ima	Now is the time
ame ga shita shiru	To rule all under heaven—
satsuki ka na	It's the fifth month! (Keene 1981, 126).

But the most admired literary daimyo of the age was undoubtedly Hosokawa Yūsai. After early service to the last of the Ashikaga shoguns he served as advisor first to Nobunaga, then Hideyoshi, and finally Tokugawa Ieyasu, who made him lord of Tanabe Castle. He practiced the tea ceremony and calligraphy but was best known for his poetry and criticism. He inherited and passed on a body of aesthetic lore concerning the poetry of the *Kokinshū*, the tenth-century anthology of *waka* poetry, compiled his own collection of *waka*, and wrote a travel diary and several poetic commentaries. Devoted to poetry, he participated in *renga* sessions with Jōha and others. Yūsai was unusual in being a warrior whom courtiers, as well as other warriors, could admire for his literary abilities and excellence in the ways of *bun*.

No discussion of daimyo culture in the sixteenth century would be complete without at least some reference to Christianity. Between 1549 and 1551 Francisco Xavier was received favorably by the Shimazu, Ōuchi, and Ōtomo. Other early missionaries found equal favor among the western daimyo. The Jesuits' policy was to win over the rulers and assume that the ruled would follow. For their part many daimyo responded favorably in the hope that the Portuguese merchant ships that brought guns and other precious commodities from the West would visit their ports. Whatever their reasons, some daimyo were converted, and others at least allowed proselytization in their domains. When daimyo were sympathetic their wives, family members, samurai, and even the farmers in the domain quickly followed suit, as the Jesuits had anticipated. Nobunaga set an example by entertaining Christian missionaries and allowing the building of a seminary at Azuchi. Christian daimyo sponsored the building of churches, colleges, and seminaries. They entertained missionaries and imported books, paintings, and religious objects from Europe. They commissioned screens and paintings showing scenes of the "southern barbarians." By mid-century there was a fad for things Portuguese, including the costumes of the padres. Daimyo and young blades, most of whom had made no spiritual commitment to Christianity, decked themselves out in Portuguese styles and sported rosaries and crucifixes as fashionable accessories. But if some daimyo accepted Christianity easily, most abjured it quickly when Hideyoshi and Ieyasu proscribed it and ordered the eradication of the alien teaching. An exception was Takayama Ukon (1553–1614), who was exiled for refusing to relinquish his faith.

The transition from war to peace: daimyo in the Tokugawa political system

Hideyoshi had dreamed of establishing an enduring dynasty. Shortly before his death he set up a council of powerful daimyo to serve as regents for his heir, the child Hideyori. Not surprisingly, these daimyo had political ambitions of their own. The council quickly broke up into rival factions that drew other daimyo into the conflict. One group led by Ishida Mitsunari, Mōri Terumoto, and Uesugi Kagekatsu supported the cause of the Toyotomi. Another faction, including Maeda Toshiie and Date Masamune, supported the powerful and wily Tokugawa Ieyasu. The battle took place at Sekigahara, near Kyoto, in October 1600. Many daimyo, expecting a Tokugawa victory, made their peace with Ieyasu before the battle, or refrained from active participation. The Toyotomi supporters were routed and fell back on Osaka Castle, where they were finally eliminated in the siege of 1614–1615.

By his victories at Sekigahara and Osaka, Ieyasu had achieved an even more extensive control over the country than Nobunaga or Hideyoshi. He was, in the fullest sense, the master of the realm. Unification was complete. But it was a unification that had been achieved by military conquest based upon the utilization of the feudal loyalties of the daimyo who became Ieyasu's vassals. Ieyasu, a daimyo himself, was therefore not in a position to eliminate the daimyo, even had that notion ever entered his head. His problem was to bend them to Tokugawa authority and integrate them into a "centralized feudal system" of rule. He immediately set about enlarging his great fortress garrison town at Edo, articulating enduring institutions of warrior government, and reordering the structure of feudal society. In 1603 he had himself appointed *Seiitaishōgun* by the court, thus formalizing the establishment of a new *bakufu*. Although Ieyasu could not know it, his victory and the hegemony he established was to endure. The Tokugawa shogunate would survive through fifteen generations until 1868 and provide Japan with two and a half centuries of stability. There were intermittent disturbances by masterless samurai (*rōnin*), sporadic peasant uprisings, and urban riots, but on the whole Japan under Tokugawa rule enjoyed what has been called Great peace throughout the realm (*Tenka taihei*).

The enduring stability was not fortuitous. In large part it derived from policies deliberately adopted by Ieyasu and his immediate successors in the Tokugawa *bakufu* toward the daimyo and other sectors of society. Some of these policies, such as the taking of hostages or the separation of status groups, had been initiated by Nobunaga or Hideyoshi but were extended and systematized by the Tokugawa. Other policies, including the drastic reduction of external contacts and the requirement of periodic residence by all daimyo in the shogunal capital, were, if not entirely new, at least adopted as new by the Tokugawa. Behind all of the major policies enforced by the early Tokugawa shoguns we can clearly see a paramount interest in stability and order, and a concern with the control of volatile factors that might upset a carefully structured political system and contribute to its downfall.

The long period of peace was to bring other benefits. Although in the interests of security and domestic stability trade with the outside world was virtually restricted to Dutch and Chinese trade through Nagasaki, Korean trade via Tsushima, and Satsuma's trade with the Ryukyu Islands, domestic trade and commerce flourished. The rebuilding of Edo, Osaka, and Kyoto and the construction of the several hundred daimyo castle towns created a national demand for materials and financial services. Population increased and urban centers flourished. The population of Edo reached one million by the eighteenth century, while Osaka, the great commodity market, and Kyoto, a city of palaces, temples, and townspeople, each had populations of nearly half a million. In the Tokugawa social hierarchy, artisans and merchants ranked beneath the samurai rulers and the peasants whose labor fed the country, but the merchant's role as broker, provisioner, banker, and moneylender became increasingly central and a wealthy merchant class developed. Although looked down upon, the merchant was indispensable to shogun and daimyo alike.

The long *Pax Tokugawa* had another important consequence. As the prospect of warfare faded from the political consciousness, shoguns, daimyo, and samurai were imperceptibly but steadily transformed from warriors into civil officials and patrons of learning and the arts. The separation of samurai from their village roots and the legal limitations of mobility among the four classes reinforced the conversion of the warrior class into civilian administrators based in castle towns. These salaried or stipended samurai became more dependent on their superiors for their livelihood than their ancestors had been, and therefore their freedom of action was more circumscribed. The Tokugawa regime, fully aware of the dangers posed by unemployed warriors in peacetime, redirected samurai ideals and energies toward loyal administrative service and the arts of peace. The right to bear arms remained the defining characteristic of the *buke*, but the administration of the state became their function.

In dealing with the daimyo, Tokugawa Ieyasu extended Hideyoshi's policy of indirect rule through a daimyo system. The daimyo were more or less autonomous in the internal administration of their own domains and served also as appointed senior advisors and administrators in the central government. However, where Hideyoshi had been content to operate as the head of a small confederation of daimyo advisors, Ieyasu imposed a tighter vassalage hierarchy and a more systematic bureaucratic structure on the daimyo. The Tokugawa shoguns regulated castle repair and construction, controlled intermarriage among daimyo houses, and made use of spies and inspectors. Thus, it was in the Edo period that the role of the daimyo was most fully institutionalized.

The Edo-period definition of a daimyo comprised several vital elements. First, a daimyo was generally the lord of a domain (*han*), responsible for effective rule over the lands and people in that domain. As a symbol of this responsibility a daimyo took an oath of loyalty to the shogun on appointment and was entrusted with the registers of lands and people in the domain. Second, a daimyo in the Edo period, by definition, had to have a nominal stipend of at least 10,000 *koku*, derived from the domain. From the sixteenth century the *koku* became the basic module for measuring income from land, feudal stipends, and the relative standing of samurai, daimyo, temples, and shrines. Third, a daimyo was a direct vassal of the shogun. But not all shogunal vassals with incomes over 10,000 *koku* were daimyo. Some shogunal retainers known as bannermen (*hatamoto*) had incomes of more than 10,000 *koku* but were not ranked as daimyo because they did not head a domain. Moreover, senior retainers of some powerful daimyo such as the Mōri and Maeda had stipends of more than 10,000 *koku* but were not regarded as daimyo. In the Edo scheme of things, sheer military prowess no longer made a warlord a daimyo, and in fact was almost irrelevant to daimyo status. The daimyo houses may have come to power through warfare and military service, but they were increasingly defined in administrative and institutional terms.

Although headship of a domain, direct vassalage ties with the Tokugawa, and a minimum fief of 10,000 *koku* were common features to all Edo-period daimyo, there were considerable differences among the 250 or so daimyo. Ranks and gradations sprang from relative closeness to the ruling Tokugawa house or from the type or scale of the domain. Depending on closeness to the Tokugawa family, daimyo were categorized as collateral or blood-related houses (*shinpan* daimyo) who had become Tokugawa vassals before the Battle of Sekigahara in 1600, vassal daimyo (*fudai* daimyo), and outside daimyo (*tozama* daimyo) who had not sworn allegiance to the Tokugawa until Sekigahara or after. Depending on the scale and coherence of the domain, daimyo were also categorized as holders of whole provinces, parts of provinces, or castles. Most types of Edo-period daimyo are represented in the exhibition.

Closest by blood to the Tokugawa were the collateral daimyo, known as *kamon* or *shinpan*. All of these claimed some blood connection with the main house of the Tokugawa. There were some twenty in this category but the most prominent members of this group were the so-called "three houses" of Kii (555,000 *koku*), Owari (619,000 *koku*), and Mito (350,000 *koku*), all of which had been established by younger sons of Tokugawa Ieyasu. These families provided heirs, if necessary, for the shogunal house. They were powerful and respected and provided advisors to the Tokugawa shoguns. Their large domains were strategically placed to guard the approaches to Edo and Kyoto. At the same time, they were held at a distance as potential rivals and not employed in the exercise of *bakufu* rule.

For officials to staff their huge bureaucracy the Tokugawa shoguns relied on a group of trusted hereditary vassal daimyo known as *fudai*. These were generally relatively small in scale, ranging from 10,000 *koku* to 150,000 *koku*. Informally they were ranked according to the length of their service to the Tokugawa family. At Ieyasu's death there were 90 *fudai* daimyo. There were some 130 by the end of the Tokugawa period. The core of the *fudai* were families like the Sakai, Ōkubo, and Honda who had served the Tokugawa from its early days in Mikawa Province in the late fifteenth or early sixteenth century. Other *fudai*, including the Ogasawara and Ii, had sworn allegiance to the Tokugawa during Ieyasu's lifetime. *Fudai* daimyo and the non-daimyo retainers of the *bakufu* known as bannermen ran the *bakufu* on a day-to-day basis. The senior *fudai* were appointed to the *bakufu's* senior council of elders (*rōjū*) while lesser *fudai* served on the junior council that concerned itself with matters affecting the Tokugawa house. Throughout Japan *fudai* domains were interspersed among those of the less trusted *tozama* daimyo with the duty of reporting to the *bakufu* anything untoward in the actions of the *tozama* daimyo. The larger *fudai* were placed on the perimeters of the Tokugawa domains while smaller *fudai* were generally located closer to Edo.

One very prominent *fudai* family represented in this exhibition was the Ii family of Hikone. Through their history we can see something of the rise of a *fudai* daimyo. They traced their ancestry to a branch of the Fujiwara noble family that was paramount during the late Heian period. Through the medieval period they were local magnates in the village of Iinoya, from which they took the name Ii, in Tōtōmi near the Pacific coast. They were vassals of the Imagawa in the sixteenth century. With the defeat of the Imagawa, Ii Naomasa gave his allegiance to Tokugawa Ieyasu in 1575. When Ieyasu entered the Kanto (eastern Japan) in 1590 Naomasa was rewarded with the largest fief, 120,000 *koku*, in the Kanto. After Sekigahara, where Ii Naomasa was a leader of the Tokugawa forces, the Ii were appointed castellans of Sawayama Castle (180,000 *koku*). Ii Naotaka served in the siege of Osaka Castle. For their services they were raised to 300,000 *koku* and appointed to a new castle at Hikone, which was built by forced contributions on a site selected by Tokugawa Ieyasu overlooking Lake Biwa and close to the imperial court in Kyoto. The Ii were placed to serve as a bulwark of *bakufu* influence in western and central Japan. Throughout the Edo period the family was always active in *bakufu* councils; five Ii daimyo served the *bakufu* in the office of Great Councillor. The last of them, Ii Naosuke, was assassinated in 1860 by antiforeign daimyo for trying to reach an accommodation with the encroaching western powers. During the Meiji Restoration the Ii fief was reduced to 100,000 *koku* before the abolition of the feudal domains in 1871.

The daimyo with the weakest ties to the Tokugawa shoguns were known as outside daimyo, or *tozama* daimyo. The *tozama* had not been vassals of the Tokugawa prior to Sekigahara. They were independent lords, large and small, who had sometimes allied with the Tokugawa, and sometimes opposed them. Some fought with Ieyasu at Sekigahara, others remained aloof or fought against him. Many were loyal to the Toyotomi until that cause was crushed. While those *tozama*, like the Hosokawa, that joined Ieyasu at Sekigahara or gave their allegiance were well rewarded in the Tokugawa political scheme, others like the Shimazu and Mōri who had fought against the Tokugawa were regarded with suspicion. They were treated with deference, but excluded from political decision-making and assigned reduced domains on the periphery of the country. Nevertheless, the more than one hundred *tozama* domains included some of the largest and most populous fiefs in Japan. Those like

32

Satsuma of the Shimazu family and Chōshū of the Mōri family that had been defeated in battle and had been stripped of some of their earlier holdings had relatively large numbers of samurai in their populations. The mid-nineteenth-century challenge to Tokugawa rule that led to the collapse of the *bakufu* and the Meiji Restoration was mounted by samurai from these powerful *tozama* domains that had been excluded from power by the Tokugawa.

Of the great *tozama*, the Maeda (Kaga domain, Honshu), Shimazu (Satsuma domain, Kyushu), Hosokawa (Higo domain, Kyushu), and Date (Sendai domain, Honshu) are all represented by objects in the exhibition. The Maeda were second only to the Tokugawa in scale of fief (102,000,000 *koku*). Their castle town of Kanazawa was renowned for Kutani pottery, fine lacquer, and the painted silk fabrics known as *kaga yūzen*. Their great wealth enabled them to be major patrons of the arts, especially the tea ceremony and Nō, and it is said that they sponsored craft workshops within Kanazawa Castle itself. The Shimazu were a long-established warrior family from Satsuma in southern Kyushu. While many domain economies languished under heavy debts in the Edo period, Satsuma enjoyed profitable control of the Ryukyu Islands, which gave it a monopoly of the precious commodity sugar. Satsuma was famous for its ceramics, a tradition developed by Korean craftsmen captured during Hideyoshi's invasions. Several Shimazu daimyo were noted administrators, scholars, and patrons of the arts. Shimazu Shigehide (1745–1833) was interested in Dutch studies and botany. Nariakira (1809–1858) developed this interest in Western learning into naval and industrial innovations.

The Hosokawa also flourished during the Edo period. For his services on the Tokugawa side at Sekigahara, Hosokawa Sansai was awarded the 359,000-*koku* fief of Kokura. In 1632 his son was appointed castellan daimyo of Higo (Kumamoto) Castle, a larger fief with an assessed yield of 540,000 *koku*. Placed in a position to block any threat from Satsuma to the south, the Hosokawa, although *tozama*, enjoyed the trust of the Tokugawa. Hosokawa Shigekata (1720–1785) was an administrator and scholar who reformed domain finances, instituted land surveys, encouraged local craft industries, and established a domain school for the education of samurai. Date Masamune (1567–1636), known as the "one-eyed dragon," also fought with the Tokugawa at Sekigahara, where he defeated Uesugi Kagekatsu, and in the Osaka campaign. The Date had built up their power in northeastern Japan, and during the sixteenth century Masamune was awarded a fief of 605,000 *koku* by Ieyasu and from 1603 began building a new castle in Sendai. The northeast produced some of the finest horses and swords in Japan. Masamune was a flamboyant figure, famous for his military prowess and elaborately worked armor. Sendai quickly became a northern outpost of cultural style derived from Kyoto and Edo. In 1868 the Date led an alliance of northern daimyo in support of the Tokugawa against the anti-*bakufu* forces led by samurai from Satsuma and Chōshū. Like the Tokugawa, the northern alliance was crushed and the Sendai *han* reduced to 280,000 *koku* before its abolition in 1871.

Having won a clear-cut victory on a national scale, Ieyasu was in a position to reward or punish every daimyo in the realm. In the interests of Tokugawa hegemony and long-term political stability he and his immediate successors completely transformed the political map of Japan. The Tokugawa held as their direct domain (*tenryō*), a huge block of territory (with one quarter of the assessed yield of the whole country) centering on Edo and the Kanto region. They also directly controlled the great cities of Kyoto, Osaka, and Nagasaki and held the major gold and silver mines. Other parts of the country were allocated to daimyo in a carefully graduated and elaborated system. In assigning domains care was taken to reward the Tokugawa vassals and allies, and to ensure the docility and loyalty of the *tozama* lords. *Tozama* daimyo like the Shimazu and Mōri who had fought against the Tokugawa at Sekigahara and Osaka were physically separated from potential allies by loyal *fudai*. The *bakufu* retained the power of confiscating domains, expropriating daimyo, or reassigning them. It used this power of attainder fiercely in the first fifty years of the seventeenth century, in the process promoting Tokugawa vassals within the system and displacing daimyo whose loyalty or administrative ability was questionable. The daimyo were bound by precedent and regulation and surveillance over them was maintained through a system of inspectors (*metsuke*). Daimyo families were forbidden to consort with the imperial court or to arrange marriages with other daimyo without approval of the *bakufu*. Major *tozama* daimyo houses were encouraged to take wives from the Tokugawa family or its loyal vassals. From 1634 a system of leaving family members as hostages in Edo was established and this was quickly expanded into a system of compulsory alternate-year residence in Edo (*sankin kōtai*).

The *sankin kōtai* system was one of the most characteristic features of the joint *bakufu*-daimyo system. It had profound economic, social, and cultural implications for the daimyo, their families, and their domains. All daimyo were required to spend alternate years in Edo in attendance upon the shogun. Even when they returned to their domains they had to leave wives and other family members as hostages in Edo. On a complicated schedule daimyo processions slowly wended their way to and from Edo along the major roads of Japan. They were a frequent sight, especially along the Tōkaidō, and provided the subjects of many Edo-period prints, such as those depicting the *Fifty-three stages of the Tōkaidō* by Andō Hiroshige. Guards on the lookout for any sign of rebelliousness at the checkpoints along the routes were warned to watch for "guns heading for Edo and women leaving." *Bakufu* regulations laid down precisely, on the basis of the *koku* yield of each domain, how many samurai and what kinds of accoutrements were to accompany each daimyo procession.

The implications of this elaborate, ceremonial hostage system were profound. In addition to their castles and administrative headquarters in their *han*, each daimyo had to build, maintain, and staff several residences (*yashiki*) in Edo. Since the daimyo's function in Edo was to attend upon the shogun, or serve in the shogunal government, rigid standards of dress and protocol had to be met, and domains, however poor, had to keep up appearances or risk official displeasure. The enormous costs of this system, with residences in the domain and in Edo and the expense of a large entourage traveling ceremoniously between the two—it took nearly two months for the Shimazu retinue to reach Edo—all fell on the domains, and most heavily on the peasantry whose job it was to produce the tax rice that supported the whole *baku-han* power structure. In order to meet the huge ceremonial expenses of *sankin kōtai*, domain administrations heavily taxed their peasants and even pared down the stipends of their samurai. In many cases they went heavily into debt with Osaka merchants, pledging future crops against loans to pay for the expenses of *sankin kōtai*. Intentionally, or by design, the Tokugawa had developed an elaborate hostage system that also added dignity to shogunal rule, drained many domains of resources that might otherwise have been turned against the Tokugawa, and—by bringing daimyo households into close proximity with one another in Edo—fostered social competition among daimyo that kept their attention away from thoughts of war.

Sankin kōtai also contributed to the massive growth and to the centrality of Edo in the Tokugawa political and cultural world. With more than 250 daimyo retinues coming and going and with hundreds of daimyo *yashiki* carefully arranged around the shogun's castle, Edo became a hub of economic and cultural as well as political life. The vast castle-city demanded a huge service population to meet its needs: temples and shrines were built, and the finest artists and craftsmen throughout the land were commissioned to work in Edo Castle or the residences of the daimyo. The city drew hungrily on the whole Kanto region for produce to feed its population and depended on the two great cities of Osaka and Kyoto to keep it supplied with rice, and other commodities and financial services. And whereas the most vital cultural centers in the seventeenth and early eighteenth centuries were Kyoto and Osaka, by the mid-eighteenth century Edo, with its Kabuki theaters, print shops, booksellers, and entertainment quarters, was setting the cultural pace. While *sankin kōtai* and the focus on Edo contributed to centralization, the continued existence of the *han*, which numbered some 290 at the beginning of the Edo period and gradually sank to 240 or so, meant a continuance of local diversity. This contributed to cultural vitality. But the *han* were closely linked with Edo by the daimyo and his retinue constantly coming and going. Local culture was carried along the highways to Edo, while metropolitan culture was diffused throughout the domains.

As the *sankin kōtai* system took hold, daimyo heirs were born and brought up with their mothers in Edo. In some cases they might not visit the domain until they were young men and had inherited the title of daimyo. They thus grew up sharing the common experience and cultural values of the daimyo residences and the shogunal court in Edo. The domain, which in any case could be rescinded by the Tokugawa, ceased to be home for them and became instead a place of periodic administrative responsibility. Daimyo quickly began to vie culturally in the decoration of their Edo *yashiki*, in bringing local products and craftsmen to Edo, and in employing artists and craftsmen from Kyoto or Edo in their home castles. The frugality and toughness that had been the mark of warrior leaders in the sixteenth century soon began to give way to refinement and ostentation. They also came to share certain Confucian intellectual and cultural values, long maintained by the nobility and Buddhist priesthood but newly relevant to a nation at peace and requiring principles of social conduct and civil administration. The hereditary descendants of the warrior leaders who had fought on the battlefields of Nagashino, Nagashima, Korea, and Sekigahara were thus transformed into an urbanized feudal aristocracy who ruled not by force of arms or demonstrated personal ability but at the pleasure of the shoguns and by an institutionalized, inherited authority. Domains tended to undergo a process of pacification and bureaucratization. Daimyo, as well as their samurai, were transformed from warlords into rulers and administrators, men of culture and local patrons of the arts. Local domain loyalty was shown less to the daimyo for his unique personal qualities of military leadership than to the institutionalized office of daimyo as head of the fief (*hanshu*).

As long as they pleased the *bakufu*, daimyo were entrusted to rule the territories assigned to them. With the approval of the *bakufu*, their heirs might inherit and, after the first fifty years or so, daimyo status tended to become hereditary. In their domains, they maintained governments that were smaller versions of the Tokugawa *bakufu*. The daimyo, as head of the domain (*hanshu*), used his senior samurai officials to govern the domain from a central castle town. Daimyo governance was directed at maintaining peace and drawing tax (*nengu*) from the farmers. Daimyo generally left villages and urban wards to govern themselves under the periodic supervision of samurai retainers. Historians generally describe this joint system of *bakufu* and *han* rule as the *baku-han* system, pointing at once to its centralized and decentralized aspects. While the *bakufu* represented the centralized power of the Tokugawa the *han* represented the local feudal and bureaucratic authority of daimyo. Although subject to oversight and occasional interference from the *bakufu*, the *han* tended to become semi-autonomous local units. Although daimyo were forced to bear the burdens of attendance and residence in Edo and were subject to levies, at the pleasure of the shogun, for the building and repair of castles, roads, and bridges, the *bakufu* lived off the taxes from its own domain and did not tax the fiefs. In return it was relieved of the burdens of local government outside its own direct domain (*tenryō*). Within the *han*, daimyo and *han* governments were relatively free to rule as they thought fit. A few large *han* had natural resources or were able to develop monopolies that kept them out of debt. Most were financially hard-pressed by a rising population and standard of living and by an increasingly monetized economy, and found it difficult to provide adequate stipends for their samurai. Some *han* governments were lax and quickly ran into debt, some were harsh and provoked peasant uprisings and insurrections. Some daimyo were indolent and given only to leisure. Others, however, acquired reputations as diligent, concerned administrators of their domains (*meikun*).

Among these model daimyo were Ikeda Mitsumasa (1609–1682) of Okayama, Tokugawa Mitsukuni (1628–1700) of Mito, Hosokawa Shigekata of Kumamoto, Uesugi Harunori (1751–1822) of Yonezawa (150,000 *koku*), Matsudaira Sadanobu (1758–1829) of Shirakawa (100,000 *koku*) in northeastern Japan, and Shimazu Nariakira (1809–1858) of Satsuma. Common to all of them was devotion to scholarship and Confucian moral standards of rule, to the building of schools and the encouragement of education for samurai, and to efforts to restore *han* finances, bring new lands under cultivation, promote local craft industries, and alleviate some of the suffering created by natural disasters. Matsudaira Sadanobu, for instance, gained a reputation for solicitous government when it was said that nobody in his domain died of starvation during the bitter Tenmei famine that struck northeastern Japan between 1781–1787. As a result, he was called upon by the *bakufu* to serve as councillor of State (*rōjū*) and led a reform of *bakufu* finances and administration. These men could be harsh in their judgments and bear down heavily on the peasantry but they also represented the Edo-period tradition of ethical Confucian-inspired feudal rule at its best.

Daimyo culture under the *Pax Tokugawa*

Throughout the Edo period shoguns and daimyo participated in an elite cultural milieu that expressed the political power realities of the age. This high feudal culture maintained and refined the traditional elite samurai virtues of *bu* and *bun*, with the emphasis shifting increasingly in the direction of *bun*, as expressed in bureaucratization, scholarly activity, and the cultivation of the arts. As the daimyo settled down under the *Pax Tokugawa*, and the rash of attainders of the early decades ended, they came to enjoy a relatively sheltered and comfortable existence within the Tokugawa power structure. The poorer among them may have found it hard to keep up appearances, with the result that they grievously exploited their domains or went heavily into debt. Those with larger disposable incomes, however, had both the leisure and the wherewithal to enjoy peace and the performance of the cultural rituals demanded by their status. Lords of their domains, bureaucrats, and men of culture, they moved in comfortable state, cossetted and guarded, from their Edo residences to their castle towns, and back to Edo. The palanquins in which they were carried were in many ways fitting symbols for the Edo-period daimyo, ferried between Edo and his domain, whose twin *raisons d'être* were attendance upon the shogun and management of his Edo *yashiki*, and administering his local domain. Many daimyo gradually became detached from the social and political realities about them, from the problems of their poorer samurai living on meager stipends, as well as from the hardships faced by the peasantry of their domains. With daimyo periodically in attendance in Edo, actual administration was left in many domains to samurai officials. In a society based on hereditary privilege, daimyo and higher-ranking samurai in the domains were worlds apart from lesser samurai and frequently lorded it over them. They had more in common with shoguns and courtiers and their fellow daimyo than with the mass of samurai or commoners in their domains. A feudal elite, they intermarried with other daimyo families or branches of the shogunal family, whose cultural values they shared, rather than with merchants or lower samurai.

Daimyo culture in the Edo period naturally reflected the political position of the daimyo themselves under the umbrella of Tokugawa power. The manifestations of culture were frequently resplendent and powerful, refined and cultivated. They were also conservative in character, traditional and somehow wanting in the energy and creativity that had been so evident in the Muromachi and Momoyama periods. Although powerfully expressive of the Edo age, daimyo culture was not the most vibrant aspect of Edo-period culture. That accolade belongs to the popular culture of the merchants, craftsmen, entertainers, and ordinary townspeople of the great cities. Daimyo were certainly aware of the vitality of popular culture around them and drawn to the world of the Kabuki theatre, popular literature, and woodblock prints. They were not active contributors to the popular realm, however. Their principal cultural role was that of inheritors and patrons of a traditional and classical Chinese and Japanese aesthetic.

We might suggest that just as the imperial court clung to the cultural style of its halcyon days in the Heian period, so the daimyo tended to idealize aesthetic modes of the Muromachi era. The cultural tone for Edo-period daimyo was set by the Tokugawa shoguns in their edicts and directions to the warrior order. We can distinguish a creative tension. One vital requirement was to preserve that military tradition on which the whole edifice of Tokugawa power rested, to reiterate constantly the samurai traditions of valor, honor, loyalty, and military preparedness. Another requirement was to modulate the military tradition, to tame it, to turn the daimyo and their samurai from the ways of war to those of peace. The path of *bu* was never relinquished in the Tokugawa period but under the *Pax Tokugawa* the inclination to promote the ways of *bun* tended to gain the upper hand.

Preservation of the martial tradition

The *Buke shohatto* (Regulations for military houses), the basic Tokugawa *bakufu* code for the warrior order, opens by urging daimyo to cultivate both the ways of *bun* and *bu*. But it clearly gives primacy to the martial arts, even in an age of peace:

The arts of peace and war, including archery and horsemanship, should be pursued singlemindedly. From of old the rule has been to practice the 'arts of peace on the left hand and the arts of war on the right'; both must be mastered. Archery and horsemanship are indispensable to military men. Though arms are called instruments of evil, there are times when they must be resorted to. In peacetime we should not be oblivious to the danger of war. Should we not then prepare ourselves for it? (Tsunoda, de Bary, and Keene 1964, vol. 1, 326)

The ideal standard for members of the samurai class was to excel in both the literary and military arts, and the shogun and daimyo strove to live up to this ideal. As leaders of the warrior class, they were still required to train in military arts. Ieyasu and his successors could not advocate the complete abandonment of military skills by warriors. There was no knowing when these skills might be needed in support of the Tokugawa or in defense of the nation, the primary responsibility of the *bakufu*. Daimyo and their samurai were encouraged to maintain the samurai tradition of spartan outdoor living, with training in the military skills of archery, musketry, horsemanship, swordsmanship, falconry, and hunting. They were required to keep their castles in repair, and their weapons ready.

The cult of *Bushidō*, the Way of the warrior, emphasizing loyalty and honor, was strengthened by the injection of Confucian notions of proper reverence for superiors and single-minded dedication to the service of one's lord. One of the clearest statements of the Edo period samurai ideal was made by Yamaga Sokō (1682–1685), a teacher of Confucianism and military science, in his moral exhortation for samurai, *Shidō*, in 1665:

> The business of the samurai consists in reflecting on his own station in life, in discharging loyal service to his master if he has one, in deepening his fidelity in association with friends, and, with due consideration to his own position, in devoting himself to duty above all. However, in one's own life one becomes unavoidably involved in obligations between father and child, older and younger brother, and husband and wife. Though these are also the fundamental moral obligations of everyone in the land, the farmers, artisans, and merchants have no leisure from their occupations, and so they cannot constantly act in accordance with them and fully exemplify the Way. The samurai dispenses with the business of the farmer, artisan, and merchant and confines himself to practicing the Way; should there be someone in the three classes of the common people who transgresses against these moral principles, the samurai summarily punishes him and thus upholds proper moral principles in the land. It would not do for the samurai to know the martial [*bu*] and civil [*bun*] without manifesting them. Since this is the case, outwardly he stands in physical readiness for any call to service and inwardly he strives to fulfill the Way of the lord and subject, friend and friend, father and son, older and younger brother, and husband and wife. Within his heart he keeps to the ways of peace, but without he keeps his weapons ready for use. The three classes of the common people make him their teacher and respect him. By following his teachings, they were enabled to understand what is fundamental and what is secondary.
>
> Herein lies the Way of the samurai, the means by which he earns his clothing, food, and shelter; and by which his heart is put at ease, and he is enabled to pay back at length his obligations to his lord and the kindness of his parents (Tsunoda, de Bary, and Keene 1964, vol. 1, 390).

For some, though not all, samurai advocates of Confucianism, a true samurai, if faced with the excrutiating choice between demonstrating filial piety toward a father and loyalty to a lord, would give primacy to loyalty over filial piety. And that classic of Edo-period *Bushidō*, the *Hagakure*, compiled by a samurai from the Nabeshima domain in Hizen in 1716, states repeatedly that the true samurai should think only of dying in service to his lord, and live constantly with the thought of death:

> Wherever we may be, deep in mountain recesses or buried under the ground, any time or anywhere, our duty is to guard the interest of our Lord. This is the duty of every Nabeshima man. This is the backbone of our faith, unchanging and eternally true.
>
> Every morning make up thy mind how to die. Every evening freshen thy mind in the thought of death . . .
>
> Bushidō, the way of the warrior, means death' (Bellah 1970, 91–92).

Bushidō thus became a cult of loyalty, a one-way ethic of loyalty based on an enhanced sense of moral obligation to one's lord. That obligation could be fulfilled on the battlefield or, in the peaceful world of eighteenth-century Japan, by self-denying service and devotion to the most petty details of administration or ceremonial performance.

Although largely untested for two centuries, the samurai martial tradition survived and resurfaced in the mid-nineteenth century when young samurai from *tozama* fiefs, angered at the *bakufu's* inability to expel the Western intruders, took up their swords and turned them against their enemies, whether supporters of the *bakufu*, foreign residents in Japan, or punitive expeditions sent by the Western powers.

Promotion of the arts of peace

While the Tokugawa were stressing the martial ideal for the whole samurai class, they clearly needed to tame the daimyo and their samurai, and to wean them from attitudes and behavior appropriate to a state of war toward a more controlled and institutionalized exercise of power and loyalty. To this end, the number of castles was controlled and the military forces that any daimyo could maintain were strictly limited in proportion to the scale of his domain. Moreover, the building or repair of castles, the making of marriage alliances, and the adoption of heirs were all closely supervised.

Even loyalty to feudal lords, which was officially emphasized on the one hand as the greatest samurai virtue, was increasingly circumscribed. During the early seventeenth century many samurai committed ritual disembowelment (*seppuku*) on the death of their lords, to follow them in death (*junshi*). Many of these acts of *junshi* were sincere expressions of devoted loyalty. Some, however, may well have been performed under considerable peer pressure. Whatever the motivation, the *bakufu* frowned on such expressions of extreme personal loyalty to daimyo and put an end to the practice by threatening to punish the families of any samurai who resorted to *junshi*. The *bakufu* was also troubled by another expression of intense feudal loyalty—the vendetta. The most famous vendetta, as the undiluted expression of the samurai ideal, was the revenge of the forty-seven *rōnin*, rendered masterless by the suicide of their lord, who stormed the residence of the man who had engineered that suicide and killed him. *Bakufu* officials were faced with a dilemma. The *rōnin* had behaved as exemplary samurai in killing the man who had wronged their lord, but the vendetta was a rejection of *bakufu* authority and a threat to public order. The matter was settled by sentencing the *rōnin* to death, but permitting them an honorable death according to the code of *Bushidō* by *seppuku*. This incident found dramatic expression in the Kabuki play *Chūshingura*.

In the interests of stability and order, the Tokugawa encouraged daimyo to devote themselves to the efficient administration of their domains and to arts of peace (*bun*). Tokugawa Ieyasu set the example. Like some of his warrior predecessors, he realized that successful government required equal attention to civilian as well as military arts. He also saw that daimyo absorption in civilian affairs reduced the risk of war and consequent threats to Tokugawa hegemony. According to the *Tokugawa jikki* (Records of the Tokugawa shoguns), Ieyasu was brought up surrounded by battle:

> And he naturally had no time to read and study. He took the empire on horseback, but his natural brilliance and his superhuman character were such that he early recognized that the empire could not be ruled on horseback. He always had great respect for the Way of the Sages and knew that it alone could teach how to rule the kingdom and fulfill the highest duties of man. Consequently, from the beginning of his reign he gave great encouragement to learning (Dore 1965, 16).

Ieyasu seems to have realized that if his regime was to endure, the martial spirit had to be controlled though not extinguished, and the arts of peace, especially scholarship, government, and administration, had to be promoted as appropriate to the samurai. Ieyasu and the Tokugawa had no desire to encourage their vassals in frivolity—daimyo and samurai were officially discouraged, not always successfully, from frequenting popular entertainments and from consorting with actors, entertainers, and courtiers—but they did wish them to devote time to serious scholarly pursuits. Ieyasu himself became late in life an assiduous scholar, or patron of scholarship, who collected books, gathered scholars to lecture to the shogunal court, studied the biography of Yoritomo, and had the *Azuma kagami* reprinted. Just as Yoritomo had gathered scholars from the Kyoto court, Ieyasu employed the Zen monk Ishin Sūden and the Tendai monk Tenkai and the Confucian scholar Hayashi Razan (1583–1657) as his advisors.

As the clamor of battle receded it was natural that samurai should devote themselves not only to the military arts, but also to learning and the fine arts. The shogun and daimyo assimilated and embodied several cultural traditions. From the point of view of heightening the authority of the shogunate it was essential to adopt elements of the aristocratic culture of the Kyoto court, Chinese scholarship, and the teachings of Confucianism as well as traditional Japanese samurai culture. Ieyasu recognized that a new system of values, order, and morality was necessary for the consolidation of the nation under the shogunate. For this, he and his successors encouraged the promotion of scholarship and education for samurai and the cultivation of men of talent. They turned especially to Neo-Confucian teachings, which posited a moral order above the shogun that at the same time legitimated the shogun's position as the just ruler carrying out the will of heaven; it sanctified the Tokugawa hierarchy of classes as being "according to nature," and it offered a code of conduct appropriate to each class. Most daimyo followed suit and patronized Neo-Confucianism, while maintaining a personal interest in Buddhism in the family temple, or in Shinto and National Learning, an intellectual movement developing in the eighteenth century that revived interest in the Japanese classics as the purest expression of Japanese identity. In keeping with Ieyasu's admonition to excel in literary as well as martial arts, the shoguns and daimyo studied painting and calligraphy, as well as the Confucian classics and ancient Japanese literature and history. Ieyasu studied the calligraphic style of the Heian court noble Fujiwara Teika (1162–1241) and painting styles under Kano masters. A few daimyo showed some talent as painters and calligraphers, though most were content to remain patrons and collectors, rather than practitioners of the arts. One of the important contributions of Edo-period daimyo was the cultivation and categorization of a cultural legacy that had been developing in Japan since the medieval period. Enthusiastic daimyo sponsorship of *chanoyu*, Nō, Confucian studies, poetry, and calligraphy, led to the refining of traditions or art and scholarship, and the stabilization of a shared cultural vocabulary.

Peace and relative prosperity in some domains, combined with this encouragement of *bun* by the *bakufu* and daimyo, and stimulated by the coming and going of *sankin kōtai* and the influence of merchant prosperity and urban culture, encouraged many different manifestations of daimyo culture in the Edo period. Nor did daimyo confine their cultural interests simply to Confucian scholarship. Aside from Confucian studies, other fields of study included Chinese and classical Japanese literature including the *Kokinshū*, and the *Tale of Genji*. Daimyo were still expected to be able to compose poetry and to quote with authority from the Chinese and Japanese literary classics.

The daimyo's pattern of life in the Edo period contributed to the patronage of and participation in a variety of traditional arts and cultural activities. Within the castle precincts, the residence of the daimyo was built in the *shoin* domestic style of residential architecture. Here the daimyo held council with his retainers, gave banquets, and entertained guests. Castles and *yashiki* required large numbers of paintings on folding screens and sliding partitions, metalwork, furniture, lacquer and ceramic utensils, and accoutrements. Artists of the Kano, Tosa, and other schools of Japanese painting were kept busy with daimyo commissions. Some daimyo had a particular fondness for expansive screens depicting battles, or such martial accomplishments as falconry, riding, or equestrian dog-shooting. Others collected prized Chinese art objects (*karamono*), especially those that had belonged to the Ashikaga shogunal collection, including celadons, lacquer, incense utensils, books, inkstones, water droppers, brushes, and calligraphy. Others were particularly attached to Muromachi-style *suibokuga* or illustrated handscrolls in the revived *yamato-e* tradition. Genre paintings and scenes of everyday life in and around Kyoto were much in demand in provincial castle towns. Zen painting and calligraphy were still prized, but in general traditional Buddhist iconographic painting and sculpture languished in the Edo period when compared with the medieval period. Daimyo tastes, like those of the country at large, were shifting in more secular directions.

Although daimyo had no opportunities to appear on the battlefield, they still needed swords, armor, muskets, and other military equipment for drills, ceremonial occasions, and as symbols of personal status. In the Edo period only samurai were permitted to bear arms, and the sword, in particular, remained the symbol of the samurai. Daimyo commissioned swords and armor from the finest makers to reflect their rank, status, and artistic taste.

Daimyo were participants in an elite cultural world in which Nō and the tea ceremony were the highest expressions of political as well as cultural preeminence. In this respect they continued to cloak themselves in the cultural trappings that had earlier added prestige to the Ashikaga shoguns. Culture and politics mingled in the tearooms and the Nō performances held in Edo Castle or the daimyo residences, or in the provincial castle towns. Although the Kabuki and the puppet theaters were flourishing among the townspeople of Edo and Osaka and were attractive to many samurai, Nō and its comic counterpart Kyōgen remained the official dramatic form patronized by shoguns and daimyo. Ieyasu adopted it, carrying on the enthusiastic patronage of Hideyoshi, Nobunaga, and the Ashikaga shoguns. Just as *bugaku* had served for centuries as the formal music of the imperial court, Nō filled this role for shogun and daimyo. Daimyo were expected to be able to chant Nō. Ieyasu and Tsunayoshi (the fifth shogun), for instance, performed Nō dances and urged the daimyo to do the same. Annual competitions of chanting and dancing (*utai-hajime*) were held. Every daimyo household was required to maintain a full set of robes, masks, and musical instruments for the performance of Nō. The Hosokawa family had a particularly fine collection, from which many robes and accessories have been lent to the exhibition. Frequent ceremonial performances of Nō were held in Edo and the provincial castle towns. Daimyo vied in sponsoring Nō actors, building stages, and acquiring robes and masks.

During the Edo period the passion for tea (*chanoyu*) spread through all sectors of society. Descendants and students of Sen no Rikyū established the major schools of tea, including the Ura Senke, Omote Senke, and Mushanokōji Senke that are still popular today. Professional tea masters made their livings instructing shoguns, daimyo, samurai, townspeople, and even wealthy farmers in the intricacies of tea and the subtleties of the tea aesthetic. For everybody, the enjoyment of tea was a participatory aesthetic in which some of the more rigid social barriers were temporarily set aside in the small world of the tearoom and all the guests could share in the appreciation of a welcoming tearoom or the host's thoughtfulness in choosing utensils.

For shoguns and daimyo, tea had added associations. Because of its enthusiastic patronage by the Ashikaga shoguns, Nobunaga, and Hideyoshi, *chanoyu* had also become an expression of wealth and power, a vehicle of elite interaction, and one of the central social rituals of warrior society. While shoguns and daimyo in the Edo period patronized tea masters of the various lineages descended from Sen no Rikyū, they also maintained their own traditions of tea, appropriate for the imposing chambers of castles and *yashiki*. Ieyasu himself was a passionate enthusiast of tea and collector of fine utensils. He received instruction from the tea master and man of culture Kobori Enshū, who also instructed Hideyoshi as well as the second and third Tokugawa shoguns. Formal and informal tea gatherings were held in Edo Castle, in the Edo residences of the daimyo, and in their provincial castles. No daimyo could afford to be ignorant of the niceties of correct etiquette or be unable to entertain his fellow daimyo in his own tearoom. Shoguns and daimyo competed in the elegant simplicity of their tearooms and gardens, in their collection of precious utensils, and in calligraphy, to display the *tokonoma* of the tearoom. Most prized were those that had belonged to the Ashikaga shoguns, or to the sixteenth-century tea masters Takeno Jōō (1502–1555), Murata Shukō (1421–1502), and Sen no Rikyū. The daimyo passion for tea also provided a vigorous stimulus for the artists and craftsmen of their own day. The work of the finest carpenters, garden designers, potters, metalworkers, bamboo craftsmen, and papermakers was all in high demand.

The traditions of daimyo tea were established by daimyo like Furuta Oribe (1544–1615), Kanamori Sōwa (1584–1656), and Katagiri Sekishū (1605–1673). The daimyo tea master Furuta Oribe, a 30,000 *koku* daimyo and disciple of Rikyū, is said to have instructed Tokugawa Hidetada, the second shogun, in the art of tea. He was suspected of treason by Ieyasu at the siege of Osaka Castle and forced to take his own life. His students in the art of tea included Kobori Enshū, Hon'ami Kōetsu (1558–1637), and many daimyo. Oribe had innovative tastes in ceramics, garden, and teahouse design, which he transmitted to the daimyo who studied within him. Kanamori Sōwa, the daimyo of Takayama Castle in Hida, was a connoisseur of tea utensils who studied tea and Zen at Daitokuji in Kyoto. In the capital he became familiar with court nobles as well as Zen monks. His tastes in tea aesthetics combined Zen simplicity with courtly elegance and refinement. Katagiri Sekishū, daimyo of the Koizumi domain in Yamato Province, served as tea master to the fourth Tokugawa shogun, Ietsuna. He practiced the more studied, plain, and rustic Rikyū tradition of *wabicha* but was on close terms with Sōwa, Enshū, and other daimyo tea devotees. Sekishū had many daimyo as his students and was particularly influential in shaping daimyo taste.

Some later daimyo devoted such interest to *chanoyu* that they came to be known as *sukiya* daimyo, or literati daimyo. Among these were Matsudaira Fumai (1751–1818) of the Matsue domain, Sakai Sōga (1755–1790), of the Himeji domain, as well as Matsudaira Sadanobu and Ii Naosuke, already mentioned. The enthusiasm for tea was particularly strong in certain daimyo houses such as the Owari branch of the Tokugawa family, the Maeda of Kaga, the Hosokawa of Kumamoto, the Matsudaira of Takamatsu, and the Date of Sendai. As in other fields, daimyo patronage of tea encouraged the refinement and categorization of cultural traditions related to tea. These daimyo patrons were serious students who recorded their tea gatherings, utensils, and aesthetic ideals in tea diaries (*o cha kaiki*). This was part of a much larger phenomenon of daimyo contribution to the elaboration of the cultural vocabulary of the Edo period.

Chanoyu was a major stimulus for the development of daimyo-sponsored kilns as well as for interior design and the codification of flower arrangements for tearooms and for formal arrangements on ceremonial occasions. While Chinese- and Korean-inspired high-fired, glazed porcelain and stoneware remained highly prized throughout the Edo period, the tastes of Sen no Rikyū and other tea masters ran to rougher, humbler Japanese or Korean ware. Rikyū patronized the potter Chōjirō, who made hand-formed, thick-walled bowls. Many daimyo took pride in the kilns and potters within their domains and, in an effort to develop local products, introduced their work to Edo and Osaka. The Ikeda family of Okayama, for instance, took an active interest in the Bizen kilns within their domain. Among the daimyo of western Japan the Shimazu, Kuroda, Nabeshima, Gotō, Matsuura, and Mōri all controlled kilns headed by Korean potters brought back forcibly during Hideyoshi's invasions of Korea. The Nabeshima family of Hizen province in Kyushu, for instance, was engaged in foreign trade, with their own licensed ships plying between Japan and southeast Asia. Nabeshima Naoshige (1538–1618) and his son Katsushige (1580–1657) both participated in the Korean invasions and brought back Korean artisans. Establishing their kilns around Arita, they produced blue and white underglaze and brilliantly colored overglaze wares that won fame throughout Japan and were carried to Europe by Dutch traders. The technological skills of these groups of Korean potters contributed to the great variety and fine aesthetic quality of Edo-period ceramics.

The tradition of flower arrangement was an ancient one in Japan and China but it was given new impetus under Rikyū's instruction that "flowers should be as they are in nature." In the early seventeenth century, Ikenobō Senkō revived the fortunes of the Ikenobō school and other schools quickly developed as the Way of flowers appealed to townspeople, samurai, and daimyo alike. Many of the schools and family traditions in the contemporary arts of tea, flowers, music, and traditional dance owe much to daimyo patronage in the Edo period.

Throughout the exhibition are reminders that a daimyo's life had its private, family side as well as its public and ceremonial aspects. The wives and children of samurai and daimyo did not have easy lives in a feudal society. In the medieval centuries, a samurai woman learned not only to keep house but to use a halberd and exercise a horse. A woman would also be taught how to take her life, if necessary, by stabbing herself in the jugular vein. Women were subject to all the hazards of an unstable age of war. Married in childhood to a youth she might never have met before her betrothal, a wife became the charge of her husband's family and was expected to produce strong sons to carry on the house. In the best of circumstances she might be a partner to her husband in the face of shared dangers. More commonly she would be abused, widowed early, cast adrift, or treated with scant respect by her in-laws. The property rights and political influence enjoyed by noblewomen and the women of influential warrior families in the Heian and Kamakura periods were whittled away under the pressures of war and the spreading of feudal values.

The *Pax Tokugawa* did not bring substantial improvements to the status of women. If anything, their situation worsened. Like the samurai bound more tightly in a Confucianized ethic of single-minded loyalty to a lord, women of all classes were bound by Confucian admonitions of threefold submission: to her husband's parents, to her husband, and to her adult male offspring. This ideal of a *Bushidō* for women found its most vigorous assertion in the *Onna daigaku* (Great learning for women) written by Kaibara Ekken (1630–1714), or by some accounts by his wife:

> However many servants she may have in her employ it is a woman's duty not to shirk the trouble of attending to everything herself. She must sew her father-in-law's and mother-in-law's garments and make ready their food. Ever attentive to the requirements of her husband, she must fold his clothes and dust his rug, rear his children, wash what is dirty, be constantly in the midst of her household, and never go abroad but of necessity. . . (Chamberlain 1905, 506).

The wives and daughters of daimyo in the Edo period were spared some of the worst of the chores, which they could pass on to a retinue of maidservants and wet nurses, but their lives were still extremely circumscribed. Married to men chosen for them by their parents, regarded in many cases as little more than fruitful wombs, they were held as hostages in the Edo *yashiki*. Travel beyond the *yashiki* was infrequent, uncomfortable, and called for special permission. The system of *sankin kōtai*, whereby the daimyo alternated between Edo and their domains, while their women were held in Edo, involved prolonged periods of separation between the daimyo, his senior retainers, and their wives. Inevitably, wives had to cope with insecurity, loneliness, and their husbands' infidelity. Even when a woman enjoyed the devotion of her husband, the Confucian and samurai traditions forbade open expression of those feelings. A samurai like Nakae Tōjū (1608–1648) could earn universal respect by expressing his filial piety to his aged mother by quitting his lord to care for her. Less independent-minded samurai and daimyo were constrained from expressing such devotion to their mothers, much less to wives who, in Confucian thinking, owed them submission. Devotion to a woman could only be a distraction from more important feudal loyalties. There were, of course, samurai as well as shopkeepers who put human affection (*ninjō*) ahead of obligation (*giri*). Such cases were turned into brilliant fiction by Edo dramatists and storytellers like Chikamatsu Monzaemon (1653–1724) and Iharu Saikaku (1641–1693). In real life and in fiction stern duty took a heavy toll on human affection. The Japanese social anthropologist Nakane Chie has argued that the demands of feudal loyalty and male bonding were so intense in Edo-period samurai society that a samurai had "little room left for a wife or sweetheart. . . . [His emotions should be] completely expended in devotion to his master" (Nakane 1970, 71). Women in the upper reaches of Edo-period samurai society therefore had to find what enjoyment they could in their children, in the companionship of other women in the household, in self-cultivation, and in occasional trips for pilgrimage or entertainment beyond the narrow confines of the *yashiki*. Although self-indulgence in any form was frowned upon under the samurai code, sexual dalliance with courtesans was not serious cause for censure and marital fidelity was not expected of a man. Wives, however, were held to higher standards of virtue. For a woman to disgrace the honor of her husband and his family carried the gravest consequences.

The private, or family, aspect of daimyo life also contributed to the arts. Robes for the daimyo, their wives, and family members frequently flew in the face of *bakufu* sumptuary prohibitions against excessive luxury. Ceremonies for the birth of an heir, coming of age (*genpuku*), or marriage of sons and daughters called for elaborate robes, cosmetic cases, new armor, swords, writing utensils, and lacquerware. No expense was spared in commissioning objects from the finest craftsmen, who were encouraged to produce work of extreme refinement. Many of these objects incorporated a pervasive and complex symbolism of design that made them subtle advertisements for their user's level of literary cultivation. Among objects of this kind displayed in the exhibition is a sumptuous lacquer dressing case belonging to the Mōri family. In samurai society, as in Japanese society at large, gift-giving was always an important cultural and political ritual. Daimyo were expected to shower lavish gifts on the shoguns and were rewarded with precious items in return. Elaborate gifts were given at marriage and on accession to power. For these gifts daimyo frequently exploited the special skills and products of artisans in their domains.

The abolition of the feudal order and the legacy of daimyo culture

Probing by Western vessels and the arrival of Commodore Perry's squadron off the coast of Japan in 1853 presented a major challenge to the Tokugawa *bakufu* and the whole Tokugawa power structure, including the daimyo. The *bakufu's* inability to fulfill its mission and expel the foreign menace created a volatile political situation in which younger samurai activists from some of the southwestern *tozama* domains challenged the Tokugawa bakufu and eventually overthrew it in the name of a restoration of imperial rule. Within a few years the new leadership, most of whom were samurai, had embarked on a process of rapid nation building that was to involve a total dismantling of the old feudal order, including the daimyo domains. In the race to modernize and strengthen Japan by introducing institutions, ideas, and technology from the West, the daimyo and the welter of domains they had headed were seen as part of a backward, divisive, and repressive *ancien régime*, too closely associated with the discredited Tokugawa shogunate. It was suggested that the daimyo might be incorporated in a great council of state, but in the first flush of Meiji enthusiasm with calls for rationalization, centralization, the promotion of talent, and "civilization and enlightenment" from the West ringing in the air, the daimyo seemed out of place. They were not subjected to violence and were not eliminated overnight. Some daimyo were called upon to advise the Tokugawa *bakufu*, the court, and the new Restoration government. Gradually, however, between 1868 and 1871 their domains were reduced and their powers shifted to the new government. Distinctions between the various categories of *han* were first reduced, together with the many subdivisions in rank within samurai society. In 1869 the daimyo of those domains that had led the Restoration—Satsuma, Chōshū, Saga, and Tosa—set an example to other daimyo by petitioning to be permitted to return their domain registers to the imperial court. This began the process of preempting daimyo and samurai claims to a land settlement in the Restoration. The new government would buy them out and coopt them politically, but with bonds or cash, not with land. No longer daimyo, they were named "Governors" of their territories and granted one-tenth of the former domain income for their own use.

Within a few years all court nobles and former daimyo would be ordered to live in Tokyo. So that they should not be demoted to commoner status overnight the government created a new peerage in which the old court nobility and the former Tokugawa family and daimyo were given the rank of peer (*kazoku*), that is to say, they were incorporated into a new Meiji elite around the emperor, made up of former court nobles, daimyo, and new peers drawn from the oligarchs who had carried through the Meiji Restoration. This creation of a new aristocracy in modernizing Meiji Japan was clearly intended to conform to European example, but perhaps even more important, to fortify the position of the imperial house and serve as a bulwark against excessive political change or undue radicalism. With the abolition of domains and creation of prefectures in 1871 all daimyo were pensioned off with government bonds scaled as fractions of their former *kokudaka* income. The bonds were later commuted into cash. Those daimyo that had enjoyed the largest incomes in the Tokugawa structure, therefore, tended to fare best under the new Meiji dispensation. Mōri of Chōshū and Maeda of Kaga received bonds worth over a million yen, which at five percent interest annually would have given them annual incomes of more than 50,000 yen, a very large income in Meiji Japan. Most daimyo fared much less well, perhaps enjoying incomes from their bond of between 2,000 and 5,000 yen a year. These were still substantial incomes in the 1880s and 1890s, especially now that they were freed from the responsibility of providing for their retainers as well as their families. As peers the former daimyo had capital and were free to invest in land, railroads, or other enterprises. Some did so very astutely and became among the wealthiest members of late Meiji society; others were less successful. On the whole, however, the former daimyo were very much more favorably treated than the mass of former samurai who were classed as commoners and granted meager financial settlements, most of which were quickly depleted. Politically, the former daimyo made less of an impact. A few entered provincial or national politics. For the most part, however, political leadership was taken by lower-ranking figures, many of whom had connections with Satsuma and Chōshū. By the close of the nineteenth century the early Meiji elite, of which the daimyo were part, was being bypassed by a new leadership that emerged from former samurai or commoner backgrounds.

What of daimyo culture in the post-Restoration era? In the full flush of enthusiasm for things Western in the 1860s and 1870s, the cultural interests of the Tokugawa elite were largely disregarded or discredited. Like all samurai, daimyo gave up their swords, formal robes, and palanquins and took to walking sticks, Western dress, and the railway. Obligatory *sankin kōtai* and attendance upon the shogun had been replaced by freedom of travel and freer social intercourse. In the abolition of the domains they lost their castles and many of their Tokyo residences. In many cases they sold off family treasures. Lesser mortals no longer bowed at their passage and they lost the power to command service from farmers and craftsmen. Where once the classical learning of Japan and China had provided their intellectual framework, they now had to come to terms with new ideas and notions from the West. Prized tea utensils, Buddhist statues, and other works of art were temporarily devalued as attention turned to the assimilation of artistic models from the West.

But not everything had been destroyed and with time came a reassessment of cultural values. Many works of art were acquired cheaply by Western collectors and museums but others were bought by Japanese who were finding new value in their own cultural tradition. Some daimyo retained substantial collections and added to them during the late nineteenth and twentieth centuries. After the fever for things Western subsided somewhat in the mid-Meiji period, Japanese and Westerners alike began to rediscover the qualities of artistic and cultural attainment that had been enjoyed and prized by the former daimyo. Nō and *chanoyu* began to regain attention, ceramics found export outlets, and painters began to revive traditional styles. Many of the elements associated with that elite feudal society that seemed at risk of being completely lost or discredited in early Meiji have since been recognized as among the finest examples of Japanese cultural attainment.

Daimyo and art

YOSHIAKI SHIMIZU

O N THE NIGHT OF THE TWENTY-EIGHTH day of the twelfth month of the fourth year of Jishō, which corresponds to 1180, the sky over Nara, the ancient capital of Japan and center of old Buddhism, turned red. Daibutsuden, the Great Buddha Hall of Tō-daiji, was burning. Taira Kiyomori (1118–1181), the head of the Taira warrior clan (Heike) and Prime Minister who controlled the imperial house and court, had sent his son Shigehira (1156–1184), to confront the hostile monks of Tōdaiji and Kōfukuji, who were sympathetic to the rival Minamoto clan (Genji). Shigehira's men set fire to houses along the roads approaching the monasteries, and eventually to the buildings within. Some 1,700 women, children, and elderly who had sought refuge in the Great Buddha Hall were engulfed by the raging fire and swirling smoke. The head of the colossal bronze Buddha, thirty-two meters high, and then the huge wooden hall, crashed to the ground. The nearby monastery of Kōfukuji met the same fate. Miraculously, the Shōsōin, which housed the imperial art collection amassed by the eighth-century emperor Shōmu (701–756) and which stood only a few hundred yards behind the Great Buddha Hall, survived.

Since the founding of Tōdaiji in the mid-eighth century, the Great Buddha and its hall had been symbols of Japanese Buddhism, which had been supported by the imperial court. The court was now devastated by the loss of the great edifices, inestimable Buddhist icons, and treasures housed within the monasteries. The imperial treasury was empty and its power eroded. There was little reason to expect the Heike usurpers to channel resources into rebuilding Tōdaiji and Kōfukuji. Not until Minamoto Yoritomo (1147–1199), given a mandate by the former emperor Go-Shirakawa (1127–1192) and freed from a twenty-year banishment in Izu, amassed an army of more than twenty thousand men, were the Heike routed. The Genji troops, led by Yoritomo's impetuous half brother Yoshitsune (1159–1189), repulsed the Heike at the decisive Battle of Dannoura in the spring of 1185.

Yet, even before the Heike had been driven from power, and within a month after the burning of Tōdaiji and Kōfukuji, the court of Kyoto had ordered the reconstruction process to begin under the leadership of a monk of Tōdaiji, Shunjōbō Chōgen (1121–1206). Chōgen energetically pursued the task, raising much-needed funds and traveling to China to engage an expert Chinese bronze caster. He also found timbers in Suō and brought them to Nara. A replica of the bronze colossus was dedicated in the eighth month of 1184, in the presence of both the cloistered emperor Go-Shirakawa and Yoritomo, who traveled from Kamakura to attend the ceremony. Ten years later, the reconstruction of the Great Buddha Hall also was completed. It was the first major public project accomplished by a new coalition that included the court, the Genji warriors, and the clerics, and a symbol of the new era of stewardship of the affairs of the state by the warriors.

When the Genji warrior clan established its government at the end of the twelfth century, many Japanese artistic traditions already had been in place for more than two centuries. Buddhist temples and Shinto shrines had their own workshops of painters called *edokoro*, the name based on the earlier and more official body within the imperial palace. Sculptural traditions had been firmly based in Nara as well as in Kyoto. Out of the new creative impetus generated by the reconstruction projects at Tōdaiji and Kōfukuji emerged the Kei school and its new style. Its stylistic influence extended to the east, centered around Kamakura, the seat of the warrior government. The sculptor Unkei (d. 1223), who along with his father, Kōkei, led the campaign to restore the Buddhist icons at Nara, propagated a style that took root under the patronage of Hōjō Tokimasa (1138–1215), the warrior chieftain in the east.

Meanwhile, new Buddhist monasteries were being built in Kamakura. Zen temples with new architectural features based on Chinese models were founded during the period of renewed, sustained contact with mainland China encouraged by the Hōjō regents in Kamakura. In the fourteenth century, especially, hundreds of Japanese Zen pilgrims went to China, many for sojourns of ten to fifteen years. Chinese monks also visited Japan at the invitation of the patrons of Zen monasteries, the Hōjō family members (cats. 47, 54, 55). The Chinese emigré monks were great teachers of sinology as well as religion. The cultural fringe benefits that Chinese Chan (Zen) Buddhism brought to Japan were enthusiastically received by the new warrior elite, who as patrons had found something new, something that had not been handed down to them by the old régime.

Renewed contacts between Japan and China led to the adoption of two Chinese painting traditions: the Song Dynasty portrait tradition, and an ink painting tradition that incorporated new subject matter and techniques. Chinese paintings at Butsunichian, a sub-temple Engakuji and the mortuary chapel of Regent Hōjō Tokimune (1251–1284) included, according to an inventory made around 1365, two new categories of painting: portraits of Chinese Chan (Zen) masters, and ink paintings of Daoist and Buddhist saints, landscapes, and flowers and birds.

When Yoritomo accepted the title *Seiitaishōgun* in 1192 he probably was uncomfortable with the idea that he had also inherited the stewardship of the arts and culture, which had always been the province of the aristocrats. His painted portrait, perhaps the single most important painting in this exhibition, presents him in courtly attire (cat. 1). The painting is part of a set of three portraits at Jingoji that survive from an original set of five: Go-Shirakawa at the center; a courtier; two Taira clan members, one of them Shigemori (1138–1179); and Yoritomo. Yoritomo appears aristocratic, despite evidence that he was in fact anything but that. His occasional complacency toward the arts is demonstrated by his refusal, during the ceremony to dedicate the reconstructed Great Buddha at Nara, to view paintings from Go-Shirakawa's extraordinary personal collection. Without seeing even a single work, Yoritomo returned the paintings to Go-Shirakawa.

Yoritomo's response to art contrasts strongly with Kiyomori's attitude toward it. In 1170 Kiyomori and Go-Shirakawa together visited the Shōsōin collection in Nara to view the art treasures amassed since the time of the emperor Shōmu. The history of the warrior-rulers' relation to art collecting from the time Yoritomo became shogun to about 1615, when the Tokugawa shogunate was formed in Edo, in fact reveals a pattern of emulation by each ruler of earlier precedents. Each daimyo referred to examples set by his antecedents and superiors, always conscious that mastery of both *bun* and *bu* were expected of a warrior. Through the thirteenth century, the shogun did not make official visits to the Shōsōin, but in the late fourteenth century and throughout the fifteenth century, when the Ashikaga shoguns established their government in Kyoto, the official visit once again became an important event. Ashikaga Yoshimitsu (1358–1408) and the courtier Regent Nijō Yoshimoto (1320–1388) viewed the Shōsōin treasures that were especially selected for a display at a Nara temple in 1385, and it was Yoshimitsu, followed by his successors, who amassed the Ashikaga shogunal collection of Chinese paintings and other art objects. Both Ashikaga Yoshinori (1394–1441) and Yoshimasa, whose portraits are included in this exhibition (cats. 5, 6), payed homage to the Shōsōin and viewed its treasures in 1429 and 1465 respectively. Later, in 1574, Oda Nobunaga (1534–1582), the daimyo of Owari, made a special visit to the famous collection. Art collecting played an important role in that it reminded rulers to attend to the arts as well as to political and military business. From Ashikaga Yoshinori's collection of Chinese art, some twenty works survive, each stamped with his collection seal, *Zakkashitsuin* (cat. 100). Ashikaga Yoshimasa's collection of Chinese painting at Higashiyama was so prestigious that even after its dispersal, items from his collection continued to be called *gyomotsu* or "honorable objects," as late as the eighteenth and nineteenth centuries.

The upper-class warriors had close connections with the Zen establishment, and maintained relationships at various levels. For example, the Ōuchi family of Suō patronized Nanzenji in Kyoto as well as Zen temples in their home province. Warrior families would also send their sons to Zen monasteries for sinological education. Some daimyo families would actively patronize a particular sub-temple, or even found one; the sub-temple would usually become the family mortuary temple. The Jukōin at Daitokuji for the daimyo family of Miyoshi and the Shinjōin sub-temple at Tenryūji for the Hosokawa are two such examples.

Their patronage of the Zen establishment naturally led some daimyo to become accomplished poets and men of letters, worthy of being commemorated in paintings inscribed by a host of erudite Zen monks. Inscriptions on an early fifteenth-century painting of a mountain villa (cat. 85) praised Ōuchi Morimi (1377–1431), constable of Suō, for his wisdom as a ruler and for his talent as an accomplished poet. Another daimyo, Yamana Tokihiro (1367–1435), was a regular member of a poetry salon organized by Zen monks of Nanzenji in Kyoto under the patronage of the Ashikaga shogun Yoshimochi (1386–1428; cat. 83). Yoshimochi himself was an inspired amateur painter, and some of his surviving works show a high artistic level (cat. 80). Among the artistic daimyo of the fifteenth century some showed an understanding of art surpassing that of their ecclesiastical counterparts. Hosokawa Shigeyuki (1434–1511), daimyo of Sanuki Province, was a collector of Chinese paintings. Upon his retirement from military and administrative duties he became a Zen priest. When Ōsen Keisan (1429–1493), a scholar-monk, visited Shigeyuki, the aging warrior told the monk that he wished to show him a landscape that he himself had painted on his recent trip to Kumano and other scenic spots on the Kii peninsula. When the scroll was opened there was nothing but a blank sheet of paper. The monk, struck by the emptiness of the painting, offered these words of praise:

> Your brush is as tall as the Mount Sumeru
> [cosmic mountain in Buddhism]
> Black ink large enough to exhaust the great earth;
> The white paper as vast as the void that swallows up all illusions.

For a daimyo to outwit a Zen monk, as Hosokawa Shigeyuki did, or to join a literary salon, as other Muromachi-period warriors did, was to partake of a private experience. By the second half of the sixteenth century, however, the artistic activities of warriors began to take on public character. Especially when warrior patrons employed painters to decorate their houses, the paintings were meant to be displayed in a large room that had a social, public function. From the second half of the sixteenth century through the early part of the seventeenth, professional painters' ateliers emerged independent of establishments such as the Buddhist temples and Shinto shrines; in order to meet effectively the needs of different clients that included a growing number of warrior families. Foremost among the ateliers was that of the Kano, who were employed by military hegemons such as Oda Nobunaga and Toyotomi Hideyoshi to decorate the interiors of their mansions and castles, as well as the Buddhist temples they patronized. This period, called the Momoyama, saw a turning point in Japanese history, away from the medieval to the pre-modern age. The art of the Momoyama period eloquently illustrates this transition.

Throughout Japan, the second half of the sixteenth century was marked by a great surge of construction, as warriors built fortified castles. Few castles survive from the sixteenth century, known as the Age of the Wars, and the interior paintings also were destroyed. Castles still extant are mostly from the Edo period. Sliding door panels from Nijō Castle in Kyoto (cat. 125) and from Nagoya Castle (cats. 126, 127) are included in the exhibition, but they are about a generation or two later than typical Momoyama sliding doors.

Two important sixteenth-century castles that were destroyed were Azuchi Castle on Lake Biwa, to the east of Kyoto, and Fushimi Castle, to the southeast of Kyoto. Azuchi Castle was built in 1576 for Oda Nobunaga, and Fushimi Castle in 1594 for Nobunaga's trusted vassal Toyotomi Hideyoshi (1537–1598). The two men brought military leadership and political unification to Japan during the second half of the sixteenth century, and also were the major patrons of painting. In 1576, Nobunaga ordered his vassal Akechi Mitsuhide (d. 1582), the man who would kill Nobunaga six years later, to superintend the construction at Azuchi. A detailed description of the building and decoration campaigns was recorded by a chronicler who compiled Nobunaga's biography. The lengthy description of the paintings distributed throughout the castle includes mention, in the seven-story-high central structure, of numerous paintings by Kano Eitoku (1543–1590), his son Mitsunobu (c. 1565–1608), and their assistants.

Kano Eitoku was the fourth-generation head of the Kano family of professional painters. Since the late fifteenth century the family had served powerful patrons, including the Ashikaga shoguns. Masanobu, (1434–1530) the founder, painted for Ashikaga Yoshimasa, and was employed in exclusive service by the shogunate. The Kano painters specialized in what their contemporaries called "Chinese mode" painting. Motonobu, Eitoku's grandfather and the son of Masanobu, was the champion of this tradition during the first half of the sixteenth century.

A typical example of Kano Motonobu's work is the set of four sliding door panels from Reiun'in exhibited here (cat. 97). During the Momoyama period, the various studios operated by the Kano family members contracted to execute specific projects, and Eitoku's studio was very much in demand. In fact Eitoku was so busy with the commissions that came from Nobunaga and Hideyoshi that the artist could hardly take care of his own household. At Azuchi, Eitoku, Mitsunobu, and assistants executed panel paintings in ink and gold. The paintings of Buddhist subjects and Chinese Confucian, and Daoist narrative themes were on the upper floors. Landscapes and paintings of flowers and birds and animals were distributed throughout the lower floors. Although the Azuchi paintings have been destroyed, the evidence of other surviving works contemporary with Eitoku, including the set of sliding door panels from Myōrenji (cat. 121), permits us to speculate that the Azuchi panels must have been monumental, brilliant due to the lavish use of gold, and dynamic in design. In 1582 Nobunaga was assassinated, and Hideyoshi assumed control of military affairs and the government. In 1583 he began the construction of Osaka Castle and commissioned Eitoku and his atelier to decorate its interior. None of the panels survived the fall of the castle to the Tokugawa forces in 1614 and 1615, but Eitoku's legacy is unabashedly reflected in the style of a monumental composition by Kano Tan'yū (1602–1674), Eitoku's grandson and painter in service to the Tokugawa shogunate. The Kano style patronized by the shogunate in turn became a model emulated by the various daimyo who caused artistic styles to be disseminated in the provinces during the Edo period.

The monumental and heroic style of painting associated with Eitoku cannot be separated from the mood of the age and the personality of his major patron, Hideyoshi. Hideyoshi's personality and artistic temperament were complex and even contradictory; he aspired to be stoic, but could not resist epicurean pursuits. On one hand he sought the rusticity of a humble tearoom, and on the other, he displayed ostentatiously a gold tea house in his castle mansion in Osaka, of which a description survives: "from the *tatami*-matted floor to the ceiling, from pillar to the cross beams, all were covered with gold; teabowls, kettle, spoon, everything was gold." Yet Hideyoshi was an enthusiastic patron of indigenous Raku wares, characterized by simplicity and directness of form and color (cats. 285, 286). In Hideyoshi the timbre and behavior of the ruthless military hegemon seem to have been conditioned by the famous art objects he owned.

Particularly during the last quarter of the sixteenth century, many famous art treasures once in the collections of the fifteenth-century Ashikaga shoguns had been broken up. Individual paintings and artworks fell into the hands of daimyo in the provinces or entered the collections of wealthy merchant-aesthetes and tea adepts in Sakai, Nara, Kyoto, and Hakata. Written records document the movement and pedigrees of some of the most coveted tea ceremony utensils and Chinese paintings. Both Nobunaga and Hideyoshi had inherited some of the prized works from the Ashikaga collections. A collection inherited by Nobunaga was destroyed by fire in 1582, though some artworks were handed to Hideyoshi who, known for his shrewd and level-headed demeanor during fierce battles, also set up a tea room where he served tea between battles. On the very spot where one's life might vanish like the morning dew, he used and admired the famous teabowls and Chinese ink paintings he inherited from Nobunaga.

In the seventeenth century, when the peaceful Tokugawa shogunate was established, the warrior class continued to serve as custodians, practitioners, and patrons of the arts. Later, following Hideyoshi's example, the Edo shogunate had tea masters in place for generations. The tea master Kobori Enshū (1579–1647) developed his own set of rules of tea aesthetics; he amassed his own collection of art, some of it traceable to the Ashikaga collections and therefore extremely valuable. Such works came to be called *meibutsu* or "renowned pieces." The daimyo and collector Matsudaira Fumai (Harusato) (1751–1818) of Izumo Province built his own art collection. The works that survived from it are called *Unshū meibutsu*, or the masterpieces of Izumo Province. This tradition of recording the pedigree of an object also led collectors to treasure boxes, inner and outer, for paintings; inscriptions on the boxes, either exterior or interior, by a known connoisseur; certificates written by connoisseurs; letters of appreciation by a famous connoisseur, and so on.

For the warrior, the balancing of *bun* and *bu* was easier said than done. In the Muromachi period the arts of *bun* were related to religious devotion or the practice of tea, Nō, or painting, and were more or less confined to private life; thus no conflict existed between *bun* and *bu*. In times of unrest, the public image of Muromachi daimyo like Ōuchi Morimi and Hosokawa Shigeyuki (1434–1511) was based almost exclusively upon their activities as warriors and men of *bu*. The Edo period was a time of specialization. Maeda Tsunanori (1643–1724), daimyo of Kaga Province, gathered samples of handicrafts from throughout Japan, which resulted in an encyclopedic collection known as *Hyakkō hishō*, now in the Maeda Foundation, Tokyo. In times of peace, however, the reconciliation of *bu*, to maintain the warrior's public responsibility, and *bun*, to sustain and embellish the warrior's private world of the spirit, often resulted in tension. Peace itself undermined the very existence of warriorhood and the concept of *bu*. Eventually, the eighteenth century saw the emergence of a group of daimyo whose activities were totally in the realm of *bun*: Satake Shozan of Akita (1748–1785; cats. 136, 137), Hosokawa Shigekata of Higo (1720–1795; cat. 139), and Masuyama Sessai of Ise (1734–1819; cat. 138). All three were natural scientist-artists whose path to their exclusive devotion to *bun* had been paved in the late seventeenth century, when peace was at last assured. In that period of transition, ironic anecdotes surfaced about Hosokawa Sansai (1563–1646), a daimyo and a man of cultivation, who was both a great collector and an armor designer. One story describes Sansai's meeting with Hotta Masamori (1608–1651), who had asked to see the daimyo's collection of tea utensils. Sansai showed Masamori only arms and armor, however. Later, Sansai explained that since one warrior had been visited by another, none other than warrior's utensils could possibly have been shown (*Kansai hikki*, 196). According to a second story, a daimyo from another province sent a messenger to ask Sansai to design a crested helmet for him. Sansai specified that it should be made from paulownia wood in the shape of water buffalo horns. The messenger was puzzled by the choice of such fragile materials. Sansai explained that a helmet crest should break easily rather than distract the wearer, yet the messenger persisted in questioning Sansai, asking how such a fragile helmet could ever be mended. Sansai replied that a warrior in battle should not expect to live another day, and that this was the ultimate law of the military man:

> If a warrior is preoccupied with the breaking of his helmet ornament, how can he handle his own life, which he lives only once? Besides, a crest broken in combat will be truly magnificent to look at. But once life is lost, it can never be replaced.' Having heard this, the messenger asked no more questions, and left (*Okinagusa*, 588–589).

Contributors to the catalogue

AMW Andrew M. Watsky
AY Ariga Yoshitaka
HY Hiroi Yūichi
JIK Janet Ikeda Kohatsu
KS Kawakami Shigeki
MK Matsushima Ken
MR Miriam Ricketts
MS Miyajima Shin'ichi
NK Nedachi Kensuke
NYA Nakamura Yoriaki
NYS Nakamura Yasushi
SH Soejima Hiromichi
SN Suzuki Norio
SY Satō Yasuhiro
TY Takahashi Yūji
WA Watanabe Akiyoshi
YK Yuyama Ken'ichi
YS Yoshiaki Shimizu

Dimensions of all works are in centimeters, followed by inches within parentheses.

All Japanese and Chinese personal names appear in the catalogue in traditional style, with surnames preceding given names.

"Left" and "right" mean the viewer's left and right when referring to paintings, proper left and right when referring to sculpture and robes.

The following words are not defined in the text:

kaō: cipher or stylized signature
shakudō: alloy of copper and gold, patinated black
shuji: character symbolizing a deity (in Esoteric Buddhism).

Chronology

Early historical period
Asuka 552–710
Nara 710–794
Heian 794–1185

Medieval period
Kamakura 1185–1333
Muromachi 1333–1573
  Nanbokuchō (Northern and Southern Courts) 1333–1392
  Sengoku jidai (Age of Wars) 1467–1573

Early modern period
Momoyama 1573–1615
Edo 1615–1868

Modern period
Meiji 1868–1912
Taishō 1912–1926
Showā 1926–present

Chinese Dynasties
Tang 618–907
Five Dynasties 907–960
Northern Song 960–1127
Southern Song 1127–1279
Yuan (Mongol) 1279–1368
Ming 1368–1644
Qing 1644–1911

PORTRAITURE

1 Minamoto Yoritomo

hanging scroll; ink and color on silk
139.4 x 111.8 (54 7/8 x 44)
Kamakura period,
1st quarter of 13th century

Jingoji, Kyoto
National Treasure

A courtierlike figure wearing tailed ceremonial headgear (*kōburi*), carrying a ceremonial sword, and clad in starched formal silk attire (*kowasōzoku*) is seated on a three-layered *tatami* mat. He holds a *shaku*, a wedge-shaped, thin wooden slat, on which the program for a ceremony would be written. His blue sash (*obi*), ornamented with a gold phoenix design, terminates in strands of gold and blue. Its outer borders are decorated with parallel bands of green, yellow, blue, and red and a zigzag pattern in gold. The eyes look sharply toward the right, and the lightly bearded face and neck of the sitter are white, slightly tinted with thin brown washes, starkly contrasting with the red of the robe's lining.

The black outer robe (*hō*), which dominates the composition, is intricately ornamented with floral patterns in lustrous black paint over a ground of matte black, a feature that has become more readable from the recent cleaning and remounting of the scroll. The peony roundels on the white silk undergarment (*shitagasane*) are rendered in pale ink. The hem of the sitter's silk trousers is ornamented with intricate floral and checked patterns of silver leaf, now tarnished. Along the borders of the tailpiece of the headgear are four rhomboid patterns. The painting has suffered damage along the upper border and in the right half of the *tatami* mat, including its sheathing cloth. The green malachite pigment of the *tatami* surface has flaked off considerably, exposing the silk support underneath.

Executed in the consummate pictorial technique of the courtly tradition of *yamato-e* indigenous to Japan, this painting is one of the earliest extant examples of formal secular portraiture. The sitter is traditionally identified as Minamoto Yoritomo (1147–1199), the first shogun who, after defeating the rival Heike, or Taira, clan at Dannoura in 1185, ruled Japan from Kamakura as the chieftain of the Minamoto clan. In 1192, soon after the death of the formidable retired emperor Go-Shirakawa (1127–1192), Yoritomo received from the court the coveted title of *Seiitaishōgun* (Great General Who Quells the Barbarians). Yoritomo became the supreme commander of the warriors and the head of the military government, and concurrently was appointed to Senior Second Rank, a prestigious court rank from which he could claim legitimacy and exert influence. Although medieval military chronicles portray Yoritomo as a suspicious, brutal, and ruthless warrior, the portrait here represents him as a courtly official rather than as a mighty military chieftain.

This painting is part of a set of four surviving portraits at Jingoji; the others are of the retired emperor Go-Shirakawa; the courtier Fujiwara Mitsuyoshi (1132–1183); and Taira Shigemori (1138–1179), the eldest son of Kiyomori (1118–1181), the warrior chieftain of the defeated Taira clan. These four in turn are believed to correspond to four paintings from an early set of five that was once at Sentōin, Jingoji, as recorded in an early fourteenth century document of Jingoji. The fifth portrait of the set, that of Taira Narifusa (fl. 1157–1177), a chamberlain of Go-Shirakawa, has long been lost.

How the ensemble was formed and came to be at the Esoteric Buddhist sanctuary of Jingoji may be partially explained by several interconnected circumstances of the politics played out around the person of the ex-emperor Go-Shirakawa during the second half of the twelfth century. Sentōin was built in 1188 to prepare for an imperial visit by Go-Shirakawa, which took place two years later. Go-Shirakawa and Yoritomo were both associated with the temple through the priest Mongaku (fl. c. 1173–1203), a former warrior who was responsible for much of the extensive rebuilding campaign at Jingoji in 1182, and whose painted portrait also survives at the same temple. Mongaku had angered Go-Shirakawa by plying him with excessive requests for funds for the rebuilding campaign, and was exiled to Izu Province (part of present-day Shizuoka Prefecture). There he met Yoritomo, who had been exiled there also, and their close association began. Later, it was through Yoritomo's support and the eventual funding from Go-Shirakawa that Jingoji was successfully rebuilt.

The courtier Mitsuyoshi played an intermediate role between Go-Shirakawa and Yoritomo when the latter became the power to be reckoned with and an ally in Go-Shirakawa's ploy to be rid of the political influence of the Taira clan. Mitsuyoshi's portrait, in composition a mirror image of Yoritomo, faces to the left. Taira Shigemori, the subject of the fourth portrait, was, unlike his father, favorably treated by Go-Shirakawa and became the Inner Minister of the old regime, but he was dismissed by Kiyomori and died young, before his father. Shigemori's portrait also faces to the left, counterbalancing that of Yoritomo. The entire set when assembled as a group exudes a strong commemorative character and can be seen as an expression of political symbolism.

The surviving four paintings at Jingoji are by different hands, although since the early fourteenth century they have been attributed to Fujiwara Takanobu (1142–1205), a low-ranking courtier serving the re-

1

2

3

tired emperor Go-Shirakawa. A painter with a considerable reputation, Takanobu is remembered as an expert in the art of *nise e* (semblance picture), which often meant depiction in a small format of people in real life. The Takanobu attribution of the Jingoji portraits, however, is not well accepted today. The portraits probably date from the first quarter of the thirteenth century. YS

2 Hōjō Sanetoki

hanging scroll; ink and color on silk
74.0 x 53.7 (29 ⅛ x 21 ⅛)
Kamakura period, c. 1275

Shōmyōji, Kanagawa Prefecture
National Treasure

Hōjō Sanetoki (1224–1276), Hōjō Kanetoki (1248–1301), Kanesawa Sadaaki (1278–1333), and Kanesawa Sadamasa (1302–1333) were members of the Hōjō clan, whose leaders controlled the Kamakura shogunate. The

Hōjō also included the most highly cultured people then in Kamakura. Portraits of these four clan members have been handed down at Shōmyōji; the portrait of Sanetoki, painted around 1275, and that of Sadamasa (cat. 3), painted around 1345, are included in this exhibition. These portraits, divided by approximately seventy years, exemplify the changes in portrait painting of upper-class warriors that occurred during that time.

Hōjō Sanetoki was the grandson of Yoshitoki (1163–1224), the second regent of the Kamakura shogunate. Sanetoki served in various important posts of the shogunate and was assistant to Yasutoki (1183–1242), the third regent, and Tokiyori (1227–1263), the fifth regent. Erudite in Confucianism, he was a strong cultural figure in the Kamakura area. He not only founded the Kanesawa Bunko (Kanesawa Library) and collected books, but also founded Shōmyōji. In 1275 he retired to Kanesawa (present-day Kanazawa, Yoko-

hama) due to illness, and he died the following year. It is not certain when he became a priest, but it seems to have been around the time when he retired to his villa in Kanesawa.

The portrait of Sanetoki is of the type known as a *hottaizō* (clerical portrait). Sanetoki has a shaven head, wears a *kesa* (priest's mantle) over a *hōi* (priest's robe), holds a fan in his right hand and a rosary in his left, and sits on a *tatami* mat. The sitter's countenance is beautifully captured with fine flowing lines, while the straight lines used for his robes display a dynamic movement of the brush. Judging from the lively expressiveness of the portrait, it was most likely painted in Sanetoki's last years or not long after his death, perhaps for such an occasion as an anniversary of his death. AY

5

4

3 **Kanesawa Sadamasa**

hanging scroll; ink and color on silk
77.1 x 53.1 (30 3/8 x 20 7/8)
Nanbokuchō period, c. 1345

Shōmyōji, Kanagawa Prefecture
National Treasure

This portrait of Kanesawa Sadamasa
(1302–1333) is one of four portraits at Shōmyōji representing four members of the
powerful Hōjō family (cat. 2). The youngest of the four depicted, Sadamasa was the
son of Kanesawa Sadaaki (1278–1333). After
serving as shogunal deputy in Kyoto and
as governor of Musashi Province, he
moved to Kamakura and headed the shogunate's office of justice in charge of territorial disputes. In 1333, together with his
father, he fought against Nitta Yoshisada's
(1301–1338) forces and was killed at Yamanouchi in Kamakura.

    In this portrait Sadamasa sits on a *ta-
tami* mat. Formally dressed, he wears a

tate eboshi (erect black headgear) on his
head, a *kariginu* (hunting robe), and
sashinuki (baggy pants tied at the ankles).
In format this is an idealized portrait of a
military leader, more stylized than the portrait of Sanetoki. The carefully painted
face has a thick layer of pigment over
which light vermilion lines are drawn and
vermilion shadows added. Stylistically, this
is a transitional work anticipating warrior
portraits of the Muromachi period. It was
probably painted around 1345, the thirteenth anniversary of his death, long after
the Kanesawa family line had come to an
end and when Shōmyōji had regained its
former influence.

    The inscription in the lower right
corner reads, *Sadamasa, former ruler of
Musashi.*   AY

4 **Ashikaga Yoshimochi**

hanging scroll; ink and color on silk
113.6 x 59.0 (44 3/4 x 23 1/4)
Muromachi period, no later than 1414

Jingoji, Kyoto
Important Cultural Property

Ashikaga Yoshimochi (1386–1428) was the
fourth shogun of the Muromachi shogunate. Yoshimochi is seated on a raised *tatami* mat wearing a headgear known as a
kōburi and a courtier's robe. This portrait
depicts him as the *Naidaijin*, a high official
of the imperial court who assisted the ministers of the Right and the Left, rather
than as the *Seiitaishōgun* (Great General
Who Quells the Barbarians), the head of
the military class.

    His depiction here strongly resembles
that of Minamoto Yoritomo (cat. 1),
painted two centuries earlier: both men
wear the formal regalia of an imperial aristocrat, and the designs on their robes are
Chinese-inspired. Both have their faces set

off by the touch of red at the collar. The comparison of Yoshimochi, in the eulogy, to a "golden phoenix and jade dragon" also reflects the ardent sinophilia of the Ashikaga shoguns and of their times. The eulogy above the figure is dated to 1414, when Yoshimochi was twenty-eight:

> *Portrait of the Seiitaishōgun, Junior First Rank, Administrative Position of Inner Minister, painted from life:*
> *An accomplished man who responds to this world, a golden phoenix, a jade dragon;*
> *Neither common nor saintly; at once a man of the world and a man of the spirit. The brush-tip* [of this writing] *makes an ardent vow for the Diamond Eyes—for a revelation of the Body of the Victory Bodhisattva* [Jizō Bosatsu].
> *Sixth day, ninth month, twenty-first year of Ōei* [1414]
> *Respectfully inscribed by Taiun* [Jaku]*gin of Butsunichisan.*
> [illegible square relief seal]
> *Taiun* [square relief seal]

Taiun Jakugin, who inscribed this eulogy, presumably was a priest of the temple Butsunichisan. Neither the priest nor the temple has been identified. This portrait is at Jingoji, the temple that Yoshimochi patronized.

A small circle surrounded by red appears above the inscription, a symbol, perhaps, of the sun. The circle recurs in another version of Yoshimochi's portrait at Jisaiin, which is dated to 1412. Similar symbols are found also in portrait paintings of the god Hachiman, the titular deity of warriors, suggesting that Yoshimochi, as the head of the Ashikaga family and as shogun, saw himself as vested with military authority and even divinity. MS

5 Ashikaga Yoshinori
hanging scroll; ink and color on silk
74.8 x 38.8 (29 1/2 x 15 1/4)
Muromachi period, c. 1458

Myōkōji, Aichi Prefecture
Important Cultural Property

Ashikaga Yoshinori (1394–1441) left the abbacy at Shōren'in in 1428 to return to the lay world and became the sixth shogun. On the tenth day of the ninth month, 1432, Yoshinori left Kyoto for a visit to Mount Fuji. The inscription on this work, by Zuikei Shūhō (1391–1473), the abbot of Rokuon'in, recounts this trip. Yoshinori stopped on the twelfth day at Myōkōji, Aichi Prefecture, a major regional Zen monastery, founded in 1348, where he stayed half a day. The temple, in preparation for the shogun's visit, reportedly relandscaped its humble garden and pond. On the eighteenth day he reached Mount Fuji, where he stayed at the estate of Imagawa Norimasa, the *shugo* (constable) of

Suruga Province (part of present-day Shizuoka Prefecture), and visited Seikenji.

When Ashikaga Yoshimasa (1436–1490) succeeded to the shogunate in 1443, *shōen* (private manors) formerly belonging to temples were restored to their owners in compliance with Yoshinori's orders. According to the inscription, this portrait of Yoshinori was painted in commemoration of that event, a fact supported by documents at Myōkōji. Also, beneath Shūhō's signature (on the extreme right), Yoshimasa himself added a short inscription and his *kaō* saying that the painting is a treasure of Myōkōji.

In the portrait Yoshinori is formally dressed; he wears an *eboshi* (black headgear) and a warrior's robe with a *koshigatana* (short sword) tucked into his sash, holds a *chūkei* (a type of folding fan), and sits barefooted on a two-tiered *tatami* mat. MS

6 Ashikaga Yoshimasa
hanging scroll; ink, color, and gold leaf on silk
44.2 x 56.0 (17 3/8 x 22)
Muromachi period, 15th century

Tokyo National Museum

Unusual in its detailed description of a room's interior, this portrait is believed to be of the eighth Ashikaga shogun, Yoshimasa (1436–1490). The figure is shown seated on a mat on a raised *tatami* mat in full ceremonial court dress, his feet bare. White, green, red, and blue pigments are used to portray the figure and his surroundings, as well as black ink and gold leaf. Some areas of gold leaf have flaked off.

Unlike some of the more famous portraits of shoguns and high-ranking warriors, such as cat. 1, this portrait is not a monumental one. The painting diminishes rather than enlarges the stature and bearing of the figure by placing it within specific surroundings. Yoshimasa's shogunate (1443–1473) was a troubled one, and he was not known as a great warrior or ruler. During the Ōnin Revolt (1467–1477), a struggle between rival factions for succession of the shogunate, Yoshimasa abdicated his position. He preferred a life of retirement, practicing and patronizing the arts, including Nō drama, painting, calligraphy, and tea. The active cultural life espoused at his villa in the Higashiyama area of Kyoto (later to become Jishōji, popularly known as Ginkakuji) gave rise to one of the most productive artistic eras in Japanese history.

It is probably because of this unique aspect of Yoshimasa's retirement that he is depicted in such an artistic interior setting. In front of him and to his side is a lacquered mirror stand. Behind him are four panels of a *fusuma* (sliding door) painting, which shows a body of water flanked on

either side by banks on which pine trees grow. Tiny figures appear, one on a bridge at the right and another in a fishing boat on the left. In the distance across the water, hills and buildings—perhaps a temple complex—are faintly visible. The style of the painting is after the Chinese Song Dynasty academic mode. Its theme is thought to be the famous Eight Views of the Xiao and Xiang Rivers. Kano Masanobu (1434–1530) was known to have painted this theme for Yoshimasa's Higashiyama villa in 1483. In addition, Masanobu was thought to have made sketches of Yoshimasa during his lifetime, one of which he used as the basis for a posthumous portrait employed in Yoshimasa's funeral service. Although the painting exhibited here has not been identified with that posthumous portrait, its style, especially in the landscape, suggest that it could be a Kano school work, if not by Masanobu himself. MR

7 Mounted warrior
hanging scroll; ink and color on silk
100.3 x 53.3 (39 1/2 x 21)
Nanbokuchō period, 14th century

Agency for Cultural Affairs, Tokyo
Important Cultural Property

In the fourteenth century, Japanese painting reflected reality by depicting the elite in their military capacity. Here we see a high-ranking warrior on a fine horse, his *tachi* sword unsheathed for action but the broken arrow in his quiver perhaps suggesting that he is coming from battle. He has traditionally been identified as Ashikaga Takauji (1305–1358), head of his clan and founder of the Muromachi shogunate who lived most of his life on the battlefield.

The *kaō* above the figure's head both supports and contradicts this identification. It is by the hand of Yoshiakira (1330–1367), Takauji's son and successor as shogun, and a portrait of Takauji bearing Yoshiakira's *kaō* is recorded as having once belonged to the powerful Asakura family of the Muromachi period. But it has also been argued that for a son to place his *kaō* prominently *above* his father's image would have been a grave breach of decorum, and that this must therefore be a portrait of one of Yoshiakira's vassals, perhaps Hosokawa Yoriyuki (1329–1392). Based on the family crest engraved on the horse's fittings, it has also been proposed that this is a portrait of Kō Moronao (d. 1351), a warrior who once served Takauji. MS

6

8 Hosokawa Sumimoto
hanging scroll; ink and color on silk
119.7 x 59.7 (47 ⅛ x 23 ½)
Muromachi period, no later than 1507
Eisei Bunko, Tokyo
Important Cultural Property

Hosokawa Sumimoto (1489–1520), born to a branch of the Hosokawa family, was adopted by Masamoto. In the sixth month of 1507, when his stepfather, Masamoto, was killed by his vassal Kōsai Mataroku Motonaga, Sumimoto escaped to Ōmi (present-day Shiga Prefecture). Kōsai Motonaga supported Hosokawa Sumiyuki, Masamoto's other adopted son who had come from the Kujō family, but in the eighth month of the same year, Hosokawa Takakuni, Miyoshi Yukinaga, and others came to Kyoto with their forces and killed Hosokawa Sumiyuki and Kōsai Motonaga. Sumimoto then succeeded to the leadership of the Hosokawa family. The inscription on this portrait was added by the scholar-monk Keijo Shūrin (1444–1518) in the tenth month of 1507, when Sumimoto was at the peak of his career. Half a year later, on the ninth day of the fourth month of 1508, Sumimoto was driven away by Hosokawa Takakuni and fled once again to Ōmi; he continued to fight against Takakuni until his death in 1520, though he never regained his position.

According to the Hosokawa family history and lineage record, Sumimoto had a certain Kano artist with the Buddhist rank Hōgen (Eye of the Law) paint this portrait after the example of a "victorious portrait" of Ashikaga Takauji (1305–1358), founder of the Muromachi shogunate; Keijo Shūrin added an inscription, and the painting was handed down in Shinjōin, a subtemple of Tenryūji, the Zen temple founded in Kyoto by Ashikaga Takauji. Shinjōin, the mortuary temple of the Hosokawa clan, was also Sumimoto's Buddhist title; the temple no longer exists.

Sumimoto wears a type of armor called *haramaki* (cats. 150, 151) and a helmet with a large *kuwagata* (hornlike projection). A *tachi* hangs from his belt, and a *koshigatana* (short sword) is tucked into his belt. He holds a halberd and a whip in his right hand and, in his left, the reins. Typical of portraits of mounted warriors, the horse is shown from the side, lifting its front right and rear left legs. The depiction of the horse suggests that this portrait was painted by an artist of the Kano school.

Keijo Shūrin's inscription, which is included in his collected literary works, reads, in part:

. . . Long ago the Genji clan subjugated the east of the capital. Military leaders rose in the eastern provinces. From Hosokawa Yoriharu to his son Yoriyuki, they were first called Kanrei [deputy shogun]. . . .

Hosokawa Sumimoto, a great archer and horseman, is far above other humans. He is also versed in waka [Japanese poetry] and appreciates the moon and the wind. . . . Outside the citadel he takes bows and ar-

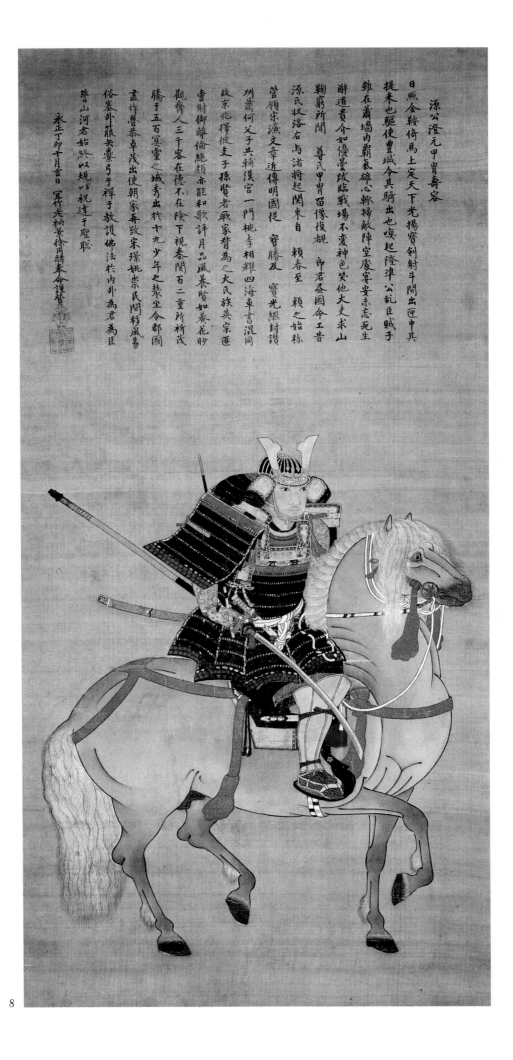

9

10

rows; in meditation and reading of sacred books he protects Buddhism. Inside and outside, pledging to the mountains and rivers for the sake of the rulers and vassals, always with propriety and benevolence, he attains saintly wisdom.

An auspicious day in the tenth month of the fourth year of Eisei [1507], Keijo Shūrin was ordered to and respectfully added an inscription.

Keijo [tripod-shaped relief seal]
Shūrin [square intaglio seal]   MS

9 **Andō En'e**
hanging scroll; ink and color on silk
120.0 x 58.0 (47 1/4 x 22 7/8)
Kamakura period, no later than 1330

Nara National Museum
Important Cultural Property

This portrait of the lay Zen Buddhist Andō En'e was painted during his lifetime. En'e is the Buddhist name of Andō Suke-yasu, son of Andō Renshō (1240–1330), who was a military leader of the late Kamakura period and a patron of Kumedadera, a temple that belonged to the Esoteric Shingon school of Buddhism in Izumi Province (part of present-day Osaka Prefecture). Little is known about the sitter.

In this portrait, formerly in Kumeda-dera, En'e is tonsured and wears a *kesa* (priest's mantle). As in *chinsō* (portraits of Zen priests), he sits on a clerical chair, his shoes on the footstool. He rests his folded hands in his lap, unlike Zen priests who in their portraits usually hold a *hossu* (Zen monk's whisk) or *shippei* (bamboo staff).

The painting portrays a robust physique, capturing the sturdy and dignified appearance of the warrior with even lines in light ink. The drapery, too, is depicted with an economy and directness of brush line.

Above the figure are three square seals and an inscription written by the Chinese Zen monk Ming-ji Chu-jun (1262–1336) on the first day of the second month of 1330.

His eyebrows long like a tree trunk, and his nose straight like a zhong [bell].

11

12

His appearance dignified and majestic, and his spirit brilliant and heroic.
He is incomparably knowledgeable in the martial arts, like the ancient Chinese military books Liu Tao and San Luo.
As to his cultivation in arts and scholarship, he is peerlessly learned like the ancient Chinese books Pa Su and Jiu Qhiu.
"Western Valley Stream" [Xi-jian Zi-tan (1249–1306), a Chinese monk] created a drop of rough waves and it caused in the eastern sea a thousand yards of billows.
He is solemn and thoughtful, dignified yet not fierce.
His retreat is noble, and he enjoys a long-lasting pleasure in the mountains.
In a hundred generations of glory, he stirs a [benevolent] breeze upon the sea.
Breaking the bind of the net of religious teaching, he is loyal to Zen Buddhism.

He is worthy of being a model of all human relationships for myriad ages.

Ming-ji was a friend of the sitter's father, Renshō, whose portrait painting is also at Kumedadera. At the request of En'e, the Chinese monk added an inscription to that portrait five days after he had written this inscription, both of which are important rare examples of Ming-ji's calligraphy.   AY

10 **Musō Soseki**
Mutō Shūi (fl. mid-14th century)
hanging scroll; ink and color on silk
120.0 x 64.5 (47 ¼ x 25 ⅜)
Nanbokuchō period, 14th century

Myōchiin, Kyoto
Important Cultural Property

Musō Soseki (1275–1351) was born in Ise Province (part of present-day Mie Prefecture). His association with monastic establishments began when he was three years old. He first studied the Tendai and Shingon schools of Buddhism but converted to Zen, and, after studying with the distinguished Zen master Kōhō Kennichi (1241–1316), he became his successor.

Musō was a figure of the greatest prominence in his own time. He moved easily among the powerful of both the imperial court and the shogunate, serving both as spiritual adviser, political adviser and go-between, and scholarly eminence. That Emperor Go-Daigo and Shogun Takauji were enemies did not prevent Musō from accepting the patronage of both. In 1325, supported enthusiastically by the emperor Go-Daigo (1288–1339), he became abbot of Nanzenji in Kyoto. He also was the founding abbot of Rinsenji, a Rinzai Zen temple in Kyoto. After the death of Go-Daigo, he founded Tenryūji through the patronage of Ashikaga Takauji (1305–1358) and his brother, Tadayoshi (1306–1352), and revived Saihōji, thus fostering the golden age of the Rinzai school of Zen in Japan. Many prominent priests were disciples of Musō Soseki, including Shun'oku Myōha (1311–1388), Mugoku Shigen (1282–1355), Zekkai Chūshin (1336–1405), and Gidō Shūshin (1325–1388). Together they contributed to the peak of the literary movement known as Gozan Bungaku (Literature of the Five Mountains, compositions in classical Chinese by Japanese Zen priests). Musō was also a significant calligrapher, poet, and designer of gardens.

The inscription on this painting, in Soseki's hand, reads from left to right:

The lower extremities from hips to heels cannot expound a theme,
So only half a torso is visible within the Kenka gate.

(translated in Boston 1970, 60)

There is a signature at the lower right in small calligraphy: *Painted by Mutō Shūi.* This portrait probably corresponds to the one recorded in 1678 in *Honchō Gashi* (History of Japanese Painting) as a painting by Mutō Shūi for Mugoku Shigen, Musō's disciple and the second abbot of Tenryūji, with an inscription by Musō Kokushi (Musō, the National Teacher). Mutō Shūi, also Musō's disciple, was a painter who specialized in portraiture.

Descriptively rendered, Musō's face is outlined with thin lines, and light vermilion shading is added. The contours and folds of the drapery are drawn with great economy of line.   AY

11 Ikkyū Sōjun

hanging scroll; ink and color on silk
98.0 x 43.0 (38 5/8 x 16 7/8)
Muromachi period, no later than 1481

Shūon'an, Kyoto
Important Cultural Property

Ikkyū Sōjun (1394–1481), known for his penetrating mind and wildly unconventional behavior, was an exceptional Zen priest of the Muromachi period. Son of

the emperor Go-Komatsu (1377–1433), at age six Ikkyū became a child attendant of Shōgai Zenkan at Ankokuji in Kyoto. Later he mastered Zen of the Rinzai school under the distinguished master Kasō Sōdon (1352–1428), who lived at the hermitage Zenkōan in Katada, Ōmi Province (present-day Shiga Prefecture). Ikkyū led a peripatetic life, training a handful of disciples without regard to their class origins. Finally in 1474, in response to an imperial summons, he became the forty-seventh abbot of Daitokuji and led the rebuilding of the temple, much of which had been destroyed in the Ōnin War (1467–1477). In the following year he erected a tomb for himself, which he named Jiyōtō, in Kokyū, Takigi village of southern Yamashiro Province (part of present-day Kyoto Prefecture), and lived in a hermitage that he built by its side. The hermitage, Shūon'an, still stands in Takigi, known by its more popular name Ikkyūji (Ikkyū's temple). A notable poet and calligrapher as well as a priest, Ikkyū criticized and vehemently despised the contemporary Zen hiearchy.

In this portrait Ikkyū sits in a chair holding a bamboo staff in his right hand, as in a traditional *chinsō* (portrait of a Zen priest). Even in this conventional clerical portrait, however, his unconventional and rebellious personality is expressed by his unshaved head, the mustache, and the informal way he sits, his right foot on his left knee with his shoes still on. The haunting face is drawn with simple brush lines; Ikkyū looks at the viewer from the corner of his eyes while his face is turned slightly away.

The inscription is in Ikkyū's hand:

Lin Ji's posterity does not know Zen
Facing Mad Clouds, who can teach Zen?
For the past thirty years it's been heavy on the shoulders
Alone bearing the Songyuan school of Zen.

Sōben, the Zen practitioner and great patron, after getting my vulgar portrait painted, asked me to write an inscription, so I complied with his request.
Formerly at Daitokuji of Murasakino [area north of Kyoto], Jun Ikkyū [over Ikkyū's seal], Old Priest under heaven.

Lin Ji is Linji Yixuan (d. 867), the Chinese monk who founded the Linji (J: Rinzai) school of Zen. "Mad Clouds" is a reference to Ikkyū's sobriquet, "Kyōunshi," Child of Mad Clouds." Songyuan is the school of Zen taught by the Chinese priest Songyuan Chongyue (1132–1202). Ikkyū signed *formerly at Daitokuji*, referring to his involvement in 1474 with the rebuilding of the monastery followed by his brief abbacy there. The inscription says that the portrait was painted for Sōben, a success-

ful merchant who made his money in the China trade and gave financial support to the rebuilding of Daitokuji. Thus the portrait can be dated after 1474 and before 1481, the year of Ikkyū's death.   AY

12 Sakugen Shūryō

hanging scroll; ink and color on silk
126.0 x 49.4 (49 5/8 x 19 1/2)
Ming, no later than 1541

Myōchiin, Kyoto
Important Cultural Property

Sakugen Shūryō (1501–1579), an erudite Zen priest of the Rinzai school in the late Muromachi period, was the third-generation abbot of Myōchiin, a subtemple of Tenryūji. He was also an important figure in the history of Ming-Japanese relations. He visited Ming Dynasty China twice, not as a Buddhist pilgrim or student but as a government envoy, first as the vice-envoy from 1539 to 1541 and later as the chief envoy. He wrote excellent prose and poetry in Chinese, and during these trips he associated with Ming scholars and painters.

In this painting Sakugen, wearing a Confucian scholar's cap and a Buddhist monk's robe and *kesa*, is seated on a bench, books by his side. He holds a book and seems to be reciting from it, conveying the image of Sakugen the literary man.

The inscription above the figure was written in the first month of 1541 (the twentieth year of the Jiajing reign-period of the Ming Dynasty) by Ke Yuchuang, a literary man in Ningbo, at the request of San'ei, a priest who accompanied Sakugen to China. Sakugen would have just returned to Ningbo after completing his first mission in the north. The inscription testifies to the affection between Sakugen and Ke Yuchuang, a friendship also recorded in *Shodoshū* (Collected works: the first mission), one of Sakugen's Ming journals (entries of 1/30/1541, 8/21/1539, and 10/10/1539). Ke Yuchuang's inscription, written in formal (or regular) script, signed by him and followed by five square seals, reads:

Encomium for the Portrait of Isai Sakugen, the Zen Master

The master is a lofty priest from Japan. Sent as an envoy to China, he lives temporarily in the district of Mingzhou. He has a sense of decorum; he is versed in literature and scholarship, and I am fortunate to know him. His junior companion San'ei, the prelate, happened to take out this small portrait of the

13   14

master, and showed it to me. I composed
an inscription for this portrait:

His appearance is peaceful; his forehead
   contains jewels inside
In a scholar's hat and a priest's robe, he sits
   solemnly with legs crossed
His letters are richly written; his religious
   mind is refreshing
Though his appearance can be beheld, his
   erudition is unfathomable
His brush flows beautifully, whether in
   Japanese or Chinese poetry
A diplomatic envoy to the emperor, in old
   temples and guest halls
His clear voice reverberates; he receives great
   imperial favor
After journeying through beautiful places,
   he tires and rests in Japan
His body will be ever healthier, and he will
   live a long life.   AY

13 Asakura Toshikage

hanging scroll; ink and color on silk
81.5 x 44.0 (32 x 17 3/8)
Muromachi period, 15th century

Shingetsuji, Fukui Prefecture
Important Cultural Property

Asakura Toshikage (1428–1481) was a powerful daimyo of the mid-Muromachi period. During the Ōnin War (1467–1477), he
ousted Shiba Yoshitake as *shugo* (constable) of Echizen Province (present-day Fukui Prefecture), routed all challengers,
and, based in Ichijōdani, laid a firm foundation for the fortune of the Asakura family. The principles of his ruthless but
competent management of the province
are reflected in the seventeen-article
house laws of the Asakura family. An excellent archer and horseman, he was also
something of a scholar, poet, and patron of
the arts, as well as a pious Buddhist. He
was acquainted with the Zen priest Ikkyū
and donated wood at Ikkyū's request for
the rebuilding of Daitokuji. Toshikage became a priest in his later years under the
Buddhist name Eirin Sōyū.

Toshikage is shown here seated on a
raised *tatami* mat, wearing a warrior's
robe, a *hōi* (priest's robe), and a *kesa* (Zen
priest's stole), indicative of both his secular
and his religious aspirations. He holds a
chūkei (a type of folding fan) in his right
hand and prayer beads in his left. The
pose is formal and generic, but the features are specific and individualized and
the personality of the sitter is subtly and
penetratingly revealed, much as in contemporary portraits of Zen ecclesiastics.

前龍寶峡嶺忠宗新
采禄歳今而衰則初四日
日咸瓦歴葉来
頼麗紫挨成一劍定天下今
参前南京禅詰極平常作略
大祥定門之肖像
聚光院疑前画作職堂進公

15

16

Judging by the degree of realism, this portrait is likely to have been painted during Toshikage's lifetime or soon after his death.

The portrait has been at Shingetsuji, a temple founded by Toshikage in Ichijō-dani, which later became the mortuary temple of the Asakura family.

14 Hōjō Sōun
    hanging scroll; ink and color on silk
    93.5 x 50.7 (36 7/8 x 20)
    Muromachi period, early 16th century
    Sōunji, Kanagawa Prefecture
    Important Cultural Property

The warrior Hōjō Sōun (1432–1519) first went by the name Ise Shinkurō Nagauji.

On becoming a Buddhist monk, he took the name Sōun'an Sōtan. His career closely paralleled that of his contemporary, Asakura Toshikage (cat. 13): beginning as a daimyo's retainer, he proceeded to seize land and usurp power wherever the occasion permitted, controlling Izu and Sagami provinces (Shizuoka and Kanagawa prefectures) from Odawara before he died. His son and grandson continued the work, and the Later Hōjō (to distinguish them from the Hōjō regents of the Kamakura period) ruled the Kantō region until their overthrow by Hideyoshi in 1590.

Like Asakura Toshikage, Hōjō Sōun was a ruthless and treacherous man, but an able administrator as well as fighter, and the house laws known as "Twenty-one Articles of Sōunjidono" reflect his determination to preserve his descendants from the kind of overthrow that had made him a daimyo. (Sōunjidono is a posthumous title taken from Hōjō Sōun's mortuary temple.)

In this powerful portrayal, Hōjō Sōun sits barefooted on a raised *tatami* mat, wearing a *hōi* (priest's robe) and *kera* (Zen priest's stole) over a warrier's robe, holding a *chūkei* (a type of folding fan) in his right hand and clenching his left. The facial expression reveals the resolute nature of the sitter. This portrait was probably painted in Sōun's lifetime, after he became a priest, or else soon after his death.   AY

68

17

15 Miyoshi Nagayoshi

hanging scroll; ink and color on silk
107.0 x 50.0 (42 1/8 x 19 3/4)
Muromachi period, no later than 1566

Jukōin, Kyoto
Important Cultural Property

At the height of his power Miyoshi Naga-yoshi (1523–1564) ruled eight provinces, stretching from Kyoto to Shikoku. Like Asakura Toshikage and Hōjō Sōun, he began as retainer of a great lord whose power he seized, but did not succeed in founding a daimyo family. He was himself overthrown by a retainer and died at the age of forty-one; the process of *gekokujō* (low overthrowing the high) was a double-edged sword.

Nagayoshi was a cultivated leader, especially skilled in *renga* (linked verse). Late in his life he was ordained a priest and given the Buddhist name Jukōin. His commemorative tomb is at the subtemple Jukōin of Daitokuji, the family mortuary temple erected by Nagayoshi's son, Yoshitsugu, in 1566.

Nagayoshi's depiction contrasts in every point with those of Toshikage and Sōun. Seated on a *tatami* mat, he is in secular and quite colorful dress, wearing a sa-murai eboshi (black headgear worn by warriors), a blue robe with his family crest, and an underrobe of contrasting blocks or stripes of bright color. A *koshigatana* (short sword) is tucked in his sash, and he holds a fan in his right hand and clenches his left fist. In place of the chilling determination in the expressions of the two earlier war-lords, Nagayoshi reveals a smooth urbanity.

The inscription above the figure, by Shōrei Sōkin (1490–1568) of Daitokuji, is dated to 1566, the third anniversary of Nagayoshi's death. The portrait was therefore a commemorative one. Two seals follow Sōkin's signature. The inscription reads, in part, from left to right:

Portrait of the late Jukōin

Thoroughly trained in the Southern school of Zen, Zen is his topic
His day-to-day disposition is likened to that of Pang and Fei [ideal laymen Zen adherents in Tang China]
With a single sword, he subjugated the land
He acquired today's dignified stature at a steady pace.   AY

16 Mōri Motonari

hanging scroll; ink and color on silk
97.0 x 50.0 (38 1/8 x 19 5/8)
Muromachi period, no later than 1562

Toyosakajinja, Yamaguchi Prefecture
Important Cultural Property

Mōri Motonari (1497–1571), a high-ranking military leader and daimyo in the Age of Wars (*Sengoku Jidai*), first served Amako Haruhisa (1514–1560), and then Ōuchi Yoshitaka (1507–1551), both daimyo of western Honshū. After Yoshitaka was killed by his retainer Sue Harutaka (1521–1555), Mōri Motonari defeated Harutaka at Itsukushima and brought Suō, Nagato, and Aki Provinces under his rule. He went on to subjugate Bingo, Iwami, Izumo, Inba, and Hōki Provinces, eventually possessing ten provinces in San'yō (present-day Yamaguchi, Hiroshima, and Okayama Prefectures) and San'in (present-day Shimane and Tottori Prefectures) as well as portions of Buzen (present-day Ōita Prefecture) and Iyo (present-day Ehime Prefecture).

In this portrait Motonari sits on a *tatami* mat wearing a *samurai eboshi* (black headgear worn by warriors) and a warrior's robe bearing the Mōri crest. A *koshigatana* (short sword) is tucked in the sash. He is holding a folding fan in his right hand and clenching his left fist. A long *tachi* sword is placed at his left. With slender face, wide-open eyes, and well-trimmed beard, Motonari is depicted without the idealization evidenced in later portrait paintings of military leaders.

According to the inscription above the sitter, the portrait was painted during Motonari's lifetime at the order of his first son, Takamoto. The inscription, dated 1562, was written by Ninnyo Shūgyō (d. 1574, the ninety-first abbot of Shōkokuji and forty-second abbot of Rokuon'in) at the request of a certain Jiku'un Eshin, presumably a monk of Nanzenji, the monastery that Motonari patronized.

The long inscription lauds the ancestral lineage of the Mōri family, tracing it back to the Ōe family, descendants of the emperor Kanmu (737–806), and mentioning the virtues and merits of one Ōe Masafusa (1041–1111), a distinguished scholar, poet, and civil administrator, from whom Motonari was directly descended. Replete with allusions to Chinese history and literature, and embellished, in the best sense of the word, with purple prose, this inscription accords Motonari the stature of a sage-warrior. The inscription reads in part (starting with the second half of the eleventh line from the right):

Now, Mōri Motonari, the ruler of Aki, Courtier Ōe, and Honorary Ruler of Mutsu province, converted early to the Three Jewels [i.e., Buddhism]. His Buddhist name is Nichirai, and his title is Dōshun. As to his power, he rules over a dozen provinces and controls over ten thousand troops. In the past, Courtier Ōe Masafusa ruled nine provinces, two islands, and western regions under Dazaifu [regional capital in Kyushu], where he lived for five years. To think, Motonari's lineage must also be Masafusa's posterity. Slowly but steadily progressing for five hundred years, how right it is—the root is big with thriving foliage; the source is high and full of water. Indeed they are well called the Ōe [Big River] family, and it is well called Jōshun [Perpetual Spring]. Ah, what prosperity!

Zen Master Jiku'un, formerly of Nanzenji, because Motonari is the monastery's patron, conveyed the order of Takamoto, Motonari's heir, to have a portrait of Warrior Motonari painted during his lifetime. Master Jiku'un asked this rustic to write a word above the portrait. Although I have not met Warrior Motonari, because I know the Zen master I dare not decline. Thus I give a few words of praise:

His power expanding over the sea, his fame reaching the clouds, in full solemnity he attends the present emperor's royal ceremonies. He assists his emperor to rule like Emperors Yao and Shun [rulers of ancient China]. He fathoms his master's teachings and penetrates the profound thoughts in

them. *He has close contacts with all people and selects talents to administer his territory. . . .*

When he holds the Mōri family sword and subjugates the enemy, his wisdom tempers the best of swords, such as the famous pair forged by the Chinese smiths Ganjian and his wife, Moxie [of the 3rd century A.D.]. When he waves a fan and commands garrisons, it is as if he consults with Sun Wu and Wu Qi [ancient Chinese military strategists of the 4th and 3rd centuries B.C. respectively]. . . .

He loves to praise courageous men of loyalty and valor. His brave tiger face recalls the ambition of Ban Chao [famous Chinese general of 1st century A.D.]. His porcupine hair resembles the beautiful beard of Commander Huan Wen [fl. 2nd half of 4th century A.D.]. The triple stars [the Mōri family crest] add brightness to his beautiful abode. The family crests of the generations of the powerful and rich decorate his military tent . . . .

He recites and composes Japanese poems. As a connoisseur of old books, he enjoys many different editions of poetry anthologies to visit the ancient steps of early Japanese poetry. With devotion, he makes the reading of Indian Buddhist scriptures his daily task, a sign of sincere faith in the Buddha.

His allies always believe in his words. "Being good to neighbors is a precious virtue, a man of virtue will never be alone" are indeed the right words for him. He has given the family headship to Takamoto and lives in retirement on Juzan. I cheer loudly for his long life.

Written in the fall of the fifth year of Eiroku [1562], humble priest, formerly of Rokuon'in, Nanzenji.

Ninnyo [square relief seal]
[illegible tripod-shaped relief seal] AY

17 Takeda Shingen
Hasegawa Tōhaku (1539–1610)
hanging scroll; ink and color on silk
42.0 x 63.0 (16 1/2 x 24 3/4)
Momoyama period, late 16th century

Seikeiin, Wakayama Prefecture
Important Cultural Property

Takeda Shingen (1521–1573), a daimyo during the Age of the Wars, began his career by supplanting his father as lord of Kai Province (present-day Yamanashi Prefecture). He brought Shinano and Suruga Provinces under his control and captured portions of Kōzuke, Tōtōmi, and Mikawa Provinces. Advancing on Kyoto, the ultimate goal in his military strategy, he died. As a youth he was a passionate student of Chinese and Japanese poetry. He was also deeply religious, with special devotion to the Tendai school of Buddhism and to Zen priests of the Myōshinji school. Shingen's wife, Tenhōrin Sanjō, was the daughter of a courtier.

Shingen had a monumental build, as can be seen in this work, an unusual portrait with an outdoor setting. The painting is accompanied by a letter written by Shingen's son, Katsuyori, which says that it was painted in Shingen's lifetime and that it was to be offered to Seikeiin. The seal *Nobuharu*, stamped at the lower left, identifies the painter as Hasegawa Tōhaku, who was then known as Nobuharu. The painting was done when Tōhaku was in his early thirties.

The warlord and his highly decorative garments are delineated in precise and colorful detail, following the *yamato-e* tradition considered appropriate for depictions of great men. In the suggestion of landscape the painter reveals his interest in the freer ink-painting style derived from China. MS

18 The emperor Go-Yōzei
Kano Takanobu (1571–1618)
hanging scroll; ink and color on silk
107.0 x 60.1 (42 1/8 x 23 5/8)
Momoyama period, early 17th century

Sennyūji, Kyoto

The emperor Go-Yōzei (1571–1617) sits on a mat placed over a large *tatami*. He wears an *eboshi* (black headgear) and an informal courtier's robe. As the 107th emperor, Go-Yōzei reigned from 1586 to 1611, during the period when Toyotomi Hideyoshi (1537–1598) subjugated the entire country and Tokugawa Ieyasu (1543–1616) gradually established political power, a time when aristocratic society was regaining relative stability. Go-Yōzei not only made efforts to revive public events and ceremonies, but was committed to learning: he studied classical literature, including *The Tale of Genji*, and enjoyed Japanese poetry, calligraphy, and painting. He was instrumental in persuading the scholar-poet and daimyo Hosokawa Yūsai (1534–1610;), when Yūsai faced a siege by enemy troops in 1600, to pass on his knowledge of the poetics of the *Kokinshū* to the imperial prince Hachijō (1579–1617), Go-Yōzei's younger brother. Through Go-Yōzei's interest in the art of printing, movable wooden type was used to publish many Chinese and Japanese classics.

Two seals are stamped at the left of Go-Yōzei's portrait, an oblong relief seal, *Kano*, and a tripod-shaped relief seal, *Takanobu*, identifying the artist. Kano Takanobu was the second son of Kano Eitoku (1543–1590). Following the death of his elder brother, Mitsunobu, in 1608, he became the central figure in the Kano school and painted a wide variety of Buddhist and literary subjects. When the imperial palace was built in 1613, he presided over its decorations, executing sliding door panels and wall paintings, some of which are preserved in Ninnaji in Kyoto. The

18

19

surviving panels, originally installed behind the emperor's seat, represent thirty-two Chinese historical luminaries, including famous ministers up to and during the Tang Dynasty.   SY

19 The emperor Go-Mizunoo
Gen'yō Shōnin (1634–1727)
hanging scroll; ink and color on silk
100.6 x 55.8 (39⅝ x 22)
Edo period, no earlier than 1680

Unryūin, Kyoto

The emperor Go-Mizunoo (1596–1680), the third son of the emperor Go-Yōzei (cat. 18), acceded to the throne in 1611 and in 1620 married a daughter of Tokugawa Hidetada (1578–1631), the second shogun. Go-Mizunoo had a penchant for scholarship and was versed in *waka* (Japanese poetry), *renga* (linked verse), *kanshi* (Chinese

poetry), calligraphy, tea, incense appreciation, and flower arrangement. Striving for a renaissance of cultural activities, he set for the members of the court special days for scholarly pursuits and published, in 1621, *Kōchō Ruien*, a Japanese edition of the mid-twelfth-century Chinese *Huang-chao Leiyuan* (Classified quotations of works by courtly scholars). Endowed with artistic talent, he painted and also designed the garden for the Shugakuin Detached Palace in northeastern Kyoto.

Though he was an intelligent and capable man Go-Mizunoo as emperor endured repeated frustrations and humiliations at the hands of Tokugawa Ieyasu and Hidetada (particularly Hidetada), who were determined to assert their authority over all spheres of Japanese life. After one too many heavy-handed shogunal interventions, Go-Mizunoo registered his disgust by abdicating in 1629. A

lifelong devout Buddhist and avid student of Zen, in 1651 he took the tonsure and adopted the Buddhist name Enjō. He became a patron and student of many cultured Zen monks, most particularly Takuan Sōhō (cat. 20), who shared his anger at shogunal interference with imperial and clerical prerogatives.

Two portraits of the emperor Go-Mizunoo were painted during his lifetime. One, in Hanjuin, Kyoto, painted by Kano Tan'yū (1602–1674), bears an inscribed *waka* composed by the emperor himself. The other, in Sennyūji, also in Kyoto, has two Japanese poems inscribed and dated to the nineteenth day of the second month, 1673. The portrait exhibited here, painted after Go-Mizunoo's death, is based on these precedents.

This portrait was painted by Go-Mizunoo's granddaughter, Gen'yō, a Zen

Buddhist nun, also known as Ringūji no Miya. Two of the artist's seals can be seen at the lower left. Genyō, who was named Ake no Miya at her birth, was a daughter of Hōshunmon-in, the seventh daughter of Go-Mizunoo. After the death of the emperor, she took the tonsure and became a nun, changing her name to Gen'yō and adopting the Buddhist title *Shōzan*. Like her grandfather, she was a strong advocate of Zen. She learned painting from Kano Yasunobu (1613–1685), son of Kano Takanobu (cat. 18).

The two poems, written on *shikishi* (square poetry sheets) and attached to the scroll, were copied from the inscriptions on the Hanjuin and Sennyūji portraits of the emperor, one from each. Deep melancholy and world-weariness is expressed in these poems:

Painful, this
withered tree fence hidden
in the deep mountain;
would that at least my heart's
flowers were fragrantly abloom.

My life being thus,
in this world that I will never revisit
the thought of leaving a trace
of my calligraphy for a moment—
even that is sad. WA

20 **Takuan Sōhō**
hanging scroll; ink and color on silk
99.0 x 46.3 (39 x 18 1/4)
Edo period, no later than 1644

Eisei Bunko, Tokyo

Takuan Sōhō (1573–1645) was a Zen priest of Daitokuji during the early Edo period, celebrated in his own time and after, as a scholar, painter, calligrapher, and tea adept. Through tea he came to be associated with the shogun and various daimyo, and he taught Zen to Miyamoto Musashi (1582–1645; cat. 128) and Yagyū Munenori (1571–1646), two formidable swordsmen. In 1629, because he objected to the shogunate's policy of control over Buddhist establishments, he was banished to the north to Dewa province, but was pardoned in 1632. During the 1630s he was friend and spiritual adviser not only to Emperor Go-Mizunoo, but also to Iemitsu (1604–1651), the third Tokugawa shogun, and in 1639 he became the founding abbot of Tōkaiji in Shinagawa, whose patron was Iemitsu.

This portrait, executed in the *chinsō* (Zen priest's portrait) mode, bears an inscription by Takuan himself dated to the sixteenth day of the sixth month, 1644:

This world of desire, form, and formlessness
is like a house on fire;
Inside a bag is an old crow,
It tries to get out but can't.
A child, skinny, worries about his father;
To this stubborn fellow both right and
wrong are lost.

20

There is vacuity, concealing nothing.
Inside his eyes is no longer any shade,
Vacuity shows no illusory flowers;
The bamboo staff still in his hand,
The hossu brush only seeks idiocy. Ah.

Sixteenth day, sixth month, the twenty-first
year of Kan'ei [1644]
Takuan, formerly of Daitokuji, in mock
self-accusation.
Sōhō [seal]   Takuan [seal]

Takuan studied poetry (*waka*) with Hosokawa Yūsai (1534–1610) around 1603. Yūsai's son, Hosokawa Sansai (1563–1646), became daimyo of the Kumamoto domain, Higo Province, and his grandson Mitsunao became an ardent patron of Zen under Takuan's influence and tutelage. These circumstances explain why this portrait was handed down in the Hosokawa family. SY

21 **Toyotomi Hideyoshi**
hanging scroll; ink and color on silk
109.0 x 51.0 (42 7/8 x 20)
Momoyama period, no later than 1600

Saikyōji, Shiga Prefecture
Important Cultural Property

Toyotomi Hideyoshi (1537–1598) died at the age of sixty-one. In accordance with his will, a mortuary shrine was built atop Amidamine in Higashiyama, Kyoto. The court bestowed the title *Toyokuni Daimyōjin* (Great Deity of the Rich Country) on Hideyoshi as deity of this sanctuary and posthumously granted him Senior First Rank. A memorial ceremony was held annually at the shrine on the anniversary of his death.

Many portraits of the deified Hideyoshi were painted. The earliest known ex-

仰瞻

豊國大明神應用參方自在身
照徹絲支日東空爍迦羅眼碧纖

慶　右

山中城州大守橘長俊公繪
豊國寺像需贊詞同辭不謹賦一偈云
慶長壬子庚子夏五十三ㅅ日
見南禪玄圃叟靈三...

元來非鬼又非人權出現
稱天下神日域朝鮮胸次
苓西乾東土眼中塵
慶子夏五吉辰
野釋惟杏叟燒香拜贊

右為山中二城守從五位豊臣朝臣橘長俊

21

22

23

ample, dated to 1598, the year of his death, and inscribed by the monk Nanka Genkō, is at Kōdaiin, the mortuary temple of Hideyoshi's wife. Portraits of Hideyoshi apparently continued to be painted until the Toyotomi family was exterminated by Ieyasu in 1615. However, no portrait dated later than the fourth month of 1601 is known.

This portrait was painted for Yamanaka Nagatoshi (Chōshun; 1547–1607), a daimyo and retainer of Hideyoshi. The Zen priests Genpo Reisan and Ikyō Eitetsu added the inscriptions, both dated to the fifth month of 1600. This date indicates that the painting was made during the uneasy period shortly before the Battle of Sekigahara (cat. 104), which confirmed the hegemony of the Tokugawa. Yamanaka Nagatoshi was originally a retainer of Sasaki Yoshikata of Ōmi Province, but served under the Oda, Shibata, and Tanba fami-

lies before taking service with the Toyotomi. At Sekigahara he neither aided nor opposed Ieyasu, remaining instead in Osaka with the Toyotomi. Ieyasu deprived him of the rank of daimyo but granted him a small fief.

In this portrait Hideyoshi sits on a *tatami* mat, wearing the court headgear called *kōburi*, a white courtier's informal robe, and bluish black *sashinuki* (baggy pants tied at the ankles). Like his fellow warlords Hōjō Sōun (cat. 14), Miyoshi Nagayoshi (cat. 15), and Mōri Motonari (cat. 16), he is shown with his right hand holding a folding fan and his left clenched in a fist. Behind him is an ink landscape. Hideyoshi is portrayed here as seated in a shrine. On a stylistic basis, the painting can be assigned to the Kano school.

The first inscription, by Genpo Reisan, reads:

We lift our eyes to Toyokuni the Great Deity
When called upon a free being which can

appear whenever and wherever
He shines all over India, China, and Japan
His steadfast eyes catch even the smallest
 speck of dust.

Tachibana Nagatoshi, the ruler
Yamanaka of Yamashiro Province, asked
us to write an inscription for the
honorable portrait of Toyokuni. We firmly
declined but he was not satisfied, so I
respectfully wrote this short poem.
 Eighteenth day of eighth month, the
third year of Keichō [1598].
 Old Genpo, Reisan of Nanzenji
 Genpo [tripod-shaped relief seal]

The second inscription is by Ikyō Eitetsu:

By nature neither a devil nor a human
A reincarnation, a god under heaven
In his thoughts, Japan and Korea are as
 small as mustard seeds
India and China are dust in his eyes.

24

25

*Fifth month of the fifth year of Keichō
[1600]*
*Humble monk Ikyō burns incense and
respectfully adds this inscription.*
Ikyō [square relief seal]
*This inscription is for Tachibana Nagatoshi,
ruler of Yamanaka Castle, Junior Fifth
Rank, Toyotomi's vassal and a member of
the court.* MS

22 Oichi no Kata

hanging scroll; ink and color on silk
96.0 x 40.9 (37 3/4 x 16 1/8)
Momoyama period, 1589

Jimyōin, Wakayama Prefecture
Important Cultural Property

Oichi no Kata (1547–1583), a younger sister
of Oda Nobunaga (1534–1582), married Asai
Nagamasa (1545–1573), a ranking warrior
from Ōmi Province (present-day Shiga
Prefecture) when she was seventeen. Nagamasa was first an ally of Oda Nobunaga,
but later turned against him and was defeated by Nobunaga's forces at the Battle
of Anekawa in 1570. Three years later Nagamasa stood siege in Otani Castle in
Ōmi, his garrison headquarters, and he
died in action at twenty-eight. Oichi no
Kata escaped death, having been sent to
Nobunaga's encampment. She then married Shibata Katsuie (1522–1583). When
Toyotomi Hideyoshi (1537–1598) attacked
Katsuie at Kitanoshō Castle in Echizen in
1583, she entrusted her three daughters to
Hideyoshi and, when Katsuie committed
suicide, took her own life as an expression
of loyalty to her husband. She was then
thirty-six. Her daughters became wards of
Hideyoshi, and one of them, Yodogimi, became his favorite consort. Another married Hidetada, the second Tokugawa
shogun.

In this portrait Oichi no Kata sits on a
tatami mat wearing a white *kosode* and
over it a patterned red *koshimaki* (waist
wrap). She holds a Buddhist sutra scroll in
her right hand, indicating that the portrait
commemorates her death. The painting is
an idealized portrayal of one who was reputed to be "the most beautiful woman
under heaven."

This painting joins two others—a portrait of Oichi no Kata's first husband, Nagamasa, and a portrait of Nagamasa's
father, Hisamasa—at Jimyōin, the Asano
mortuary temple on Mount Kōya. The
portraits of Nagamasa and Oichi no Kata
are assumed to have been painted in 1589
to commemorate the seventeenth anniversary of Nagamasa's death and the seventh
anniversary of Oichi no Kata's. They were
probably then offered to Jimyōin to join
the portrait of Hisamasa, which was
painted in 1569. AY

23 Maeda Toshiharu
hanging scroll; ink and color on silk
78.8 x 39.4 (31 x 15 1/2)
Momoyama period, late 16th century

Chōreiji, Ishikawa Prefecture
Important Cultural Property

Maeda Toshiharu, the head of a group of wealthy farmers in Owari Province (present-day Aichi Prefecture), was the father of Toshiie (1538–1599), the first-generation head of the Maeda clan, which ruled Kaga Province (present-day Ishikawa Prefecture). This portrait was reportedly offered by Toshiie to Chōreiji (in Nanao City, Ishikawa Prefecture) at the time of its founding in commemoration of his father. A later portrait of Toshiie's mother (cat. 24) is also at Chōreiji.

The painting presents Toshiharu at the moment of a religious experience. His head shaven, he is portrayed as a Buddhist priest seated on a *tatami* mat and wearing a Zen priest's stole over a priest's robe, which partially covers a sword lying on the *tatami*. His right arm resting on his knee, Toshiharu holds a fan in his right hand and rests his left hand on the *tatami* as he looks up at the stylized purple clouds on which Amida Buddha will descend to receive his soul at the moment of death. In front of him is a *tenmoku* teacup on a lacquer stand. On the floor in front are a page, who sits ceremoniously, and a servant holding a ewer. The style of the painting is provincial, and the composition is unique for a commemorative portrait.

AY

24 The wife of Maeda Toshiharu
hanging scroll; ink and color on silk
69.2 x 40.7 (27 1/4 x 16)
Momoyama period, late 16th century

Chōreiji, Ishikawa Prefecture
Important Art Object

Very little is known about the life of Maeda Toshiharu's wife, whose portrait, though painted somewhat later, forms a pair with that of her husband. Wearing a white nun's robe, she holds prayer beads in her hands. She was from the Takeno family and had one son, Toshiie. She died in 1573. Her posthumous Buddhist title is Chōreiin Myōkyū Daishi.

Chōreiji in Nanao City, Ishikawa Prefecture, where these portraits come from, is a temple that belongs to the Sōtō school of Zen. In 1581, with the area under his control, Maeda Toshiie built the temple, named Hōenji at the time of its founding, and invited the monk Daitō Keijo from a temple with the same name at Takase, Echizen Province (part of present-day Fukui Prefecture), to be its abbot. In 1583, when Toshiie moved to Kanazawa, Daitō went also to head a new Hōenji there. In

27

1594 Daitō returned to the temple in Nanao and renamed it Chōreiji after the posthumous Buddhist name of Toshiie's mother.

AY

25 Maeda Kikuhime
hanging scroll; ink and color on silk
70.6 x 34.5 (27 3/4 x 13 5/8)
Momoyama period, 1584

Saikyōji, Shiga Prefecture
Important Art Object

Maeda Kikuhime (1578–1584) was the sixth daughter of Maeda Toshiie, the first ruler of Kaga province. Her mother was Toshiie's consort, Ryūkōin (daughter of Kasama Yoshichi). Kikuhime lived with

the Nishikawa family of Ōtsu, near Kyoto, and was later adopted by Toyotomi Hideyoshi (1537–1598). She died in 1584 at the age of seven and was buried in Saikyōji.

In this portrait she sits on a *tatami* mat wearing a *kosode*, holding chrysanthemums in her right hand, a reference to her name, Kiku, which means chrysanthemum. Toys are by her side, including a *papier-mâché* dog, a top, and dolls, as well as an incense container. This commemorative portrait was painted soon after her death.

At the top of the painting in two squares intended to resemble *shikishi* (square poetry sheets), is an inscription dated to 1584, the year of her death. It was

26

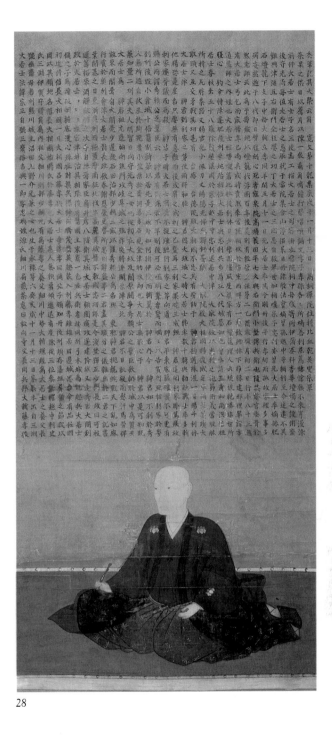

28

written by the priest Shinchi, the eighth abbot of Saikyōji. Saikyōji, devastated by a battle waged by Oda Nobunaga, was restored through Hideyoshi's contributions. It is probably because of this relationship that his adopted daughter, Kikuhime, was buried in Saikyōji and her portrait placed at that temple. Another version, presumed to be a copy of this portrait, is at Saihōji in Kanazawa.

The inscription, a poem in Chinese, is read from left to right:

Portrait of Kinkei Kūgyoku Dōjo [Golden Cascade Heavenly Jewel Young Girl, the posthumous Buddhist title of Kikuhime]
Fall wind blows over grass and flowers
Death is inevitable still

Hang the portrait painting for now
And recite the sutras to honor her soul

Twenty-first day, eighth month of the twelfth year of Tenshō [1584]
Shinchi, the High Priest [kaō]   AY

26 **Hosokawa Yūsai**
   hanging scroll; ink and color on silk
   104.0 x 51.0 (41 x 20)
   Momoyama period, no later than 1612

   Tenjuan, Kyoto
   Important Cultural Property

Hosokawa Fujitaka (1534–1610), better known by his Buddhist name Yūsai, was a retainer of the fifteenth Ashikaga shogun Yoshiaki (1537–1597), but left him in 1573 to serve Oda Nobunaga (1534–1582). Nobunaga later awarded Yūsai the Province of Tango (the northern part of present-day Kyoto Prefecture). After Nobunaga's death during the Honnōji Incident, an unsuccessful coup instigated by his vassal Akechi Mitsuhide, Yūsai took the tonsure and became a priest, leaving the leadership of the family to his son Tadaoki (Sansai, 1563–1646). After the Battle of Yamazaki, in which Hideyoshi defeated and killed Mitsuhide, Yūsai became a close confidant of Toyotomi Hideyoshi (1537–1598). In 1600, he sided with Tokugawa Ieyasu (1543–1616) at the Battle of Sekigahara (cat. 104) against the Toyotomi. An astute military leader, Yūsai was also a gifted poet and scholar of poetry: he received the *Kokin denju* (secret teachings on the poetics of the early-tenth-century *Kokinshū* poetry anthology) from the Sanjōnishi family (cat. 66). He also became an important figure among the literary men around Hideyoshi who pursued the art of *renga* (linked verse).

In this portrait the seated Yūsai appears relaxed, with a Chinese-style fan in his right hand. Another portrait with an identical composition was transmitted in the Hosokawa family and is now in the Eisei Bunko. A clan document indicates that it was painted by a certain Tashiro Tōyū, commissioned by Yūsai's widow (cat. 27) on the third anniversary of his death. Tashiro Tōyū may in fact be a misinterpretation of the name of Tashiro Tōho, a painter who served the Hosokawa clan. Since the Tenjuan portrait is executed in the same style as the Eisei Bunko version, the two may have both been painted by Tōho. The inscription on the painting exhibited here, read from left to right, was written by the Zen priest Ishin Sūden (cat. 53), abbot of Nanzenji, in the fifth month of 1612. His inscription is followed by an illegible tripod-shaped relief seal. Yūsai, in 1602, restored Tenjuan, which was the *hōjō* (abbot's quarters) in Nanzenji. Excerpts from the inscription read as follows:

. . . Renowned for his elegant pursuits, he is a complete man combining arts [bun] and arms [bu]. A man of nobility, a descendant of the sixth grandson of the emperor Seiwa, he was a ruler endowed with awesome dignity and inspiring decorum. . . . He built a splendid castle, which was majestic, beautiful and high. . . . When he lectured on The Tale of Genji, the big river and the ocean took in small rivers, like the River Min entering Chu [name of an ancient country in China]. He could argue right and left and up and down. . . . He discussed Chinese poetic styles and recited by heart the secret teachings of Japanese poetry, that is, Kokinshū, Man'yōshū [Anthology of myriad leaves], and the Tale of Ise. He recited sitting down or walking. . . . The round fan in his hand sweeps away the muggy heat. The sharp sword he wears on his waist cut off human passions and ties. Try to paint him; it can't be done. Try to draw him; it can't be achieved. The more one looks up, the higher he is; the more one tries to delve, the harder he is to penetrate . . . . The late Hosokawa Yūsai passed away suddenly on the twentieth day of the eighth month of the fifteenth year of Keichō [1610] at age seventy-seven. His bereaved wife, Kōjuin, commissioned an artist to paint a portrait of his benign face, and asked me to write an inscription. My refusal was unheeded, so I have written useless words and wasted statements. . . . MS

29

27 Kōjuin

hanging scroll; ink and color on silk
104.0 x 51.0 (41 x 20)
Edo period, 1618

Tenjuan, Kyoto
Important Cultural Property

Kōjuin (1544–1618) is the posthumous Buddhist title of the wife of Hosokawa Yūsai (1534–1610); she was a daughter of Numata Mitsukane, ruler of Kumagawa Castle in Wakasa Province (part of present-day Fukui Prefecture). For a while she had followed the Christian faith, with the name of Maria, having been baptized early in the Keichō era (1596–1615).

The inscription on this portrait, written by Reikei Ungaku in the eleventh month of 1618, says that it was requested by Takayuki, one of her sons. Ungaku's signature is followed by his square relief seal. The painting now forms a pair with that of her then-deceased husband, painted a few years earlier. The sitter faces her husband, her palms joined in prayer and one knee raised. This work, like cat. 26, also has a counterpart in the Eisei Bunko. The Eisei Bunko version has an inscription written in the eighth month of the same year by Yūsetsu Zuihō, which says that Hosokawa Tadaoki (Sansai, 1563–1646) had commissioned it.

The inscription on this portrait eulogizes Kōjuin for her Buddhist faith and her knowledge of Chinese literature, qualities that would have made her particularly compatible with her husband. It reads, in part:

. . . Her grace is bountiful, her courteousness

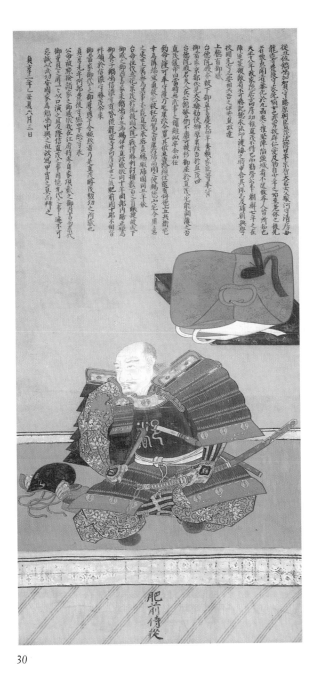

30

31

knows no bounds. . . . Her late father continued the Numata family, and served as a retainer at the shogun's camps [where he found her] a perfect match, marrying her to a Hosokawa. [She] retired to a splendid mansion with colorful beams, and her eldest son succeeded to the headship of the family. . . . Once she saw the cherry blossoms in the capital and realized how Buddhism viewed all myriad things as ephemeral. Another time she stopped at cascades and understood how the pines . . . kept their color with unshaken constancy. When she recited from the [Chinese] Book of Songs, she would dip the brush in ink, ponder for a while, and compose a tanka [thirty-one-syllable Japanese poem] on such themes as the rain on Mount Fu and the waves of the Xiang River. Again, following Chinese metric poems, she would spontaneously play the

twenty-five stringed zither. . . . She loved books by [the Chinese Tang-dynasty poet] Du Fu, and would write down [the Chinese Tang-dynasty poet] Hanshan's poem Maple Grove when she heard the theme of the Tatsuta River in a Japanese poem. . . . Her memory will benefit from all her goodness, and lovely leaves and branches [her descendants] will be countless. . . .   MS

28 Hosokawa Sansai

hanging scroll; ink and color on silk
107.5 x 51.5 (42¼ x 20¼)
Edo period, 1670

Eisei Bunko, Tokyo

Seated on a tatami mat with a hossu (Zen monk's whisk) in his right hand is Hosokawa Sansai (Tadaoki; 1563–1646), a distin-

guished warrior and tea practitioner of the late Momoyama and early Edo periods. The oldest son of Hosokawa Yūsai (Fujitaka, 1534–1610), Sansai was an astute and loyal vassal who served three military hegemons in their relentless quest to unify the nation: Oda Nobunaga (1534–1582), Toyotomi Hideyoshi (1537–1598) and, at the Battle of Sekigahara in 1600 (cat. 104), Tokugawa Ieyasu (1543–1616). In this portrait, Sansai wears a robe with the paulownia mon, the family crest of the Toyotomi.

This commemorative portrait was commissioned in 1670 by San, an adopted daughter of Sansai, around the time of the twenty-fifth anniversary of his death. It was presented to Kōtōin, a subtemple of Daitokuji that was the mortuary temple Sansai had built for his father Yūsai. The long dedicatory inscription, dated to 1670 and written by the monk Ken'ei Sōtan (1511–1672) of Kōtōin, summarizes the events of Sansai's life. In the inscription, Sansai is called *Daikoji* (Great Buddhist Layman). It makes special mention of the suicide of Sansai's Christian wife Gracia, daughter of Nobunaga's assassin, Akechi Mitsuhide. Before the Battle of Sekigahara (1600), in which her husband supported Tokugawa Ieyasu, Gracia had been taken hostage by the leader of the opposing forces. To preserve her husband from wavering in loyalty to Ieyasu out of concern for her safety, Gracia committed suicide.

Ieyasu rewarded Sansai's loyalty and military support by giving him in fief Buzen Province (parts of the present-day Prefectures of Fukuoka and Ōita), which he ruled from the refurbished Kokura Castle. Ieyasu also presented him with a coveted Chinese *chaire* (tea container) named *Rikyū shiribukura* (Rikyū's fat bottom; cat. 277), as well as swords and Chinese Zen calligraphies.

In 1621, Sansai retired to Nakatsu Castle in Buzen Province, leaving the position of head of the family to his son Tadatoshi. Tadatoshi became daimyo of Higo (present-day Kumamoto Prefecture) in 1632, and Sansai moved to Yatsushiro, also in Higo. With the nation at peace, Sansai spent the remainder of his life between Yatsushiro, Kyoto, and Edo (present-day Tokyo), devoting much of his time to the pursuit of tea and the supervision of kilns that he had established for the production of tea wares. He died in 1645 and was buried at Kōtōin, where his grave was marked by a stone lantern that he had received from his tea master, Sen no Rikyū (1522–1591). YS

29 Hosokawa Hasumaru

hanging scroll; ink and color on silk
66.4 x 34.0 (26⅛ x 13⅜)
Momoyama period, 1587

Chōshōin, Kyoto
Important Cultural Property

Almost all of the portraits of children from the Momoyama period were of deceased sons or daughters, painted at the request of the grieving parents. Behind every child's face is the profound sorrow experienced by those left behind. The sitter depicted here, Hosokawa Hasumaru, was the ninth child of Hosokawa Yūsai (1534–1610). On the eighth day of the seventh month of 1587, the gravely ill Hasumaru arrived in Kyoto from Tango for medical treatment and curative prayer, to no avail. Yūsai learned the sad news of his son's death upon his return from a military venture in Kyushu for Toyotomi Hideyoshi (1537–1598).

The inscription above the figure was written by Baikoku Genpō; two of his seals

can be seen in the column at the far right of the inscription. It is dated to 1587, when Genpō was abbot of Nanzenji; the portrait is from Chōshōin, a subtemple of Nanzenji. Genpō was the spiritual mentor of Baiin Genchū, Yūsai's younger brother. According to the inscription, Hasumaru died at age twelve. He is described as a conscientious student of classical learning, poetry, and music, as well as of the sword and the crossbow.

In the portrait, Hasumaru still wears bangs, indicating that he had yet to perform the coming-of-age ceremony. Nevertheless, he is depicted wearing the formal dress of the Momoyama-and Edo-period samurai; the sleeveless jacket with extended shoulders (*kataginu*) and full trousers (*hakama*) over a *kosode*. The samurai's standard long (*Katana*) and short (*wakizashi*) swords are thrust through his sash. His pose is also that of the adult samurai: right hand holding a folding fan, left hand clenched (see cats. 14, 15, 16). The pale blue and gold brocade of the *kataginu* and *hakama*, and the chrysanthemum-and-lattice design on the *kosode* reflect the sumptuous fashions favored in the Momoyama period. MS

30 Nabeshima Naoshige

hanging scroll; ink and color on silk
84.5 x 41.0 (33¼ x 16⅛)
Edo period, no later than 1685

Kōdenji, Saga Prefecture

Warriors in full battle dress are seldom portrayed in Japanese art. A portrait such as this is especially rare in that the sitter is captured at the moment just before leaving for battle, with his ceremonial robes and cap removed and laid behind him. His helmet is placed beside him on the *tatami* mat. He firmly grasps a fan in his right hand and a *tachi* sword in his left. He bends slightly forward, with a determined gaze. On the front of the cuirass the character *miyako* (capital) is written in archaic script; its significance remains unknown.

The sitter is Nabeshima Naoshige (1538–1618). At one time, he was a retainer of Ryūzōji Takanobu of Hizen Province (parts of the present-day Prefectures of Nagasaki and Saga), a local warlord who died in action during the 1584 Battle of Shimabara and fought against the powerful Shimazu forces. Naoshige then supported Takanobu's son Masaie. In 1590 Masaie retired and Naoshige succeeded to the leadership of the Ryūzōji clan. After the Battle of Sekigahara in 1600 (cat. 104), on the order of Tokugawa Ieyasu (1543–1616), he subdued the forces of the Tachibana clan in Chikugo Province (part of present-day Fukuoka Prefecture), and the Saga domain was officially recognized as his.

This painting is kept at Kōdenji, the Nabeshima family's mortuary temple,

which belongs to the Sōtō school of Zen Buddhism. The inscription, whose author remains unknown, gives Naoshige's biography, highlighting his military and civil accomplishments. Chief among them are his valor as a leader of Hideyoshi's expedition forces in Korea, his establishment of a school and the Buddhist temple Enkōji upon his return from Korea, and his loyalty, and his son's, to the Tokugawa shogunate.

The last five columns of the inscription tell of the circumstances in which the portrait came to be painted:

. . . In the first year of Jōkyō [1684], when Abe, Bungo no kami, and Hotta, Shimousa no kami, were ordered [by the fifth shogun Tsunayoshi] to check letters of thanks [from the past shoguns] kept in various daimyo families, I was in Edo, and took to the castle those given to our family. I explained [to the shogun] orally the honor of the manifold favors [our family had received in the past] referring in particular to [Ryūzōji] Takanobu and Naoshige. I recalled things about the latter, our forebear, that are not to be forgotten. Indeed, bringing peace to the nation through military feats, he became the founder of the Nabeshima clan, which is now being revived. Thus, here is a portrait [of Naoshige] clad in armor and I bow deeply to it.

The third day of the sixth month, the second year of Jōkyō [1685].

At the bottom of the painting is written *Hizen jijū* (Chamberlain from Hizen), an honorific court title. MS

31 Honda Tadakatsu

hanging scroll; ink and color on paper
124.0 x 64.0 (48¾ x 25¼)
Momoyama period, early 17th century

Honda Takayuki, Tokyo
Important Cultural Property

Honda Heihachirō Tadakatsu (1548–1610) was a famous military leader who served Tokugawa Ieyasu (1543–1616). Along with Sakakibara Yasumasa (1548–1606) and two others, he is one of the so-called *Shitennō* (Four Deva Kings) of Ieyasu. He followed Ieyasu into more than fifty battles and, in 1601, as a reward for his long service, became daimyo of a domain in Ise Province (most of Mie Prefecture).

Tadakatsu sits on a folding chair, wearing black armor; the actual armor worn by the sitter is included in this exhibition, (cat. 160.) A set of prayer beads hangs from Tadakatsu's right shoulder across his chest. He wears a long *tachi* sword and a shorter *wakizashi* and holds a *saihai* (commander's baton). The forms in this portrait—the sitter's face, the *hakama* (trousers), even the sandal cords and most remarkably the armor—are angular and abstracted. Although there is no direct relationship, this quality recalls the portrait of Minamoto Yoritomo (cat. 1).   SY

32 Kuroda Nagamasa

hanging scroll; ink and color on paper
126.0 x 59.5 (49 5/8 x 23 3/8)
Edo period, no later than 1624

Fukuoka Art Museum,
Fukuoka Prefecture
Important Cultural Property

Kuroda Nagamasa (1568–1623), a prominent daimyo, was the ruler of a large domain at Fukuoka in Chikuzen Province (part of present-day Fukuoka Province). He first served Toyotomi Hideyoshi (1537–1598) and then Tokugawa Ieyasu (1543–1616). Nagamasa fought in many battles, including the 1583 Battle of Shizugatake, the 1584 battles of Komaki and Nagakute, the Korean expeditions of 1592 and 1597, and the 1600 Battle of Sekigahara (cat. 104). He was at one time an enthusiastic supporter of Christianity, and used a seal written in the roman alphabet.

Nagamasa is shown mounted on a dappled horse wearing an Ichinotani helmet and, under a *jinbaori* jacket, a set of black armor (cat. 162). He is prepared to go to the front, holding a *saihai* (commander's baton) in his right hand and the reins of the horse in his left. The upper half of the painting is filled with two inscriptions. The shorter one, in large characters at the left, contains a poem. It was requested by Nagamasa's vassal Kuroda Kazunari and was written by the Zen scholar-monk Kōgetsu Sōgan (1574–1643); two of Kōgetsu's seals follow his signature. At the right is a long epitaph in smaller characters dated to 1624, written by Hayashi Razan (1583–1657), a distinguished Confucian scholar.

Kōgetsu's poem, read from left to right, follows:
With armor and arms the battlefield round
No one ever argues the merit of a sweating
    horse.
If overt power is likened to a plant
It is the plum blossom, that which first
    tastes the winds of spring.   SY

33 Sakakibara Yasumasa

hanging scroll; ink and color on silk
112.0 x 46.0 (44 x 18 1/8)
Momoyama period, early 17th century

Agency for Cultural Affairs, Tokyo
Important Cultural Property

Sakakibara Yasumasa (1548–1606) was a distinguished high-ranking warrior who, with Honda Tadakatsu (1548–1610), was counted among Tokugawa Ieyasu's (1543–1616) four most devoted retainers, his *Shitennō* (Four Deva Kings). Since the time of his father, Nagamasa, the family had served Ieyasu.

32

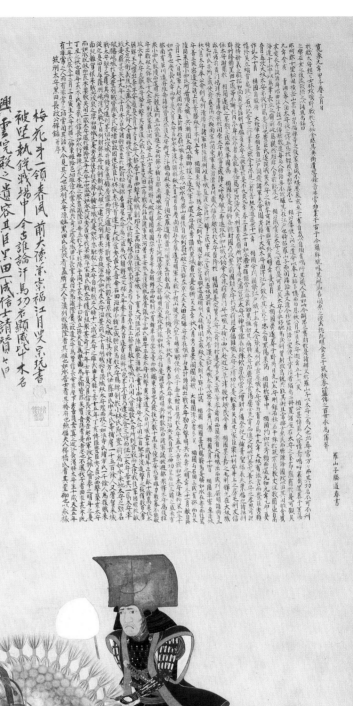

33

34

The name Yasumasa includes the character *yasu*, which he received from Ieyasu in appreciation of his loyalty. He achieved fame for his valor in battles, but after Ieyasu's triumph at the Battle of Sekigahara in 1600 (cat. 104), he found himself in opposition to the more bureaucratic group of military leaders around Ieyasu. Realizing that the age of battles was over, Yasumasa retired.

In this portrait Yasumasa sits on bear fur, wearing black armor, also shown in this exhibition (cat. 159). He wears a long *tachi* sword and a shorter *wakizashi* at his left waist and holds a *saihai* (commander's baton) in his right hand. A banner stands behind him. On it is a circle, symbolic of the sun, and the character *mu* (nothingness). A banner with the same design exists today, but the sun and the character *mu* are in gold leaf on an indigo ground. The portrait, the armor, and the banner were all in the Sakakibara family until recently.   SY

34 Inaba Ittetsu
hanging scroll; ink and color on silk
94.0 x 54.6 (37 x 21½)
Momoyama period, probably 1589

Chishōin, Kyoto
Important Cultural Property

Inaba Ittetsu (1516–1588) was the youngest child of Inaba Michinori, a military leader of Mino Province (part of present-day Gifu Prefecture). First he became a priest at Sūfukuji, built by Saitō Toshiyasu, the *shugodai* (acting military governor) of Mino, with Dokushū Kansai as the founding priest. In 1525, when the Asai family of Ōmi advanced on Mino, his father and five brothers died in action. Ittetsu (Single Iron) returned to the lay world and assumed the position of head of the family. He served as a retainer under military chieftains of four different clans—the Toki, Saitō, Oda, and Toyotomi. Ittetsu died in Shimizu Castle in Mino on the

nineteenth day of the eleventh month of 1588.

The inscription on this portrait was written by Gyokuho Shōsō (1546–1613) of Daitokuji in the tenth month of 1589; two of Shōsō's seals follow his signature. Although Ittetsu is presented as a priest, tonsured and clad in a dark outer robe, a *tachi* is at his side, reflecting his status as a warrior. According to the *Lineage of the Inaba Family*, Ittetsu's son Sadamichi asked an artist from Kyoto to paint this portrait. The style of the painting suggests that the painter may have been Hasegawa Tōhaku (1539–1610); who also painted a *chinsō* (portrait of a Zen priest) of Gyokuho Shōsō.

Portions of the inscription read as follows:

He was a brave soldier in the martial world, a loyal retainer of the family and country. In him the mortal and the saintly coexisted. His image combined the spiritual and the worldly, the two realities not interfering with each other....

壽像石田隠州太守梅岩道圓居士壽像寶
臘殿

才黄文武心養聖賢江花謝混幸風單名德化
稱第一溪家工參運選栝計咸儀目心三千端
筍遙大夫爵把槍撹晶士權鼓奪捉旗横揮
三亭者卧弘諸蕎別床異被保暮齡者呉
亀影笑常早文章遊藝園軒揺歌非
雅進喜對洛陽彫日心萬葉集窓繭潮水
月照看百家編李浄逸傳諸則博淵日郎
慶彙官晴則耕石田加二嘉尚智者宗師古
被自德止観教道釘由居士今呈高量
壽聖禅慨必言外妙心即躰中玄新披得
雲山納衷女端坐四大輔圏室則
不有貫小斗踵久昌宣中三桂此夫沸外
三梅啄

要見真相處

月明常惡御楼前
    壽二至皆囲居士海幻賀求寶里雄
    推綽不許以級早語塞其請云

維時文禄第三甲午菊月吉辰

前妙心現住雲山小此丘伯蒲叟誌暑

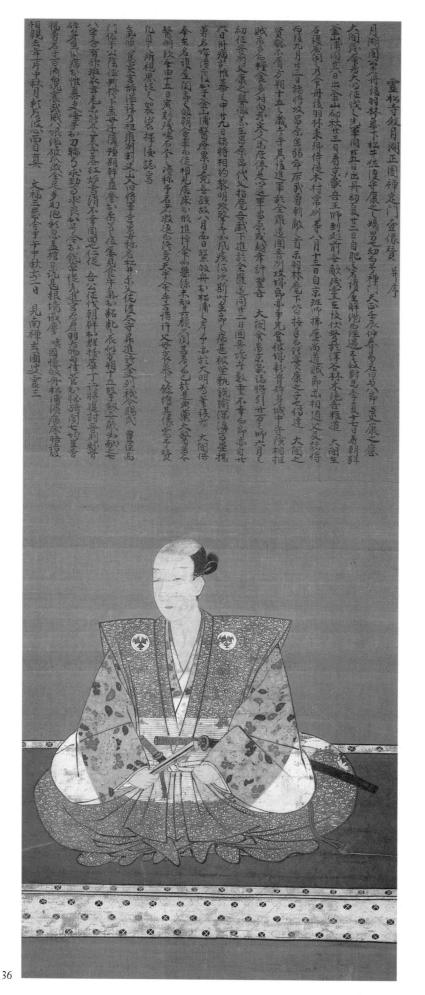

36

37

Here is my clumsy eulogy:

*In good virtue and fragrant name he had no
peer
Cutting the sky horizontally, his treasured
sword flashed as if with new snow and
frost
Sitting grand in this house, what is it that
he knows?
Ironwood blossoms [a reference to his
name and metaphor for something rare]
and spring are in heaven and earth.
Ah! . . .*   MS

35 Ishida Masatsugu

hanging scroll; ink and color on silk
61.0 x 35.8 (24 x 14)
Momoyama period, no later than 1594

Jushōin, Kyoto
Important Art Object

Ishida Masatsugu (d. 1600) was the father
of the warrior Ishida Mitsunari (1560–
1600), who led a coalition of daimyo
against Tokugawa Ieyasu (1543–1616) at the
decisive Battle of Sekigahara in 1600 (cat.
104). Mitsunari had gained power as an important retainer of Hideyoshi, and Masatsugu's skills as a warrior and administrator
also came to be in demand. He served as
daikan (deputy governor) of Sakai (near
present-day Osaka), the area under the
Toyotomi's direct rule. After Mitsunari's
defeat at the Battle of Sekigahara and the
fall of his garrison castle at Sawayama in
Ōmi (present-day Shiga Prefecture), Masatsugu and the rest of his family committed suicide. Mitsunari was beheaded on
the banks of the Kamo River in Kyoto.

In this painting, the tonsured Masatsugu is presented as a Buddhist cleric; his
warrior status, though, is represented by
the short *koshigatana* sword at his waist.
His outer robe is richly patterned with
paulownia blossoms. The artist has captured Masatsugu's imposing presence and
his sharp, determined expression, conveyed through the eyes and furrowed
brow.

The inscription was written by Ha-
kuho Eryō, one-time abbot of Myōshinji.
It is dated to 1594, indicating that the portrait was painted during Masatsugu's lifetime. Two of Eryō's seals follow his
signature. The inscription says that it was
written at the request of Masatsugu himself, and that Masatsugu had come under
Eryō's spiritual influence. The portrait
comes from Jushōin, a subtemple within
Myōshinji founded by Eryō and named after Masatsugu's Buddhist title.

The inscription reads in part:

*. . . Talented both in arts [bun] and arms
[bu], his heart nourishes saintliness and wisdom. . . . His body grand and robust; his decorum awesome and full of dignity. . . . A*

*valiant warrior with a spear . . . waging a
battle totally under his control, this is like
[the Chinese general] Zhuge Liang, though
in a different seat and a different robe. . . .
He swings his poetry fan lightly and dances
in an elegant gathering. In spring he sees
cherry blossoms in the capital, and daily recites poems from the Man'yōshū. Through
his window is the changing scene of the lake
under the moonlight, and he looks at the
books by one hundred poets. . . . He left his
place of living and threw away his office.
Now he tills the Fields of Stones [that is,
Ishida, his family name] . . . .*   MS

36 Matsui Yohachirō

hanging scroll; ink and color on silk
90.0 x 37.0 (35 3/8 x 14 1/2)
Momoyama period, probably 1594

Hōsenji, Kyoto

Matsui Yohachirō (d. 1593) was the first-
born son of Matsui Yasuyuki (1550–1612).
Yasuyuki was a *karō* (elder) who served Hosokawa Yūsai (1534–1610) and his son Sansai (1563–1646). Yohachirō served with
distinction during the 1592 Korean expedition. He returned home with an illness,
however, and died on the fifteenth day of
the eighth month of the following year.
His grief-stricken parents commissioned
this posthumous portrait. The inscription,
focusing on Yohachirō's military feats in
Korea, is dated the day before the first anniversary of Yohachirō's death and was
written by Genpo Reisan of Nanzenji; two
seals are impressed below his signature.

Yohachirō is sumptuously dressed in a
green *Kosode* with gold and dark green
flower and leaf designs, and over it the formal dress of a samurai (sleeveless jacket
and full trousers) with a design of scattered
white pine needles. He is seated on a *tatami* mat and wears two swords. His right
hand holds a fan and the left is clenched,
as in so many warrior portraits of the time.
The composition is close to that of the
portrait of Hosokawa Hasumaru (cat. 29).
The oval face, delicate eyes and nose rendered with sinuous lines, and small, thin
lips contribute to an overall gentle facial
expression not unlike those seen in contemporary genre paintings.   SY

37 Sakuma Shōgen

Kano Tan'yū (1602–1674)
hanging scroll; ink and color on silk
63.8 x 28.4 (25 1/8 x 11 1/8)
Edo period, c. 1636

Shinjuan, Kyoto

Sakuma Shōgen Sanekatsu (1570–1642) was
a warrior who first served Toyotomi Hideyoshi (1537–1598), and then three successive generations of Tokugawa shoguns:
Ieyasu (1543–1616), Hidetada (1578–1631),

and Iemitsu (1604–1651). He also was renowned as a tea adept, and had built a tea
house named *Sunshōan* in 1617 within the
precinct of Ryūkōin, a subtemple of Daitokuji. He used *Sunshōan* as his artistic sobriquet and was a great collector of art.
Among the treasures included in his collection at Sunshōan were twelve fragments from a codex of eleventh-century
calligraphy transcribing poems from the
Kokinshū anthology. Known as the *Sunshōan shikishi* (Sunshōan poem sheets),
they are now dispersed among various collections. The tea house no longer survives.

Kōgetsu Sōgan (1574–1643), a Zen
monk of considerable expertise in arts and
letters who had been instrumental in the
restoration of Daitokuji, inscribed this
scroll as follows:

*Inscription beckoned by the portrait of
Tokusōsaishu San'in Sōka Koji [Sakuma
Shōgen] painted during his lifetime
A breeze of fresh wind sweeps away the
worldly dust
Hiding in the thicket is a man growing old
Around his waist he still has a house and
rare treasures
Polishing them with a three-foot hossu
[Zen monk's whisk] won't make them
clean.
Written by Yawning Man
Kōgetsu [tripod-shaped relief seal]
Sōgan [square relief seal]*

Sakuma Shōgen sits in front of a
screen painting of a dragon in a bamboo
grove, opposite a boy attendant with a
Chinese hair style. He himself is wearing
the informal loose gown and soft cap of
the Chinese gentleman-scholar in retirement or at leisure. Both the painting and
the inscription compare Shōgen to a high-
minded Chinese recluse. This portrait is
similar to another work depicting Shōgen,
painted by Kano Tan'yū (1602–1674; cat.
42) and also inscribed by Kōgetsu, in 1641.
A note written on the back of the Shinjuan painting says that on the original
wooden roller of the scroll, now lost, was a
date corresponding to 1636. It is assumed
that the painting dates from around
1636.   SY

38 Sen no Rikyū

attributed to Hasegawa Tōhaku
(1539–1610)
hanging scroll; ink and color on silk
80.6 x 36.7 (31 3/4 x 14 3/8)
Momoyama period, no later than 1595

Sen Sōsa collection, Kyoto

Sen no Rikyū (1522–1591) was born into a
merchant family in Sakai, a bustling port
city south of Osaka. After studying tea
with Kitamuki Dōchin (1504–1562) and Takeno Jōō (1502–1555), he became the leading exponent of *wabi* (simple, or rustic)

文禄第四乙未歳台春�日
上毛春供養
宗慶興之請贊伽陀一絶係
利休居士肖像當題信男
斯一翁手跡知
旧時姿趙州且盤喫茶底方不
頭上申兼手中頼儲與遺儀

三玄齋宗quad園

後学羅浮散人賛

庭帥生に意思中
背山別業似瀟水
高標清節嘯松風
道學勃興桑海東

印是先生樂景春
四垣松市一庭亭
本朝怡然六経真
北囿峯頭世外身

香巖西堂
拜賛

38

39

style tea in his own time, and perhaps the most important (certainly the best known) figure in the whole history of tea. He served as personal tea instructor to Oda Nobunaga (1534–1582) and then Toyotomi Hideyoshi (1537–1598). This position enabled him to become a close confidant of Hideyoshi and to acquire the substantial political influence inherent in such a relationship. In 1591, however, for reasons now unclear, Hideyoshi ordered him to commit suicide.

Tanaka Sōkei, thought to be related to Rikyū and one of the founders of the Raku kiln (cats. 285, 286), commissioned this portrait. The Raku wares were developed under Rikyū's close aesthetic supervision. The inscription was written by Shun'oku Sōen (1529–1611) of Daitokuji, the spiritual successor to Shōryō Sōkin; both priests instructed Rikyū in Zen.

Rikyū is portrayed in this painting as a lay Buddhist, wearing a black robe and holding a fan. The style of the painting, especially in the face, recalls that of Hasegawa Tōhaku who frequently painted for Rikyū and Sōen. Tōhaku was commissioned by Rikyū to execute the ceiling painting of the gate of Daitokuji. He also painted sliding door panels in Sangen'in, a subtemple that was Sōen's residential quarters. There is, thus, a strong possibility that Tōhaku painted this portrait.

The inscription reads, from left to right:

Hat on his head and fan in his hand
The solemn image he left behind captures
*   what he always was*
Like Zhao Zhou [a Chinese Zen priest famous for his intuitive approach] *he sits*
*   awhile and drinks tea*
This old man seems to gain knowledge
*   without struggle.*
Sōkei showed me Layman Rikyū's portrait
*   and asked me to write an inscription, so I*
*   have written a four-line verse and offer*
*   this with incense.*
Fourteenth day, ninth month, fourth year of
*   Bunroku* [1595]
Sangen, Old Shun'oku Sōen
Sōen [square intaglio seal]

MS

39 Fujiwara Seika living in leisure
Kano Sansetsu (1589–1651)
hanging scroll; ink on paper
119.5 x 31.3 (47 x 12⅜)
Edo period, early 17th century

Nezu Institute of Fine Arts, Tokyo

Fujiwara Seika (1561–1619) was a Confucian scholar whose teachings were of great significance in the early Edo period; Seika was the name of his residence. He was descended from the aristocratic Reizei family, guardians and perpetuators of one of the traditions of classical Japanese poetry.

While still in his teens, Seika entered Shōkokuji, one of the five major Zen monasteries of Kyoto, where he studied Zen as well as classical Chinese literature and Song Neo-Confucianism. Seika eventually returned to lay life and led a renaissance in Song Confucian scholarship.

In the Edo period, Confucianism became the official teaching of the governing samurai class, and daimyo employed prominent scholars to assist them in governing. Hayashi Razan (1583–1657), Seika's student and one of the inscribers of this painting, served the shogunate, but Seika himself refused official engagement, and in his later years retired to a mountain retreat at Ichiharano north of Kyoto. That retreat is the setting for this painting. Although the retreat no longer stands, an old well remains.

The painter of the portrait, Kano Sansetsu, was the leading student and adopted heir of Kano Sanraku (1559–1635), whom he succeeded as head of the Kano studio; he was also an admirer of Seika. The regular geometric composition is both characteristic of Sansetsu's work and idiosyncratic within the Kano school. Sansetsu's signature can be seen at the lower right, followed by his seal.

Razan wrote the lower inscription, read from left to right, with a seal following his signature; in his collected works, this poem is dated to 1639. Hori Kyōan (1585–1642), another close disciple of Seika, wrote the upper inscription, read from left to right and with two seals underlying his signature at the right. Both inscriptions eulogize Seika's retreat and his studies of Confucianism.

WA

40 Ishikawa Jōzan
Kano Tan'yū (1602–1674)
hanging scroll; ink and color on silk
100.6 x 38.3 (39⅝ x 15)
Edo period, mid–17th century

Jōzanji (Shisendō), Kyoto

Although Ishikawa Jōzan (1583–1672) fought with distinction in many military engagements for Tokugawa Ieyasu (1543–1616), in 1615, during the summer battle of Osaka, he disobeyed his commanders out of excessive zeal and was severely reprimanded. Jōzan relinquished his domain and went to Kyoto where he took the tonsure and became a monk at Myōshinji. Later, in order to support his mother when she became seriously ill, Jōzan entered the service of the daimyo Asano Nagaakira, lord of Kii and later of Aki domains; upon his mother's death, he returned to Kyoto. At the age of fifty-eight, he built a retreat in Ichijōji village, in northeastern Kyoto, and asked Kano Tan'yū, the foremost painter of that time, to paint portraits of thirty-six Tang and Song Chinese poets. Hanging them on the walls, Jōzan called his retreat Shisendō (Hall of Immortal

40

41

42

Poets), and lived there in retirement. Shisendō, also known as Jōzanji, still stands today.

Jōzan studied Confucianism from Fujiwara Seika (1561–1619). He was accomplished in Chinese poetry and *reisho* (C: *li shu*), the archaic, clerical style of calligraphy, and also painted in the Chinese mode. He was a friend of Hayashi Razan (1583–1657) and Hori Kyōan (1585–1642), both also students of Seika.

In this portrait, signed and sealed by Tan'yū at the lower left, Jōzan leans on an armrest in a relaxed manner. The pose is reminiscent of imaginary portraits of such famous literary figures as the Tang Chinese poet Li Bo and the Nara-period Japanese poet Hitomaro. The brushwork and use of colors are refined, and the sitter is presented as a man of lofty thoughts and of purity of mind. The inscription, written in clerical-style script by Jōzan himself, is followed by his seal:

*He reclines on the armrest at ease, wearing a
   dark brown cap
His face quiet and eminent, his spirit bright
   and lofty
He communes with nature, nourishes his
   inner spirit
His thoughts stubborn at age eighty, a
   hermit of three spirits
Who is this hermit but Rokuroku Sanjin*
[Jōzan's artistic pseudonym].

WA

41 **Kaihō Yūshō and his wife**
   attributed to Kaihō Yūchiku
   (1654–1728)
   hanging scroll; ink and color on paper
   114.7 x 44.0 (45⅛ x 17¼)
   Edo period, early 18th century

   Kaihō Hiroshi Collection, Kyoto
   Important Cultural Property

Kaihō Yūshō (1533–1615) was one of the most prominent painters of the Momo-

yama period. In this posthumous, commemorative portrait, Yūshō and his wife Myōtei look at a painting of the Tang Chinese poet Li Bo viewing a waterfall.

The greater part of the inscription at the top of the portrait, written by Yūshō's grandson Yūchiku in 1724, gives an account of Yūshō's life. In the shorter section at the right, Yūchiku has transcribed a letter written in 1608 by a Korean government official named Pak Tae-gǔn who sought a painting by Yūshō, whom he called "number one under heaven."

Because the painting is stamped with the seals *Kaihō* and *Dōki* at the lower right, the seals of Yūshō's son Yūsetsu (1598–1677), it has long been attributed to Yūsetsu. Recent scholarship has determined that these seals were added later, however, and the painting is now believed to have been painted by Yūchiku.

Myōtei wears a *kosode* robe and an *uchikake* (outer *kosode* worn without a

90

43

sash). According to the history of the Kaihō family written in Yūchiku's time, this *kosode* and *uchikake* were gifts from Iemitsu (1604–1651), the third Tokugawa shogun, whom Myōtei and Yūsetsu met after Yūshō's death. The meeting was arranged by Iemitsu's wetnurse Kasuga no Tsubone, the youngest daughter of Saitō Toshimitsu, a military leader and close friend of Yūshō. In this painting, Myōtei is portrayed with her back to the viewer, giving prominence to the *kosode* and the *uchikake* decorated with the Tokugawa *mon* of three hollyhock leaves, thus recording for posterity the honor bestowed on the Kaihō family.   SY

42 **Kano Tan'yū**
Momota Ryūei (1647–1698)
hanging scroll; ink and color on paper
66.4 x 47.9 (26 1/8 x 18 7/8)
Edo period, late 17th century

Kyoto National Museum
Important Cultural Property

The painter Kano Tan'yū (1602–1674), the eldest son of Takanobu (cat. 18), not only cemented the prestigious reputation of the Kano school of painting, but also established the official painting style of the Edo period. This work is thought to be a preparatory sketch for a finished painting, now lost, which was in the Kajibashi Kano family of Edo, founded by Tan'yū and one of the four Kano families that served the shogunate.

With concentrated gaze, Tan'yū holds a paintbrush in his right hand. He was probably in his last years when this portrait was painted; he has lost much of his hair, he is flabby around the mouth, and

his face is deeply wrinkled. The sharp eyes, prominent hooked nose, tightly closed lips, and square jaw nevertheless convey the strength of the aging artist, who was to painting what Tokugawa Ieyasu was to politics.

Although there is no seal on the painting, an inscription, *Painted by Ryūei*, identifying the artist, is written on top of the lid of the box that contains the scroll. Momota Ryūei was one of four close disciples of Tan'yū. He served the Shimazu family of Satsuma Province (part of present-day Kagoshima Prefecture) as a painter, and also practiced medicine.   AY

44

43 Minamoto Yoritomo
polychromed wood
h. 70.6 (27 3/4)
Kamakura period, 2nd half of 13th
century
Tokyo National Museum
Important Cultural Property

Minamoto Yoritomo (1147–1199), a late
Heian warrior, rose to political power by
destroying the rival Taira clan, and all potential competitors within his own lineage.
In 1192 he was appointed by the emperor
seiitaishōgun (Great General Who Quells
the Barbarians) and, as the first shogun of
the Kamakura shogunate, initiated a
warrior-class regime.

This statue of Yoritomo purportedly
was enshrined at Shirahatasha in the
Tsurugaoka Hachimangū in Kamakura. In
1180 the Tsurugaoka Hachimangū was
moved by Yoritomo from Yuigahama to its
present location, and it thrived under government support in the following years.

Perhaps for this reason the statue of Yoritomo was placed in a building inside the
shrine complex. Shirahatasha was destroyed by fire in 1280 and reconstructed
soon after. This statue dates to the period
of Shirahatasha's reconstruction.

The figure holds a *shaku* (wooden ceremonial slat) in his right hand, and he
wears the informal court dress of the
Heian aristocrat: an *eboshi* (black headgear), a *kariginu* (hunting robe) on the upper body, and *sashinuki* (baggy pants tied
around the ankles) on the lower body. This
apparel, also found on the statue of Hōjō
Tokiyori in Kenchōji (cat. 44), is typical of
warriors' statues in the Kamakura period.
The head and torso were carved from separate pieces of wood, front and back, with
additional pieces for the face and knees.
The interior of the statue is hollow, and
the eyes are inlaid crystal. Much of the
original polychromy has been lost.   NK

44 Hōjō Tokiyori
polychromed wood
h. 68.9 (27 1/8)
Kamakura period, late 13th century
Kenchōji, Kanagawa Prefecture
Important Cultural Property

This statue of a fully dressed warrior is
said to be of Hōjō Tokiyori (1227–1263),
who as *shikken* (regent for the shogun) between 1246 and 1256 exercised supreme
power in the Kamakura shogunate. The
construction of Kenchōji, where this work
is enshrined, began in 1249 at Tokiyori's
initiative and was completed in 1253. Its
first chief priest was Lanqi Daolong (J:
Rankei Dōryū; 1213–1278), a Chinese Chan
(Zen) priest of the Rinzai school. The temple has been destroyed by fire several
times; hence no contemporary written
documents concerning this statue are extant.

Numerous works based on close ob-
servation of the subject were made during

45

the Kamakura period. This trend toward realism resulted in many fine portraits of well-known personalities from the last half of the thirteenth century on. Like the figure in cat. 43, Tokiyori wears an *eboshi* (black court headgear), a *kariginu* (hunting robe), and *sashinuki* (baggy pants tied around the ankles). The small eyes, which gaze into the distance, mouth turned slightly down at the outer corners, and upturned nose capture the individuality of the artist's model. The technical execution seems to place this work in the later half of the thirteenth century.

The head and body are made of two pieces of Japanese cypress (*hinoki*), one each for front and back; separate pieces are attached for the sides of the body, legs, and the robe, and the eyes are inlaid crystal. Cloth was glued onto the surface of the statue, then coated with *sabi urushi* (thick raw lacquer mixed with pulverized stone) and over this undercoating black lacquer was applied followed by white pigment, and finally colored pigments. The surface has deteriorated, however, expos-

ing the brown *sabi* lacquer. The wooden ceremonial slat (*shaku*) in the right hand is a later addition.   SH

45 Miura Yoshiaki
polychromed wood
h. 99.5 (39⅛)
Kamakura period, 13th–14th century
Manshōji, Kanagawa Prefecture

The warrior Miura Yoshiaki (Ōsuke, 1092–1180) wielded great power in the Miura Peninsula (Kanagawa Prefecture) and surrounding areas in the late Heian period. When Minamoto Yoritomo (1147–1199) rose to attack the Taira clan, Yoshiaki led the Miura clan in support of Yoritomo. He was defeated by the Taira, and he died in battle. Yoritomo, having become shogun in 1192, built Manshōji in honor of Yoshiaki near the site of his death in 1194. An inscription inside the head of the statue states that Minamoto Yoritomo built Manshōji for Yoshiaki.

The figure wears the formal attire of a high aristocrat of the Heian period: a *kanmuri* (formal hat indicating court rank), a *tachi* (slung sword), and in his right hand a wooden ceremonial slat (*shaku*). The face is old and wrinkled, but the concentrated, severe gaze and the tightly closed lips convey inner power.

The head and body were made from two separate pieces of wood, front and back, and the head was separated from the body at the neck for further hollowing-out and then reattached. The eyes are crystal. Though the interior was hollowed out, the walls remain thick, making the statue very heavy.

This portrait statue occupies a shrine called Goryō Myōjin in the Manshōji complex. Goryō Myōjin was purportedly built in 1212. The striking degree of stylization of the body suggests that the portrait was made much later, toward the end of the Kamakura period. Inside the body are three wooden tablets documenting, among other things, the restoration of the statue in 1719.   NK

46

46 Itchin

Kōshun (fl. 1334)
polychromed wood
h. 79.0 (31⅛)
Nanbokuchō period, 1334

Chōrakuji, Kyoto
Important Cultural Property

This is one of seven portrait sculptures of Jishū-school patriarchs from Konkōji, the Jishū training temple on Shichijō Street in Kyoto. When Konkōji was closed in 1908, all seven statues were moved to Chōrakuji in Kyoto. Jishū is a populist branch of the devotional Jōdo (Pure Land, or Amidist) sect of Buddhism. It was founded by the monk Ippen (1239–1289) in the mid-Kamakura period and remained a considerable force in Japanese religious life through the fifteenth century, patronized especially by common people and by the tough and unsophisticated warriors from eastern Japan.

According to temple tradition, this statue depicts Donkai (1265–1327), the fourth patriarch of the Ji sect, the first ab-bot of Konkōji, and the founder of Shō-jōkōji in Kanagawa Prefecture, the head-quarters of the Jiji sect. However, in the course of the recent restoration, writing was found inside the statue, stating that Kōshun sculpted this portrait of the fifty-seven-year-old Yo Amidabutsu (the Buddhist name of Itchin). Itchin (1278–1355), the sixth patriarch of the Jiji sect, was the abbot of Shōjōkōji and also later became the first abbot of the training temple Kōshōji, on Ichijō Street in Kyoto.

The statue wears a simple *kesa* (priest's mantle) over a priestly robe. The palms, joined in front of the chest, are common to seated portraits of Jishū priests. The face, with crystal eyes, is descriptively rendered. This portrait is the finest and oldest of the group of seven Chōrakuji sculptures, and it is significant as a rare *juzō*, that is, a portrait made during the subject's lifetime. (Most Japanese "portraits" were posthumous, sometimes by many generations.)

Details about the artist Kōshun are unknown. However, like Kōshu, the sculptor of a 1420 portrait of Ippen, also formerly at Konkōji, Kōshun is thought to be a Kei-school sculptor and later follower of the famous Unkei (d. 1223). NK

47 Yishan Yining

polychromed wood
h. 76.0 (29⅞)
Kamakura period, c. 1317

Nanzen'in, Kyoto

Yishan Yining (1247–1317), known in Japan as Issan Kokushi (National Teacher), was an erudite priest of Chinese Rinzai Zen Buddhism who came to Japan in 1299 carrying a diplomatic letter from Emperor Chengzong of the Yuan dynasty of China. Although suspected by the Kamakura shogunate of being a Yuan spy, this deeply cultured man had a strong spiritual impact on many people, including Hōjō Sadatoki (1271–1311), the shogunal regent from 1284 to 1301. Yishan became the abbot of Ken-chōji, Engakuji, and Jōchiji, renowned

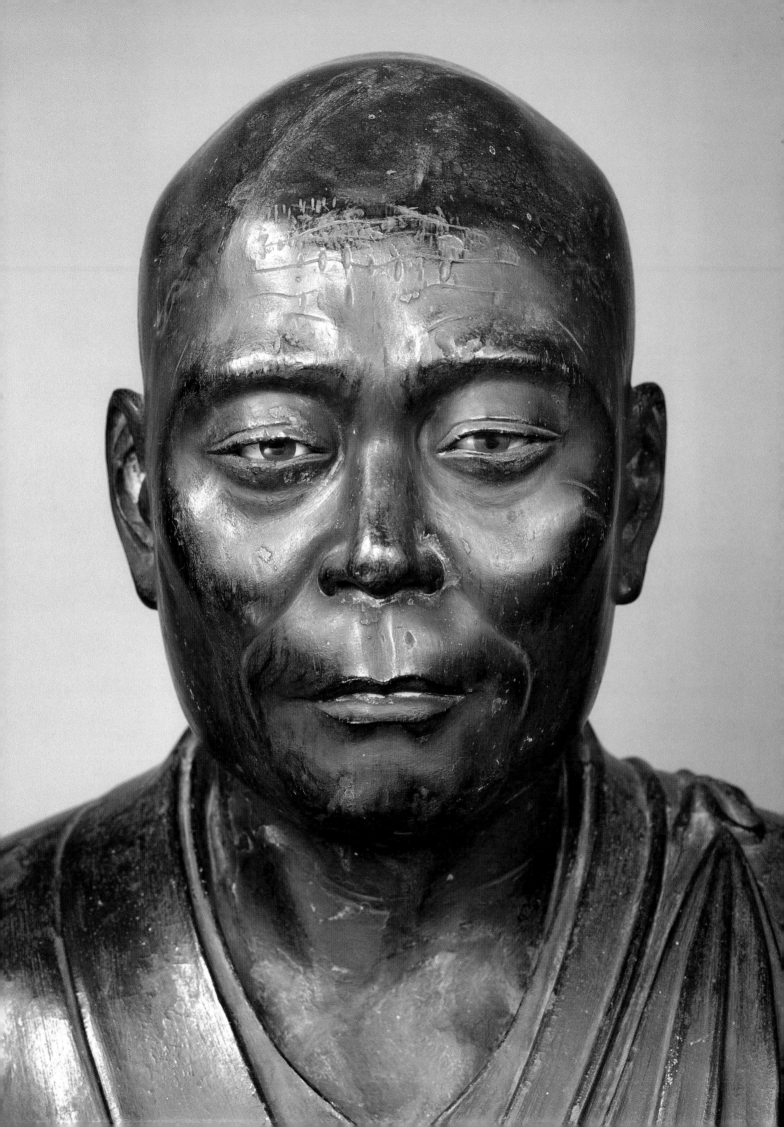

Zen monasteries of Kamakura. His fame reached finally to Kyoto where he was invited by the retired emperor Go-Uda (1267–1324), and was appointed the third abbot of Nanzenji. Go-Uda, devoted to Yishan's faith, posthumously bestowed on the priest the title *Kokushi* and built a mausoleum for him beside that of the emperor Kameyama (1249–1305), Go-Uda's father. Yishan is known as the father of *Gozan Bungaku* (Literature of the Five Mountains), the literary movement espoused by the scholar-monks of Japanese Zen in the fourteenth and fifteenth centuries. He was also instrumental in transmitting from China to Japan the Zhu Xi school of Confucianism.

An excellent example of *chinsō* sculpture (portraits of Zen priests), this statue, probably made soon after Yishan's death in 1317, is enshrined at Nanzen'in, a subtemple of Nanzenji and the site of the mausoleums of Kameyama and Yishan. Made of Japanese cypress (*hinoki*), the main part of the head and torso are made of two hollow pieces joined front to back. The eyes are crystal. Yishan holds a stick called a *keisaku* (a disciplinary stick used on monks whose attention wandered during meditation) in his right hand, and his robe and *kesa* (priest's mantle) draped over the chair (not exhibited).   NK

48 Mujū Ichien
polychromed wood
h. 79.4 (31¹⁄₄)
Kamakura period, c. 1312

Chōmoji, Aichi Prefecture
Important Cultural Property

Mujū Ichien, born in 1226 in Kamakura, was probably a member of the Kajiwara family, which served the Kamakura shogunate. After taking the tonsure in Hitachi Province (present-day Ibaraki Prefecture), he studied the doctrines of the older schools of Buddhism. He also studied Zen as a disciple of Enni Ben'en (1202–1280) at Tōfukuji, a major Zen monastery in Kyoto. He thus acquired a wide range of Buddhist learning. In 1262 Mujū became the founding abbot of Chōmoji, where he lived for fifty years, during which time he wrote many books, including *Sasekishū* (A Collection of Sand and Pebbles), a famous anthology of Buddhist stories in ten volumes. In 1282 he declined an invitation to become the second abbot of Tōfukuji. He died in 1312 at the age of eighty-six at Rengeji in Ise (Mie Prefecture), which he also headed. He left the following parting verse:

A seagull floats over the sea
Seven and eighty years
The wind rests, the waves are still
Calm as in the days of yore.

Mujū's portrait is enshrined in the Founder's Hall at Chōmoji. As is common

with *chinsō* sculpture (portraits of Zen priests), he holds a *hossu* (whisk with long white hairs, symbolic of priestly office and the brushing away of worldly thoughts) in his right hand and sits on a chair (not exhibited). *Chinsō* sculpture typically captures the realistic appearance of the model, including such details as the large mole on the left eyelid. The result is that the person's spirit also is conveyed. The mild expression, the relaxed pose, and the clothing, which is more or less symmetrical, capture the unruffled state of mind of the model. This fine *chinsō* was probably made around the time of Mujū's death in 1312.

The head and body are made of two hollow pieces of wood, joined front to back. The *Hōkyōin dharani*, a set of Esoteric Buddhist incantations, is written inside, in Sanskrit. Most of the polychromy that originally covered the entire surface is now lost, exposing the underlayers of *sabi urushi* (raw lacquer mixed with pulverized stone) and black lacquer.   SH

49 Myōan Eisai
polychromed wood
h. 60.3 (23³⁄₄)
Kamakura period, 13th–14th century

Jufukuji, Kanagawa Prefecture

Myōan Eisai (1141–1215) owes his eminence in Japanese history to two accomplishments: the propagation of Rinzai Zen as an independent school of Buddhism, and the reintroduction (from China) of tea drinking and tea cultivation after several centuries of disuse. Born in present-day Okayama Prefecture, he began religious life as a student of Esoteric doctrines, especially Tendai. But in the course of two trips to China to study Buddhist doctrine he became persuaded of the greater validity of Rinzai Zen teachings. Zen doctrines had been known in Japan since the seventh century, but only as elements in the teachings of other Buddhist schools; it was Eisai who established Rinzai Zen as an independent school, which soon acquired a great and influential following.

On his return in 1191 from the second of his two trips to China, Eisai preached for a time in Kyushu, where he founded Shōfukuji (near Hakata, present-day Fukuoka) and cultivated the tea seeds he had brought with him. He expressed his conviction of the life- and health-giving properties of tea in *Kissa yōjōki* (On Drinking Tea and Maintaining Health). His Zen teachings met with opposition from the established schools, and the court in Kyoto enjoined Eisai to silence on the subject of Zen. But in 1199 he was in Kamakura, where his converts among the shogunate and the warriors included Hōjō Masako and Minamoto Yoriie, widow and son of Yoritomo. In Kamakura in 1200 he became founding abbot of Jufukuji, and in 1202 he

returned to Kyoto with the backing of the shogunate and there, under the auspices of the shogun Yoriie, converted Kenninji to the practice of Rinzai Zen. The affinity of the warrior class for Zen, and the close relationships between members of the *bakufu* and Zen prelates, which characterized the following several centuries, had their beginnings in the work of Eisai.   NK

50 Toyotomi Hideyoshi
polychromed wood
h. 73.8 (29)
Momoyama period, c. 1598–1615
Osaka City

Toyotomi Hideyoshi (1537–1598), the second "great unifier" of Japan, began his career in the service of the first, Oda Nobunga (1534–1582), whose military genius carried him from a minor domain in Owari Province to the mastery of most of Japan. Hideyoshi's rise was even more dramatic: this son of a peasant farmer was Nobunaga's equal as a strategist and his superior as a diplomat. By 1590 he had reduced all of Japan to peace and fealty, had taken the title of Imperial Regent, and could turn his attention to legitimating and controlling what he had won. Though his notion of civil administration was a simple and quite sketchy extension of the domainal administration of a daimyo, his land survey (begun in 1585) transformed Japanese social and cadastral organization to the forms that prevailed throughout the Edo period. His territorial ambitions extended to the (unachieved) conquest of China; he understood the value of manufacturing and commerce and controlled them for his benefit; and his patronage of the arts was, by contemporary accounts, both grandiose and knowing.

As this sculpture suggests, he was apparently an exceedingly homely man. Nobunaga, who greatly valued his abilities, called him "Monkey" (*saru*). Much of the extant portrait sculpture of Hideyoshi, like the painted portraits of him, was produced for the shrines built after his death. When the Toyotomi family was destroyed by Tokugawa Ieyasu (1543–1616) in 1615, these shrines, which deified Hideyoshi, were destroyed or closed. Thus this sculpture can be dated to the period between 1598 and 1615.

Although its history is not known, this work is one of the most idiosyncratic examples of sculpted portraits of Hideyoshi. While the face reflects the stylized expression of the Nō mask of an old man, it still retains a sense of realism and individuality. The work is made with the *yosegi zukuri* technique (hollow joined woodblock), and the coloring and pedestal are later additions.   NYS

48

49

50

51 **Toyotomi Sutemaru**
polychromed wood
h. 56.0 (22)
Momoyama period, c. 1591

Rinkain, Kyoto
Important Cultural Property

Toy boat
polychromed wood
l. 200 (78¾); w. 69.7 (27½)
Momoyama period, c. 1591

Gyokuhōin, Kyoto
Important Cultural Property

Toyotomi Sutemaru (Tsurumatsu, 1589–1591), the first son of the hegemon Toyotomi Hideyoshi (1537–1598), and Yodogimi, died when he was just two years old. The grieving father, Hideyoshi, built Shōunji in eastern Kyoto as the child's memorial temple. This portrait was enshrined there. When the Toyotomi family fell and the Tokugawa ruled the nation, Shōunji was de-

stroyed, and Sutemaru's portrait was moved to Rinkain, a subtemple of Myōshinji, a large Zen monastery in Kyoto. The portrait was probably moved there because this was the place where Nange Genkō, the first abbot of Shōunji, lived in retirement.

Sutemaru sits on a pedestal wearing a long-sleeved kimono, tied in back with a sash. The surface is richly polychromed in white, vermilion, and gold. Perhaps because Hideyoshi loved his son very deeply, it is strikingly idealized and stylized, almost doll-like.

The boat is said to have been one of Sutemaru's toys. It was offered by Hideyoshi to Myōshinji, where Sutemaru's funeral took place. It is now in the possession of Gyokuhōin, another subtemple of Myōshinji. Resembling a real boat, it has a small cabin at the helm and another at the stern. A board with wheels is attached to the bottom of the boat so that it can be pulled. The hull of the boat is gilded, and the rest is polychromed.   NK

52 **Jigen Daishi**
polychromed wood
h. 75.1 (29½)
Edo period, c. 1644

Enichiin, Shiga Prefecture
Important Cultural Property

The monk Tenkai (1536–1643), or Jigen Daishi, was a distinguished priest of Tendai Buddhism who was active from the Momoyama to the early Edo period. Born in Aizu Province (part of present-day Fukushima Prefecture), Tenkai trained at Enryakuji, Onjōji, Kōfukuji, and other Buddhist temples. He enjoyed the confidence and favor of the first three Tokugawa shoguns—Ieyasu, Hidetada, and Iemitsu—and, like many Zen monks of the Momoyama period, was often their advisor in secular as well as religious matters. In 1624, by order of the shogun family, he constructed Kan'eiji, the headquarters of Tendai Buddhism in the east, and became its founding abbot. Tenkai is also famous

51

as the person responsible for the great cultural enterprise of block-printing the *Issaikyō* (complete collection of Buddhist scriptures). Having lived to the old age of one hundred seven years, he received from the emperor the posthumous title *Jigen Daishi*.

Tenkai was instrumental in reconstructing many buildings at Enryakuji, the headquarters of the Tendai school outside Kyoto. This portrait of Tenkai is the main icon of Enichiin, built in 1644 as a subtemple of Enryakuji, and probably dates from that time—that is, one year after his death.

The head and torso are made of several pieces of Japanese cypress (*hinoki*), with crystal eyes. The figure wears a cloth draped over its head, a vermilion priestly robe, and over it a *kesa* (priest's mantle) decorated with polychromy and cut gold leaf. Tenkai is seated, holding prayer beads in both hands and a *gokosho* (five-pronged ritual instrument symbolizing a thunderbolt) in the left hand. NK

101

52

53 Ishin Sūden

polychromed wood
h. 32.7 (12⅞)
Edo period, 17th century

Nanzenji, Kyoto

Ishin Sūden (1569–1632) was an early Edo Zen Buddhist priest of the Rinzai school. He was born to a retainer of the Muromachi shogunate, which collapsed when he was a child, and he entered the Zen monastery of Nanzenji and became a priest. He became abbot in 1605, reinvigorated the monastery, and lived at Konchiin, a subtemple. Serving Tokugawa Ieyasu (1543–1616) from 1608 on, he drafted the shogunate's diplomatic correspondence. Eventually he supervised a wide range of diplomatic and religious activities, and he participated in the drafting of laws for the shogunate, including the *Buke*

shohatto (Rules for the Military Houses, that is laws governing the daimyo and samurai) and the laws prohibiting Christianity. Also wielding tremendous influence with Ieyasu's successor, Hidetada, he was called *Kokue no Saishō*, or the premier who wore the black robes of a priest. He lost power during the reign of Iemitsu (1604–1651), the third Tokugawa shogun.

This small portrait sculpture is placed in the upper floor of the gate of Nanzenji, which was rebuilt by Sūden in 1628. Sūden, seated on a chair, wears a hat, a priestly robe, and, over it, a *kesa* (priest's mantle). His left hand is palm down, while the right hand originally held either a *shippei* (bamboo whip used for Zen training) or a *hossu* (whisk with long white hairs symbolically used to brush away worldly thoughts), now lost. The sleeves and the hem of the robe hang deeply in front, and a staff is placed at the side.

Although this hollow statue is small for a *chinsō* (Zen priest's portrait), the

joined-wood (*yosegi*) structure of the head and body is no different from typical examples. The eyes are crystal. The coloring of the hat, the chair, and the staff is well preserved. Although the face is somewhat lacking in liveliness and the body is generalized, this sculpture demonstrates the technical mastery of the era.   NYS

53

CALLIGRAPHY

54 Letter

Wuxue Zeyuan (1226–1286)
hanging scroll; ink on paper
35.8 x 69.4 (14 x 27 3/8)
Kamakura period, 1283

Engakuji, Kanagawa Prefecture
Important Cultural Property

Wuxue Zeyuan (Mugaku Sogen in Japanese), also known as Zeyuan (Shigen in Japanese), was a Chinese monk of the Rinzai (Linji) school of Zen (Chan). A native of Mingzhou on the southeastern coast of China, he came to Japan in 1279, the year the Chinese Southern Song Dynasty was overthrown by the Mongols, at the invitation of Hōjō Tokimune (1251–1284), regent of the Kamakura shogunate. Appointed abbot of Kenchōji in Kamakura, Zeyuan taught Zen to Tokimune and many other warriors. When Tokimune founded Engakuji in 1282, Zeyuan was appointed its founding abbot.

This letter from Wuxue Zeyuan to Hōjō Tokimune was written in 1283, the year after the founding of Engakuji, though dated only to the eighteenth day of the seventh month. Demonstrating the friendship between the regent and the Chinese monk, the letter thanks Tokimune for the *shōen* (manors) offered to the temple, including the Tomita manor of Owari Province, and for the *migyōsho* (writ) that designated the temple as the shogunate's place of worship.

Zeyuan, who had a large number of followers among Kamakura warriors, played an important role in transmitting to Japan the contemporary Chinese calligraphic style of the Song Dynasty, which was strongly influenced by the great calligrapher of the Tang Dynasty, Yan Zhenqing (709–784). NYA

55 Preface to poems

Daxiu Zhengnian (1214–1288)
hanging scroll; ink on paper
32.4 x 110.0 (12 3/4 x 43 1/4)
Kamakura period, 1274

Gotō Museum, Tokyo
Important Cultural Property

A Linji Chan (Rinzai Zen) priest from the Zhejiang province in southeastern China, Daxiu Zhengnian (J:Daikyū Shōnen) came to Japan in 1269 at the invitation of the regent Hōjō Tokimune (1251–1284), as had his countryman Wuxue Zeyuan (cat. 54). Zhengnian lived at the monasteries of Zenkōji, Kenchōji, Jufukuji, and Engakuji, and became the founding abbot of Jōchiji, all in or around Kamakura. For nearly twenty years he promoted the Chinese Song dynasty style of Zen among Kamakura warriors. His cultural as well as religious influence on Hōjō Tokimune and Sadatoki (1271–1311) was profound.

This document, dated to the fourth month of the eleventh year of Bun'ei

(1274), is a recollection of the Chinese priest's friendship with his Japanese disciple Muzō Jōshō (1234–1306), a relative of the regent Hōjō Tokiyori (1227–1263). Muzō, originally from Sagami province, went to China as a Zen student-pilgrim in 1252, and there in 1254, while studying at Wanshouchan Si, on Mount Jing near Hangzhou, he met Daxiu Zhengnian in 1254. Muzō returned to Japan after fourteen years of traveling in China, and was followed not long after by Daxiu Zhengnian.

The text recounts their first meeting at the place of their master Shiji Xinyue (d. 1254), their ensuing friendship, and their reunion after Zhengnian's arrival in Japan. It also relates Muzō's visit in 1274 to Hōgenji in Sagami Province, where Zhengnian was abbot: Muzō asked Zhengnian to add a preface to a scroll of poems by Chinese monks on the theme of the Stone Bridge at Mount Tiantai, the great Buddhist center in Zhejiang Province that Muzō had visited. The poem scroll itself is lost, though the first half of the poems are known through a later copy. Zhengnian's calligraphy is an elegant version of the *kaisho* (regular, or standard) mode. The taut but dynamic structure of individual characters reflects the tradition of the great Northern Song Chinese calligrapher Huang Tingjian (1045–1105). In the quality of the brushstrokes, however, Zhengnian, like Wuxue Zeyuan, was influenced by the style of Yan Zhenqing (709–784) of the Tang Dynasty. NYA

56 The sobriquet *Shun'oku* and a dedicatory poem

Musō Soseki (1275–1351)
hanging scrolls; ink on paper
sobriquet, 34.0 x 77.7 (13 3/8 x 30 5/8);
poem, 35.2 x 74.4 (13 7/8 x 29 1/4)
Nanbokuchō period, 1346

Rokuōin, Kyoto
Important Cultural Property

Musō Soseki (cat. 10) from Ise Province was famous as a Zen priest, adviser to the great and powerful of the shogunal and imperial courts, calligrapher, painter, poet, scholar, and garden designer. He first studied the Tendai and Shingon schools of Buddhism, and later converted to the Rinzai school of Zen. As a young Zen novice, he was briefly a student of the Chinese scholar-monk Yishan Yining (1247–1317), an association that was instrumental in Musō's later scholarly and literary eminence and leadership of the Gozan Bungaku, the Sinophile literary movement centered around the Zen monasteries. He lived in the major monasteries of Nanzenji in Kyoto and Engakuji in Kamakura, but also founded many temples and retreats in remote areas. In addition to establishing a

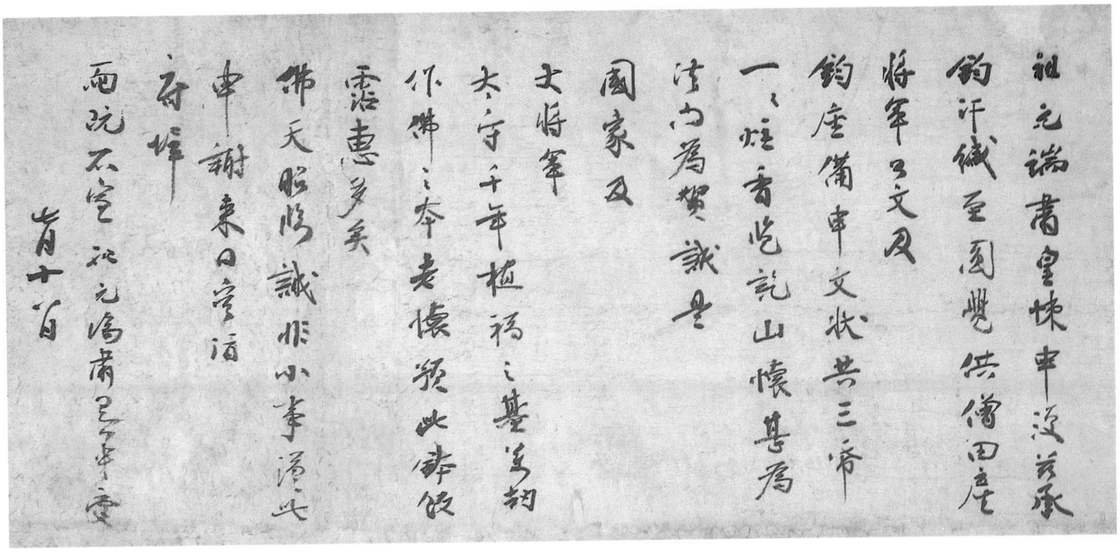

54

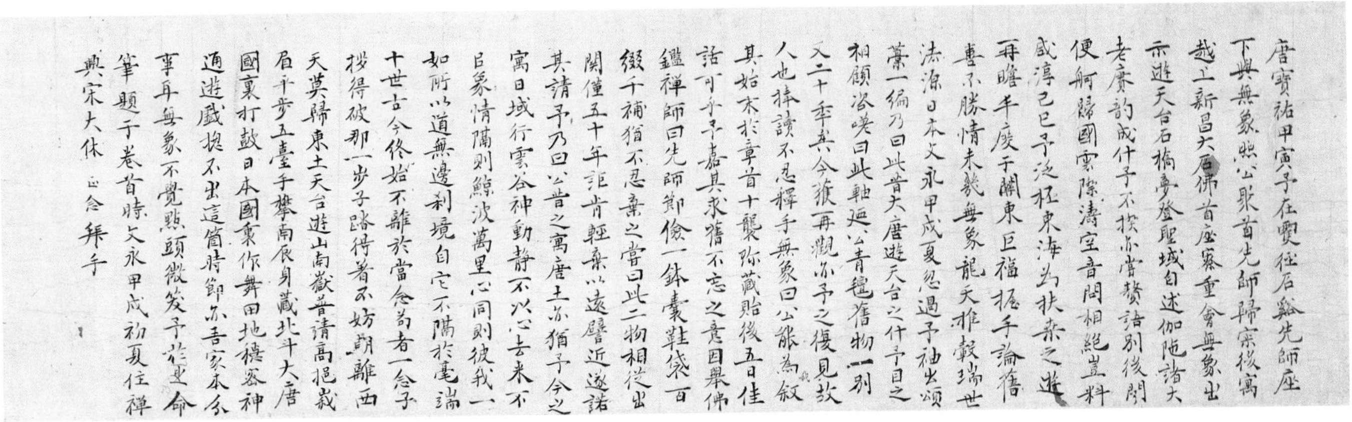

55

lineage of disciples who dominated Rinzai Zen and its cultural tradition for many generations, Musō enjoyed the confidence of the political leaders of his time. His converts included such luminaries as the emperor Go-Daigo (1288–1339), the regents Hōjō Sadatoki (1271–1311) and Takatoki (1303–1333), and the shogun Ashikaga Takauji (1305–1358) and his brother, Tadayoshi (1306–1352). With Musō's encouragement, Ashikaga Takauji, who had first been Go-Daigo's ally and then his bitter enemy, built Tenryūji in Kyoto for the welfare of the deceased emperor's soul, and he made Musō its founding abbot. A master of garden design, Musō created the gardens of several Kyoto temples, including Saihōji and Tenryūji.

The calligraphy with the two semicursive (gyōsho) characters shun and oku is the sobriquet given to Musō's disciple Shun'oku Myōha (1311–1388); the calligraphy with smaller characters, also in semicursive script and in columnar

arrangement, is a dedicatory poem that accompanies the first:

A hundred flowers are originally flowers of one branch
In the end I see that all fragrant flowers are connected to my house
Suddenly opening the door, the peaceful air spreads
Spring scene from here reaches all over the river and sand.

The name Shun'oku means "spring house," and the poem, written at Nishiyama, is dated to the spring of 1346. In the third month of that year, Musō retired from the abbacy of Tenryūji to live in its subtemple Ungoan. Musō was seventy-one then and Shun'oku thirty-five. Musō's signature, Bokutotsusō (simple and artless old man), and his seal appear between the two large characters; two seals and his signature are at the left of the poem. NYA

57 **Fugen, Shukuryū, Keishō**
Ashikaga Yoshimitsu (1358–1408)
hanging scrolls; ink on paper
Fugen, 33.4 x 80.2 (13 1/8 x 31 5/8);
Shukuryū, 33.5 x 80.2 (13 1/8 x 31 5/8);
Keishō, 33.5 x 80.3 (13 1/8 x 31 5/8)
Muromachi period, late 14th century

Engakuji, Kanagawa Prefecture
Important Cultural Property

Ashikaga Yoshimitsu, the third shogun of the Muromachi shogunate, was the grandson of Takauji (1305–1358) and the son of Yoshiakira (1330–1367), the first and second shogun, respectively. Succeeding his father as shogun in 1366, Yoshimitsu built a residence called Hana no Gosho (Palace of Flowers) in 1378 in the area of Kyoto called Muromachi, thus giving rise to the name Muromachi shogunate. In 1392, after fifty-six years of bitter division within the imperial family, Yoshimitsu succeeded in unifying the Southern and Northern courts. He became Dajō Daijin (prime

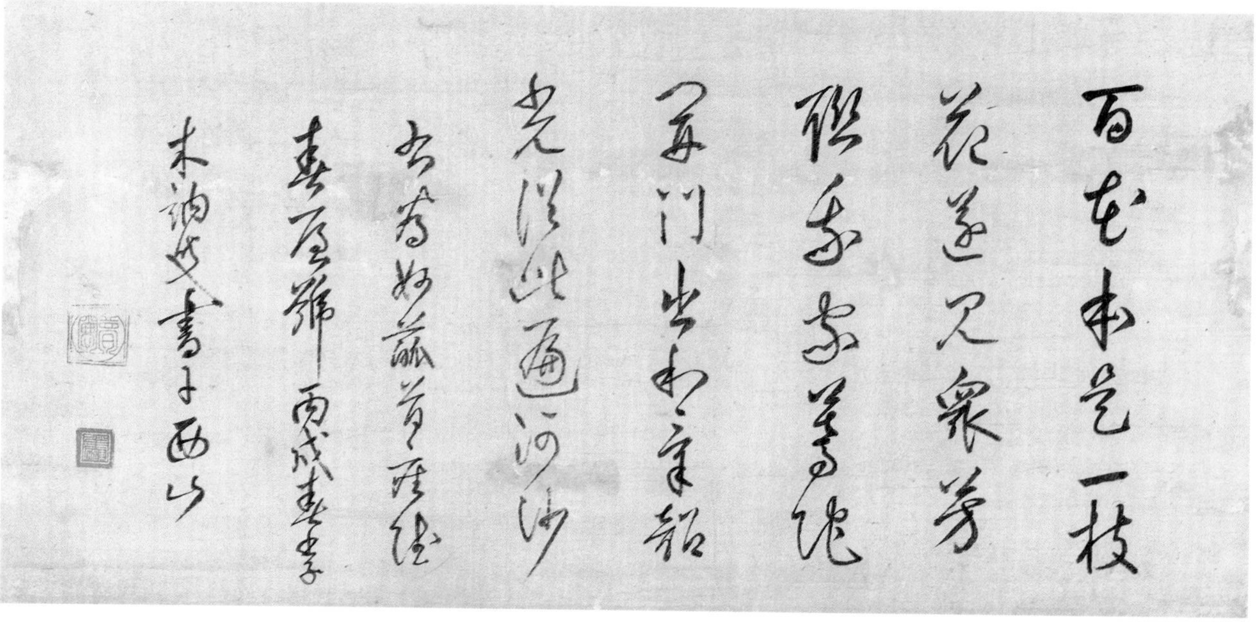

56

minister, the highest post in the imperial bureaucracy) in 1394, and the following year entered the Buddhist priesthood, assuming the Buddhist name Dōyū; he also used another Buddhist name, Tenzan. Taking the tonsure, however, was not an abdication of power but a means to wield it more effectively. He suppressed the Ōuchi family and other powerful *shugo* daimyo in the provinces and opened diplomatic relations with China under the Ming Dynasty, calling himself *Nihon kokuō* (King of Japan). He also built a residential villa at Kitayama in northwestern Kyoto, which is now Rokuonji, famous for its pondside Golden Pavilion (Kinkaku). In addition to his political and military abilities,

Yoshimitsu is noted for his enthusiastic and discriminating patronage of art and scholarship.

These three calligraphic works of two characters each bear Ashikaga Yoshimitsu's seals. Each work is stamped with a vermilion square seal, *Dōyū*, and a vermilion tripod-shaped seal, *Tenzan*, referring to Yoshimitsu's Buddhist names.

Calligraphies of this type are known as *gakuji*, or "forehead characters." Incised wooden plaques based on them were hung above the central entrances of temple buildings. These three—*Fugen, Shukuryū,* and *Keishō*—identify three buildings in Shōzokuin, originally a subtemple of Kenchōji, which was moved in 1335 to Enga-

kuji as the mortuary temple of Wuxue Zeyuan (1226–1286), who was the latter's founding abbot. In keeping with their function, the characters are written in the regular, or standard mode (*kaisho*), with great attention to balance and legibility. They are dignified and monumental.

According to the historical document *Kamakura Gozanki* (Record of the Kamakura Zen temples), *Fugen*, meaning "universal revelation," refers to the Tochidō, or Hall of the Local Deity; *Shukuryū*, meaning "lodging dragon," refers to the guest hall; and *Keishō*, meaning "cassia tree and sunlight," refers to the Soshidō, or founder's hall.

NYA

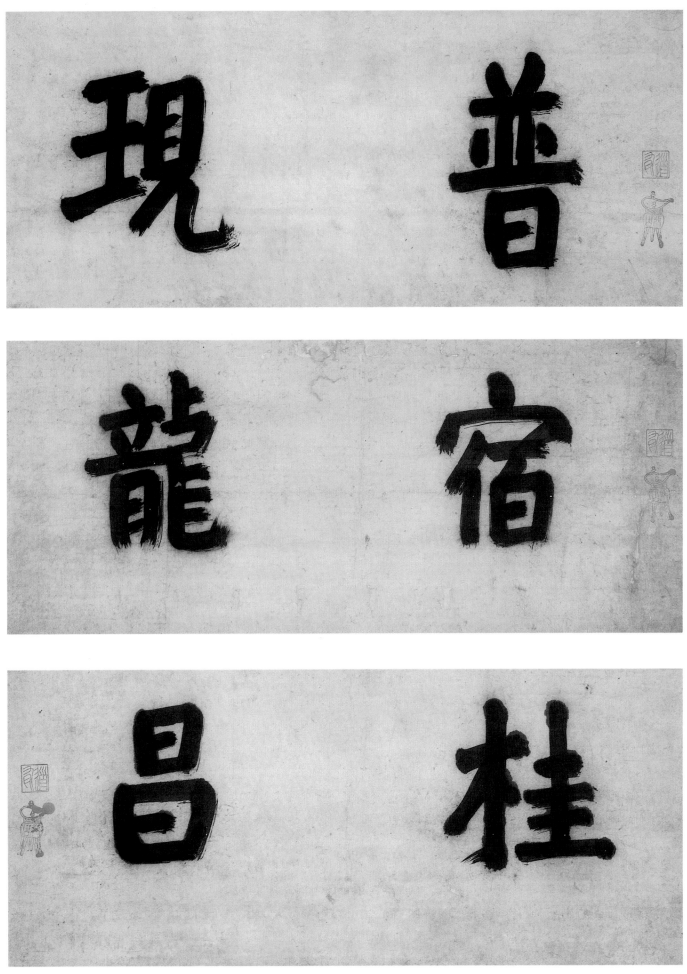

普現

龍宿

昌桂

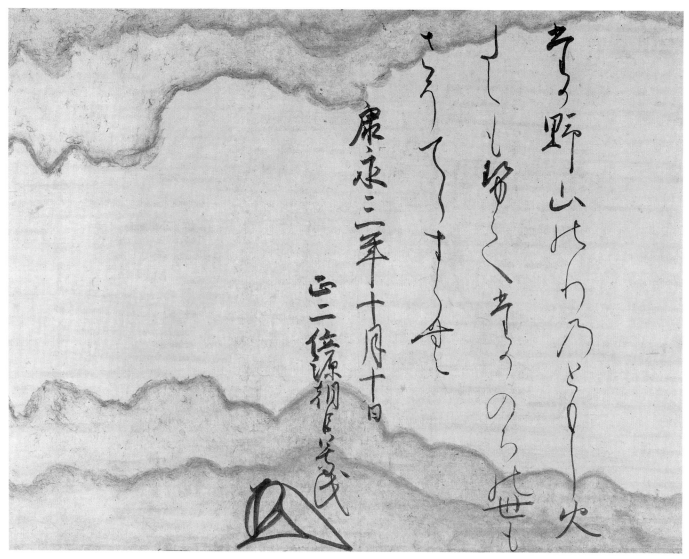

58

58 *Wakagaishi*

Ashikaga Takauji (1305–1358)
hanging scroll; ink on decorated paper
31.2 x 52.0 (12¹/₄ x 20¹/₂)
Nanbokuchō period, 1344
Sekai Kyūseikyō (MOA Art Museum),
Shizuoka Prefecture

Kaishi is folded paper on which poems are written at formal occasions, such as a banquet. The term literally means paper kept in the breast of the kimono ready to be used when prompted. When *waka* (Japanese poems) are written, they are called *wakagaishi*; when *renga* (linked verses) are written, they are called *rengagaishi*.

This *wakagaishi* was composed and written by Ashikaga Takauji, the clan chieftain and successful warlord, who in 1338 was appointed *Seiitaishōgun* (Great General Who Quells the Barbarians), the first shogun of the Muromachi shogunate in Kyoto.

Though his entire adult life was spent in battle, intrigue, and the pursuit of power, Takauji was also deeply religious, a follower of the Zen priest Musō Soseki (1275–1351). For the soul of the deceased emperor Go-Daigo (1288–1339), Takauji founded Tenryūji at Musō's urging and with Musō as its founding abbot. In his efforts to unify the country, he built in each province a temple as a place of prayer for national peace and for the souls of the war dead (whether they had fought with him or against him). This *wakagaishi* was reportedly offered to Kongōbuji, the Esoteric Shingon headquarters temple atop Mount Kōya in Wakayama Prefecture.

Takauji was also a poet. Eighty-five *tanka* (short poems) by him are included in the poetry anthology *Zoku Goshūi Wakashū* and other imperial anthologies. The *Tsukubashū* of 1357, an anthology of linked verses, contains sixty-seven of his *renga*. In this example of *wakagaishi*, Takauji praises the long tradition of the Buddhist faith on Mount Kōya. A colophon following the poem reads, *tenth day, tenth month, third year of Kōei* [corresponding to 1344], *Minamoto no Ason Takauji, Senior Second Grade* followed by Takauji's *kaō*. Two days before this date, the Buddhist text *Hōjaku-*

kyō Yōhon—copied by Takauji; his younger brother, Tadayoshi (cat. 60); and Musō Soseki—was offered to Kongō Zanmaiin, a subtemple of Kōyasan. Attached to the backs of the pages of the text are 120 poems, each written on *tanzaku* (narrow strips of poetry paper), including twelve by Takauji.

The paper in this example, known as *kumogami* (paper decorated with cloud patterns), creates an illusion of space suitable to the spirit of the poem. The poem itself, occupying the three right-hand columns, is fluidly written in the Japanese *kana* syllabary. The colophon occupies the two lines at the right and is written in semicursive (*gyōsho*) characters. The poem expresses Takauji's devotion to Kōyasan:

Atop Mount Takano [that is, at Kōyasan]
the religious candle
will never be extinguished;
in the future world, whoever the ruler,
it will shine as brightly. TY

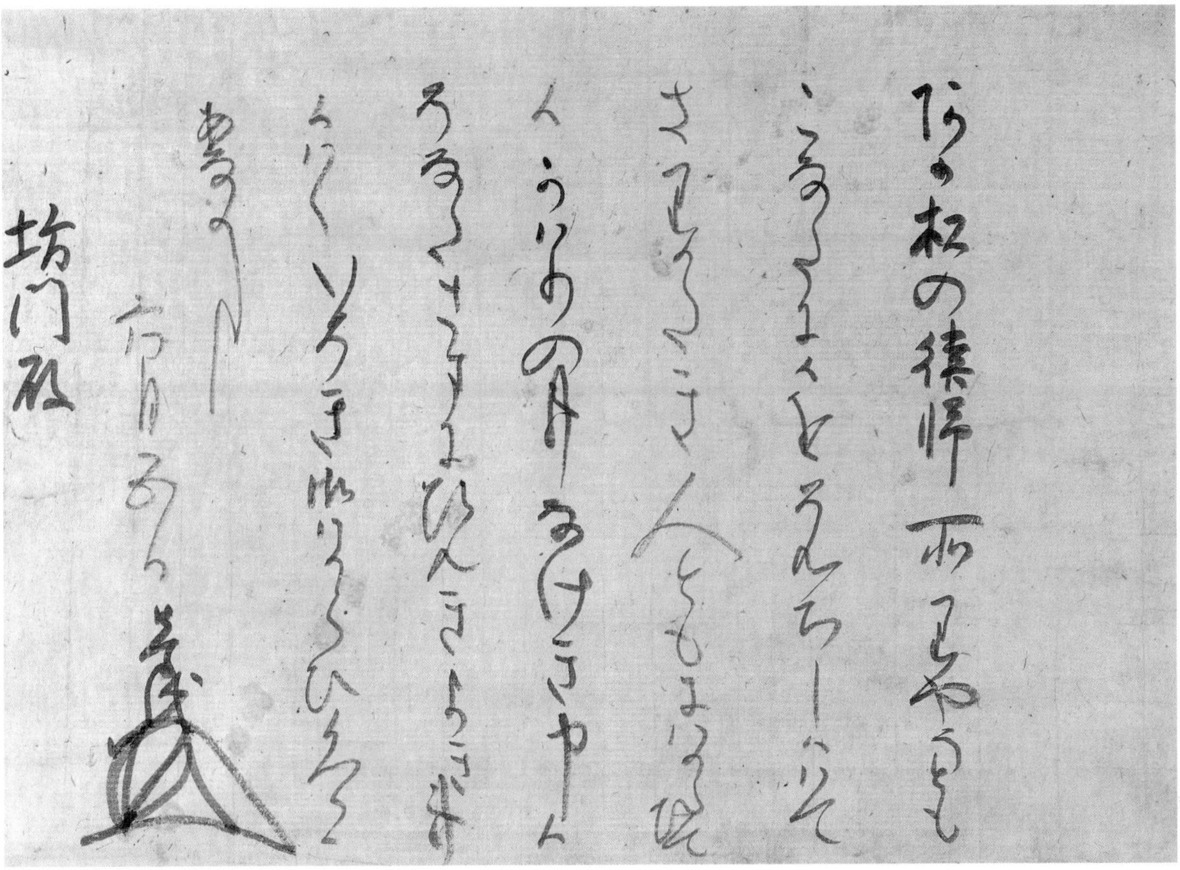

59

59 **Letter**
Ashikaga Takauji (1305–1358)
hanging scroll; ink on paper
31.0 x 44.0 (12 1/4 x 17 3/8)
Nanbokuchō period, mid-14th century

Tokyo National Museum

As the emperor Go-Daigo's chief military supporter, Ashikaga Takauji overthrew the shogunate and was instrumental in exterminating the Hōjō family, which had controlled the shogunate for over a century. But the two allies soon fell out, as each discovered the other's determination to be master of the realm. Not without much hard fighting, Takauji drove Go-Daigo from Kyoto and set up in his stead an emperor of the rival line, who obligingly appointed Takauji shogun.

Takauji wrote this letter to his son and heir, Yoshiakira (1330–1367), the second shogun. He has unwittingly given away, the letter says, a portion of the land once owned by Akamatsu Norisuke (d. 1351), a powerful daimyo of Harima and Bizen provinces who supported the Ashikaga. Since Norisuke had demanded land for re-placement, Takauji asks that Yoshiakira arrange it quickly if he has an appropriate piece of land. The spontaneous calligraphy (*sōsho*) and the subject of the letter reflect the affable and evenhanded side of Takauji's character. The letter was probably written in 1353 while Takauji remained in Kamakura, entrusting Kyoto to Yoshiakira. It is addressed to Bōmondono, a familiar name of Yoshiakira, after the name of his residence at Bōmon.   TY

60 **Writ**
Ashikaga Tadayoshi (1306–1352)
hanging scroll; ink on paper
35.0 x 57.0 (13 3/4 x 22 1/2)
Nanbokuchō period, 1349

Kyōto Furitsu Sōgō Shiryōkan
Important Cultural Property

This document, one of over twenty-four thousand known as the Tōji documents, is a *gechijō* (warrior's order given to his retainers) by Ashikaga Tadayoshi in response to the complaint of a certain Kōshin, the *zasshō* (temple representative) of Tōji (popular name for Kyōō Gokokuji) in Kyoto. From the time the shogunate was established in 1338, there was a division of authority between Ashikaga Takauji (1305–1358), who took military leadership, and his younger brother, Tadayoshi, who supervised daily political affairs, including lawsuits. This writ was issued to convey a court decision based on Tadayoshi's authority.

The management of some privately owned manorial land in Harima province had been turned over to Tōji by the emperor Go-Uda (1267–1324) in the twelfth month of 1313, as were other similar properties in 1317. However, in 1349 the temple appealed to the shogunate against the *jitō* (estate stewards) of the original owners, who since 1340 had occupied the land and diverted the temple's lawful revenues. Despite the government's summons, the stewards had not come to Kyoto to justify their actions. Therefore, Ashikaga Tadayoshi ordered in this writ that their illegal

111

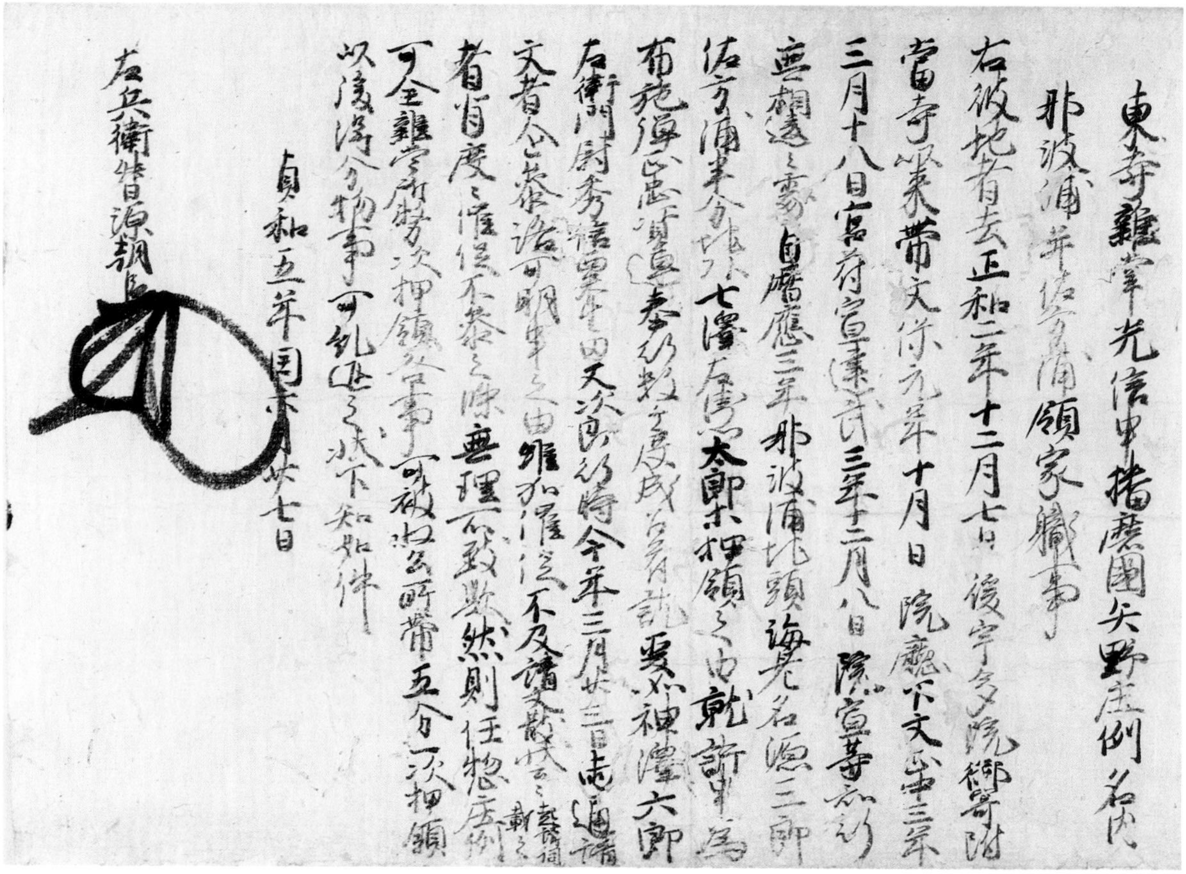

東寺雑掌光信申播磨国矢野庄例名内
那波浦并使名浦領家職事

右彼地者去正和二年十二月七日後宇多法院領家職奇附
當寺収来帯文永九年十二月七日院廳下文并三年
三月十八日官符以宣下三年十二月八日院宣等旨
無相違之處自嶋應三年那波浦地頭海老名源三郎
佐方浦先分地者七澤左衛門太郎未押領之就訴申為
右衛門尉秀清使罷向之時今年三月廿三日注進状
布苑浦光貞遵行之條無所致歎然則任惣庄例
文者旨度之催促不參之源無理致歎然則任惣庄例
者旨度之催促不參之由雖被加下知不及承引之間
可全難堪所勘次押領之事可被止所帯五ヶ次押領
以後漸ヶ分物事可処ヶ状下知状件

　　貞和五年閏六月廿七日

左兵衛督源朝臣（花押）

60

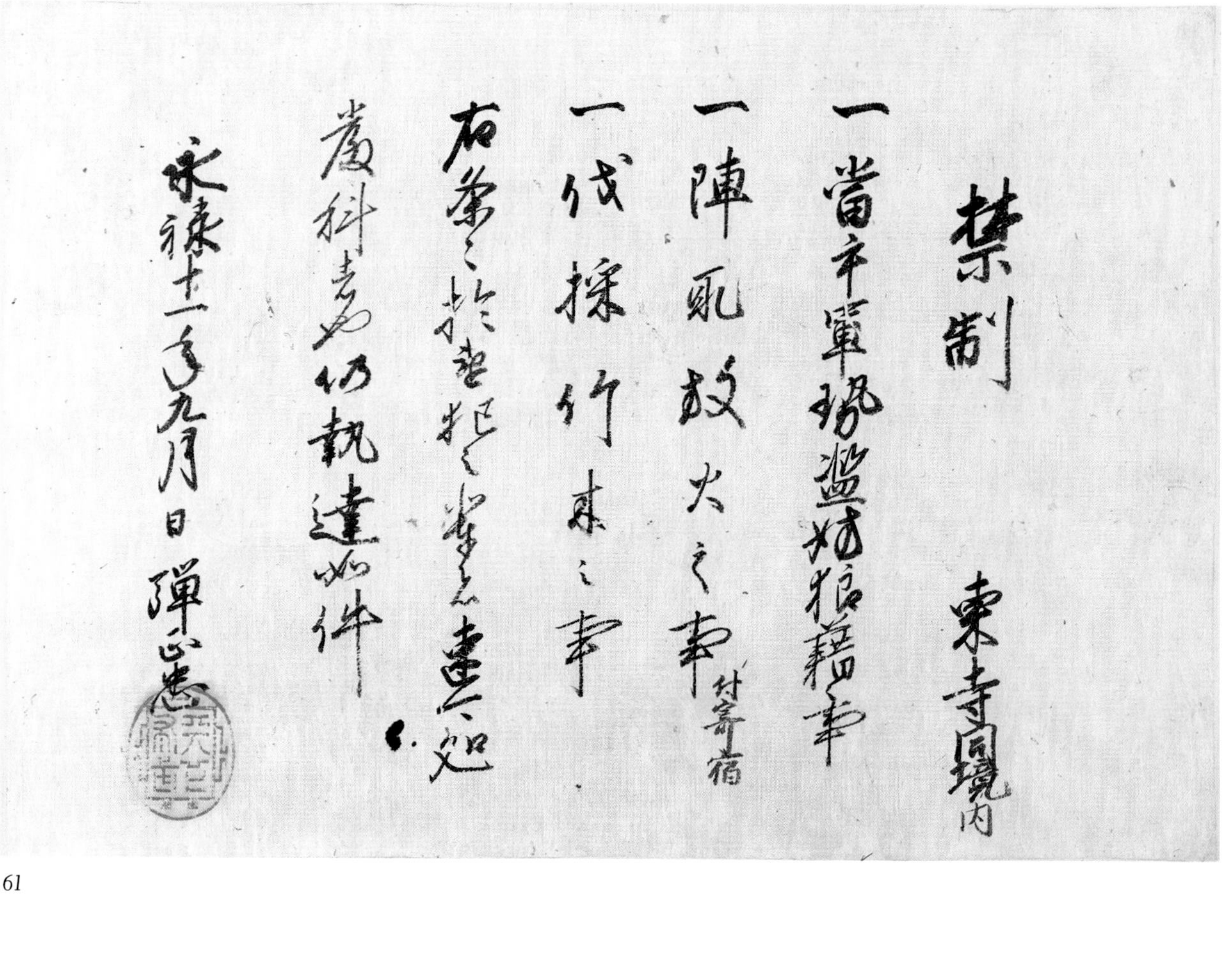

禁制
　　　　東寺境内

一当手軍勢濫妨狼藉事
一陣取放火之事　付寄宿
一伐採竹木之事

右条々於違犯之輩者速可処厳科者也仍執達如件

永禄十二年九月日　弾正忠（印）

61

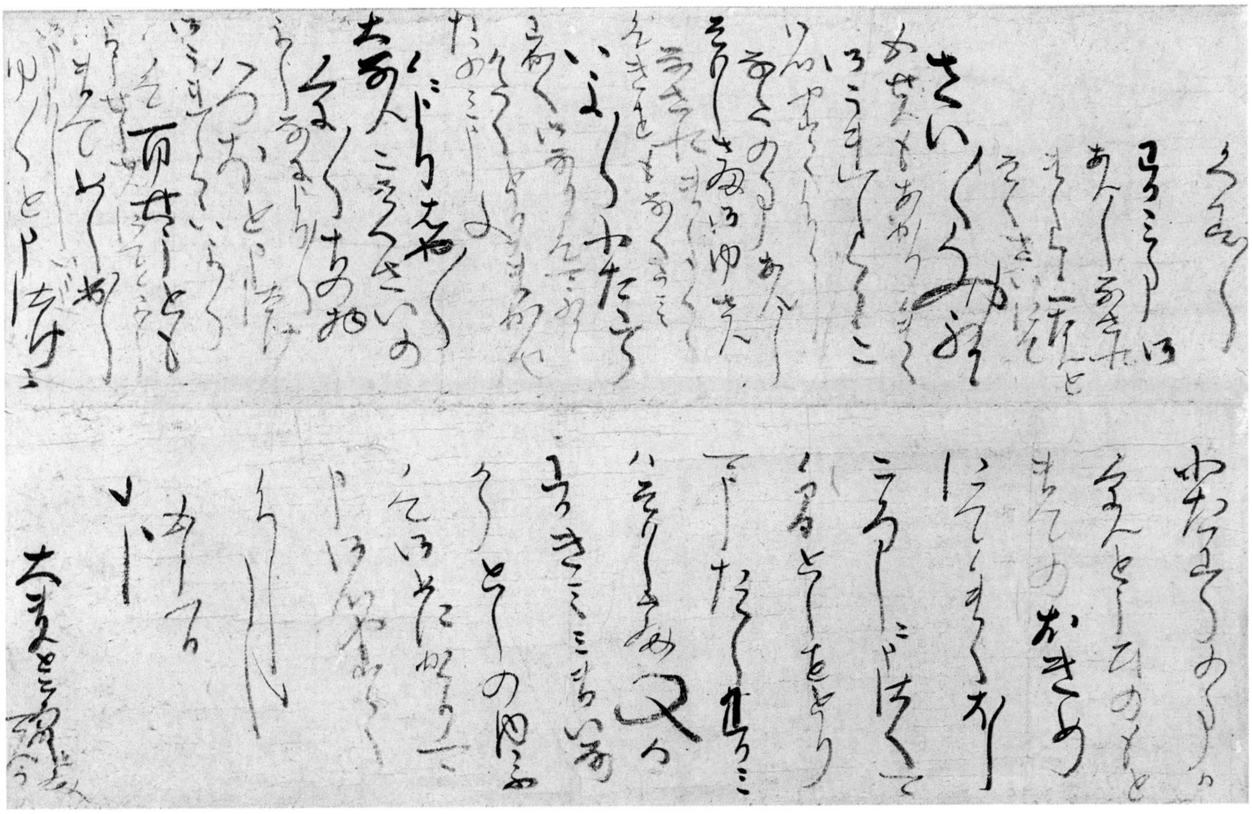

62

occupation be stopped, one-fifth of their land be taken away, and the management of the areas returned to Tōji. The writ is dated to the twenty-seventh day of the intercalary sixth month of the fifth year of Jōwa (1349). Although the document may have been written by a scribe serving Tadayoshi, the writ is official, since Tadayoshi added his *kaō* at the end.   TY

61 Prohibitions

Oda Nobunaga (1534–1582)
hanging scroll; ink on paper
35.5 x 53.0 (14 x 20 7/8)
Muromachi period, 1568

Kyoto Furitsu Sōgō Shiryōkan
Important Cultural Property

Oda Nobunaga is remembered in Japanese history for his attempts in the latter part of the sixteenth century to unify under his aegis a nation torn by civil strife among many contending barons. Having first unified Owari and Mino provinces, he entered Kyoto on the twenty-sixth day of the ninth month of 1568, as a supporter of Ashikaga Yoshiaki (1537–1597), who became shogun under his auspices. Upon taking control of the capital, Nobunaga at-

tempted to reassure the court and the townsmen by preventing pillage and general lawlessness on the part of his troops. To this end he issued under his seal specific orders of protection and prohibitions against violence to persons or property.

The document illustrated here was issued for the protection of Tōji, and consists of three articles of prohibition:

Prohibited in the Tōji complex
Item: Violence and disturbance by our
  forces
Item: Unlawful taking of land and arson
Item: Cutting down bamboo and trees
Those who violate these rules will be swiftly
  and strictly punished. This is ordained
  from above.
The ninth month of the eleventh year of
  Eiroku [1568], Danjō no Jō [Judge of the
  Office of Justice]

Tōji was the Kyoto headquarters of Esoteric Buddhism, and the document is among the twenty-four thousand and more historical documents that constitute the "Tōji documents." The oval vermilion seal, *Tenka Fubu* (military rule throughout the nation), at the bottom of the left column is a seal Nobunaga began to use around the eleventh month of 1567, when he moved his garrison from Owari Prov-

ince to Gifu in Mino Province; it signals his intention to unify Japan under his own rule through military power. Nobunaga used this seal until the first month of 1570; thereafter he used the same characters in a horseshoe-shaped vermilion seal.   YK

62 Letter

Toyotomi Hideyoshi (1537–1598)
hanging scroll; ink on paper
28.6 x 48.5 (11 1/4 x 15 1/8)
Momoyama period, 1590

Myōhōin, Kyoto

Toyotomi Hideyoshi, one of Japan's most powerful military leaders, was the son of an unknown peasant. He served Oda Nobunaga (1534–1582), and after Nobunaga was assassinated in 1582 by his vassal Akechi Mitsuhide (1528–1582), Hideyoshi defeated and killed Mitsuhide in just nine days. In the following year Hideyoshi destroyed his rivals Oda Nobutaka (1562–1583), the third son of Nobunaga, and Shibata Katsuie (1522–1583). Between 1585 and 1590 he conquered or brought to terms the following powerful rivals: the Chōsokabe family of Shikoku, the Shi-

63

mazu family of the Satsuma domain in Kyushu, and the Later Hōjō family, who controlled the Kanto from their garrison town of Odawara. After these tremendous victories, he subjugated the other daimyo without a fight, thus achieving national unification and laying the foundation for Japan's early modern society.

This personal letter, written in a loose, informal cursive (*sōsho*) by Hideyoshi, is dated to the first day of the fifth month of 1590, during Hideyoshi's siege of Odawara Castle, the headquarters of Hōjō Ujimasa (1538–1590) and his son Ujinao (1562–1591), the leaders in the east. Addressing his mother, Tenzuiin (referred to in the letter by her title *Ōmandokoro*, or mother of the *Sesshō* (regent, that is Hideyoshi's mother), Hideyoshi inquires after her health and reports the military situation:

Please, please do not worry about me. I am very healthy and am fed well, so I would like you to feel at ease. I beg you to take a trip and divert yourself so you will feel young. Also, more than anything else I am happy to hear that Dainanko is healthy. Please tell him to concentrate on his health all the more.

I am delighted to hear from you again and again. Please do not worry about me.

Now that I have at last had Odawara tightly besieged, I control eighty percent of what goes on in the provinces, and even summoned peasants so that they would follow my strict orders. Since Odawara is the key to the Kanto and to the entire nation, I have to starve them out, so it will have to take time. However, as for myself, I will return to Kyoto before the year is over, partly to inquire after you and the young prince, so I will see you. Please feel at ease. Farewell.

First day of the fifth month.

"Dainanko," a dialectical variant of *dainagon* (Grand Councilor), refers to Hidenaga, Hideyoshi's half brother. Hidenaga was ill in Kyoto that spring but seems to have regained his health and returned to his castle at Yamashiro in Yamato Province (part of present-day Nara Prefecture). The "young prince" refers to Hideyoshi's first son, Toyotomi Sutemaru (cat. 51), who was born in the fifth month of the previous year. In this one letter two sides of Hideyoshi's character are revealed: the inexorable conquerer, and the affectionate son.

The paper was originally folded in half along the crease that runs across it. The letter was begun with the fold underneath, then the paper was flipped to continue the text on the other side, the fold still at the bottom; when the paper was unfolded, one side of the letter was upside

down. At a later date the letter was cut in half along the crease and rejoined so that both parts are right side up.   YK

63 **Letter**
Tokugawa Ieyasu (1543–1616)
hanging scroll; ink on paper
30.2 x 51.5 (11 7/8 x 20 1/4)
Edo period, 1615

Tokyo National Museum
Important Art Object

After the death of the military leader Toyotomi Hideyoshi (1537–1598), Tokugawa Ieyasu and his allies defeated a great coalition of daimyo led by Ishida Mitsunari (1560–1600) at Sekigahara in 1600 (cat. 104), and in 1603 he was appointed by the emperor *Seiitaishōgun* (Great General Who Quells the Barbarians), thus formally establishing the Edo shogunate. Passing on the charge of the shogunate to his son, Hidetada (1579–1632), in 1605, Tokugawa Ieyasu came to be called *Ōgosho*, an honorable title for a former shogun or shogun's father. He destroyed Toyotomi Hideyori (1593–1615), the son of Hideyoshi, in the battles at Osaka in the winter of 1614 and the summer of 1615, and laid the foundations for the two hundred and fifty years of the Edo shogunate.

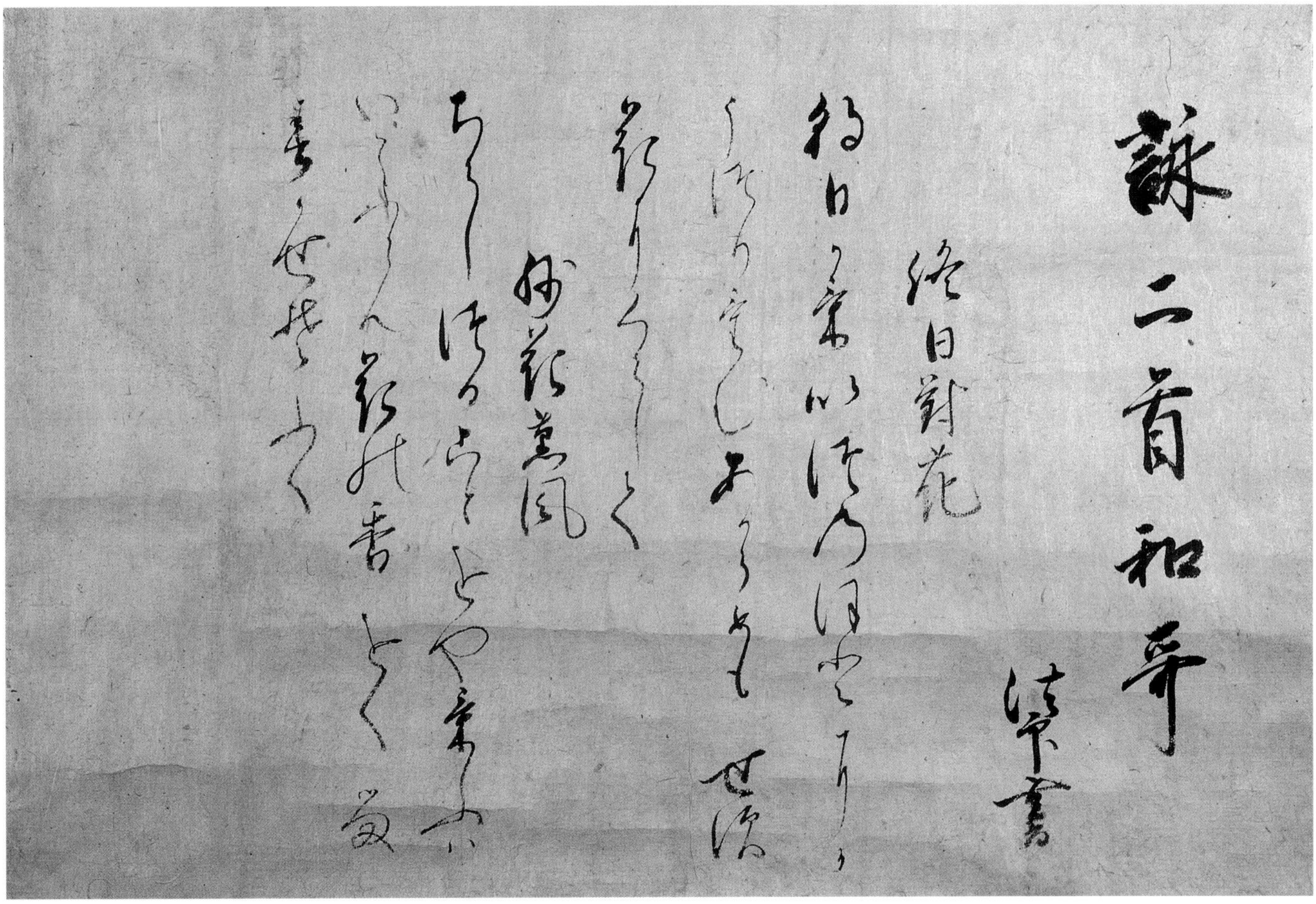

詠二首和歌　　草書

終日對花

64

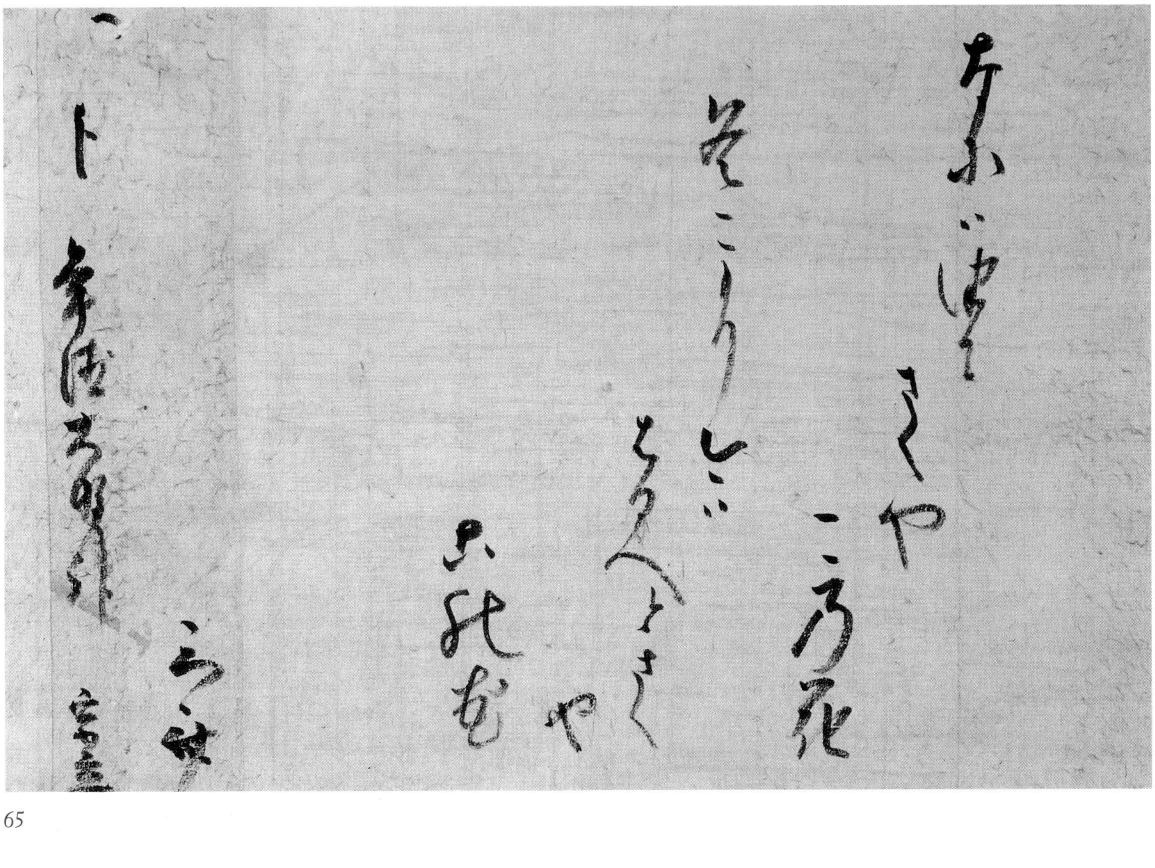

65

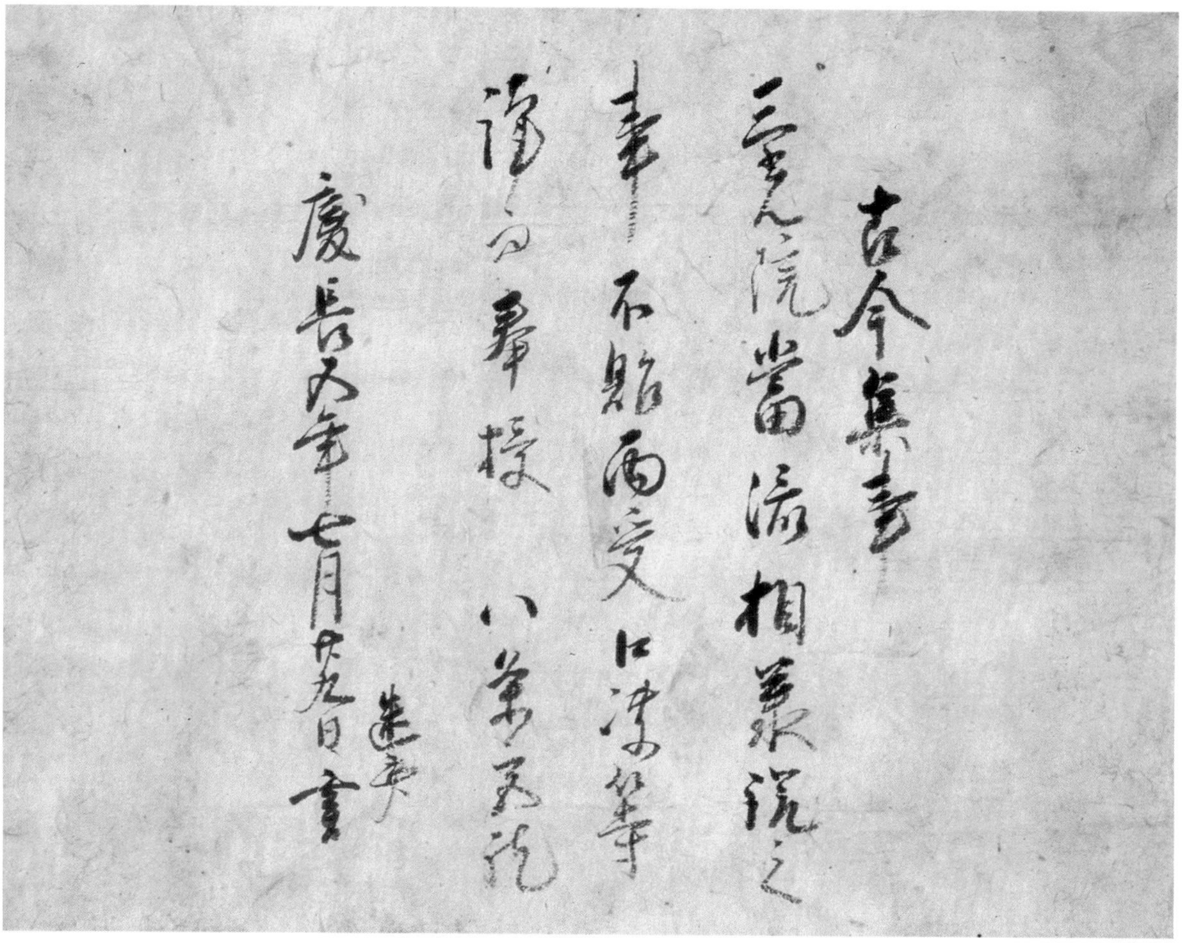

66

This letter, in Ieyasu's informal cursive (sōsho) writing style, is addressed to Chobo, maid of his granddaughter Senhime, and inquires after Senhime's health. He says that he is sending a certain Tōkurō as a messenger to bring him news of his granddaughter:

I am truly concerned about her illness, and caringly I write the following.

Since I worry about how she is feeling in her illness, I am sending Tōkurō. How is she doing? I want to know the particulars. Tōkurō should report back in detail.

> To Chobo   Daifu

Senhime, the daughter of the second shogun, Hidetada, lived at Osaka Castle as the wife of Toyotomi Hideyori until the castle fell in the fifth month of 1615. She then married Honda Tadatoki. After Tadatoki died in 1626, she lived in Edo under the name Tenjuin. The maid Chobo served Senhime, changed her name to Matsuzaka Tsubone, and lived until the age of ninety. The letter is signed *Daifu* (Inner Minister), referring to Ieyasu. Several other letters from Ieyasu to Senhime

or Chobo are known, each of them reflecting his tender affection for his granddaughter.

YK

64 *Wakagaishi*
Hosokawa Yūsai (1534–1610)
hanging scroll; ink on paper
27.1 x 41.0 (10 5/8 x 16 1/8)
Momoyama period, late 16th–early
17th century
Eisei Bunko, Tokyo

Hosokawa Fujitaka, or Yūsai, his better-known Buddhist name, was a high-ranking warrior and daimyo whose life spanned the late Muromachi and Momoyama periods. The second son of Mibuchi Harukazu, he was adopted in 1540, at the age of six, by Hosokawa Mototsune. He served Ashikaga Yoshiharu (1511–1550), the twelfth shogun, and after his death became an ally of Oda Nobunaga (1534–1582), supporting Yoshiaki (1537–1597), the fifteenth shogun. Later he served Toyotomi Hideyoshi (1537–1598) and became the daimyo of Miyazu Castle in Tango Province, with a fief of 120,000 *koku*.

This *wakagaishi* (paper of poems; cat. 58), brushed by Yūsai, contains two poems he composed on cherry blossoms, each poem based on one line of a Chinese couplet: *I face flowers all day long / Remaining flowers are fragrant in the wind.* The poems convey the peaceful thoughts on a spring day of an old poet who has lived through the vicissitudes of a world torn by incessant warfare:

Two Compositions

Hōin [Seal of the Law; the highest
    Buddhist rank given by the court]
    Genshi [alternative Buddhist name of
    Yūsai]

I face flowers all day long [in Chinese]

Here since the morning sun—
when at all
did the light shift?
I have not even looked aside
being with flowers all day till dusk.

Remaining flowers are fragrant in the wind
    [in Chinese]

116

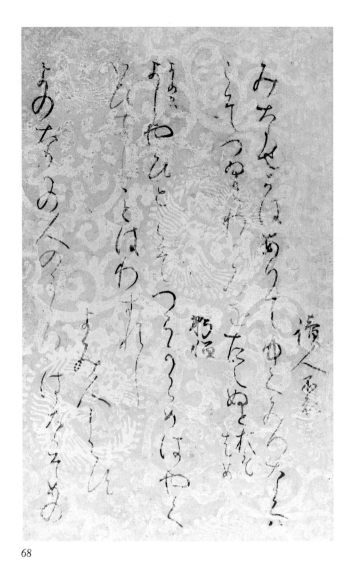

67   68

*That it has already
scattered them
perhaps it regrets today;
sending flowers' fragrance
spring wind blows.*

Yūsai is a very model of the cultivated daimyo: competent in warfare and administration, a famous poet of the arts and literature of antiquity. He left many works on classical literature, including *Hyakunin isshushō* (Annotations on *A Poem Each by One Hundred Poets*) and *Ise monogatari ketsugishō* (Annotations on *Tales of Ise*) as well as an anthology of poems, *Shūmyōshū*.   YK

65 *Wakagaishi*
Hosokawa Sansai (1563–1646)
hanging scroll; ink on paper
31.0 x 47.0 (12 1/4 x 18 1/2)
Edo period, early 17th century
Eisei Bunko, Tokyo

Hosokawa Sansai (Tadaoki), son of Hosokawa Yūsai (1534–1610), served Oda No-bunaga (1534–1582) as the daimyo of Miyazu Castle in Tango Province. When Akechi Mitsuhide (d. 1582) assassinated Nobunaga, he tried to persuade Sansai, who was his son-in-law, to join his cause. In spite of the marriage alliance, Sansai threw his support to Toyotomi Hideyoshi (1537–1598), Nobunaga's trusted vassal, who defeated and killed Mitsuhide. Later Sansai served Tokugawa Ieyasu (1543–1616) and became the daimyo of Kokura Castle in Buzen, northern Kyushu. Sansai was a cultured man well versed in Japanese poetry and painting. He is remembered as an important disciple of the tea master Sen no Rikyū (1522–1591).

Sansai wrote this *wakagaishi* (paper of poems; cat. 58) in the semicursive (*gyōsho*) mode, arranging the characters on the paper in the style called *chirashigaki* (scattered writing):

*Flowers on the trees
in bloom at Naniwazu
say, 'Now the winter
yields its place to the springtime!'
Flowers blooming on the trees.*

(Translated in McCullough 1985b, 319.)

Sansai was not the author of this poem, which appears in one of the prefaces to the tenth-century *Kokinshū* (Anthology of ancient and modern Japanese poems). Sansai copied out the text of this well-known poem partly as a prayer, partly as an exercise in calligraphy.

The note attached to the left edge addresses this copy of the poem to Nentoku Daimyōjin (Great God of the Year), because it was written on the New Year's Day as a prayer to the guardian god of the coming year. It is signed *Sansai Sōryū*, Sōryū being Sansai's Buddhist name.   YK

66 Concerning *Kokinshū*
Hosokawa Yūsai (1534–1610)
hanging scroll; ink on paper
29.0 x 38.0 (11 3/8 x 15)
Momoyama period, 1600
Eisei Bunko, Tokyo

Much knowledge of all kinds, including that in the realm of *bun* (arts) and *bu* (arms), was in Japan considered secret, or privileged, and was transmitted orally from a master to a worthy pupil—a process known in traditional Japan as *denju* (literally, "to transmit and impart"). Knowledge of how to read and understand poems of antiquity, too, was handed down that way. This document is about *Kokin denju*, the transmission of criticisms and interpretations of the poems in *Kokin wakashū* (*Kokinshū* for short; Anthology of ancient and modern Japanese poems), an early-tenth-century compilation. Knowledge of the *Kokin denju* tradition, which was begun by the poet Sōgi (1421–1502) of the Muromachi period and passed on within the Nijō school of poetry, was considered a supreme achievement in the Japanese poetry tradition of the middle ages.

Hosokawa Yūsai, the calligrapher of this document, was a member of the Nijō school and learned in the art of *Kokin denju*. The document is a certificate of *Kokin denju* from Yūsai to the imperial prince Hachijō (Prince Toshihito, 1579–1629), the younger brother of the emperor Go-Yōzei (1571–1617). On the eighteenth day of the seventh month of 1600, just before the Battle of Sekigahara (cat. 104), the forces of Ishida Mitsunari (1560–1600) laid siege to Yūsai at Tanabe Castle in Tango Province (part of present-day Kyoto Prefecture). On the twenty-seventh day, Go-Yōzei, gravely concerned that the *Kokin denju* tradition might end with Yūsai, had Prince Hachijō send Ōishi Jinsuke, his councilor, to persuade Yūsai to make peace. As a military man, Yūsai declined. This certificate, dated the twenty-ninth day of the seventh month, 1600, indicates that Yūsai, facing the possibility of death, had decided to make Prince Hachijō his successor in the *Kokin denju* tradition. Signed at the end *Yūsai* and *Genshi*, both of them Buddhist names, the document records three generations of Yūsai's line of transmission of *Kokin denju*: first Sankōin, a courtier also known as Sanjōnishi Saneki (1511–1579), who transmitted *Kokin denju* to Yūsai; second, Yūsai himself; and third, Prince Hachijō, to whom Yūsai passed on the tradition. YK

67 *Shitae Shūishōgire*

hanging scroll; ink on decorated paper
26.3 x 18.5 (10 3/8 x 7 1/4)
Heian period, early 12th century

Tokyo National Museum

Beginning in the late sixteenth century, the connoisseurship and collecting of old Japanese calligraphies, particularly to adorn the *tokonoma* of the tea hut during tea ceremonies, led to the systematic dismembering of old Japanese books and scrolls, particularly those of thirteenth-century date or earlier. These fragments (*kire* or -*gire*, literally, "cut pieces") are known as *kohitsugire*, *kohitsu* being a shortened form of *kojin no hisseki*, or

"brush traces of men of antiquity." (By contrast, the Chinese or Chinese-inspired calligraphy produced by Zen monks was known as *bokuseki*, or "ink traces.")

This is a fragment from an early-twelfth-century transcription of the late-tenth-century *Shūishō* (Selected gleanings), a private (as opposed to imperial) anthology in ten volumes said to have been compiled by Fujiwara Kintō (966–1041), a courtier and poet of the mid-Heian period. The fragment is called a *shita-e* (underdrawing) because there is a delicate drawing on the paper, in silver paint, of plants and birds.

Originally from the first of a set of scrolls, this fragment presents seven lines on the theme of spring. The first three columns from the right are a headnote to the poem, which composes the next two columns. The remaining two columns are the headnote to the next poem, which is not transcribed here. The text reads:

Priest Ekei, on cherry blossoms in bloom in a dilapidated house which nobody was expected to visit:

*On a field of wild grass
in an uninhabited house
cherry blossoms are in bloom;
will they perhaps peacefully
scatter in the wind?*

Composed while regretting the falling cherry blossoms at the house of Yoshichika, Junior Middle Councilor.

The beautiful, fluent *kana* calligraphy is ascribed to Minamoto Toshiyori (1055–1129), an attribution that cannot be accepted with certainty. Several calligraphic works by the same hand are known, including *Gen'eibon Kokinshū* (the Gen'ei-era edition of the *Kokinshū*), *Gosenshū-gire* (Fragments of the later anthology of ancient and modern Japanese poems), and *Sujigire* (Fragments of the *Kokinshū*) all of the early twelfth century. YK

68 *Minbugire*

hanging scroll; ink on decorated paper
25.4 x 17.0 (10 x 6 3/4)
Heian period, early 12th century

Sekai Kyūseikyō (MOA Art Museum), Shizuoka prefecture
Important Art Object

Besides being cut up into fragments to adorn the *tokonoma* during the tea ceremony, fine old calligraphies might also be dismembered to be pasted into albums known as *tekagami*, or "mirrors of [skilled] hands." These albums of *kohitsugire* (cat. 67) were collectors' items, or copyists' models, or both together. They became popular during the seventeenth century.

The piece shown here is a fragment of a transcription from the early-tenth-century compilation *Kokin Wakashū* (or *Kokinshū*, Anthology of ancient and mod-

ern Japanese poems). The twenty-volume *Kokinshū*, in which the emperor Daigo (885–930) had contemporary and recent poets' *waka* (31-syllable Japanese poems) collected by imperial edict, is the oldest anthology of such poems of Japan. Along with *Shin Kokinshū* (New anthology of ancient and modern Japanese poems), it is the most famous imperial anthology.

This fragment is from a *kohitsugire* called *Minbugire*—supposedly so called after an owner who bore the title *Minbu* (Officer of the Department of Finances). Originally the *Minbugire* was in book form. The poems were written in two columns each, with eight to ten columns on a page. The fragment here, a single page, contains two poems and half of a third copied from the *Kokinshū*, one poem by Ōshikōchi Mitsune (fl. c. 900), a compiler of the *Kokinshū*, and two by anonymous poets. The transcribed poems are numbered 793, 794, and 795 in the fifteenth volume of the *Kokinshū*, entitled "Love":

Anonymous

*If there were never
the slightest flow of water
in the dry river
of our love, then I would think
the channel doomed to vanish.*

Mitsune

*Has your love then cooled?
Well and good as Yoshino,
River of Good Fields:
I will still bear in memory
the words we spoke at the start.*

Anonymous

*In this world of ours,
what is it that resembles
the human heart?
Dyestuffs from the dayflower
(all too quick to fade away).*
(Translated in McCullough 1985a, 174.)

The flowing calligraphy suggests a slow movement of the brush, with attention to even spacing between characters and some characters linked with a consistent leftward tilt. The imported Chinese paper is decorated with a design of arabesques, roundels, and phoenixes printed in mica. Although the calligraphy is commonly ascribed to Minamoto Toshiyori (1055–1129), a poet of the late Heian period, there is no evidence for this attribution. Judging from the calligraphic style, the poems appear to have been copied in the twelfth century. YK

69

69 Precepts of the Seven Buddhas

Ikkyū Sōjun (1394–1481)
hanging scroll; ink on paper
125.3 x 32.2 (49 3/8 x 12 5/8)
Muromachi period, 15th century

Eisei Bunko, Tokyo

A single line of bold calligraphy fills the narrow paper:

Do not commit evil deeds;
Strive to do good deeds.

These are the first two of four verses known as *Shichibutsu tsūkai no ge*, or *Verses of Precepts of the Seven Buddhas*, from the early Buddhist sutra *Zōichi-agon-kyō* (*Ekottara-agama-sutra* in Sanskrit; translated into Chinese during the Eastern Jin Dynasty, AD 317–420), which summarizes the essential teachings of the Buddhas. The remaining verses, not transcribed here by Ikkyū, read:

Purify your thoughts—
This is what the Buddhas teach.

The calligraphy is by the famous Zen monk Ikkyū Sōjun (cat. 11). A work like this, written in a single column, is known as *ichigyōsho*, or a single line of calligraphy that often transcribes revered names or epithets or extracts from sacred texts—a kind of written icon. This form is distinctly Japanese, being unknown in China. A calligraphy with four large characters, *Sha Ka Nyo Rai* (the Buddha Sakyamuni), written by Tettō Gikō (1295–1369), the second abbot of Daitokuji, is an early Japanese example of *ichigyōsho*. It is possible that Ikkyū, in his deep veneration of this master, followed the same format. Another well-known work in this format by Ikkyū is an epithet, *The First Patriarch, Great Master Bodhidharma*, in a private collection in this country.

Ikkyū was born on New Year's Day, 1394, the son of the emperor Go-Komatsu (r. 1392–1411); because he was born outside the palace he was never acknowledged as an imperial son. Ikkyū was a passionate and outspoken iconoclast—a harsh critic of received pieties, ceremonious practices, and the contemporary Zen establishment, which thrived through the patronage of the Ashikaga government and powerful daimyo. His fulminations against most of the Zen hierarchy were vitriolic, and he refused all clerical appointments, choosing instead to move from one small hermitage to the next, training only a handful of disciples. Ikkyū finally became abbot of Daitokuji, in 1474, at the age of eighty-four, but only in response to an imperial summons to rebuild the devastated Daitokuji, and he retained the post for less than a year.

The calligraphy here is somewhere between the regular (*kaisho*) and semicursive (*gyōsho*) modes, executed in bold, rough, and swift brushwork that conveys something of the tempestuous nature of the calligrapher. The brush was apparently made of a piece of bamboo, finely split at one end. The brush movement was so quick that Ikkyū inadvertently omitted the character "good" from the second verse. This character was added later in small, precise calligraphy, to the right of Ikkyū's text. On the lower left is stamped a square relief seal, *Ikkyū*.   YS

RELIGIOUS SCULPTURE

70 **Fudō Myōō with two attendants**
    Unkei (d. 1223)
    polychromed wood
    h. Fudō Myōō, 136.8 (53 7/8); Kongara
    Dōji, 77.9 (30 5/8); Seitaka Dōji, 81.8
    (32 1/4)
    Kamakura period, 1186

    Ganjōjuin, Shizuoka Prefecture
    Important Cultural Property

Unkei, the foremost Japanese sculptor of
Buddhist images during the early Kamakura period, had a wide and long-lived influence. Along with his father, Kōkei, and
his father's other leading disciple, Kaikei
(fl. c. 1185–1223), Unkei led the Buddhist
sculptors of Nara in the work of reconstructing the ancient Nara temples, which
were burned in the course of civil war in
1180. The work included the restoration of
the great Buddha of Tōdaiji and the many
Buddhist images that surrounded him.
When this task was completed in 1203, the
court granted Unkei the title *hōin* (Seal of
the Law), the highest rank accorded to artists.

    In 1186, before beginning work at
Nara, Unkei made the three Buddhist images shown here for the Ganjōjuin; the patron who commissioned them as an act of
piety was Hōjō Tokimasa (1138–1215), a warrior cheftain of Izu Province in the northeast and father-in-law and ally of the newly
made shogun, Minamoto Yoritomo (1147–
1199).

    Traditional Buddhist iconography
gives Fudō eight youthful attendants, of
whom the pair seen here are the two most
commonly shown: the mild and devout
Kongara and the more brutish and violent
Seitaka.   NYS

70

71 Senju Kannon

gilt bronze
h. 104.5 (41¹/₈)
Kamakura period, c. 1237–1247
Nagoji, Chiba Prefecture
Important Cultural Property

This gilt bronze Buddhist image, with forty-two arms cast separately and attached to its body, represents the typical form of Senju Kannon (literally thousand-armed Kannon, though most images were made with "many" arms representing the canonical thousand). The thousand arms stand for the infinite number of means that Kannon, Bodhisattva of Compassion, employs to save suffering creatures. Originally this image also represented Eleven-Headed Kannon, each head symbolizing a vow to save the world. But the eleven small heads and the image of Amida, Buddha of Compassion, to whom the bodhisattva Kannon pertains, have been lost. Portions of fingers and accessories are also missing.

A *kaō* carved in the joint of one of the hands indicates that this image was made for Chiba Tanetoki, a descendant of Chiba Tsunetane who was a supporter of Minamoto Yoritomo (1147–1199). Tanetoki was a minor ruler in the northeast section of present-day Chiba Prefecture. Following the custom of warriors of eastern Japan, who typically built a place of worship inside their residences to enshrine a Buddhist image, Tanetoki probably placed this Senju Kannon in a corner of his dwelling. This piece probably was made between 1237 and 1247, when Tanetoki served the Kamakura shogun, before the Kamakura area became the center of sculpture in the Eastern provinces.

The protruding abdomen adds a note of realism to the otherwise columnar form. The style of this powerful figure derives from Unkei's (d. 1223; cat. 70), which set the standard for sculpture in the eastern provinces. A delicate expression in the slanting eyes under long arching eyebrows, the narrow hips, and the elaborately draped garment, though, are less characteristic of Unkei, and suggest the influence of Higo Jōkei, a sculptor of Buddhist images who was then active in Kyoto and who adopted the style of Song dynasty Buddhist paintings.   NYS

72 Anteira Taishō and Santeira Taishō

polychromed wood
h. Anteira Taishō, 91.5 (36);
Santeira Taishō, 81.7 (32¹/₈)
Kamakura period, 13th century
Honzan Jionji, Yamagata Prefecture

Anteira Taishō (Divine General Anteira) and Santeira Taishō (Divine General Santeira) are two of the Twelve Divine Generals (Jūni Shinshō), attendants of Yakushi, Buddha of Healing. The twelve divine generals, presented as armored warriors, are said to protect devotees of the Yakushi Buddha. In the Yakushi Hall at Honzan Jionji, the twelve generals flank the principal images, the triad of Yakushi and his bodhisattvas Nikkō (Solar Radiance) and Gakkō (Lunar Radiance).

Each general represents one of Yakushi's vows to save humankind. In addition, the twelve generals correspond to the twelve horary animals who represent the twelve divisions of heaven in ancient Chinese astronomy: rat, ox, tiger, rabbit, dragon, snake, horse, sheep, monkey, rooster, dog, and boar. Each animal represents one year of a twelve-year cycle; it also represents a day in a twelve-day cycle, a two-hour period in each day, and a compass direction. Each general would protect the time periods and direction ruled by his corresponding animal. Anteira Taishō corresponds to the rabbit, Santeira Taishō to the snake.

Among the twelve pieces, the statue of Santeira Taishō is particularly fine. He strikes a vigorous pose, with his left arm raised, and wind-blown hair and sash. His upturned face expresses anger through the knitted brows and the down-turned mouth. The image is made of Japanese cypress (*hinoki*) in the joined woodblock technique (*yosegi zukuri*), in which the main part of the figure—head and torso—is assembled from more than two pieces of separately carved and hollowed-out wood. Cloth is pasted on the surface of the sculpture, which is then coated with *sabi urushi* (a paste of raw lacquer and pulverized stone), black lacquer, and white pigment. Over this, flower designs and dragons are carefully drawn with shaded colored pigments. For the hair and the cuirass, cut gold leaf is applied.

Sagaeshō, where Jionji is located, was a manor famous from the Heian period for its fine horses, which were sent to Kyoto for the use of the courtiers. In the main hall of Jionji are a number of statues, including the five aspects of the Bodhisattva of Wisdom and Intellect (Monju Goson), which were made in Kyoto in the late twelfth century. This indicates the existence of an early and strong tie between the temple and Kyoto. The statues of the Twelve Divine Generals were probably made by a Buddhist sculptor in Kyoto.

SH

124

71

72

73 Aizen Myōō in shrine
Jōin and Shūkichi (fl. 1297)
gilt bronze
h. figure, 7.9 (3¹/₈); shrine, 30.0 (11³/₄)
Kamakura period, 1297
Shōmyōji, Kanagawa Prefecture
Important Cultural Property

Aizen Myōō (Lord of Passions), like Fudō, is one of the Kings of Bright Wisdom, guardians of Buddist truth. He symbolizes the transformation of the human passions, particularly lust and greed, into Enlightenment. He is customarily shown, as here, wearing a lion crown, with a third eye of wisdom in the center of his forehead, with six arms, and with an Esoteric Buddhist symbol in each hand. Since the *myōō* are fierce aspects of the Buddha, his hair stands up in anger. Behind him is a sun halo, and he sits, like most Buddhist deities, on a lotus throne. Beneath the lotus blossom seat is a vase, traditionally containing treasures; these are depicted on the base of the lotus throne, closely following the iconographic prescriptions of Esoteric Buddhist sutras. Much care has been lavished on the realistic modeling of the angry face and the exaggerated folds of the hem of the garment.

The lion crown, hair, arms, and accessories were each made separately. Each of the many tiers of the pedestal is made of cast bronze, hammered bronze plate, and cast silver, and decorated with gold and silver gilt and inlay. The wooden *zushi* (miniature shrine) may have been made at the same time as the image, or shortly after. An inscription on the back of the pedestal indicates that this small, elaborately cast image was made at Shōmyōji in 1297.

The names of the sculptors, Jōin and Shūkichi, father and son, are recorded in the inscription. Calligraphy on other extant items in Shōmyōji reveals that Jōin and Shūkichi were metalworkers from the Eastern provinces and were active at Shōmyōji and at Gokurakuji in Kamakura, another Esoteric Buddhist temple. This image has a simplicity and directness that bespeaks the style of provincial artisans.

NYS

73

74 **Jizō Bosatsu**
polychromed wood
h. 167.5 (66)
Kamakura period, late 13th century

Jufukuji, Kanagawa Prefecture
Important Cultural Property

Jizō Bosatsu (*bosatsu* is the Japanese for
bodhisattva), which was introduced into
Japan in the eighth century, became toward the end of the Heian period an object of popular faith as the particular deity
who intervenes for the sake of those suffering in Hell. As in most extant images of
Jizō, he is depicted here as a monk,
shaven-headed and clad in monastic robes.
He holds a "wish-granting" jewel in his left
hand, and in his right the characteristic
monk's staff, not pictured, topped by loose
rings whose jingling announced his
approach.

Jufukuji was built in 1200 by Minamoto Yoriie, the second shogun of Kamakura, and Hōjō Masako, the widow of
Minamoto Yoritomo (1147–1199), the first
shogun. Eisai (or Myōan Yōsai, 1141–1215;
cat. 49) was its founding priest.

The well-focused oval face and proportion between the head and body indicate that this piece was probably made by
an accomplished sculptor toward the end
of the thirteenth century. The front and
back of the head were carved in two parts
and joined behind the ears. The crystal
eyes enhance the realism of the figure. Although life-size wooden sculpture from
the late Heian period and later typically
employed the *yosegi zukuri* technique (hollow joined blocks), using material from different trees, here the body, excluding the
hands but including the upper half of the
pedestal, was made from a single block of
Japanese cypress (*hinoki*). Over the pasted
cloth and *sabi urushi* (thick raw lacquer
mixed with pulverized stone), which still
remain, black lacquer and pigment seem
to have been applied to the entire surface.
The staff in the right hand and the bottom
section of the pedestal are later additions.

SH

74

75

75 Dainichi Nyorai in shrine
lacquer and gold leaf on wood
h. figure, 32.1 (12⅝); *shrine*, 83.7 (33)
Kamakura period, late 12th century

Kōtokuji, Tochigi Prefecture

Dainichi Nyorai (or Dainichi Buddha) was the principal deity of the Esoteric Tendai and Shingon schools of Buddhism, which exalted him as the source of all existence. Esoteric Buddhism, which originated in India, reached Japan via China in the ninth century. This new form of Buddhism, into which elements of Hinduism had been merged, emphasized magical cult practices, mystical formulas, an enormous pantheon of vastly empowered and intricately related deities, religious ecstasy, and the conviction that only the initiate could participate actively in the faith. As often happened with Buddhist deities translated to Japan, in the late Heian and Kamakura periods Dainichi the cosmic principal acquired also the role of protector and provider of such secular benefits as health and various forms of worldly success, though as an Esoteric deity he could be appealed to by the lay devotee only through the mediation of exotic ceremo-nies performed by learned Esoteric monks.

Dainichi is shown seated cross-legged on a lotus throne in the standard posture of Buddhist meditation. His hand gesture (S: *mudrā*) is specific to Esoteric Buddhism: the right fist clasps the index finger of the left hand, symbolizing all-encompassing and cosmic wisdom. The hand gesture and the golden Wheel of the Buddhist Law identify him as Ichiji Kinrin—*ichiji* being the magical "single syllable" that expresses Dainichi's power, *kinrin* being the "golden wheel" symbolic of Buddhism's universality. The pedestal, made of lacquered and gilded wood, forms a lotus throne, supported by eight wooden gold-painted lions, of which four are extant. Crystal pendants hang from the tips of the lotus petals. X-ray examination of the figure of Dainichi has revealed that on the inside are a round jewel (*shingetsurin*, ring of the moon-clear heart), probably of crystal, and a miniature five-tier *stupa*, a pagoda of a type specific to Esoteric Buddhism (*gorintō*), probably of wood. Part of the surface of the miniature shrine has recently been restored.

Although the statue of Dainichi is small, details of the face are precisely rendered and the body is well balanced. This image is said originally to have been enshrined in Hokkaiji, built in the late twelfth century by Ashikaga Yoshikane (d. 1199), an important figure in the Kamakura shogunate in the northern part of Ashikaga. Yoshikane's wife was a younger sister of Hōjō Masako, wife of Minamoto Yoritomo (1147–1199), the founder of the shogunate. Around that time, the Hōjō family placed Buddhist images by Unkei in Ganjōjuin, Shizuoka Prefecture. Considering the close kinship of the Ashikaga to the Hōjō, it is possible that this statue of Dainichi was indeed made by Unkei (d. 1223, cat. 108), who worked for the Hōjō family.   SH

76

76 Hachiman with two attendant deities

Kyōkaku (fl. 1326)
wood
h. Hachiman, 72.3 (28½); Okinaga
Tarashihime, 44.3 (17½); Himegami,
45.2 (17¾)
Kamakura period, 1326

Akana Hachimangū,
Shimane Prefecture
Important Cultural Property

The triad is composed of Hachiman (the god of war) in the center wearing a courtly robe (*hō*) and holding a wooden ceremonial slat (*shaku*), with Okinaga Tarashihime (Empress Jingū) to his right and the goddess Himegami (often identified as Hachiman's consort) to his left. The style of their clothing is modeled after that of the court of the Heian period.

Hachiman has been worshiped at least since the Nara period. His oldest extant shrine is located in Usa (present-day Ōita Prefecture, Kyushu), where he seems to have been a local and relatively minor Shinto deity. In the mid-eighth century Hachiman was dramatically elevated to Shinto tutelary deity of Tōdaiji, the imperially commissioned Buddhist temple in Nara. This set a precedent for the building of Hachiman shrines, both independently and within the precincts of Buddhist temples; the Hachimangū, built at Iwashimizu south of Kyoto, exemplifies the former status, the Hachiman shrine at Tōji in Kyoto

exemplifies the latter. The association of Shinto deities with Buddhist temples, and indeed their conflation with Buddhist deities, was a characteristic phenomenon of the Heian period.

The Iwashimizu Hachimangū had been built by Minamoto Yoriyoshi (999–1075). Following his ancestor's example, Minamoto Yoritomo (1147–1199) established a Hachimangū at Tsurugaoka in Kamakura, site of his newly created warrior government. Because of Yoritomo's veneration of the god, Hachiman became widely revered as the patron deity of the Minamoto lineage as well as the guardian of the military class and hence "god of war."

Akana Hachimangū is located in the mountainous area of Shimane Prefecture near the border of Hiroshima Prefecture. As a branch of Iwashimizu Hachimangū, it has been in existence since at least the twelfth century. In 1965, when this triad of Hachiman with two attendants was restored, inscribed wooden tablets were discovered inside the image of Hachiman. The tablets greatly clarified the circumstances of its creation. According to the inscription, in 1326 the *jitō* (estate steward) of the area, joined by several others, commissioned the triad from Kyōkaku of Yamashiro Province (present-day Kyoto), a great sculptor of Buddhist images.

Hachiman is made of Japanese nutmeg (*kaya*, Torreya nucifera); while Japanese cypress (*hinoki*) is used for the other

two figures. The main part of each image is made of two separate pieces, one for the front and one for the back; the hair and eyebrows are painted.　　　SH

77 **Bishamonten with two attendants**
Tankei (1173–1256)
polychromed wood
h. Bishamonten, 168.0 (66⅛);
Kichijōten, 79.2 (31⅛); Zen'nishi Dōji,
71.2 (28)
Kamakura period, 13th century

Sekkeiji, Kōchi Prefecture
Important Cultural Property

Bishamonten is one of the Four Heavenly Kings (Shitennō) who guard the Buddha's Law in the four quarters of the universe, the north being Bishamonten's special responsibility. The Shitennō originated in India as Hindu deities, were early absorbed into the Buddhist pantheon, and were transmitted with the faith to Central Asia, China, and Japan. In the course of this eastward passage they acquired their military characteristics: armor and weapons in the style of China's Tang dynasty (618–907), and expressions and gestures of fierce determination or even menace. Of the Four Heavenly Kings, Bishamonten (also called Tamonten) is the most powerful, possibly because East Asian geomancy makes the north the direction of greatest danger; he is also the only one worshiped independently. Images of Bishamonten that have not lost their arms are identifi-

able by the miniature pagoda that Bishamonten characteristically holds on his upturned left palm while brandishing a weapon in his right hand.

Pursuant to their protective function, images of the Four Heavenly Kings were usually placed at the corners of a temple altar whose center was occupied by Buddhas and bodhisattvas. In a central altar triad, Bishamonten would often flank an image of Sakyamuni Buddha, with the goddess Kichijōten, also of Hindu origin, on Sakyamuni's other side. In time Kichijōten came to be regarded as Bishamonten's wife. As a principal image, Bishamonten would himself be flanked, as here, by Kichijōten and Zennishi Dōji, a young boy regarded as the divine couple's child (and sometimes as an incarnation of Bishamonten himself). The best-known example of the Bishamonten triad, dating from the late Heian period, is at Kuramadera in Kyoto.

An inscription on the tenon connecting the left foot of Bishamonten with the base records that this triad was made by the great priest Tankei, with the rank of *hōin* (Seal of the Law). Tankei, the first son of Unkei (d. 1223), was born in 1173 and participated with his father around 1212 in sculpting the Buddhist images for the Hokuendō of Kōfukuji in Nara. In 1213 he was given the rank *hōin*, the highest honor awarded to sculptors of Buddhist images. In 1254 he made his best-known work, the wooden Senju Kannon (Thousand Armed Kannon) for Myōhōin in Kyoto.

Each of the figures in this triad is naturally posed and has small, well-modeled features. Bishamonten's build is formidable, his stance unyielding, and his expression adamant, but he is in no respect contorted or grotesque. The expressions of Kichijōten and Zennishi are calm and mild. In all these respects the figures are typical of Tankei's style. Each of the images is made of Japanese cypress (*hinoki*). The right and left halves of Bishamonten's head and torso were carved from separate hollowed-out blocks, as were the back and front halves of the other two figures. The eyes are inlaid crystal. Bishamonten's pedestal is a small earth demon whom the deity is often shown subduing. The pedestals for Kichijōten and Zennishi Dōji are later additions.　　　SH

78 **Amida Nyorai**
Kaikei (active c. 1185–1223)
lacquer and gold leaf on wood
h. 266.5 (104⅞)
Kamakura period, 1201

Jōdoji, Hyōgo Prefecture
Important Cultural Property

This is the 8-*shaku* (approximately 240-centimeter, or 8-foot) image of Amida described in documents as made by Kaikei in

1201 for a *raigōe* ceremony. Also extant at Jōdoji, founded by the priest Shunjōbō Chōgen (1121–1206), who restored Tōdaiji of Nara in the Kamakura period, are twenty-five of the original twenty-seven bodhisattva masks made at the same time for the same ceremony. In Jōdoji's Amida Hall is a colossal wooden Amida triad, also by Kaikei. Jōdoji was an Amidist temple founded by the enormously influential monk Shunjōbō Chōgen, who supervised the restoration of Tōdaiji in Nara after its destruction during the civil war of 1180–1185, and who became both patron and religious mentor of the sculptor Kaikei.

Raigō-e is a ritual that reenacts the descent of Amida Buddha from his Pure Land (Jōdo; popularly called Western Paradise because it was believed to be in the western part of the cosmos), accompanied by the bodhisattvas Seishi and Kannon and often by a heavenly host of lesser deities, to take the soul of a dying devotee to the Pure Land of immeasurable bliss, where it awaits rebirth to a high state of being. This Amida image was probably dressed in an actual costume and placed on a wagon leading a procession of people wearing the bodhisattva masks to represent the heavenly host. An armature would have been inserted inside the image to support it during the procession. The deity's hands form the gestures iconographically specific to the "welcoming descent." The names of the contributors are written inside the image, as well as *An* (Sanskit), followed by *Amidabutsu*, the Buddhist name of Kaikei.

Kaikei was active in the early Kamakura period, along with Unkei (d. 1223) and others, in the restoration of the Nara temples. His earliest extant work is a wooden statue of Miroku Bosatsu (Bodhisattva of the Future), which is dated 1189 (Museum of Fine Arts, Boston). There are approximately forty extant works by Kaikei, making him especially important for the study of the history of Japanese sculpture, since it is possible to trace the continuous development of his style. His most typical work, known through many versions, is the standing statue of the descending Amida Nyorai, which is noted for its refinement and detailed idealization.

Made in 1201, the work exhibited here dates approximately to the middle stage in Kaikei's stylistic development. Although a portion of the surface is damaged, most of the original gilt lacquer remains intact. Parts of Amida's halo have been restored.　　　SH

77

78

133

PAINTING

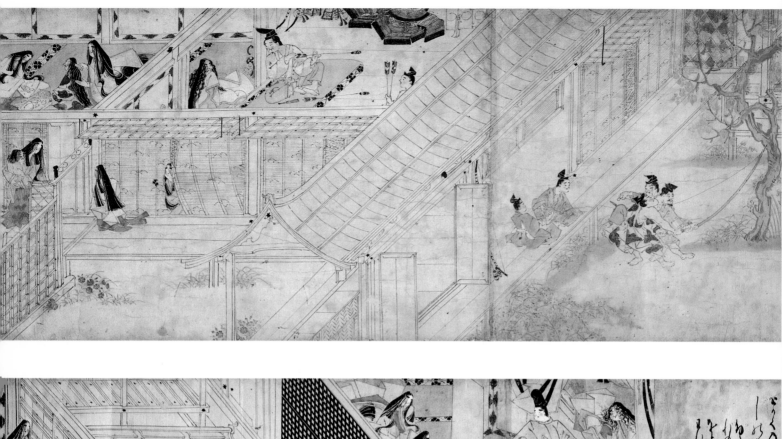

79 Tale of Obusuma Saburō

handscroll; ink and color on paper
28.8 x 1123.5 (11 3/8 x 449 1/2)
Kamakura period, late 13th century

Tokyo National Museum
Important Cultural Property

This illustrated tale is about two warriors, Yoshimi Jirō and Obusuma Saburō, both sons of a powerful daimyo in Musashi Province in the east (parts of present-day Tokyo, Saitama, and Kanagawa prefectures). The alternating sections of text and pictures that survive tell only a portion of

what must have been a longer tale, and even the scroll shown here is missing one section of painting.

Jirō, the elder brother was an aesthete who pursued music and poetry and sought the amenities of a life of artistic accomplishment (*bun*) modeled after the artistocratic way of life pursued in Kyoto. He took a wife, a former lady-in-waiting at court, who bore a daughter, Jihi (Compassion). Jihi grew into a stunningly beautiful young woman, and her reputation spread far and wide, resulting in offers of mar-

riage from many provinces. A betrothal to Naniwa no Tarō was arranged; their marriage was to take place after a three-year period.

The scroll opens with a scene of Jirō's domestic life. His men play the game of *go*; women view a painting and play musical instruments, all within courtly buildings, complete with gardens and ponds—quite unlike the typical home of a rugged eastern warrior. Jirō, wearing a casual white robe, converses with his wife in a chamber. Behind the chamber is an unattended space for storage of armor (section one).

The younger brother, Saburō, was a gruff warrior disciplined in the martial arts (*bu*). He married a robust woman described in the text as "seven feet tall [with] curly hair, all spirals when tied. There was nothing in her face so prominent as the long nose. Her lips were curved downward. There was no redeeming quality in whatever she said or did." She bore three sons and two daughters. The picture that follows the text depicts the activities at Saburō's residence, where his retainers practice riding and archery, and examine their weapons. Saburō's wife, recognizable by her curly hair and large nose, is inside, where a child is held by one of the maids (section two).

When the two brothers were called to the capital to serve as military guards at the emperor's palace, Saburō set out first with his men, passing a group of brigands who, aware of Saburō's martial prowess, allowed Saburō to pass. Jirō and his retinue followed; but they were attacked by the brigands. At the lower right Jirō, dressed in casual clothes of dappled patterns of blue against white, unarmed and ill-prepared, squats on the ground before a helmet and a box containing the rest of his armor. His men are getting it out. A bloody battle ensues, ending in slaughter of many men on both sides (section three).

Jirō died in the battle; Saburō had returned from the capital too late to rescue his brother. Before Jirō died, he asked Saburō to make sure that his possessions, including lands, be distributed among his vassals. He asked in particular that his mansion be left to his wife and daughter Jihi. Ietsuna, one of Jirō's faithful men, took Jirō's head home, but on his way the Buddhist deity Kannon appeared before him. The deity told him that, in compassionate response to Jihi's cries of grief, Jirō's soul would be assured of rebirth in paradise. The painting depicts the miracle of the deity Kannon over an ocean. The rays of divine light emanate from the crown of the deity and shine upon the head of Jirō, which, wrapped in the clothes he wore, lies by Ietsuna, who dozes on the shore (section four).

Meanwhile, at home, Jirō's wife and Jihi anxiously awaited the news. Earlier, Jihi dreamed of Ietsuna, carrying a hawk perched on his left hand and a helmet in his right. The hawk flew toward the west and the helmet fell to the ground—a premonition. The hawk was the soul of her father and the helmet his head. The painting depicts Ietsuna, now back at Jirō's mansion, delivering the head to Jirō's wife and daughter (section five).

The next text relates the fate of Jirō's family after his death. Saburō, ignoring Jirō's parting request, steals his lands and the mansion, evicts Jirō's wife and Jihi, and makes them his servants. The next painting in this sequence, now lost, probably included a scene of the takeover of Jirō's mansion by the unruly Saburō and his ugly and ambitious wife, and the ousting of Jirō's wife and Jihi. A fragment believed to be a part of the missing section was discovered and published in 1962. It depicts Jirō's wife and daughter, clad in humble rustic clothes, drawing water from a well for Saburō's horses. From this section on, then, the tale turns to the fortune of Jihi and her mother.

Jihi and her mother have become the servants of Saburō. The house is visited by the provincial governor, who notices Jihi's beauty and proposes marriage to her. Through trickery, Saburō's wife substitutes one of his ugly daughters, thwarting Jihi's marriage to the governor, who departs, brokenhearted. The last painting shows the governor dressed in courtly robe, preparing for a meeting with Jihi. To his right, the curly-haired daughter of Saburō, excited by her prospect of marriage, tries to draw the attention of the guest,

who turns his head away from her (section seven).

The tale narrated in this scroll is incomplete. Although it begins with the story of the two different brothers, the heart of the story seems to be Jihi's misfortune and eventual compensation through her marriage to Naniwa no Tarō, and the intercession of Kannon, the Buddhist deity. Although the painter of the scroll is unidentified, the painting is stylistically comparable to another work, *Ise shinmeisho utaawase* (Poetry contest on the themes of the newly selected places-with-names around Ise), dated to c. 1295, now in the collection of the Ise Shrine.　　YS

80 Hotei

Ashikaga Yoshimochi (1386–1428)
hanging scroll; ink on paper
31.0 x 56.0 (12 ¼ x 22)
Muromachi period, 1st quarter of fifteenth century

Fukuoka Art Museum, Fukuoka
Important Cultural Property

Hotei (C: Budai; cats. 99, 101), an eccentric Chinese figure with a special status among the Chinese Buddhist saints and sages, is shown grinning and leaning on a bulging sack. A wisteria wood cane lies on the ground nearby. The six-line inscription quotes stanzas of aphoristic verse from the Buddhist philosophical text, the *Diamond Sutra* (S: *Vajracchedika prajnaparamita Sutra*; J: *Kongō hannya haramitsu kyō*, or the "Perfection of Wisdom which cuts like a thunderbolt"). At the lower right of the sack is the square intaglio seal of the artist, *Kenzan no shō* (seal of Kenzan), and a *kaō* is brushed below it. The cipher is that of the fourth Ashikaga shogun, Yoshimochi (1386–1428), and *Kenzan* (Prominent Mountain) is Yoshimochi's Buddhist title (*dōgō*).

The name Hotei literally means "cloth bag," a reference to the sack, his only possession aside from the cane. In Chinese and Japanese Zen Buddhist hagiology, Hotei is considered an extraordinary figure, revered for his eccentric behavior and cryptic sayings. Hotei's legend can be traced to the biography of Qici, an early tenth-century Chinese Buddhist (though not of the Zen school) priest. He is said to have walked around city marketplaces carrying his cloth bag and cane, at times begging for money, and putting just about everything he came across into his bag, including pickled fish. He uttered strange, incomprehensible words. Among his supernatural attributes were the ability to forecast the weather and to defy the cold and even death—after he died at Fengchuan he was mysteriously seen in another province.

By the eleventh century AD Hotei had become widely recognized as a truly enlightened being outside the traditional

transmission line of the Zen (C: Chan) school. In the most important canonical collection of biographies of Zen partriarchs, *Transmission of the Lamp* (J: *Keitoku dentōroku*; C: *Jingde quandong lu*) (1002 AD), Hotei is included among ten "who reached the gate of Zen," that is, enlightenment. More significantly, Hotei began to be regarded generally in Chinese Buddhism as the reincarnation of the Future Buddha Maitreya, who would appear in this world as the salvation figure after the Laws of the Buddha had lost their effectiveness. In popular Buddhism Hotei acquired additional benevolent attributes; he was revered as the bestower of wealth and the lovable companion and protector of children.

Soon after Hotei's death in 917 A. D., his colorful exploits and enigmatic character, reinforced by the belief that he had been a living Buddha, began to appear as literary and pictorial motifs in Chinese Buddhist literature and art. By the twelfth century, Hotei's image had been carved in stone and modeled in clay; he had been painted by notable artists and had become a subject of distinguished poets and official scholars such as Su Dongpo (1037–1101). During the reign of Emperor Gao Zong (r. 1127–1163) the emperor himself composed a poem on Hotei:

*In the blue sky, a small cloud; high above in
    the sky, a solitary moon,*
[He] *manages to dwell outside this world,
    secretly in a faraway place,*
*Naturally seeking to hide in the market
    place, strange is this hero.*
*Wherever he goes he carries the cane and
    cloth bag,*
*To satisfy his hunger, what's wrong with
    wine or meat fresh with dripping blood?*
*Farewell to the Jade Palace, farewell to the
    beautiful pavilion,*
Where the snow continues to fall.

Hotei's human eccentricities and his supernatural attributes were enough to establish independent pictorial themes within the artistic tradition of Zen monasteries.

The verses inscribed on this painting are not directly related to Hotei's biography nor to the literary nor artistic traditions established around the Hotei theme. Rather Yoshimochi included the verses as a way of eulogizing Hotei as an enlightened being. The verses are transcribed to form three pairs of couplets in an unusual order: they are read from the third line from the right to the last line on the left and backward from the second line to the first on the right. Edward Conze translated the verses from the Sanskrit as:

*. . . dharmas should be forsaken, still more
    so no-dharmas. . . .*

80

Self-identical (sama) is that dharma, and
  nothing is therein at variance
  (vishama). . . .
Those who by my form did see me,
And those who followed me by voice
Wrong the efforts they engage in,
Me those people will not see
. . . Everything has potential Dharma,
  even as a dream, a faulty vision,
  a bubble or a shadow;
As dew drops or a lightning flash.
So should one view what is conditioned.

In both public and private life, Yoshi-mochi showed enthusiasm for the Zen school, and he himself was tonsured in 1423. As the Ashikaga shogun he frequently issued economic policy directives favorable to the Zen monasteries. His cultural activities in Kyoto, especially after his father, Yoshimitsu, died in 1408, were closely linked to notable scholar-monks, including Gyokuen Bonpō (cat. 84). Yoshimochi often sponsored poetry gatherings for scholarly monks talented in Chinese-style poetry. The seventeenth-century biography of painters, *Honchō gashi*, mentions that Yoshimochi learned painting from the artist-monk Minchō (1351–1431), and Minchō's biography in the same source mentions the painter's close contact with Yoshimochi. There is, however, little visual evidence that Minchō directly influenced Yoshimochi's painting. In the close-knit cultural sphere of Kyoto Zen temples, Yoshimochi had opportunities to see Chinese paintings. A talented amateur, like Winston Churchill at his easel,

Yoshimochi created his own ink paintings, several of which survive in public and private collections, including some outside Japan. Yoshimochi's paintings, like the works of most amateurs, vary in quality.

Stylistically, this Hotei painting follows both the Chinese and Japanese precedents of the fourteenth century. The dynamic brushstrokes that make up Hotei's sleeves and cane are reminiscent of the style associated with Yintuoluo (c. 1350s), an Indian (or Central Asian) painter active in China. Hotei's head shape, his grinning face, and large ear recall another painting of Hotei by Mokuan Reien (active 1340s), a Japanese painter-monk and pilgrim in China.   YS

81 Daruma (S: Bodhidharma)
Bokkei Saiyo (fl. 1452–1473)
hanging scroll; ink on paper
110.0 x 58.3 (43 1/4 x 23)
Muromachi period, no later than 1465

Shinjuan, Kyoto
Important Cultural Property

Bodhidharma (J: Daruma) was an Indian prince of the early sixth century AD who went to south China to spread the practice of meditation. At first unsuccessful, he crossed the Yangzi River and went north to Mount Song, where he meditated for nine years facing the cave wall at the Shaolin monastery. Daruma's teaching subsequently evolved into a forceful religious movement, which became known as

Chan (J: Zen) Buddhism, which survives vigorously to this day. Many different types of portraits of Daruma exist, all imaginary representations of the patriarch based on various narrative accounts. Here Daruma is represented in half-length, casting a concentrated stare with bulging eyes. He is clad as a monk, in a plain cassock, and his arms are folded in front of him. The long fingernail of the left thumb marks Daruma as an ascetic; the earring on the left earlobe marks him as a princely personage. At the lower right are stamped a two-character relief seal, *Bokkei*, and a circular relief seal, *Saiyo*, below it. They are the seals of the artist of the Soga clan, Bokkei Saiyo, otherwise known as Hyōbu Bokkei.

The written history of Zen Buddhism starts with the pseudobiography of Daruma, the founding patriarch of the school, which informs us that the teaching he transmitted to China was fundamentally different from that which had been taught and practiced by other traditioinal Buddhists. Daruma taught that the Buddha's doctrine should be transmitted from mind to mind, by directly pointing at the heart of a man so that he would see his nature and attain his own Buddhahood.

The history of Daruma portraiture dates as early as the eighth century AD in China. As the commemorative portrait of the founding patriarch of the Zen school, a Daruma portrait would be displayed by the Zen adepts on the fifth day of October for the memorial ceremony honoring his

寛正六年春王正月

香至王宮梅柳芳

少林十□求何事

半身形像現全身

東土西天徒弄神

前德禅大燈章孫似一承拜賛

81

140

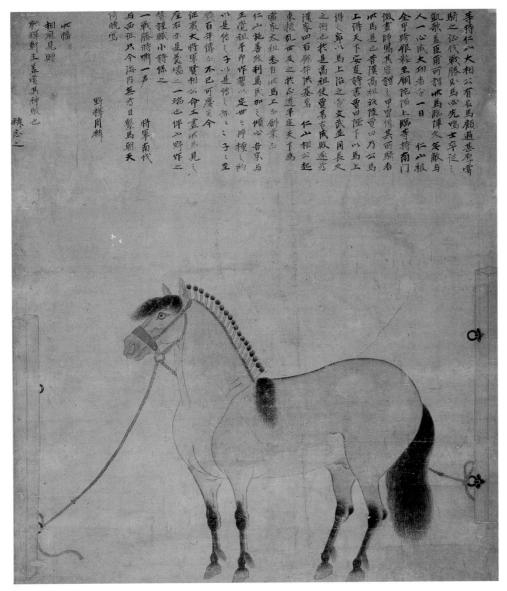

82

death. Many different types and styles of Daruma portraits were painted in both China and Japan. The half-length type had appeared already before the twelfth century in China.

The inscription above is by the famous Zen monk of Daitokuji Ikkyū Sōjun (1394–1481; see also cat. 11). As Daruma faces to the left, the inscription is written from left to right:

Followers in China and India conjure your spirit;
Half the figure, a portrait, reveals your entire body;
What did the grass mat at Shaolin [temple] accomplish?
At the Palace of King Xiangzhi, spring of plums and willows.

The sixth year of Kansei [1465], day of spring; [signed] Fifth generation descendant of Daitō [Kokushi or the National Master]

and formerly of the Tokuzen[ji subtemple], Jun Ikkyū respectfully eulogizes [stamped with a square relief seal *Ikkyū*]

The poem is recorded, with slightly different wordings, in Ikkyū's collection of literary works *Kyōun shū* (Mad Cloud Coll.). The Palace of King Xiangzhi mentioned in the last line of Ikkyū's poem is a Chinese name for the palace of the father of Bodhidharma, thought to have been situated in South India, corresponding to present-day Madras. *Fifth-generation descendant of Daitō* refers to Ikkyū's position in the transmission line of teaching; *fifth from Daitō* (Great Lamp) *Kokushi* (National Master) to the monk Shūhō Myōchō (1282–1337), the founding abbot of the Daitokuji monastery in Kyoto. Tokuzenji is a subtemple of Daitokuji, which had been refurbished by Ikkyū sometime around 1459 when he was appointed its abbot.

The artist Bokkei Saiyo was the earliest of the group of artists known by the

family name Soga, who served the warrior clan Asakura in Echizen Province (now Fukui Prefecture located on the Japan Sea coast). The Asakura, in turn, were for generations vassals of the Shiba family who, as a branch family of the Ashikaga, had been *kanrei* (deputy shogun) in control of the Echizen region. At the time this Bodhidharma painting was executed Echizen was ruled by Asakura Toshikage (also known as Takakage, 1428–1481; cat. 15), the powerful warrior and enlightened ruler of Echizen proper who controlled the area as *shugodai* (deputy constable). The Asakura family came under the influence of and actively patronized Ikkyū, and Bokkei is recorded as one of his disciples. At least two portraits of Ikkyū were painted by Bokkei Saiyo, one dated 1452 and the other 1453. On the basis of the dates of these paintings, it is assumed that this Bokkei is "Hyōbu Bokkei" who is mentioned in the collection of literary works of the scholar-

141

monk Kisei Reigen (1403–1488) as a student of the painter Shūbun, a frequent companion of Ikkyū, and who died in Ise in 1473. Not much else is known about our painter.

In this work, the bold brushstrokes that delineate Daruma's robe are the mark of a Soga painter. The half-length type of Daruma portrait, with the robe executed in sketchy brushwork, and with more carefully described facial features, was transmitted to Japan from China during the Muromachi period. The later Japanese versions are distinguished from the Chinese precedents by the bolder use of dark ink tones resulting in abstract, patterned forms, especially in the definition of the robe. The style of Bokkei, his immediate successor Soga Sōjō (cat. 87), and two generations of Soga Chokuan (cat. 129) of the sixteenth century consistently show strong individualistic brushwork and the achievement of dramatic tonal contrasts, marking them as expressionistic artists who had emerged in the provinces after the mid-fifteenth century.   YS

82 Excellent Horse

hanging scroll; ink and color on paper
66.7 x 58.0 (26 3/4 x 22 7/8)
Muromachi period, c. 1502
Kyoto National Museum
Important Cultural Property

This stately horse, tethered front and back to a pair of square posts, is described in profile with contour lines. The horse's forelock, mane, tail, and lower legs are painted in black ink. The body is colored with light ocher, the headstall with vermilion, and the posts with light reddish brown. A long inscription by the Zen monk Keijo Shūrin (1444–1518) in the top third of the scroll consists of a narrative concerning the horse, Shūrin's short poem, and a short colophon. Shūrin writes that the horse depicted is a famous one, owned by the first Ashikaga Shogun, Takauji (1305–1358), and that the current shogun had the horse portrayed in order to remind himself constantly of his ancestor's deeds. The colophon notes that the scroll was presented by the current shogun as a gift to the master of the Renkiken (annex of the Shōkokuji Zen monastery in Kyoto). The inscription reads:

The Prime Minister, Lord Jinzan [Shogun Ashikaga Takauji] [the founder of] the Tōji[in] temple, once owned a famous horse. The affectionate care [he bestowed on the horse] was quite extraordinary. When [the Lord] mounted the horse in a winning battle, chastising the enemy, the horse would neigh loudly, leading the officers' and soldiers' victorious cheers. Isn't this precisely what [the Lord's] vassals said about the

horse always being fearless at the battle ground, being one with men in spirit, thus leading a great victory? One day, Jinzan, donning gold armor, seated himself on the silver saddle and went to the South Gate of the Tōji[in] on Nijō Street of Kyoto, where he summoned a painter to paint his portrait. That painting is known as 'the armored portrait,' and the horse mounted [by the sitter] is this very horse. In antiquity, the Emperor Gao Zu of the Han dynasty told Lu Jia [from the state of Chu], 'I acquired my realm on horseback. How can I be bothered by the Book of Odes and Canon of History?' Jia replied, 'You may have acquired your realm on horseback, but how can you possibly rule your realm on horseback? [One achieves] the skill of government that endures by cultivating both arts (bun) and arms (bu).' Thereupon Gao Zu had Jia write the accounts of the rise and fall [of the past rulers], thus laying the foundation for the Han [dynasty] that lasted for more than four hundred years. Lord Jinzan['s forces] rose in the east, dispersed rebellions that brought chaos to the nation, and restored to it the Correct Path. He brought peace to the realm, establishing himself as the founding chief of this [Ashikaga] family. All of this [he] began on the back of this horse. Jinzan's rule delivered benevolent government, benefiting all people. In addition, his heart was devoted to our [Zen] school and he offered a vow in writing to [our patriarch] Shōgaku [Musō Soseki], establishing perpetual patronage of [our school], to be continued by his offspring who passed it on to their offspring, which has continued already for more than a hundred years without interruption. How felicitous this is! Now, the current wise Minister, the Barbarian-Subjugating Great Shogun, ordered a painter to paint [a picture of] this horse, which he keeps close to him to look at. This, too, is an instance of revering people of the past. [The shogun] asked this old rustic to compose a eulogy. I am obliged to do this by respectfully composing a short verse:

Victorious battle after battle the horse neighs loudly;
The shogun chastised enemies in the south, conquered rebels in the west.
Peace came to the realm;
The horse, tethered, bows to the emperor, and listens to the daybreak bush warbler.
[Signed] *Rustic monk Shūrin*

[Colophon]

This hanging scroll was presented to the master of the Renkiken [an annex of the Jōtokuin subtemple of the Shōkokuji monastery] by the shogun. The purpose is to praise the horse's divine excellence.
[Signed] [Shū]*rin recorded this.*

The Japanese tradition of depicting tethered horses dates back to at least the Kamakura period. Tethered horses are fre-

quently represented in narrative handscrolls of the medieval period in Japan, often in the stable of a warrior's residence. By the Muromachi period the subject became independent. The warrior Ogasawara Norinaga, an instructor of equestrian archery, had a portrait of his beloved horse Tanjō (Short Cane) painted in 1483, which was inscribed by the Zen monk Ōsen Keisan (1429–1493). In other instances tethered horses were often painted on large screens showing horses and grooms (cat. 105). It is likely that the artist of this painting used an existing work as a model (funpon). In fact, the type of horse, the style of the mane, the manner of tying the ropes to the halter and the two posts, and the flat, stylized form of this horse are similar to features depicted in a pair of screens of tethered horses in the Imperial Household collection. By the late fifteenth century and the early decades of the sixteenth, Kano painters such as Masanobu and his son Motonobu also began to depict this theme.

Keijo Shūrin, the inscriber of this painting, was one of the most important scholarly Zen monks in fifteenth-century Kyoto. He was born the son of Ōdate Mochifusa, a warrior and waka poet, who served several shoguns closely, but especially the eighth shogun Yoshimasa (1436–1490) during the Ōnin civil war (1467–1477). As a Zen monk Shūrin belonged to the influential school of Musō Soseki (1275–1351), mentioned in the inscription as having had Ashikaga Takauji, the first Ashikaga shogun, as his patron. Shūrin's career was intimately linked to the Shōkokuji monastery, where he attained its abbacy eight times between 1495 and 1508.

Keijo Shūrin's inscription is included in his voluminous collected literary works, Kanrin koroshū, although without the short poem and colophon. The works in the book are arranged in chronological order, and this inscription can be dated to within three years after 1501. Based upon such internal evidence, recent Japanese scholarship has reasonably established that the painting was commissioned by the eleventh Ashikaga shogun, Yoshizumi (1480–1511); that the master of the Renkiken mentioned in the colophon is the monk Juzan Eisō (1462–1508), a tonsured son of the imperial prince Fushiminomiya Sadatsune; and that the painting was executed around 1502.

The artist who painted this work was possibly Kano Masanobu (1434–1530). Masanobu was in direct service to the shogunate. He is known to have executed paintings of horses for the shogun and he could have had ready access to models on which to base this painting. In March 1489

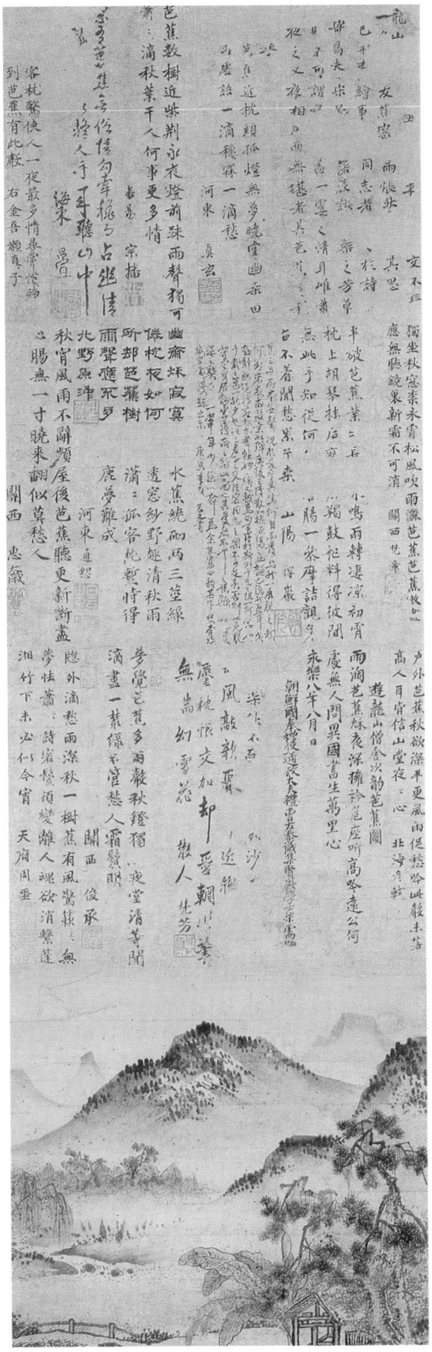

83

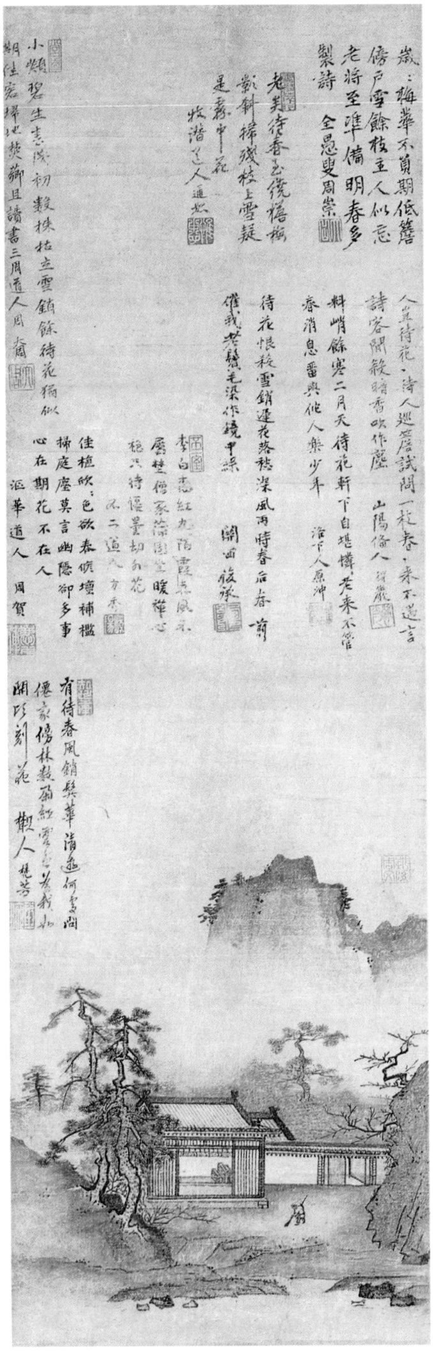

84

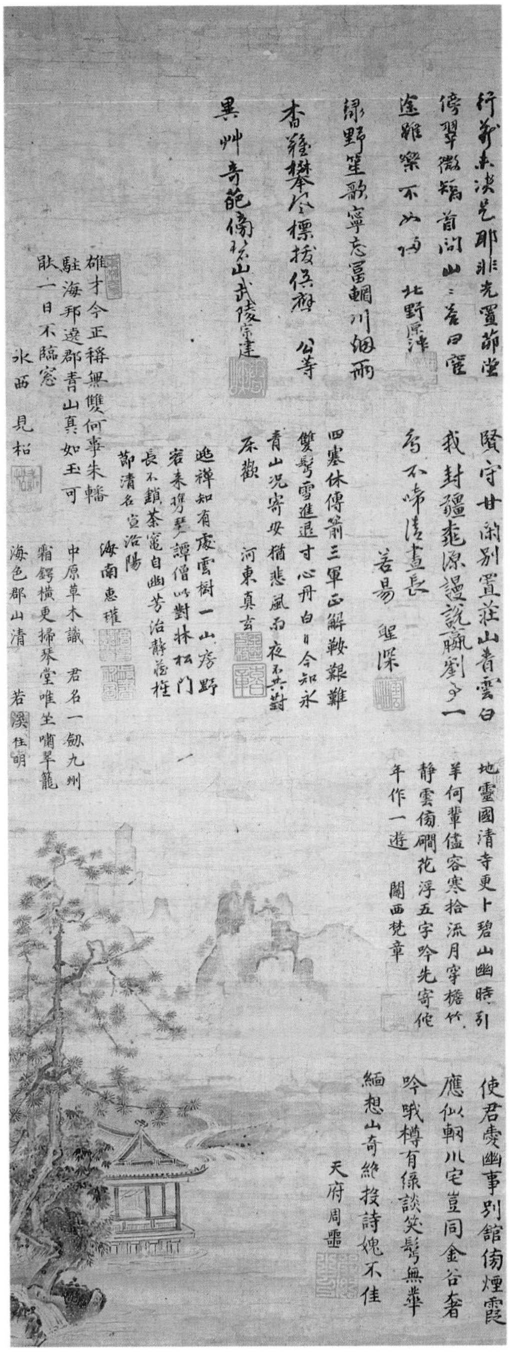

85

he painted a portrait of the ninth shogun, Ashikaga Yoshihisa (1465–1489). After the young shogun died in a battle, a commemorative portrait of Yoshihisa armed and mounted on a horse was commissioned from Masanobu by Yoshihisa's mother, Tomiko. This latter painting, in full color on silk, is preserved at the Jizōin in Aichi Prefecture.   YS

83 Banana Tree in the night rain

hanging scroll; ink on paper
95.9 x 30.9 (37³/₄ x 12¹/₈)
Muromachi period, no later than 1410

Agency for Cultural Affairs, Tokyo
Important Cultural Property

A humble hut, set in a landscape of hills and a lake, is flanked by a pine tree on the right and a banana tree on the left. On the opposite shore, water cascades into the mist-covered lake, and a grove of willow trees emerges from the mist. It is autumn, as the bare tree branches indicate. Splashes of dark ink around the banana tree and the willow trees suggest rainfall. Fifteen inscriptions identify the theme.

The painting was made on behalf of a young monk of Nanzenji, Ikka Kenpu (fl. 1410–1460). Later, poetic inscriptions were added to the painting, imbuing it with multiple meanings and making it into a *shigajiku* (see cat. 84, 86, 91), or "poetry-painting scroll," a favored format of the Muromachi period, particularly among Zen monk-litterateurs and their associates. Among those who inscribed it were: twelve prominent Zen poet-monks; the Korean scholar and government envoy Yang Su, who had come to Japan for the inauguration of Ashikaga Yoshimochi (cat. 4) to the shogunal seat succeeding his father Yoshimitsu, who had died two years earlier; and Yamana Tokihiro (1367–1435), a

143

powerful military ruler of the Provinces of Tajima (now northern Hyōgo Prefecture), Bingo (eastern Hiroshima Prefecture) and Inaba (eastern Tottori Prefecture), and director of the office of military affairs (*samurai dokoro*) of the Muromachi government. Tokihiro, like Ōuchi Morimi (cat. 85) of Suō Province, was closely associated with the literary monks of Kyoto who formed a close-knit literary salon under Yoshimochi's patronage. Two of the inscriptions were written in the year corresponding to 1410, thus dating the painting to no later than that year.

The summer banana tree in the winter snow—first versified by the poet Wang Wei (Chinese, 699–759) is a frequent paradoxical motif in Chinese poetry. Here it becomes a melancholy symbol of transience and an embodiment of ephemeral phenomena and volatility. This corresponds to the way it often is described in early Buddhist texts. Translations of the poetic inscriptions follow.
Poem by Yamana Tokihiro (top row, extreme left):

[The night rain] *jolts awake the guest from his sleep; restless: he will be up the rest of the night. Though I know well the sounds of rain, rain hitting banana leaves makes special sounds indeed.*

Poem, dated to the eighth month of the year corresponding to 1410, by Yang Su (bottom row, second from right):

[Title] *On visiting monks' quarters at [Auspicious] Dragon Mountain [Nanzenji] I add a poem to the painting Banana tree.*

Rain drops on the banana leaves, an autumn eve has deepened.
I maintain decorum, sit properly and listen to the lofty poems [of my esteemed colleagues.]
Where has the venerable Huiyuan [Chinese monk-recluse at Mount Lu, 334–416 A.D.] gone?
No one mentions him in his poem.
Scholar from a foreign country, I cast my thoughts [on Huiyuan] far into the distance of myriad miles.

Poem by monk Seiin Shunjō (second poem from left of the bottom row):

Awakened from a dream I hear many sounds of rain against banana leaves;
A hall in the autumn night lit by the faint light of a solitary lantern—the scene of purity.
Oblivious to all, the rain keeps falling on banana leaves' green, unmindful of my melancholy thought and of the beard that is white as the frost.

It is most likely that the painting was conceived as an independent hanging scroll and the inscriptions were written on a horizontal handscroll and only later cut up and mounted above the painting to make it into a *shigajiku*.   YS

84 Plum Blossom Study

hanging scroll; ink and color on paper
119.8 x 35.4 (47 1/8 x 13 7/8)
Muromachi period, no later than 1419
Idemitsu Museum of Arts, Tokyo

A stream flows in front of a scholar's study whose doors stand open. Boxes that may contain paintings or calligraphy are stacked in one corner of the room. Two pine trees soar high on the slope in the left foreground, and on the opposite side is a boulder surmounted by a pair of gnarled plum trees. A boy sweeps the ground with a long broom in front of the building, and behind it a white wall with an open door encloses a garden. In the distance a range of rocky mountains emerges out of the mist. In the upper section of the painting are Chinese poems inscribed by nine prominent Zen scholar monks of Kyoto, all contemporaries. Of these Daishū Shūchō, who brushed his poem on the upper left, was the first to die, making 1419, the year of his death, the latest possible date of the painting.

A spurious square relief seal stamped at the lower right hand corner claims the painting is by Tenshō Shūbun (fl. 1420–c. 1461), the great ink painter of the first half of the fifteenth century, but it is more likely by an unknown painter. So famous was Shūbun that many anonymous works from the fifteenth century later came to be attributed to him. Stylistically, the painting is reminiscent of Chinese paintings in the academic tradition known in Japan during the Muromachi period. The stately, deliberate forms of the pine trees, the rocks delineated by contour lines and texture dabs, and the mountains executed in both line and ink washes are some of the stylistic features of the Chinese academic tradition. The architecture of the study, the landscape imagery, and the traditional uniting of poetry and painting are all Chinese-inspired.

A scroll such as this, which combines a picture and contemporary inscriptions written by its earliest viewers, is called a *shigajiku*, or "poetry-painting scroll." When the subject is a scholar's study, real or imagined, as in numerous instances from the early fifteenth century, it is called a *shosaizu*, or a painting celebrating a study (cats. 86, 91, 85). In this example, the poems not only express the feelings of the viewers toward the study, but also name it *Taikaken* (Awaiting Blossom Study; that is, Plum Blossom Study). The suffix *ken* usually means an apartment or annex of a residential building of a subtemple within a monastery. These apartments, which were provided with *shosai*, or studies, were of-

ten used as retirement quarters for the aged Zen monks.

The inscribers of this painting were a tightly knit group of like-minded souls who shared cultural values and spiritual aspirations with the person for whom the painting was made. They are closely related to each other on more than one level: through their clerical ranks and careers within the Kyoto metropolitan monasteries, the shared benefits under the patronage of the shogun Ashikaga Yoshimochi (1386–1428), and the fellowship formed through their literary activities. Daishū Shūchō's poem reads:

The green grass growing atop the tiny peak, spring is just around the corner.
Trees, still devoid of leaves, stand amidst the lingering snow.
To wait for plum blossoms is akin to awaiting elegant guests.
I swept the ground, lit the incense; now I should turn to my books.

Another poem, the second from the right of the second row, is by monk Kengan Genchū (d. 1421), whose inscribed poem also appears in cat. 85:

The chilling gale of spring's first day against the February sky;
Being at the Plum Blossom Study is what I enjoy most.
Getting on in years, I heed little the news of coming spring;
Gladly I pass it on to others, letting the young take pleasure in it.

Finally, monk Gyokuen Bonpō (fl. 1420), the painter of orchids, wrote his poem at the lower left:

The spring wind I waited for came and went, taking with it the white of my beard;
Where should I seek pleasure away from this world? I must visit the abode of the immortals.
Near the grove of trees crimson blossoms dapple the branches,
Bursting forth all at once, it seems, for me.
                                    YS

85 Mountain villa

hanging scroll; ink and color on paper
81.8 x 32.0 (32 1/4 x 12 5/8)
Muromachi period, no later than 1415
Masaki Art Museum, Osaka

A small lakeside pavilion on stilts is partially obscured by a cluster of rocks, a pair of tall pine trees, and some bushes at the lower left. Behind the pavilion a stream flows into a lake. The rocky mountains in the central distance are flanked by pale silhouettes of still more distant mountains. Touches of light blue on the peaks, the water, the tiles of the pavilion, the bamboo leaves, and pine needles, as well as the

86

87

145

faint reddish brown of the rocks in the foreground, create subtle coloristic effects in this predominantly monochromatic painting.

Like the *Plum Blossom Study* (cat. 84), this work is a *shosaizu* (painting celebrating a scholar's study), an ink painting genre that flourished in Japan from the late fourteenth century throughout the Muromachi period. These paintings, depicting an unassuming hut in an imaginary landscape as a study or scholarly retreat, represent an ideal to which the person for whom they were made would have aspired. The significance of the landscape imagery is usually explained by a group of poetic inscriptions added directly on the painting, here by nine contemporary Zen monks. This painting and its poems celebrate the cultivated personality of the warrior Ōuchi Morimi (1377–1431), constable (*shugo*) daimyo of Suō Province (now Yamaguchi Prefecture, located on the western tip of Honshu), who in real life actually had built for himself a mountain villa to which he could retreat and pursue his studies.

During the Muromachi period, the political control of the Suō region as well as the island of Kyushu, far away from the seat of the shogunal government in Kyoto, was left to various contending local powers, including the Ōuchi family. After several years of factional battles, the Ōuchi family, chiefly through astute military and political maneuverings by Morimi, had come to control large blocks of territory, including northern Kyushu, and in 1404 Morimi was officially recognized by the shogunate as the constable daimyo of the whole region. With the central base of power firmly established within his domain and the large neighboring areas coming under his control, Morimi frequently traveled to Kyoto where he was warmly received by members of the upper-class warrior society, including the shogun, the deputy shogun (*kanrei*), and other ranking warriors. In Kyoto, Morimi befriended erudite monks of the metropolitan Zen monasteries. Morimi's personal contacts with scholar monks included the monk Ishō Tokugan (1360–1437), who was a frequent guest at Morimi's villa in Suō, and who wrote a long eulogy lauding Morimi and his villa. Ishō also wrote a dedicatory inscription for a portrait painting of Morimi. The importance of Ishō's relationship with Morimi and the Ōuchi family in Suō may also be seen in another painting in this exhibition, the *Chōshōken* (Listening to the Pines Study; cat. 86).

Among Morimi's personal accomplishments were the practice of Zen, taking the tonsure in 1405, and the pursuit of sinological studies through the reading of Confucian texts and Chinese poetry.

Morimi was also instrumental in obtaining a set of the Korean edition of the Buddhist tripitaka, the complete collection of Buddhist scriptures, through his trade with Korea. In 1410, Morimi published a woodblock-printed edition of the Chinese Buddhist text *Cang-cheng fa-shu* (J: Zōjō hossū), now known as the Ōuchi edition. From 1418 until his death Morimi helped the shogunate in the building campaign of the Shinto shrine Usa Hachimangu in Buzen (now Ōita Prefecture in Kyushu). After 1425, when he returned to Kyushu to quell an uprising there, Morimi had to concentrate his energy on controlling his domain. He died in 1431, at the age of fifty-five, in battle in Kyushu. He was buried at the Zen temple Kokuseiji in his home province of Suō.

Stylistically, this painting is linked to a number of similar works from the early part of the fifteenth century. The pine trees, rocks, and pavilion in the foreground are carefully described. Like other early ink paintings in which an attempt is made to depict an all-inclusive landscape, the spatial relationship between the foreground and the far distance remains ambivalent. The composition is probably based on a lost Chinese prototype, as is a very similar painting in the Konchi-in in Kyoto, which is dedicated to a young Zen Buddhist monk and depicts an idealized study.

More than half of those who inscribed the Masaki painting, which was completed no later than 1415 (the earliest known death date of any of the inscribers), are also authors of similar eulogies added to contemporary paintings of similar format and style. Some of their poems laud Morimi's essential virtues as a cultivated warrior. In one poem at the upper right, by the monk Genchū (d. 1421), the speaker is the warrior himself:

To serve in the world or to retire as a
*   hermit—I am yet to seek a resolution;*
So first I built a thatched hut in the
*   mountains;*
I raise my head high to gaze at the
*   mountain and ask what I should do;*
The mountain replies: 'A pleasure it will be
*   to serve in the government, but you will*
*   not be as happy as when you return home*
*   to retire.'*

Another poem, the first from the right in the second row, by the monk Shōshin (dates unknown) is addressed to Morimi:

You, Sir, wise Governor, built a villa to seek
*   repose;*
You made this realm your territory, where
*   the mountains are blue and clouds white.*
This idyllic place far surpasses the Peach
*   Blossom Spring of Yuan Chao and Liu*
*   Chen [of China];*
How peaceful is the clear day here when not
*   even a bird cries!*

Another poem, by the monk Keimei (dates unknown), just above the pine trees, reads:

Even the plants and trees of China know
*   your name;*
The sword you raised over Kyūshū, deadly
*   and chilling as the winter's frost, is now*
*   resting.*
You swept the Lute Hall, so that you just sit
*   and chant.*
The seas are all green; the hills around the
*   realm clear.*

Two of the other poems liken the villa in the painting to the famous Wang-chuan Villa of the archetypal Chinese poet-painter and scholar-official Wang Wei (699–759), revered as an inventor of landscape painting in China and Japan. One of them is by the monk Shūken (dates unknown):

Merriment of music and song in the green
*   field does not eliminate the thoughts of*
*   fame and fortune;*
Too remote to reach are the mists and rain
*   at the Wang chuan Villa.*
This otherwordly abode is the right place for
*   elegant souls;*
Unusual plants carpet the green mountains.

This painting, then, commemorates the powerful constable daimyo Ōuchi Morimi for his successful pursuit of the arts of both war (*bu*) and peace (*bun*), in the best tradition of the Japanese medieval warrior.   YS

86 **Listening to the Pines Study**
hanging scroll; ink and color on paper
103.0 x 31.8 (40 1/2 x 12 1/2)
Muromachi period, no later than 1433
Seikadō Bunko, Tokyo
Important Cultural Property

A tall, gnarled pine tree, its roots precariously clinging to a rocky bank, rises at the right. A pavilion is framed by the trunk and branches of the tree. Behind the pavilion soars a second, equally gnarled pine tree, painted in ink so pale that it appears to be almost a shadow of the first. A mountain path leads from the left side of the landscape, across a timber bridge over a cascading stream on the left, to the pavilion. A jagged mountain towers in the center, its lower portion obscured by the wafting mist.

Five inscriptions, written at different times over a twenty-five-year period, are brushed at the top of the painting in a disorderly fashion. In fact, visible seams between the inscriptions indicate that they have been reorganized. The earliest of these, the one at the upper right, is by the Zen monk Ishō Tokugan (1360–1437; see cat. 85). It contains a short preface, *Listening to the Pines Study (Chōshōken)*, poem composed for Attendant (*Jisha*) Ryūkō[ ]wa . . . , and a postscript, *On the third day of* the second month of the year Kichū [corresponding to 1433]. These relate for whom and when the poem was written. The main body of Ishō's poem reads:

I hear there is a man of high virtue in the
*   realm of the west, who lives at Nanmei;*
High above the hut soar tall pine trees,
*   offering their green canopies;*
A lamp casting spots of light behind the
*   tiny window must indeed make me long*
*   to get there.*
Sounds of the wind blend with the reading
*   voice all night long.*

Japanese scholars have recently argued that the scroll was produced in Kyoto on behalf of a certain young monk, Attendant Ryūkō[ ]wa of Nanmeizan monastery, also known as Jōfukuji, in Suō (now Yamaguchi Prefecture), located on the western tip of Honshu island. This would explain the reference in the poem to "the realm of the west." Suō was governed by the powerful Ōuchi family (see cat. 85), who also patronized the temple. Indeed, Ishō was closely associated with Ōuchi Morimi, constable daimyo of Suō. Shōgō Chōjū, whose poem is written above the right shoulder of the mountain, was from a warrior family closely allied with the Ōuchi family. Ryūkō Shinkei, who wrote the poem just across from Chōjū's, enjoyed the patronage of the Ōuchi family while in Kyoto, and later went to Suō.

While "Attendant Ryūkō[]wa" remains unidentified, he is assumed to have been a young Zen monk at Jōfukuji, whose scholarly ambitions were embodied in his study-retreat, real or imaginary, which became the theme of this scroll. The title of the painting, as well as that of the poem *Chōshōken* (Listening to the Pines Study) was appropriately chosen for the scholarly hermitage in this work, for it refers to the idea of listening to "whispers of pine winds and sounds of stream waters," a Chinese phrase well known in Japan. The term "Chōshō," a recurring literary and pictorial theme and name in China, became a model for the Japanese.

Originally the scroll had only Ishō's inscription, but through the subsequent years and presumably as the scroll was moved back and forth between Kyoto and Suō, four more inscriptions were added. It exemplifies the dissemination of the early fifteenth-century *shosaizu* (painting of a scholar's study) to the provinces by the second quarter of the fifteenth century. Ji-kuun Tōren (1391–1471) added the final inscription, written at the upper left in 1458, twenty-five years after the first. It reads:

Trek, trek up the precarious path, the road
*   through the mountains goes on and on;*
The hermit's abode between the
*   moss-covered cliff and the deep green*
*   stream;*
Hermitage, after all, is no more than a
*   trifling way of life;*

88

*Whispers of pine trees may lure you on, but
don't let leisure turn into lethargy.*

[signed] *Chōkonsō* (an alternative literary sobriquet of Jikuun) *Tōren invites those who aspire to retire by his clumsy verse. The end of the second year of Chōroku* (1458).

The five inscriptions, written at different times over the span of a quarter of a century, function differently from those of early fifteenth-century *shosaizu* (cats. 84, 85) where laudatory poems were written during a gathering of many like-minded poet-monks. The inscriptions on this work form a collection of individual poems, each a personal response to the scroll and to the idea of the hermitic practice. Tōren's poem seems to contain a measure of irony about the futility of such retirement. Such sentiment reflects a new attitude of reservation toward the practice. Occurring at the same time, in the mid-fifteenth century, was the diminution of patronage of the literary gatherings at Zen temples, which had been championed by such men as Shogun Ashikaga Yoshimochi (1386–1428), and a corresponding increase in the bureaucratic nature of the activities of the temples.

Stylistically, the painting exhibits some unusual features. The choppy brushstrokes, each showing marked thinning and thickening, suggest a stylistic model different from that which is assumed to have been behind earlier *shigajiku* examples. The model may have been a Chinese painting or a Korean work done in the Li Cheng (919–967)-Guo Xi (c. 1020–1090) tradition. The rocks in the foreground, the pine trees, and the mountain above are rendered by contour lines that consist of a series of twisting brushstrokes that reveal the choppy, nervous movement of the hand. Along with monochromatic ink washes, reddish browns and blue-greens have been extensively used, though much of the original pigment has been lost.   YS

87 Landscape
attributed to Soga Sōjō (fl. after c. 1491)
hanging scroll; ink on paper
60.2 x 29.5 (23 3/4 x 11 5/8)

Muromachi period, late 15th century
Fujii Akira Collection, Tokyo

A large rock surmounted by three bamboo trees tilts sharply to the right in the middle of the foreground at the water's edge. Between it and a rocky precipice to the left topped with two low pine trees are a path, a brushwood fence, and a gate with thatched roof. Behind the foreground rock, spits of land bordered by water plants extend into the lake, where an empty boat is moored. Behind the boulder, steps ascend the mountainside, where a thatched hut on stilts is situated. Two

89

men, presumably a host and his guest, converse inside; one of them turns his head to catch a view of the lake. A mountain with spindly trees along its ridges rises beyond the hut. Behind the mountain's left shoulder stands a solitary distant peak. A square relief seal that reads *Sekiyō* or *Akabae* (Red Fly), the seal of a painter of the Soga school, is stamped at the lower left hand corner of the painting.

The painting shares expressive characteristics with the *Daruma* portrait by Bokkei Saiyo (cat. 81), another Soga school painter. Dramatic contrasts of ink tones and the abstract rendering of the rock and tree forms distinguish this painting. The jagged rocks are made up of angular forms rendered by the blunt tip of the brush. The abstract shading and texturing of the rocks, as well as the twisting and turning zigzag shapes of the branches and trunks of the pine trees, are far removed from the restrained forms seen in the contemplative landscape paintings from the first half of the fifteenth century (cats. 84, 85, 86).

Two other ink landscapes carrying the seal *Sekiyō*, now in the collection of the Gunma Prefectural Museum of Modern Art, depict autumn and winter landscapes. These originally belonged to a set of four paintings on the theme of the Four Seasons, but the spring and summer landscapes were destroyed in the Tokyo

earthquake of 1923. The name Sekiyō, unusual for a painter, is not recorded in contemporary sources, but two other works with this seal are cited in the nineteenth-century reference *Koga bikō*, under the artist Soga Dasoku. Stylistically the Sekiyō paintings are comparable to the landscapes on a set of eight large sliding door panels (*fusuma*) in the abbot's *hōjō* (living quarters) of the Shinjuan, a subtemple of the Daitokuji monastery in Kyoto. Built in 1491 to commemorate a Zen monk of Daitokuji, Ikkyū Sōjun (1394–1481), the Shinjuan contains three sets of sliding door panels installed in three rooms representing *Birds and Flowers in a Landscape Setting, Landscapes of the Four Seasons,* and *Landscape,* all traditionally attributed to a certain Dasoku. The set *Landscapes of the Four Seasons* is stylistically close to the Sekiyō paintings. The third set, *Landscape,* has been reattributed to Soga Sōjō in recent years. Scholars in Japan all agree on the dates of the Shinjuan panels and active years of Soga Sōjō. But uncertainty continues about the identity of Dasoku, whether more than one painter bore this name, his/their dates, whether Soga Dasoku and Soga Sōjō were the same person, the identity of the artist who used the seal *Sekiyō,* his dates, and whether he was the same person as Soga Dasoku and/or Soga Sōjō.   YS

148

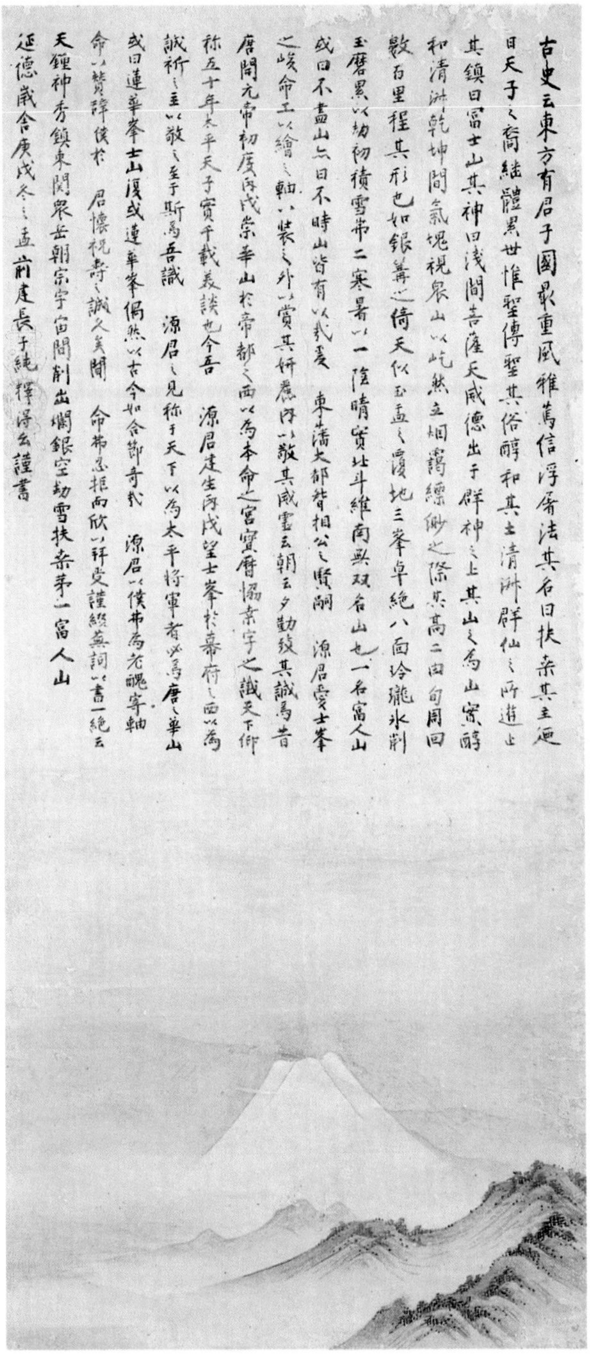

90

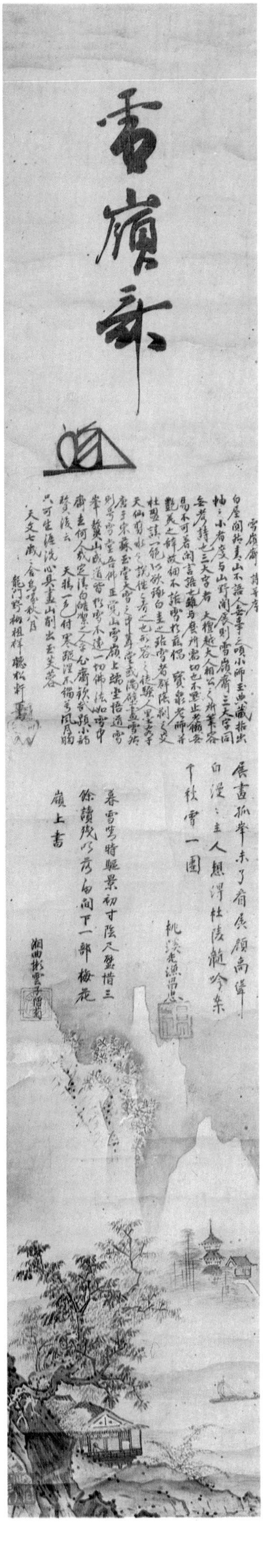

91

88 Sugawara Michizane in his deified form as Tenjin crossing to Song China
Sesshū Tōyō (1420–1506)
hanging scroll; ink and color on silk
112.3 x 56.5 (44¼ x 22¼)
Muromachi period, 1501

Okayama Prefectural Art Museum

A lightly bearded man clad in a Chinese scholar's robe is seated on the trunk of a gnarled pine tree. The tree rises diagonally from a flat, uncluttered terrain. Pine and plum branches echo the contours of the man's upper body. He faces toward blossoming plum branches, which twist and turn and seem about to embrace him. The figure looms large against the bare background. At the lower right is an inscription, *Gyōnen hachijūni sai Sesshū hitsu* [Brushed by Sesshū, current age eighty-two], followed by the artist's square relief seal, *Tōyō*. The painting was executed in 1501 by the foremost ink painter of the second half of the fifteenth century, Sesshū Tōyō.

The figure in the painting is Tenjin (Heavenly God), the Japanese courtier and scholar Sugawara Michizane (845–903) who was deified soon after his tragic death in exile at Dazaifu in northern Kyushu. A victim of trumped-up political charges, Michizane was stripped of his high government rank and deprived of the civilized life he enjoyed as a talented poet in the capital. Before his departure from Kyoto, Michizane composed a poem to a plum tree in his garden, reminding it not to forget the arrival of spring after he was gone; the plum tree followed Michizane, flying all the way to Dazaifu. The plum blossom motif became associated with Michizane, who came to be revered as the god of plum blossoms. He also was worshipped as the god of scholarship, calligraphy, and poetry, especially of *renga* (linked verse). By the thirteenth century, Tenjin joined the ranks of the Buddhist pantheon; he was believed to be a reincarnation of Bodhisattva Kannon (C: Guanyin).

Although the Tenjin cult essentially was a tradition rooted in Japan's courtly culture, in time it was absorbed by the sinophile culture of the Zen monastic establishment. By the end of the fourteenth century a fantastic story circulated among the Zen monks in Japan about Tenjin, in which he appeared in a dream of the monk Enni Ben'en (Shōichi Kokushi, "National Master Shōichi," 1202–1280), founding abbot of the Tōfukuji monastery who had just returned from China. Tenjin asked the monk to suggest a teacher from whom he could receive instruction in Zen and be given a robe as certification. Enni told Tenjin that he should go to his own teacher, the Chinese Zen master Wuzhun Shifan at Jingshan. Subsequently, Tenjin again appeared in Enni's dream and said he had indeed received instruction and

the robe from the Chinese master. To prove it Tenjin, holding a plum branch, showed Enni a Zen pilgrim's satchel, saying it contained the robe. The Tenjin image based on this story is known as *Totō* [or *Tosō*] Tenjin (Tenjin crossing to Tang [or Song] China. The association of Tenjin with China probably owes much to the Zen monks' penchant for Chinese poetry, especially their familiarity with Su Dongpo's (1036–1101) poem "The flight of the plum blossoms." Many portraits of Tenjin as a scholar, dressed in Chinese robes and wearing a cap, carrying a monk's satchel and holding a plum branch, were painted and inscribed by poet monks of the early Muromachi period. Most of the extant Tenjin portraits show a figure standing upright against a neutral background, like a religious icon. In Sesshū's painting, the informally posed Tenjin has the satchel at waist level (mostly concealed by his sleeves) on a shoulder strap, but does not hold the plum branch. Instead he looks at the plum tree, which, along with the pine tree, is a part of a credible natural space.

The style of the painting is remarkably close to that of Sesshū's famous pair of screens of birds and flowers (cat. 96). The crisp, dynamic lines that define forms, the twisting and turning of the branches, and the convincing spatial depth find readily recognizable counterparts in the monumental screens.

The painter Sesshū Tōyō was born in Bitchū Province (part of today's Okayama Prefecture). Very little is known about Sesshū's early years. He was a student monk at Hōfukuji in Bitchū and went to the Shōkokuji monastery in Kyoto while he was still young. Around 1451, at age thirty-two, Sesshū formally became a disciple of the monk Shunrin Shūtō (d. 1463) and eventually became the *shika* (monk who screens guests seeking interviews with the abbot) of the monastery. It is assumed that at Shōkokuji he studied under the painter Tenshō Shūbun (fl. c. 1420–c. 1461), who was the Controller of the monastery, and whom Sesshū later acknowledged as his mentor.

By the mid-1460s, Sesshū left for Yamaguchi in Suō Province (part of present-day Yamaguchi Prefecture), and established his studio. Sesshū's move to Suō is indicative of the tendency of artists and poets in the late fifteenth century, a time of civil disturbance, to move away from metropolitan centers such as Kyoto to the provinces in search of reliable sources of patronage. The Suō region was then under the control of the powerful Ōuchi daimyo family, whose control extended as far west as northern Kyushu and occasionally east to central Japan. More important, the Ōuchi, exceeding the power of the Ashikaga *bakufu*, controlled the lucrative China trade and even main-

tained their own diplomatic relations with China and Korea. The economically and culturally affluent city of Yamaguchi came to be called "Little Kyoto." In 1467 Sesshū traveled to Ming China with a trade mission dispatched by the Ōuchi family. The trip, which lasted until 1469, took Sesshū from the port city of Ningbo to Beijing, affording numerous opportunities to see not only China's scenic spots, but also many paintings, some of which he copied. Sesshū's direct knowledge of the paintings of contemporary Ming artists unknown in Japan set him apart from other Japanese artists of the Muromachi period.

After returning to Japan in 1469, Sesshū led a peripatetic existence, moving between Suō, Bungo (today's Ōita Prefecture), and Kyoto, as well as traveling to central and northern Japan. In 1486, he was back in Suō where he executed the *Landscape of the Four Seasons*, a masterpiece in a style that translates the Chinese academic style of Xia Gui in a dynamic and expressive manner. In 1495 Sesshū made a painting in the "broken ink" or *haboku* style of the Chinese painter Yujian of the Southern Song Dynasty, which he gave to his pupil Josui Sōen (dates unknown) as certification of his having mastered the style. In or shortly after 1501 he painted a view of *Amanohashidate*, an important scenic spot on the Japan Sea coast, in a naturalistic style different from his previous works. Sesshū died either at Masuda in Iwami Province (part of present-day Shimane Prefecture) in 1502 or at Unkokuan in Yamaguchi in 1506, the latter possibility being more widely accepted. This *Tenjin* painting of 1501 is one of Sesshū's late works, painted at age eighty-two.

Sesshū left many disciples. His style spread widely in Japan to Kamakura in the east and Satsuma (the western part of today's Kagoshima Prefecture in Kyushu) to the south. Among the later followers who closely emulated Sesshū's art was Unkoku Tōgan (1547–1618), a warrior's son in the service of the Mōri, the militant daimyo family of Aki Province (part of today's Hiroshima Prefecture) who overthrew the Ōuchi and took control of the Suō territory. YS

89 "Huang Zhuping" after Liang Kai
Sesshū Tōyō (1420–1506)
hanging scroll; ink on paper
30.2 x 30.6 (117/8 x 12¹/6)
Muromachi period, late 15th century

Kyoto National Museum
Important Cultural Property

Sesshū Tōyō, an important artistic personality of the Muromachi period, made copies of Chinese paintings from the Song and Yuan periods after he returned from a journey to China between 1467 and 1469. The intent was to supplement his recent

92

92

exposure to the art he had seen in China, by studying the earlier Chinese masterpieces that were already in Japan. This sketch is one of six original ink sketches extant today. It is signed *Sesshū*, to the left of a pine tree trunk. The name Liang Kai is brushed outside the frame at the lower right, indicating that the picture is a copy based on a Chinese work, now lost, by Liang Kai (fl. c. 1195–c. 1224), an accomplished painter of the conservative Chinese Imperial Academy of the Song dynasty and a highly expressive ink painter as well. Six other related sketches are now lost, but are known through seventeenth-century copies contained in a single handscroll by Kano Tsunenobu (1636–1713), now in the Tokyo National Museum.

A man under a pine tree, pointing with his outstretched right arm, shouts at a pair of rocklike forms on the ground. The subject is Huang Zhuping, a legendary Daoist of the Han Dynasty, who is turning rocks into sheep. The story of the sage is from an early Chinese collection of tales of eighty-four Daoist saints and sages (*Shenxian zhuan*), compiled by the Daoist scholar and alchemist Ge Hong (known also as Bao Puzi), who was active 326–334 AD. Huang Zhuping, at age fifteen, was herding sheep when he met a Daoist master who took him to Mount Jinhua in Zhejiang Province. After more than forty years, Zhuping's older brother Zhuqi came looking for him, and asked where his sheep were. Zhuping replied that they were in Shandong Province (northeastern

part of China). In Shandong Zhuqi saw nothing but white rocks. Zhuqi went back to Shandong accompanied by Zhuping, who, by shouting at rocks, turned thousands of them into sheep.

At the lower left of the painting is a white sheep just transformed, and next to it another with its legs emerging from a dark rock. Dynamic brushstrokes define the pine tree trunk, branches, terrain and, most expressively, Huang's costume. The kinesthetic quality of the brushstrokes in this work conveys something of both Sesshū's own artistic style and the spontaneity associated with Liang Kai's ink paintings.   YS

151

90 Mount Fuji

attributed to Kenkō Shōkei
(fl. 1478–1506/1518)
hanging scroll; ink and color on paper
66.0 x 30.0 (26 x 11 3/4)
Muromachi period, no later than 1490

Tokyo National Museum

Mount Fuji stands against a gray sky in the center of the composition. In the right foreground is an undulating range of hills; two other ranges recede toward Fuji. Trees and vegetation dot the crests and valleys of the two closest ranges. A filmy blue wash defines the most distant range, which floats like a wafting band of mist at the foot of Fuji. Apart from this blue and the faint reddish brown and green on the other two ranges, the painting is monochromatic. The white pigment applied to the stylized, three-pinnacled form of Mount Fuji creates visual contrast with the surrounding ink-washed sky. The reverence felt for Mount Fuji is evident in the frequent depictions of it in Japanese art, from thirteenth-century narrative paintings to the dramatic woodblock prints by Hokusai and Hiroshige in the nineteenth century.

The long inscription, dated to 1490, is by the Zen monk Shijun Tokuyū (dates unknown). The first half of the text describes how, for centuries, Fuji has been regarded as the sacred mountain of the nation; the second half explains that the painting was executed for a certain "sagacious Lord Minamoto, the heir to the shogunal deputy in Kamakura." Shijun was the 159th abbot of the Kenchōji monastery in Kamakura before he wrote the inscription, signed *Shijun, the monk Tokuyū, a former* [abbot] *of Kenchō*. Recent Japanese scholarship has astutely established that this work was painted for the warrior Ashikaga Masauji (1466–1531), who "loved the loftiness of Mount Fuji, ordered an artist to paint it and had it mounted as a hanging scroll." Masauji personally sent the scroll to Shijun requesting that he write an inscription.

Masauji was a member of a branch family of the Ashikaga in the east and the grandfather of Haruuji (see cat. 91). He was based at Koga in Shimōsa Province (now Ibaragi Prefecture) during the last decade of the fifteenth century, when the entire eastern region was embroiled in military conflicts among several contending powers attempting to unify the area. In 1490, Masauji was twenty-four years old and on his way to attaining the post of deputy shogun (*kubō*) of the Kanto region, which he achieved seven years later, in 1497. His ambition to unify the region, however, was never realized, and the armed conflicts went on for another several decades. In the inscription Shijun expressed his sincere hope that Masauji would become the unifier.

Although unsigned and without seals, the painting has been attributed to Kenkō Shōkei a painter-monk of Kenchōji. He was sometimes called Kei Shoki, or Kei the Secretary, from his monastic position of *shoki*, whose role it was to keep the official records of the monastery. The attribution is not entirely unreasonable, for the artist was closely connected with the inscriber Shijun who, around 1493, wrote a poem for the artist about "*Hinrakusai*" (Joy in Poverty Study). This was the name of the artist's study as well as his artistic pseudonym. Early accounts of the artist's career at Kenchōji are not verifiable from contemporary sources, but he is traditionally believed to have been a student of Chūan Shinkō, another painter-monk at Kenchōji who was active around the middle of the fifteenth century. Chūan Shinkō executed a painting of Mount Fuji in ink, now in the collection of Nezu Institute of Fine Arts in Tokyo. In 1478, during a lull after the Ōnin civil war (1467–1477), Shōkei went to Kyoto to study painting under Geiami (1431–1485), then a leading painter in the capital, who was also an artistic consultant (*dōbōshū*) to the Ashikaga shogun and the curator of the shogunal collection. In 1480 Shōkei returned to Kamakura, but in 1493 he was again back in Kyoto. By 1499, he had returned to Kamakura where he was active through 1506 or 1518. His death date is unknown.

In the dotted forms of the vegetation, the schematic tree shapes, and the parallel brushstrokes that describe the ranges of hills, the style of the painting recalls that of Kenkō Shōkei's landscapes, though many of these are stylistically datable to his late years, almost two decades after this Mount Fuji painting was executed. The most convincing evidence for the attribution of this painting to Kenkō Shōkei, however, is the form of the mountain itself. In its stylization, it recalls a Mount Fuji painted a few decades earlier by Chūan Shinkō, the artist's earlier mentor at Kenchōji.   YS

91 Snow Peak Study

Senka (fl. 16th century)
title calligraphy by Ashikaga Haruuji
(d. 1560)
hanging scroll; ink and color on paper
97.5 x 17.0 (38 3/8 x 6 7/8)
Muromachi period, no later than 1538

Gotō Museum, Tokyo
Important Art Object

Two deciduous trees rise atop a rocky slope at the lower left, their branches hanging over a craggy lakeside embankment. A narrow path leads toward the water's edge, where a scholar's study stands with *shōji* open. A gentleman seated inside gazes across a lake at a temple gate and a pagoda, which rise above the wafting mist at the right. A sailboat heads toward the near shore under the darkening sky against which, like a tall white screen, a range of snow-covered mountains looms. On the roof of the study a sheet of snow inches toward the eaves. Trees atop the cliff above still glisten under the chilling snow.

At the lower left corner is a square intaglio seal, which reads *Senka*, the name of an artist active during the first half of the sixteenth century in the Kamakura region, near present-day Tokyo. Very little is known about the painter Senka. The format of the painting is archaistic in that it is a *shigajiku*, a type that by this time had lost its vitality in Kyoto, where innovative, large-scale painting formats were being explored by the Kano artists (cat. 97). This painting lacks the atmospheric spatial recession typical of the earlier Shūbun style. Despite the small size of the scroll, the foreground trees, rocks, bamboo bushes, and pavilion, and the temple buildings across the lake are clearly legible. This work shows the influence of Ming-period Chinese landscape painting, which had been actively studied by Japanese artists such as Sesshū Tōyō (cat. 88, 96) and Kenkō Shōkei (cat. 90) since the third quarter of the fifteenth century.

An inscription in three sections occupies the upper two-thirds of the scroll. It consists of the title of the painting, a preface, and poems typical of the *shosaizu* (painting celebrating a scholar's study). At the very top are three large characters *Setsu-rei-sai* (Snow Peak Study), which is both the name of the pavilion depicted in the painting and the title of the painting. These large characters were written by Ashikaga Haruuji (d. 1560), a deputy shogun in the Kanto region (*Kantō kubō*), whose *kaō* appears at the lower left. The middle section of the inscription comprises a long prose preface and a short poem, dated to the autumn of 1538, by the Zen monk Rinchū Soshō, at one time the abbot of the Kenchōji Zen monastery in Kamakura. The preface, which was written in the *Chōshōken* (Listening to the Pines Study) of the abbot's living quarters of Kenchōji, gives a brief history of the inscribing of the scroll and elaborates on the lofty symbolism of snow and the snowy landscape depicted in the scroll. In the bottom row are two more poems by Zen monks who were contemporaries of Rinchū Soshō:

Setsureisai
poem and preface

No sound was heard in the humble dwelling and no voice came from the blue mountains—a moment of repose—when my disciple Gyoku, Head of the Kitchen, brought out a scroll, a small one, which he handed to this rustic. As the scroll was unrolled there were three large characters, setsu rei sai [Snow Peak Study] *accompanying a voiceless poem,* [that is, a painting]. *These*

93

臨濟裁松次黃檗問
深山裁許多生什ㄆ
濟云一作山門境致二
作後人標榜遮了打地
三下㕔鑱偃嘘之春

94

characters are by the brush of the Grand Minister and our Great Patron [Ashikaga Haruuji; d. 1560], to which no idle words should be casually added. That notwithstanding, the request [to have my inscription] was pressing enough to break my reticence. I, being old and lazy, am a man of few flattering words. Thus, without elaborating on snow, here I offer a lead poem and ask the Venerable Master of the Hōsen [the Hōsen'an subtemple] and his companion to join me with their poems, so that, like burnishing chipped white jade, theirs would improve mine.

Snow, in the diagram of the Book of Changes, is explained as a multitude of Ying elements, easily changeable; it is also said that snow was made by the Creator who divided water into myriad icy flowers. Those who would represent snow were poets and painters of the Tang and Song dynasties. Scholar Su [Dongpo] built a hall with a thatched roof amidst deep snow; he covered its walls with a painting of snow and called the building Snow Hall. Our Buddha Sakyamuni had reached the Right State of Consciousness atop the snow-covered mountain peak, where he sat and meditated in order to attain Enlightenment. Our Patriarch Seppō [Xuefeng or Snow Peak; 822–908] had attained the Way atop Ao-shan [in Hunan]. All of these occurred within close proximity of snow. All that Buddha Dharma [embraces] is likened to being amidst snow. Who is the master of this study? Isn't he surely a person of impeccable purity and simplicity of heart? Admirable indeed is his steadfast heart. Here is my humble poem or, rather, an afterthought:

Under the clear sky the chilling white sheet;
Incorruptible is the purity of heart that knows elegant things;
May he always put to use [the thought of snow] to cleanse his heart;
The picture of the mountains yields white lotus blossoms.

The Seventh year of Tenmon [1538]; the Year dwells Under the 24th Constellation Hydra; Autumn, the 8th month. Rustic Zen Monk Soshō; written at Chōshōken [Listening to the Pines Study]. [followed by a tripod-shape seal]

At the lower right is a poem by the monk Teihō Shōchū (dates unknown), also at one time the abbot of Kenchōji and referred to in the preface as the "Venerable Master of the Hōsen." Hōsen or Hōsen'an is the name of a subtemple of the Kenchōji monastery, to which the monk Shōchū is likely to have retired when he wrote this poem. Very little is known about this monk. The poem, which directly responds to the snow landscape and the study, is in the form of seven-character quatrain:

*One cannot see enough of the solitary peak
  once the scroll is unrolled;
Craggy and lofty, the mountain soars in the
  ceaseless snow;
The study's master must surely know the
  marrow of Du Fu's poetry;
A view of eternal snow from where the
  poetry is born.*
[by] *Tōkei Tōgyo Shōchū*
[followed by a square relief seal *Shōchū*]

The poem on the left, also a seven-character quatrain, is by the monk Kyūsei Sōkiku (d. 1567), who also served as abbot at Kenchōji, probably Shōchū's "companion" in the preface:

*Snow cleared at dusk hurrying a calendar's
  turn;
The precious jade disk, short are winter's
  hours reserved for study;
The book remains half-read when the sun
  sets over the western quarters.
A bunch of plum blossoms—more books on
  the peak.*
[by] *Shōkyoku Ran'unshi Sōkiku*
[square relief seal *Yōshi*]

YS

92 **Summer landscape; Winter landscape**
   Sesson Shūkei (c. 1504–c. 1589)
   pair of hanging scrolls; ink and slight
   color on paper
   each 102.0 x 40.5 (40¼ x 16)
   Muromachi period, mid-16th century
   Kyoto National Museum

Massive rocks crowned with trees, a waterfall in the distance, and a cascading stream in the summer scroll at right contrast with snow-covered mountain paths amidst leafless trees, icy peaks, and a pale moon in the winter scroll at left. The artist's square intaglio seal, *Sesson*, is stamped at the outer edge of each painting, above the mountain peaks. The oddly shaped foreground rocks and boulders in the summer scroll, the contrasting dark and light surfaces of the rocks and cliffs conveying an eerie, nocturnal atmosphere in the winter scene, and the diminutive hunched figures are all characteristic of the work of Sesson Shūkei.

Sesson Shūkei was the last of the major painters to develop the two-hundred-year-old Japanese ink landscape tradition. Even more remarkable, Sesson, who lived

to the age of about eighty-six, produced almost all of his most important paintings not in Kyoto, the capital, but in the eastern and northeastern provinces under the patronage of various local daimyo. The peripatetic Sesson was a truly creative painter whose art diverged from the established aesthetic norms of fifteenth century artists such as Shūbun and Sesshū, who used Chinese paintings as their models. Sesson not only reinterpreted the works of these artists, but injected his own sense of thematic eccentricity and graphic expressiveness. Whether he painted figures, animals, or landscapes, Sesson invented highly personalized forms imbued with a energy, humor, and passion.

The facts of Sesson's early biography are unknown, but it is believed that his birthplace was near Ōta in Hitachi Province (part of today's Ibaraki Prefecture), a territory then ruled by the Satake family residing at Ōta Castle. Sesson became a Zen monk, most likely taking the tonsure under the auspices of the Satake family. In the 1550s he is believed to have gone to Kamakura, the city of important Zen monasteries such as Kenchōji (where Kenkō Shōkei had been) and Engakuji. He also went to Odawara, a castle town and headquarters of the regional hegemons, the powerful Hōjō family. Odawara under the Hōjō in the sixteenth century was the veritable cultural center of the east. The Hōjō had amassed a sizable collection of art, including a number of Chinese paintings of legendary renown. Among these were Southern Song works such as those by Muqi and Yujian that had been in the Ashikaga shogunal collection in the fifteenth century. In the 1560s, Sesson is believed to have been in Aizu in Iwashiro Province (part of today's Fukushima Prefecture), where he enjoyed the patronage of Ashina Moriuji (1521–1580), a powerful daimyo to whom he had offered a painting earlier.

By the mid-1570s, however, the entire Kanto had become embroiled in fighting among the contending powers of the region. This eventually resulted in the rise of Date Masamune (1567–1636), who in 1589 put an end to the Ashina family power and took over their territory. It is speculated that at this point the artist decided to retire to Miharu in Iwaki Province (an area that today includes the southeastern part of Fukui Prefecture and southern tip of Miyagi Prefecture), seeking the protection of the local power, the Tamura clan, who were related by marriage both to the Ashina and the powerful Date.

Sesson, like Sesshū and Kenkō Shōkei before him, enjoyed certain freedoms and privileges because he was a Zen monk. He had studied classical Chinese, and during his travels he was permitted to view prized Chinese paintings and more recent paintings by the Japanese painters in Kamakura, including works by Kenkō Shōkei

and Senka. His journeys to Kamakura and Odawara in the 1550s may have taken him as well to the Ashikaga Gakkō, or Ashikaga School, the great learning center for sinology in Shimotsuke Province (in present-day Tochigi Prefecture) in the sixteenth century. By the 1540s, Sesson, still under Satake patronage, had probably established his reputation as an artist. In 1542 he wrote a painting treatise, *Setsu monteishi* (Advice to students), in which he articulated his theories on style, especially the methods of brushwork and the techniques of discriminating ink tones, as well as on the importance of observing nature and learning by copying earlier paintings. He emphasized the importance of an individual style that demonstrated the ability to transcend the model.

The style of these two paintings indicates a date earlier than the more personalized, later landscapes. His bulky mountain forms reflect Sesson's response to Chinese Ming landscapes, which were known to Sesshū in the 1460s. Yet, the crisp, clearly delineated motifs of the summer and winter landscapes are more closely linked to the style of Kenkō Shōkei, active in Kamakura in the last decade of the fifteenth century and early part of the sixteenth. In the summer painting, the overall composition and the craggy precipices share an affinity with cat. 93, a landscape by the warrior-painter Nagao Kagenaga (1469–1528). The chilling white mountain peaks looming against the nocturnal sky in the winter painting recall cat. 91, the *Snow Peak Study* by Senka (fl. mid-sixteenth century and after), also shown here. This pair of landscapes probably dates from the 1550s, when the artist was in his late forties or early fifties and in Kamakura and Odawara. YS

93 **Landscape**
   Nagao Kagenaga (1469–1528)
   hanging scroll; ink and color on paper
   99.0 x 47.5 (39 x 18¾)
   Muromachi period, early 16th century
   Private Collection,
   Important Art Object

This painting of a craggy mountain landscape towering above a lake bears the artist's square relief seal, *Kagenaga*, at the lower left corner. The artist, Nagao Kagenaga, was a warrior and head of the Nagao family who, as *shugodai* (assistant constable), ruled the region of Ashikaga in the southwestern sector of Shimotsuke Province (part of today's Tochigi Prefecture to the north of Tokyo). This was the area in which the Ashikaga warrior family had originated.

Through its mannered, intense brushwork, this painting is related to the pictorial style associated with Kenkō Shōkei (fl.

mid-fifteenth–early sixteenth century), a painter-monk of Kenchōji. Shōkei had studied with Geiami (1431–1485) in Kyoto between 1478 and 1480 and transmitted his style to Kamakura. From Kamakura the style spread in the eastern provinces through the works of the artists around Shōkei, including Senka, whose *Snow Peak Study*, also shown here (cat. 91) is roughly contemporary with Kagenaga's work. The light blue, clearly outlined forms of the distant precipices, the short, angular brushwork defining the jagged cliff, and the densely textured rock surfaces of the tall peaks are some of the common stylistic features also seen in the works of Shōkei's followers such as Keison and Kōboku. This style was instrumental in shaping one of the modes of landscape painting by Sesson Shūkei (c. 1504–c. 1589), who worked in the northern and eastern regions of Japan during the second half of the sixteenth century.

The Nagao in Ashikaga were a branch of the main family based at Shirai in neighboring Kōzuke Province, and served the powerful Uesugi, the deputy shogun in the East (*Kantō kanrei*), who was based at Kamakura. In addition to political and military interests, similar cultural interests bound the Nagao in Ashikaga and the Uesugi. Throughout the fifteenth century, the Uesugi, especially Norizane (1410–1466) and Noritada (1433–1454), supported the Ashikaga Gakkō or Ashikaga School, one of the earliest formal Confucian schools in Japan, by donating sinological books. Some of these evidently had been pilfered from the Kanesawa Bunko, or Kanesawa Library established by Hōjō Sanetoki (1224–1276) in Yokohama. By the mid-sixteenth century the school was described by the Jesuit missionary Francis Xavier in his letters to the headquarters in Goa and Rome as "the university in eastern Japan."

The Nagao in Ashikaga also had an artistic connection with the Kano family, also of Shimotsuke. The father of Kano Masanobu (1434–1530), the founder of the Kano school of painting in Kyoto, had married a woman from the Ashikaga Nagao family. Both the father and the son therefore had been retainers of the Nagao clan. In addition, a seventeenth-century account of Nagao Kagenaga written by a Kano school painter, Shōun (1637–1702) reports that Masanobu's son Motonobu (1476–1559) had once studied painting under Kagenaga. The Kano connection with the Nagao family can also be illustrated by the fact that Kagenaga's son Norinaga (1503–1550), a painter in his own right, donated a landscape painting by Masanobu to the Chōrinji temple in Ashikaga. Masanobu's painting, executed in a style not unlike Geiami's, is still extant. Chōrinji, a Zen temple of the Sōtō school, was the Nagao family's mortuary temple in Ashi-

95

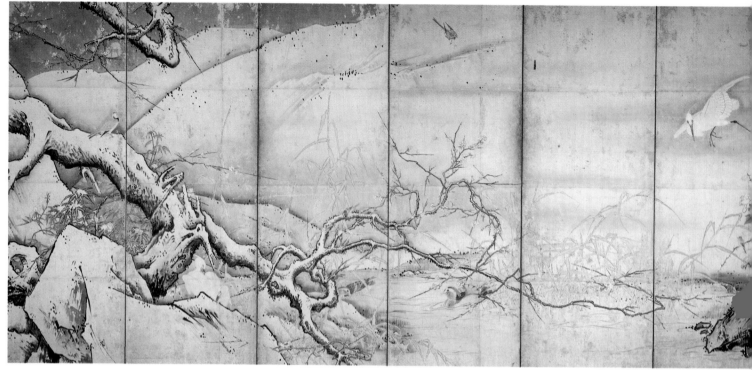

96

kaga. The temple also owns self-portraits of three successive generations of the Nagao warrior-artists, Kagenaga, Norinaga, and Norinaga's son Masanaga (1527–1569). Later in his life, Masanaga adopted his grandfather's name Kagenaga, thus often causing confusion between the two. This landscape painting by Kagenaga, before it came into the possession of the present owner, was also at Chōrinji.   YS

94 Patriarch Rinzai (c: Linji) planting a pine tree

Yamada Dōan (d. c. 1573)
hanging scroll; ink and color on paper
81.2 x 34.0 (32 x 13⅜)
Muromachi period, mid-16th century

Tokyo University of Arts

An old man clad in ragged cassocks, his left shoulder exposed, carries over his right shoulder a hoe with a young pine sapling tied to its handle. The pale outer garment, which identifies the figure as a Buddhist, is punctured by two gaping holes, indicating his indifference to external appearance. He is white-haired and bearded, with a facial expression that conveys something of his otherworldliness, not unlike that of an aged and ascetic Lohan, a follower of the Buddha Sakyamuni. The artist's rectangular relief seal, *Yamadashi Dōan* (Dōan of the Yamada family), is stamped at the lower left. A five-line inscription by a certain as yet unidentified Genyō, whose circular seal is stamped at the end of the last line, incompletely quotes a passage from the famous collected sayings of the Zen patriarch Linji Yixuan (d. 867):

When Linji was planting pine trees [his teacher] *Huangbo asked him, You plant so many pine trees deep in the mountains, but what are they for?* [Lin-]*ji replied, First, for the scenery of the temple gate; second, as a road sign for those who will come here in the future. When finished speaking* [Linji] *dug at the ground three times with the hoe he was carrying on his shoulder, and drew a deep sigh.*

The iconographic attributes of this figure ordinarily would identify him as the Fifth Zen Patriarch Hongren (601–675) who is said to have been a pine planter at Potou before being chosen Patriarch. It is difficult to say whether Genyō misinterpreted the painting or whether Dōan intended it to be Linji. The problem of identifying the figure exemplifies how the identifying characteristics of one iconic figure were often applied to another.

Although many questions remain about the identity of Yamada Dōan, it is certain that he was a warrior-painter of the sixteenth century. Three different painters with the name Dōan are known in the Yamada family. Extant works purported to be by Dōan carry different kinds of seals, including the rectangular relief stamped on this painting. Although no definitive biography of the artist has been established, our Dōan is widely identified as Dōan I, or Yamada Junchi [or Toshitomo], whose probable death date was c. 1573. He was ruler of Iwakake Castle in Yamada city, Yamato Province (in present-day Nara Prefecture). He held a second-level position (*taiho*) in the department of finance (*min-*

bushō), and therefore was an official of the lower junior rank. As to his artistic activities, the seventeenth-century source *Honchō gashi* says that he followed Shūbun and Sesshū, and that he studied Song painting and used its ideas. About the style of Dōan the same source says that his brushwork is rough and abbreviated. From various scattered references, we know that he actively patronized Buddhism. He contributed funds to the restoration of the Great Buddha of Tōdaiji at Nara shortly after 1567, and he donated a lantern to the Kasuga Shrine, also in Nara.

A number of fine paintings stamped with a rectangular seal identical to the one on this painting are now accepted as works by Dōan. They are *Hotei* (C: Budai) in the Cleveland Museum, *Shōki* (C: Zongkui) in Kenchōji, Kamakura, and *Eggplants and melons*, a pair of hanging scrolls in the collection of the Museum of Fine Arts, Boston.   YS

95 White hawk

Toki Tomikage (Fukei; fl. mid-16th century)
hanging scroll; ink on paper
100.7 x 49.5 (39⅞ x 19½)
Muromachi period, mid 16th century

Fujii Akira Collection, Tokyo
Important Art Object

A noble white hawk, its sharp claws firmly grasping a plum branch, is silhouetted against a wintry sky. Its deadly bill closed, the bird of prey casts an alert gaze to the left. White plum blossoms bud and bloom on the branch. The stately shape of the

hawk is rendered in reserve, by saturating the background of the paper with gray ink. Except for the wing and the tail sections, the bird's plumage is described in a pale tone of ink, with careful attention given to the feather patterns. At the right, on the white part of the branch, is the signature *Mino no kami, Tomikage hitsu* (Brushed by Tomikage, Constable of Mino Province), followed by the square relief seal *Tomikage*.

Hawk images and scenes of falconry were painted in Japan as early as the fourteenth century. During the Muromachi period, Chinese paintings of hawks were avidly collected by the Japanese; for example, contemporary documents record a notable group in the Ashikaga shogunal collection in Kyoto. Although the Chinese paintings probably were made by Ming dynasty painters, in Japan they were associated with earlier Chinese painters renowned for their hawk paintings, such as the artistic Emperor Hui Zong (1082–1135) of the Northern Song dynasty, whose paintings of birds were noted for their detailed realism. In Japan, hawks were painted on large screens and sliding door panels as well as on smaller hanging scrolls. Each format required a different type of depiction, and each was executed in a variety of mediums—ink, color, or ink and color together: a hawk in the wilderness going after a pheasant; a hawk tethered to a perch (a vestige of falconry practiced among the warriors); or a hawk perched freely on a tree branch. Tomikage's hawk belongs to this third type.

Hawks were favored by warrior-class painters for their fierceness and fearlessness. A hawk overtaking its prey was an apt symbol for the martially trained members of a warrior family. This painting, however, is unique, as it combines the image of the heroic white hawk and the white plum blossoms. The plum blossoms, particularly those rendered in monochrome ink, were, in the Confucian traditions in China and Japan, symbols of the high-minded purity and integrity of the ideal scholar; they represented the spirit of cultivated men. Thus this painting unifies the traditions of *bun* (cultivation of arts) and *bu* (martial prowess).

Tomikage, or Fukei, was a member of the recalcitrant Toki family of warriors, who vied with the central power of the Ashikaga government through their preeminent control over Mino Province (today's Gifu Prefecture in central Japan). Various members of the Toki family held the position of constable (*shugo*) from the middle of the fourteenth century through the middle of the sixteenth century, when the eleventh-generation head, Yoriyoshi (or Raigei; d. 1583), was driven out of the territory by one of his vassals, terminating the family hegemony over the territory. The Toki family members were astute warriors as well as cultivated advocates of poetry and arts. Tobun (active 1520s), Yoritaka (dates unknown), and Yoriyoshi are some of the other known artistic personalities of the Toki clan. The Toki family genealogy, however, does not record Tomikage, though he is cited in the seventeenth-century *Honchō gashi* (History of Japanese

Painting) as a painter who emulated the brush method of Shūbun and who showed consummate skill in painting hawks. The hawk was a popular subject among the Toki painters ever since the family's fifth-generation head, Yoritada (d. 1397) first painted one. The Toki family was particularly well known for its family tradition of falconry. The prominent Zen monk of Shōkokuji, Keijo Shūrin (1444–1518), who inscribed a long eulogy for the commemorative painting of a tethered horse (see cat. 82), composed a eulogy for a now-lost hawk painting in which he specifically praises the Toki family's pursuit of the art of falconry:

Constable Lord Toki loved hawks all his life. His family preserved a [special] method of hawk-keeping which always worked. [According to it] falconers of Japan should put a hawk in a cage only after it is fed a female pheasant captured in its eastward flight on the eighth day of the fourth month. Earlier, Lord [Toki] acquired a fabulous hawk which he loved very much. One day he was about to go hunting with the bird perched on his arm when a female pheasant was seen over the garden. It flew in circles and descended to the ground. Lord [Toki] ordered a certain Sadayasu of the Tajimi family to fetch a dog and go after the pheasant. Sadayasu caught it with no less bravery than that of [the hero] Zi Lu [of China's antiquity]. Then the pheasant was fed to the hawk. Sure enough, that was the eighth day of the fourth month. So pleased was Lord [Toki] that he asked a painter to

97

*paint the picture of the hawk and had me
write an inscription. . . .*

   Who this Lord Toki was is a matter of
conjecture. If he was of exactly the same
generation as the monk Shūrin, Toki Masafusa (1467–1519), the ninth head of the
family, might have been the falconer.
Other Toki family members known as
painters of hawks include Toki Yoritaka
(dates unknown) and the eleventh figurehead of the Toki family and Constable of
Mino, Yoriyoshi (d. 1583), who during the
family's downfall in the 1540s escaped to
Kai Province (now Yamanashi Prefecture)
to seek protection under the warrior
Takeda Shingen (1521–1573). In a portrait
also included here, Shingen is depicted
with a hawk (cat. 17).   YS

96 **Flowers and Birds**
      attributed to Sesshū Tōyō (1420–1506)
      pair of six-fold screens; ink and color
      on paper
      each 179.0 x 365.5 (70¹/₂ x 143⁷/₁₀)
      Muromachi period, c. 1483

      Kosaka Zentarō Collection, Tokyo
      Important Cultural Property

On the right screen is a summer scene
with a pair of cranes near a waterfall; on
the left screen, a winter scene of egrets
and mandarin ducks in a snowy landscape.
Rocks, a gnarled pine tree, a crane, and a
waterfall are all crowded into the lower
right of the summer screen; another crane
at the center is framed by overhanging
pine branches. In the winter screen, distant snowy hills stand against a darkened
sky; the lower left-hand corner is filled
with snow-covered rocks and an old plum
tree that extends its twisting branches

across the foreground toward a lake. Both
screens emphasize the tactile forms in
their lower registers, which sharply contrast with the uncluttered space of the
middle and far distance.
   Sesshū Tōyō, to whom these screens
are attributed, was a pivotal figure in the
development of Japanese ink painting, especially of landscapes. Although these
screens are unsigned, they are the best in
artistic quality and the earliest in date
among some two dozen sets of screens of
this subject attributed to Sesshū. This pair
was once owned by the Masuda family in
Shimane Prefecture, descendants of Masuda Kanetaka (d. 1485), a local military
steward (*jitō*) who ruled the territory of
Masuda in Iwami Province (part of today's
Shimane Prefecture); the Masuda territory
lay immediately to the north of Suō, the
territory under the Ōuchi's control during
the fifteenth century. Sesshū painted a

portrait of Kanetaka before 1479, presumably when the artist visited the warrior's domain during his peripatetic years after he returned from Ming China in 1469. According to Masuda family tradition, Sesshū presented these screens to the family when Kanetaka's grandson Munekane (fl. 1512–1544) was installed as the territorial steward in 1483.

These screens, which show Sesshū's characteristic handling of solid forms and space in a monumental format, are consistent with the style of his *Landscape of the four seasons* (Tokyo National Museum), painted while he was in China between 1467 and 1469. The descriptive, dynamic forms of the pine tree and its branches as well as the plum branches find parallels in cat. 88, made in 1501. The style also shares features with works by Ming Academic painters such as Lü Ji (fl. c. 1497 and later), indicating that Sesshū closely observed the style of bird-and-flower paintings in

contemporary China. Sesshū, however, dramatized spatial expression in terms of its lateral expansion in the monumental screens. For example, the corner mass contrasts with the void at the center, an example of a compositional formula he inherited from his mentor Shūbun (fl. c. 1420–c. 1461), and which would be carried on by Kano Masanobu (1434—1530) and his son Motonobu (1476–1559).   YS

97 Flowers and Birds of the Four Seasons

Kano Motonobu (1476–1559)
set of four hanging scrolls; ink and slight color on paper
each h. 177.5 x w. 118.0 (69 7/8 x 46 1/2)
Muromachi period, 1543

Reiun'in, Kyoto
Important Cultural Property

These four hanging scrolls, which compose a set, were originally mounted on sliding doors. They were part of a series, depicting flowers and birds of the four seasons, which decorated the central chamber (*shitchū*) of the abbot's residential quarters (*hōjō*) of Reiun'in in Kyoto. The residential section of a Muromachi-period Zen temple was usually designed on a rectangular grid, facing a garden to the south, and divided into six rooms: the *shitchū*, the largest and most formal room, in the

98

center front; a chapel, at center rear; and adjoining rooms, the *jōkan* and *gekan*, on either side. At Reiun'in the *shitchū* had twelve sliding doors in all. Eight wide panels, four on the east side and four on the west side, depicted summer and spring, and four narrow panels on the north side depicted fall and winter scenes (shown here). All of the forty-nine paintings decorating the walls and doors of the *hōjō*, were remounted as hanging scrolls in 1683. In 1693, the entire building was restored, and still exists.

Reiun'in, established in 1526 as a subtemple within Myōshinji, was founded by the nun Seihan (d. 1534), who was widowed in 1504 when her husband, Yakushiji Moto-

kazu, a high-ranking warrior, was put to death following an unsuccessful rebellion against his master, Hosokawa Masamoto (1466–1507). The nun Seihan studied Zen with Daikyū Sōkyū (1468–1549), three times abbot of Myōshinji, and asked him to oversee the subtemple as its resident priest. In 1543 Daikyū purchased a monks' dormitory at Toganoo, west of Kyoto, and moved it to Reiun'in as its residential quarters. At Reiun'in, the painter Kano Motonobu (1476–1559), who then was receiving Zen training under Daikyū, painted sliding door panels and walls of four rooms of the building, including the *shitchū*. The paintings depicted landscapes with figures, moonlight, snow, and flowers and birds. These were executed in

the modes of the Song Chinese painters Xia Gui, Yujian, Muqi, and Ma Yuan as well as in the style of the Japanese painter Sōami, a senior contemporary of Motonobu. The set shown here, executed in soft brushwork and muted ink tones, reflects the Muqi mode. The tradition of basing pictorial designs on Chinese prototypes had already been firmly established by the time of Motonobu. In 1485, for instance, Motonobu's father Masanobu (1434–1530) had decorated the sliding door panels for the private chapel of the retired Ashikaga shogun Yoshimasa (1436–1490; cat. 6) and used several Chinese paintings as models.

The Reiun'in paintings show more

than one hand, and it is believed that the decoration campaign involved Motonobu and his entire workshop of assistants and apprentices. Most of the artists in the workshop, which was the most prolific group working in Kyoto at that time, were family members. This assured continuity and growth, along the family line. The Kano school was founded by Masanobu during the closing decades of the fifteenth century, and lasted some four hundred years. By the late eighteenth century nine branch family studios were operating in Kyoto and Edo (present-day Tokyo). Under Motonobu's astute leadership and management it became the most sought-after professional painters' group, producing

monumental screen paintings and sliding door panels for warriors, Buddhist temples, and the court. Motonobu's screens were also sent to China as official gifts from the Japanese government to the Ming court.

Motonobu's art drew not only on ink painting, but also on colorful *Yamato-e* (cat. 120). The principal motifs are placed toward the front of the composition, thus minimizing spatial depth and creating an illusion of slow but steady lateral movement in space. Motonobu's style of painting flowers and birds became a standard formula employed by several succeeding generations of Kano painters.   YS

98 **Miho no Matsubara**
    set of six hanging scrolls
    ink and color on paper
    each of two outer scrolls 154.2 x 54.7
    (60 3/4 x 21 7/8)
    each of four inner scrolls 154.2 x 59.0
    (60 3/4 x 23 1/4)
    Muromachi period, mid-16th century

    Egawa Art Museum, Hyōgo Prefecture
    Important Cultural Property

This set of six hanging scrolls, which originally decorated a six-fold screen, presents a panoramic bird's-eye view of Miho no Matsubara (Pine Grove at Miho), a famous, scenic spot on Suruga Bay, in Shizuoka Prefecture. The view includes a long stretch of sandbar with a pine grove that extends through the middle sections of the first four scrolls from the right, and a Buddhist temple said to be Seikenji, in the bottom section of the last scroll on the left. Behind the pine grove stretches the mist-filled Suruga Bay, which merges with the sky above the horizon.

Since the Heian period, *meisho*, or famous sites, have been used as both literary and pictorial themes. The earliest extant view of Miho no Matsubara dates from the late thirteenth century. Because most views of this site would include Mount Fuji either alongside the pine grove or behind it, it is generally thought that this work originally must have been accompanied by another screen, now lost, representing the sacred mountain.

The painting is unsigned and without seals, but has traditionally been attributed to Nōami (1397–1471), a distinguished *renga* (linked verse) poet, connoisseur of art, advisor to the Ashikaga shogunate in cultural affairs, and painter. Only one painting, a *White-Robed Kannon* (private collection, Japan), is firmly accepted as by Nōami. Despite its evocative ink washes and generally soft brushwork, reflecting the style associated with the Ami school of painters around Nōami, his son Geiami (1431–1485), and grandson Sōami (d. 1525), this work cannot be attributed to Nōami on either stylistic or documentary grounds. However, Sōami's remarkable ink painting *Eight Views of Xiao and Xiang,* 1513, on sliding door panels at Daisen'in in Kyoto, is the stylistic source of this view of *Miho no Matsubara.* Seikenji, a walled Buddhist temple complex, is visible in the lower left corner, buried in thick mist and surrounded by trees; it has been borrowed from Sōami's *Evening Bells from a Temple in Mist,* one of the Eight Views mentioned above. The scalloped forms of the floating distant clouds, painted in gold, also have a precedent in the Daisen'in panels. The painting thus must postdate Sōami; a mid-sixteenth-century date is a likely possibility.   YS

99 **Budai**
   Zhiweng Ruojing (fl. mid-13th century)
   hanging scroll; ink on paper
   91.8 x 29.0 (36 1/8 x 11 3/8)
   Southern Song, c. 1256–1263

   Umezawa Kinenkan, Tokyo
   Important Cultural Property

Budai (J: Hotei) is a semi-legendary figure from the pantheon of Zen Buddhist saints and sages. The artist of this work is Zhiweng Ruojing, whose two seals appear at the lower left. Although unrecorded in Chinese painting history, Zhiweng is known in Japan through a handful of paintings of Zen Buddhist subjects dated in the mid-thirteenth century. In this painting Budai is depicted without a back-

99

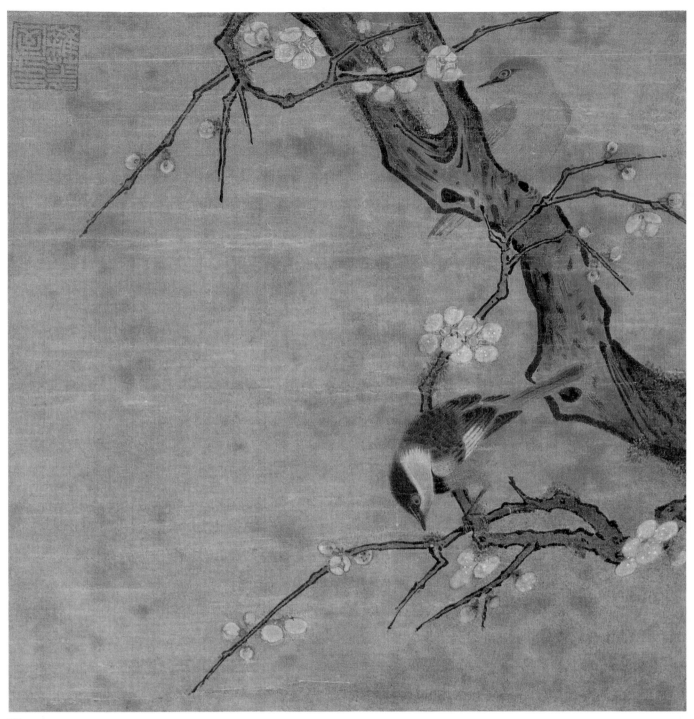

100

ground, in abbreviated lines of ink with varying thickness and tonality. In the tradition of *mōryōga* (*wang-liang-hua* in Chinese), or "apparition painting," some of the pale ink lines seem to vanish, creating a figure that appears to float on the paper.

The inscription, by Yanqi Guangwen (1189–1263), a Chinese Chan (J: Zen) monk and abbot of the monastery of Jingshan in Hangzhou, was requested by a Zen monk, a certain Chan-liao, who cannot be identified:

Having walked far and wide,
Having been running back and forth,

Shaking your brain and turning your head,
You are getting old and senile in front of the
*   Jeweled Pavilion.*
After Sudhana is gone,
Do you know if the grass is still green or
*   not?*

Yanqi became abbot of Jingshan in 1256 and remained there until his death. Thus the painting can be dated between 1256 and 1263. Zhiweng's works were brought to Japan from China during the Muromachi period, a time when many Chinese paintings were brought over by Japanese Zen pilgrims and avidly collected by the

Ashikaga shogunate. This painting was later examined and approved by the Edo connoisseur and painter Kano Tan'yū (1602–1674), who left his seal on the box in which the painting is stored.   MR

163

101

102

100 **Birds in a plum tree**
attributed to Ma Lin (fl. c. 1250–1260)
hanging scroll; ink and color on silk
27.6 x 28.0 (10 7/8 x 11)
Southern Song, mid-13th century

Gotō Museum, Tokyo
Important Cultural Property

This intimate view of two small birds perched in a plum tree forms a pair with another painting of two sparrows in a tree, now in a private collection. The two are assumed to have been cut from a larger painting and made into smaller, unobtrusive images suitable for viewing at tea gatherings or for a space in a private study. Cutting up or cropping imported Chinese paintings, though not condoned today, was practiced by the Ashikaga shoguns. A well-known instance is the handscroll *The Eight Views of Xiao and Xiang* in the collection of the shogun Ashikaga Yoshimasa; each of the eight views was cut and mounted as a separate hanging scroll.

This painting is stamped at the upper left with a square intaglio seal, *Zakkashitsu-in*, which has been identified as the collection seal of the sixth Ashikaga shogun, Yoshinori (1394–1441). Thirteen other Chinese paintings now dispersed in various Japanese collections have this seal.

Ma Lin, to whom this painting is attributed, was active in the reigns of the emperors Ning Zong (r. 1195–1224) and Li Zong (r. 1224–1264). A son of Ma Yuan, the famous artist of the Southern Song Painting Academy, Ma Lin is described in Chinese accounts as a painter less gifted than his father. Extant works by Ma Lin are few. A landscape painting entitled *Landscape at sunset* in the Nezu Institute of Fine Arts, Tokyo, signed *Chen Ma Lin* (His majesty's servant Ma Lin), is perhaps the finest work by him.   YS

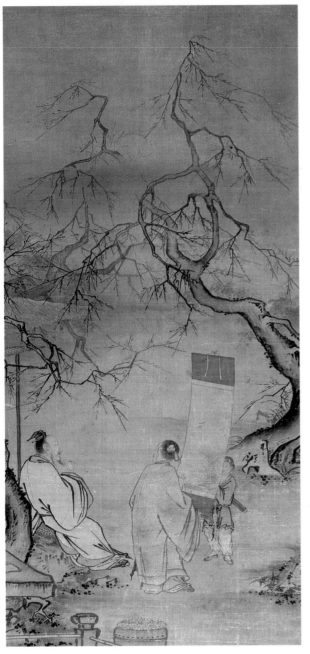

103

102 **Snow landscape**

Sun Junze (fl. mid-14th century)
hanging scroll; ink and color on silk
126.0 x 56.1 (49⁵/₈ x 22¹/₈)
Yuan, mid-14th century

Tokyo National Museum
Important Art Object

This winter landscape depicts a snowy lake shore with a scholar's pavilion. It bears the signature at the lower left of Sun Junze, a Chinese painter active during the Yuan Dynasty (1279–1368). The monumental painting typifies the fourteenth-century Chinese development of the academic style associated with Southern Song-period (1127–1279) painters Ma Yuan and Xia Gui. The landscape is devoid of the evocative, mist-filled space typical of Southern Song landscapes; instead it is described in a prosaic three-part perspective—near, middle, and far distances—encouraging the viewer to traverse the space logically. The motifs from near to far are given local clarity. The peak at the upper left is rendered as a flat silhouette, a two-dimensional effect that would become a marked stylistic feature of landscape painting in the subsequent Ming Dynasty. The positioning of key motifs such as the pavilion, the lake, the precipice, and the distant range of hills resembles elements found in later Japanese landscape paintings (for example, cat. 91), but on a reduced scale. The later Japanese painters in fact were influenced by the style of Chinese landscape artists of the Ming Dynasty (1368–1644).

The facts of Sun Junze's early biography are not known. The fourteenth-century Chinese source *Tu hui bao jian* informs that he was a native of Hangzhou, that he was skilled in painting landscapes and figures, and that he emulated Ma Yuan and Xia Gui. The limited Chinese collection catalogues from the Ming Dynasty mention his works, but little is known in China about him or his works. In Japan, however, Sun Junze's landscape paintings were very well known in the fifteenth century. The *Onryōken nichiroku*, a daily record kept by priests of the Shōkokuji monastery in Kyoto, provides the most direct documentation of Sun Junze's landscapes, which were seen by such contemporary figures as the Ashikaga shogun Yoshinori (1394–1441) and the painter Oguri Sōkei (fl. 1490s). In this daybook a set of four landscapes (presumably Landscapes of the Four Seasons) by Sun Junze is mentioned several times between 1436 and 1491. Although none of the four can be identified with extant Sun Junze works, they were very highly regarded by their owners, including the warrior-aesthete and deputy shogun (*kanrei*) Hosokawa Shigeyuki (1434–1511). The paintings were in the shogunal collection in 1465, and in 1491 the painter Oguri Sōkei, then working on a set

101 **Budai**

hanging scroll; ink on paper
77.1 x 30.9 (30³/₈ x 12¹/₈)
Southern Song, or early Yuan, 4th quarter of 13th century

Agency for Cultural Affairs, Tokyo

This remarkable Chinese ink painting of the slumbering Budai (J: Hotei) has been in Japan since at least the fifteenth century. It is known through the gourd-shaped relief seal *Zen'a* stamped at the lower right, which is believed by some to be a collection seal of a certain Zen Ami, a garden specialist serving the Muromachi shogunate; and by others to be a seal of a Chinese copyist; and by still others to be

that of a poet specializing in linked verse. Stylistically, the painting is unmistakably Chinese. Unlike the *Budai* by the mid-thirteenth-century Zhiweng, the artist of this painting uses dynamic and kinesthetic broad brushwork for the drapery contrasting with the carefully rendered face, torso, and left hand. The coexistence of the two modes in figure rendition is a stylistic feature of dated examples from the fourth quarter of the thirteenth century.

The painting has been attributed variously to a few of the Chinese painters known to the Japanese. The Edo connoisseur and painter Kano Tan'yū (1602–1674) made a close copy of the painting and added an inscription attributing it to Muqi of the late Southern Song.   YS

104

of sliding door paintings at Shosenken, a subtemple of Shōkokuji, used them as models for his work.   YS

103 **Scholars viewing paintings**
hanging scroll; ink and color on silk
118.5 x 58.4 (46 5/8 x 23)
late Song–early Yuan
late 13th–early 14th century

Egawa Art Museum,
Hyōgo Prefecture

Playing the *koto* (a stringed instrument), playing chess and practicing and enjoying calligraphy and painting were essential pursuits for the cultivated person in the Song Dynasty, and these four activities, called *qin qi shu hua* in Chinese, were often a theme of Southern Song painting. Many Japanese artists also employed this theme from the Muromachi period on.

Originally one of a set of four *qin qi shu hua* hanging scrolls, this work, on the theme of painting, is the only one remaining. It was handed down in the Asano family of daimyo of Aki Province (part of present-day Hiroshima Prefecture). This painting, in the style of Ma Yuan (fl. c. 1190–c. 1225), the famous Southern Song academic painter, dates to the late Southern Song or early Yuan Dynasty. In the Muromachi period there was a particular interest in the Southern Song style, and this work was already well known in Japan. In the screen painting by the Muromachi painter Sesshū Tōyō (1420–1506) of Flowers and Birds (cat. 96; see also cats. 88, 89), there are plum branches very similar to those in this painting. Furthermore, the man at the left in the work exhibited here recalls a figure in *Three Teachings* (Museum of Fine Arts, Boston) by the lesser-known Sessō Tōyō (fl. c. 1460–c. 1488), who was possibly a disciple of Sesshū or perhaps even the same person.   WA

104 **The Battle of Sekigahara**
attributed to Tosa Mitsuyoshi
(1539–1613)
pair of eight-fold screens; ink, color, and gold-leaf on paper
each 194.0 x 594.0 (76 3/8 x 233 4/5)
Edo period, no later than 1611 or 1612

Private Collection

When Toyotomi Hideyoshi died in 1598, the nation's political leadership was left to a Council of Five Elders (*Gotairō*) and a Five-Man Council of Commissioners (*Gobugyō*). From these two councils emerged two rival leaders, Ishida Mitsunari (1560–1600), a commissioner who had been a confidant and a favored vassal of Hideyoshi, and who championed the cause of the hegemony of the Toyotomi; and Tokugawa Ieyasu (1543–1616), warlord and sometime ally of Hideyoshi, who had been consolidating his military power and his landholdings in the east, and maneuvering through grants of fiefs and marriage alliances to create a daimyo coalition loyal to himself.

The commissioner Mitsunari, who also had formed an alliance with daimyo loyal to the Toyotomi, attempted to strengthen his own position by making Toyotomi Hideyori, the young son of Hideyoshi, his *cause celebre*. The struggle between Mitsunari and Ieyasu culminated in the most famous battle in Japanese history, the Battle of Sekigahara in Gifu, on the fifteenth day of the ninth month of 1600. Mitsunari's troops, totalling approximately 82,000 men, comprised the western army; the eastern army, or Ieyasu's alliance, consisted of about 75,000 men. Ieyasu emerged victorious from the battle to decide the rule of the realm. Mitsunari fled, but later was captured and executed in Kyoto.

The right-hand screen depicts events of the day before the final battle from a vantage point north of the village of Seki-gahara. Fragmentary views of the village, desolate rice fields and a few farm houses, now occupied by troops, can be seen in panels two, three, and four from the right. In the upper area of the screen Ieyasu's troops march along Nakasendō Highway (panels two through six) to join his camp at Akasaka, where the coalition of the eastern army welcomes his arrival (panels five through eight). Among the troops in the upper portion of panel four is the gray-bearded Ieyasu, well-protected by his men. He rides a white horse, and wears black armor and a white headband. Panels one and two depict Ōgaki Castle, the garrison headquarters of the western army, two miles west of Akamatsu. Skirmishes are taking place in front of the entrance to the castle, where some of the over-zealous troops of the eastern army had been lured away from Akamatsu and were thoroughly beaten by the western army on the eve of the battle.

The left screen depicts Sekigahara from the south. With Ieyasu's men close at their heels (panels one through three), the defeated troops of Mitsunari's army flee from their burning camps (panels two through three) toward Ibukiyama (Mount Ibuki; panels five through eight), which lies to the northeast of Ōgaki Castle. Some are engaged in sword-to-sword combat, others in spear and sword combat. In the lower sections of panels four through six, riflemen aim at the fleeing soldiers. These riflemen belong to the twenty-thousand-man force led by the turncoat Kobayakawa, who began the battle supporting Mitsunari and ended it, probably by prearrangement, on the side of Ieyasu. In other scenes in this screen, ranking warriors of the western army are about to commit *seppuku*, or self-inflicted disembowelment.

This pair of screens is the largest and most detailed pictorial treatment of the Battle of Sekigahara, containing more

than two thousand figures. Although the right and left screens are not continuous, they represent the temporal sequence of events at Sekigahara. Many of the pasted-down rectangular cartouches (nineteen on the right screen and eight on the left) erroneously identify places, and the specific identities of troops, the garrison camps of individual daimyo, and the individual persons engaged in combat cannot be established with certainty. The painting and written accounts also disagree on particulars such as Ieyasu's outfit. According to one historical record, Ieyasu rode into the final battle wearing a European-style cuirass (*nanbandō*), mounted on a white stallion. Yet he appears here among the victorious eastern troops (center of panel one, left screen) wearing indigenous black armor and a helmet with a large hornlike *kuwagata*. (Ieyasu also appears in panel four of the right screen.)

These screens are attributed to Tosa Mitsuyoshi (1539–1613) on the basis of style, and are known as the *Tsugaru byōbu* (screens) because they were transmitted in the Tsugaru family, the castellans of Hirosaki Castle in Aomori Prefecture. The screens were part of a trousseau taken to the family by Tokugawa Ieyasu's adopted daughter, Matehime, when she became the bride of Tsugaru Nobuhira (1586–1631), in 1611 or 1612. According to a Tsugaru clan document, Ieyasu owned four screens depicting Sekigahara, of which Matehime took the two shown here. The composition of the original set of four screens may have been continuous, showing the scenes from the beginning of the battle to the aftermath, but because Matehime probably picked the first and third screens to form a new pair, there are gaps in the narrative. The place names contained in pasted-down cartouches mentioned above may in fact correspond to places in the missing screens.

Apart from the political significance

of Ieyasu's victory at Sekigahara, the battle also was a contest between old and new weapons. A study by the late George Sansom provides the following statistics on the army of 3,000 men dispatched by Date Masamune (1567–1636), daimyo of Sendai, to aid Ieyasu: 420 were cavalry men, 1,200 carried firearms (matchlock guns), 850 carried spears, and 200 carried bows. Clearly, by 1600 the most effective weapons were firearms, followed by spears, bows, and last, swords, the least effective.   YS

105 Horse stable

pair of six-fold screens; ink, color, and gold leaf on paper
each 149.5 x 355.5 (58 7/8 x 140)
Muromachi period, c. 1560

Tokyo National Museum
Important Cultural Property

These screens depict six well-bred and well-groomed horses tethered in six stable compartments, each corresponding to one of the three inner panels of the screens. The stable, seen from the back, is set in a well-kept garden with exotic pitted rocks and blue ponds with cranes and white herons; a pine and a cherry tree flank the gable ends of the building. A group of courtiers, warriors, and monks relax playing the games of *go*, *shōgi*, and *sugoroku* (double six) in a *tatami*-matted seating area. Saddles and stirrups rest on racks, and a monkey—believed to keep evil spirits away from the horses—toddles toward a young attendant who is carrying a teabowl on a stand. Grooms, one of them stealing a nap, are in a corridor that separates the front from the rear of the stable.

The tradition of painting horses in a stable was first seen in handscroll form as early as the Kamakura period, in a depiction of veterinary surgeons and medicinal herbs before a stable. A late fifteenth-century narrative scroll, *Seikōji engi emaki*,

in the Tokyo National Museum, shows a horse stable and may be seen as a precursor of horse stable screens like this work. This set of screens is stylistically attributed to the Kano studio, although to no specific artist. The stylized silhouettes of the horses recall a painting of a single horse, datable to no later than 1521 (cat. 82). Judging from the number of surviving works, this type of screen painting of horses in a stable was popular throughout the sixteenth century among upper-class warriors. These screens inform us how horses, important properties of the warrior class, were kept in a residential setting.   YS

106 Training horses and horse stable

pair of six-fold screens; ink, color, and gold leaf on paper
each 154.0 x 355.0 (60 5/8 x 139 3/4)
Edo period, early 17th century

Taga Taisha, Shiga Prefecture
Important Cultural Property

In the right screen three horses are being tried out by the trainers; another horse, held by three grooms, nervously awaits its turn. Two others, tethered to posts, anxiously rub the ground with their forehooves. From a room in a sizable mansion, the scene is observed by a man, perhaps a daimyo or a high-ranking warrior, who leans against an armrest, relaxed, and attended by boy servants. On the veranda of the adjoining room are other spectators. In the back of the room, his back turned toward the garden, is a tea master preparing tea. A young attendant bringing a bowl of tea to the spectators is distracted by the excitement in the garden.

In the left screen a stable is shown with six horses in compartments, each corresponding to one panel. Unlike the Tokyo National Museum screens of the same subject (cat. 105), this view does not include any animating genre scenes. This work represents a second type of stable

105

106

107

screen current in the seventeenth century, focused solely on the horses. The front of the stable is marked by a row of curtainlike pieces of cloth, dyed dark blue in the lower half. These are *noren* that hang above the entrance to each stable. The horses, all well groomed, are tied by two reins, the ends of which are fastened to metal rings imbedded in posts. A thick, braided rope with a fluted pattern hangs from above and goes around each horse's belly (save the horse in panel seven). This is a *hara-kake*, used to prevent the horse from lying on its belly and from violent movements. The rope's ends (here invisible) are tied to two horn-shaped projections on the lateral beam. Gold clouds cover the right half of the roof, the left half of the veranda, and a part of the *tatami*-matted space. Behind the stable grow disproportionately large bamboo trees, a decorative device.

The right screen shows stylistic elements that are close to the work of Kano Mitsunobu (1565–1608) around 1600, especially in the tree motifs and their spatial handling. These screens, therefore, may date from the first decade of the seventeenth century. Mitsunobu was already an important artist of the Kano school as early as 1581 when he and his father, Eitoku, were employed by Oda Nobunaga to decorate the interiors of his Azuchi Castle. It was in this same year that Nobunaga held a grand dressage of his several hundred horses, which was viewed by the emperor Ōgimachi. These screens, especially the one on the right, no doubt reflect memories of that great event on a modest scale. YS

107 **Dog-chasing event**
attributed to Kano Sanraku (1559–1635)
pair of six-fold screens; ink, color, and gold on paper
each 152.0 x 348.5 (59⅞ x 137⅕)
Momoyama period,
late 16th–early 17th century

Tokiwayama Bunko,
Kanagawa Prefecture
Important Cultural Property

The rise and maturation of the Japanese warrior class were accompanied by the development of activities reflecting the concern with military skill and social conduct befitting a warrior. Among the sports contests that incorporated mounted archery were *yabusame*, *kasakage*, and *inuoumono*, illustrated here. In *yabusame* and *kasakage* archers on galloping horses shot at immobile and inanimate targets. In *inuoumono*, the targets were live dogs.

Inuoumono consisted of two distinct phases of activity, *nawa no inu*, the "dog inside the rope," and *soto no inu*, the "dog outside the rope." In *nawa no inu*, a group of mounted archers waited just outside a large circle marked by a thick rope. At the center of the circle was a smaller circle of sand. A dog was released inside the sand ring, and as it crossed over the rope boundary, the archers would try to hit it with blunt large-headed arrows. When the dog passed into the area outside the circle, the contest would shift to the *soto no inu* phase, in which the mounted archers chased the dog and attempted to strike it with the blunt arrows. These proceedings were closely observed by the *kenmi*, a judge who rated the contestants on their

archery form, the way they handled their horses, and their success in hitting a dog. Other men were responsible for releasing the dog within the ring, handling the dogs to be used later in the event, and recording the scores from their post within the *nikkijo*, a roofed enclosure at one end of the playing field. Important spectators also sat in the *nikkijo*, while others would watch from outside the fenced precinct.

The earliest textual reference to *inuoumono* known is found in the *Azuma kagami*, a historical compliation of the late thirteenth century comprising both private and shogunal records. It describes an event that took place in the south garden of the shogun's residence, with the young lord in attendance. A number of documentary references to *inuoumono* are known from the ensuing Muromachi period and, despite an imperial edict in 1350 that temporarily banned it, texts were written on this popular sport. Different schools espoused different methods for conducting *inuoumono*. One event in 1489 included the participation of thirty-six archers in three teams of twelve, which seems to have been standard, and more than one hundred and fifty dogs. A decrease in documentary evidence of *inuoumono* from the end of the Muromachi period through the early Edo period probably reflects a decline in its popularity, though in the middle Edo period a revival in interest seems to have occurred. For example, a grand event was organized by the Shimazu family on the seventh day of the fourth month of 1646.

The earliest depictions of *inuoumono*,

aside from illustrations in texts from the Muromachi periods, date from the end of the Muromachi period. The event usually was painted in a lively and straightforward manner, as one component of a larger picture. Eventually, the theme was treated on a grander scale, expanded to fill the broad expanse afforded by a pair of six-fold screens as well as *fusuma* (sliding door) panels. More than a dozen Momoyama- and Edo-period *inuoumono* screens, in pairs and singly, are known today.

The screens shown here are generally regarded as the oldest extant *inuoumono* screens, and are considered by many to be the finest. It has been argued on stylistic grounds that this set was painted by Kano Sanraku, an artist active during the Momoyama and early Edo periods, when the practice of *inuoumono* had waned. A passage in the late seventeenth-century art historical text, the *Honchō gashi*, relates that Sanraku first painted *inuoumono* after hearing how it had been practiced from an old man named Sasaki Genyū. This confirms that Sanraku's *inuoumono* paintings were produced after the actual practice of *inuoumono* had waned in popularity.

In this painting many of the conventions of *inuoumono* are portrayed. The *nawa no inu* area is carefully depicted with a large circle of rope bordered with a ring of sand in which the mounted archers wait, and an inner circle of sand. On the left-hand screen, in the *nikkijo* is the man responsible for recording the events poised with ink and brush at hand. On the right-hand screen, fifty-one participants

are divided equally into three teams of seventeen; one group dismounted at the top, one at the bottom, and one on horseback around the rope circle. Great attention is given to the robes of the attending figures; those of the mounted participants are depicted with sleeves billowing from extended arms to achieve maximum decorative effect against the gold background.

The composition is contrived to achieve a contrast of action and inaction. The two aspects of the event, *nawa no inu* and *soto no inu*, are clearly divided, one to each six-panel screen. The artist has emphasized a highly charged stillness in the *nawa no inu* scene. The dog is yet to be released and the participants wait expectantly atop their horses who paw the ground with energetic anticipation. In the *soto no inu* scene, the potential for activity is given full play, as the mounted archers and attendants converge on the fleeing dog in a galloping wedge of movement.   AMW

108 **Cherry blossom viewing and falconry**
attributed to Unkoku Tōgan
(1547–1618)
pair of six-fold screens; ink and color on paper
each 157.0 x 345.5 (61⅘ x 136)
Momoyama period, late 16th century
Sekai Kyūseikyō (MOA Art Museum), Shizuoka Prefecture
Important Cultural Property

Seasonal images from spring and winter decorate this pair of screens. The spring scene of cherry blossom viewing is painted in a polychromatic style, while the winter scene of falconry is depicted in subdued tones. In the spring screen, women and children enter into a festive dance as their palanquin and luggage bearers relax. The colorfully dressed women and children are gathered in what appears to be a temple compound on a hill, in an area separated from the temple buildings by green curtains hung between cedar trees. Under the shade of a giant pine tree, the luggage bearers squat by the palanquins and talk among themselves; one prepares tobacco leaves for his long pipe. The scene is illuminated by sunlight filtering through the golden spring mist. In the winter screen, samurai and their attendants are engaged in hunting. The hunters intently pursue pheasants that are being chased and attacked by hawks and dogs in a desolate winter field. A steep, overhanging cliff and rustic, thatched-roofed houses behind a brushwood fence fill the last two panels at the left.

Although the artist is not identified by a signature or seal, these screens have

108

109

110

been attributed to Unkoku Tōgan (1547–1618), a third-generation follower of Sesshū Tōyō (1420–1506). Stylistic features associated with Tōgan are the manner of depicting the jagged rock outcroppings, the linear textures of the rocky terrains occupying the landscape setting in the left screen, and the faces of the people depicted in both screens (cat. 119).

What is known of Tōgan's life comes from fragmentary contemporary writings by the artist himself and from later but more complete accounts compiled by his descendants. One reliable biography says that Unkoku Tōgan, whose earlier name was Hara Chibei, was born in 1547 as the second son of a warrior, one Hara Naoie, a retainer of a minor daimyo of Nokomi Castle in the northern Kyushu province of Hizen. After his father's death in 1584 in the Battle of Arima, the artist became a retainer of the powerful daimyo Mōri Terumoto (1553–1625), with an annual stipend of 200 koku. In 1593, the artist copied the Landscape of the Four Seasons, a long handscroll by Sesshū and a treasure of the Mōri family. The same source says that Terumoto was so impressed by the copy that the artist was allowed to use as his artistic name Unkoku, after the name of Sesshū's studio, and to adopt the character tō of Tōyō as his own, and also that on this occasion Tōgan took the tonsure. A colophon brushed by Tōgan at the time the copy was made, and which accompanies the original by Sesshū, says that Terumoto gave the scroll to the artist in token of Tōgan's succeeding to Sesshū's artistic tradition and that the artist was also given Sesshū's studio, Unkokuken.

Art historical sources compiled in the seventeenth century and later also note that before Tōgan inherited Sesshū's artistic tradition, he had studied painting under Kano Shōei (1519–1592), or his more famous son Eitoku (1543–1590). This connection is supported by stylistic evidence found in some of Tōgan's works. Shōei and Eitoku, and the painters who worked in their studios, were the pioneers of the colorful Momoyama style of painting. Elsewhere Tōgan is recorded as a practitioner of tea and a participant in renga (linked verse) gatherings. In 1611, Tōgan was given the rank of hokkyō (Bridge of the Law), the lowest of the three honorific ranks (the others are hōgen or Eye of the Law, and hōin or Seal of the Law) given by the Imperial court to clerics and gifted artists.

This pair of screens can be said to show both of Tōgan's styles: the spring screen displays the buoyant, colorful mode typical of the Momoyama-period genre style related to the Kano tradition, and the winter screen shows Tōgan's conservative and archaistic mode reflecting Tōgan's debt to the Sesshū tradition.   YS

109 **Scenes from the Tale of the Heike**
attributed to Yano Saburōhyōbei Yoshishige
(fl. 1632–1653)
pair of six-fold screens; ink, color, and gold leaf on paper
each 174.7 x 375.0 (68³/₄ x 147³/₅)
Edo period, first half 17th century

Eisei Bunko, Tokyo
Important Art Object

The conflicts between the two warrior families of the late twelfth century, the Minamoto (Genji) and Taira (Heike), were shaped into a major epic battle narrative, the Tale of the Heike, during the early thirteenth century. The Tale's themes of rise and fall of the mighty, of duty and compassion, of the sublime and the earthly, are cast in an essentially Buddhist view that the affairs of this world are transient and volatile. Thus the Tale has inspired poetry, Nō librettos, and paintings throughout the medieval period and well into the Edo period.

Two episodes from the Tale are shown here. The right screen depicts the Battle of Uji, south of Kyoto (site of the famous Buddhist temple of Byōdōin), on the twentieth day of the first lunary month of 1184. At the Battle of Uji the Genji troops, 60,000 strong and led by Minamoto Yoritomo, surprised the army of his own cousin Yoshinaka. Yoshinaka's victorious campaigns against the Heike had aroused Yoritomo's suspicion, and hence the attack. Yoshinaka's garrisons removed bridges and positioned themselves on the northern shore of the Uji River, which the Genji army hesitated to cross. Then, from a corner of Byōdōin, two high-ranking war-

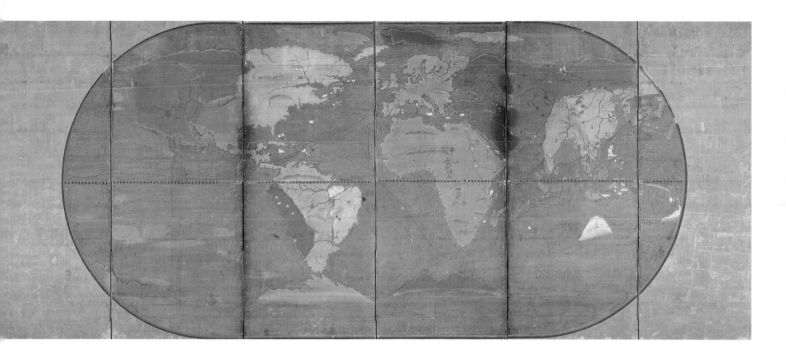

riors of the Genji clan, Sasaki Shirō Taka-
tsuna and Kajiwara Genta Kagesue,
emerged and raced each other on horseback across the churning water. Each
hoped to be the first to reach the other
shore in order to launch the attack on
Yoshinaka's garrisons. Both warriors were
mounted on horses that had been personal
gifts from Yoritomo, in recognition of their
valor. Sasaki rode a dark chestnut horse
named Ikezuki and Kajiwara a black horse
named Surusumi, both Yoritomo's most
coveted horses. The two warriors plunged
into the river, Kajiwara with a slight head
start, but Sasaki, by clever trickery, outdis-
tanced Kajiwara.

In the screen the two horses trot toward the water's edge. Between the gold
clouds a section of the ruined Uji Bridge is
visible. Kajiwara's black horse braved the
churning water first, eighteen feet ahead
of Sasaki who from behind shouted that
Kajiwara's horse's girths needed tightening. While the gullible Kajiwara, in mid-
stream, attended to this problem, Sasaki
overtook him and reached the opposite
shore first.

The left screen depicts an episode
soon after the battle at Ichinotani, Harima
Province (part of Hyōgo Prefecture, near
Kobe), which occurred one month after
the Uji River episode. The Genji defeated
the Heike at Ichinotani, and the Heike survivors fled the shore toward the fleets.
One of the ablest ranking warriors of the
Genji troops, Kumagae Nobuzane, pursued them. The painting depicts the subsequent events, described in the *Tale*.

*As he was riding to the beach, he
caught sight of a fine-looking warrior urging
his horse into the sea toward a boat an-*
*chored a little offshore. The warrior wore ar-
mor laced with light green silk cords over a
twilled silk battle robe decorated with an
embroidered design of cranes. On his head
was a gold-horned helmet. He carried a
sword in a gold-studded sheath and a bow
bound with red lacquered rattan. His quiver
held a set of black and white feathered arrows, the center of each feather bearing a
black mark. He rode a dappled gray horse
outfitted with a gold-studded saddle. He was
swimming at a distance of five or six tan
[that is, more than 100 feet] when Nobuzane roared at him: You out there! I believe
you are a great general. It is cowardly to turn
your back on your enemy. Come back!*

*Naozane beckoned to him with his fan.
Thus challenged, the warrior turned his
horse around. When he reached the beach,
Naozane rode alongside, grappled with him,
and wrestled him to the ground. As
Naozane pressed down his opponent and removed his helmet to cut off his head, he
saw before him the fair-complexioned face
of a boy no more than sixteen or seventeen.
Looking at this face, he recalled his son,
Naoie. The youth was so handsome and in-
nocent that Naozane, unnerved, was unable
to find a place to strike with the blade of his
sword. . . . He thought to himself: The
slaughter of one courtier cannot conclusively effect this war. Even when I saw that
my son, Naoie, was slightly wounded, I
could not help feeling misery. How much
more painful it would be if this young warrior's father heard that his son had been
killed. I must spare him! Looking over his
shoulder, he saw a group of his comrades
galloping toward them. He suppressed his
tears and said: Though I wish to spare your
life, a band of my fellow warriors is approaching, and there are so many others
throughout the countryside that you have*
*no chance of escaping from the Genji.
Since you must die now, let it be my hand
rather than by the hand of another, for I will
see that prayers for your better fortune in
the next world are performed.*
(Translated in Kitagawa and Tsuchida 1975, vol.
2, 561–562.)

When the youth was beheaded,
Naozane found a flute in a brocade pouch
tucked around the youth's body. The
youth was soon identified as Atsumori, an
outstanding flute player, only seventeen
years of age, and a son of Tsunemori, the
chief of the department of construction at
the Imperial Palace. The flute was the famous flute named Saeda (Small Branch),
originally owned by Emperor Toba (r.
1107–1123). Kumagae, deeply disturbed by
the event, later took the tonsure and spent
the remainder of his life as a Buddhist
evangelist.

The screens are traditionally attributed to a minor painter, Yano Saburōhyōbei Yoshishige, who served Hosokawa
Sansai (1563–1646) at Kokura, Kyushu, and
his son Tadatoshi (1586–1641), daimyo of
Higo Province (now Kumamoto Prefecture). The painting shows technical mastery reminiscent of the professional Kano
studio tradition, which far exceed our ex-
pectations of a provincial painter.   YS

110 **Maps of the world and of Japan**
pair of six-fold screens; ink, color, and
gold leaf on paper
each 163.8 x 379.6 (64½ x 149½)
Edo period, after 1632

Jōtokuji, Fukui Prefecture
Important Cultural Property

This striking pair of screens, one a map of
the world and the other a map of Japan, re-

111

112

113

veals how the Japanese perceived the shape and space of the world outside their own during the early decades of the seventeenth century. The elliptically shaped map of the world, like a view of the earth from outer space, is isolated by the gold surface into which the map is set. A tripod-in-circle seal of the painter Kano Eitoku (1543–1590) is stamped on the lower section of the gold ground of panel six. The attribution to Eitoku is not accepted.

Of some two dozen examples of maps surviving from the seventeenth century, this work is one of the earliest produced by Japanese artists. Although the map of the world was undoubtedly inspired by European prototypes, no corresponding model has been found in Japan. Since Portuguese traders and the Jesuits were already in Japan by the 1540s, we may speculate that European maps were familiar to the Japanese. The Jesuits report that Nobunaga owned a globe in 1580 and hung a map of the world in his room in 1581.

In the map of the world, oceans are painted in dark blue and the strangely shaped land masses in ocher, browns, pink, and white, creating impressive coloristic effects. In the map of Japan, the island nation is surrounded by blue seas with carefully drawn schematic wave patterns and by wafting gold clouds that, like the islands themselves, float on the seas.

These maps are both informative and decorative. The map of the world is beribboned by the equator, a decorative straight band of alternating black and orange. The tropics of Cancer and Capricorn are lines of gold, as are the latitudinal parallels drawn across the two polar regions. Four continental land masses—Europe, Africa, and North and South America—and the Atlantic Ocean are on the third and fourth panels, the center of the screen, while what must be Mexico and Alaska are on

panel five. Eastern Europe and Asia stretch toward the right. Japan, a tiny cluster of strangely shaped pink islands—a miniature of the fully blown version in the other screen—is at the upper right of the map, rendered larger than its relative size, but nonetheless dwarfed by the vastness of the rest of the world.

The inordinately large land masses near the polar regions in the map of the world indicate that this map is based generally on a cartographic projection devised by the Flemish mathematician and geographer Gerhardus Mercator (1512–1594), whose navigational map was published in 1569 and refined in 1590 by an English geographer, Edward Wright, but was not in general currency until about 1630. In this Japanese version, to maintain visual harmony, the regions of the South Pole, which would have filled the lower areas of the map, are mostly painted over by the blue of the ocean.

Both maps are inscribed with place names. Indeed, an inscription on the map of the world has been cited as evidence for the earliest possible date of 1592. The inscription, written on the right edge of panel two in *hiragana* (Japanese syllabic letters), reads *Orankai*, which is the Japanese reading of the Chinese name of a nomadic tribe, reported for the first time by a Japanese warrior and close vassal of Hideyoshi, Katō Kiyomasa (1562–1611), when he led a northern expedition during the Korean campaign in 1592. The tribe was known to the Jesuits by 1594. The name is used in this map for an area northeast of Korea.

Except for the names of provinces in China and Southeast Asian countries, which are written in Chinese characters, the rest are in *hiragana: Inkiresu* for England, *Furansa* for France; *Hatagonun* for Patagonia, the southernmost of South America; and *Nowakineya* for New

Guinea, which is rendered like an iceberg bobbing in the south Pacific, on panel two. These names represent Japanese orthography approximating the Latinized place names in Portuguese or Spanish, agreeing with the fact that the map shows the Portuguese and Spanish trade routes in red lines issuing from two ports of the Iberian peninsula, Lisbon in Portugal and Sanlúcar de Barrameda in Spain.

North America, including Canada, has three inscriptions on the fourth panel. Below the left tip of the shortest of three green mountain ranges is *Furorita* for Florida, which actually lies considerably farther south. *Amerika* is inscribed to the left of the middle mountain range, identifying the entire continent. And most significantly, *Nowafuransa* is inscribed at the upper right of the land mass, for "New France," an earlier name for Canada in currency after around 1632 when, after sporadic control by the British during the Thirty Years' War (1618–1648), the region's predominantly French settlement was restored to France by the treaty of Saint-Germain-en-Laye. The name New France continued to be used until 1763, when the territory was ceded to Great Britain. If the inscriptions were written at the time the map was produced, then the map postdates 1632.

The names of provinces (*kuni*) are inscribed on the screen depicting the islands of Japan. The snow-capped sacred mountain, Mount Fuji, marks the center of Honshu, while a range of green mountains runs along the center of the northeastern section of the island.

It has been asserted that this type of map of Japan could have been produced as early as 1592. The date is based on the convoy route drawn in red between the northwestern tip of Kyushu and the Korean peninsula, on panels five and six. This

route was used by Hideyoshi's army before and during his Korean expedition of 1592. This date, too, is problematic. The shapes of the islands, as conceptual as the land masses of Europe, are also based on a European model, possibly the Dutch cartographer William Blaeu's map of Asia of 1635. The strangely shortened Honshu island and the abstract shapes of the islands of Shikoku and Kyushu are in fact closer to a map of Japan published by the Jesuits in the 1640s than to any European precedents that the Japanese might have seen in the sixteenth century. The earliest possible date for this type of map, therefore, would be the 1630s or 1640s, later than the proposed Momoyama-period date by almost half a century.   YS

111 Twenty-eight cities and myriad countries

pair of eight-fold screens, ink and color on paper
each 194.8 x 516.3
Momoyama or Edo period, 17th century

Imperial Household Collection

In the Momoyama period, folding screens showing maps of the entire world or detailed representations of particular distant places were made to satisfy a fascination with an outside world that until then had been unknown.

This set is the largest among such extant screens. Along the top of each panel of one screen are eight mounted figures in four opposing pairs. They have been identified as, from the right, the rulers of Persia, Abyssinia, Tartary, Moscow, France (Henry IV), Spain (Philip II), Turkey, and the Holy Roman Empire (Rudolf II). The third and fourth, seventh and eighth figures appear also, only minutely altered, in catalogue 112. In vertical rows beneath the

figures, twenty-eight cities are depicted, from top to bottom, right to left: Goa, Paris, Prague, Calcutta, Mexico City, Aden, Frankfurt, Sofala, Venice, Amsterdam, Cologne, Cuzco, Rome, Ormuz, Bantam, Mozambique, Istanbul, London, Genoa, Hamburg, Seville, Antwerp, Stockholm, Moscow, Lisbon, Dantzig, Bergen, and Alexandria. A map of Portugal, in place of cities, occupies part of the first and second panels from the right. The depictions of these cities and figures are derived primarily from a map of the world by Willem Blaeu (1571–1638), published in 1606–1607. The rulers of England and China represented in Blaeu's map are missing in the Imperial screen, however; the view of Rome comes from *Vita Beati patris Ignatii Loyolae*, a biography of Saint Ignatius published in Antwerp in 1610. The map of Portugal can be traced to *Theatrum Orbis Terrarum* by Abraham Ortelius (1527–1598), first published in 1570 and reprinted four more times by 1612.

On the two outer panels of the other screen are pairs of men and women from forty-two countries, in native dress, and on the six panels in between, a map of the world; these depictions are close to the 1606–1607 Blaeu map. In the Blaeu map, however, scenes from only thirty countries are included, though couples from forty-two countries can be seen in another map by Blaeu, in which the world is divided between two circles, published either in 1619 or around 1645. In the lower part of the fourth panel of this screen is a framed inset containing an allegorical representation of the Four Continents: Europe (a seated woman) is flanked on the left by the New World (two figures wearing feathered headdresses) and on the right by Asia (two figures with a camel) and Africa (a figure with a crocodile). In another framed inset, at the bottom of the sixth panel, are cannibals from Brazil.   AY

112 Four equestrians in combat

four-fold screen; color and gold leaf on paper
166.0 x 338.0 (65 3/8 x 133)
Momoyama period, early 17th century

Kobe City Museum of Nanban Art, Hyōgo Prefecture
Important Cultural Property

European trade with Japan in the sixteenth century brought with it more than Chinese silks and other foreign goods bought with Japanese silver. With the merchants came Catholic missionaries, and the propagation of the new faith required sacred images for instruction and devotion. Japanese interest in Western painting did not, however, focus only on devotional images. Instructed by Jesuit artists, Japanese painters began to explore techniques and materials by copying the European art made available to them. Although the subject is foreign, the martial theme and lavish coloring of this work are in keeping with the tastes of a Momoyama-period daimyo.

The screen consists of two facing pairs of equestrian rulers of Christian and Muslim nations. The figures have been tentatively identified as (from right to left) a Tartar ruler, a Russian czar, a Turkish sultan, and the Holy Roman emperor Rudolph II. With only minor deviations, four figures correspond to the third (from right), fourth, seventh, and eighth rulers depicted in the upper portion of one of the pair of screens in the Imperial Household (cat. 111). Models for these figures were drawn from different, unrelated sources, such as the small prints of *Twelve Roman Emperors*, c. 1590, by Adriaen Collaert (c. 1560–1618), and the figures of rulers on a map of the world by Willem Blaeu (1571–1638), which was brought from Holland and known in Japan during the first decade of the seventeenth century.

114

115

116

This painting, now mounted as a four-fold screen, was originally part of a set of eight sliding-door panels. The remaining four have been mounted as an eight-fold screen, now in a private collection. These works were reportedly in the Aizu-Wakamatsu Castle, the home of Leon Gamō Ujisato (1556–1595), a Christian daimyo, and his son Gamō Hideyuki (1583–1612), and remained there until 1644, when they changed hands and were kept by the Matsudaira family until the Meiji Restoration in the nineteenth century. MR

113 European musicians
pair of six-fold screens; color and gold on paper
each 102.5 x 308.0 (40 3/8 x 121 1/4)
Momoyama period, early 17th century

Eisei Bunko, Tokyo
Important Cultural Property

This work is one of many extant paintings of Western genre scenes. Interest in European dress, lifestyle, and landscape, as illustrated in imported copies of European engravings, explains the great appeal of these screens in Momoyama and Edo Japan. The brilliant colors and gold would have catered to the extravagant tastes of the Momoyama-period daimyo.

In the right screen two women are playing the viol and the harp to ardent listeners. Other figures in the foreground are immersed in conversation. The sea, dotted with ships, stretches behind the main figures. The left screen is less centered, with pairs of men conversing in the foreground and an expanse of water to the left. In both screens distant figures and buildings in the mountainous landscape create small, isolated scenes. Details such as the European dress and musical instruments are well executed; however, the artist was not adept in the Western technique of perspective, contributing to a lack of unity between the figural groupings. A hint of professional training in the Kano-school style is evident in the red peonies in the foreground and the mountains in the background, both frequently depicted by artists of the Kano school.

The themes depicted derive from the Catholic missions in Japan. The musicians in extravagant dress and the attendants at the small Temple of Love in the right-hand screen are clearly related to the theme of profane love. Christian symbolism is evident in the wine press in panel six of the same screen, signifying the Sacrifice. Jesuits not only taught Japanese artists how to paint using Western techniques, but also tried to impart something of their Christian message through what seemed to be secular themes. The daimyo who commissioned works such as these were largely Christian converts or at least supporters of commerce and communication with Europeans. MR

114 Arrival of the southern barbarians
attributed to Kano Mitsunobu (1565–1608)
pair of six-fold screens; ink, color, and gold leaf on paper
each 164.0 x 365.0 (64 1/2 x 143 3/4)
Momoyama period, c. 1593

Nanban Bunkakan, Osaka

Portuguese traders were the earliest Europeans to come to Japan, followed by the Jesuits in the 1540s. The foreigners were called *nanbanjin*, or "southern barbarians," and the art that deals with them is called *nanban* art. This pair of screens, the earliest-known example of this type, depicts the arrival of Portuguese traders in Nagasaki.

In the right screen, behind a row of shops and partially hidden by gold clouds, is a view of the Catholic mission situated high on a hill. Included are a *tatami*-matted chapel, its altar marked by a roundel containing a three-nail design, a symbol of Christ's Passion; a confessional with a circular map of the world on its outer wall; and a smaller building, probably an oratory, its roof surmounted by a gold cross-shaped finial. From the gate issues a party of missionaries to greet the traders, who, led by the elegantly dressed captain under a red parasol, proceed from the left. The two parties meet at the center of the screen.

In the left screen a galleon with a high prow and stern sails into the harbor, dwarfing a small boat on its starboard side, which is unloading cargo to the shore. The blue water contrasts with the white spray of waves, as do the fanciful colors of the crews' costumes with the gold clouds.

An early genre painting, this work is attributed to Kano Mitsunobu, who, in 1593, was called from Kyoto to Nagoya in northern Kyushu to decorate the castle headquarters Hideyoshi had built during his Korean expedition of 1592–1593. Mitsunobu reportedly observed the Portuguese in Kyushu; thus the details such as the costumes in this work are believed to have been based on life. YS

115 Sights in and around Kyoto
pair of six-fold screens; ink, color, and gold leaf on paper
each 160.5 x 323.5 (63 1/8 x 127 3/8)
Edo period, after 1620

Osaka Municipal Museum, Osaka

Sights in and around Kyoto (Rakuchū raku-gai) as a subject originated in urban landscape paintings of Kyoto done in the 1470s. The earliest extant screens, however, postdate the first quarter of the sixteenth century and were painted by Kano-school painters: by Motonobu in the 1530s; by Motonobu's grandson, Eitoku, in the 1560s; and by Eitoku's son, Mitsunobu, in the 1580s. A forerunner of genre painting, their focus shifts from a view of the

city with the changing seasons and monthly events to one that highlights specific sites, architecture, both public and private, and the individual activities of citizens of this fast-growing city. This trend toward thematic changes became even more marked during the first quarter of the seventeenth century, the period to which this set of screens belongs.

This pair of screens depicts Kyoto shortly after 1620. In the right screen, divided by the Kamo River, is the area along Higashiyama, or Eastern Hills, seen from the west. The view includes Toyokuni Jinja, which enshrines Toyotomi Hideyoshi, in the upper portion of panel one; the colossal Buddha Hall of Hōkōji, the focus of this screen, on panel two; Yasaka Jinja, or Gion Shrine, on panels three and four; Yoshidayama, a hillock in the northeastern part of the city, on panels five and six; and the Shinto sanctuary of Kamo Jinja on panel six. Two large bridges, Sanjō and Gojō Ōhashi, span the river. Town blocks stretch northward along the river's west bank, with floats and processions of the Gion Festival depicted along a main street. On panel six is the precinct of the Imperial Palace, only partially visible.

The left screen presents the western part of the city bordered by two rivers: the Horikawa, which runs north and south, is depicted at the bottom; the Ōigawa, which meanders southward to become the Katsura River, is on panels four and five. The port town of Yodo, where the Katsura River ends and the Yodo River begins its flow southwest toward Osaka, is depicted on panel six. The focus of this screen is Nijō Castle, completed shortly after 1603, the Kyoto headquarters for the garrisons of the shogun Tokugawa Ieyasu. From its gate issues a procession, observed by warriors along its path, which has been interpreted to be the procession of Kazuko, the daughter of the second shogun, Tokugawa Hidetada, on her way to the Imperial Pal-

ace to wed the emperor Go-Mizunoo, which took place on the eighteenth day of the sixth month of 1620.   YS

116 **Amusements at Higashiyama**
pair of six-fold screens, ink, color and gold leaf on paper
each 84.0 x 276.0
Edo period, 17th century

Kōzu Kobunka Kaikan, Kyoto

Higashiyama, the eastern section of Kyoto, remains today a popular spot for visitors on pleasure trips and pilgrims to the shrines and temples. This small-scale continuous composition gives the viewer a miniaturized look into various scenes in the Higashiyama area, focusing on spring cherry-blossom viewing. Unlike many other Higashiyama compositions, in this version the Yasaka Jinja appears on the left-hand screen, with the temple of Kiyomizu on the right-hand screen at the very top. Between these two stretches a long avenue filled with travelers and merrymakers. Vendors of food and various wares throng the road. Interesting scenes include the banquet being held under the cherry trees at the far right, where dancers perform. In the left screen groups of women stroll in colorful kimono, while nearby samurai admire them.

Because among the figures in these screens warriors predominate, it is believed to have been commissioned by a daimyo. In the left screen, members of the warrior class rest in tearooms outside the shrine's gate. Some warriors engaged in archery practice are shown in the middle of the right screen. The lively style of the figures and the lavish use of color suggest that it is a work of the Kano school. Brilliant green, red, blue, and yellow pigments enhance a beautifully decorative surface dominated by gold. The clouds that weave in and out of the trees are first patterned

in relief with *gofun* and then painted over with gold. The richly textured result is in keeping with the extravagant tastes typical of the Momoyama period.   MR

117 **Matsushima**
pair of eight-fold screens; ink, color, gold, and gold leaf on paper
each 185.0 x 488.6 (72 7/8 x 192 3/8)
Edo period, late 17th century

Fukuoka Art Museum, Fukuoka Prefecture

Transmitted in the Kuroda family of Fukuoka, the daimyo of a domain in northern Kyushu, these screens depict the scenic cove of Matsushima, a part of Sendai Bay on the Pacific coast of today's Miyagi Prefecture in northern Honshū. The bay at Matsushima, with its widest span of a little over ten kilometers (eight miles), is a *meisho* ("famous place" or "place with a name") of long standing in Japanese history. It attained national prominence in the Edo period as one of the three most beautiful sites of Japan (*Nihon sankei*); the two others are Amanohashidate on the Japan Sea coast, and Itsukushima, renowned for a Shinto shrine of the same name, on the Inland Sea. Visiting Matsushima in the fifth month of 1689 on his famous journey to the north, poet Matsuo Bashō (1644–1694) remarked that Matsushima was the most beautiful spot in Japan, comparable to Dongting Lake and West Lake of China, and that its churning waves at high tide were as dramatic as the Hangzhou bore on the Qiantang River.

The sheer geographic wonder of the site alone invites awe. Over 260 fantastically shaped rocky islets, large and small and crowned with pine trees, are scattered around the cove. (Matsushima means "pine islands.") The scenes represented in these screens are viewed from the ocean side. The focus of the right screen is the

117

precinct of the Rinzai Zen monastery of Zuiganji, located behind the town of Matsushima that lies in the center of the arc of the shore. One of the Main Provincial Monasteries (*shosan*), Zuiganji was restored in 1604 under the patronage of an enlightened local daimyo, Date Masamune (1567–1636), lord of the domain of Sendai. In the left screen the focus is the precinct of the local Shinto sanctuary of Shiogama Jinja, which enshrines a salt deity, and the nearby fishing town of Shiogama at the south end of the shore. Shiogama literally means saltpan; in the yard of one of the houses, four saltpans are prominently displayed. The two screens together thus take in the whole view of the shore of Matsushima, from northeast to southwest.

The water of the bay is painted in deep blue, and the schematic mists that float over it are rendered in gold and sprinkled with flakes of gold leaf. The view contains as many boats, as islets: cargo ships and fishing boats with full sails are returning to the shore; others, like the large pleasure boats, are moving out to sea. There is a veritable regatta of ships, barges, boats, dinghies, and skiffs, the details of which are startlingly exact. Places on shore and islets in the bay, as well as sites of local shrines and temple buildings, are identified and named individually by some eighty small rectangular paper cartouches pasted directly on the panels.

The depiction of the towns of Matsushima and Shiogama is not unlike those in cats. 115 and 118, representing microcosms of urban human activities in all their specificity. Technically and stylistically, the painting represents the combined traditions of *yamato-e* of the Tosa school, in its coloring and miniature de-

tails, with elastic distortion of the rock forms and expressive brush lines that contour the islets. This ink-painting style is likely to have been inspired by Sesson Shūkei (c. 1504–1589) who was active in northern Japan one hundred years earlier. What is new in this late-seventeenth-century work is the merging of genre scenes with views of actual topography—an approach totally different from the more abstract and conceptual views of Matsushima painted by Sōtatsu (fl. 1602–1639) and his later follower Ogata Kōrin (1658–1716).   YS

118 **Scenes of Edo**
ink, color, and gold leaf on paper
two six-panel screens, each 162.5 x 344.0 (64 x 135²/₅)
Edo period, after 1641

National Museum of Japanese History, Chiba Prefecture

This pair of six-fold screens illustrates selected aspects of the city of Edo (present-day Tokyo) in the mid-seventeenth century. Visual weight is overwhelmingly given to the architectural symbols and leisure-time activities of Iemitsu (1604–1651), the third Tokugawa shogun. The six panels of the left-hand screen present a relatively contiguous panorama of the city, from a high vantage point to the east, facing west; occasionally, more distant views, such as that of Mount Fuji in the upper left corner, are included. The three left-hand panels of the right screen, seen from a high western vantage point turned toward the east, continue this broad sweep of the city. The three panels at the right, though, clearly break with the continuous view and incorporate scenes of the northern outskirts of Edo.

Architectural elements reflect the Tokugawa hegemony. The focal point of the screens is Edo Castle, on the two right-hand panels of the left-hand screen, consisting of a multi-storied donjon and numerous subsidiary buildings encircled by two moats. The castle is flanked by two great temple complexes, both prominent Buddhist institutions closely associated with the *bakufu*, Zōjōji on the left-hand screen, and Kan'eiji on the right-hand screen. Directly above Edo Castle are the residences of the *gosanke*, the three Tokugawa branch families from the provinces of Owari, Mito, and Kii. Across the moat from the castle are daimyo residences built under the *sankin kōtai* system. Iemitsu formalized the system in 1634, requiring daimyo to maintain a domicile in Edo and alternate a period of residence in their domains with a period in Edo; their families lived continuously in Edo as hostages. Cartouches identify the various residences, including those of the Matsudaira, Ii, and Nabeshima families.

Iemitsu is known to have loved hunting and military events, many of which are depicted in the screens. A boar hunt can be seen on the right-hand screen, and to its right, a scene of *muchi uchi*, in which warriors do battle with bamboo weapons. Iemitsu seems to be present as a spectator in many of these scenes, though his face is not shown. Below Mt. Fuji on the left-hand screen is another scene of *muchi uchi*. A red chair, facing away from the viewer and surrounded by retainers carrying lances, is most certainly that of the shogun. A passage at the top of the adjoining panel illustrates a scene of pheasant hunting, and seated at the most advantageous viewing point is a figure, probably Iemitsu, surrounded by retainers; his feet

are spread imperiously apart and he is shielded by a red umbrella. The burgeoning merchant class, though not completely ignored, is of relatively minor importance in this painting.

Almost five thousand figures appear in this set of screens and, not surprisingly, the artist has employed a formulaic approach in drawing their individual features. Nonetheless, their movements are skillfully rendered. Meandering, stylized gold clouds form a low relief frame around the individual scenes, helping to define each one while simultaneously unifying them and linking them to Edo Castle, the center from which they radiate. Embedded within the gold clouds are roundels filled with butterflies in low relief, in pairs and singly. As this was a crest used by many daimyo during this period, it may have been an indication of the status of the patron of these screens.

The date of the screens probably is no earlier than 1641, when the Shiba Tōshōgū (the red-roofed building in the upper-right corner of the Zōjōji temple complex) was built. The precise dating is still a matter of debate.   AMW

119 Seven Sages of the Bamboo Grove
Unkoku Tōgan (1547–1618)
pair of six-fold screens; ink and slight color on paper
each 156.3 x 359.6 (61½ x 141½)
Momoyama period, late 16th century

Eisei Bunko, Tokyo

A mountain landscape setting links this pair of screens of seven Chinese scholars engaged in a variety of activities. In the right screen an empty valley separates the foreground terrain from a distant rocky

hill topped by sparse trees. In the fifth panel of the right-hand screen the moon (or sun?) rises in a darkened sky. In the foreground of the second panel of two men under gnarled pine trees discuss a handscroll held by the man on the right. In the sixth panel, another man with a cane followed by two young attendants walks past a bamboo grove.

In the left screen two men converse in front of a stone bridge over a mountain brook. On the other side a twisting tree extends like a canopy from a huge precipice. Beneath the cliff is a rustic retreat with a thatched roof, its finial visible through a large, pitted hole in the rock. Inside the hut, two men sitting at a Chinese chess table are distracted by a waterfall in the background. An attendant sits outside the hut, his back turned toward the two scholars. The artist's square intaglio seal, *Tōgan*, is stamped on the upper outer edge of each screen.

The screens represent the Seven Sages of the Bamboo Grove, a semilegendary group of Chinese scholars (Shan Tao, Ji (or Xi) Kang, Yuan Ji, Wang Rong, Liu Ling, Yuan Xian, and Xiang Xiu) who periodically retreated from the mundane world to the seclusion of a bamboo grove during the political and military tumult of the mid-third century. There the sages freely pursued a life of reclusion, drinking wine, listening to *qin* (Chinese zither), and holding *qing tan* ("pure talk," that is, philosophical discussions). They also danced, sang, and disported themelves as the spirit moved them. The idea of the gentleman-scholar retreating to the wild to enjoy a respite from Confucian decorum and the constraints of duty, and then returning to duty, refreshed in spirit, formed an almost archetypal theme in Chinese art. It had appeared as early as the mid-fifth century

AD on the tiled walls of a tomb interior. In Japan the story apparently was known by the eighth century, since it is referred to in a poem in the *Man'yōshū* anthology. The subject was familiar to erudite courtiers of the Heian period, and became a theme for painters during the Muromachi period. An early example of a painting of the Seven Sages is the now-lost hanging scroll by Gakuō Zōkyū (fl. c. 1482–1515). During the second half of the sixteenth century, artists such as Kaihō Yūshō (1533–1615) and Hasegawa Tōhaku (1539–1610) in Kyoto, Keison (dates unknown) in Kamakura, and Sesson Shūkei (c. 1504–c. 1589) in northeastern Japan began to paint monumental sliding door panels and screens with this subject.

Unkoku Tōgan (cat. 108) painted the Seven Sages of the Bamboo Grove on sliding door panels at the Ōbaiin subtemple of Daitokuji monastery. The dates of these panels are now thought to be c. 1595–1596. At Ōbaiin the figures are considerably more monumental and the landscape setting eliminated. On the reverse of the Ōbaiin panels, however, Tōgan painted a panoramic landscape that is stylistically more developed than the landscape in the Eisei Bunko screens. Here the figures are situated in a carefully depicted landscape setting, and the rocks and tree forms are crisply contoured and given texture dabs in an orderly manner. The artist is self-consciously formulizing the brushwork modes that originated in the works of Sesshū Tōyō (1420–1506). It may be assumed that Tōgan executed these screens earlier than the Ōbaiin sliding door panels.   YS

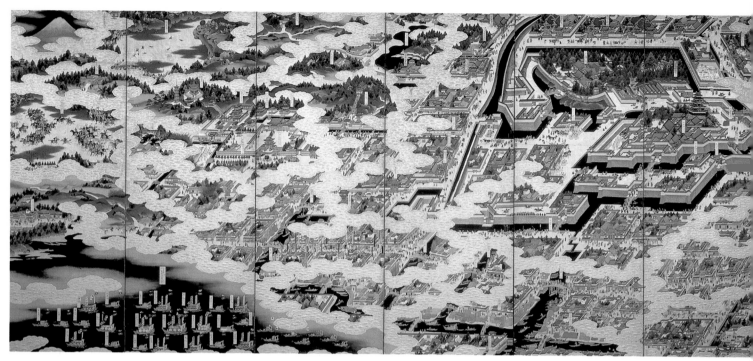

118

119

193

120

121

122

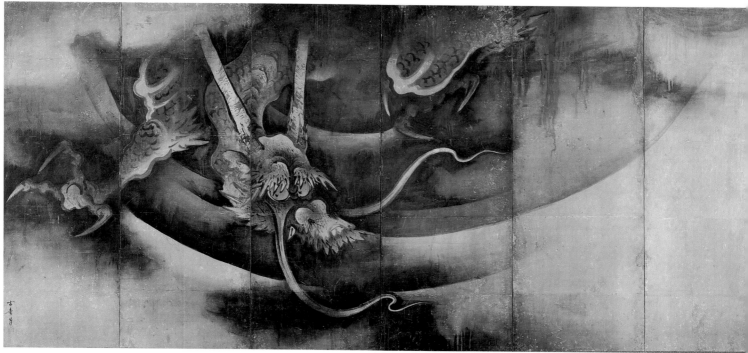

123

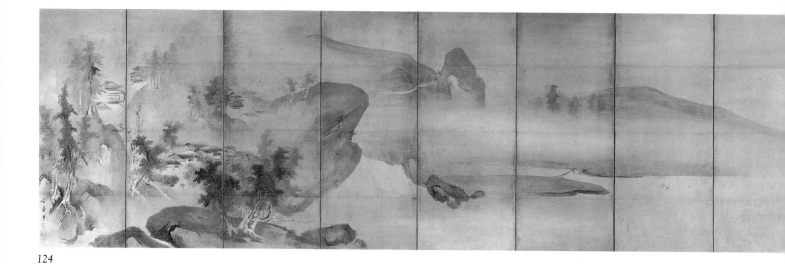

124

120 Flowers and Birds of the Four Seasons
Studio of Kano Motonobu (1476–1559)
pair of six-fold screens; ink, color, and gold leaf on paper
each 158.2 x 355.6 (62¼ x 140)
Muromachi period, first half of 16th century

Agency for Cultural Affairs, Tokyo

This extraordinary pair of screens in gold and colors represents flowers, birds, and insects of the four seasons. Set in a languorously spreading space, their world takes the form of an idealized garden—a paradise—sprawling from right to left. Although the two screens are not continuous, seasonal progression is indicated. Spring and summer flowers dominate the right screen, while autumn and winter flowers are depicted on the left screen. The cascade feeding into the pond is associated with spring and summer, while the snow-capped mounds announce winter. An encyclopedic array of some twenty-four different flowers and grasses and thirty-one birds native to Japan populates this garden, which is more like a man-made palace garden or the interior of an aviary than a natural landscape.

The screens are known as *kinbyōbu*, or "gold screens," a term that was in currency from around 1440. Decorative in function, these screens were in great demand in Japan, and they were exported to Ming China in the sixteenth century. They were also used by the shogunal family at funeral services because of the paradisal associations evoked by them.

This work is executed in *yamato-e*, the indigenous mode of painting characterized by details rendered in opaque colors and conceptualized forms. But there are features of the Chinese *kanga* mode of painting, as in the descriptive forms of flowers and tactile shapes of the rocks placed in the outer lower corners of the screens. The combined style of *yamato-e* and *kanga* is a specialty of Kano Motonobu and his studio. A recent study has firmly attributed this work to Motonobu's studio and dated it to the first half of the sixteenth century. It is a precursor of the Imperial Household screens from the late sixteenth century (cat. 122). YS

121 Pine and cherry trees
sliding door panels, ink, color and gold leaf on paper
each 184.0 x 138.0 (72½ x 54⅜)
Momoyama period, c. 1615

Myōrenji, Kyoto
Important Cultural Property

Cherry trees blossoming deep in the mountains, unknown to anyone, and pine trees are heavily painted on a gold background. The style employed to describe the rocks and trees indicates that this is the work of an artist of the school founded by Hasegawa Tōhaku (1539–1610).

The bold composition, with branches extending beyond the frames of the four sliding door panels, would suggest that this work dates from the mid-Momoyama period. The history of Myōrenji indicates that the painting may be properly placed toward the end of the period, though. The temple was moved to its present location in 1587, and rebuilt during the Keichō era (1596–1615), with construction completed in the fifth month of 1615. These paintings probably date from the time of the Keichō reconstruction, probably around 1615, when the generation of younger artists who succeeded Tōhaku were active. MS

122 Autumn flowers and grasses
attributed to Kano Eitoku (1543–1590)
pair of two-fold screens; ink, color, and gold leaf on paper
each 175.0 x 198.4 (70 x 79⅜)
Momoyama period, 16th century

Imperial Household Collection

This set of screens originally formed part of a series of sliding-door panels on the theme of autumn flowers and grasses or flowers of the four seasons. The screens, probably owned by the Hachijō no Miya family, are not contiguous, indicating that they were not adjoining in the original sequence of panels.

In the center of the right screen rise tall blades of pampas grass, chrysanthemums, *fujibakama* (purple trousers), and bellflowers. The weathered rocks typical of Kano painting are at the bottom, and at the top, a glimpse of distant mountains through the clouds. On the left screen are more rocks, a range of distant hills, and chrysanthemums and ivy turning red in the autumn chill. Beyond the hills are distant snow-covered peaks.

Although this painting has traditionally been attributed to Kano Eitoku, written evidence documenting the making of new sliding door paintings for the reconstruction of the Hachijō no Miya residence in 1599 suggests that the artist might have been Eitoku's younger brother, Sōshū (1551–1601). The gold clouds and gold ground and the elegance of the composition are typical of Sōshū's manner. In terms of technique and style, however, an argument can be made for attributing the paintings to Eitoku's son Mitsunobu (c. 1565–1608). AY

123 Dragons and clouds
  pair of six-fold screens, ink on paper
  Kaihō Yūshō (1533–1615)
  each 149.5 x 337.5 (58⁷/₈ x 132⁴/₅)
  Momoyama period,
  late 16th–early 17th century

  Kitano Tenmangū, Kyoto
  Important Cultural Property

In East Asian art, dragons often appear as
protectors of Buddhism or as rain deities.
In this painting, however, the dragon is a
symbol of heroic kingship, embodying the
spirit of the Momoyama period. In contrast to Chinese dragon paintings, these
dragons are a trifle antic as well as awesome.

 Typically in East Asia, the dragon was
paired with the tiger as cosmological symbols of East and West, water and metal, respectively. On a pair of paintings in
Daitokuji by the Song painter Muqi is
the inscription, *When the dragon rises,
clouds appear* and *When the tiger roars,
wind blasts*. In the Daitokuji paintings the
dragon coaxing the rain from the clouds
and the tiger calling forth the wind form a
metaphor for the enlightened emperor
seeking an equally enlightened minister.

 Kaihō Yūshō also executed a pair of
paintings with the dragon and tiger,
though he more often depicted a pair of
dragons, as seen here.   MS

124 Landscape of the Four Seasons
  Kaihō Yūshō (1533–1615)
  pair of eight-fold screens, ink and
  color on paper
  each 111.0 x 368.0 (44¹/₂ x 147¹/₄)
  Momoyama period, early 17th century

  Sekai Kyūseikyō (MOA Art Museum),
  Shizuoka Prefecture
  Important Cultural Property

Kaihō Yūshō was born in Ōmi Province
(present-day Shiga Prefecture), where his

father was a retainer for Asai Nagamasa
(1545–1573), the last great daimyo of the
Asai family. As a child Yūshō was sent to
live at Tōfukuji, an important Zen temple
in Kyoto. He later became a lay priest and
served the abbot of the temple. Yūshō's
talent as a painter was recognized by the
priests at Tōfukuji, who encouraged him
to study the painting of Kano Motonobu
(1476–1559). Later Yūshō turned to the
works of Chinese monochrome ink painters of the Song and Yuan dynasties, particularly that of Liang Kai (fl. c. 1195–c. 1224).
After mastering the techniques of monochrome ink painting he began also to paint
in the highly colored, lavish Momoyama
decorative style, and eventually achieved
an interesting synthesis of various styles.
Among his patrons were Toyotomi Hideyoshi (1537–1598) and Emperor Go-Yōzei
(1571–1617). His most famous paintings are
the large-scale works at Kenninji and the
screens at Myōshinji.

 Yūshō's residency at Tōfukuji was fortuitous, not just for the opportunity to
study painting, but because he was not required to participate in the fighting between the Asai clan and Oda Nobunaga,
which led to Nagamasa's suicide at Odani
Castle in 1573, following his defeat.

 This work follows the compositional
conventions of Muromachi-period screen
paintings, characterized by the concentra-
tion of the foreground mass at the far sides
of the screens. The center is an open expanse of water and mist. The painting is
Yūshō's interpretation of scenes from the
famous Chinese poetic theme, *Eight
Views of the Xiao and Xiang Rivers*. This
combination of poetic themes with seasonal allusions was a popular device in Japanese screen painting. Two scenes from
the *Eight Views* are the *Mountain Market*
scene on the left screen, and the *Wild
Geese Descending onto a Sandbar*, faintly
visible to the left of the right screen. Sea-

sonal allusions include the plum blossoms
of early spring and distant snowy mountains. Such close juxtaposition of different
seasons was commonly found in landscape
paintings. Yūshō created patterns by contrasting areas of dark and light with generous ink washes. The high level of skill and
sense of unity in this work suggest that it is
a later work by Yūshō.   MR

125 Pine and hawk
  Kano Tan'yū (1602–1674)
  set of four sliding doors; ink, color, and
  gold leaf on paper
  each 207.0 x 159.5 (81¹/₂ x 62³/₄)
  Edo period, 1626

  Kyoto City
  Important Cultural Property

This set of four sliding doors is from the
Fourth Chamber of the building that contains the *Ōhiroma* (Audience Room) of the
Ninomaru Palace precinct at Kyoto's Nijō
Castle. The interior measures about
twenty-one feet wide, forty feet long, and
thirteen and a half feet high. The chamber
was used as the guards' quarters, next to
the audience room proper, the most formal room of Nijō Castle, and is thus also
known as *Yari no ma* (Chamber of the
Lances). It is enclosed by sliding doors,
intercolumnar wall panels, and friezes
above, all gold-leafed and decorated with
paintings of massive pine trees and hawks.
The four panels shown here, with a design
of a monumental pine tree and a hawk in
front of a waterfall, were installed at the
south end of the chamber, facing north.

 Nijō Castle was begun in 1601 and
completed in 1603. It was originally built as
the garrison quarters for Tokugawa Ieyasu
(1543–1616), the first Tokugawa shogun,
who used it during his residency in Kyoto.
After Ieyasu's death in 1616 the buildings
went through several rebuilding and refurbishing phases, the most notable being a

125

1624 rebuilding campaign in preparation for the 1626 visit of Emperor Go-Mizunoo (1596–1680; cat. 19). The Ninomaru Palace dates from this period. Thereafter much of Nijō Castle was extensively renovated; and in the course of this work some buildings were removed from the site.

The interiors of the Ninomaru Palace precinct, consisting of three architectural blocks, were decorated in 1626 by a team of painters of the Kano school, headed by the twenty-four-year-old Kano Tan'yū (1602–1674). Over the years, the paintings have been damaged and extensively repainted, especially in their details, but the overall composition has retained the style of the young Tan'yū, who was inspired by the heroically monumental style associated with his grandfather Kano Eitoku (1543–1590).

At the age of ten, accompanied by his father, Kano Takanobu (1571–1618; cat. 18), the talented Tan'yū was granted an audience with shogun Tokugawa Ieyasu at Sunpu (currently Shizuoka City) in 1612. This event signalled the advent of the Kano school's monopoly over official painting commissions from the shogunate as well as the imperial court, and including the daimyo. Five years later, in 1617, at age

fifteen, Tan'yū was appointed painter-in-service to the Tokugawa shogunate (goyō eshi) in Edo. In 1619, assisting his cousin Kano Sadanobu, Tan'yū played a leading role in the decoration of the newly refurbished Empress' Quarters at the Imperial Palace in Kyoto. Two years later Tan'yū was given a sizeable tract of land in the Kajibashi district in Edo (present-day Tokyo), which became his home and studio. In 1623, at age twenty-one, he began the decoration of the sliding doors at Osaka Castle. The Ninomaru decoration campaign followed soon after, from 1624 to 1626, and marked the beginning of Tan'yū's rise to preeminence among mid-seventeenth-century Japanese painters.

The commanding form of the pine tree and the hawk, symbol of endurance, fortitude, and martial prowess (cats. 95, 129), may be a pictorial expression of the political power at the top of the social hierarchy, proclaiming the new era of Japan that had just been inaugurated under the effective rule of the shogunate and the daimyo.   YS

126 **Exemplary emperors**
Kano Tan'yū (1602–1674)
set of four sliding door panels; ink, color, and gold-leaf on paper
each 192.0 x 140.5 (75⅝ x 55¼)
Edo period, 1634

Nagoya City, Aichi Prefecture
Important Cultural Property

This set of four sliding door panels originally was installed in the Jōrakuden or "Guest house" built in 1634 as an annex to the main complex of Nagoya Castle, the headquarters of the Matsudaira, the daimyo of Owari Province (now Aichi Prefecture) and a branch family of the Tokugawa. The construction of the Jōrakuden (literally "building for a journey to the capital") started in the fifth month of 1633 and continued through the first six months of 1634. The intention was to provide lodging for the third Tokugawa shogun, Iemitsu (1604–1651), and his entourage on their trip to Kyoto in the seventh month of that year. Along with numerous other buildings that constituted the Nagoya Castle complex, the Jōrakuden survived well into the twentieth century. On 14 May 1945, the entire castle structure, including more

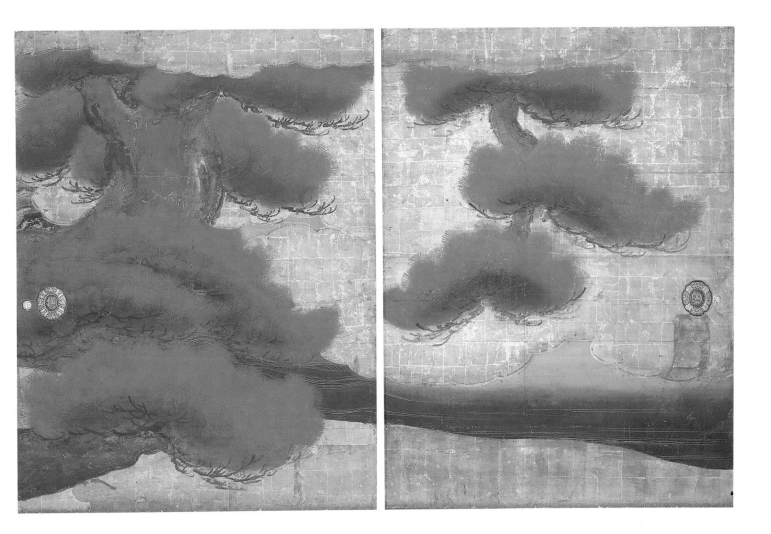

than 144 painted doors and wall paintings, was destroyed by aerial bombardment. More than 662 moveable sliding door paintings, painted wooden doors, and ceiling panels had previously been evacuated, and thus escaped destruction. The doors shown here originally were installed in a southwestern room, the First Chamber (*Ichi no ma*), of the Jōrakuden, as part of a sequence painted by Kano Tan'yū (1602–1674; illustrating a Chinese theme, *Exemplary Emperors* (*Teikan*, or literally "Mirrors of Emperors"). These panels were on the east side of the chamber, facing west.

The theme of the Exemplary Emperors, with its characteristic Confucian, didactic overtone, was introduced from China sometime during the third quarter of the sixteenth century through a woodblock-printed book, *Illustrated tales of Exemplary Emperors (Di jian tu shuo)*, compiled in 1572 and presented to the Wan Li emperor (r. 1573–1620) in the following year by Zhang Juzheng (1525–1582), a scholar and senior Grand Secretary of the Ming court. It contained a total of 117 illustrated didactic tales, of which 81 depicted the good deeds and the remaining 36 the

bad deeds of Chinese emperors. Through the efforts of Toyotomi Hideyori (1593–1615), a son of Hideyoshi (1537–1598), a Japanese edition appeared in 1606. Painters began to take up the theme, basing their compositions on the printed versions. Kano Sanraku's (1559–1635) ink paintings pasted onto a pair of six-fold screens (private collection, Japan) are the earliest extant Japanese example of painted translations of the Exemplary Emperors theme.

The sliding doors shown here illustrate the Han-Dynasty Emperor Xuan Di (r. 73–49 BC) generously rewarding provincial civil magistrates, so that they would be encouraged to stay on in their posts and effectively and benevolently administer the affairs of the populace. The emperor, seated on the throne, entertains two kneeling magistrates by offering food on large plates carried by chamberlains. Apart from the red throne and the green robes of three figures—the emperor, one of the chamberlains, and one of the magistrates—the overall monochromatic composition contrasts with the extensive application of gold flakes and paint used to produce an atmospheric effect. The surging pine tree, the bulky rock at the lower

right, and the evocative landscape at the left are executed in Tan'yū's typical ink painting style. Tan'yū was thirty-two years old when he executed this work, some seven years after his work at Nijō Castle (cat. 125). YS

127 **Bamboo grove, leopards, and a tiger**
set of four sliding door panels, ink, color, and gold leaf on paper
each 185.0 x 140.0
Edo period, c. 1614

Nagoya City, Aichi Prefecture
Important Cultural Property

The four sliding door panels shown here once separated two chambers of the formal *omote shoin* nucleus of the main building (*honmaru*) of Nagoya Castle, one on the west side, the other on the east side facing the entrance (*genkan*). The *honmaru* was built for a branch family of the Tokugawa, the Matsudaira of Owari Province (now Aichi Prefecture). It was completed in 1614. Its interior decoration included more than one thousand paintings mounted on the walls and on sliding doors. In 1945 the Nagoya Castle complex was destroyed by aerial bombing. Fortu-

126

nately, the movable paintings such as the sliding doors had been evacuated, and 662 works survived the bombing. All are registered as Important Cultural Properties. The First Room (*ichinoma*) and the Second Room (*ninoma*) were decorated with twenty paintings of tigers, leopards, and bamboo on gold-leaf grounds mounted on the sliding doors and intercolumnar walls. This set of paintings is from the smaller *ichinoma* and is among the eighteen extant works from those rooms.

Two different hands are identifiable in the two rooms. The artist of the *ichinoma* is the more experienced of the two, possibly Kano Kōi (d. 1636). He was the mentor of the much younger but more famous Kano Tan'yū (1602–1674), to whom is ascribed a set of twenty sliding door panels of tigers, leopards, and bamboo in the smaller residential quarters at Nanzenji, executed around 1637 or 1638. The style of the Nanzenji sliding doors compares closely to that of this set, and thus its attribution to Kōi may be accepted. The artist of the *ninoma* remains unidentified.

The theme of the tiger, often paired with the dragon, appeared in ink paintings throughout the Muromachi period. Although the theme was Chinese and Daoist in origin—the forces that cause clouds and winds to rise—the Japanese fascination with the subject was largely inspired by the famous *Tiger* paired with the *Dragon* by the Chinese painter Muqi of the late Southern Song, once in the shogunal collection. In the sixteenth century a Kano school painter, perhaps Shōei (1519–1592), made a monumental ink painting of a tiger and a leopard to decorate the walls of chambers adjacent to the chapel at Jukōin, a subtemple of Daitokuji. To portray the animals against a gold-leaf ground in a large public space, was new in the seventeenth century. Here the tigers, and no less the leopards, are no longer an embodiment of the mysterious force of the universe that causes the wind to rise, but down-to-earth, tactile symbols of the warrior class. YS

128 **Reeds and geese**
Miyamoto Musashi (1584–1645)
pair of six-fold screens; ink on paper
each 155.5 x 361.5 (61¼ x 142⅜)
Edo period, after 1640

Eisei Bunko, Tokyo
Important Cultural Property

Unsigned and without the artist's seals, this pair of screens can be attributed to Miyamoto Musashi, or Niten, his artistic sobriquet. Musashi, perhaps the greatest swordsman of his time, was known for his invincible martial art using two swords. Born in Harima (part of today's Hyōgo Prefecture) in 1584 (or 1582), he was a youth during the turbulent years that saw warfare ravaging the countryside and the appearance of the military hegemons, including Toyotomi Hideyoshi and Tokugawa Ieyasu. In 1600 Musashi fought on the losing side of the Western Army at the Battle of Sekigahara (cat. 104) and became a masterless samurai, or *rōnin*. He spent the next thirty-seven years as a wanderer. He is said to have won over sixty duels during these peripatetic years, including

one in 1610 with Sasaki Kojirō, another famous swordsman, at Kokura, in northern Kyushu, the domain of the Hosokawa. In 1637 Musashi joined the Tokugawa garrisons to chastise the Christian daimyo of Shimabara, also in Kyushu. His art of the swords recognized, he was offered the position of sword instructor to serve Hosokawa Tadatoshi (1586–1641), son of Sansai and the daimyo of Kumamoto. This pair of screens, which has long been in the Hosokawa family, was reportedly commissioned by Tadatoshi, which may explain the absence of Musashi's signature or seals as a sign of humility.

Where Musashi studied painting is unknown. It is likely that he was self-taught, as were other warrior painters, such as Ashikaga Yoshimochi of the Muromachi period. Over twenty-five ink paintings of various subjects by Musashi exist, many of them stamped with his seals, including Bodhidharma and other Zen-inspired themes. This pair, by far the best work by Musashi, shows that he was directly inspired by the style of Kaihō Yūshō's (1533–1615) sliding-door panels at

Reitōin and Zengoan, subtemples of Kenninji in Kyoto, datable to the late sixteenth century. The stylistic affinity between Yūshō and Musashi is more than accidental: Yūshō was a warrior turned painter. The brushstrokes of Yūshō, and especially of Musashi, as in these screens, are charged with decisiveness, speed, and spontaneity not unlike the traces of a sword swung in space.   YS

129 Plum trees and pair of hawks

Soga Nichokuan (fl. mid-17th century)
pair of six-fold screens, ink and color on paper
156.2 x 363.0 (61½ x 143)
Edo period, mid-17th century

Takamori Shigeru Collection, Kumamoto Prefecture

Soga Nichokuan was the son of Soga Chokuan, an artist active during the Momoyama period in the port city of Sakai (south of present-day Osaka). Although Nichokuan's dates are unknown, there is evidence that he was active in 1656. The evidence is in the form of an inscription

by Takuan Sōhō (1573–1645), himself a painter and calligrapher of note as well as a Zen monk, written on folding screens listed in the nineteenth-century art historical reference book *Koga bikō*. There also exists a family lineage and history in the artist's own hand, now at Hōryūji.

Soga Chokuan specialized in paintings of chickens and even more of hawks, which were especially favored by military leaders in the Muromachi period. Chokuan's conservative style, characterized by formalized brushwork and hardened forms, satisfied this demand. Although Nichokuan carried on his father's subject matter and style, he eventually developed his own eccentric forms while absorbing the current style of Edo-period ink painting. The work shown here reflects this transformation.   WA

127

128

129

130

208

209

130 **Bush clover and deer**

attributed to Sakuma Sakyō
(1581–1657)
pair of four-fold screens; ink, color,
and gold leaf on paper
159 x 346.8 (62 ½ x 136 ½)
Edo period, 1628

Sendai City Museum,
Miyagi Prefecture
Important Art Object

This pair of four-fold screens is from a set
of twelve sliding door panels probably installed in a chamber of Wakabayashi Castle, completed in 1628, in southeastern
Sendai. The castle was built as a private
residence for Date Masamune (1567–1636),
daimyo of Sendai, so that he could spend
his later years in privacy, away from Sendai Castle where he administered affairs of
government. The panels, now remounted
as three folding screens, depict autumn
themes of chrysanthemums, bush clover,
and deer. (The chrysanthemum screen is
not included in the exhibition.)

    Opaque green, blue, and brown mo-
tifs are painted against a brilliant surface
of gold-leafed clouds, a longstanding stylistic feature of *yamato-e*. According to the
Date clan record, this work is attributed to
Sakuma Sakyō (1581–1657), formerly of
Kyoto, a leading artist of the clan's painting bureau (*edokoro*). While still in his
teens, Sakyō reportedly assisted the Kyoto
painter Kano Mitsunobu (1565–1608),
known for the wall and sliding door paintings that he executed in the richly colored
yamato-e style, and who worked at
Fushimi Castle from 1594 on. At that time
Date Masamune, then a vassal of Toyotomi Hideyoshi (1537–1598) and in 1596, a
supervisor of the castle construction, recognized Sakyō's talent.

    Very little is known about Sakyō and
other artists who worked under the patronage of seventeenth-century provincial
daimyo. The date when Sakyō entered
Masamune's employ is a matter of conjecture, but it could have been 1601 or 1602,
when Masamune was visiting Fushimi.
The Date clan document records that Sakyō was a member of a team of lacquer artists and builders employed for large-scale
refurbishing and reconstruction campaigns for the domain's public buildings.
Sakyō worked at Ōsaki Hachiman Jinja,
the Date clan shrine, in 1607; the Rinzai
Zen temple of Zuiganji at Matsushima
(cat. 117) in 1609; the Audience Hall at Sendai Castle in 1610; and Wakabayashi Castle
in 1628.

    Sakyō, also called Kano Sakyō, appar-
ently headed a workshop, though it had
far fewer members than the major schools
in Edo and Kyoto. The names of Sakyō's
son Gentoku, a disciple by the name of
Kurōta, and a certain Kano Sadakichi, are
recorded. Stylistically, while this painting

131

reflects the fashionable mode of Kano Mitsunobu's painting in Kyoto around 1600, the clarity of the composition and the open handling of space make Sakyō's work unique among seventeenth-century screens of the Edo period.

Date Masamune himself brushed the inscriptions in cursive writing on the panels. They are poems chosen from various poetic anthologies, including the *Kokinshū* and *Shin kokinshū*; two are Zen-related sayings, one by the Chinese scholar and poet Su Dongpo (1036–1101) on panel four of the right screen, the other at the top of panel three of the left screen, referring to an answer in verse form made by the great Chinese Chan (Zen) patriarch Maozu Daoyi (709–788) to a question put to him by Layman Pang (c. 740–808). Selected translations follow:

[right screen, third panel]
O cord of life!
Threading through the jewel of my soul,
If you will break, break now:
I shall weaken if this life continues,
Unable to bear such fearful strain
(translated in Brower and Miner 1975, 301).

[right screen, fourth panel]
Not a thing is;
it stores everything without limit;
there is a flower;
there is the moon;
there is a pavilion.

[left screen, second panel, top]
It is in winter
that a mountain hermitage
grows lonelier still,
for humans cease to visit
and grasses wither and die
(translated in McCullough 1985a, 77).

[left screen, third panel]
While you contemplate
swallowing the water of the West
in one gulp,
The river continues to flow East,
day and night,
without ceasing or waiting.   YS

131 **Mythological scene**
Kano Tan'yū (1602–1674)
hanging scroll; ink and color on paper
109.0 x 31.9 (42 7/8 x 12 1/2)
Edo period, after 1638

Tokyo National Museum

The title of this painting, *Ugayafukiaezu no Mikoto kōtanzu*, translates literally as "The picture of the birth scene of the Prince-cormorant-rush-thatch-unthatched." This long, dangling name, which first appears in a mythological narrative in *Kojiki* (Records of Ancient Matters, c. 712 AD) refers to the father of the now legendary first emperor of Japan, Jinmu Tennō. The narrative is about Hikohohodemi no Mikoto, who, having lost a fishhook he had borrowed from his brother, goes to the palace of the sea in order to look for it. There he marries Toyotama no Mikoto, who is the princess of the sea god. When his return home is imminent, the princess asks Mikoto to build a hut on the beach, where she will be delivered on the day when the wind is rough and waves churn high. Mikoto had hardly completed thatching of the roof of the hut with cormorant feathers when the princess went into labor. The princess, turning into a serpent, is seen by Mikoto and then vanishes with the newborn wrapped in rushes. In the painting the infant is on the beach, and the stunned Mikoto, his back to the viewer, stands in front of the hut, whose roof is incompletely thatched.

A more elaborate narrative painting of this theme dating from the late twelfth century was in the collection of Tan'yū's patron, the third shogun, Tokugawa Iemitsu (1604–1651). A set of two handscrolls, originally owned by a Shinto shrine in Wakasa province (in present-day Fukui Prefecture), was presented to Iemitsu as a gift from Sakai Tadakatsu (1587–1662), the daimyo of Wakasa, but not before being copied by Kano Daigaku (fl. 1659), who, like Tan'yū, worked for the shogunate. Tan'yū must surely have seen the twelfth-century version or its copy by Daigaku, from which this synoptic version came into being. On the lower right is the artist's signature, *Tan'yū hōgen hitsu* (Brushed by Tan'yū, the Eye of the Law), followed by two of his seals: a large circular relief seal, *Hōgen Tan'yū*; and a small square relief seal, *Tan'yū*. The painting postdates 1638, when Tan'yū received the title "Eye of the Law." YS

132 **Hotei**
   Iwasa Katsumochi (1578–1650)
   hanging scroll; ink on paper
   101.3 x 33.6 (39 7/8 x 13 1/4)
   Edo period, c. 1624–1633
   Tokyo National Museum

A plump, grinning dwarf of a man carrying a cane and a bag is Hotei, an eccentric figure familiar in Zen Buddhism as a reincarnation of the Buddha Maitreya (cat. 80). In China and Japan, Hotei represents spiritual freedom from the conventions and rules of the world. Executed in pale ink and rendered in spontaneous brushwork, the figure stands against a neutral ground. On the lower right are stamped two seals: one a small square relief seal, *Dōun*; the other, a large circular relief seal, *Katsumochi*. The artist, Iwasa Katsumochi, is better known as Matabei.

Matabei was born into a warrior's family. His father, Araki Murashige, the castellan of Itami Castle in Settsu Prov-

ince (part of today's Osaka Prefecture), served Oda Nobunaga, against whom he later rebelled. The consequence of the rebellion was annihilation of the family by execution. Matabei, still an infant, was smuggled out by a wet nurse to escape the tragedy and was raised until he was about fifteen years old in Kyoto, reportedly under the protection of the Buddhist sanctuary of Honganji. He is said to have studied painting with Kano Naizen (1580–1616), an artist of considerable repute in genre painting, which was emerging as a major art form in Kyoto. Little is known about Matabei's life until he was forty years old, when, around 1617, he went to Echizen Province (Fukui Prefecture), where he was to remain for twenty years. He established a reputation as a versatile painter that reached as far as Kyoto. In 1637, he was summoned to Edo to produce trousseau articles for a daughter of the third Tokugawa shogun, Iemitsu. He died in Edo thirteen years later.

This painting was done during Matabei's mature years in Fukui, between about 1624 and 1633. The inscription by the Zen monk Zenshitsu Sōshū (1572–1640), at one time an abbot of Daitokuji, reads:

*Carrying a bag and a cane you appear
   even more enlightened;
Why do you beg with a grin on your mouth?
Instead of wandering, lost in the
   realm of the humans,
The better it will be the sooner
   you go back to the Tushita Heaven.*

YS

133 **Court ladies viewing chrysanthemums**
   Iwasa Katsumochi (1578–1650)
   hanging scroll; ink and slight color on paper
   132.0 x 55.0 (52 x 21 5/8)
   Edo period, c. 1623–1624
   Yamatane Art Museum, Tokyo
   Important Art Object

A warrior's son, the artist Iwasa Katsumochi, popularly known as Matabei (cats. 132, 134), spent twenty years between about 1617 and 1637 in Echizen (Fukui Prefecture), at the invitation of its ruler, Matsudaira Tadanao, a grandson of Tokugawa Ieyasu. Matabei, when he went to Fukui, must have already established a reputation as a major artist in Kyoto, where he had spent his earlier years. During his sojourn in Fukui, Matabei produced an enormous number of paintings, both of Japanese and Chinese subjects and in versatile styles.

This painting was originally pasted on a pair of six-fold screens, known as the *Kanaya byōbu*, along with eleven others of various themes and styles, and kept in the Kanaya family of Fukui. All the paintings

were subsequently removed and mounted as individual hanging scrolls, now dispersed in various collections. One of Matabei's seals in square intaglio, *Hekishōgūzu*, is stamped at the lower left. The box that holds this painting is accompanied by a transcript of an oral history of the *Kanaya byōbu*, which says that the screens were given to the wealthy Kanaya family of Fukui as a gift after about 1624 by Matsudaira Naomasa, a younger brother of Tadanao and the castellan of Ōno Castle in Echizen Province, as a token of gratitude for his childhood custody by the family. The painting accordingly can be dated to no later than 1624.

Executed in a disciplined mode of painting known as *hakubyō*, or plain drawing, which became fashionable as an archaistic mode within the conservative Tosa school from the late sixteenth century to the early decades of the seventeenth, the painting depicts a scene of elegant court ladies viewing chrysanthemums from the rear of their carriage. The exact narrative origin of the subject is yet unidentified. This work employs the tradition of *yamato-e* in its preoccupation with precision and refinement in rendition, markedly contrasting with Matabei's ink painting of Hotei (cat. 132). The oblong-shaped faces of the court ladies, with full cheeks, are a signature feature of Matabei's style, readily noticed in many of his works. YS

134 **Poet Saigyō viewing the moon**
   Iwasa Katsumochi (1578–1650)
   hanging scroll; ink on paper
   101.3 x 33.0 (39 7/8 x 13)
   Edo period, c. 1637
   Gunma Prefectural Museum of Modern Art, Gunma Prefecture

Saigyō (1118–1190) was a member of the aristocratic Fujiwara family with a promising career at court. In 1140, for reasons that are not clear, he gave up his successful life and took the tonsure, retiring to a humble hut in the outskirts of Kyoto and taking up the life of a recluse, wanderer, and poet. He traveled extensively around the country, going as far north as the province of Mutsu (part of today's Iwate Prefecture); Mount Yoshino and Mount Kumano are two of the many places that he celebrated in poems composed on site. Some ninety-four poems by Saigyō are included in the *Shin kokinshū*, the imperial anthology of *waka* compiled by Saigyō's younger contemporary, Fujiwara Teika.

In this painting by Iwasa Katsumochi, or Matabei (cats. 132, 133), the itinerant Saigyō, clad in monk's garb and holding a cane and a straw hat, is viewing the moon, half hidden by a cloud. The style of this painting differs from the *Hotei* (cat. 132) in its descriptive features. The contours and folds of the cassock worn by Saigyō are de-

133

134

scribed with deliberation, as is the book box he carries on his back. Executed in ink, the painting shows Matabei's stylistic versatility. At the lower left is a large circular relief seal of the artist, *Katsumochi*. This work can be dated stylistically to about 1637, when Matabei was still in Echizen (Fukui Prefecture), just before he set out on his journey to Edo. The inscription, assumed to be by Matabei, transcribes Saigyō's famous poem about viewing the moon:

"When we see the moon . . . " were our
*   parting words*
* on those future thoughts of each*
*   other;*
I wonder if the sleeves of those I left at
*   home*
* are wet with tears tonight.*

YS

135 Flowers and plants of the first, fifth, and ninth months
Yanagisawa Kien (1704–1758)
three hanging scrolls; ink and color on silk
each 99.0 x 41.0
Edo period, 18th century

Imperial Household Collection

Yanagisawa Kien, who served the clan that ruled the Kōriyama domain in Yamato Province (present-day Nara Prefecture), was known as a man of cultured pursuits and many talents. In particular, he excelled since his youth at painting flower-and-bird subjects. Unsatisfied with the works of the Kano school, he copied Yuan and Ming paintings and studied with Yoshida Shūsetsu of the Nagasaki school. His works generally combine descriptive drawing and rich colors, though he also executed finger paintings and monochrome ink paintings of bamboo. Along with Gion Nankai (1677–1751) and Sakaki Hyakusen (1697–1752), he is one of the pioneers of Japanese literati painting, or *bunjinga*.

The theme of this set of three scrolls, one of his finest works, is related to the first, fifth, and ninth months of the lunar calendar, considered to be months of misfortune. Traditionally, on the seventh day of the first month one ate a rice gruel with seven herbs for good health during the coming year. On the fifth day of the fifth month one hung a *kusudama* (medicine pouch) in one's home. On the ninth day of the ninth month one drank a special *sake* to avoid illness.

The painting for the first month depicts a footed hexagonal celadon vase ornamented with a floral scroll. A miniature plum tree and two other plants, known in Japanese as *fukujusō* (literally, "Long Life Plant," a kind of ranunculus often used as a New Year's decoration) and *shirabachi*, grow in the vase. The painting for the fifth

month represents a *kusudama*, suspended with a vermilion and gold rope, trailing threads of five different colors and festooned with blue irises, pink azaleas, white camellias, and morning glories. The painting for the ninth month shows a red woven basket containing Japanese pears, pomegranates, roses, and orchids. Each painting is inscribed with Kien's own Chinese poem, signed and sealed by the artist, conveying appropriate thoughts on the corresponding lunar month.

AY

136 Iris and knife
Satake Shozan (1748–1785)
hanging scroll; ink and color on silk
112.5 x 40.0 (44 1/4 x 15 3/4)
Edo period, 2nd half of 18th century

Private collection
Important Art Object

During the second half of the eighteenth century there was a renewed interest in the Western mode of image-making among the Japanese, not simply as an artistic practice, but also as a practical science. Inspiration came from books of anatomy, botany, medicine, and zoology, brought by the Dutch, from which *Rangaku* (Dutch studies) soon emerged as a new branch of learning. Sugita Genpaku (1733–1817) and Hiraga Gennai (1728–1779) were two of the champions of this new tradition: the former was a medical doctor serving the Obama clan (in today's Fukui Prefecture), who translated *Tafel Anatomia* (1734) and published the first Japanese book of anatomy; and the latter was a natural scientist and expert on herbal medicine. Genpaku's anatomy book, published in 1774, was illustrated by a student of Gennai, a samurai from the domain of Akita in northern Japan. Gennai himself was called to Akita in 1773 for a geological survey of the domain that produced copper, where he laid the foundation for *Akita ranga*, the school of Western-style painting based in Akita. The school flourished under the patronage of the daimyo of Akita, Satake Shozan, the artist of this painting. Shozan's theories on Western-style painting are contained in two treatises he wrote in 1778, *Gahō kōryō* (Summary of the laws of painting) and *Gato rikai* (Understanding paintings).

This painting is signed *Minamoto Yoshiatsu*, Shozan's personal name following the ancestral origin of his family, Minamoto. A circular relief seal below the signature is in the roman alphabet, *Zwarr Wit*.

YS

137 Studies of lizards, tortoises, and insects
Satake Shozan (1748–1785)
album; ink and color on paper
34.0 x 28.3 (13 3/8 x 11 1/8)
Edo period, 2nd half of 18th century

Private collection
Important Art Object

Two other similar albums are included in this collection, and all three were treasured by their creator, Satake Shozan (cat. 136). One album includes Shozan's 1778 treatises *Gahō kōryō* (Summary of the laws of painting) and *Gato rikai* (Understanding painting). Shozan wrote admiringly about western painting, explaining the laws of perspective, shading, and various pigments. He also included illustrations of painting techniques, foreign copper-plate prints, and floral studies. Another album contains studies of birds. The album exhibited here consists primarily of studies of insects.

In the album shown here, in addition to reptiles and amphibians, almost 300 types of insects are depicted, including caterpillars, butterflies, moths, and dragonflies. The drawings were not necessarily all executed by Shozan himself; on stylistic grounds, many of the works can be attributed to Shozan's retainer Odano Naotake (1749–1780), an artist trained in western-style painting.

In eighteenth-century Japan, interest in natural history was on the rise, and many albums of studies were produced. The studies in this album, however, were not drawn from live models. Almost half of the insects depicted are copied from collections of studies compiled by Hosokawa Shigekata, such as the one shown here, *Studies of Insects* (cat. 139); it is possible that other drawings in the album are also copied from other works.

Whether or not these studies are from life does not affect their value as art objects. Each is carefully drawn and conveys a fascination with the forms and substance of nature. At times, the artist seems to have attempted to make associations between disparate things; for example, the beehive illustrated here resembles some deep-sea fish. These studies differ from Shigekata's counterparts; for Shozan, the exterior forms are objects of fascination. The studies in Shozan's albums served as source material for his full-fledged western-style paintings and those of other artists in the Akita domain.

SY

214

玉
堂
頌
吉
一
年
之
連

斗
建
寅

嚴
昌
辰

洪
園
士

135

重
子
亥
之
日
云
云

誰
家
始
試
浥
塵
瓶

鄧
山
洪
園

九
月
九
日
望
鄉
臺
他
席

化
鄉
遥
容
杯
入
情
乞
顧

南
中
吉
鴻
雁
那
從
北
地

來

洪
園
客
僑
士

215

136

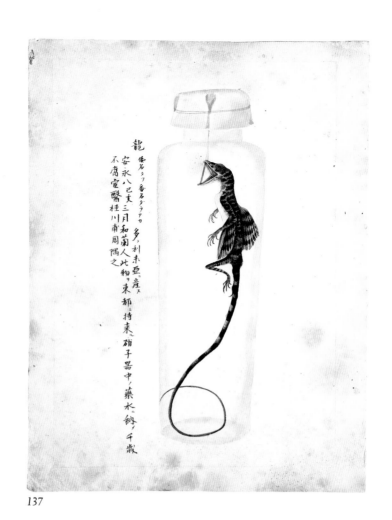

龍
番名タフ番名タラアカ
安永八己亥三月和蘭人此物ヲ東都ニ持来硝子器中ノ藥水ニ納ノ千歲
不腐宣醫桂川甫周隔之
多ノ利末亞産入

137

138

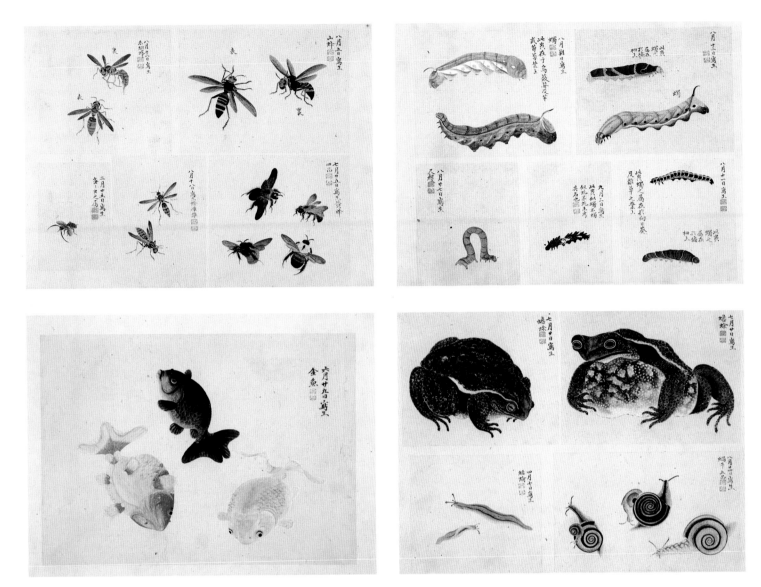

138

138 **Studies of insects, amphibians, and fish**
Masuyama Sessai (1754–1819)
four albums; ink and color on paper
each 21.8 x 29.9 (8 5/8 x 11 3/4)
Edo period, 1808

Tokyo National Museum

Contained in these four albums are pages of finished studies of insects, amphibians, fish, and other small creatures that inhabit the natural world, pages of which ten are illustrated here. These discerning studies were made by Masuyama Sessai, the artistic daimyo of the domain of Nagashima in Ise Province (part of Mie Prefecture). Each study is inscribed meticulously, recording the name of each species and where, when, and by whom it was collected. Some insects are viewed from three angles. The finished works are grouped and mounted according to the months in which they were collected, and the four albums are divided according to the four seasons, butterflies of the spring in album one; dragonflies of the summer in album two, and so forth.

Masuyama Sessai in his private life was a student of Chinese herbal medicine and a painter of considerable talent inspired by Chinese Ming and Qing paintings. He was interested in natural history, a field first explored by Hiraga Gennai (1728–1779), also a student of herbal medicine, and by Satake Shozan (cats. 136, 137), the daimyo of the domain of Akita in the north and one the harbingers of Western-style painting. Sessai was especially important as a patron of such artists as Kimura Kenkadō (1736–1802) and Kuwayama Gyokushū (1746–1799), who painted in the style of Chinese scholar-amateurs.   YS

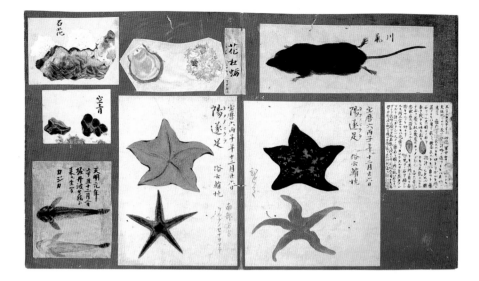

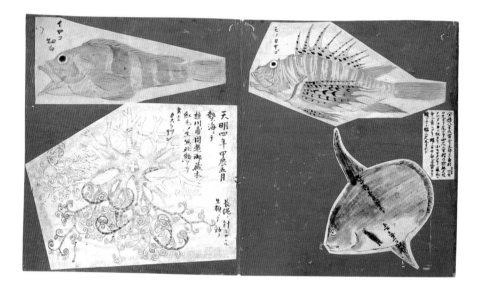

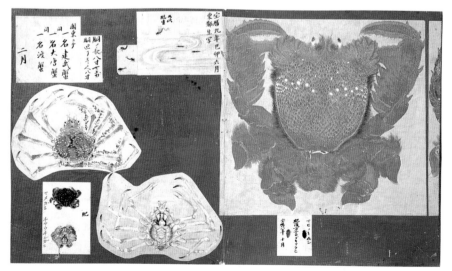

139

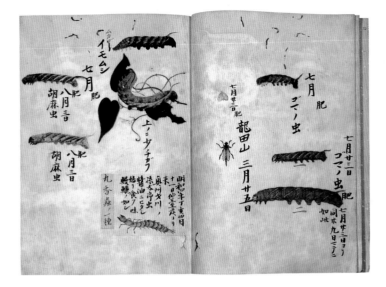

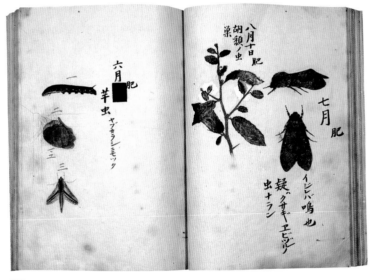

139

139 Studies of animals and insects
attributed to Hosokawa Shigekata
(1720–1785)
two albums; ink and color on paper
animal album 22.0 x 30.0 (8 5/8 x 11 3/4);
insect album 27.3 x 20.4 (10 3/4 x 8)
Edo period, 1756–1785

Eisei Bunko, Tokyo

Hosokawa Shigekata, an eighteenth-century daimyo of Higo Province (today's Kumamoto Prefecture), is credited with enlightened and humanitarian policies during his thirty-nine–year rule. In 1754 he established two schools within the Kumamoto Castle precinct, one for martial arts and one for Confucian studies. He abolished harsh corporal punishment for criminals and instituted a humane penal code. He founded a medical school and culti-

vated an herbal garden. In private life, he was a poet, calligrapher, and, in particular, an artist known for his carefully drawn studies of the natural world. Like his contemporaries Masuyama Sessai, daimyo of a domain in Ise (cat. 138), and Satake Shozan, daimyo of the Akita domain in northern Honshu (cats. 136, 137), Shigekata left albums of studies of animals, insects, and plants. Ten such albums are kept in the Eisei Bunko, two of which are shown in this exhibition.

The larger album contains studies of animal species. The illustrations have been cut from either a booklet or a handscroll and pasted on the album's leaves, which are dyed reddish brown with persimmon juice. Each work is accompanied by an inscription, either written directly on the work or on an attached piece of paper, identifying the species and giving the date and place where it was seen or

captured and sketched. These sketches were made between 1756 and 1785. Three leaves are illustrated here. Pages of the smaller album are filled with studies of insects, thirty-seven species in all, each showing different stages of growth.   YS

140

141

140 Album of assorted paintings

Sakai Hōitsu (1761–1828)
album; ink and color on silk or paper
each 25.1 x 20.0 (9 7/8 x 7 7/8)
Edo period, before 1797

Seikadō Bunko, Tokyo

This accordion-type album contains seventy-two individual paintings of various subjects, in different mediums on either silk or paper, mounted on both the front and back of the paper, thirty-six to each side. The covers are elaborately made, with the corners capped by a silver open-work design of pine, bamboo, and plum. In the center of the front cover is pasted a paper label that reads *Tekagami* (Mirrors of calligraphy), which usually designates model examples of calligraphy. The album, however, is a collection of paintings, and has been rightly called *zatsugachō*, or "album of assorted paintings," by the present owner. The paintings serve as a response by the artist Sakai Hōitsu to the various painting styles current in his time. Seven different seals are used throughout the album, and occasionally the artist's signature accompanies a seal. The seal *Tōkakuin' in* (seal of Tōkakuin) on the painting *Beetle and corn* illustrated here may give the earliest possible date to this group of paintings. Tōkakuin is an ecclesiastical title earned by Hōitsu when he took the tonsure in 1797, a date after which the art-

ist is likely to have selected the paintings to be assembled into the present album.

Hōitsu was born in Edo into the family of Sakai Tadamochi, the daimyo of Himeji Castle in Harima Province (today's Hyōgo Prefecture), whose ancestor Tadataka was the patron of Ogata Kōrin (1658–1716) in Edo. The various styles in this album reflect Hōitsu's artistic background. He was taught by Kano Takanobu (cat. 18); Utagawa Toyoharu (1735–1814), the *ukiyo-e* artist; and Sō Shiseki (1712–1786), the realist of the Nagasaki school in Edo. The historical significance of these works is evident in the nine paintings (four illustrated here) that emulate the style of Itō Jakuchū (1716–1800), a decorative naturalistic artist of Kyoto.

The album is contained in two boxes. On the back of the lid of the outer box is a dedicatory inscription, dated the third month, spring of the year corresponding to 1893, by Sakai Dōitsu (1845–1913), the fourth-generation head of Hōitsu's studio, Ukaan, and the son of Suzuki Kiitsu (1796–1858), the immediate pupil of Hōitsu. The back of the lid of the inner box is inscribed and signed by Hōitsu himself.   YS

141 Birds in fruit trees

Bian Wenjin (fl. 1403–1435)
pair of hanging scrolls; ink and color on silk
each 31.0 x 31.5 (12 1/4 x 12 3/8)
Ming, 1st quarter of 15th century

Eisei Bunko, Tokyo

In the Edo period small, intimate Chinese paintings executed in color, rather than large, imperious ones, were often used to decorate the *tokonoma*. This pair of small paintings of birds perched in fruit trees exemplify the taste.

Two seals are stamped on both paintings: one an unidentifiable square intaglio, and the other a square relief, *Bian Wenjin shi*. The signature *Daizhao Longxi Bian Jingzhao xie* (Painter in attendance Bian Jingzho of Longxi painted this) accompanies the two seals of the painting on the right. Jingzhao is a personal name of Bian Wenjin, a painter and a member of the Painting Academy of the Ming court, who, as a painter in attendance, served three emperors in succession. The style of calligraphy of the inscription is close to another, identically phrased inscription on a painting in a Japanese collection, which is widely accepted as a major work of Bian. The second seal, however, is different from the accepted version.

An outstanding naturalist painter in the Song academic style, Bian earned a

142

224

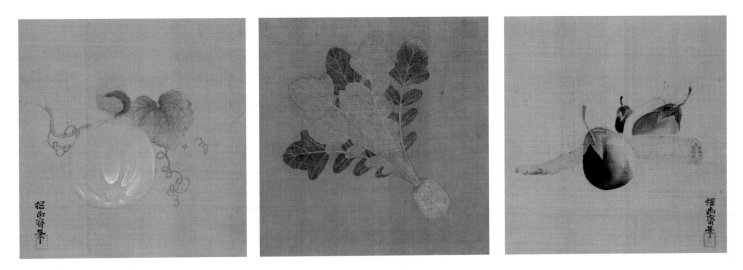

143

reputation for paintings of flowers, fruits, and birds that are as beautiful and charming as they are carefully detailed and lifelike. Bian is considered the last of the painters who followed the tradition of the Song academic style before the emergence of another academy painter, Lü Ji of the late fifteenth century-early sixteenth, whose monumental style is reflected in the triptych by Li Yihe in this exhibition (cat. 142).   YS

142 **Flowers and birds**
      Li Yihe (?)
      hanging scrolls, triptych; ink and color
      on silk
      each 128.1 x 62.5 (50 3/8 x 24 5/8)
      Ming, late 17th century (?)
      Eisei Bunko, Tokyo

This triptych, consisting of three large paintings of flowers and birds, has been transmitted since the eighteenth century in the Hosokawa daimyo family of Higo (today's Kumamoto Prefecture). It was painted by an elusive artist, Li Yihe of Shanhan (in Fujian Province), as signed on the upper left of the center scroll. Although Li Yihe is unrecorded in Chinese sources, he has been identified as either a Ming Dynasty Chinese painter or, as in the nineteenth-century Japanese art-historical source *Koga bikō*, as a Korean painter of the Yi Dynasty. Paintings bearing the signature of the artist have been known in Japan since the seventeenth century. The painter and connoisseur Kano Tan'yū (1602–1674) reportedly made a sketch of a painting by this artist.

In subject matter and general style, these paintings are related to the Chinese Ming academic tradition established by the court painter Lü Ji (fl. c. 1497 and after), whose influence in Japan can be seen in the screens of Sesshū Tōyō (1420–1506) of the late fifteenth century and Kano Motonobu (1476–1559) of the sixteenth century. Strictly, however, Li Yihe's paintings hardly reflect the kinesthetic contour lines or the tactile forms of the Lü Ji tradition. The forms are evenly flat, and the overall compositions more decorative. Monumental hanging scrolls of flowers and birds like this triptych would have graced the walls of a large alcove of a daimyo's residence in the eighteenth and nineteenth centuries.   YS

143 **Turnip**
      attributed to Hu Tinghui (fl. 1st
      quarter of 14th century)
      hanging scroll; ink and color on silk
      21.9 x 20.7 (8 5/8 x 8 1/8)
      Yuan, 14th century
      Ueyama Ikuichi collection, Nara
      Prefecture

Lotus root with eggplants/Melon
      Kano Tan'yū (1602–1674)
      pair of hanging scrolls; ink and color
      on silk
      each 21.9 x 20.7 (8 5/8 x 8 1/8)
      Edo period, after 1635
      Ueyama Ikuichi collection, Nara
      Prefecture

These three works form a triptych assembled by Kano Tan'yū, the artist of the two flanking paintings. The center painting, *Turnip,* is said to be by the Chinese artist Hu Tinghui, an early Yuan Dynasty painter. The square relief seal at the upper right cannot be identified; it may be a collector's seal. Hu Tinghui's works were among Chinese paintings in the Ashikaga shogunal collections, and were valued during both the Muromachi and Edo periods. During the latter period *Turnip* was known by another title, *Kyakurai ichimi* (Guest arrives, shares one taste), which comes from an inscription on a famous ink painting coveted by the Edo tea adepts entitled *Vegetable,* by the great Chinese artist Muqi (fl. mid-13th century).

Tan'yū's companion pieces are signed *Tan'yū sai,* the artistic sobriquet given him in 1635 by the Zen monk aesthete Kōgetsu Sōgan (1574–1643) of Daitokuji, followed by an oblong relief seal, *Tō* or *Fuji,* referring to the Fujiwara clan from which Tan'yū claimed his family descent. This triptych can thus be dated to after 1635. The triptych, an embellishment for tea, may have been formed during the 1640s when Tan'yū was deeply involved with tea adepts of Daitokuji such as Kōgetsu himself and the warrior aesthete Sakuma Sanekatsu (also known as Shōgen; 1570–1642), whose portrait, inscribed by Kōgetsu, was painted by Tan'yū around 1641 or 1642 (cat. 37).   YS

144

144 Western dogs

Sakai Hōitsu (1761–1828)
votive plaque, ink, color and gold leaf
on wood
118.5 x 148.7 (46⅝ x 58½)
Edo period, 1814

Sōjiji (Nishiarai Daishi), Tokyo

This *ema* (votive plaque) of two Western dogs is signed at the lower right, *Painted by Hōitsu Kishin*, followed by a round relief seal, *Bunsen*. Along the left edge is written, *An auspicious day in the third month of the eleventh year of Bunka; donor Yaoya Zenshirō*, recording that this plaque was offered to the temple in 1814 by Zenshirō, master of Yaozen, the renowned restaurant then in the Asakusa area of Edo (present-day Tokyo). Hōitsu often went to Yaozen and was a good friend of Zenshirō, who was born in the year of the dog. According to the zodiacal cycle, 1814 was the year of the dog, and to commemorate it, Zenshirō probably commissioned Hōitsu to paint this plaque. Another work by Hōitsu, *Pair of dogs*, was transmitted in the restaurant.

The dogs in this work were derived from those in a pair of hanging scrolls by Mitani Tōshuku (1577–1654), a student of Unkoku Tōgan (1547–1618). The Tōshuku scrolls are now lost, but an 1816 copy by a Kano school painter now in the Tokyo National Museum confirms the connection. In addition, Hōitsu's close friend Tani Bunchō (1763–1840) reproduced one of the two Tōshuku scrolls in his book *Honchō gasan* (published around 1810), also noting that Tōshuku's paintings were at the Shōshōin of the Tsurugaoka Hachimangū in Kamakura. It is likely that Hōitsu copied the works at the Shōshōin and used them for this votive plaque.

In the early seventeenth century, Europeans probably brought the custom of walking a dog with a collar and leash to Japan. This sparked the curiosity of the Japanese, and the Western dog became a frequent motif in genre works such as *nanban* (southern barbarian) screens (cat. 114). Tōshuku's paintings of Western dogs, and others like them, were made against this historical background. In the Sōjiji plaque the dogs have been placed in an abstracted space. The chain on the larger dog has been elongated to the edge of the plaque, suggesting that the dogs' owner stands outside the painting space. SY

145

145 Tethered horse

Kano Sanraku (1559–1635)
ink, color, and gold leaf on wooden panel
88.7 x 125.0 (34⅞ x 49¼)
Edo period, 1614

Myōhōin, Kyoto

As late as the Kamakura period live horses were offered to Shinto shrines as gifts to deities by those who believed in their protective power. In the Muromachi period life-size wooden horses were sometimes substituted for the live ones, soon followed by less expensive paintings of horses. Named *ema* (votive paintings of horses), usually of modest size, they form a category of their own in Japanese art; some *ema* were painted by major artists.

This work, impressive for its size and no less so for its expressive quality, was painted by Kano Sanraku, a former warrior turned painter who headed the studio of the famous artist Kano Eitoku when the latter prematurely died in 1590 at the age of forty-seven. Along the right edge of the painting is an inscription: *By the brush of Kano Shūri* [member of the Shūridokoro, or Department of Repair and Construction of the Imperial Palace, an honorific title; i.e., Sanraku], *First day of the sixth month of the nineteenth year of Keichō* [corresponding to 1614]. Along the left edge is another inscription: *To hang as votive offering; the donor* [Kibei Ujichika] *of An'yōji.* The painting was originally offered to Hōkoku Jinja, a mortuary shrine of Toyotomi Hideyoshi (1537–1598), whom Eitoku and Sanraku had served as painters. YS

227

ARMS AND ARMOR

146 *Ōyoroi* armor
iron, leather, lacquer, silk, gilt metal
cuirass h. 33.3 (13 1/8)
Kamakura period,
late 13th–early 14th century

Kushibiki Hachimangū,
Aomori Prefecture
National Treasure

Ōyoroi (literally "great armor") was the loose-fitting defensive armor of mounted archers that was developed late in the Heian period. This set from the Kamakura period, remarkable for its abundant and highly accomplished decoration, represents the finest efforts of the metalworking and armor-making traditions of that time.

Typical of *ōyoroi*, it is constructed chiefly of leather and iron lames bound together to form horizontal tiers. The lamellar tiers are covered with lacquer to lend strength and rigidity and then laced together vertically, with distinctive, thick, red silk lacing in this example, to create large sections. These sections are then joined with smaller, solid iron or leather parts.

The conventions followed in composing this set are standard for *ōyoroi* armor. The upper part of the cuirass consists of a small solid iron *munaita*, or chest plate, and the *tateage*, two lamellar tiers in the front and three tiers in the back. The lower part of the cuirass, a four-tiered *kabukidō*, protects the front, back, and left side of the lower part of the torso. The right side of the body is protected by a completely separate section called the *waidate*. The *kusazuri*, a protective skirt suspended from the cuirass, is divided vertically into four large sections of five tiers each; the right section, a part of the *waidate*, is separate from the other three sections. The *ōsode*, or large upper-arm guards, are seven tiers each. Two smaller independent protective plates hang down from the shoulders, one over each side of the chest: on the right, the *sendan no ita* made of three lamellar tiers, and on the left, the *kyūbi no ita* of one solid iron plate.

A *tsurubashiri* of soft leather covers the lamellar tiers of the front of the cuirass to provide a smooth surface for drawing the bow. It is stencil-dyed with a design of *shishi*, mythical lionlike creatures, on a background of peonies. The peony is traditionally associated with refinement and the *shishi* with valor, both qualities to which the members of the warrior class aspired. The two motifs often appeared together on armor, particularly in the Kamakura and Muromachi periods.

The helmet, typical of those worn as part of a set of *ōyoroi* during this period, is of the *hoshi kabuto* type, literally "star helmet," a reference to the hundreds of rivets that punctuate its surface. The helmet bowl is made from trapezoidal plates of black-lacquered iron. A large, flaring, five-tier lamellar *shikoro*, or neck guard, is suspended from the bottom of the bowl, its upper four tiers folded back sharply at the front to form the *fukikaeshi*. The peak at the front of the helmet provides a base for the great hornlike projection, the *kuwagata*.

This set of armor is unusual in its lavish use of high-relief gilt metal decoration. The motif of the chrysanthemum appears throughout on many of the constituent parts of the armor. Reflecting a tendency toward realism in the Kamakura period, the perfectly formed flowers are modeled with close attention to fine detail, viewed from the front, side, and back, in carefully orchestrated clusters. The overall extravagance of this set is apparent in the *kyūbi no ita* and the *munaita*, generally only wrapped with a piece of ornamental leather, which are here covered with the chrysanthemum metalwork. The *ōsode* provide a surface for a more expansive treatment of the motif, as the chrysanthemums branch up and outward from a bamboo fence toward stylized clouds at the top. The hole at the top of the helmet, the *tehen no ana*, is encircled with the gilt-metal interweave. Four plates radiating from the *tehen no ana* along the four cardinal axes to the base of the helmet bowl are encrusted with the gilt chrysanthemum metalwork, as are other parts of the helmet such as the *fukikaeshi* and the base of the *kuwagata*.   AMW

147 *Ōyoroi* armor
iron, leather, lacquer, silk, gilt metal
cuirass h. 33.3 (13 1/8)
Nanbokuchō period, 14th century

Eisei Bunko, Tokyo
Important Cultural Property

According to Hosokawa family tradition, this set of *ōyoroi*, the oldest armor in the Hosokawa collection, was worn in a 1358 battle in Kyoto by Hosokawa Yoriari (1332–1391), the founder of the family. Much of the original assemblage that protects the body has survived: the cuirass and its pendant *kusazuri* (protective skirt), including the entire *waidate* (right side guard), and the *kyūbi no ita*, which is suspended from the left shoulder over the chest. The lacquer-coated tiers are made from iron and leather lames. The front of the cuirass was originally covered by a *tsurubashiri*, now lost, of soft deerskin with stenciled designs. The two expansive *ōsode* (large upper-arm guards) are replacements dating from the sixteenth century and the *sendan no ita*, which would have been suspended from the right shoulder over the chest, is missing.

The *hoshi kabuto* (star helmet) is made of narrow trapezoidal iron plates

146

231

147

148

fixed with rows of neatly assembled rivets. The rim band is pierced to receive studs that fasten the peak in front and the *shikoro* (neck guard), made of five lacquered lamellar tiers joined with white and red silk lacings, along the sides and back. The peak is ornamented with a high-relief design of gilt chrysanthemums, on which the now-lost *kuwagata* was mounted. At the top of the helmet, the *tehen no ana* opening is circumscribed by the *hachimanza*, a multi-layer gilt metal ring. The front of the helmet has three spatulate ornaments known as *shinodare*. The four upper tiers of the neck-guard extend forward and fold back to form *fukikaeshi*, the helmet's pair of flaps. Each of these flaps, covered with dyed leather with stenciled designs of *shishi* and peonies (cat. 146) is decorated with a single, large, gilt chrysanthemum, also found on the *kyūbi no ita*. The right-hand flap of the *shikoro* has lost several of its lacquered lames, the vivid reminder of a sword blow during a fierce battle. YS

148 **Dōmaru** armor
iron, leather, lacquer, silk, gilt metal
cuirass h. 29.5 (11 5/8)
Muromachi period,
first half 16th century

Kagoshima Jingū,
Kagoshima Prefecture
Important Cultural Property

Dōmaru is a type of armor characterized by a continuous sheathlike cuirass that is wrapped around the body of the wearer and fastened at the right side. It is thought to have been developed as the armor of the common foot soldier roughly during the same period as *ōyoroi*, from about the middle of the Heian period. During the fourteenth century, however, as combat tactics shifted the emphasis from mounted archers to formations of foot soldiers wielding the halberd and the long sword, higher-ranking warriors began to prefer the more manageable *dōmaru* to the bulky *ōyoroi*, adding a helmet and pair of *ōsode* (large upper-arm guards). This set of unusually well-preserved *dōmaru* has survived the centuries with its helmet and *ōsode* intact.

The construction of this set is absolutely standard for the Muromachi period. Small protective parts of solid iron wrapped in stencil-dyed leather edge the top of the cuirass. Each of the tiers beneath is composed primarily of small leather lames that are tied together and coated with lacquer. These horizontal tiers are then laced together vertically. To protect important parts of the body, iron lames are interspersed with the leather ones in some portions of the lamellar tiers. The upper lamellar part of the front of the cuirass is a two-tier section, while that the back is a three-tier section; below this, a

four-tier section fits around the body. Suspended from the shoulders is a pair of *gyōyō*, made of iron plate wrapped in stencil-dyed leather, which protects the cords that fasten the shoulder straps to the front of the cuirass. A *kusazuri*, the protective skirt, hangs from the cuirass in eight small sections of five lamellar tiers. Dividing the *kusazuri* into a larger number of smaller sections made *dōmaru* more flexible than *ōyoroi*. The pair of *ōsode* have seven lamellar tiers each. The lack of a *tsurubashiri*, the sheet of leather that covers the lamellar-tiered front of the cuirass in *ōyoroi* armor, reflects the shift away from the use of the bow and arrow.

Several colors of silk lacing are used to join the lamellar tiers together. The lacing pattern of the central portion of the armor, the cuirass and the *kusazuri*, is reflected in the lacing of the *ōsode*. The uppermost tiers of the central portion are joined by red, white, and red lacings. Below are rows of green lacing, and then tiers joined with red and white; at the very bottom is a cross-stitched section of red. To accommodate this sequence in the seven-tiered *ōsode*, only one lacing of green in the middle is needed.

The lacquered helmet is of the *suji kabuto*, or "ridged helmet," type; here the ridges are covered with gilt metal. Its shape, called *akoda* after a kind of oblong gourd, was especially popular in the Muromachi period. Attached to the helmet bowl is a *shikoro*, or neck guard, of three lamellar tiers, the upper two turned back at the front to form the *fukikaeshi*. The front of the helmet holds an elaborate gilt openwork section of chrysanthemums, the base for the gilt-metal hornlike projection, the *kuwagata*, which flanks a central sword-shaped projection.

A shrine legend records that this armor was used by Shimazu Takahisa (1514–1571), ruler of a large domain in southern Kyushu, whose son Yoshihiro (1535–1619) was responsible for starting the first Satsuma ware kilns (cat. 252). The Kagoshima Jingū owns another set of *dōmaru* similar to this one except in the colors of the lacings used to join the tiers together. AMW

149 **Dōmaru** armor
iron, leather, lacquer, silk, *shakudō*, gold
cuirass h. 29.0 (11 3/8)
Muromachi period, 16th century

Kōzu Kobunka Kaikan,
Kyoto Prefecture
Important Cultural Property

Like cat. 148, this set of *dōmaru* is well preserved: the original *akoda*-shaped *suji kabuto* helmet, the pair of *ōsode* (large upper-arm guards), and the cuirass, including the *kusazuri* (protective skirt), are intact. In addition, it has retained a set of *suneate* (shin guards), each made from

three curved plates of iron. Although the construction of the armor as a whole is basically standard for the Muromachi period, the *fukikaeshi* of the helmet stands up more than is typical and the monochromatic use of light aqua lacing is unusual.

A number of decorative techniques often used by armorers are employed, including openwork, high relief, *iro-e* (the application of gold or silver onto a background of another metal for color contrast), and *nanako* (in which the metal is given a raised-dot surface). The *shakudō* leaves and branches that hold clusters of chrysanthemums on several parts of the armor are executed in openwork. *Nanako* can be found on the toggles that fasten the shoulder straps to the front of the cuirass. The *iro-e* technique is used in combination with high relief to emphasize the writing on the plaque of the helmet, which reads *Hachiman Daibosatsu* (the Great Bodhisattva Hachiman), the patron god of the warrior. *Iro-e*, sometimes with high relief and sometimes alone, is also used in a number of places throughout the armor to describe a *mon*, or family crest, that includes a chrysanthemum and a horizontal stroke signifying the Japanese numeral *one*. This *mon* was used by the Nasu, a warrior family of Shimotsuke Province (present-day Tochigi Prefecture). Indeed, in the *Shūko jisshu*, an illustrated nineteenth-century compendium of famous antiquarian objects, this same set of armor is listed as a possession of the Nasu clan. AMW

150 *Haramaki* armor
iron, leather, lacquer, silk, gilt metal
cuirass h. 30.3 (11 7/8)
Muromachi period,
first half 16th century

National Museum of Japanese History, Chiba Prefecture
Important Cultural Property

This set of armor is of the *haramaki* type, in which the cuirass is wrapped around the front and fastened at the back. The close-fitting *haramaki* originally was the armor of the common foot soldier. In response to changes in military technique that required more mobility than the cumbersome *ōyoroi* armor allowed, high-ranking warriors began to wear the more flexible *haramaki* with a helmet and pair of *ōsode* (large upper-arm guards). It is thought that these warriors adopted *haramaki* somewhat later than *dōmaru*, during the fifteenth century, and their patronage encouraged the production of high-quality *haramaki*; this set is a well-preserved example from the sixteenth century.

The cuirass, the *kusazuri* (protective skirt), and the *ōsode* are constructed of thickly lacquered tiers of small lames. The

149

235

150

cuirass and top two rows of the *kusazuri*
and the top three rows of the *ōsode* are
made of alternating leather and iron lames
to protect vital areas; the remaining tiers
are made completely of leather lames.
Typical of *haramaki*, the five-tiered *kusazuri* is divided into seven sections, as compared with the four sections in *ōyoroi*, and
the eight sections common in *dōmaru*.

The tiers have been joined together
with lacings of different colors, as in cat.
148. The lacing pattern of the central portion of the set, consisting of the cuirass
and the pendant *kusazuri*, is echoed by
that of the *ōsode*. On both, the upper tiers
are bound by, in descending order, white,
red, and then white lacings. Below are
tiers joined together with indigo-dyed
leather thongs. At the bottom are lacings

of white and then cross-stitchings of red.
As was common in the earlier *ōyoroi*, mul-
ticolored lacing borders many of the parts.
The metalwork of gilt chrysanthemums
and the leather stencil-dyed with *shishi* on
a background of peonies are similar to
those in cat. 146, though on a much-
reduced scale.

Although partially repaired in the Edo
period, this set of armor is complete in its
constituent parts and represents a classic
example of Muromachi-period *haramaki*.
It is said to have been used by Hosokawa
Yorimoto (1343–1397), and was passed
down through generations of the Nabeshima family, daimyo of a domain in Hizen Province in Kyushu. The Nabeshima
were closely involved with the development of the ceramic industry in their fief,
including Karatsu ware (cats. 248, 249) and
Nabeshima ware (cats. 258, 259). AMW

151 *Haramaki* armor
iron, leather, lacquer, silk, gilt metal
cuirass h. 26.1 (10 1/4)
Muromachi period,
first half 16th century

National Museum of Japanese History,
Chiba Prefecture
Important Cultural Property

In its general construction, size, and in
most of the details, this set of *haramaki* is
similar to cat. 150. Differences between
the two include the color of the lacing of
some of the tiers and the slightly more narrow form of the cuirass. This set is also extremely well preserved, though some of
the lacing is damaged and a few of the
small pieces of gilt metalwork are missing. AMW

236

151

152 *Haramaki* armor
iron, leather, lacquer, silk, gilt metal
cuirass h. 32.0 (12½)
Momoyama period, late 16th century,
with later additions
Eisei Bunko, Tokyo

An example of *haramaki*, literally "belly
wrapper" this set of armor was worn by
Hosokawa Yūsai (Fujitaka, 1534–1610). The
upper-arm guards are flared in shape, a
type known as *hirosode*, and are contemporary with the cuirass. The helmet, also
probably of contemporary date but possibly a later addition, is of the *suji kabuto*
type, constructed from iron plates with
standing ridges. The sword-shaped decorative element at the front was originally
flanked right and left by the horn-shaped
elements of a *kuwagata*, now missing. The
base of the *kuwagata* is marked with the

kuyō mon, the crest of the Hosokawa family, a design of one large circle surrounded
by eight smaller circles. The *kote* (armored
sleeves), whose gloves are also decorated
with the *kuyō mon*, as well as the *haidate*
(protective apron) and *suneate* (shin
guards), were added when the set was
handed down to Hosokawa Tsunatoshi
(1643–1714). YS

153 *Tōsei gusoku* armor
iron, leather, lacquer, silk, wool,
shakudō, silver leaf, bear fur,
gold leaf, wood
cuirass h. 32.5 (12¾)
Momoyama period, late 16th century
Sendai City Museum,
Miyagi Prefecture
Important Cultural Property

Tōsei gusoku, literally "modern equipment," was innovative in materials and
construction. It was first produced during
the latter half of the sixteenth century. Responding to the needs of battle techniques
that employed large groups of foot soldiers, *tōsei gusoku* was made to maximize
the potential of the warrior to move easily
in battle as well as to give the wearer a distinctive appearance. Originally owned

152

153

by the warlord Toyotomi Hideyoshi (1537–1598), this set is a representative Momoyama-period example. The extensive use of silver leaf, white satin, red woolen cloth, and white silk lacing gives it an overall striking visual effect, and details are rendered in *maki-e* lacquer. Hideyoshi is recorded to have given the set in 1590 to Date Masamune (1567–1636), daimyo of Sendai, and it was passed down through subsequent generations of the Date family.

The *tōsei gusoku* cuirass took one of a number of new forms: it was often divided into two (*nimaidō*) or five (*gomaidō*) hinged sections; it could be made of large sheets of iron, or tiers of lames or long horizontal panels. The tiers in this set are made of large, notched silver-leafed leather lames. Typical of *tōsei gusoku*, the total number of tiers is greater by two than that of earlier armor, and the system of lacing the tiers together is greatly simplified. Reflecting a debt to the earlier *dōmaru* type of armor, though, the bottom portion of this cuirass is a continuous tiered section that is tied on the right. The *kusazuri*, made from five silver-leafed lamellar tiers, is divided into seven sections.

Helmets of the *tōsei gusoku* were often fashioned in a wide range of idiosyncratic forms. Here, the helmet is made from sheets of iron, covered on the outside with bear fur. A pair of gold-leafed wood fan-shaped appendages are attached to the front and back. The small *shikoro*, the neck guard suspended along the sides and back of the rim of the helmet, consists of two silver-leafed tiers, one a long horizontal iron plate and the other a horizontal plate divided into three sections. The top tier is bent up at the front to form small *fukikaeshi*. A mask, the *hohoate*, is beaten from a sheet of iron into the shape of the lower jaw, lacquered red and attached to the helmet, and from it is suspended a three-tier throat guard made of red-lacquered, narrow iron panels. Two tiers of silver-leafed leather lames, suspended below the iron throat guard from a silver-leafed iron collar, provide further protection for the throat.

Tōsei gusoku included a number of specialized protective parts such as the *kote* (armored sleeves), *haidate* (protective apron), and *suneate* (shin guards). Here, the *kote* protect the arms with parallel iron splints and the hands with gloves hammered from sheets of iron. These silver-leafed parts are all connected with a latticework of iron chain mail, and the whole is attached to a ground of white figured satin. In addition to the *kusazuri*, the legs are protected by two other component parts related to the rest of the set in their materials and composition. The *haidate* is made of silver-leafed, vertical iron splints divided into three sections and combined with iron chain mail, which

runs both horizontally and vertically to form a gridlike pattern. The shins are encased in *suneate* of five silver-leafed vertical iron splints. Both the *haidate* and *suneate* are grounded on the same white figured satin used in the *kote*.   AMW

154 *Tōsei gusoku* armor
iron, leather, lacquer, silk
cuirass h. 36.5 (14 3/8)
Momoyama period, late 16th century

Kunōzan Tōshōgū,
Shizuoka Prefecture
Important Cultural Property

This set of *tōsei gusoku*, said to have been worn by Tokugawa Ieyasu (1543–1616) during his great triumph at the Battle of Sekigahara in 1600 (cat. 104), was treasured as a symbol of Tokugawa dynastic power. According to shrine records, Ieyasu had the armor made after a dream in which he saw Daikokuten, a god associated with wealth and war. In Japanese the helmet shape is described as being in the style of a headdress traditionally worn by Daikokuten in sculptural and pictorial representations. The armor became known as the "dream-inspired form" and served as the model for many copies made by succeeding generations of Tokugawa rulers, of which cat. 155 is one example. Following Ieyasu's death, the armor was transferred to Kunōzan Tōshōgū, a mortuary shrine dedicated to Ieyasu, in Shizuoka Prefecture. In 1647, it was moved to a storage site within the Edo Castle precinct and, in 1882, was returned to Kunōzan Tōshōgū where it remains today.

The set is constructed from lamellar tiers. It is distinguished as an early and well-documented example of *tōsei gusoku* and by the overall high quality of its workmanship. A sheet of cloth-backed chain mail, in three sections, is suspended from the underside of the *shikoro*, providing extra protection for the neck and illustrating the practical nature of this set. This quality is also reflected in the layer of chain mail beneath the *kusazuri* (protective skirt) and in the construction of the substantial *suneate* (shin guards), each made of three hinged sections of iron plate. The *haidate* (protective apron) is made of card-shaped, hard leather lames. A decorative element for the front of the helmet, consisting of a gold-leafed leather fern wreath, a circle, and a wood *shigami* (cat. 160), has survived with the armor, though the fittings necessary to secure it to the helmet are lacking. The entire set was covered with black lacquer, which has altered over time to its present brown hue.   AMW

154

155

155 ***Tōsei gusoku* armor**
iron, leather, lacquer, silk, wood,
gold leaf
cuirass h. 39 (15 3/8)
Edo period, mid-17th century

Kunōzan Tōshōgū,
Shizuoka Prefecture

This set of *tōsei gusoku* is a copy of cat.
154, the greatly treasured armor owned by
Tokugawa Ieyasu (1543–1616). It is said to
have been made for the fourth-generation
Tokugawa shogun Ietsuna (1641–1680) in
1656, when the original was still being
stored within the Edo Castle precinct.

Overall, this is a faithful reproduction of
the earlier set, though the fittings necessary to attach the decorative element to
the front of the helmet have been added.

AMW

156

156 **Tōsei gusoku armor**
iron, leather, lacquer, silk, hemp,
bear fur, gilt metal
cuirass h. 37 (14½)
Edo period, 19th century

Kunōzan Tōshōgū,
Shizuoka Prefecture

This set of *tōsei gusoku* was owned by the
twelfth Tokugawa shogun, Ieyoshi (1793–
1853). The lacquered iron cuirass consists
of two hinged parts. The upper part is
laced. The bottom tier of the seven-
sectioned *kusazuri* (protective skirt) is
edged with bear fur. The *sode* (upper-arm

guards) are black-lacquered iron, and the
kote (armored sleeves) are made of iron
chainmail and blue hemp cloth. The iron
helmet is of the *hoshi kabuto* (star helmet)
type, unusual for the armor of the Tokugawa shogunate.   HY

157 Tōsei gusoku armor
iron, leather, lacquer, silk, gilt metal
cuirass h. 37 (14½)
Edo period, 18th–19th century
Kunōzan Tōshōgū,
Shizuoka Prefecture

When a son in the Tokugawa shogunate household celebrated his coming of age, it was customary for the Iwai house, overseers of the shogunal armor, to present him with a set of armor. This set is one such example. Although six similar sets are extant and their provenance is unclear, this one is traditionally said to have belonged either to the ninth shogun, Ieshige (1711–1761), or the eleventh shogun, Ienari (1773–1841). It is made of two hinged halves, with lamellar tiers laced in red, and the helmet is of the *suji kabuto* (ridged) type.   HY

158 Tōsei gusoku armor
iron, leather, lacquer, silk, yak hair
cuirass h. 45.0 (17¾)
Momoyama period,
late 16th–early 17th century
Agency for Cultural Affairs, Tokyo
Important Cultural Property

The powerful influence exerted by European armor on the development of "modern equipment" is reflected in this set of *tōsei gusoku*. Along with firearms, which altered the nature of Japanese warfare, sets of Western armor began to arrive in Japan from the end of the Muromachi period. Japanese warriors adapted them by adding typical Japanese parts: *kusazuri* (protective skirts) were suspended from the cuirass and *shikoro* (neck guards) from the helmet. Japanese armorers then started to produce entire sets of Western-style armor, known in Japanese as *nanbandō gusoku*, of which this set is representative.

According to the *Tokugawa jikki* (Records of the Tokugawa shoguns), this set was presented by Tokugawa Ieyasu (1543–1616) to his important ally Sakakibara Yasumasa (1548–1606), daimyo of a domain in Kōzuke Province (present-day Gunma Prefecture). The cuirass is made from two single sheets of hammered iron, one for the front and one for the back, hinged on the left side and fastened together with cord at the right. The rims of the cuirass are finished with lacquer, and the interior is lined with black-lacquered leather. Iron shoulder straps serve as the base for a pair of hinged *gyōyō*, which protect fastening cords and a pair of horn toggles. Also attached to the shoulder straps are a set of *kobire*, tiny shoulder guards often used in *tōsei gusoku*, here three tiers of narrow iron panels bound with blue lacing. The *kote* (armored sleeves) are made from metalwork patches, some in the shape of

gourds and chrysanthemums, all connected by a weave of chain mail to iron gloves and attached to a ground of blue silk cloth richly brocaded with a design of peonies.

The lower half of the body is protected by the standard set of several well-integrated parts. The *kusazuri* is made of five tiers of small black-lacquered leather lames divided into nine sections. The tiers are bound together with blue silk lacing. Below the *kusazuri* is the *haidate* (protective apron), made of five tiers of card-shaped small, black-lacquered leather lames, also bound with the blue silk lacing. The *haidate* is backed with the same richly brocaded blue cloth that was used for the *kote*. The shins are protected by a pair of *suneate*, made of six iron splints and iron chain mail.

The helmet is formed from two sheets of hammered iron and lined with heavily stitched linen cloth. Twelve decorative rivets encircle the base of the helmet, and cart wheel designs are depicted in *maki-e* lacquer at the sides. A *shikoro* of five tiers of long horizontal iron panels is suspended from the base of the helmet, as is a hammered iron mask with a detachable nose. A plume of white yak hair trails from the rear of the helmet, reflecting the tendency for the projecting element of the *tōsei gusoku* helmet to be made of unusual materials and to be positioned more freely than in earlier periods.   AMW

159 Tōsei gusoku armor
iron, leather, lacquer, silk, gilt metal,
silver
cuirass h. 39.0 (15⅜)
Momoyama period,
late 16th–early 17th century
Agency for Cultural Affairs, Tokyo
Important Cultural Property

This set of *tōsei gusoku* was owned by Sakakibara Yasumasa (1548–1606), the daimyo of a domain in Kōzuke Province (present-day Gunma Prefecture). Lavish use is made of *maki-e* lacquer to depict the gold and silver dragon that winds around the lower tiers of the cuirass, and the gold waves that churn along the bottom two tiers of the *kusazuri* (protective skirt). Silver is used to trim both the cuirass and the *kusazuri*. Gold *maki-e* lacquer and gilt metal cart wheel designs are dispersed over many parts of the set, including the small *fukikaeshi* of the helmet, the top of the cuirass, and the iron gloves.

The set, composed of tiers made from black-lacquered horizontal iron panels, is of the *nimaidō* type, with the front and back forming two discrete hinged sections. The five-tiered *kusazuri* is divided into seven sections. Below this is the *haidate* (protective apron), made of iron chain mail

with chrysanthemum-shaped medallions attached to a light brown cloth ground brocaded with a design of clouds. The black-lacquered *suneate* are made from three hinged curved sections of iron lined with linen. The *kote* (armored sleeves), are a grid of iron chain mail with gourd and floral medallions, backed with the same brocaded cloth as the *haidate*.

The helmet is a *suji kabuto*, or "ridged helmet," somewhat similar in construction and shape to that of the Kagoshima Jingū *dōmaru* (cat. 148). In this *tōsei gusoku* helmet, however, the *shikoro*, or neck guard, is formed of five iron panels tiered to curve sharply downward. A sword-shaped projection stands alone at the front of the helmet, a popular Momoyama-period style. In the Muromachi period, similar projections were usually combined with a horn-shaped *kuwagata*, whose twin prongs would flank it on either side, as in the Kagoshima Jingū helmet. The interior of the helmet is inscribed, *Made by Yoshimichi*. The hammered iron mask is lacquered on the interior and is equipped with a set of silver-plated teeth; a four-tiered throat guard is attached to the mask.

An early seventeenth-century portrait of Sakakibara Yasumasa depicts the warrior wearing this armor (cat. 33). In the painting, Yasumasa sits cross-legged on a bear skin cushion, and the dragon and wave design on the armor is recognizable. It is interesting to note, though, that in the painting, the armor is equipped with a set of *sode*, upper arm-guards, also decorated with the wave designs. The mask has been removed, allowing a clear view of the sitter's face.   AMW

160 Tōsei gusoku armor
iron, leather, lacquer, silk, paper,
wood, gold leaf
cuirass h. 39.0 (15¾)
Momoyama period,
late 16th–early 17th century
Honda Takayuki Collection, Tokyo
Important Cultural Property

This massive set of *tōsei gusoku* was originally owned and worn by Honda Tadakatsu (1548–1610), one of Tokugawa Ieyasu's most trusted generals and a powerful daimyo of Ise Province (a large part of present Mie Prefecture). Attached to the sides of the distinctive helmet is a striking pair of antlers, large but lightweight, made of wood and layers of paper hardened with coats of black lacquer. The grimacing horned head (*shigami*) at the front of the helmet, carved from wood, covered with black lacquer and gold-leafed, was a type of ornament popular from the Momoyama through the Edo periods. This set includes a string of gold-leafed wood prayer beads (not pictured here) reflecting the Buddhist faith of the warrior.

157

158

159

161

162

249

The set is complete, with all of the component protective parts, and the cuirass is of the *nimaidō* type, with two hinged sections. The tiers are made of long, horizontal panels—iron for the cuirass, leather for the *kusazuri* (protective skirt)—shaped and lacquered to give the appearance of tiers of individual lames. Accompanying the set is a portrait of Tadakatsu wearing the armor, including the prayer beads, and sitting confidently spread-legged on a stool (cat. 31).   AMW

161 *Tōsei gusoku* armor
    iron, leather, lacquer, silk, gold leaf
    cuirass h. 38.0 (15)
    Momoyama period,
    late 16th–early 17th century

    Sendai City Museum,
    Miyagi Prefecture

The impressive *tōsei gusoku* armor of the Date clan of Sendai was marked by an insistence on both functional pragmatism and severe elegance. This example, one of three similar sets ordered by Masamune (1567–1636), the first of the Date daimyo and a patron of the arts, was given to a retainer; a second set remained in the Date family while the third has been excavated from the foundation of Masamune's mausoleum. Copies of the armor were produced by subsequent generations of the Date daimyo.

Like the Kuroda armor in the Fukuoka Art Museum (cat. 162), the cuirass is of the *gomaidō* type, constructed from five hinged sections, though here each section consists of a single black-lacquered iron plate. Characteristic of Masamune's armor, the *kusazuri* (protective skirt) is divided into nine sections, each with six tiers of single, black-lacquered iron plates. The tiers are bound together with blue silk lacing. The other parts maintain this insistence on black and functional severity: the *haidate* (protective apron) is made of six rows of card-shaped, black-lacquered iron on a ground of black figured silk; each of the tubular *suneate* (shin guards) are two full sections of black-lacquered iron; the black-lacquered *kote* (armored sleeves) are made of iron chain mail backed with black figured silk, with six iron splints at the forearm and gloves of iron plate.

The black-lacquered, ridged *suji kabuto* helmet continues the austere elegance typical of the whole set. It lacks any decorative embellishment around the hole at the top of the crown. The *shikoro* is made of four tiers of thin horizontal iron strips and the top tier is turned back to form small *fukikaeshi* tabs, each with a simple openwork decoration of a five-petaled plum blossom. The grimacing

hammered iron mask extends down from the top of the cheek and nose to a three-tiered iron throat protector, while the full peak of the front of the helmet shields the upper part of the face. A sleek, gold-leafed leather crescent moon, elegantly poised off-center, balances on the front of the helmet. Not atypically, the helmet bowl was recycled from an older helmet; it is engraved with the name of its maker and the date: *Myōchin Nobuie, one day in the eleventh month of the fourth year of Tenbun* [1535].   AMW

162 *Tōsei gusoku* armor
    iron, leather, lacquer, silk, wood,
    silver leaf
    cuirass h. 35.8 (14 1/8)
    Momoyama period,
    late 16th–early 17th century

    Fukuoka Art Museum,
    Fukuoka Prefecture
    Important Cultural Property

This set was originally owned by Kuroda Nagamasa (1568–1623), daimyo of a domain in Chikuzen Province (part of present-day Fukuoka Prefecture). It is an example of the *gomaidō* type of *tōsei gusoku*, in which the cuirass is divided into five hinged sections, one section each for the front, back, and left sides, and two sections for the right side, where the armor is fastened. The cuirass is formed from tiers made of single, long, horizontal panels of iron wrapped with rough-grained, black-lacquered leather. Small iron parts, trimmed with gold embedded in lacquer, border the top of the cuirass. A four-tiered *kusazuri* (protective skirt) constructed from large lames made of lacquered, smooth leather is divided into seven sections, bound with dark brown silk lacing and suspended from the cuirass.

The helmet is in the Ichinotani style. Ichinotani is a place name, the site at which the twelfth-century tragic hero Minamoto Yoshitsune (1159–1189) achieved his greatest military triumph. The broad, silver-leafed appendage is formed from a thin sheet of wood attached to the back of the iron helmet bowl. The four-tiered *shikoro*, unlike the rest of the armor, is lacquered in reddish-brown. Kuroda family records indicate that when Kuroda Nagmasa participated in Hideyoshi's Korean expeditions, he received the helmet from Fukushima Masanori (1561–1624), a warrior who became daimyo of the Hiroshima domain, as an offering to help mend their strained relations. Nagamasa treasured the helmet and is recorded to have worn it in the Battle of Sekigahara in 1600 (cat. 104) and at the Siege of Osaka in 1614–1615, which may account for the many repairs. In an early seventeenth-century portrait (cat. 32) Nagamasa is

shown wearing the armor with a jacket over it, as well as an Ichinotani helmet.   AMW

163 *Tōsei gusoku* armor
    iron, leather, gold leaf, lacquer, silk,
    wood, bear fur, wool
    cuirass h. 39.0 (15 3/8)
    Edo period, 19th century

    Eisei Bunko, Tokyo

This set of *tōsei gusoku* is said to have been owned by the thirteenth-generation Hosokawa daimyo Yoshikuni (1835–1876). It reflects the influence of a tradition of armor design followed within the Hosokawa family known as the "*Sansai ryū*," or the Sansai mode, in which innovations conceived by Hosokawa Sansai (1563–1646) were standardized. Sansai believed that the colors of silk lacing on the cuirass should be limited to black, brown, dark blues, and purple; in this set, the cuirass is laced with dark blue, which subtly contrasts with the chestnut hue of the cuirass. Another distinctive characteristic of the Sansai mode, not always used but featured in this set, is the construction of the left portion of the *kusazuri* (protective skirt), the side that would be turned toward the enemy, from gold-leafed panels and crimson lacing. The bottom of the *kusazuri* is edged with bear fur, as is sometimes the case in Hosokawa armor. A *jinbaori* (battle jacket) of white wool with gold brocade facing is worn over the cuirass; the left sleeve is made of red wool, matching in color the lacing of the left portion of the *kusazuri*.

Sansai is reported to have said that he preferred a fragile helmet ornament, for when it broke in combat it would do so easily, without distracting him; he thought that the sight of a helmet ornament breaking on a battleground was something truly heroic and beautiful. Although this set was not made for use in battle, the enormously long and gracefully curved, black-lacquered wood ornaments of Yoshikuni's helmet seem to reflect this attitude.   YS

163

164

165

166

164 **Tōsei gusoku** armor
iron, leather, lacquer, silk, wood, gold leaf, yak hair
cuirass h. 42.8 (167/8)
Momoyama period, late 16th century

Ii Naoyoshi Collection,
Shiga Prefecture

165 **Tōsei gusoku** armor
iron, leather, lacquer, silk, wood, gold leaf
cuirass h. 40.2 (157/8)
Edo period, 17th century

Ii Naoyoshi Collection,
Shiga Prefecture

166 **Tōsei gusoku** armor
iron, leather, lacquer, silk, gilt metal, wood, gold leaf
cuirass h. 39.9 (155/8)
Edo period, mid-18th century

Ii Naoyoshi Collection,
Shiga Prefecture

167 *Tōsei gusoku* armor
iron, leather, lacquer, silk, wood,
gold leaf
cuirass h. 40.2 (15 7/8)
Edo period, mid-19th century

Ii Naoyoshi Collection,
Shiga Prefecture

168 *Haramaki*
iron, leather, lacquer, silk, gilt metal,
wood, gold leaf
cuirass h. 29.6 (11 5/8)
Edo period, mid-19th century

Ii Naoyoshi Collection,
Shiga Prefecture

169 *Tōsei gusoku*
iron, leather, lacquer, silk, silver leaf
cuirass h. 29.7 (11 3/4)
Edo period, 17th century

Ii Naoyoshi Collection,
Shiga Prefecture

These six sets of *tōsei gusoku,* covered
with brilliant red lacquer, are among the
more than fifty that have been passed
down through successive generations of
the Ii family, the Edo-period daimyo of Hikone, a city in present-day Shiga Prefecture. Historical tradition traces the Ii clan
back almost one millennium, to the birth
in 1009 of its founder Tomoyasu who became *kami* (governor) of Tōtōmi Province
(part of present-day Shizuoka Prefecture).
Tomoyasu took the family name *Ii* from
Iinoya, the Ii Valley, where he lived. The
similarities among the sets of Ii armor
from the end of the sixteenth century
onward—in color, construction, and in the
pair of tall, hornlike elements (*wakidate*)
projecting upward from the sides of the
helmets—reflect the tendency during the
peaceful Edo period for families to copy
the sets of armor that had served their ancestors in battle.

The prototype for the armor identified with the Ii family is said to have been
worn by Ii Naomasa (1561–1602), twenty-
fourth head of the Ii family in the ancestral line descending from Tomoyasu and
the first Ii daimyo of Hikone; cat. 164 was
owned by Naomasa. Early in his career,
Naomasa is said to have adopted from
Yamagata Masakage, a general celebrated
for his military prowess, the practice of
lacquering his armor red. The cuirass,
which fastens at the right side, is made
from tiers of iron sheets, each scalloped
along the top edge. Suspended from the
cuirass is a five-tiered leather *kusazuri* (protective skirt), divided vertically into seven
sections, beneath which is a *haidate* (protective apron) of chain mail, and then, to
cover the shins, *suneate* of chain mail and
iron splints. Typical of many sets of Ii ar-

167

168

169

mor, the arms are protected by a five-tiered pair of small *sode* (upper-arm guards) and *kote* (armored sleeves) of chain mail with iron gloves. Displayed prominently in relief on the gloves is the Japanese character *i*, first of the two characters that form the name Ii. The distinctive red-lacquered iron helmet became a model followed especially closely in the later Ii armor; it is fitted with a shallow, five-tiered iron *shikoro* (neck protector) and the *wakidate*, the pair of long gold-leafed wood decorative elements attached to the sides. White yak hair cascades from the top of the helmet.

Although slight modifications are apparent, the armor of the second-generation daimyo of Hikone, Ii Naotaka (1590–1659), as represented by cat. 165, follows closely that of his father, Naomasa. Among other minor changes, the cuirass is bound with leather cords in a more complex and decorative manner and the number of tiers in the small *sode* is increased to

seven, but the debt to the earlier armor is obvious. Even at this early stage in the history of the daimyo rulership of the Ii family in Hikone, the distinguishing characteristics of their family style of armor were established. This style would continue to be used throughout the Edo period.

By the time of the brief sixty-day reign of the ninth-generation daimyo, Ii Naoyoshi (1727–1754), when peace had blessed Japan for more than a century, the tendency toward the decorative elaboration of armor unrelated to practical need became increasingly noticeable. For example, the cuirass of cat. 166 comprises a busy combination of variously textured tiers, bound with white, light green, and red silk lacings. Nevertheless, the distinctive, well-established features of Ii armor, such as the coat of red lacquer and the

tall *wakidate* on the helmet, are duly employed.

The girth of cat. 167, largest among the Ii sets, reflects the physical size of its owner, Ii Naosuke (1815–1860), the thirteenth daimyo of Hikone and an imposing political figure during the turbulent era leading up to the Meiji Restoration of 1868. Recognizing the futility of efforts to maintain Japan's self-imposed isolation, Naosuke played a pivotal role in bringing about change from 1858 to 1860, when he served as *tairō*, literally "great elder," for the weakened Tokugawa shogunate. Seeking to direct his country into the international arena, he engineered the signing of a trade agreement with the United States, antagonizing conservative Japanese and thereby provoking his assassination in 1860 at the Sakurada Gate in front of Edo Castle.

The two remaining sets of red-lacquered Ii armor were made for children

255

170

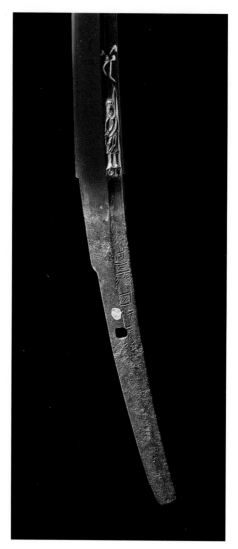

of the Ii daimyo: cat. 168 for a daughter of Ii Naosuke, and cat. 169 for Ii Naoshige, a son of the second-generation Ii daimyo, Naotaka. Cat. 168 takes the form of *haramaki* (cats. 150, 151, 152), and reflects the Edo-period practice of making copies of earlier armor, though the copies often sacrificed authenticity to decorative elaboration. On cat. 169 can be seen the *tachibana mon*, the Ii family crest, depicting the fruit and leaves of the mandarin orange on a stem enclosed in a circle; this or a more simplified version was often used by the Ii clan on their personal belongings, such as saddles, clothing, and sword mountings (cat. 191). Small-scale sets of armor typically were made for younger members of warrior families. They served as visual reminders of the social status of the child and were worn at important occasions, such as the coming of age ceremony.

In all, fourteen successive generations of the Ii family held the position of daimyo of Hikone until it was abolished shortly after the Meiji Restoration in 1868.   AMW

170   ***Tachi* blade**
Yukihira (fl. early 13th century)
steel
blade length 79.9 (31½)
Kamakura period, 13th century

Eisei Bunko, Toyko
National Treasure

The swordsmith Yukihira of Bungo Province (most of present-day Oita Prefecture) is said to have been a disciple of Teishū, a late Heian-period monk and sword maker at Hikosan, a mountain center of Buddhism. Yukihira's known works include a *tachi* dated to 1205, so it is understood that he was active in the Kamakura period. The *tachi* is a type of sword slung from the waist with the edge facing down. This slender example, representing the finest

qualities of Yukihira's style, has an elegant arched shape. The surface texture of the blade is of a type described by sword connoisseurs as *itame*, or wood grain. The temper line along the edge of the blade is almost completely straight. Engraved on the front side of the blade is a *shuji* representing the fierce-looking but benevolent Buddhist guardian deity Fudō Myōō as well as a depiction of the Kurikara dragon, a symbol of Fudō, coiled around a sword and about to swallow it from the tip. On the reverse side of the blade is the *shuji* for Bishamonten, another Buddhist guardian deity, especially adopted by warriors, as well as a Buddhist image that can be taken for either Bishamonten or Fudō Myōō. On the tang is inscribed, *Made by Yukihira of Bungo province.*

Long a celebrated work, this *tachi* blade was given by the daimyo and literary figure Hosokawa Yūsai (also known as Fujitaka, 1534–1610) to Karasumaru Mitsuhiro (1579–1630), to whom he also transmitted a highly valued secret teaching passed orally from teacher to select disciple, on the tenth-century poetic anthology *Kokinshū*. The accompanying leather mounting dates from that time.   HY

171   ***Katana* blade**
Mitsutada (fl. 13th century)
steel
blade length 68.5 (27)
Kamakura period, 13th century

Eisei Bunko, Tokyo
National Treasure

Originally a long *tachi* measuring over 90 centimeters (c. 35½ inches), this blade was made into a *katana* in the Momoyama period. Unlike the *tachi*, which was slung from the waist with the edge down, the *katana* was worn edge up, thrust through the belt. The tang of this blade holds two gold-

171

inlaid inscriptions. On one side is, *Mitsu-tada*, followed by the *kaō* of Kōtoku. "Mitsutada" is the name of the Kamakura-period master swordsmith of Osafune in Bizen Province (part of present-day Oka-yama Prefecture) who originally forged the *tachi*. The name Kōtoku and the *kaō* be-long to Hon'ami Kōtoku (active late sixteenth–early seventeenth century), the great sword connoisseur in the service of Toyotomi Hideyoshi (1537–1598), who treated the blade. The other side of the tang is inscribed, *Owned by Ikoma, Sanuki no kami*, referring to Ikoma Kazumasa, daimyo of a domain in Sanuki Province (present-day Tokushima Prefecture). The blade has thus come to be known as *Ikoma Mitsutada*.

A characteristic Osafune blade, it ex-emplifies the bold, broad-bodied form pop-ular in the mid-Kamakura period. The sur-face texture of the metal is a fine *itame* (woodgrain), faintly clouded. As described in the rich Japanese vocabulary of sword-related language, the temper line is a combination of irregular "clove" shapes (*chōji midare*) and small pointed curves (*gunome*). HY

172 **Katana** blade
Yosōzaemon no Jō Sukesada
(fl. 16th century)
steel
blade length 64.3 (25 1/4)
Muromachi period, 1534
Sword Museum, Tokyo

In the Muromachi period the Bizen smith-ery was the largest sword-making commu-nity in Japan; it became especially active after 1500, and the name Sukesada figured prominently. More than ten Bizen sword makers called themselves by that name, but the key figure was the man who forged this sword, Yosōzaemon no Jō Sukesada. In this period *tachi* were not made; instead many *katana* of about 63 centimeters (c. 24 3/4 inches), worn thrust through the sash with the edge up, were produced. A specialty of Sukesada swordsmiths' work was a temper line with irregular pointed curves (*gunome midare*) mixed with Fuji-like mountain shapes. Such a pattern can be seen in this fine, somewhat longer-than-average example with an *itame* (woodgrain) surface texture. On one side of the blade the *shuji* for Fudō Myōō is en-graved, and on the other side is the *shuji* for Marishiten, a guardian goddess of the warrior. The tang is inscribed, *Osafune Yosōzaemon no Jō Sukesada of Bizen prov-ince. An auspicious day in the second month of the third year of Tenmon* [1534]. HY

171   172

173 *Wakizashi* blade
Yasutsugu (d. 1646)
steel
blade length 34.9 (13 3/4)
Edo period, 17th century

Tokyo National Museum

The first of many swordsmiths to use the name Yasutsugu was born in the village of Shimosaka in Ōmi Province (present-day Shiga Prefecture) as Shimosaka Ichizaemon, and studied with Ōmiya Kanetomi (fl. late sixteenth century), signing his works Shimosaka. He later moved to Echizen Province (part of present-day Fukui Prefecture), where he served the Matsudaira family. Around 1606 he was granted the honor of using in his name the Japanese character *yasu*, from the given name of Tokugawa Ieyasu. Thereupon he changed his name to Yasutsugu and began to serve the Tokugawa shogunal house as swordsmith. Successive generations of swordsmiths who went by the name Yasutsugu were active until the late Edo period; the first two generations served both the shogunate in Edo and the Matsudaira family of Echizen, but during the third generation the family divided into the Edo and Echizen branches. Reflecting the influence of Masamune (fl. late thirteenth–early fourteenth century), the famous swordsmith of the Kamakura period, and his son Sadamune, the Yasutsugus style is characterized by an irregular temper line (*midareba*). Carvings in the blade of such themes as dragons, Buddhist figures, and trees are also typical of his work, mostly executed by Kinai Tomosuke (fl. early seventeenth century) and his disciples.

This fine *wakizashi* blade, about 30 to 60 centimeters (c. 12 to 24 inches) long, was made by the second-generation Yasutsugu, who died in 1646. The *itame* (woodgrain) surface texture recalls the work of Masamune and Sadamune, and the temper line is described with large undulations (*notare*). On the front side of the blade are carvings by Kinai Tomosuke depicting the Buddhist deities Jizō Bosatsu, Fudō Myōō, and Bishamonten; on the reverse is a carving of the Kurikara dragon about to swallow a ritual sword. Engraved on the front of the tang is a depiction of the hollyhock *mon*, which the Tokugawa allowed the Yasutsugu smiths to use; below it is an inscription that reads, *With foreign iron, at Edo, Bushū,* and on the reverse is inscribed *Echizen Yasutsugu,* meaning that Yasutsugu of Echizen Province made the blade at Edo in Bushū (Musashi Province) using, along with native iron, rare imported iron from the West.   HY

174 *Tantō* blade
Sagami no kami Masatsune
(1534–1619)
steel
blade lenth 28.5 (11 1/4)
Momoyama period, 16th century

Sword Museum, Tokyo
Important Art Object

Sagami no kami Masatsune was a swordsmith employed by the Tokugawa of Owari province, one of the three Tokugawa branch houses (*gosanke*). He was born in 1534 in Mino Province (part of present-day Gifu Prefecture), where he studied under Kanetsune of Seki and was given the name Kanetsune, which was later changed to Masatsune; in 1592 he received the honorary title *Sagami no kami*. In 1600 he accompanied the fourth son of Tokugawa Ieyasu (1543–1616), Matsudaira Tadayoshi (1580–1607), when he moved to Kiyosu in Owari Province (present-day Aichi Prefecture). After Tadayoshi's death, Masatsune lived near Nagoya Castle and served the Owari Tokugawa.

Masatsune's work belongs to the Seki tradition of Mino province. The surface texture is usually a mixture of *itame* (wood grain) and *masame* (straight grain), as can be seen on this fine blade. Typically his blades have a straight temper line (*suguha*), as in this example, or an undulating temper line (*notareba*). On this *tanto*, a short blade less than 30 centimeters (c. 12 inches) in length, has been carved a vivid openwork depiction of the Kurikara dragon, coiled around and about to swallow a ritual sword. The tang is inscribed with the name of the smith, *Sagami no kami Fujiwara Masatsune*.   HY

175 *Katana* blade
Musashi Daijō Tadahiro (1572–1632)
steel
blade length 58.9 (23 1/8)
Edo period, 1629

Tokyo National Museum
Important Art Object

This blade, somewhat shorter than the typical *katana*, was forged by Musashi Daijō Tadahiro, born Hashimoto Shinzaemon Tadayoshi. Employed as a clan craftsman in the Nabeshima domain of Saga in Hizen Province, northern Kyushu, he was sent to Kyoto in 1596 on clan order to study with Umetada Myōju (1558–1631), a famous carver of swords and maker of swords and metal fittings. Following his return to Saga in 1598, his school prospered and *Hizen tō*, or swords of Hizen Province, became well known. He received the title *Musashi Daijō* in 1615 and changed his name to Tadahiro. Hizen swords are characterized by a fine *itame* (woodgrain) surface and temper lines that are either straight (*suguha*) or have irregular "clove"

shapes (*chōji midare*), as on this blade. Carvings are often by Umetada Myōju, as here, or by one of his disciples. The inscriptions on the tang reads: *Musashi Daijō Fujiwara Tadahiro. Tadahiro is a disciple of Umetada Myōju. The twenty-fourth day of the ninth month of the sixth year of Kan'ei* [1629], *carving by Myōju at age seventy-two*—indicating that this work was a joint effort of master and student.   HY

176 *Katana* blade
Echizen no kami Sukehiro (1637–1682)
steel
blade length 69.6 (27 3/8)
Edo period, 1677

Tokyo National Museum
Important Art Object

Echizen no kami Sukehiro was apprenticed to the Osaka swordsmith Tsuda Sukehiro; he was adopted by his teacher and inherited his name. In 1657 he received the honorary title *Echizen no kami* from the court, and ten years after that he entered the service of Aoyama Inaba no kami, a Tokugawa retainer who served as warden of Osaka Castle.

At first Sukehiro made temper lines with irregular "clove" shapes (*chōji midare*), like those of his teacher, but eventually he pioneered a beautiful and distinctive style of temper line reminiscent of the shape of ocean waves known as *tōran midare*, as can be seen in this example. The shape of the blade, with a rather slight curve, was common in the Edo period, and it has a fine *itame* (woodgrain) surface texture. The inscription on the front of the tang identifies the swordsmith, *Tsuda Echizen no kami Sukehiro*, and the date is recorded on the reverse, *A day in the eight month of the fifth year of Enpō* [1677].   HY

177 *Katana* blade
Ōsumi no Jō Masahiro (fl. early 17th century)
steel
blade length 70.5 (27 3/4)
Momoyama period, 1606

Agency for Cultural Affairs, Tokyo
Important Cultural Property

Ōsumi no Jō Masahiro was an apprentice of the famous Kyoto swordsmith Horikawa Kunihiro (active late sixteenth–early seventeenth century). Masahiro's style is based on the style of the fourteenth-century smith Sadamune of Kamakura. This fine example of Masahiro's work, typical of the Momoyama-period blade, is wide with a slight curve and large point. It has an *itame* (woodgrain) surface texture, and the temper line consists of small undulations (*konotare*). Inscribed on the front

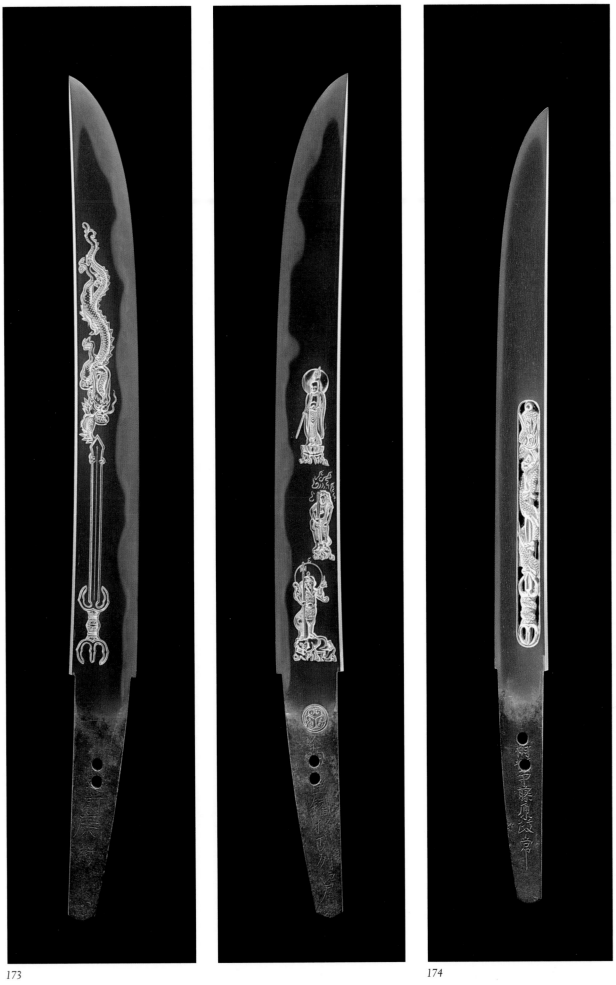

173

174

of the tang is, *Ōsumi no Jō Fujiwara Masa-hiro,* and on the reverse, *An auspicious day in the third month of the eleventh year of Keichō* [1606]. HY

178 **Hyōgo gusari no tachi** mounting
wood, rayskin, silver, iron, gilt metal
length 103.8 (40 7/8)
Kamakura period, 13th century

Tokyo National Museum
Important Cultural Property

The name for this type of mounting refers to the chains of woven wire, *hyōgo gusari,* used for the pair of hanging straps. Magnificent yet austere, this mounting was popular among high-ranking warriors from the late Heian period into the Kamakura period. After the middle of the Kamakura period, however, *hyōgo gusari no tachi* began to assume a more ceremonial function and came to be produced exclusively for dedication to temples and shrines.

This example is known as *Hōjō Tachi* since it was dedicated to the Mishima Taisha in Shizuoka Prefecture by a member of the Hōjō family, regents of the Kamakura shogunate. The hilt is covered with rayskin, and its edges are rimmed with silver. On each side of the hilt, along the lower edge, are four pairs of the *mitsu uroko mon,* the design of contrasting triangles that forms the Hōjō family crest. The *menuki* (metal ornaments on the side of the hilt) consist of the *mon* on an openwork ground. The wooden sheath is covered with silver, which is incised and gilt with a design of three sets of the *mon* and held in place with other silver fittings; the chains are also made of silver. The iron *tsuba* (sword guard) is wrapped with thin silver plate. Although not included in the exhibition, the mounting usually holds a steel Bizen blade dating from the mid-Kamakura period. HY

179 **Hyōgo gusari no tachi** mounting
wood, rayskin, gilt copper, silver
length 97 (38 1/8)
Kamakura period, 13th century

Niutsuhime Jinja,
Wakayama Prefecture
Important Cultural Property

Niutsuhime Jinja in Wakayama Prefecture has long been venerated as the Shinto protective shrine of Mount Koya, south of Kyoto, a center of Shingon Buddhism since the early ninth century. Among the many sword-related items dedicated to the shrine since the Heian period is this *hyōgo gusari no tachi,* an excellent example thought to date from the late Kamakura period. Its hilt, made of wood covered with rayskin, is edged with gilt copper decorated with a high-relief peony design on a *nanako* (raised-dot) ground. The *kabuto-*

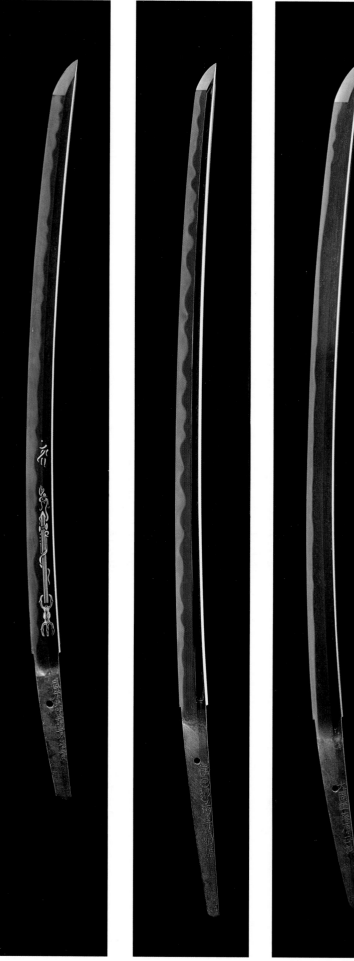

175   176   177

260

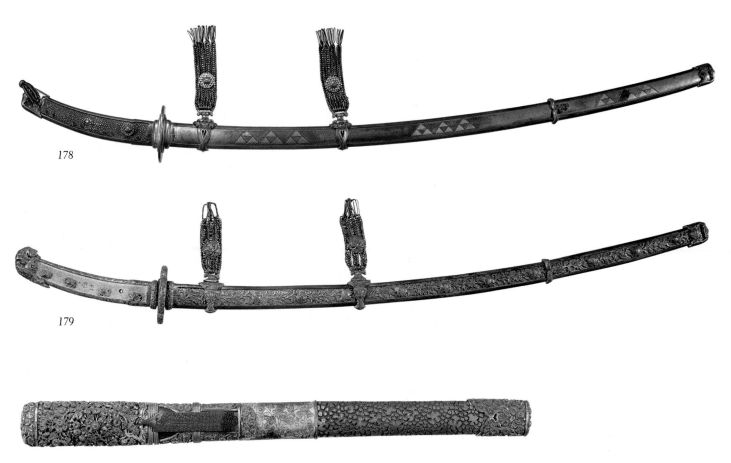

178

179

180

gane (metal fitting covering the pommel) takes the shape of a *shishi*, a mythical lion-like animal, and the *fuchi kanagu* (metal collar at the blade end of the hilt) is covered with a peony design; along the length of the hilt are hammered decorative peony studs. All the metal hilt fittings are gilt copper. The silver-covered wooden sheath is overlaid with a gilt openwork floral-scroll and peony design, and the long edges are gilt rimmed. The chains are attached to "legs" decorated with the peony design in high relief on a *nanako* ground. The blade contained within this mounting, not shown in this exhibition, is far removed from practical use.   HY

180 *Koshigatana* mounting
wood, silver, gilt copper
length 42 (16 1/2)
Muromachi period, 15th century

Tokyo National Museum

The *koshigatana*, a short sword worn at the waist usually without a sword guard, was carried in combination with the slung sword, or *tachi*. The length of the blade varies from 25 to 35 centimeters (10 to 13 3/4 inches). The typical mounting features extensive metal fittings distributed over its length. Sometimes short swords were fitted with a *kozuka* (small knife) and a *kōgai* (a skewerlike implement carried in special pockets on the side of the sheath). From the late Kamakura period, the reinforcing metal fittings on the hilt came to cover the

hilt entirely, a fashion that continued into the Muromachi period and which is typified by this ornate example. The wooden hilt is covered with silver, over which is laid an extensive gilt copper openwork weave with high-relief chrysanthemums. The wood sheath is covered with gilt copper given the appearance of rayskin and metal fittings with high-relief and engraved chrysanthemums. A gilt copper dragon-and-wave design is depicted on the *kozuka* in high relief and engraving, while the *kōgai* is decorated with a ruler and bracken sprout design.   HY

181 *Itomaki no tachi* mounting
wood, silk, lacquer, *shakudō*, gold, leather
length 110 (43 1/4)
Momoyama period, early 17th century

Sword Museum, Tokyo
Important Cultural Property

Ornate *itomaki no tachi* were produced from the end of the Muromachi period. Daimyo used swords of this type for ceremonial purposes, as rewards or gifts, and as dedicatory gifts to temples and shrines. The *itomaki no tachi* characteristically had metal fittings of *shakudō* (or sometimes gold) decorated with family *mon* (crests) on a *nanako* (raised-dot) ground. The length of the sheath was decorated with the same *mon* and with auspicious motifs such as paulownia and phoenix in *maki-e* lacquer. The hilt was covered with rich

brocade, to which were fastened *menuki* (metal ornaments) with the family *mon*, and the whole was then intricately wrapped with brown or purple silk cord. The same cord was continued on the upper part of the sheath, and leather and silk hanging straps were attached.

In this mounting, handed down in the Uesugi family, daimyo of Yonezawa (in present-day Yamagata Prefecture), and probably given to them by Toyotomi Hideyoshi (1537–1598), the hilt is covered with gold brocade and wound with brown silk cord; the cord is continued onto the sheath. The sheath is covered with amber lacquer sprinkled thickly with gold particles; this kind of lacquer ground is called *nashiji* (pear-skin ground), for the ruddy speckled pear that it resembles. Against this ground, on each side of the sheath, are seven paulownia *mon* in *maki-e* lacquer. The metal fittings are also decorated with paulownia crests, crafted in high relief and thinly covered with gold using the *iro-e* technique on a *nanako* (raised-dot) *shakudō* ground. Not included in the exhibition, the Kamakura-period steel blade normally in this mounting was made by a swordsmith of the Ichimonji school of Bizen Province.   HY

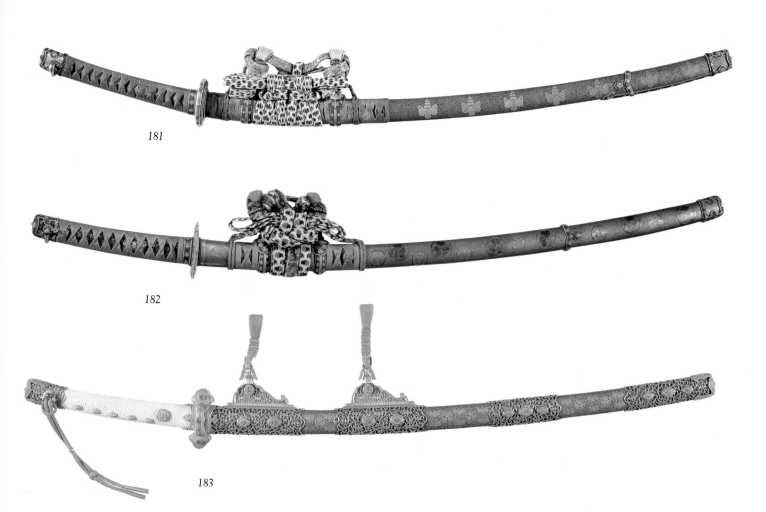

181

182

183

182 Itomaki no tachi mounting
wood, silk, lacquer, *shakudō*, gold,
silver, leather
length 105.5 (41½)
Edo period, 17th century

Tokyo National Museum

The hilt of this classic early Edo-period *ito-maki no tachi* (cat. 181), covered with a gold brocade cloth, is wrapped with brown silk cord. This same wrapping is also used on part of the sheath. Along the length of the sheath are many hollyhock *mon*, the crest of the Tokugawa clan, in gold and silver *maki-e* and thin sheets of metal. The various metal fittings distributed over the sword are also decorated with the hollyhock *mon* in high relief thinly covered with gold (*iro-e*) on a *nanako* (raised-dot) *shakudō* ground. Although its provenance is unknown, the use of the hollyhock *mon* suggests that this *itomaki no tachi* was owned by a family with connections to the Tokugawa shogunate.   HY

183 Kazaritachi mounting
wood, rayskin, copper, gold, enamel,
lacquer, leather
length 102 (40⅛)
Edo period, early 17th century

Watanabe Kunio Collection, Tokyo

The *kazaritachi*, developed in the Heian period as a more ornate version of the *karatachi* (Chinese sword) of the earlier Nara period, was the most important sword used on ceremonial occasions at the imperial court. *Kazaritachi* mountings are characterized by the extensive use of openwork metal fittings in colorfully inlaid floral scroll designs, and by the prominent "feet" with appendages to which the hanging straps are attached. The hilt is typically covered with white rayskin and punctuated with a row of ornamental studs. As on the earlier *karatachi*, the *tsuba* (sword guard) is made in the stylized shape of a *fundō* (balance weight). From the Mo-moyama period, members of the imperial court aristocracy used *kazaritachi* with a slim, straight sheath that encased only a perfunctory blade; warriors with a court rank, however, used one in which the sheath was broad and arched to accommodate a practical blade.

The sheath of this example is some-what broad and curved. The hilt is covered

with white rayskin and has a row of orna-mental studs shaped like *tawara* (straw rice bags) and *menuki* (hilt ornaments) with a paulownia *mon*. The sheath is decorated with a floral-scroll design of paulownia and hollyhock *mon* in gold *maki-e* lacquer on a *nashiji* lacquer ground. Along the sheath are four gilt copper fittings with paulownia crests and red and green enamel flower motifs against an intricate *nanako* (raised-dot) and openwork background. The *tsuba* is inlaid with green enamel.

Representative of the refined style and outstanding craftsmanship of the early modern era, this *kazaritachi* is said to have been given by Emperor Go-Yōzei to Tokugawa Hidetada (1579–1632), the sec-ond shogun, on the occasion of his being awarded the court title *seii tai shōgun* on the sixteenth day of the fourth month of the tenth year of Keichō (1605).   HY

184 Kazaritachi mounting
wood, rayskin, lacquer, copper, gold,
enamel, leather
length 101 (39¾)
Edo period, late 17th century

Takahashi Toshio Collection, Tokyo

This *kazaritachi* mounting (cat. 183) has the characteristic features of its type, such

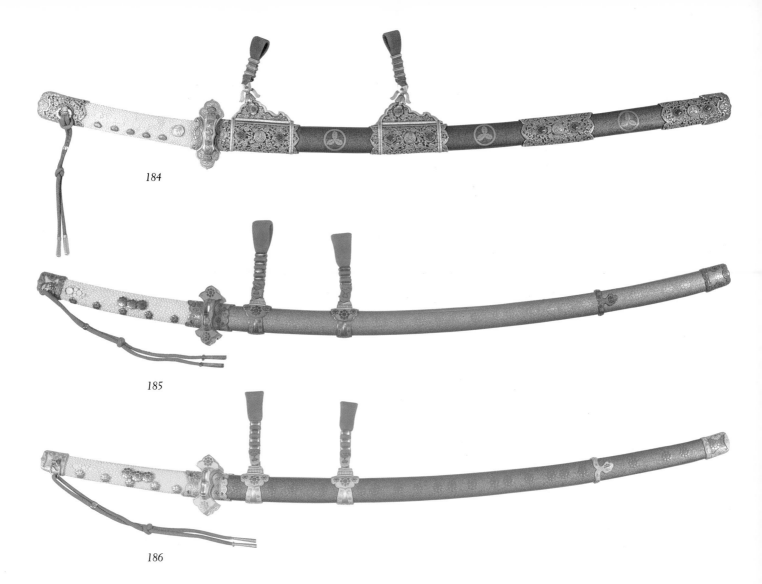

184

185

186

as prominent "feet," a *fundō*-shaped *tsuba*, and extensive metal fittings with colorful enamel inlay distributed over the length of the sheath. The curve and breadth of the sheath indicate that it was owned by a warrior. It was transmitted in the Maeda family of the Daishōji domain, a branch of the powerful Maeda clan of the Kaga domain (cats. 260, 261). The oak-leaf *mon*, dispersed over the sheath in *maki-e* lacquer on a *nashiji* ground and also on the metal fittings, was the crest used by the Yamanouchi daimyo of Tosa, on the island of Shikoku. This mounting was presented to one of the Maeda lords to mark some occasion.   HY

185 **Silver *maki-e no tachi* mounting**
     wood, rayskin, lacquer, silver, leather
     length 98 (38 5/8)
     Edo period, late 18th century

     Eisei Bunko, Tokyo

186 **Gold *maki-e no tachi* mounting**
     wood, rayskin, lacquer, gold, leather
     length 96 (37 3/4)
     Edo period, late 18th century

     Eisei Bunko, Tokyo

As the ceremonial *kazaritachi* mounting (cat. 183) was expensive and time-consuming to manufacture, simplified styles gradually came to be used. One such substitute was the *hosodachi*, or slim *tachi*. Another was the even more simplified *maki-e no tachi* type, of which this pair, transmitted in the Hosokawa family and thought to date from the late Edo period, is a representative example. They are identically made except that one has metal fittings of gold, to be used on festive occasions, and the other has metal fittings of silver, to be used on solemn occasions.

The hilts are covered with white ray-skin. Along the lower part of the hilts are rows of five cherry blossom–shaped ornamental studs, and at the center are *menuki* consisting of three *kuyō mon*, the Hoso-kawa family crest of eight small circles around a single large circle. The sheaths are decorated with the *kuyō mon* in *maki-e* lacquer on a *nashiji* lacquer ground. The metal fittings encircling the mounting at various points are also decorated with the *kuyō mon* on a *nanako* (raised-dot) ground. The "feet" are those of an ordinary *tachi*, without the prominent appendages seen in the *kazaritachi*. The *tsuba*, shaped like a *fundō* (balance weight), and the hanging cords bound with seven metal rings, how-ever, represent traces of the *kazaritachi* style retained in these otherwise simplified ceremonial swords.   HY

187 **Set of *daishō* mountings**
     wood, rayskin, silk, lacquer, *shakudō*,
     gold, silver, horn
     length top, 92 (36 1/4); bottom, 56 (22)
     Edo period, 18th century

     Watanabe Kunio Collection, Tokyo

From the Muromachi period, warriors are known to have worn long *katana* and short *wakizashi* swords together as a pair, but in the Edo period combinations of long and short swords with identical mountings were standardized and were known as *daishō goshirae*, or large and small mount-ings. For formal occasions sets were worn in which the sheath of each sword was covered with black lacquer, with the metalwork made of *shakudō*, either unor-namented or with the family *mon* on a *nanako* (raised-dot) ground. Lacquered horn was typically used for some of the small parts, such as the *kashira* (pommel), the rings for the tying cords on the sheath, and the tip of the sheath of the long sword.

This pair of *daishō goshirae*, dating from the eighteenth century and unusual for its felicitous decorative motifs, was handed down in the Maeda family, daimyo of a wealthy domain in Kaga Province (part of present-day Ishikawa Prefecture). The hilts are covered with white rayskin

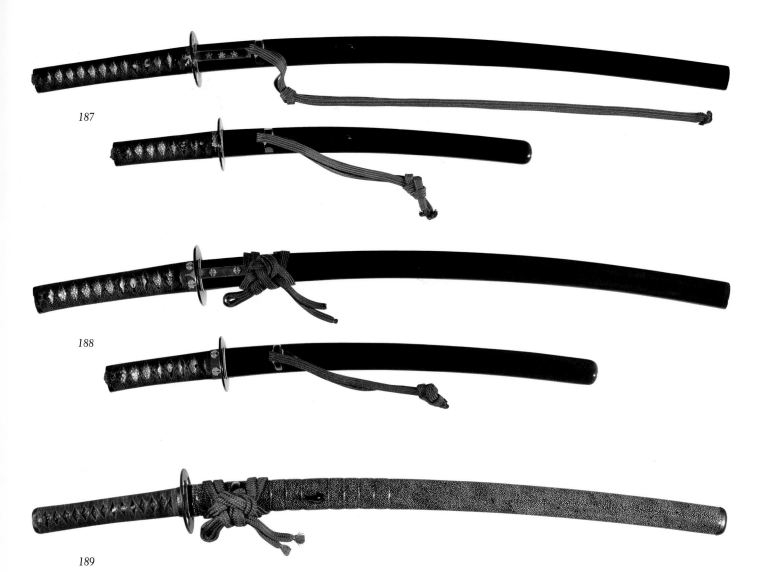

187

188

189

and wrapped with black silk cord. The *kashira* are made of horn and coated with black lacquer, while the *fuchi* (metal collars at the blade end of the hilts) are decorated with auspicious designs in gold and silver on a *shakudō* ground. The *menuki* (hilt ornaments) are modeled with a phoenix design. The sheaths are coated with black lacquer and, typically, the tip of the long one is cut straight across while the short one is rounded. A *kozuka* (small knife) and a *kōgai* (skewerlike implement) are attached to the longer sword, while the shorter one has only the *kozuka*. These accessories are decorated with the stylized plum blossom crest of the Maeda family, in high-relief gold on a *nanako* (raised-dot) *shakudō* ground; the reverse is inscribed with the name and *kaō* of the maker of these fittings, Gotō Kōrei (fl. late eighteenth century), a metalworker who served the Maeda family. The round *tsuba*, or sword guards, are decorated with conventional symbols of good fortune, such as a mallet, symbol of the god of wealth, a money pouch, jewels, and scrolls in gold on a *shakudō* ground.   HY

188 **Set of *daishō* mountings**
wood, rayskin, lacquer, silk, *shakudō*, gold, horn
length top, 89 (35); bottom, 63 (24 3/4)
Edo period, 18th century

Sword Museum, Tokyo

This set of black-lacquered *daishō goshirae* (cat. 187), made according to the established conventions, was owned by the Nabeshima family, rulers of the Saga domain in northern Kyushu. The hilts of both swords are covered with white rayskin and wound with black silk cord. The *kashira* (pommels) are made of horn covered with black lacquer, and the *fuchi* (metal collars at the blade end of the hilts) are inset with high-relief gold *mon* of contraposed *myōga* sprouts on a *nanako* (raised-dot) *shakudō* ground. Typical of *daishō* sets, the tip of the longer sword is cut straight across, while that of the shorter sword is rounded. The longer sword is fit with a *kozuka* (knife) and a *kōgai* (skewer) with the same *myōga* crest, gold on a *nanako shakudō* ground. The round *tsuba*, or sword guards, are made of undecorated *shakudō*.   HY

189 ***Katana* mounting**
wood, lacquer, rayskin, sharkskin, leather, gold, iron, copper, silk, horn
length 88 (34 5/8)
Momoyama period, 16th century

Eisei Bunko, Tokyo

This mounting, made for a sword that was forged by Seki no Kanesada (fl. late sixteenth century) and owned by Hosokawa Sansai (Tadaoki, 1563–1646), came to be treasured as the *Kasen Goshirae*, or "Immortal Poets Mounting." The reason for the name, some say, is that Sansai struck down some traitorous thirty-six retainers, the same number as the Thirty-six Immortal Poets, so designated in the eleventh century. The name of the mounting may simply reflect Sansai's love of poetry. The hilt is covered with black-lacquered rayskin and wound with brown leather over gold bean-shaped hilt ornaments *(menuki)*; the *kashira* (pommel) is made of blackened copper. The sheath is decorated by a technique in which sharkskin is covered with black lacquer and polished so that the

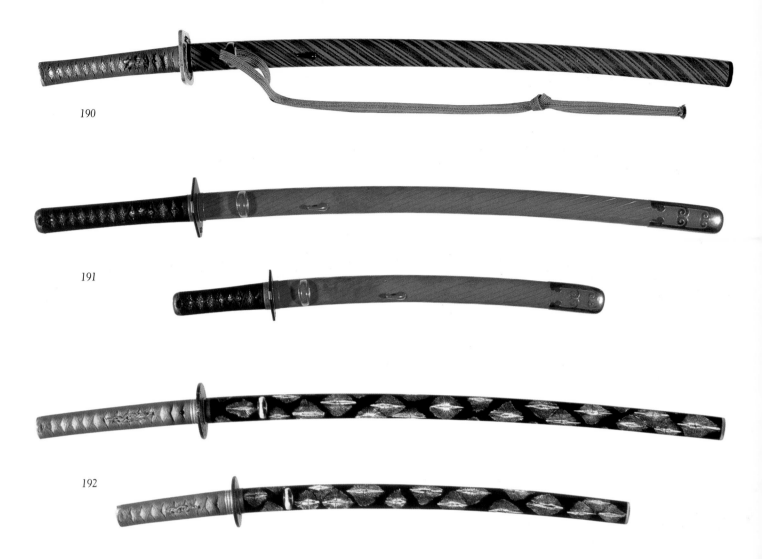

190

191

192

white stubble of the skin is exposed; rings are engraved on the section near the *tsuba*, or sword guard. The tip of the sheath, made of iron, tapers like "the bottom of a boat." The round *tsuba*, also made of iron, is decorated right and left with elegant openwork of silhouetted butterflies. This dignified and subtly detailed mounting conveys well the taste of the cultivated Sansai.   HY

190 **Katana mounting**
      wood, lacquer, rayskin, sharkskin,
      rattan, gold, copper, brass, *shakudō*
      shell, horn
      length 96 (37 3/4)
      Edo period, mid-18th century

      Sword Museum, Tokyo

The hilt, covered with white rayskin, is wrapped in brown-lacquered rattan. The *menuki*, copper with gold details, take the form of a horse. The *kashira* (pommel) and the *fuchi* (metal collar at the blade end of the hilt) are made of brass with a paulownia design in gold, *shakudō*, and shell. The sheath is covered with what appears to be black-lacquered sharkskin, upon which are

spiraling stripes of red lacquer and silver plate. The sheath opening, the ring and hook to which the tying cord is fastened, and the tip are made of black-lacquered horn.

On the brass *tsuba* is a large openwork moon; in the bottom half, in gold and copper, stands Zhang Guolao, the Chinese Daoist immortal of the Tang Dynasty who was said to have traveled immense distances on a white mule, which he kept in a gourd, at his waist, when not needed.

The metal fittings are by Tsuchiya Yasuchika (cats. 210, 211).   HY

191 **Set of daishō mountings**
      wood, rayskin, silk, lacquer,
      shakudō, gold, silver, brass, horn
      length top, 101 (39 3/4); bottom, 63.8
      (25 1/8)
      Momoyama period, 17th century

      Ii Naoyoshi Collection,
      Shiga Prefecture

Ii Naomasa (1561–1602), a close ally of Tokugawa Ieyasu, was famous for the red-lacquered armor and swords that he wore to battle; this style was carried on by subsequent generations of the Ii clan (cats.

164–169), as in this pair of *daishō goshirae* (cat. 187). High-relief *menuki* in the form of mandarin oranges (*tachibana*), the family crest of the Ii, are placed on the red-lacquered rayskin-covered hilts, which are then wrapped with black silk cord. The *kashira* (pommels) are made of undecorated silver; the *fuchi* (collars at the blade end of the hilts) are made of brass and inset with the mandarin orange crest in *shakudō*. The rounded tips of both sheaths are also made of silver, fashioned with a scroll motif. Red lacquer is applied to the sheaths so as to look like cord wrapped diagonally. The *tsuba* are made of *shakudō*.   HY

192 **Set of daishō mountings**
      wood, rayskin, silk, lacquer, iron, gold,
      horn
      length top 105.8 (41 5/8); bottom 79.5
      (31 1/4)
      Edo period, 18th century

      Ii Naoyoshi Collection,
      Shiga Prefecture

On both swords, large and small, the hilts are covered with white rayskin etched

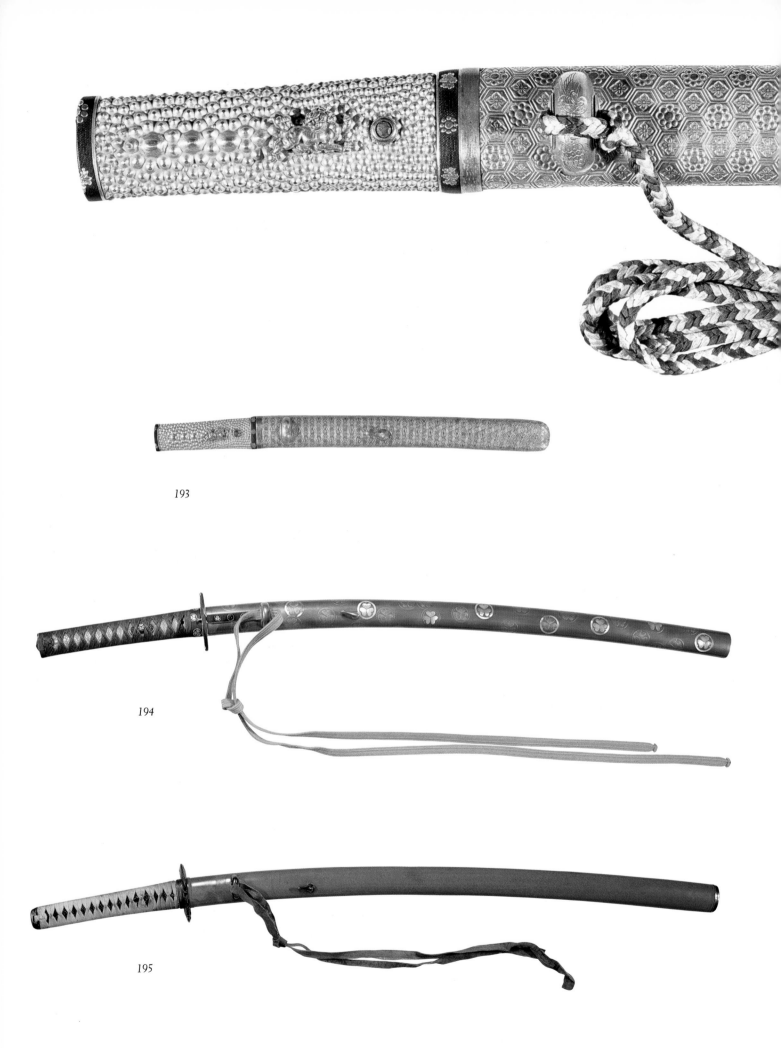

193

194

195

with an allover hexagonal tortoise-shell pattern, on top of which are gold *menuki* with a dragon design, the whole then wrapped with brown silk cord. The *kashira* (pommels) and *fuchi* (metal collars) at either end of the hilts are made of gold-covered iron. The smaller sword is fit with a *kozuka* (small knife) that is decorated with a high-relief depiction of a dragon.

In the mid-Edo period many different methods were used to decorate sword sheaths. Here diamond-shaped pieces of rayskin are placed on the sheath, covered with black lacquer, and then polished, resulting in a pattern that suggests butterflies.

It was also common at this time to take themes for the decoration of the sword fittings from traditional Chinese narratives. The iron *tsuba* of the large sword refers to the *Tanxi* tale from the *Romance of the Three Kingdoms*, in which Liu Bei of the Shu kingdom, riding the horse called Dilu, was chased by his enemy Cai Mao to the waters of the Tanxi; miraculously, Dilu jumped the stream and Liu Bei was saved. This *tsuba* is engraved *Otsuryūken Miboku*, the artist name used by Hamano Shōzui, active from the mid to the late Edo period, in his late years. The *tsuba* of the small sword is decorated with a depiction of Mencius and holds an inscription that reads *Eishun*, the artist name used by the mid-eighteenth-century metalworker Nara Jōi during his earlier years. HY

193 *Koshigatana* mounting
    wood, silk, *shakudō*, gold
    length 47 (18 ½)
    Momoyama period, 16th century

    Watanabe Yoshio Collection, Tokyo
    Important Cultural Property

Although subdued Muromachi-period-style *koshigatana* (cat. 180) continued to be made, the sword mountings of the Momoyama period, reflecting the spirit of the times, were often ornate, with the hilts and sheaths covered with such materials as rayskin or thin sheets of gold. Transmitted in the Hosokawa family, daimyo of the Kumamoto domain (in present-day Kumamoto Prefecture), this is one such example, traditionally said to have been used by Hosokawa Yūsai (1534–1610) and Sansai (1563–1646).

The hilt is covered with a thin sheet of gold, patterned like rayskin; the sheath is covered with sheet gold in a hexagonal (tortoise-shell) pattern, each section filled with either a floral design or the *kuyō mon*, the crest of the Hosokawa family. The *kashira* (pommel) and *fuchi* (metal collar on the blade end of the hilt) metal fittings on the hilt are decorated with high-relief paulownia and *kuyō mon*, both in thin sheets of gold (*iro-e*) on a raised-dot ground. Gold *shishi*, lionlike mythical beasts, form the hilt ornaments (*menuki*), the work of a Gotō school craftsman (cat. 215). A *kozuka* (small knife) attached to the reverse of the sheath is decorated with a high-relief gold depiction of *shishi* with peonies. HY

194 *Katana* mounting
    wood, lacquer, rayskin, shell, silk, gold, *shakudō*, horn
    length 97.3 (38 ¼)
    Edo period, 18th century

    Tokyo National Museum

The Tokugawa had this mounting made in the late Edo period for a famous *tachi* blade that was forged by Ichimonji Sukezane (active late thirteenth century) and owned by the Tokugawa family of Kii Province. The hollyhock *mon*, crest of the

Tokugawa, is distributed over the entire length of the mounting, suggesting that it originally belonged to a *daishō* set; the short sword was probably lost during or after the Meiji period. The hilt is covered with white rayskin and wound with light green silk cord, beneath which are placed hilt ornaments (*menuki*) with the hollyhock *mon*. The *kashira* (pommel) and *fuchi* (collar) at either end of the hilt are decorated with gold high-relief hollyhock *mon* on a *nanako* (raised-dot) ground of *shakudō*. Scattered on the sheath are hollyhock *mon* in gold *maki-e* and shell. The ring for the tying cord is horn. Both sides of the round sword guard hold the hollyhock *mon* in gold on a *nanako* (raised-dot) ground of *shakudō*, as do the *kozuka* (small knife) and *kōgai* (skewer) attached to the sheath. HY

195 *Katana* mounting
    wood, lacquer, rayskin, leather, copper, iron, horn
    length 93.0 (36 ⅝)
    Momoyama period, 16th century

    Tokyo National Museum
    Important Cultural Property

This Momoyama-period mounting was owned by Yūki Hideyasu (1574–1607), son of Tokugawa Ieyasu and daimyo of a domain in Echizen Province (part of present-day Fukui Prefecture). The hilt is covered with black-lacquered rayskin and wrapped with brown leather. The *kashira* (pommel) and the *fuchi* (collar on the blade end of the hilt) are made of blackened copper and engraved with a zigzag "mountain road" design. The sheath is completely covered with red lacquer. On the iron *tsuba*, or sword guard, are two oxen facing counterclockwise, boldly sculpted in the round. HY

196

197

198

196 Sword guard
iron
diam. 9.3 (3 5/8)
Muromachi period, early 16th century
Fukushi Shigeo Collection, Tokyo

This mid-Muromachi-period iron sword guard, carved in the round with an openwork design of a *rinbō*, can be said to reflect the Buddhist faith of the warriors. The *rinbō* design typically consists of eight swords, radiating out like the spokes of a wheel, through a lotus-shaped ring, which also symbolizes Buddhism. This sword guard has, on either side of the tang hole, openings through which the *kozuka* (small knife) and *kōgai* (a skewerlike implement) would be passed.   HY

197 Sword guard
iron
diam. 10.5 (4 1/8)
Muromachi period, mid-15th century
Kishida Eisaku Collection, Gunma Prefecture

Probably crafted by an armor maker in the mid-Muromachi period, this iron *tsuba* is thin with a hollow rim. On one side of the tang hole is a three-story pagoda and on the other crossed sickles, both in skillfully executed openwork. The sickle probably represents a sharp sword and the pagoda a memorial to warriors who died in battle. HY

198 Sword guard
iron
diam. 8.9 (3 1/2)
Muromachi period, 16th century
Tokyo National Museum

Owari *tsuba* were a type of iron sword guard made from the end of the Muromachi period through the Edo period in the province of Owari (presently part of Aichi Prefecture). As reflected by this well-known example, the iron typically had fine color and the distinctive designs were executed in openwork. Here a single crab facing to the right is depicted, the right claw large and the left one small. When the *tsuba* is worn, the crab faces away from the wearer's body.   HY

199 Sword guard
iron
diam. 9.2 (3 5/8)
Muromachi period, 16th century
Tokyo National Museum

This iron *tsuba* is decorated with a broad openwork design of a vertical bow and two horizontal arrows; two geese are in flight at the top and a roll of bow string can be seen at the bottom. Until the mid-fourteenth century, the bow and arrow were the warrior's primary weapons, and from the Kamakura period, when the Minamoto clan took control of the country and implemented warrior rule, they were offered to Hachiman shrines, such as the one at Iwashimizu south of Kyoto, in veneration of Hachiman Daibosatsu, the patron god of the warrior. The bow and ar-

268

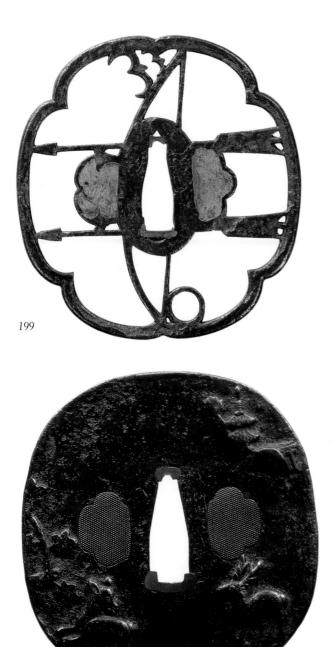

199

200

201

row were often depicted in combination with Hachiman Daibosatsu, decorating armor, sword blades, and metal fittings; although Hachiman Daibosatsu is not depicted on this *tsuba*, the design implies that motif. The color and hardness of the iron and the design suggest that this was the work of a late-Muromachi-period *tsuba* maker of Owari.   HY

200 **Sword guard**
    iron
    diam. 8.0 (3 ¹/₈)
    Muromachi period, 16th century

Yamada Hitoshi Collection, Tokyo

From the Muromachi period, *Kyōsukashi*, or Kyoto openwork, iron *tsuba* were made, it is said, on the order of the sixth Ashikaga shogun, Yoshinori (1394–1441); they

continued to be made in Kyoto throughout the Edo period. They are characterized by delicate openwork designs of natural motifs, such as floral subjects and birds. This example is shaped like a four-petalled flower; its fine openwork interior consists of two large *myōga* sprouts to the right and left of the tang hole, a plum blossom above and below the tang hole, other motifs such as clover, a bamboo hat, and plovers. The *myōga* plant, an unlikely seeming decoration for armor and weapons, nevertheless appears often, since its name is a homonymn for words meaning "divine protection."   HY

201 **Sword guard**
    Kaneie (fl. late 16th–early 17th century)
    iron with inlaid copper, silver, and gold
    diam. 8.3 (3 ¹/₄)
    Momoyama period, early 17th century

Eisei Bunko, Tokyo
Important Cultural Property

Kaneie, a *tsuba* maker who lived near Kyoto in Fushimi, Yamashiro Province, is credited as the first to make sword guards with pictorial decoration. He was active from the late Muromachi period into the Momoyama period. Strongly influenced by Muromachi-period ink paintings, he depicted such subjects as landscapes and figures. The designs on his relatively thin iron *tsuba* were carved in relief, shaving

202

203

204

off the background portions, and subtly inlaid with contrasting colored metals such as gold, silver, and *shakudō*.

Depicted on the front of this elegant iron *tsuba* is an autumn view of Kasuga Shrine near Nara, with its identifying deer, a maple branch at the left edge, and at the upper right a pagoda and *torii* gate behind rolling hills. Inlays pick out the details, such as the copper *torii* and touches of silver on the deer and gold on the maple leaves. On the reverse a maple tree is carved. Flanking the central opening through which the tang of the blade is passed are two holes for the *kozuka* (small knife) and *kōgai* (skewerlike implement), here filled with *shakudō*. On the front, flanking the tang hole, is an inscription that reads *Resident of Fushimi, Jōshū* [Yamashiro province]; *Kaneie*.   HY

202 Sword guard
Kaneie (fl. late 16th–early 17th century)
iron with inlaid gold and silver
diam. 7.9 (3 ⅛)
Momoyama period, early 17th century

Eisei Bunko, Tokyo
Important Cultural Property

Also by Kaneie (cat. 201), this fist-shaped iron *tsuba* is crafted so that a *kozuka* (small knife) can be inserted through the single hole to the left of the tang opening. On the front are the Buddhist deity Bishamonten and two old cedar trees, the details picked out with subtle inlays of gold and silver. The reverse side shows two old cedar trees and a pair of wild geese. On the front, flanking both sides of the open-

ing for the tang, is an inscription that reads, *Resident of Fushimi, Jōshū* [Yamashiro province]; *Kaneie*. Despite the irregular shape and rough finish of the surface, this masterpiece by Kaneie is technically accomplished; it reflects the sophisticated simplicity of medieval ink painting and the Buddhist faith of the warrior.   HY

203 Sword guard
Umetada Myōju (1558–1631)
brass with inlaid *shakudō*
diam. 8.0 (3 ⅛)
Momoyama period, early 17th century

Kawabata Terutaka Collection, Kanagawa Prefecture

Umetada Myōju, one of the most famous swordsmiths of the Momoyama and early

205

206

Edo periods, was equally well known for metal fittings. He made a great many *tsuba*, using materials such as brass, *shakudō*, and copper. Designs included depictions of such motifs from nature as oak trees and grapes. His skill at delineation, composition, and use of color evokes the Rinpa style of painting.

This round *tsuba*, made of brass with a slightly raised edge, is a representative work by Myōju. On both sides, rendered in inlaid *shakudō*, is an oak tree with leaves and acorns surrealistically large for its trunk—an example of the common use of dislocation and disjunction as decorative devices in Japanese art. Flanking the tang hole on the front the artist's name is engraved: *Umetada* on the right, and *Myōju* on the left. The *shakudō* fillings in the

holes for the *kozuka* (small knife) and *kōgai* (skewer) are later additions.   HY

204 **Sword guard**
Hayashi Matashichi (fl. mid-17th century)
iron with inlaid gold
diam. 8.4 (3¼)
Edo period, 17th century
Eisei Bunko, Tokyo
Important Art Object

The metalworking industry of Higo Province (present-day Kumamoto Prefecture) developed under the protection and patronage of the Hosokawa daimyo of Kumamoto, producing objects for the sword mountings for which Higo was famous. Various types of metal fittings were made,

especially openwork iron *tsuba*, and most were decorated with inlay work. Throughout the Edo period such important schools as the Hayashi, Hirata, Nishigaki, and Shimizu flourished; at the end of the Edo period the famous Kamiyoshi Rakuju appeared.

Following the move of the Hosokawa clan to Kumamoto in 1632, Hayashi Matashichi, the founder of the Hayashi school, was engaged as an official clan craftsman. This fine flower-shaped iron *tsuba* by Matashichi is decorated with crisply executed openwork depictions of cherry blossoms and the *kuyō mon*, the Hosokawa family crest, all detailed with inlaid gold. The artist's name, *Matashichi*, is inlaid in gold between the tang hole and the *kozuka* (knife) hole at the left.   HY

271

207

205 **Sword guard**
Hayashi Matashichi
(fl. mid-17th century)
iron with inlaid gold
diam. 8.0 (3⅛)
Edo period, 17th century

Eisei Bunko, Tokyo
Important Art Object

On this flower-shaped iron *tsuba* are five
openwork cherry blossoms. An inlaid gold
rope pattern encircles the inner portion,
and beyond this in a concentric circle, fine
threadlike openwork lines represent mist.
Evenly spaced around the scalloped pe-
rimeter are four heart-shaped perforations.
The blossoms of this powerful work are
carved in slight relief, and the gold harmo-

nizes well with the color of the iron. To the
left of the tang hole the artist's name, *Matashichi*, is inlaid in gold.   HY

206 **Sword guard**
Hayashi Matashichi
(fl. mid-17th century)
iron with inlaid gold
diam. 8.0 (3⅛)
Edo period, 17th century

Eisei Bunko, Tokyo

The *tsurumaru*, literally "round crane," is a
type of dancing crane motif in which the
tips of the widely spread wings meet above
the head, forming a circular cartouche.
This red-tinted black iron *tsuba* is decorated with the *tsurumaru* motif in skillfully
executed openwork. The eyes are deli-

cately inlaid with gold. Among the extant
tsuba of Hayashi Matashichi, this is a particularly fine work.   HY

207 **Set of sword guards**
Kamiyoshi Rakuju (1817–1884)
iron with inlaid gold
diam. left, 7.5 (3); right, 8.4 (3¼)
Edo period, 19th century

Eisei Bunko, Tokyo

A verdant growth of dew-laden pampas
grass, with the moon shining through it,
has long symbolized Musashino, the broad
grassy plain where the warriors of eastern
Japan created the shogunal capital, Edo.
As early as the Heian period Musashino
served as a theme for literature and paint-

208

210

209

ing, and in the Momoyama period the bending, swaying, moonlit grasses became commonplace in the decorative arts as well.

This pair of iron *tsuba*, large and small for a *daishō* set of swords, is finely decorated with the requisite pampas grass, dew, and crescent moon in openwork, and further ornamented with a hammered-gold inlaid floral scroll. The artist's name, *Rakuju*, is inlaid in gold to the left of the tang holes. Kamiyoshi Rakuju was a famous late-Edo-period craftsman who studied the traditional techniques of the Hayashi school from Hayashi Tōhachi (fl. first half of the nineteenth century).

HY

208 **Sword guard**
Attributed to Hirata Dōjin (1591–1646)
iron with inlaid cloisonné enamels and gold
diam. 8.2 (3¼)
Momoyama period, 17th century
Watanabe Kunio Collection, Tokyo

Hirata Dōjin, born Hikoshirō, is said to have learned the cloisonné enamel technique in Korea when he accompanied the Japanese armies at the end of the sixteenth century. His son, Narikazu, served the Tokugawa shogunate as a craftsman specializing in cloisonné, a position that subsequent generations of Hirata held throughout the Edo period. This ornate and technically accomplished iron *tsuba*, traditionally attributed to Dōjin, is exe-

cuted with openwork as well as extensive inlaid cloisonné enamel and gold-wire decoration of stylized clouds and floral motifs; even the thick edge is embellished with enamels.

HY

209 **Sword guard**
Gotō Ichijō (1791–1876)
shakudō with inlaid gold
diam. 8.0 (3⅛)
Edo period, 19th century
Tokyo National Museum

Gotō Ichijō was born in Kyoto, the son of Gotō Jujō, a member of a collateral branch of the main Gotō family that served the shogunate; later, Ichijō also served the *ba-*

273

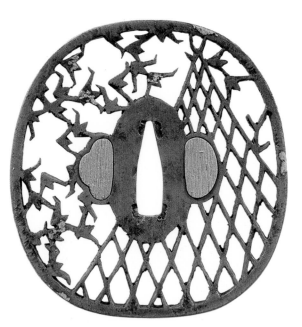

211

212

kufu in Edo. For his artistic achievements he received in 1834 the honorary rank *hokkyō* and in 1863, *hōgen*. For his finely executed works Ichijō employed a wide range of subject matter, including naturalistic floral motifs, landscapes, and figures, in addition to motifs typical of earlier Gotō work, such as *shishi* (mythical lionlike animals) and dragons.

This *tsuba*, made from *shakudō*, is decorated with a depiction of Futamigaura, a *meisho* (famous scenic spot) in Mie Prefecture where the so-called husband and wife rocks stand in the ocean close to the shore, linked with ropes; on top of the larger rock is a *torii*. Here the large pair of rocks is situated at the lower right, surrounded by lapping waves; in the upper part are several sailboats and distant

mountains, behind which peaks the sun. The rocks are depicted in high relief and gold, the sun with inlaid gold, while the other motifs are rendered in low relief. Futamigaura has long been a popular place to visit on the first day of the year; appropriately, the reverse of this *tsuba* is decorated with cranes and the sacred *sakaki* tree, both of which have auspicious associations with New Year's. Flanking the tang hole is the inscription, *Gotō hokkyō Ichijō* [*kaō*].

HY

210 **Sword guard**
Tsuchiya Yasuchika (1670–1744)
iron with inlaid gold
diam. 7.7 (3)
Edo period, 18th century
Tokyo National Museum

Tsuchiya Yasuchika was born in Shōnai in Dewa Province (presently most of the prefectures of Yamagata and Akita.) He studied with Satō Chinkyū (fl. late seventeenth century) and then moved to Edo, where he apprenticed with Nara Tokimasa (active late seventeenth century). Yasuchika used a great variety of metals in his work, including brass, *shakudō*, and copper for backgrounds, though here iron is employed. A figure stands in a mountainous

background by a stream, holding a sickle and a rope of inlaid gold, with rushes at the left and the openwork moon half covered by clouds above. The reverse is decorated with similar motifs, without the figure. The tang hole is flanked by openings for the *kozuka* (small knife) and *kōgai* (skewerlike implement); to its left on the front is inscribed the name *Tōu*, one of the artist names Yasuchika used in his later years, when he lived in the Kanda area of Edo. HY

211 **Sword guard**
Tsuchiya Yasuchika (1670–1744)
copper with inlaid gold
diam. 8.5 (3 3/8)
Edo period, 18th century

Miyazaki Kazue Collection,
Kanagawa Prefecture
Important Cultural Property

This oblate copper *tsuba*, an excellent example of Tsuchiya Yasuchika's (cat. 210) late work, has a skillfully carved openwork design of a flock of plovers flying diagonally across the right with a drying fishnet at the left. The design is given variety with the touches of inlaid gold, and the *kozuka* (small knife) and *kōgai* (skewer) holes are filled with plugs of gold. To the

right of the tang hole, *Tōu*, one of Yasuchika's artist names, is engraved in seal form characters. HY

212 **Sword guard**
Nara Toshinaga (1667–1736)
iron with inlaid gold
diam. 7.4 (2 7/8)
Edo period, 18th century

Eisei Bunko, Tokyo
Important Cultural Property

Nara Toshinaga is considered one of the three great metalworkers of the Nara school, the other two being Tsuchiya Yasuchika (1670–1744; cats. 210, 211) and Sugiura Jōi (1700–1761). He was active in the city of Edo during the mid-Edo period,

213

creating powerful works characterized by the thickness of the background metal and the designs carved in high relief. The design on this iron *tsuba* concerns a story from the war between the Taira and Minamoto clans in which Minamoto Yoshitsune (1159–1189), the brother of Yoritomo, chased the Taira troops and advanced to Mure Takamatsu on the opposite shore from Yashima. On the front is an armored and mounted high-ranking warrior, Yoshitsune perhaps, depicted in high relief with gold details. The branch of a pine tree is engraved at the top, and a pool of water is carved out in openwork at the bottom. On the reverse is a retainer holding a flag beneath a high-relief pine tree, its needles incised. On the front, between the opening for the *kozuka* (small knife) on the left and the tang hole, is engraved the artist's name, *Toshinaga*, and his *kaō*.　HY

213　*Daishō* sword fittings
Ishiguro Masayoshi (b. 1774)
shakudō, gold
diam. left *tsuba*, 7.6 (3); right *tsuba*, 7.4 (27/8)
Edo period, 18th century
Private Collection

Ishiguro Masayoshi, an accomplished metalworker who apprenticed with Ishiguro Masatsune of Edo, produced ornate sword fittings, often depicting flower and bird subjects on a *nanako* (raised-dot) *shakudō* ground in high relief, inlay, and gold applied with the *iro-e* technique. This set of fittings is comprised of a pair of *tsuba*, the *kashira* (pommels), and the *fuchi* (metal collars at the blade end of the hilt) for a pair of *daishō* mountings. All are given a *nanako shakudō* ground and decorated with a pine tree and gold long-tailed bird motif. The *tsuba* are engraved, *Jugakusai Ishiguro Masayoshi* [*kaō*], and the *fuchi*, *Ishiguro Masayoshi* [*kaō*].　HY

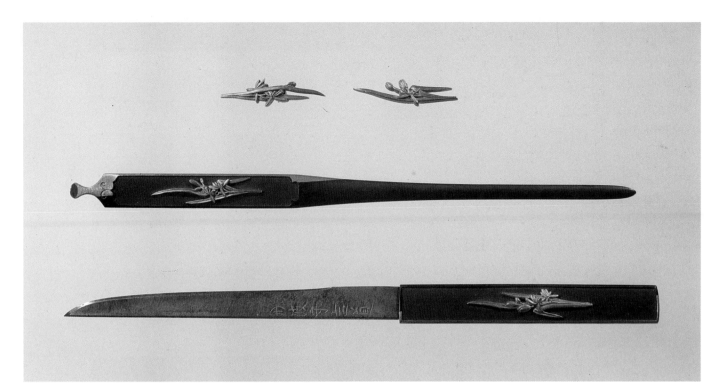

214

214 *Mitokoromono*
Gotō Tsūjō
(fl. c. 1690)
shakudō and gold
length   *kōgai,* 21.2 (8⅜); *kozuka* (not including blade), 9.7 (3⅞); *menuki,* 3.0 (1⅛) each
Edo period, late 17th century

Hiroi Akihisa Collection, Tokyo

The *mitokoromono*, literally "things for three places," is a set of metal sword fittings with matching decorative schemes; the set is composed of a small knife *(kozuka)*, a skewer *(kōgai)*, and a pair of hilt ornaments *(menuki)*. The small knife and skewer slide into their separate openings on either side of the sheath. The long tapered end of the *kōgai* was used to fix a warrior's hair, while its spoon-shaped end was shaped to be used as an ear cleaner. *Menuki,* positioned on either side of the

sword hilt, aided the grip and provided decoration. In the Muromachi period only the Gotō family produced matching *mitokoromono* sets, but by the middle of the Edo period other craftsmen began to produce them as well. This set was made by the eleventh-generation Gotō metalworker Tsūjō (Mitsutoshi), and is characteristic of the work of the Gotō school (cat. 215.) Both the *kōgai* and *kozuka* are decorated with gold orchids in high relief on a *nanako* (raised-dot) *shakudō* ground; the gold *menuki* take the form of orchids.   HY

215 Sword fittings by nine consecutive generations of the Gotō family
shakudō, gold, silver
length c. 9.6 (3¾) each
Muromachi period–Edo period, 15th–18th century

Fukushi Shigeo Collection, Tokyo

The founder of the Gotō family of sword ornament makers was Gotō Yūjō (given

name, Masaoku, fl. c. 1460), who served the eighth Ashikaga shogun, Yoshimasa (1436–1490), in the Muromachi period. Assimilating and building upon standard metalworking techniques, Yūjō established a distinct Gotō style, primarily expressed in *mitokoromono,* the set of sword fittings consisting of the *kozuka, kōgai,* and *menuki* (small knife, skewer, and hilt ornaments; cat. 214). The Gotō subsequently flourished, with successive generations serving the Ashikaga shogunate, Toyotomi Hideyoshi, and the Tokugawa shogunate. In the Edo period the Gotō products became known as *iebori,* literally "house carvings," referring to the official status of the Gotō as craftsmen to the shogunate, as distinguished from other "town carving" metalwork, or *machibori.* In all there were seventeen generations of Gotō, listed below by artist name, followed by the given name in parentheses and approximate period of activity:

1. Yūjō (Masaoku),
   fl. c. 1460
2. Sōjō (Mitsutake),
   fl. c. 1500
3. Jōshin (Yoshihisa),
   fl. c. 1530
4. Kōjō (Mitsuie),
   fl. c. 1570
5. Tokujō (Mitsumoto),
   fl. c. 1600
6. Eijō (Masamitsu),
   fl. c. 1610
7. Kenjō (Mitsutsugu),
   fl. c. 1620
8. Sokujō (Mitsushige),
   fl. c. 1630
9. Teijō (Mitsumasa),
   fl. c. 1650
10. Renjō (Mitsutomo),
    fl. c. 1680
11. Tsūjō (Mitsutoshi),
    fl. c. 1690
12. Jujō (Mitsumasa),
    fl. c. 1720
13. Enjō (Mitsutaka),
    fl. c. 1730
14. Keijō (Mitsumori),
    fl. c. 1740
15. Shinjō (Mitsuyoshi),
    fl. c. 1750
16. Hōjō (Mitsuaki),
    fl. c. 1820
17. Tenjō (Mitsunori),
    fl. c. 1850

This set consists of nine *kozuka* (small knives) with ornaments made by the first nine Gotō generation heads; the character of the Gotō style is maintained throughout, and typically only gold, silver, and *shakudō* are employed.

The first example (*a*) is a slender high-relief gold dragon executed by Yūjō, the first-generation head of the Gotō. Jujō (Mitsumasa), the twelfth Gotō master, made the *sao* (base) of *shakudō* with a *nanako* (raised-dot) ground and set the dragon on it. Recording this history, the reverse, covered with a thin sheet of gold, is engraved, *mon* [referring to the ornament] *Yūjō; Mitsumasa* [*kaō* of Mitsumasa]. The Gotō lineage was skilled at the depiction of dragons; in particular, those by Yūjō are known for their sense of movement.

The high-relief *shakudō* Kurikara dragon of the second example (*b*) was made by Sōjō, the second-generation Gotō head. The *sao* was again made by Jujō (Mitsumasa), the twelfth-generation head, as his inscription on the back describes, *mon Sōjō; Mitsumasa* [*kaō* of Mitsumasa]. The Kurikara dragon, wound around a sword and about to swallow it, was often used as a motif in sword-related decoration (cat. 170.)

The stout high-relief gold dragon of the third example (*c*) is a characteristic work of Jōshin, the third Gotō head. The

a.

b.

c.

d.

e.

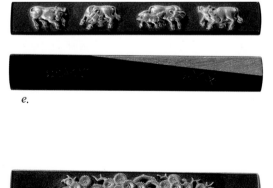

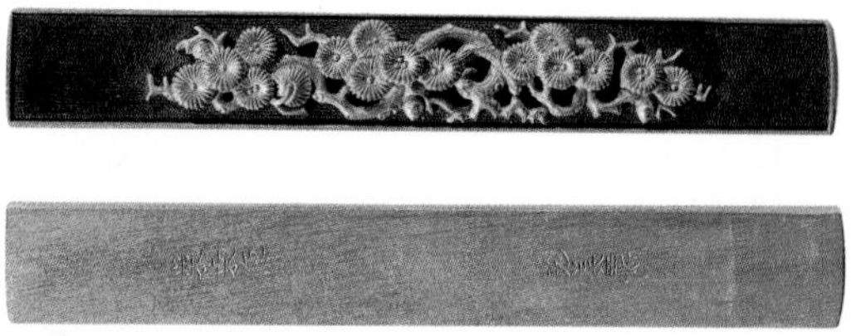

f.

215

278

g.

i.

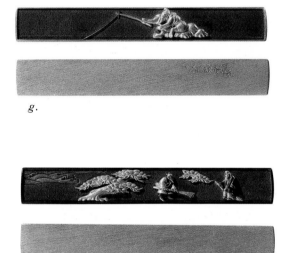

h.

sao was made by Renjō (Mitsutomo), the tenth-generation Gotō head. The inscription on the reverse reads, *mon Jōshin; Mitsutomo* [*kaō* of Mitsutomo].

The fourth example (*d*) holds a closely described gold high-relief depiction of Fudō Myōō executed by the fourth-generation Gotō head, Kōjō. The *sao* was again made by Jujō (Mitsumasa), the twelfth-generation Gotō head, whose inscription on the reverse reads, *mon Kōjō; Mitsumasa* [*kaō* of Mitsumasa].

The fifth example (*e*) consists of five gold high-relief oxen in a variety of postures by the fifth-generation Gotō head, Tokujō. The ox is one of the twelve animals of the zodiacal cycle, a theme often used by the Gotō school. The ninth Gotō head, Teijō made the *sao* and inscribed the reverse, *mon Tokujō; Teijō* [*kaō* of Teijō].

The sixth-generation Gotō head, Eijō, made the high-relief gold pine tree of the sixth example (*f*); the pine, treasured as a

symbol of long life, endurance, and loyalty, and often used as a motif in the arts, spreads widely right and left across the horizontal plane. The pine needles are depicted as wheels of needles, typical of the traditional Gotō style. Shinjō (Mitsuyoshi), the fifteenth-generation head, made the *sao*, as inscribed on the reverse, *Made by Eijō; Mitsuyoshi* [*kaō* of Mitsuyoshi].

The seventh example (*g*) was made entirely by Kenjō, the seventh-generation Gotō head. The plump high-relief gold figure of Ebisu, revered as one of the seven gods of good luck, sits on a rock holding a fishing pole. The reverse is inscribed, *Gotō Kenjō* [*kaō*].

The eighth example (*h*), a motif known as *Takasago*, was decorated by the eighth-generation Gotō head, Sokujō. The motif, often depicted by the Gotō school, consists of an old pine tree, here in gold, and an old man holding a rake and an old woman holding a broom. Here the pine tree is in gold and both figures are made of

shakudō and detailed with gold and silver. Takasago is a place in the province of Harima (present-day Hyōgo Prefecture). In legend, and in the Nō play also called *Takasago*, an ancient and mutually devoted couple named Jō and Uba are revealed as the spirits of the pine trees, one at Takasago, one at Sumiyoshi. The *sao*, with a silver wave pattern at the upper left on the front, was executed by the twelfth-generation head, Jujō (Mitsumasa), who inscribed the edge, *Made by Sokujō; Mitsumasa* [*kaō* of Mitsumasa].

The ninth example (*i*) is decorated with a scene of fishing, a motif often employed in the arts from the Muromachi period, here consisting of high-relief mountains on the left and a fisherman rowing a small boat at the right, bobbing among the carved waves; details are added in gold and silver. This work was made by the ninth Gotō head, Teijō, who inscribed the reverse, *Teijo* [*kaō*].   HY

279

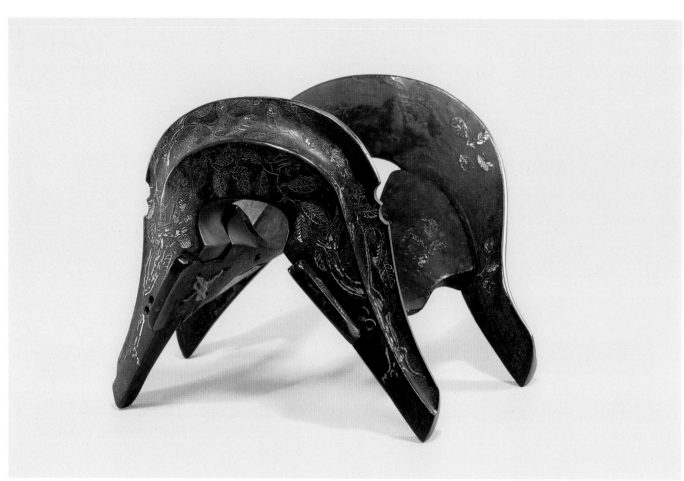

216

216 **Saddle**
lacquer on wood with shell
30 (11¹³/₁₆)
Heian period
Eisei Bunko, Tokyo
National Treasure

The arched pommel and cantle of this saddle are red oak, and the bars, which form
the saddle's seat, are soft paulownia. The
ends of the bars that join the pommel and
cantle are exposed in front and back, revealing the saddle's basic structure. This
type of saddle is called *wagura* or *yamato-
gura* (Japanese-style saddle) to distinguish
it from the earlier *karakura* (Chinese-style
saddle), in which the bar ends are concealed. The pommel has a scalloped
groove on either side for a rider to grasp
when needed. Small slits on the bars allow
a cinch to be passed through and tied
around the belly of the horse.

The saddle is finished with black lacquer and ornamented with a design of oak
branches and leaves; on the outer faces of
the pommel and cantle are pairs of horned
owls. All these designs are executed in the
technique called *raden* (inlaid iridescent
seashell), usually that of the *yakōgai* (turbo
marmoratus) or *awabi* (abalone). The lacquer surface, worn and chipped in some
places, has lost much of its original bril-
liance and has been partly retouched.

Many of the shell pieces have fallen off,
leaving only the grooves that held them.
The edges of the pommel and cantle, as
well as the underside of the seat, are
painted gold, which is a later addition.

This type of saddle, unlike the
karakura-style saddles used only for ceremonial occasions, actually was used in
battle. One tradition has it that this saddle
belonged to the illustrious general Minamoto Yoritomo (1147–1199). Thirteenth-
century epic narratives that describe
battles of the late twelfth century mention
saddles with similar designs of oak and
owls, suggesting that this design was
widely used in the twelfth century. An excellent pictorial record survives today in a
masterly late twelfth-century ink drawing,
the *Animal caricature scrolls* at Kōzanji,
Kyoto.

This saddle has been in the Hosokawa
family since the mid-sixteenth century,
when the thirteenth shogun, Ashikaga
Yoshiteru (r. 1546–1565) presented it to Hosokawa Fujitaka (Yūsai, 1534–1610), who
gave it to his fourth son, Takayuki. After
Takayuki's death in 1647 it was owned by
one Arisaka Sadaifu, presumably one of
the Hosokawa's vassals.   YS

217 **Saddle**
lacquer on wood with shell
29.8 (11³/₄)
Kamakura period
Eisei Bunko, Tokyo
National Treasure

This saddle, made of red oak and paulownia wood, would have provided the rider
with a secure, stable seat. Saddles of this
type are called *suikangura* (informal saddle), or sometimes *gunjingura* (military
camp saddle), which in the thirteenth century meant easy to mount but unfit for
ceremonial use. This distinction reflected
new developments in Japanese saddlery
that brought subtle changes in shape as
well as decor. Compared with cat. 216, the
rims of the pommel and cantle are thinner
(0.7 cm and 1.0 cm, respectively) and the
decoration more elaborate. The rims may
have been covered by metal (perhaps silver) ridges, now lost.

The saddle is finished with black lacquer, and its pommel and cantle are extensively decorated with inlaid iridescent
seashell in the *raden* technique. Originally,
the seat also was richly decorated with inlaid shell. Except for a few sprinkles for
the pine leaves, most of the shell in this
area has been lost through abrasion caused
by repeated contact with a rider's armor.
The pommel and cantle are decorated

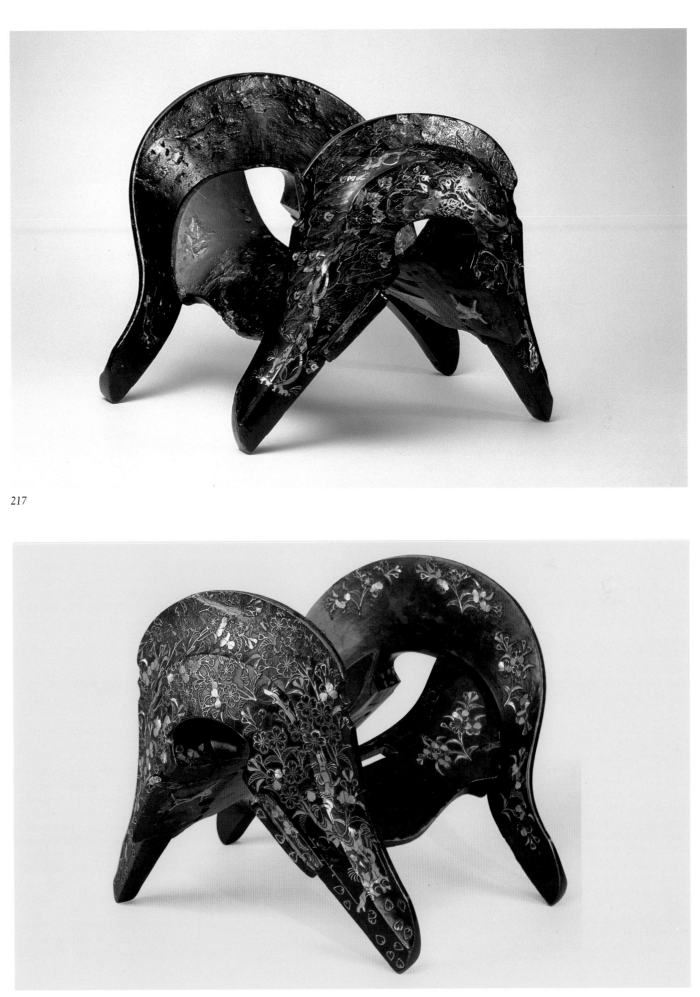

217

218

219

with a design of rain-soaked, wind-blown leaves and vines of the *kuzu* (arrowroot) plant juxtaposed with pine needles. Among the maze of plant forms are several Japanese characters, also in the *raden* technique, written in cursive script. The characters are from a famous *waka* (thirty-one-syllable poem) on the theme of love, by Jien (1155–1225). This poem was included in the imperial anthology, *Shin kokin wakashū* (New collection of ancient and modern poems).

Waga koi wa
matsu o shigure no
somekanete
Makuzugahara ni
kaze sawagunari

This love I feel—
    powerless to change her mind,
    like the drizzle the pine's hue;
My heart like the wind
    that stirs the leaves on Kuzu Plain.

The poem's rich, elusive symbolism derives from long-established poetic conventions. Puns based on Japanese homonyms give certain words hidden meanings. For example, the wind exposing the whitish undersides of the *kuzu* leaves (*urami*, or "to see the back") in the poetic language creates a pun on a homonym that means "to hate." The word "pine" or *matsu* is a pun on another word pronounced *matsu*, which means "to wait."

The pictorial equivalents of the plant imagery in the poem mesh with the char-

acters written on the saddle. The characters are superimposed over the plant forms, and serve as keys to the identification of the poem. This convention, known in the Japanese calligraphic tradition as *ashide* (literally "reed-script"), in which characters are written as if part of the reed plant on an embankment, was one of the most frequently used artistic forms in the twelfth and thirteenth centuries. The characters are:

shigure (drizzle of autumn), in the lower center of the pommel's outer faces;
some (to dye or change hue), on the lower right edge of the pommel;
ni (particle indicating "at" or "in") on the lower left edge of the pommel;
shigure, in the upper center of the cantle;
waga (my), in the lower center of the cantle;
koi (love), on the lower right edge of the cantle; and
hara (field), on the lower left edge of the cantle.

The inlaying technique used for this saddle is very elaborate. The two sides of the *kuzu* leaves are depicted in two different ways: the white undersides are represented by inlaid cut pieces of shell simulating the general shape of the leaves, and by dark spaces left between the leaves to indicate the veins; the faces of the leaves are defined by lines made of extremely fine pieces of shell. The pine needles are rendered in herringbone patterns. The lacquer surfaces have suffered consid-

erable damage and some parts show traces of later repair. On the peak of the pommel the damage and subsequent repairs have been most extensive.

Since the early seventeenth century it has been believed that this saddle was owned by Minamoto Yoshitsune (1159–1189), the younger brother of Yoritomo (1147–1199). This provenance is spurious, however, because the date when the poem was first included in the Imperial anthology, *Shin kokinshū*, 1205, post-dates Yoshitsune's death date.   YS

218 **Saddle**
    lacquer on wood with shell
    30.0 (11 13/16)
    Kamakura period
    Agency for Cultural Affairs, Tokyo
    Important Cultural Property

Like cats. 216 and 217, this *gunjingura*, or military camp saddle, is among the most famous examples in Japan. Such *wagura* (Japanese-style) saddles with a rounded shape and hand grooves in the pommel were used by military commanders from the late Heian through the Kamakura periods. Lacquered saddles were considered very precious articles, and some were exported to China; one was even presented to an emperor of the Song Dynasty.

Gnarled mountain cherry trees (*yamazakura*) extend up and across the outside faces of the pommel and cantle. The roots

220

of the cherry trees begin at the bottom of both legs of the saddle, while their branches then arch toward the center, paralleling the saddle's curved shape and create a symmetrical design. The branches on both legs are adorned with cherry blossoms, leaves, and tiny ferns growing along the tree's trunk. Even the seat of the saddle, which would have been covered by a saddlecloth, is decorated with a delicate design of scattered leaves and sprays of blossoms. Roots and tree trunks are filled in with full pieces of shell, while most of the flower petals are delicately outlined with a thin line of shell. The stylized treatment of natural motifs such as these cherry blossoms is characteristic Kamakura-period arts and crafts. The intricacy and complexity of the cherry blossom design is comparable to that of the *shigure* saddle (cat. 217), suggesting that both saddles were created during the same period.

This saddle formerly belonged to the Asano family, overlords of Aki Province (present-day Hiroshima Prefecture).   MR

219 Saddle and stirrups
maki-e and black lacquer, gold and silver on wood
saddle 27.5 (10⅞)
Momoyama period, 16th century
Tokyo National Museum
Important Cultural Property

The bold decoration on the front and back wheels of this saddle is typical of Momoyama-period design. It consists of

large reed stalks in gold *takamaki-e* (relief *maki-e*) lacquer and sheet gold on a black lacquer ground; silver drops of dew cling to the reeds. The two wheels are rimmed with gold. The stirrups, of black lacquered wood mounted on iron, are similarly decorated with reeds.

This saddle is said to have belonged to Toyotomi Hideyoshi (1537–1598). An ink drawing of the saddle is inscribed, *Middle of the first month, fifth year of Tenshō* [1577], *Hideyoshi* [kaō]. However, on the reverse of the saddle seat is an inscription that reads, *A day in the ninth month, second year of Bun'an* [1446], indicating that this was an old saddle newly decorated in 1577.   SN

220 Saddle and stirrups
maki-e lacquer and gold on wood
27.8 (10¼)
Edo period, 17th–18th century
Tokyo National Museum

The front and back wheels are decorated with a plum tree and hawk design in *takamaki-e* (relief *maki-e*) lacquer and cut gold leaf on a pear-skin ground (*nashiji*); the hawks' eyes are glass. An inscription on the reverse of the saddle seat reads, *Tenth day of the second month, seventh year of Meiō* [1498]. As seen in cat. 219, and as was often the case in the Edo period, an old saddle was newly decorated.   SN

LACQUER

221

221 **Set of shelves with designs based on The Tale of Genji**
maki-e and black lacquer, gold, silver, tin, and mother-of-pearl on wood
65.5 x 72.5 x 33.0 (25³/₄ x 28¹/₂ x 13)
Momoyama period, 17th century

Agency for Cultural Affairs, Tokyo
Important Cultural Property

Formerly owned by the Hachisuka family, daimyo of Awa Province (present-day Tokushima Prefecture), this three-tiered set of *zushidana* type shelves includes a cabinet on the middle level in which the doors swing out and another on the lower level with a sliding door. The decorative motifs are based on the Heian-period romantic classic, *The Tale of Genji*. The motif of two young pines on the top shelf is associated with the twenty-third chapter, *Nenohi*, by which name this set is known. The designs on the other levels— moonflowers on a fan, a carriage, and a fan with a picture of a bridge—are all related to other chapters in *Genji*. A fence runs diagonally across the doors, and maple leaves and pine needles are scattered on the interiors of the cabinets and on the sides and back of the set.

   Maki-e is the term used to describe a group of Japanese lacquer techniques in which powdered metal, usually gold or silver, and lacquer are used to create designs. The motifs in this set of shelves are depicted in *takamaki-e* (relief *maki-e*) lacquer, in which the *maki-e* motifs are executed on a surface raised with such materials as raw lacquer and pulverized stone. In addition, inlaid mother-of-pearl (*raden*), and gold, silver, and tin are employed. The bold composition and techniques are characteristic of the group of lacquerwares known as *Kōetsu maki-e*, associated with Hon'ami Kōetsu (1558–1637, cats. 254, 255). SN

222

222 **Set of shelves with design based on**
Kokei sanshō
maki-e and black lacquer, gold, silver,
tin, and mother-of-pearl on wood
65.5 x 72.8 x 32.7 (25¾ x 28⅝ x 12⅞)
Momoyama period, 17th century

Tokyo National Museum
Important Art Object

This set of shelves, similar in form to cat.
221, is decorated on the top with a design
of a plum tree, and on the lower two tiers
with packages of incense and an incense
burner. On the upper shelf is a depiction
of three men on a bridge, based on the
apocryphal Chinese allegorical tale known
in Japanese as *Kokei sanshō* (Three laugh-
ers of Tiger Stream). Long ago, according
to the tale, the monk Huiyuan retired to
the Donglin Temple at Mount Lu in
Jiangxi Province and pledged never to
cross the tiger stream into the secular
realm. Once, his friends the poet Tao
Yuanming and the Daoist Lu Xiujing visited him; the three became so engrossed in
conversation that in seeing his two friends
off, Huiyuan inadvertently crossed the
bridge, and they burst into laughter. The
front doors are decorated with a brushwood fence and the sides and back with dianthus. The decoration is executed in gold

and silver *takamaki-e* (relief *maki-e*) lacquer
with cut gold and silver leaf, tin plate, and
inlaid mother-of-pearl (*raden*).

The daimyo and tea master Furuta
Oribe (1544–1615) ordered a set of shelves
with the *Kokei sanshō* motif from Kōami
Chōgen, younger brother of Kōami
Chōan, the seventh head of the Kōami
school of *maki-e* craftsmen who served the
Tokugawa shogunate. Seven such sets are
extant today, although it is not clear which
is the original.   SN

223

223 Writing table

11.2 x 58.2 x 34.2 (4³/₈ x 22⁷/₈ x 13¹/₂)
maki-e and black lacquer, gold and
silver on wood
Momoyama period, 16th century

Myōhōin, Kyoto
Important Cultural Property

This type of *bundai*, or writing table, is associated particularly with *renga* (linked
verse) gatherings. The *bundai* was not actually used as a support for writing but
rather to hold the paper on which poems
would be brushed. This example is said to
have been owned by Toyotomi Hideyoshi
(1537–1598); its top is decorated with autumn flowers and grasses in *takamaki-e* (relief *maki-e*) lacquer and cut gold and silver
leaf on a black lacquer ground. The sides
are covered with *hiramaki-e* (level *maki-e*)
chrysanthemums and paulownia *mon*.
The style of the decoration is reminiscent
of the so-called Kōdaiji *maki-e*, popular in
the Momoyama period, which was associated with Kōdaiji, a Zen temple in Kyoto
established in 1605 by the widow of Toyotomi Hideyoshi. The techniques actually employed are mostly traditional
Muromachi-period ones, however, so this
work may be considered a transitional
piece.   SN

224 Writing table and writing utensil box

bundai 9.2 x 59.2 x 35.0 (3⁵/₈ x 23¹/₄ x
13⁷/₈)
suzuribako 6.1 x 23.1 x 24.6 (2³/₈ x 9¹/₁₆
x 9¹¹/₁₆)
maki-e lacquer, gold, silver, and gilt
silver on wood
Momoyama period, 16th century

Suntory Museum of Art, Tokyo
Important Cultural Property

Both the *bundai* (writing table) and the *suzuribako* (writing utensil box) are decorated with a combination of bamboo,
paulownia, and the phoenix. In China, the
phoenix was believed to signal the imminent appearance of a virtuous emperor.
The bird eats bamboo seeds, rests on a
type of paulownia tree, and drinks from
the fountain of nectar, said to spring only
in an age of perfect peace. This is representative of the lavish Momoyama-period
style, in which the *takamaki-e* (relief
maki-e) technique, cut gold and silver leaf,
and thick gilt silver plate were lavishly
used. The background is executed in a
technique known as *nashiji* (pear-skin
ground), a *maki-e* ground treatment, similar in appearance to the skin of the *nashi*,
or Japanese pear, in which metal flakes,
usually gold, are suspended in lacquer.   SN

224

225

225 **Writing utensil box**
4.6 x 22.5 x 24.5 (1¹³⁄₁₆ x 8⁷⁄₈ x 9⁵⁄₈)
maki-e lacquer, metal, and
mother-of-pearl on wood
Edo period, 17th century

Ishikawa Prefectural Museum of Art

In the Edo period, the arts prospered under the Maeda family, daimyo of a rich domain in Kaga Province (part of present-day Ishikawa Prefecture). During the reign of the third-generation Maeda daimyo, Toshitsune (1593–1658), the Kyoto *maki-e* artist Igarashi Dōho was invited to Kanazawa, the castle town of the Maeda, and the *Kaga maki-e* style of lacquer was developed. This *suzuribako* (writing utensil box), remarkable for its elaborate *maki-e* technique, is attributed to Dōho. It is decorated with a field full of such grasses and flowers as chrysanthemums, pampas grass, Chinese bellflowers, and *fujibakama*, or "purple trousers." The designs are executed in *takamaki-e* (relief *maki-e*) lacquer, sheet metal, and inlaid mother-of-pearl (*raden*). The ground is in the *maki-e* technique known as *ikakeji*, in which fine gold or silver filings are densely spread over wet lacquer. The reverse of the lid and the removable tray inside are decorated with flying cranes, some holding pine branches in their beaks.   SN

226 **Writing utensil box**
4.0 x 21.3 x 23.8 (1⁹⁄₁₆ x 8³⁄₈ x 9⁵⁄₁₆)
maki-e, red and black lacquer, gold, tin, and mother-of-pearl on wood; copper
Edo period, 17th century

Eisei Bunko, Tokyo

With the advent of a period of peace at the beginning of the early modern era, the working life of the commoner became a popular theme in both painting and crafts, supplementing the traditional subjects related to the court and warrior classes, and landscapes. This trend is reflected in the decoration of this *suzuribako* (writing utensil box), with seven women transplanting rice shoots in slightly raised *takamaki-e* (relief *maki-e*) lacquer, inlaid mother-of-pearl (*raden*), and sheet-gold and tin. Black lacquer is used for the women's eyes and hair and red lacquer for their lips. A regular, diagonal wavelike pattern in gold *maki-e* forms the ground on the top and sides of the overlapping lid and the sides of the box. The interior is decorated with a dianthus design and holds a round copper water-dropper, an inkstone, and a removable tray. Not shown in the photograph is an inkstick, decorated with a design of scattered chrysanthemums.   SN

226

227

227 **Bridal trousseau**
maki-e, red and black lacquer on wood; gilt copper, silver and nickel
zushidana 75.8 x 101.9 x 39.7 (29³/₄ x 40¹/₈ x 15⁵/₈)
kurodana 71.2 x 77.5 x 38.4 (28 x 30¹/₂ x 15¹/₈)
shodana 103.9 x 100.0 x 44.0 (407/₈ x 39³/₈ x 17³/₈)
Edo period, 19th century

Hōfu Mōri Hōkōkai,
Yamaguchi Prefecture

The Edo-period daimyo bride brought to her new home an elaborate set of household furnishings reflecting the power and prestige of the daimyo family. The contents of the trousseau were established by the early Edo period. A typical trousseau centered around three sets of shelves, the *zushidana* (right), the *kurodana* (black shelves) (center), and the *shodana* (book shelves) (left). Included are most of the things required for personal use, such as, on top of the *zushidana*, a large box containing smaller boxes of cosmetic items.

On the first shelf is a set of utensils for the incense game (cats. 233, 234) and on the bottom shelf is a *suzuribako* (writing utensil box; cats. 224, 225, 226). A clothes rack and wash basin are displayed in front. Set out before the *kurodana* are a *kushidai* (comb stand), and to the left, a set of *ohaguro* equipment for blackening the teeth (cats. 229, 230); the distinctive redcornered box on the *kurodana* contains cosmetic paraphernalia. The *shodana* holds articles related to reading and writing; in front is a cast nickel mirror on its folding holder, with the storage box to the right.

This set was used by the daughter of Narihiro (1783–1836), the tenth-generation Mōri daimyo of the Hagi domain in present-day Yamaguchi Prefecture, when she married into the Mōri branch family of Tokuyama. The many constituent parts are decorated with a plum blossom floral scroll and latticework design, and the water plantain *mon*, a family crest used by the Mōri. These motifs are executed in gold and silver *hiramaki-e* (level *maki-e*) lacquer. The arabesque plum blossom design is executed in alternating *hiramaki-e* and *enashiji*, in which designs are depicted with *nashiji* (pear-skin ground). The fittings are gilt copper, engraved with the water plantain *mon* and a floral scroll.   SN

228

228 **Bridal trousseau**
maki-e, red and black lacquer on
wood; silver
zushidana 79.7 x 99.1 x 39.7 (31 3/8 x 39
x 15 5/8)
kurodana 68.2 x 77.7 x 39.1 (26 7/8 x
30 5/8 x 15 3/8)
Edo period, 18th century

Kōzu Kobunka Kaikan, Kyoto

This set of bridal furnishings belonged to a
daughter of the Nanbu family, daimyo of a
domain in present-day Iwate Prefecture.
Centered around a *zushidana* (right) and
kurodana ("black shelves,"), it contains
washing basins, cosmetic utensils (cats.
229, 230) including teeth-blackening (*ohaguro*) equipment, a set of utensils for the
incense game (cats. 233, 234) and writing-
related objects. The design consists of a
peony floral scroll and the *tsurumaru* (circular crane) *mon* of the Nanbu clan in gold
maki-e lacquer on a pear-skin ground
(*nashiji*). The fittings are made of silver. SN

229

229 Cosmetic set
maki-e and black lacquer on wood;
nickel, gilt silver
mirror holder h. 63.3 (24 7/8)
kushidai 37.5 x 36.4 x 25.3 (14 3/4 x 14 3/8 x 10)
Edo period, 19th century
Eisei Bunko, Tokyo

The wife of the tenth-generation Hoso-kawa daimyo, Narimori (1804–1860) is believed to have owned this set of cosmetic utensils. It includes a folding mirror holder and two mirrors cast from nickel engraved with the name Fujiwara Iesato, a famous mirror-maker of the late Edo period (right). At the center of the set is the *kushidai*, literally "comb stand," which holds not only combs but also various brushes and boxes of powder and oils. On the left is a set of equipment for *ohaguro*, or blackening the teeth, a custom popular among both men and women in the court class from the Heian period, and practiced by women after they had come of age or married in the Edo period; the metal objects in this set are made of gilt silver. The design consists of gold *maki-e* lacquer chrysanthemums on a black lacquer ground.   SN

230 Cosmetic set
maki-e lacquer on wood
kyōdai h. 62.7 (24 5/8)
kushidai 26.1 x 29.4 x 21.8 (10 5/16 x 11 9/16 x 8 9/16)
Edo period, 19th century
Tokyo National Museum

This cosmetic set is part of the bridal furnishings owned by the daughter of Tokugawa Harutomi (1771–1852), the tenth-generation daimyo of the Wakayama domain in Kii Province. In 1816 she was married to Nariyori, the sixth son of Tokugawa Ienari (1773–1841), the eleventh shogun. Included here are a *kyōdai* (mirror-holder on a chest of drawers) and its mirror, many containers and the utensils they hold, a *kushidai* (comb stand) with its various combs, brushes, and boxes of powders and oils, and a set of equipment for tooth blackening (*ohaguro*). The decoration consists of the hollyhock *mon*, associated with the Tokugawa family, and a bamboo trellis fence in gold and silver *maki-e* lacquer on a pear-skin ground (*nashiji*).   SN

230

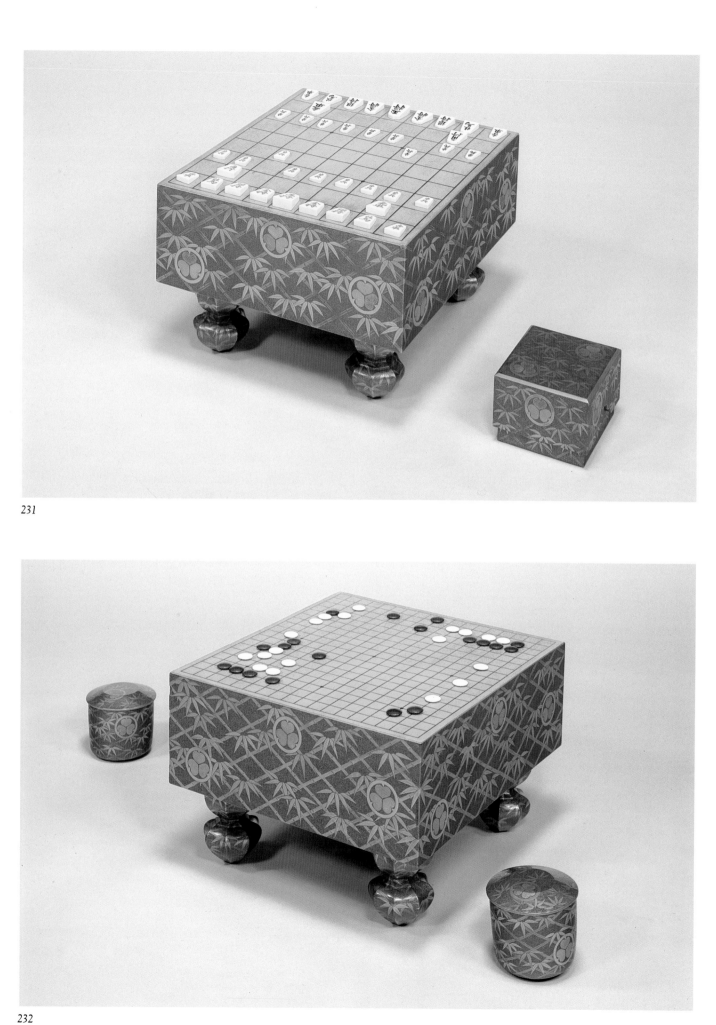

231

232

233

231 Shōgi set
maki-e lacquer on wood
h. 23.0 (9¹/₁₆)
Edo period, 19th century
Tokyo National Museum

232 Go set
maki-e lacquer on wood
h. 28.2 (11¹/₈)
Edo period, 19th century
Tokyo National Museum

These two sets of board games, one for shōgi, sometimes called Japanese chess (cat. 231), and the other for go (cat. 232), were made as part of the bridal furnishings for the daughter of Harutomi (1771–1852), the tenth-generation Tokugawa ruler of the Wakayama domain in Kii Province (cat. 230). Although it is not typical for these games to be decorated with maki-e lacquer, these are decorated like the other components of the set, with the maki-e hollyhock mon. The game pieces for the shōgi set, usually made of wood, are made of ivory, reflecting the high position of the Kii Tokugawa house.

Go (also called igo) is thought to have originated in ancient China, arriving in Japan during the Asuka period (552–645). It

was popular in both court and temple circles, and eventually was embraced by the warrior class. Shōgi is believed to have originated in India, though it spread widely and developed in a number of different forms. Japanese shōgi is related to the Chinese form. Although it is not clear when it arrived in Japan, by the Kamakura period it was enjoyed by members of the court class. In cat. 105, warriors can be seen playing both games. A total of six types of shōgi are known; the type known as shōshōgi (small shōgi), which eclipsed most of the others from the Sengoku period, is the type illustrated in the screens. The boards of both games are usually made from the wood of either the oak or kaya (Japanese nutmeg) tree; the latter is preferred today. The black pieces used in go are made of black stone, with that from Nachi in Wakayama Prefecture especially prized.   WA

233 Set of utensils for the incense game
maki-e lacquer on wood; silver, ebony
box 13.2 x 24.0 x 18.0 (5³/₁₆ x 9⁷/₁₆ x 7¹/₈)
Edo period, 18th century
Eisei Bunko, Tokyo

In the Heian period, the fragrance of aromatic wood was enjoyed by members of court society. The appreciation of incense became formalized in the Muromachi period, much like tea drinking and flower arranging, and many varieties of monkō, literally "listening to the incense," were established. Throughout the Edo period, enthusiasts of this widely popular game included members of the warrior class. This set of incense utensils, handed down in the Hosokawa family, is decorated with the kuyō mon, the Hosokawa family crest, and a floral scroll in maki-e lacquer on a pear-skin ground (nashiji); the metal implements are made of silver. The wife of Shigekata (1720–1785), a mid-Edo-period Hosokawa daimyo of Kumamoto, is said to have used this set.   SN

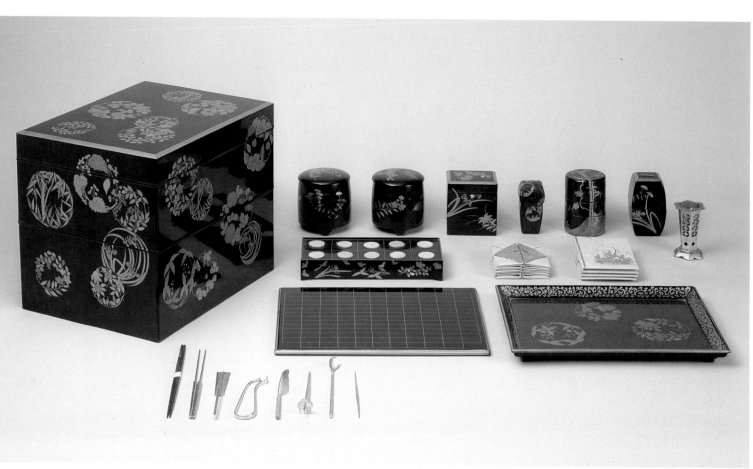

234

234 Set of utensils for the incense game
maki-e and black lacquer, gold on
wood; silver
box 20.5 x 24.3 x 18.8 (8¹/₁₆ x 9⁹/₁₆ x
7³/₈)
Edo period, 18th century
Eisei Bunko, Tokyo

Like cat. 233, this set of incense utensils
has been handed down in the Hosokawa
family and the wife of Shigekata (1720–
1785), a mid-Edo Hosokawa daimyo of Kumamoto, is said to have used it. The
decoration consists of such plants and
flowers as bush clover, chrysanthemum,
peony, camelia, iris, and bamboo arranged
in circular motifs in slightly raised gold
takamaki-e (relief *maki-e*) lacquer. The
metal implements are made of silver.   SN

235 Shell matching game
shell containers 49.5 x 40.0 (19¹/₂ x
15³/₄)
maki-e and black lacquer on wood;
color on shell
Edo period, 18th–19th century
Eisei Bunko, Tokyo

The octagonal, black-lacquered containers
for this shell matching game are decorated

with the *kuyō mon*, family crest of the Hosokawa clan, in gold *maki-e* lacquer. In the
containers are stored 360 shells, each one
half of a pair with matching designs drawn
from *The Tale of Genji*, or with floral and
bird decoration. To play the game, the
shells are mixed up and participants must
find the two shell halves with the same
picture. Because the two perfectly
matched halves symbolize fidelity, the
shell matching set was regarded as one of
the most important items in a daimyo
bridal trousseau.   SN

236 Set of trays and tablewares
maki-e and red lacquer and silver on
wood
(left) 22.6 x 39.4 x 41.2 (8⁷/₈ x 15¹/₂ x
16¹/₄)
(center) 21.0 x 37.3 x 38.4 (8¹/₄ x 14⁵/₈ x
15¹/₈)
(right) 19.5 x 35.3 x 36.4 (7¹/₁₆ x 13⁷/₈ x
14³/₈)
Edo period, 17th century
Rinnōji, Tochigi Prefecture

This ensemble, comprising large, medium,
and small *kakeban* (tablelike trays for special occasions), lidded bowls, a hot water
ewer, and a rice container, is said to have
been used by Tokugawa Iemitsu (1604–

1651), the third Tokugawa shogun. The entire set is decorated with a pear-skin
ground (*nashiji*), a gold and silver *maki-e*
clove floral scroll, and the three-leaved hollyhock *mon*. The edges of the trays are
rimmed with silver, and the interiors of the
bowls are finished with red lacquer.   SN

235

236

237

237 Set of tray and tablewares
maki-e, black and red lacquer on wood
tray a 16.0 x 36.3 x 36.3 (6⁵/₁₆ x 14¹/₄ x 14¹/₄)
tray b 13.5 x 33.4 x 33.0 (5⁵/₁₆ x 13¹/₈ x 13)
tray c 11.9 x 30.7 x 30.4 (4¹¹/₁₆ x 12¹/₁₆ x 11¹⁵/₁₆)
Edo period, 17th century
Hokkeji, Gifu Prefecture

This set of trays and bowls is said to have been used by Mitsumasa (1619–1633), grandson of Katō Kiyomasa (1562–1611). Kiyomasa was a retainer of Toyotomi Hideyoshi (1537–1598) and daimyo of a domain in Higo Province (present–day Kumamoto Prefecture). On a black lacquer ground, three different *mon* (family crests) are depicted in gold *hiramaki-e* (level *maki-e*) lacquer. The paulownia *mon* was given to the Katō by Toyotomi Hideyoshi. The Chinese bellflower and *orizumi* (broken inkstick) *mon* were originally the crests of the Bitō family, daimyo of a domain in Sanuki Province (currently Kagawa Prefecture), but due to poor administration, their domain was confiscated and their armor and other personal belongings given to Katō Kiyomasa; subsequently, the Bitō *mon* were also used by the Katō family.   SN

238 Picnic set
maki-e lacquer and gold on wood
37.0 x 37.8 x 23.0 (14⁵/₈ x 14⁷/₈ x 9¹/₁₆)
Edo period, 18th–19th century
Eisei Bunko, Tokyo

This picnic set includes a multi-tiered box for food, dishes, a pair of *sake* flasks, and cups. The various items are covered with a chrysanthemum design primarily in slightly raised gold and silver *takamaki-e* (relief *maki-e*) lacquer and sheet gold on a pear-skin ground (*nashiji*). This type of set, popular from the Momoyama period onward, is known in Japanese by several names, such as *kōchū* (travel kitchen), *sagejū* (portable tiered box), and *hanami bentō* (flower-viewing lunch box).   SN

239 Picnic set
maki-e lacquer on wood
32.6 x 34.8 x 17.8 (12¹³/₁₆ x 13³/₄ x 7)
Edo period, 18th–19th century
Eisei Bunko, Tokyo

Fitted inside the outer frame of this picnic set are a lidded four-tiered octagonal box, a drum-shaped *sake* container, a box-shaped *sake* container, a square tray, a footed tray with cut corners, and *sake* cups, all decorated with motifs of the four seasons in *maki-e* lacquer. The top of the frame is decorated with a pair of carp and churning waves in slightly raised gold and silver *takamaki-e* (relief *maki-e*) lacquer on a pear-skin ground (*nashiji*). The lid of the octagonal tiered box is covered with a *nashiji* background and a framed picture from *The Tale of Genji* and the sides of each tier hold framed flower and bird designs in *maki-e* lacquer. The drum-shaped *sake* container is decorated with a phoenix design on an exposed wood-grain ground. Because the drum was indispensable for singing and dancing at parties, *sake* containers came to be made in the shapes of drums; though the earliest extant examples date from the Muromachi period, they are known from Kamakura-period paintings. Mandarin ducks on rocks are depicted on the top of the rectangular *sake* container, and landscapes are framed on the sides. The interior of the square tray has a persimmon and chestnut design on a *nashiji* background; a running water and maple design decorates the sides. On the footed tray is a plum tree and pheasant design on a *nashiji* background. The cups have a design of cherry blossoms and running water on a wood-grain ground.   SN

238

239

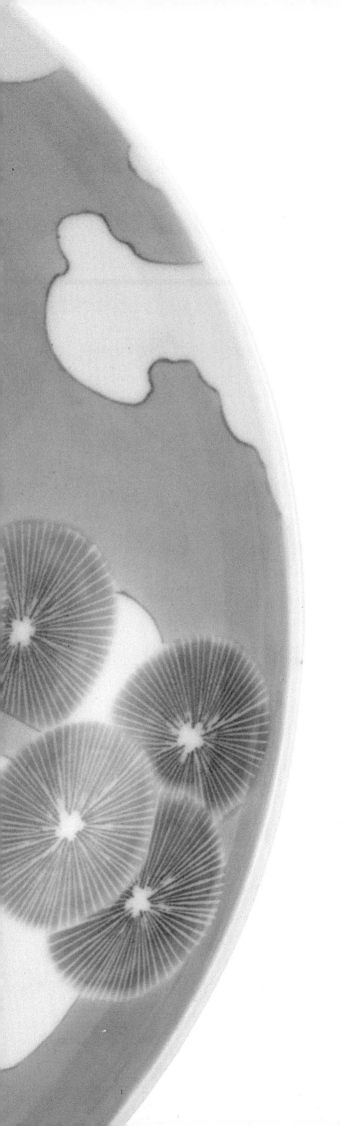

CERAMICS

240 Jar
Shigaraki ware
h. 27.5 (10 3/4)
Muromachi period,
15th–16th century

Fukuoka Art Museum, Fukuoka
Prefecture

The rustic stoneware vessels of the Shigaraki kilns (in present-day Shiga Prefecture), like those of Bizen and other similar kilns in the medieval era, were utilitarian—*tsubo* (jars), *kame* (wide-mouthed jars), and *suribachi* (grating bowls). In the late fifteenth century, the early tea master Murata Shukō (1423–1502) judged Shigaraki jars to be, in combination with fine imported objects, appropriate for use in the tea ceremony. Shigaraki wares were the first native Japanese ceramics, along with those of Bizen, to be so embraced. They came to be used in the *wabi* form of tea, which was based on the innovations of Shukō and refined during the sixteenth century by Takeno Jōō (1502–1555) and then Sen no Rikyū (1522–1591). As traced through contemporary tea journals, the most typical Shigaraki component of the range of tea utensils was the *mizusashi* (fresh water container), though *kensui* (waste water jars) and *hanaire* (flower containers) were also used. Most of these vessels were originally utilitarian, though by the late sixteenth century pieces were being made specifically for the tea context.

Among the users of Shigaraki wares were leading military figures, including Toyotomi Hideyoshi (1537–1598) who used a Shigaraki jar in 1583 at the festivities attending the construction of Osaka Castle. Katagiri Sekishū (1605–1673), the influential proponent of a formalized daimyo tea, used Shigaraki as did many daimyo, including the Date clan of Sendai who were steeped in the teachings of Sekishū and Furuta Oribe (1544–1615). Tsunamura (1659–1719), the fourth-generation Date daimyo, recorded in his tea diary the use of several Shigaraki pieces, both old and new, some treasured and used repeatedly.

The continued use of Shigaraki wares in tea was assured with the formalization of the Rikyū aesthetic of rustic simplicity by the master's grandson Sōtan (1578–1658). Of even greater importance was the designation in 1632 of the Shigaraki kilns as producers of the "official" glazed tea jars in which the famed leaves from nearby Uji were packed for presentation to the shogunate. With the resulting base of economic support, the kilns prospered throughout the Edo period, during which time they produced an expanded repertoire of mostly glazed utilitarian objects.

The unpretentious qualities of Shigaraki wares that came to be appreciated by tea men are evident in this Muromachi-period *tsubo*. Its shape is simple, broadening from a flat base to a bulging shoulder, then tapering to a narrow neck and everting again at the mouth. The incised pattern of cross-hatching between two parallel lines at the shoulder is a distinctive Shigaraki motif, especially on smaller jars. Three parallel horizontal lines, the Japanese character for the numeral three, etched just above the decoration on two sides of the jar, are thought to be some kind of kiln mark.

The firing effects characteristic of Shigaraki wares are evident. The body is stippled with white grains of feldspar present in the Shigaraki clay and drawn to the surface by the heat of the kiln. Small holes are left by other feldspar particles that have melted away, an effect known in Japanese as *ishihaze*, or "stone-burst." The kiln fires also induced the scorched coloring and the thin coat of natural wood ash glaze, which partially covers the vessel, running down past the shoulder to the middle of the body. From the late sixteenth century, smaller versions of this type of jar were produced specifically for use as flower containers in the tea setting.   AMW

241 *Sake* flask
Bizen ware
h. 30.2 (11 7/8)
Momoyama period, early 17th century

Okayama Prefectural Museum,
Okayama Prefecture

The high-fired and unglazed wares of Bizen and Shigaraki, esteemed for their austere rusticity, were the first Japanese ceramics to be deemed suitable for use in the tea context. From the mid-sixteenth century the potters of Bizen (in present-day Okayama Prefecture) supplemented their production of utilitarian wares with tea and tea-related objects, particularly *mizusashi* (fresh water containers), *hanaire* (flower containers), and fine tablewares. While utilitarian wares changed little even over long periods of time, tea wares evolved according to current fashions.

Tokkuri, or *sake* flasks, were produced in great quantity by the Bizen kilns in the Momoyama period. In this example, clean lines define the plump, barrel-shaped body, thin neck, and crisply finished

240

241

242

mouth. The neat, concise form, made from a relatively fine-grained clay, provides a sympathetic surface for the red diagonal streaks, *hidasuki*, which resulted from shielding a vessel wrapped in rice straw from direct contact with the flames during firing. The straw burns away, leaving the *hidasuki* on a background of unscorched white clay.

Hidasuki are but one of several characteristic Bizen firing effects that were highly regarded by tea patrons. Depending on the placement of an object within the kiln and its position in relation to the path of the shooting flames and the shower of ash from the burning wood, different firing effects would result. Pieces placed directly in the flames would be dramatically scorched. Light flecks of natural glaze (tea men likened their appearance to sesame seeds) could result from the ash in the kiln atmosphere. It was possible to control which parts of a piece would be affected by the flames and ash by masking with other objects.

Archaeological excavations throughout Japan have revealed that in the medieval period, the Bizen complex was only one of more than thirty in Japan where utilitarian stoneware objects, primarily *tsubo* (jars), *kame* (wide-mouthed jars), and *suribachi* (grating bowls) were fired. During the Muromachi period, production was concentrated at fewer but larger kilns, suggesting the start of cooperative efforts. Ready access to ports on the Inland Sea allowed the establishment of a distribution system to markets around central Japan. Further consolidation seems to have occurred by the late Muromachi or early Momoyama period, concentrated around three large kilns to the north, south, and west of the village of Inbe in Bizen, where production continued through the Edo period. AMW

242 **Fresh water container**
Mino ware, Shino type
h. 19.2 (7 1/2)
Momoyama period,
late 16th century
Nezu Institute of Fine Arts, Tokyo

243 Bowl
Mino ware, Shino type
diam. 27.5 (10 ¹³⁄₁₆)
Momoyama period,
late 16th–early 17th century

Suntory Museum of Art, Tokyo

244 Bowl
Mino ware, Nezumi Shino type
diam. 28.5 (11 ¼)
Momoyama period,
late 16th–early 17th century

Tokyo National Museum
Important Cultural Property

245 Bowl
Mino ware, Nezumi Shino type
diam. 24.9 (9 ¾)
Momoyama period,
early 17th century

Suntory Museum of Art, Tokyo

246 Teabowl
Mino ware, Black Oribe type
h. 8.5 (3 ³⁄₈)
Momoyama period,
early 17th century

Umezawa Kinenkan, Tokyo

243

244

245

246

247

247 **Covered dish**
Mino ware, Green Oribe type
h. 6.3 (2 ½) x l. 27.9 (11)
Momoyama period,
early 17th century

Tokyo National Museum

In Mino Province, now the southern part of Gifu Prefecture, the production of highly innovative glazed ceramics prospered at a large number of kilns from the middle of the sixteenth century through the early seventeenth century. The Mino potters, while mindful of the need to satisfy the requirements of function, experimented with glazes and decorative schemes as well as with shapes and the techniques for forming them. Their

tea-related wares were embraced by an enthusiastic group of patrons whose membership included prominent military figures, as evidenced by the recovery of Mino ceramics from excavated daimyo residences from many sites throughout Japan.

During this same period, Mino's importance as a center for ceramic activity was matched by its significance as the stage for major political personalities and events. In the sixteenth century, Saitō Dōsan (d. 1556) overthrew the Toki clan to become a daimyo of Mino. To improve relations with Oda Nobuhide (1510–1551), daimyo in the neighboring province of Owari, Dōsan married his daughter in 1548 to Nobuhide's son, Oda Nobunaga (1534–1582). Nobunaga subsequently moved

against Mino and by the mid-1560s had subjugated it, an important early triumph for the instigator of the movement toward a unified Japan. Nobunaga was interested in regulating the ceramic industry in his domain and was a practitioner of tea. He was served by the tea masters Sen no Rikyū (1522–1591), Imai Sōkyū (1520–1593), and Tsuda Sōgyū (d. 1591). In 1600, Mino was the setting for the pivotal Battle of Sekigahara (cat. 104), in which Tokugawa Ieyasu (1543–1616) won the position of preeminence that was maintained by his descendants for 250 years.

In the fifteenth century, the technology for producing glazed ceramics was introduced to the Mino area from the well-established kilns of neighboring Seto.

By the beginning of the sixteenth century, a more efficient and advanced type of kiln began to be used in Mino and Seto, leading eventually to the creation of new wares at the Mino kilns, including Shino and Nezumi Shino. At the beginning of the seventeenth century, the multichambered *noborigama* (climbing kiln) was introduced from Karatsu to the Mino area, first to Motoyashiki, enabling the artistic breakthroughs that culminated with copper-glazed Green Oribe wares. At these *noborigama*, copies of the wares of other Japanese kilns such as Iga, Shigaraki, and Karatsu were also made. Utilitarian objects were produced even at those kilns that fired the finest tablewares and tea utensils, and they assumed greater importance as the demand for Mino tea-related wares decreased.

A coat of feldspathic white glaze, typical of Shino ceramics, envelops most of the *mizusashi* (fresh water container) from the Nezu Institute of Fine Arts (cat. 242). This glaze was perfected in the 1580s, the result of earlier experiments involving ash glazes with a high feldspathic content. A simple drawing in iron oxide is visible beneath the glaze; it depicts a pair of arching reeds on one face of the vessel and a range of three low mountains and pine trees on the other. The stolid shape of the *mizusashi* conveys a great sense of weight. The form is enlivened by pronounced bulges at the top and bottom and irregular contusions, willful marks of the potter's artistic personality that foreshadow later and even more dramatic effects. The treatment of the rim was likened by connoisseurs to the notch of an arrow (*yahazu*) giving rise to the name by which this type of *mizusashi* was known. Similar *yahazu*-style *mizusashi* were also made at other Japanese kilns, including Karatsu, Bizen, and Shigaraki, reflecting a confluence of tea-ware taste.

The Shino bowl from the Suntory Museum of Art (cat. 243) was made for *kaiseki ryōri*, the meal associated with the tea ceremony. Inimitable and irregular in shape, this heavily potted dish rests on three legs. It is decorated with underglaze iron drawing and covered with a thick coat of white feldspathic glaze. In the central section, interwoven grasses, a common Shino motif, sprout from one of the four trimmed corners. Each of the four sections on the rim holds a discrete design. Two of the adjoining sections are filled with recognizable motifs depicted in an abbreviated but naturalistic manner: one with airborne plovers and a net hung to dry, the other a simple drawing of bush clover. The other two sections are filled with abstract geometric designs, the origins of which may possibly lie in imported European art forms. The design in each section is formally related to the one opposite. Both the net and bird motif and its

opposite are horizontal and without a single focal point, while the clover and its opposite are each set on a central axis from which the design bifurcates.

The irregularly shaped bowl from the Tokyo National Museum (cat. 244) is an example of Nezumi Shino, a type of Mino ware covered with iron-rich slip that fires gray, the color of a mouse (*nezumi*). Iron slip was applied with a ladle to parts of the vessel, creating soft-edged borders with the sections left uncovered. The artist etched hard-edged designs through the gray slip with a sharp tool, and then applied feldspathic glaze to the whole vessel. The areas not covered with the iron slip, such as the mass at the center of this dish and two parallel oblong shapes on the rim, fired white. The wagtail etched atop the central white form transforms it by association into a rock, while the iron slip fingers at the base of the rock become waves, with the addition of scraped lines beneath the rock. Five-leafed *kumazasa*, a type of bamboo, are incised through the slip on either side of the rock and painted on the rock with iron slip. In contrast to the decoration on the face of the dish, the exterior has been treated in an energetic, nonrepresentational manner.

Similar decorative techniques have been employed in the shallow Nezumi Shino bowl from the Suntory Museum of Art (cat. 245). Most of the wide interior of the bowl has been masked with iron slip, leaving uncovered only part of the rim and interior. The plate is dominated by a great willow, its trunk extended across the white boulderlike mass with a drawn arched line of iron slip; its branches fill the dish interior. Three birds are each formed of the same three etched marks. Non-representational decoration is also prominent.

Oribe-style Mino ware was fired at a small number of the Mino kilns. The name of the ware refers to the great Momoyama period tea master, Furuta Oribe (1544–1615), born in Mino and awarded a domain near Kyoto by Toyotomi Hideyoshi (1537–1598). Oribe's exact relationship to the Mino kilns is unclear, though the style that bears his name is thought to reflect his advanced ideas regarding aesthetics. Perhaps no shape is more representative of the tea wares Oribe is said to have favored than that of the *kutsugata*, or shoe-shaped, teabowl, here represented by one from the Umezawa Kinenkan in the Black Oribe mode (cat. 246). Its exaggerated warp was added after the basic form had been thrown on the wheel. The lacquerlike black glaze was a technical innovation made earlier at the Mino kilns at Amagane, the result of removing an ironglazed vessel from the kiln while it was still hot and rapidly cooling it. At the earlier kilns, the glaze was applied to simple cylindrical teabowls, while in the Oribe style it was just one decorative element, used in

conjunction with irregular shapes and sometimes graphic designs. Here, one side of the outer wall and the bottom of the interior of the bowl are covered with decidedly abstract images traditionally interpreted as cranes and reeds, carved through the outer coat of black glaze and filled in with white slip.

The covered dish in the shape of a fan from the Tokyo National Museum (cat. 247) is a product of the Mino *noborigama* kilns, which produced Oribe ceramics characterized by an iridescent green copper glaze and underglaze iron drawing. The design of this vessel is a blend of natural and geometric motifs. Triangular indentations inside the vessel at the base of the fan and incised lines in the lid collect glaze, creating color variations within the large mass of green.

The Oribe potters often employed molds to make complicated shapes. They experimented with a wide range of vessel forms, including sets of small shallow or tall dishes, known as *mukōzuke*, and large dishes with stepped sides and bowlike handles. This dish was designed to contain food, although the cover does not fit snugly enough to retain heat effectively. Apart from its utilitarian function, and perhaps more important, the cover was regarded as another surface for decoration and as a dramatic device, concealing not only the edible contents of the dish but its interior decoration as well. AMW

248 **Large dish**
Karatsu ware
diam. 43.9 (17 1/4)
Momoyama period,
late 16th–early 17th century

Umezawa Kinenkan, Tokyo
Important Cultural Property

249 **Jar**
Karatsu ware
h. 15.8 (6 1/4)
Momoyama period,
late 16th–early 17th century

Idemitsu Museum of Arts, Tokyo

Karatsu ware is the glazed high-fired pottery of Hizen Province, a large area in northern Kyushu that falls within present-day Saga and Nagasaki prefectures. As at other locations in western Japan, a great flourish of ceramic activity occurred in Hizen following the Korean expeditions of 1592 and 1597, the unsuccessful attempts of Toyotomi Hideyoshi (1537–1598) to subjugate the Asian mainland. Many of the military leaders in these invasions were daimyo and prominent warriors of Kyushu domains, including Matsuura Shigenobu (1549–1614), Nabeshima Naoshige (1538–

248

1618), and Gotō Ienobu of Hizen. In the early 1590s, Hideyoshi issued orders instructing his officers to bring craftsmen with them upon their return to Japan from the Korean peninsula. Accordingly, Korean potters made their way to Hizen and with the protection of the local rulers established kilns in many of its variously held territories, including the Saga, Hirado, and Karatsu domains. Even prior to the Korean invasions, such Korean-influenced glazed ceramics seem to have been made on a limited scale in Hizen at kilns near the Kishidake Castle of the Hata clan. Until they were ousted by Hideyoshi in 1594 the Hata were rulers in the area. They had long engaged in trade and piracy with Korea and China. The great expansion of ceramic production following the Korean expeditions, however, is well reflected by the excavated sites of over one hundred Hizen kilns where a variety of types of Karatsu ware was made.

Utilitarian vessels were the mainstay of the Karatsu kilns. Tea men were drawn to their unpretentious beauty and adopted them for use in the tea ceremony. Over time, vessels for the tea context were commissioned, including those in styles that can also be found at other Japanese kilns, such as *kutsugata*, or "shoe-shaped," tea-

bowls (cat. 246), popular in the early seventeenth century and associated with the prominent tea master Furuta Oribe (1544–1615). Oribe, who helped to popularize Karatsu wares by using them himself at tea gatherings, resided at Nagoya Castle in Hizen for eighteen months from 1592 to 1593. The castle was the expedition operations base, located near the port of Karatsu (not to be confused with Nagoya Castle on Honshu). Terasawa Hirotaka (1563–1633), a retainer of Hideyoshi and a tea enthusiast, also served the war effort from Nagoya Castle and after the first campaign was appointed daimyo of the Karatsu domain, where he supported ceramic production.

The two examples of Karatsu ware in the exhibition are decorated with designs painted in underglaze iron oxide. The large dish from the Umezawa Kinenkan (cat. 248) is potted from sandy clay, its shallow curving bowl stepped up to a wide undulating rim pinched at irregular intervals. Typical of many large Karatsu dishes, the ring foot is small for the size of the vessel it supports. Except for the foot and the area immediately surrounding it, the dish is completely covered with a mixed feldspathic and ash glaze. A sinuous pine tree meanders over the dish interior, throwing some of its branches up along the rim of the dish. An uneven line encircles the

outer edge of the rim, forming the ground for two triangular sections of parallel grass-like strokes at the base of the trunk.

The *tsubo* (jar) from the Idemitsu Museum of Arts (cat. 249) is of a type commonly made for utilitarian storage, though this example was probably employed as a *mizusashi* (fresh water jar). The body sits atop a ring foot, tapering from its pronounced, bulging mid-section to the mouth whose narrow rim is delicately turned out. On the upper part of the jar, a simple design of reeds, a common Karatsu motif, is rendered in fluid brushstrokes of underglaze iron.

The great prosperity enjoyed by the Hizen Karatsu kilns during the early part of the seventeenth century suffered due to the growth in popularity of native porcelains, first fired in Hizen. The number of kilns making Karatsu pottery decreased and most of those remaining made utilitarian wares. In the Karatsu domain, some kilns fired ceramics commissioned by the daimyo for presentation to the shogunate or other daimyo, a practice that is said to have begun as early as the tenure of Terasawa Hirotaka and continued despite periodic interruptions until the Meiji Restoration, even as the post of daimyo of the Karatsu domain passed from one clan to another.   AMW

249

250

Fresh water container
Takatori ware
h. 15.5 (6¹/₈)
Edo period, first half 17th century
Umezawa Kinenkan, Tokyo

The modest complex of Takatori kilns, established under the auspices of the
Kuroda family, was one of several begun in
the early seventeenth century with the
backing of Kyushu daimyo. The Kuroda
clan received control over their domain in
the northern Kyushu province of Chikuzen, part of present-day Fukuoka Prefecture, for supporting the victorious
Tokugawa Ieyasu (1543–1616) at the Battle
of Sekigahara in 1600 (cat. 104). Typically,
immigrant Korean potters were responsible for beginning production of the Takatori stonewares.

As recorded in retrospective accounts
such as the *Takatori rekidai kiroku* (Record
of the successive Takatori generations), an
1820 compilation of Takatori-related oral
tradition and written evidence, the earliest
official clan kiln was established by the
daimyo Kuroda Nagamasa (1568–1623) at
the base of Takatori mountain after his
move to Chikuzen in 1600. The operation
of this kiln, Eimanji Takuma, is attributed
to the Korean potter P'alsan (also known
by his Japanese name Takatori Hachizō)
who came to Japan following Hideyoshi's
Korean expeditions. A second clan kiln
was opened in 1614, at Uchigaso. After Nagamasa died in 1623, P'alsan and his son
fell into disfavor with the next-generation
Kuroda daimyo, Tadayuki (1602–1654), for
asking permission to return to Korea, a request that was not granted; they were banished to Yamada where they are said to
have begun another kiln.

Extensive investigations at the sites of
the first two kilns have clarified the character of their products and broadened a
once-narrow perception based on the
wares of later kilns that reflect an aesthetic
associated with Kobori Enshū (1579–1647),
the important seventeenth-century arbiter
of tea taste. The Eimanji Takuma kiln, excavated in 1982, was found to be a modest
16.6-meter multi-chambered *noborigama*
(climbing kiln). Although some tea objects
were fired, most of the wares were utilitarian. The subsequent Uchigaso kiln, examined from 1979 through 1981, was a much
larger 46.5-meter *noborigama*. The excavated sherds suggest that a great variety of
utilitarian and tea objects were produced
in a number of different styles; ranging
from simple but robust jars to teabowls in
the flamboyant style associated with
Furuta Oribe (1544–1615), which exerted a
great impact on many kilns throughout Japan during the early seventeenth century.
Sherds of pieces closely related to the
products of the later Shirahatayama kiln
were also found. These excavations also
indicate that certain types of objects

thought over the years to be Karatsu ware were also fired at the early Takatori kilns.

The Shirahatayama kiln opened around 1630, during the tenure of Kuroda Tadayuki. The Enshū-influenced wares typical of this and later kilns are characterized by understatement and subtle contrast, effectively employed in this Takatori *mizusashi* (fresh water container). The cylindrical *mizusashi*, potted from finely textured clay, is glazed with earthtones that have fired into a sleek coat. Overlaps of the smooth exterior glaze laid on in four well-considered applications create four delicate lines arcing from top to bottom. Another sweep of glaze, also a somber tone, washes the lip of the vessel, while the interior is covered with a fine, irregular, mazelike pattern. The bottom is unglazed.

The stylistic traits associated with Kobori Enshū were perpetuated at kilns established in 1665 at Koishiwarazumi. There the major output consisted of tea wares, especially great quantities of *chaire* (powdered-tea containers). The close association between the Takatori lineage of potters and successive generations of Kuroda daimyo continued with new kilns being sponsored until the end of the Edo period.   AMW

251 Flower container
Agano ware
h. 17.8 (7)
Edo period, first half 17th century
Eisei Bunko, Tokyo

Agano is another of the western Japanese ceramic wares established by immigrant Korean potters under local daimyo patronage in the early seventeenth century. It was produced in the northern Kyushu province of Buzen (parts of the current prefectures of Fukuoka and Oita) at the official kilns of the Hosokawa clan. The transfer of Hosokawa Sansai (Tadaoki, 1563–1646) from Tango Province (the northern portion of Kyoto Prefecture) to Buzen more than doubled the worth of his holdings. This was his reward for his support of Tokugawa Ieyasu at the Battle of Sekigahara in 1600 (cat. 104).

As recorded in later documents, Sansai, a daimyo reknowned as a poet, painter, and important tea disciple of Sen no Rikyū (1522–1591), began production of ceramics at a small kiln in the garden of his castle in Kokura, where he moved in 1602. The kiln is said to have been operated by Chonhae (also known by his Japanese name, Agano Kizō), a Korean potter who came to Japan after Hideyoshi's Korean expeditions, living first in the Karatsu domain and then moving to Buzen at Sansai's invitation. The possible site of this kiln, uncovered in 1982, yielded a great variety of types of glazed and unglazed ce-

251

ramics, though it is possible that not all were fired at this small kiln.

Agano ware was made on an expanded scale at the Kamanokuchi kiln, probably opened during the first decade of the seventeenth century and operated by Chonhae. Sherds recovered from this site, excavated in 1955, show that both utilitarian and tea wares were made there. The kiln was a large 41-meter *noborigama* (climbing kiln), thus similar in scale to the nearby and roughly contemporary Takatori ware Uchigaso kiln (cat. 250). Indeed, though there is a marked paucity of irregularly shaped wares at Kamanokuchi, corre-

spondences between the two kilns, and with the Karatsu kilns, can be drawn in terms of techniques and glaze types. Some sherds at Kamanokuchi show a stylistic affinity with Hagi wares (cat. 253), more than is evident at other Kyushu kilns. Nearby at Iwaya Kōrai, another kiln was also active at this time.

Sansai relinquished the post of daimyo to his son Tadatoshi (1586–1641) in 1621. Around 1625 another kiln, the Agano Sarayama Hongama, was opened. Production continued there under Hosokawa patronage until the clan was moved

252

253

southwest to Kumamoto in Higo Province in 1632. Sansai retired to Yatsushiro in Higo, accompanied by Chonhae and other potters, establishing kilns that fired tea wares. After the Hosokawa move to Kumamoto, Sarayama Hongama was continued by descendants of Chonhae as the official kiln of the Ogasawara clan, the Hosokawa replacements in Buzen.

This *hanaire* (flower container), with its simplicity of shape and earth color, is representative of the refined tea wares produced under Sansai's patronage. The box in which the flower container is stored bears an inscription stating that it was

once owned by Sansai, but it is unclear whether this piece was produced at one of the pre-1632 Agano kilns in Buzen or shortly after Sansai moved to Yatsushiro. Traditionally, it is said to have been made by Chonhae; whether this attribution is correct is impossible to verify, though later Yatsushiro wares often have less delicate forms and sometimes decoratively patterned designs. A fitting on the back of this type of container allowed it to be hung on the post of a tea room, though it could be placed on the ground. AMW

252 **Teabowl**
Satsuma ware
h. 10.8 (4¼)
Edo period, early 17th century
Fukushi Shigeo Collection, Tokyo

Satsuma ware is another of the many types of ceramics established by a daimyo following his participation in Hideyoshi's Korean expeditions. According to historical records maintained by the Naeshirogawa Satsuma ware kiln, Shimazu Yoshihiro (1535–1619), a Sen no Rikyū (1522–1591) disciple and ruler of the large

Satsuma domain in southern Kyushu, returned from Korea in 1598 accompanied by more than seventy Koreans. Among them, it is thought, were a number of potters who were responsible for operating the earliest Satsuma kilns. Tradition is that the first kiln, producing utilitarian vessels and not clan-protected, was begun while Yoshihiro fought at the Battle of Sekigahara in 1600 (cat. 104). The Uto kiln in Chōsa, the earliest clan-sponsored kiln, was not opened until around 1601, after Yoshihiro had returned to his domain. The second, Osato kiln, was begun after Yoshihiro retired in favor of his son Iehisa (1576–1636) in 1607 and moved to Kajiki, slightly east of Chōsa. Both were located near Yoshihiro's residences and are said to have been operated by the Korean Kim Hae (also known by the name he acquired in Japan, Hoshiyama Chūji). At both kilns, the chief products were tea wares.

This teabowl, probably from one of these first two clan kilns, is one of the few examples of its type known. Its shape is related to contemporary Korean porcelain or Mishima-style vessels, reflecting the roots of the early Satsuma potters. Simple and stolid, the bowl is firmly supported by a tall, ring foot, tapering from a low, protruding waist toward a wide mouth. The glaze, a forerunner of the deep black glaze that was to become a characteristic Satsuma type, has fired to an irregularly mottled surface that softens the form. Brushed in Edo-period writing on a paper cartouche on the lid of the box that holds the bowl is *Satsuma owan*, or "Satsuma bowl."

Examinations of the Uto site indicate that the kiln was small and not fired many times, a peculiarity that might be explained by the Hoshiyama family account that soon after opening the Uto kiln, Kim Hae was sent by Yoshihiro to the well-established Seto kilns for five years of training. Shortly after Kim Hae's return to the Satsuma domain and with Yoshihiro's move to Kajiki in 1607, the Osato kiln replaced Uto. The Osato kiln, also small, appears to have been fired many times, probably until Yoshihiro's death in 1619.

Yoshihiro's son Iehisa ruled from Kagoshima, south of the earlier locations. After Yoshihiro passed away in 1619, Kim Hae moved there at Iehisa's behest and operated a small-scale clan kiln in Tateno. At this kiln, continued by Kim Hae's descendants after his death, tea wares were produced that reflect the refinement of the then-current Kobori Enshū aesthetic. This kiln was replaced by a much larger one where the scale of production was expanded and new wares were developed. Subsequent generations of Shimazu dai-

myo continued to encourage the activities at Tateno through their patronage and by sending potters to other Japanese kilns to learn new techniques, as Shimazu Narinobu (1769–1841) is reported to have done at the end of the eighteenth century. Official and non-official kilns were active within Satsuma throughout the Edo period, producing a wide range of ceramics including the colorful overglaze enamel works that are, for many, the type most often associated with Satsuma. AMW

253 **Teabowl, named** *Daimyō*
Hagi ware
h. 8.5 (3 3/8)
Edo period, 17th century

Nezu Institute of Fine Arts, Tokyo

The Hagi kilns were both daimyo-sponsored and begun by Korean potters who came to Japan following the Korean campaigns. They were located on the main Japanese island of Honshu, on the northern shore of its western tip (part of present-day Yamaguchi Prefecture). This area was controlled by the Mōri, a clan whose territories were drastically reduced from eight provinces to two after Mōri Terumoto (1553–1625) opposed Tokugawa Ieyasu (1543–1616) at Sekigahara in 1600 (cat. 104). In 1604, the seat of the Mōri administration was transferred to Hagi and, according to mid-eighteenth century records compiled by the clan, a kiln was then established at Matsumoto near the Hagi castle by the immigrant Korean potter Yi Chak-kwang who was assisted by his younger brother Yi Kyŏng. The Hagi ware enterprise evolved into a closely managed organ of the clan where glazed ceramics based on Korean prototypes, chiefly tea wares, were produced.

Reflecting the ceramic ideal sought by the Mōri patrons, this Hagi teabowl recalls Korean wares, specifically Ido type bowls. Ido bowls are thought to have been employed originally for utilitarian purposes in Korea and imported to Japan in the sixteenth century for tea men who appreciated their understated beauty. The slightly irregular cone-shaped bowl, thick at the bottom and thinner near the rim, flares from a precariously small, high, ring foot, accented at the joint of the foot and body with a tooled line. Glaze covers the bowl in an uneven coat that has fired to a subtle range of colors, from white areas where the glaze is thick to pink blushes.

The extent to which the Mōri were involved in the affairs of the Matsumoto kiln, and the others that followed, can be traced through historical records. A document dated 1625 with the *kaō* of the first generation Mōri daimyo of Hagi, Hidenari (1595–1651), relates his granting of the name Kōraizaemon to a certain Saka Sukehachi, the former Yi Kyŏng. Mid-Edo

documents record that in the same year Yi Chak-kwang's son was given the name Sakunojō and assigned by Hidenari to head the Matsumoto kiln; he was given the same stipend that his father had received, while Kōraizaemon got a stipend that was slightly less. The expansion of the Matsumoto kiln operation is reflected by the growing number of stipended potters in clan records from the late 1620s to 1645.

In the second half of the seventeenth century, the number of official kilns in the domain increased. In 1657, a kiln was opened in Fukawa Sōnose, east of Matsumoto, with the help of laborers assigned by the clan and skilled potters who relocated from Matsumoto. This operation, however, had a somewhat different status than Matsumoto in that it was allowed to produce other wares in addition to those it produced for the clan. In 1663, during the tenure of the Mōri daimyo Tsunahiro (1639–1689), clan kilns producing only official wares were established as offshoots of the Matsumoto kiln, the Miwa and Sahaku kilns. In 1700, the first-generation Miwa head potter was sent to Kyoto on clan order to learn the Raku techniques, as was the fourth-generation head in 1744. By sending the potters to Kyoto, the daimyo hoped to keep the potters of the heavily Korean-influenced Hagi wares aware of other Japanese ceramics.

With clan approval, the Hagi tradition was transmitted within the extended Mōri family. A Hagi potter went to the clan kiln of Chōfu, a Mōri branch family domain, at the request of the Mōri daimyo Tsunamoto (1650–1705). As recorded in an 1815 kiln document, a Hagi potter established an official kiln in 1745 for the rulers of the small Tokuyama domain, also a branch family of the Mōri.

Throughout the Edo period, the clan continued its involvement with the Hagi kilns, both old and new, official and non-official, some of which flourished while others failed. In 1815, the clan issued an order prohibiting non-official kilns from making copies of official teabowls or using a certain type of clay; apparently, the order was not observed, as it was repeated in 1832. In the early nineteenth century, kilns were established with Mōri assistance to fire porcelain wares for daily use, to complement the pottery made by the other kilns. AMW

254 **Teabowl, named** *Juō*
Hon'ami Kōetsu (1558–1637)
h. 9.9 (3 7/8)
Edo period, early 17th century

Gotō Museum, Tokyo

255 **Teabowl, named** *Azuma*
Hon'ami Kōetsu (1558–1637)
h. 8.8 (3 1/2)
Edo period, early 17th century

Kitamura Bunka Zaidan, Kyoto

The popularity of the practice of tea stimulated the diversification of native Japanese wares. Some tea men actively joined in this process as amateur potters, without the technical skills or inhibitions of the professionals, supplying a new source of energy to the artistic flux. Typically, these amateurs employed the uncomplicated methods for forming vessels established in the mid-sixteenth century by the Raku lineage of potters (cats. 285, 286). One of the earliest and most artistically successful and influential members of this group was Hon'ami Kōetsu, the prominent early Edo-period calligrapher, designer, and student of the tea master Furuta Oribe (1544–1615).

Kōetsu's serious involvement with ceramics did not begin until he was in his late fifties. Earlier, he had been trained in sword connoisseurship, his family's traditional profession, and had attained his artistic reputation primarily through achievements in the field of calligraphy. In 1615, he moved to Takagamine, land granted to him by Tokugawa Ieyasu (1543–1616), northwest of Kyoto, where he formed an artistic community and is reported to have found "good earth." A letter dating to around 1620 from Kōetsu to Katō Akinari (1592–1661), the son of Katō Yoshiaki (1563–1631), daimyo of Matsuyama in Iyo Province (present-day Ehime Prefecture), concerns the order of a teabowl by the older Katō, reflecting the high regard accorded his ceramic work even during his lifetime.

Very few ceramic objects are currently accepted as authentic works by Kōetsu. All of these are tea-related wares, and most are teabowls. The two examples in this exhibition represent the two basic Raku glazes, red and black, and Kōetsu worked in both. *Juō* (Ten Kings) is an example of the red Raku type (cat. 254). Its globular form sits on a short foot, and the rim of the mouth curves gently inward, a tendency echoed on the carved lower part of the body. Although Kōetsu used the simple methods pioneered by the Raku potters, handbuilding his bowls from slabs of clay, he was not bound by their conceptual framework. Chōjirō (1516–1592), the founder of the Raku tradition, was en-

254

255

317

256

257

trusted by the tea master Sen no Rikyū (1522–1591) with realizing in plastic form the reserved and austere *wabi* aesthetic he espoused, and the responsibility of preserving this tradition no doubt had a constrictive effect on Chōjirō's successors. Kōetsu, on the other hand, adhered to the aesthetic theories of his own time, especially those of his tea teacher Oribe; these encouraged outgoing, idiosyncratic expressions in clay, as seen, for example, in the products of the Mino kilns (cats. 242–247).

The shape of *Azuma* (East, cat. 255) and its thick coat of black Raku glaze are reminiscent of the works of the third-generation master of the Raku lineage, Dōnyū (also known as Nonkō, 1599–1656). Letters from Kōetsu to the Raku family, in one of which he orders clay from them, and contemporary biographical accounts indicate that Kōetsu pursued his ceramic activities with the guidance of Jōkei, the second-generation Raku master, and Dōnyū. The nature of this relationship probably was one less of dependence than cross-fertilization; the revitalization of the Raku tradition that Dōnyū is credited with is attributable at least in part to his involvement with the amateur potter Kōetsu. Some of Kōetsu's most striking black bowls are characterized by their sharply defined profile, frequently with an outward-slanting rim and portions of the bowl not covered with glaze. In compari-

son, *Azuma*, one of the most reticent of Kōetsu's works, seems softened and demure. The rim of the mouth is blunt and describes a slow undulating movement. The dominant feature is the white-tinged crackled area of glaze.   AMW

256 **Large storage jar for tea leaves**
Nonomura Ninsei
(fl. mid-17th century)
h. 26.3 (10 3/8)
Edo period,
mid-17th century

Agency for Cultural Affairs, Tokyo
Important Cultural Property

257 **Fresh water container**
Nonomura Ninsei
(fl. mid-17th century)
h. 14.0 (5 1/2)
Edo period,
mid-17th century

Tokyo National Museum

Nonomura Ninsei is regarded as the pivotal figure in the early development of Kyōyaki, the ceramic wares of Kyoto, often decorated with multi-color enamels. His work reflected the refinement and luxury of Kyoto and satisfied the aesthetic requirements of Japan's political and cultural elite. By the mid-seventeenth century, Kyōyaki was being made at a number

of kilns established along the eastern and northern fringes of Kyoto. Around 1647, Ninsei established the Omuro kiln in the western part of the city at Ninnaji and began to fire his ceramics, primarily tea-related vessels. Ninsei's studio was characterized by great versatility, producing objects in both large and small scales and sometimes in styles other than the multi-colored enameled type exhibited here, including refined versions of the wares of other kilns such as Seto, Karatsu, and Shigaraki.

The angled shoulder and tall, narrow form of the *chatsubo*, or large storage jar for tea leaves, in the collection of the Agency for Cultural Affairs (cat. 256) recalls that of much smaller containers used for powdered tea in the popular *katatsuki* style. Despite the tremendous increase in size, the form has lost none of its delicacy. By appending the four loops at the shoulders that are typical of *chatsubo*, Ninsei invented a composite form that he is known to have employed in at least two other pieces.

Most immediately striking in this work is the bold decoration. Although the multi-color enamel process was probably introduced to Japan from China, Ninsei developed new techniques, experimenting with elegant harmonies of color and decorative motifs. These often speak less of China than of Japan, drawing influence from native sources such as the *yamato-e*

319

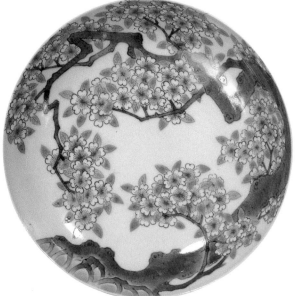

258

painting traditions and lacquer. Small pine trees in gold and light green, and red camellia and plum blossoms outlined and detailed in gold with light green leaves, stretch into the characteristic rich *Ninsei-guro* (Ninsei black) background. Low, rolling mountains, like those in Japan, loom behind in gold. The lower portion of the vessel remains undercorated, revealing the clay body, and the bottom is marked with a large seal that reads *Ninsei*.

Ninsei reaped the benefits of a tea world support system that linked him with tea masters and members of the different social classes, including court, wealthy merchant, and daimyo clients. Cat. 256 was owned by the Kyōgoku family, daimyo of the Marugame domain on Shikoku from 1658 throughout the Edo period, one of many works by Ninsei in their possession. The wealthy Maeda daimyo of

Kaga (part of present-day Ishikawa Prefecture) also owned many pieces by Ninsei, some of which are recorded to have entered their collection through the well-connected Kyoto tea master and sometime Maeda guest, Kanamori Sōwa (1584–1656). Sōwa's social influence and aesthetic guidance were of great importance to Ninsei, especially during the early part of the artist's career.

Like cat. 256, the *mizusashi* in the collection of the Tokyo National Museum (cat. 257) adapts the shape of a powdered tea container, in this case, a *natsume*, a type usually made of black lacquer. Two other slightly larger *mizusashi* in this shape are known, though this example is the most minutely and painstakingly executed. The walls are thin, elegantly curving up toward the flattened top that is stepped down at the mouth to form a ledge upon which the lid would rest. The

unglazed bottom of the vessel is stamped with the large *Ninsei* seal.

The colored decoration is a mixture of natural motifs and geometric abstractions. A weave of silver diamond-shaped lozenges, graded in size from the narrower bottom to wider top, are filled with gold floral abstractions on a red ground. Four windows are framed by the weave, each opening onto a white ground and containing green-leafed peony buds and blooms in combinations of gold and red, and red and silver. The technique employed for the flowers is that of *yamato-e*, especially that seen in the floral forms painted by the artists of Sotatsu's studio. Gold is used for the earth and clouds, and to delineate the juncture of the vertical wall with the top. The top is decorated with a billowing wave pattern in silver on a red ground. Subsequent oxidation has blackened the silver.

258 **Set of five dishes**
Nabeshima ware
diam. 20.0 (7 7/8)
Edo period,
late 17th—early 18th century
Tokyo National Museum

259 **Dish**
Nabeshima ware
diam. 29.6 (11 5/8)
Edo period,
late 17th—early 18th century
Suntory Museum of Art, Tokyo

From around 1675, the official Nabeshima clan kiln of Ōkawachi in the Arita area of Hizen Province (in present-day Saga Prefecture) produced Japanese porcelains of the highest technical quality, with refined, elegant designs. Although angular and unusually shaped objects are not unknown, the Nabeshima potters concentrated on a small repertoire of uniformly shaped tablewares, primarily round high-footed dishes, which they decorated with a palette limited to red, green, and yellow overglaze enamels, underglaze blue, and occasionally iron-brown glaze and celadon green. Examinations of the Ōkawachi site have revealed an enormous *noborigama* (climbing kiln), measuring 137 meters in length and consisting of at least twenty-seven chambers; it is thought that only three central chambers, affording optimal firing conditions, were used for the official porcelains, and the remaining chambers for utilitarian wares.

For most of its long history the kiln was administered with the close control of the Nabeshima daimyo. The examples of Nabeshima ware included in this exhibition are thought to date from the peak production period of the Ōkawachi kiln, from the end of the seventeenth century through the middle of the eighteenth century, when the Nabeshima clan's participation in administration of the kiln was at its height. A directive issued in 1693 by the Nabeshima daimyo Mitsushige (1632–1700) shows concern with the quality of the wares and makes detailed comments regarding the affairs of the kiln. He castigates the kiln administrator about a recent slippage in the quality of the official wares, complains about the repetition of designs, and demands that new, fashionable ones be found. To prevent the marketing of copies of official wares by other kilns, he prohibits outside potters from having access to Ōkawachi, and orders imperfect or otherwise unusable Ōkawachi porcelains to be disposed of properly.

The finest Nabeshima wares were used exclusively by the clan or presented to others of high social rank in the court, military, and political spheres. This prac-

Ninsei's biography must be pieced together from inscriptions on his works, contemporary temple records, diaries, and accounts by the potter Ogata Kenzan (1663–1743). At the beginning of *Tōkō hitsuyō*, Kenzan's treatise on ceramic techniques, Ninsei's name is given as Nonomura Seiemon. The family name Nonomura refers to an area in the Province of Tamba, presently in Kyoto Prefecture, where large tea storage jars were made in the early Edo period. A 1649 source calls him the "potter Seiemon," and a record in the Ninnaji archives from the following year informs us that Ninsei had been a Tamba potter. He apprenticed at the Awataguchi kiln in Kyoto, following which, according to Kenzan, he spent several years in Seto for further training. Returning to Kyoto, Ninsei opened the Omuro kiln around 1647 through the mediatory efforts of Kanamori Sōwa. By 1656,

the year Sōwa died, the potter had assumed the name Harima, as inscribed on an excavated sherd, and by the following year, the name Ninsei. The origin of the Japanese characters that make up Ninsei's name is explained by Kenzan: the first character *nin* was borrowed from Ninnaji, and the second character *sei* from his common name. Documentary evidence suggests that Ninsei's son, though not blessed with his father's artistic acumen, probably succeeded as master of the Omuro kiln during the early part of the Enpō era (1673–1681).   AMW

259

tice is documented in the personal chronicle of Nabeshima Shigemochi (1733–1770). The entry for the seventeenth day of the sixth month of the second year of Meiwa [1765] records a ten-day visit by Shigemochi to his daimyo counterpart in Odawara (currently part of Kanagawa Prefecture), during which time Shigemochi presented a gift of ceramics.

Details regarding the early history of official Nabeshima clan porcelain kilns are unclear. A mid-Meiji-period document based on older kiln-related clan materials relates that two porcelain-producing kilns predating the Ōkawachi kiln fired wares for the Nabeshima daimyo. The first, at Iwayagawachi, was superseded by a second at Nangawara. At these two early kilns, it is thought that special wares for the daimyo were produced on order, though the strict clan control over all phases of kiln activities that was so prominent at the Ōkawachi kiln had not yet been established.

Many of the typical characteristics of Nabeshima porcelains are evident in the set of five dishes in the Tokyo National Museum (cat. 258). Most Nabeshima

dishes were made in one of a limited range of sizes. The dishes in this set are medium-sized, referred to in terms of the old Japanese measurement system as seven *sun*, an especially practical and popular size manufactured in quantity and decorated in matching sets. Reminiscent of the contemporary lacquer tablewares with which they were used, the dishes have a shallow bowl fitted with a relatively tall ring foot.

The design, concentrated away from the center, depicts a cherry tree in full bloom, employing all of the typical Nabeshima colors except celadon green and brown. Fingerlike roots anchor a great trunk that throws off several twisting branches, the outline and details described with a dark underglaze blue and filled in with a lighter blue tone. The petals of the blossoms are described with a fine red line that is also used for the interior detail of the flowers, while the petals themselves are white, the porcelain left in reserve. The leaves are colored with overglaze applications of green and yellow. This design was one of many recorded in a design book maintained by the Nabeshima clan, where it is dated to 1718, though, due to the frequent repetition of designs, it cannot be assumed that this is the date of this partic-

ular set. Many Nabeshima designs were lifted from contemporary design pattern books or adapted from textiles and *maki-e* lacquer wares.

Although porcelains painted with overglaze enamels are the most renowned of the Nabeshima kiln products, extremely fine pieces decorated only with underglaze blue were also produced, such as the dish decorated with a pine tree motif (cat. 259). Its size, one *shaku*, is the largest of the most common Nabeshima dish sizes. The stylized pine adapts well to the same type of centrifugal composition seen in cat. 258. Its jagged yet gracefully twisting trunk and branches are outlined in blue and then filled in with a uniformly smooth coat of light blue. Attached to the branches are overlapping circles of precisely drawn, stiff, radiating pine needles in dark blue. In place of a ring foot, three evenly spaced projecting feet, crafted in the shape of scalloped leaves and covered with underglaze blue, support the dish. Other three-legged dishes of this type, all characterized by especially fine workmanship, suggest that these vessels were made on order for particularly important occasions.   AMW

260

260 Large dish
Ko Kutani ware
diam. 40.5 (16)
Edo period, late 17th century

Umezawa Kinenkan, Tokyo
Important Cultural Property

261 *Sake* ewer
Ko Kutani ware
h. 16.8 (6 5/8)
Edo period, late 17th century

Eisei Bunko, Tokyo
Important Cultural Property

Despite the unsettling persistence of unresolved historical issues, the artistic merit of the enameled porcelain wares known as Ko Kutani, or Old Kutani, remains unquestionable. The painted designs of Ko Kutani porcelains are as exuberant and boldly drawn as the designs of Nabeshima wares are distilled and precise. The typical Ko Kutani vessel is thickly potted from a relatively coarse grade of porcelain clay and sometimes decorated with a limited amount of underglaze blue. Designs, usually outlined and detailed first in black, are colored with richly-toned overglaze enamels, including green, purple, dark blue, yellow, and red. Most of these wares are decorated with naturalistically depicted floral motifs, landscapes with Chinese figures, and bird-and-flower themes, alone or more often in combination with abstractions and geometric patterns.

The Kutani problem focuses on the questions of where objects that have traditionally been called Ko Kutani were actually made, and what the relationship is between these wares and Kutani, an isolated village located in the Daishōji domain. Daishōji, a part of the large Kaga territory (presently part of Ishikawa Prefecture) under the control of the powerful Maeda clan, was ruled by a Maeda branch family. The sites of two porcelain-producing kilns in Kutani were examined during a series of archaeological excavations begun in 1970. The earlier kiln was a large multi-chambered *noborigama* (climbing kiln), about thirty-four meters in length, which scientific tests indicate was probably used until the latter part of the seventeenth century. The start of this kiln is accorded a date no later than that inscribed on an excavated sherd that reads *Meireki 2* [1656], *Kutani*. The second kiln, also a *noborigama*, was much smaller, less than fourteen meters long. A combination of documentary and archaeological evidence suggests that it was fired until probably the late seventeenth or early eighteenth century. The various sherds

gathered from these two sites, including white porcelains that were possibly intended to receive overglaze enamel decoration later, some underglaze blue porcelains, and celadons, have not conclusively solved the mystery, though some of the characteristic types of so-called Ko Kutani were not represented. In the nineteenth century, a revival of porcelain production took place in the Kutani area, though these later products should not be confused with Ko Kutani wares.

The earliest written record concerning the start of kilns in Kutani, dating to 1736, is retrospective in nature. It notes that during the Meireki era (1655–1658), Maeda Toshiharu (1618–1660), the first daimyo of the Daishōji domain and a son of the enormously wealthy Kaga daimyo and art patron Maeda Toshitsune (1593–1658), ordered a person by the name of Gotō to make pottery at Kutani, adding that another type of ware, similar to Chinese Nankin porcelain, had once been made there but was no longer. Two later documents present more elaborate stories. According to one from 1784, the second Daishōji daimyo Maeda Toshiaki (1637–1693) sent Gotō Saijirō to the large complex of advanced porcelain kilns at Arita in Hizen to acquire ceramic skills, after which he returned to Kutani and opened a kiln. The substance of the story, that the Kutani kilns were started on a technological foundation introduced from Arita, is supported by physical evidence. In the early seventeenth century, the ceramic industry at Arita was the first in Japan to produce porcelain, and the type of kiln and the kiln furniture excavated at the Kutani kilns are similar to those used at Arita.

The complicated Ko Kutani question has spawned a substantial body of literature and opinion. Some ceramic historians have reassigned what were originally thought to be products of the Kutani kilns to Arita, and blue-and-white sherds excavated at several Arita kiln sites are clearly of a type that has traditionally been thought of as Ko Kutani. Another theory is that Arita-made porcelain bodies were shipped to Kaga where they were decorated. Recently, fresh discussion has been sparked by the recovery of Ko Kutani sherds during examinations conducted from 1984 through 1986 at the site of the Daishōji daimyo residence in the capital city of Edo (presently Tokyo). Until this discovery, no Ko Kutani sherds had been found in any of the excavated Edo-period residential sites around Japan. The new findings, in a house occupied by the daimyo of the territory in which the village of Kutani and its Edo-period kilns are located, argue for a close connection between the Maeda clan and Ko Kutani wares; the nature of this connection, though, cannot yet be determined. A reso-

lution to the Ko Kutani debate, if there is one forthcoming, awaits further archaeological and art historical research.

The large dish from the Umezawa Kinenkan (cat. 260) has twelve hexagonals along the rim, surrounding a central roundel that contains a floral motif dominated by two large peonies. The realistically depicted flowers face away from each other, one fully open and the other just beginning to bloom, outlined and detailed in a fluid black line and densely colored with purple enamel. Green stems and leaves, one tinged with yellow, complement the flowers along with two red line drawings of butterflies, one large and the other small. On the rim, the major elements of the central design are abstracted into a motif composed of two contraposed butterflies viewed from above against a background of purple peony petals. This motif is placed in six of the hexagons, which alternate with six others filled with a maze of green geometric decoration. The overglaze enamels are applied with great freedom, allowing accidental overflows of color beyond the boundary lines. Three sections of blue enamel floral scrollwork, each with a purple peony blossom, wind around the back of the bowl.

Of the few known Ko Kutani *sake* ewers with a similar low, round form derived from metal prototypes, the example in the Eisei Bunko (cat. 261) is generally regarded as the most finely executed in both shape and decoration. The meticulously formed vessel, supported by three small legs, has a spherical bottom, a bulging register encircling the top, and a broad, knobbed lid. From a single point at the back, an arching round handle spans the top of the vessel to the front where it divides and attaches to the body just above the appended half-cylinder spout.

Colorful, animated decoration enlivens the vessel. A scroll of red peonies on brown stems with green and blue leaves forms a ground for five blue and green *shishi*, mythical lionlike creatures that frolic over the vessel, one on the lid and four distributed around the sides of the body. An underglaze blue floral scroll with three chrysanthemum flowers decorates the handle, while the spout has a decorative pattern in green and yellow. To mask an apparent kiln defect, the very bottom of the vessel is painted with a leaf in blue enamel.   AMW

261

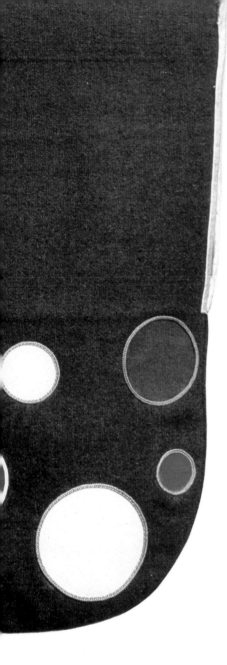

TEXTILES

262

262 *Dōbuku*

appliqué and stencil dyeing on leather
l. 89.0 (35)
w. 141.0 (55 ½)
Muromachi period, 16th century

Ueda Municipal Museum,
Nagano Prefecture
Important Cultural Property

The *dōbuku* was a short jacket worn by
high-ranking samurai from the late Muromachi to early Edo periods. This leather
example, with seven white leather paulownia crests appliquéd to the front and back,
is said to have been given in 1568 by Oda
Nobunaga (1534–1582) to Matsudaira Nobu-
kazu (1539–1624), founder of the Matsudaira family of the castle town Ueda in
Shinano Province (present-day Nagano
Prefecture).

Leather with color or designs added
by dye or smoke was often used on arms
and armor from the Heian through the
Muromachi periods; in the early modern

era, it was also used for civilian clothing.
The leather was stretched taut over a slow
fire of such materials as straw or pine needles; typically, straw produces a brown
color, as in this *dōbuku*, and pine needles
gray. The longer the smoking period, the
darker the shade that resulted, and the
background pattern of this *dōbuku* was
created by smoking the darker areas longer
than the lighter. This technique employed
a stenciled resist. The whole piece of
leather would be smoked till the lighter of
the desired shades had been achieved.
Then a stencil of the intended pattern,
with cutouts wherever the lighter color
was required, would be laid over the
leather and a resist material such as wax or
gum applied through the cutouts. This resist material prevented further darkening
of the leather beneath it. The smoking
process would then be continued until the
darker shade had been reached on the un-
resisted parts of the leather. Finally the
leather would be removed from the smoke
and the resist material picked off, reveal-

ing the lighter shade wherever it had been applied. This *dōbuku* is a fine and early example of the *komon* (small pattern) stencil technique, developed from the stencil methods used earlier on leather for armor, and often employed in the Edo period for the clothing of the warrior class.   KS

263 **Dōbuku**
shibori dyeing on silk
l. 115.0 (44 7/8)
w. 115.8 (45 1/8)
Momoyama period, 16th century

Kyoto National Museum
Important Cultural Property

This *dōbuku* is said to have been given by Toyotomi Hideyoshi (1537–1598) to Nanbu Nobunao (1546–1599), a warrior who sent horses and falcons to Hideyoshi during the Odawara campaign in 1590. The design is entirely appropriate for a gift between feudal warriors: paulownia blossoms, Hide-

yoshi's crest (*mon*), in a stiff, heraldic line across the purple-dyed shoulders and more freely disposed on the white midsection, and feathered arrow shafts, forming another rigid line, on the green lower border. The contrast of the regular, static arrangement above and below with the looser composition in the middle makes for a bold, dynamic design.

The fabric is *nerinuki*, a plain-weave silk of raw (unglossed) warps and degummed (glossed) wefts. Its characteristic crispness, soft luster, and flat surface are particularly suited to *shibori* dyeing, a reserve, or resist, technique in which parts of the fabric are protected against the dye when the piece is dipped in the dye bath. Either the background or the design may be so protected. The area to be reserved is "squeezed" (*shiboru*) away from the rest of the fabric by pinching or shirring, then tightly wound with waterproof thread, fiber, or (for larger areas) bamboo sheathing; when the fabric has been dyed and dried, these protective elements are removed.

To make the design on this *dōbuku*, the paulownia and arrow motifs were reserved in white while their respective backgrounds were dyed purple and green; in the midsection the process was reversed and the background reserved in white while the paulownia were dyed purple, blue, and two shades of green. The division of the background into contrasting color areas, the use of motifs from nature, and the overall effect of lightness, softness, and delicacy in the design are characteristics of the decorative style now called *tsujigahana*, which flourished from the latter half of the Muromachi through the Momoyama period.

Among the upper classes of earlier periods, clothing with dyed designs had been a poor second to that with woven designs. The popularity of *tsujigahana* among the daimyo of the Age of the Country at War (*Sengoku* era) must have been simultaneously a result of and a spur to advances in *shibori* techniques.   KS

263

264

264 Dōbuku
stencil dyeing on silk
l. 87.0 (34 1/4)
w. 141.0 (55 1/2)
Edo period, 17th century

Agency for Cultural Affairs, Tokyo

This *dōbuku*, shaped like a *jinbaori*, is said to have been used by Inagaki Nagashige (1539–1603) or his son Shigetsuna. Eight later consecutive generations of the Inagaki ruled as daimyo of the domain of Toba (in present-day Mie Prefecture), starting in 1725 when Inagaki Akikata (1698–1752) transferred to Toba and lasting until the Meiji Restoration, during the reign of Inagaki Nagahiro (1854–1920). Until recently, the *dōbuku* remained in the possession of the Inagaki family. Although generally similar in form to *dōbuku* decorated with small-pattern *komon* designs dating from the beginning of the early modern era, this example is reversible. The composition of the intricate design is unusual in early *komon* textiles, suggesting an early Edo-period date. The back of the *dōbuku* is decorated with the large *mon*, or family crest, of the Inagaki, depicting facing sprouts of the *myōga* plant.   KS

265 Jinbaori
kirihame and embroidery on wool
l. 90.0 (35)
w. 126.0 (49 1/8)
Momoyama period, 17th century

Sendai City Museum,
Miyagi Prefecture

This striking *jinbaori* is said to have been owned by Date Masamune (1567–1636), daimyo of Sendai. Originally the *jinbaori*'s purpose was functional; it was worn over armor for protection against cold and rain. Gradually the element of design assumed greater importance, and styles were created that reflected the personal tastes of the military elite. Horizontally centered on the back of this jacket of thin wool is the bamboo and sparrow crest (*mon*) of the Date family embroidered in gold. Using the *kirihame* technique, the prominent and variously sized circles of white, yellow, red, green, and blue wool are fitted into holes cut out of the garment and trimmed with different colors.   KS

266 Jinbaori
kirihame and appliqué on wool
l. 77.0 (30)
w. 104.0 (40 1/2)
Momoyama period, 16th century

Tokyo National Museum

Made of wool dyed bright red with cochineal, this boldly decorated *jinbaori* is said to have been owned by the daimyo Kobayakawa Hideaki (1577–1602), a nephew of Toyotomi Hideyoshi and commander in the 1597 invasion of Korea and supporter of Tokugawa Ieyasu at the Battle of Sekigahara. On the back are represented a pair of large crossed sickles. The blade of each is made in the *kirihame* technique, fitting black and white wool pieces into holes cut out of the garment and sewing them securely into place; the handles are appliquéd on top of the red wool. Woolen fabrics were brought to Japan in the Momoyama period by the Portugese, as reflected by the Japanese word for such material, *rasha*, derived from the Portugese *raxa*, meaning woolen cloth. The curved hem of this *jinbaori*, uncharacteristic of traditional Japanese clothing, shows instead the impact of the sartorial style of the Portugese and Spanish who came to Japan in the Momoyama period.   KS

267 Kosode
embroidery and *kanoko shibori*
dyeing on figured satin
l. 142.5 (55 1/2)
w. 124.0 (48 3/8)
Edo period, 17th century

Nomura Collection,
National Museum of Japanese
History,
Chiba Prefecture

The *kosode* was the principal Japanese outer robe from the sixteenth century on, having previously served as outer garment for the lower classes and as undergarment for the upper classes. From the *kosode* evolved the modern kimono. *Kosode* literally means "small sleeves," a reference not to the length or width of the sleeves themselves but to the size of the wrist openings. This *kosode* is a representative example of the Kanbun style of *kosode* decoration that was particularly popular during the Kanbun era (1661–1673) of the Edo period. In

265

266

the Kanbun style the front and back of the garment are each a single field for a markedly asymmetrical design depicted quite large, even in closeup. The primary design field was the back, on which the design formed a dramatic arc across the shoulders and down the right side, leaving the left side undecorated. *Kosode* decorated in this striking style were favored by the then-economically powerful merchant sector of society, but were also widely popular with other classes.

An order book of the Kariganeya *kosode* design house illustrates Kanbun styles ordered by Tōfukumon'in (1607–1678), daughter of the second Tokugawa shogun, Hidetada, and consort of Emperor Go-Mizunoo.

On the back of this *kosode*, large overlapping maple leaves form the arc across the shoulders to the right hem, with the red figured satin (*rinzu*) background exposed on the left. The maple leaves, outlined with gold, are of two types. Some are depicted in *kanoko shibori*, literally, "fawn-spot" *shibori*, referring to the allover dappled pattern of small white spots, each centered on a dot of the background color. These diagonal rows of tiny white circles were produced by pinching off successive bits of fabric along the bias and binding each bit tightly with waterproof thread or fiber, except at the tip, before immersion in the dye bath. Gold embroidery picks out the veins and forms tiny globes of dew on the *shibori* leaves. The remaining leaves are rendered in gold and white embroidery against brush-applied black dye (*hikizome*).

A close look at the embroidered maple leaves reveals that they are solidly paved with cherry blossoms—a kind of surreal juxtaposition much favored in *kosode* designs of the early Edo period. The combination of cherry blossoms and maple leaves evokes for the Japanese their two favorite seasons, spring and fall.

Other similar Kanbun-style decorative schemes can be seen in the *Shinsen onhiinagata,* a *kosode* design book published in 1666, the sixth year of the Kanbun era.   KS

267

335

268 *Uchikake*
embroidery and *kanoko shibori*
on figured satin
l. 171.8 (67)
w. 120.0 (46 3/4)
Edo period, 18th century
Tokyo National Museum

The *uchikake*, a woman's outer garment worn unbelted over the *kosode*, first appeared in the Muromachi period; in the Edo period women of the samurai class began to wear formal *uchikake* on an ornately embroidered background of white, red, or black. This example is made of red figured satin (*rinzu*). The design consists of cherry blossoms and bamboo screens amid conventionalized cloud-scrolls. On the back of the robe one of the screens is decorated with a kind of pomander ball known as a *kusudama*. Embroidery is the chief technique employed to execute the designs, with gold-leaf–covered thread used on the clouds and screens, although some of the cherry blossoms are depicted with clusters of dots in the *kanoko shibori* resist-dyeing process (cat. 267).

The design suggests one of the most beloved of Japanese pastimes—a cherry-blossom viewing party, with the participants protected from vulgar gazes by the lightweight bamboo screens. Clouds drifting among the cherry blossoms refer to a perennial Japanese literary conceit, expressed in scores of poems: an "elegant confusion" as to whether it is cherry blossoms or clouds one is looking at.   KS

269 *Furisode*
yūzen (resist paste) dyeing and
embroidery on silk
l. 166.3 (64 7/8)
w. 124.2 (48 3/8)
Edo period, 19th century
Tokyo National Museum

The *furisode* (swinging sleeves) is a type of *kosode* distinguished by sleeves that hang free of the main body of the garment, below the arm. Although in the early part of the Edo period the sleeves of the *furisode* were not especially long, they gradually increased in length so that by the latter half of the period, sleeves as long as ninety centimeters (c. thirty-five inches) were made. The *furisode* was worn on special occasions by children and young women. This refined example could have been worn by a woman of the samurai class. The fabric is a type of silk crepe called *chirimen*. Its textured matte surface lent itself well to the delicate detailed designs created by *yūzen* dyeing.

The uppermost portion is dyed a solid green. Beneath, a refreshing design runs diagonally across the garment: pine and maple trees occupy the upper half while in the bottom half are male and female pea-

cocks and large blooming peonies. Peacocks and peonies formed a favorite auspicious motif, symbolic of beauty and plenty. Running water flows through the design, from top to bottom. Against the green dyed background, the design is composed chiefly of a sharply defined, white reserve pattern executed by the skilled application of dye-resistant paste. This technique, known as *shiro age*, was a typical feature of *yūzen* dyeing of the latter part of the Edo period. The design is highlighted throughout with embroidery in red, gold, and other colors.   KS

270 *Kosode*
yūzen (resist-paste) dyeing and
embroidery on silk
l. 174.0 (67 7/8)
w. 126.0 (49 1/8)
Edo period, 19th century
Nomura Collection,
National Museum of Japanese
History,
Chiba Prefecture

Save for the shoulder area, a design of rafts with flowers tossed on the waves covers all of this light blue silk crepe (*chirimen*) *kosode*. The theme of rafts with flowers was favored by women of the court and samurai aristocracy for their clothing; in this example the rendering of the design is already quite stylized.

The waves and spray are depicted by the *shiro age* technique, reserved from the blue dye with dye-resistant paste; the crests of the waves are embroidered with gold-leaf–covered thread. Borne on the rafts are cherry blossoms, irises, narcissus, peonies, wisteria, and chrysanthemums, depicted by a variety of methods: reserved in white, dyed in indigo and purple in stenciled *kanoko* dots, with embroidery in red, purple, light green, and gold. The ruinous cost of *kanoko shibori*, besides placing it beyond the means even of many samurai, actually brought about its prohibition by the shogunate in sumptuary laws that were sometimes harshly enforced. Stenciled *kanoko*, being far easier to execute, was neither exorbitant nor illegal: instead of binding each spot individually with dye-proof fiber, the dyer would resist an entire motif with paste applied through a stencil; after the dye had dried and the paste had been removed, the dyer might simulate true *kanoko* by painting in the tiny central dot of background color by hand. The placement of the design on the garment, the use of the *shiro age yūzen* technique, and the densely stitched embroidery are characteristic of the later part of the Edo period. The purple embroidery floss was probably dyed with a chemical pigment.   KS

268

269

270

271 *Kosode*

embroidery and dyeing on silk
l. 155.0 (60 ½)
w. 120.0 (46 ¾)
Edo period, 19th century

Nomura Collection,
National Museum of Japanese
History,
Chiba Prefecture

A characteristic samurai-class *kosode* from the latter part of the Edo period, the decoration on this example is concentrated between the waist and the bottom hem and executed in *shiro age*, reserved white, with added embroidery. On the light green *chirimen* (silk crepe) cloth is a shore scene of plovers and pine trees, with the waves and pine trees in reserved white and embroidered in gold-leaf–covered thread. The plovers, sewn in gold, fly in a dipping line from one sleeve to the other. A hut originally embroidered at the shore in black thread is now all but gone.

Many *kosode* designs of the Edo period were based on literary themes taken from well-known Japanese and Chinese poems, a trend especially noticeable in *kosode* worn by the court and samurai classes. By long poetic tradition, plovers over water bespeak winter. The combination of plovers, a hut, and pine trees at the seashore in this example recalls the famous poem by Minamoto no Kanemasa in the early-twelfth-century poetry anthology *Kin'yōshu* (Anthology of golden leaves):

Plovers
fly to and from Awaji Island
calling;
how many nights have their cries
awakened the barrier guard of Suma? KS

272 *Katabira*

chayazome, embroidery, and pigment
on hemp
l. 165.0 (64 ⅜)
w. 129.0 (50 ¼)
Edo period, 18th century

Nomura Collection,
National Museum of Japanese
History,
Chiba Prefecture

Katabira were unlined *kosode* worn made for the most part of hemp or ramie. The crisp coolness of these fabrics made them particularly suitable for summer wear. *Chayazome*, or "Chaya dyeing," refers to the exceedingly laborious, exacting, and expensive technique whereby the areas to be reserved were paste-resisted on both sides of the fabric before the garment was dip-dyed in indigo. Several shades of blue could be achieved by paste-resisting each area of the design when its desired shade had been reached, then continuing to dip the garment for darker shades elsewhere.

Characteristically, touches of embroidery in bright gold and colors liven this cool color scheme. *Katabira* in other color schemes might be worn by men as well as women, but blue-and-white *chaya*-dyed *katabira* were worn only by women, particularly if not exclusively by women of the upper levels of samurai society.

Typically, *chayazome* designs were landscapes or waterscapes; here we have an idealized rustic landscape with a stream purling through it, fishing nets drawn up to dry (in tepeelike shapes) along the stream banks, compounds of thatch-roofed cottages behind brushwood fences, a tiny arched bridge, and everywhere flowering fields and pine groves in a boldly two-dimensional arrangement whose resemblance to a meandering stream is probably not accidental. In this magical landscape, verdure of all the seasons appear together: plum blossoms of late winter; cherry blossoms of early spring; irises, peonies, and narcissus of summer; chrysanthemums, bellflowers, bush clover, and maple leaves of fall. Bamboo grass carpets the open spaces, water lilies lift their broad leaves in the stream, and dense stands of pine offer cool shade.

As well as being aesthetically pleasing, this *katabira* is technically a tour de force. The outlines of the paste-resisted areas were flawless. The ivory background areas were probably brush-dyed, as were the touches of yellow in the pine trees, and the very fine slightly greenish blue lines in the fishing nets and the brushwood fences have probably been drawn with indigo pigment. KS

273 *Katabira*

chaya-zome and embroidery on hemp
l. 161.0 (62 ¾)
w. 123.0 (48)
Edo period, 19th century

Nomura Collection,
National Museum of Japanese
History,
Chiba Prefecture

This hemp *katabira*, or summer robe, is the canvas for a unified shore scene. Only the left sleeve is blank, and so persuasive is the design that the viewer imagines it continuing there, hidden only by distance and by mist. Unlike cat. 272, which is assertively two-dimensional and exceedingly stylized in its depiction of motifs from nature, this landscape recedes into the distance from hem to shoulder and treats each individual motif with considerable modeling and three-dimensionality. All the

271

272

342

273

blue in the design was executed in indigo in *chaya-zome* resist dyeing; when the dye had dried and the resist past had been removed, the other colors were added with embroidery.

A thatch-roofed house is seen under pine and blossoming cherry trees on the right sleeve; below is a salt-evaporating pan in a pine grove; near the bottom are thatch-roofed houses among pine and cherry trees and fishnets hung to dry. Gentle waves connect these motifs. This shore landscape, set against the slightly off-white hemp background, is appropriate for a summer robe. It is thought to have been worn by a relatively low-ranking woman of a daimyo household. Fashion dictated the red silk facings at the collar and wrist openings.   KS

274 *Katabira*
chaya-zome and embroidery on hemp
l. 175.8 (68 1/2)
w. 120.0 (46 3/4)
Edo period, 18th century
Tokyo National Museum

Like cat. 272, this *chayazome katabira* is entirely covered by an idyllic landscape, in which rustic villas await the arrival of a daimyo household escaping the oppressive urban heat. This too is a fantasy landscape, in which vegetative states of all the seasons are seen together: cherry blossoms of spring; iris and cockscomb of summer; chysanthemums, bellflowers, and maple leaves of fall; and the evergreen pines, symbols of winter. Unlike cat. 272, this landscape is mostly water, and water reeds, water plantain (with arrow-shaped leaves), and pickerel-weed grow abundantly. The viewpoint is generally closer, and the motifs slightly larger and more three-dimensional than in cat. 272.

Chaya dyeing is a lost art—the composition of the resist paste is no longer known—so it is not possible to replicate the making of such a *katabira*. It has been plausibly said, however, that the making of a *chayazome katabira* of this quality took over two years from the creation of the design, making such garments among the most luxurious dyed textiles of the Edo period.   KS

275 *Koshimaki*
embroidery on silk
l. 174.4 (68)
w. 121.4 (47 3/8)
Edo period, 18th century
Tokyo National Museum

276 *Koshimaki*
embroidery on silk
l. 163.3 (63 5/8)
w. 126.0 (49 1/8)
Edo period, 19th century
Tokyo National Museum

A part of the formal summer attire of women of the warrior class, the *koshimaki*, literally "waist wrap," was worn over the *katabira*; it was worn off the shoulders and arms, secured at the waist and loosely wrapped around the lower half of the body. In earlier times the *uchikake* had been worn in this fashion in the summer, and this was called *koshimaki sugata* (waist wrap form), but in the Edo period the style became formalized and the *koshimaki* as such was developed. Over a short-sleeved *katabira* such as cat. 273, a similarly short-sleeved *koshimaki* (cat. 275) would be worn; if the *katabira* was of the *furisode* (swinging sleeves, cat. 272) type, a long-sleeved *koshimaki* (cat. 276) would accompany it. In the late Edo period, certain colors and designs were defined for the *koshimaki*; typically, motifs with auspicious associations were finely embroidered on black or brown plain-weave silk (*nerinuki*).

On cat. 275 the pine twigs, flowering plum, and bamboo—the "Three Friends of Winter"—connote courage, purity, and resiliency; the cranes and the tortoises (symbolized by the hexagonal "tortoiseshell lozenges") connote longevity and purity; and the four-sided "coin" motif enclosing a stylized blossom stands for prosperity.

Cat. 276 offers the instantly recognizable "myriad treasures" (*takara zukushi*), singly and together the emblems of material advantage and good fortune. The "myriad treasures" assemblage can vary somewhat in its composition; here it seems to include the hat and cape of invisibility, the keys to the storehouse of good fortune, the flaming wish-granting jewel, the mallet of good fortune, the drawstring money pouch, crossed cloves (alternatively identified as rhinoceros horns, a highly esteemed restorative throughout East Asia), and the "seven jewels"—this last a category that comprises gold, silver, and a varying list of gemstones.

The plethora of connotative motifs on the *koshimaki* seems intended to compensate for the notable absence of such motifs on the *chayazome katabira* with which they were worn.   KS

274

275

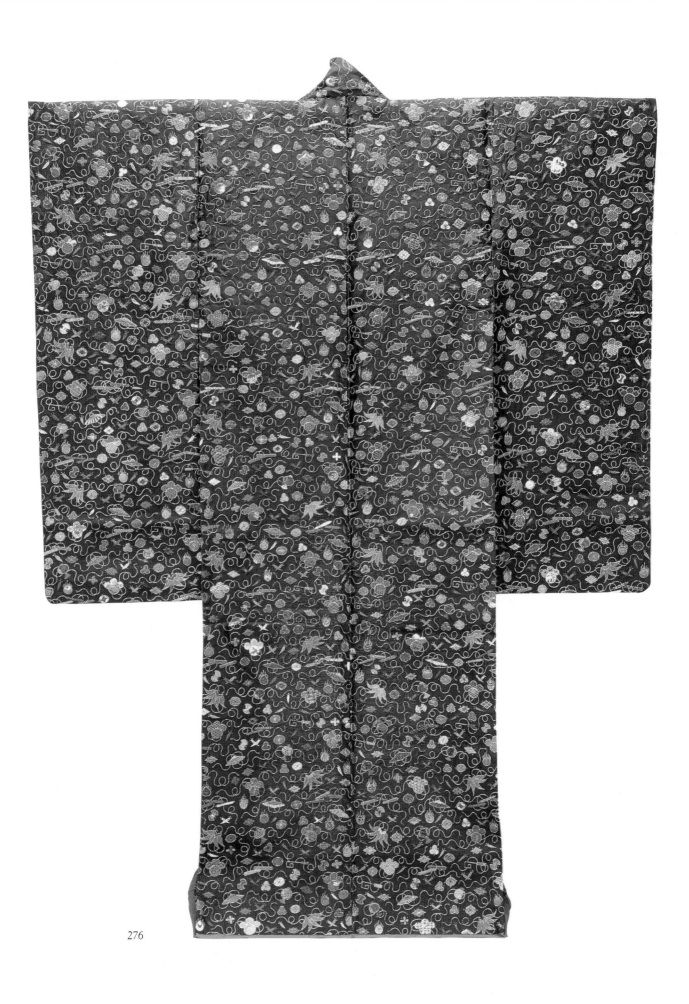

276

277 **Tea container, named *Rikyū shiribukura***
h. 6.7 (2⅝)
Southern Song

Eisei Bunko, Tokyo
Important Art Object

This small container for thick tea, or *chaire*, was probably first used as a medicine container in China, and later came to be greatly treasured by the Japanese. For warriors such as Oda Nobunaga (1534–1582), Toyotomi Hideyoshi (1537–1598), and Tokugawa Ieyasu (1543–1616), who sought to unify Japan at the end of the sixteenth century, the possession of a prize *chaire* often symbolized political and cultural power. *Chaire* were often bestowed upon daimyo as rewards for loyalty and support on the battlefield. Hosokawa Sansai (1563–1646), for instance, is said to have so desired the *chaire* shown here that he declared he would trade one entire province for it. Owners would display famous pieces boldly, in order to humble and subdue those who possessed nothing as great.

Chaire were also appreciated for their artistic value and actual use in the tea gathering. Many warriors treasured and protected their utensils because of strong sentimental attachment. In a time of constant warfare, when retainers could easily change sides, utensils proved unable to betray their owners.

Chaire were brought to Japan around the middle of the thirteenth century, during the Kamakura period. Many of the valued *chaire* were fired in China during the Southern Song and Yuan dynasties. The locations of many of these Chinese kilns are unknown, as is the name of the potter who made this small container. *Chaire* often are discussed under the rubric *karamono*, or Chinese objects, superior to Japanese objects and therefore held in high esteem by the Japanese.

This container is called the *Rikyū shiribukura*. As recorded in the *Kitano ochanoyu no ki*, the great tea master Sen no Rikyū owned and used it at the great Kitano tea gathering held by Toyotomi Hideyoshi in the tenth month of 1587. This grand tea gathering is believed to have been an attempt by Hideyoshi to invite tea connoisseurs from all over the country to come and display their most famous utensils. The latter part of the *chaire*'s name, *shiribukura*, derives from its stout shape, which slightly bulges out toward the base. Despite Hosokawa Sansai's known desire to possess this *chaire*, he was denied this privilege during Rikyū's lifetime. It was only after Rikyū's untimely death that the *chaire* found its way into the Tokugawa family. Following the important Battle of Sekigahara (cat. 104) in 1600, Sansai was invited by Ieyasu for a banquet. Hidetada, Ieyasu's son, is said to have praised Sansai

for his alliance and, remembering Sansai's earlier desire for the *chaire*, presented it to him as a reward. This dramatic provenance adds immensely to the value of a utensil that also is held in great artistic regard. In this way the *chaire* has been imbued with a lasting legacy.

Being relatively small in size, the *Rikyū shiribukura chaire* lends itself well to the tea man's gentle handling. The dark brown color of the outer glaze resembles a thin coating of molasses. The shiny glaze covers the *chaire* from the upper rim to the lower area, where it is only partially glazed. A spiralling pattern on the foot of the *chaire* indicates that it was cut from the wheel with a string.

Appreciation of a *chaire* depends to a large extent upon what the Japanese call its "scenery," or the appearance of the glaze on the outer surface. This tea container has obviously experienced a less than peaceful life, attested by the evidence of repair around the upper edge. The attitude toward preservation in the tea ceremony (*chanoyu*) illustrates the serious reverence tea people held for their utensils. A chip or crack would be lovingly repaired and the utensil would be valued even more after having suffered such a blemish. The natural weathering of the utensils provided yet another dimension that would affect its legendary worth. Appreciation depends also on the shape of the *chaire*, which is one of several designated standard *chaire* shapes. As with most utensils in the tea gathering, one also views the bottom of the *chaire*. This is done by gently tilting the *chaire* to one side to obtain a view of the foot with the mark left behind when the potter cut it from the wheel.

The mouth of this *chaire* is covered with an ivory lid. It is said that the paper-thin gold foil applied to the reverse side of the lid served as a device to signal any obvious tampering with the tea. The foil would change color if poison were present. In the world of the warrior, taking part in a tea gathering could at times be dangerous.

Three cloth bags made of different fabrics accompany this *chaire*. During the actual preparation of tea only one bag covers the *chaire*, but the *Rikyū shiribukura* can be used with any of the three interchangeable cloth bags, all of a type known as *kantō*, which is a striped cloth. The fabric of the two outer bags is labeled *jōdai* and *chūko*, pointing to the period of importation; *jōdai* objects were imported during the first half of the Muromachi period (fifteenth century and before) and *chūko* arrived in the latter half (sixteenth century). The fabric of the center bag is known as *Taishi kantō*, which is an ikat-weave cloth found in Indonesia. The

277

splashed-pattern technique of *kasuri*, which still continues to be produced, is characterized by a background of dark red, with thin, woven horizontal stripes of yellow and dark blue. A pattern of white, brown, and yellow thread weaves its way between the stripes, lending the fabric a "splashed" look. From its name, *Taishi kantō* is often mistakenly believed to be associated with another famous fabric that it closely resembles. This different and much earlier cloth was used with Buddhist artifacts and is thought to trace its origins to the Hōryūji, a temple in Nara, which is associated with the famous statesman Shōtoku Taishi (574–622). The *Taishi kantō* shown here was imported during the Momoyama period. The term probably derived from a family named Taishiya, in the city of Sakai, who greatly treasured this material.

These cloth bags were originally used to protect the ceramic utensil from harm. Gradually the bags themselves, and the way they were tied, became an aesthetic component of the tea gathering. The fabric was often taken from extremely valuable and rare bolts imported from China. Unwilling to waste even the scrap material, the Ashikaga shoguns used remnants of Chinese fabrics in the mounting

of scrolls or to be sewn into bags for *chaire*. The slender rope attached to the top is tied in a precise way to indicate whether the *chaire* contains tea. The complicated method of tying was also supposedly an additional measure intended to preclude tampering with the contents.

Throughout the development of the tea gathering the Japanese have expressed a special fondness for covers and containers, and utilitarian purposes became supplemented with ceremonial and aesthetic intentions. Likewise, the boxes for tea utensils are a coveted component of utensil ownership. The tea scoop and its accompanying tube container and the many layers of wrappings and boxes, both inner and outer, only accentuate the worth of the tea container. The boxes also serve as vital evidence in certifying the validity of its contents.

From the Momoyama period to the beginning of the Edo period, the production of native Japanese *chaire* flourished along with the development of *wabi* (rustic) tea, which sought to incorporate *kuniyaki*, or native wares, into the tea gathering. However, as seen in Sansai's desire for the *Rikyū shiribukura*, the old established taste for the Chinese *chaire*

remained strong among the daimyo and was never completely replaced by a new and overwhelming purely Japanese aesthetic. The artistic appreciation and categorization of Chinese *chaire*, which had been standardized during the Higashiyama period, remain close to the divisions and ranking seen among *chaire* today.   JIK

278 **Teabowl**
   h. 6.7 (2 5/8)
   Southern Song
   Eisei Bunko, Tokyo

Tenmoku teabowls were originally brought into Japan by monks returning from China during the Kamakura period. The Chinese term *tenmoku* refers to a type of bowl distinguished by a conical shape, a small, narrow foot, and relatively thin walls. Many of these bowls are said to have come from Mount Tianmu in Chekiang Province, where many Japanese monks were known to have been trained and introduced to tea drinking within the framework of monastic regulations. The name *tenmoku* is actually a Chinese place name.

This *tenmoku* bowl was thrown on a potter's wheel, unlike the later hand-molded native Japanese Raku bowls (cats. 285, 286). It represents an artistic expres-

278

279

sion bound to the ideal of precision, perfection, and refinement. It was almost in reaction to this type of highly refined Chinese ware that later tea men began to create native Japanese wares with more natural shapes. The almost pristine shape of this *yuteki,* or oil-spot, *tenmoku* bowl was highly valued by early connoisseurs and probably was appreciated more for its decorative value than utilitarian purpose. The glaze is appropriately named, as it resembles a film of oil sparkling on the surface of the water. Silver and blue spots glisten on the black background.

Tenmoku bowls are often compared to the half-sphere formed by the base of a lotus flower. Usually the sides of the bowl extend gradually upward in a straight line from the foot. However, the mouth of this bowl is very wide, like a morning glory in full bloom. On the sloping inside wall of the bowl, almost halfway down from the rim, are five oil drops, suggesting five crests spaced at even intervals. This intentional design indicates that the study of glazes during the Song Dynasty had progressed greatly. The thickness of the rim indicates that this bowl would probably have been a decorative piece for display on a special shelf, as it would be difficult to drink from this particular bowl.

Tenmoku bowls, when actually used at tea gatherings or displayed as decorative pieces, were presented on special *tenmoku* stands (cats. 280, 281). Due to the very narrow and seemingly precarious base characteristic of *tenmoku* bowls, the stand was an integral part of the use of these wares and valued as an artistic piece in itself. After a guest received a *tenmoku* bowl of tea, he would remove the bowl from the stand and cradle it in his hands to drink. After carefully observing the features of that particular bowl, he would return the bowl to its stand before relinquishing it to his host.

When tea drinking was first introduced to Japan, very simply decorated *tenmoku* bowls were used in Zen monasteries. In present-day Kyoto there is a special tea gathering at Kenninji every April, to commemorate Myōan Eisai (1141–1215), the founder of the temple. During the time since the introduction of tea in the twelfth century, a new Song style of preparing tea had been developed, which di-

280

281

353

282

rectly influenced tea preparation in the Japanese tea ceremony. The Kenninji gathering tries to recreate tea drinking as it was practiced in Zen temples after Eisai's time during the fourteenth century. *Tenmoku* bowls on stands are distributed to each of the guests sitting in the main temple hall. A monk carries a bronze pitcher with a long, slender nozzle, which provides a tip on which a small bamboo tea whisk rests. After removing the tea whisk, the monk then pours hot water into the already tea-filled *tenmoku* bowl and proceeds to whisk the brew. He serves each guest in turn, in this same manner.

During the fourteenth and fifteenth centuries, the Ashikaga shogun prized *tenmoku* bowls for their foreign import appeal, and included them in many of the lists of famous tea utensils and art objects. In later centuries, *tenmoku* lost much of its appeal as the growth of native Japanese wares was actively encouraged, and as a mixture of native and Chinese wares came to be used in a harmonious, subdued fashion. Finally, during the Edo period the interest in the *tenmoku* bowl was revived by daimyo tea practitioners. The *tenmoku* continued to be used as a ceremonial ware for offerings made to the gods and Buddhas. In addition, it came to symbolize the type of bowl for serving a nobleman or someone of high rank at a tea gathering. In this instance, the elaborate *tenmoku* stand, in some tea schools, was occasionally replaced by a plain wood stand, which was used only once and then discarded. JIK

279 Teabowl
h. 4.5 (1¾)
Southern Song

Eisei Bunko, Tokyo

The distinguishing feature of this Chinese *tenmoku* bowl is the leaf design in the bottom and along the side of the bowl, intended to be discovered after the tea had been finished. "Konoha" literally means tree leaf, and describes a special technique reserved for *tenmoku* bowls made with this characteristic. This bowl, made in Kiangsi Province and imported into Japan, has a disturbing yet romantic charm. It is almost as if a solitary leaf, swept up by autumn breezes, came to gently rest in the bowl just moments before firing. The outline of the veins in the leaf is clearly set off by the dark tortoise-shell brown of the glaze. Leaves with high silica content, such as the horse chestnut, are considered the best kind to use for this firing effect.

Chinese utensils such as these *tenmoku* bowls and their stands were an integral part of any daimyo's collection. The possession of Chinese utensils went hand in hand with the increased production of domestic and Korean-made tea utensils. Murata Shukō (1423–1502), known as one of the early proponents of native Japanese tea, never advised completely forsaking Chinese wares for domestic ones. He suggested that tea practitioners should assemble a harmonious grouping of Japanese

and Chinese utensils that would complement each other.

Hosokawa Yūsai (1534–1610), father of Sansai (1563–1646), was not only a renowned warrior like his son, but is especially remembered for his great literary accomplishments. He extensively studied the composition of thirty-one-syllable poems (*waka*) and wrote a poem pertaining to the warrior and his training in all fields: "Of those who dislike poetry, linked verse, dance and tea, the limitation of their upbringing is plainly obvious." However, like the delicate balance sought between Chinese and Japanese wares, a daimyo had to juggle his role as warrior and tea connoisseur. Known as a skilled tea person, Sansai never permitted his artistic calling to overshadow his profession as a warrior. When Hotta Masamori (1608–1651), governor of Kaga Province, requested that Sansai display his famous collection of utensils, Sansai evidently disappointed him by displaying, instead, warrior paraphernalia.

JIK

280 Teabowl stand
lacquer on wood with shell
diam. 16.4 (6½)
Ming

Eisei Bunko, Tokyo

Tenmoku teabowl stands were imported along with *tenmoku* bowls from China to be used as supports for the narrow-footed bowls (cats. 278, 279). The stand itself was

283

284

often valued as an independent artistic piece. This *tenmoku* stand has a floral pattern encompassed by hexagonal, or tortoise-back-shaped, crest designs, both inlaid with mother-of-pearl. This technique of applying iridescent seashell, known as *raden*, was also used earlier, on, for example, saddles of the Heian period. The use of very thin fragments of seashell is a specifically Chinese technique and is believed not to have been practiced in Japan. Most Japanese *raden* technique uses a thicker fragment of shell. Upon closer inspection of this particular *tenmoku* stand, the pieces of seashell resemble the peeled-away cross-section of a tree's growth rings. The effect is one of transparent fragments interlaced with delicate strands resembling spidery veins of mica.   JIK

281 **Teabowl stand**
lacquer on wood
diam. 15.5 (6⅛)
Ming

Eisei Bunko, Tokyo

This *tenmoku* stand, used as a support for a *tenmoku* bowl was imported from China. *Guri* refers to the spiral pattern carved in deep relief across the surface. The beauty of this stand is due to the technique known as *tsuikoku*, where layers of dark brown, almost black, lacquer are alternately applied with vermilion layers. The carved spiral pattern accentuates the stratified layers of lacquer.

The provenance and use of this particular *tenmoku* stand are undocumented. In daimyo tea culture the quality and wide variety of utensils collected by daimyo revealed his artistic knowledge and refinement. High quality utensils were essential for entertaining superiors. Before the medieval period, a subordinate was expected to pay a visit to his superior's residence, while later the custom was reversed and

the ruler began to visit his subordinates. Socializing became a means of strengthening the fragile bond between ruler and vassal. The Ashikaga shoguns regularly visited the Hosokawa and other daimyo residences. It was a heavy responsibility to provide first-rate cultural entertainment.

Special gathering places and suitably important utensils, such as this *tenmoku* stand, were required to accommodate such illustrious guests. The combination of utensils selected for a tea gathering also revealed whether careful consideration had been given to the affair. Not just any *tenmoku* bowl could be paired with this stand. Warriors wished to be recognized for their acumen, not only in the arts of war, but also in the more creative arena of art and culture. They were competing not only with other warriors, but with the old aristocrats who had lost political power to the warrior class, yet were thought to still outrank the warriors in pedigree and social refinement.   JIK

285

286

282 Square tray
lacquer on wood
diam. 18.1 (7⅛)
Ming
Eisei Bunko, Tokyo

This lacquered tray was made in China during the early Ming period. *Katatsuki chaire,* or square-shouldered thick tea containers, were customarily displayed placed in the middle of a square tray of this type. Since the purpose of the tray is to enhance the beauty of the thick tea container, an unadorned, yet tastefully lacquered tray is much preferred by tea people. Most thick tea containers, or *chaire,* are a shade of dark brown, which contrasts nicely with the red color of the tray. Visible cracks on the tray's surface are evidence of natural aging. The bottom is covered with black lacquer and marked by an unidentifiable red seal.   JIK

283 Incense container
lacquer on wood
diam. 6.2 (2¼)
Ming
Eisei Bunko, Tokyo

The plump figure of the beggar monk Budai (J: Hotei, cat. 80), one of the seven gods

of good fortune, decorates the lid of this incense container. The *tsuishu* technique, seen also on the peony and leaf incense container (cat. 284) is effectively used here. Budai is recognizable by his enormous belly and the bag that he carries to collect alms.   JIK

284 Incense container
lacquer on wood
diam. 5.5 (2⅛)
Ming
Eisei Bunko, Tokyo

Kōgō literally means "incense" and "to fit together"—a reference to the lidded container. The incense container in the tea gathering holds the incense until it is added directly to the fire beneath the kettle. This utensil should not be confused with an incense burner or censer, which were displayed in the *tokonoma* (alcove) until late in the Momoyama period. The incense container is used in conjunction with the charcoal ceremony, which, along with the serving of the meal and making of the tea, is an integral component of a complete tea gathering. Skillful placing of the charcoal encourages the successful burn-

ing of the fire needed to boil the water. The incense must be carefully aimed so that it falls close to the fire, but not too close, thus prolonging the release of the scent that permeates the tearoom.

This incense container probably was crafted in China. Using a technique known as *tsuishu* a design is carved through several layers of lacquer revealing the different colors lying below the surface. This container has layers of red, green, and yellow, which result in a variety of colors in the flowers, leaves and stems. The *tsuishu* technique was commonly used to highlight a pattern known as "red flowers and green leaves." Here the flower is a peony, which gives a distinct feeling of Chinese elegance and taste.

Materials used in making incense containers can include lacquer, wood, metal, bamboo, shell, or ceramic. Lacquer incense containers were often part of the *shoin* style of decoration. The early preference for Chinese wares was later replaced, as native and Korean wares were gradually integrated into the tea gathering and objects from everyday use were adapted. Rikyū enjoyed choosing tea utensils from among the most ordinary objects, which were often overlooked by others.

The modern-day tea gathering is of-

356

287

ten seen as a synthesis of the five senses. Often, small pieces of incense are buried under the barely lit charcoal and release their scent just as the guests arrive. Thus the guests are greeted by the lingering scent of the incense, before they see the host. The guest makes his way along the tea garden path, washes his hands in the water basin placed outside the tearoom, and symbolically cleanses his thoughts. Warriors were asked to leave their swords outside the tearoom door. The use of incense can be traced to Buddhist ceremonies. Although the ritualistic, religious use of incense has since been combined with the purely pleasurable, incense still conjures up a feeling of otherworldliness and tranquility.   JIK

285 **Teabowl, named *Otogoze***
Raku Chōjirō (1516–1592)
h. 8.2 (3¼)
Momoyama period

Eisei Bunko, Tokyo
Important Art Object

It is said that Raku teabowls perfectly capture the *wabi* spirit of Rikyū's (1522–1591) style of tea. Rikyū was responsible for introducing a native Japanese aesthetic to

tea, which broke away from the more precise, severe Chinese style that had held the fascination of Japanese tea men. In 1585 Rikyū commissioned Chōjirō, a tile maker for the Jurakudai palace, to create a new type of teabowl according to his strict specifications.

In contrast to the wheelthrown Chinese *tenmoku* bowls (cats. 278, 279), Raku teabowls are hand-modeled, with considerably thicker, straighter walls. Raku bowls are usually covered with either a somber black or red glaze. Unlike *tenmoku* bowls, Raku bowls were meant to be placed directly on the mat, rather than on a stand. For this reason a Raku bowl has a wider, more stable foot.

Chōjirō, the founder of the first generation of Raku potters, was commissioned by Hosokawa Sansai (1563–1646) to make this teabowl. Rikyū's grandson Sotan gave this bowl the name *Otogoze*, also the name of one other bowl by Chōjiro. *Otogoze* refers to a female, but not to the frail, delicate classical type of beauty. On the contrary, this term implies the coarse, homely features of a woman with a high forehead, plump and bulging cheeks, and flat nose. When viewed from above and from the side, the slight warp of the uneven rim is evident. The dull, matte glaze is

typical of Chōjiro's bowls. A dab of black lacquer has been applied to repair a blemish on the top rim of the bowl. A slight tinge of green inside *Otogoze* offers proof of its use.

Otogoze comes equipped with an impressive array of protective boxes. First, the bowl is wrapped in a cloth bag made from silk crepe. The inner box is made from paulownia wood and bears the name of the bowl in the handwriting of the seventh-generation Hosokawa. Paulownia wood is almost religiously used to store precious tea utensils. It is valued for its apparent resistance to fire and humidity. In some areas of Japan it has been the custom to plant a paulownia tree after the birth of a daughter. When the daughter is ready to marry, the tree has grown large enough to provide the wood for the trousseau containers.

To hold a teabowl cradled safely between both hands, feeling the lulling warmth through the thick clay body, is truly a sensual experience. All the senses are ignited as one lifts the bowl upward to the lips. This is followed by a savoring of the scent and taste of the tea. Unlike the handle of a western teacup, which distances one from the immediacy of the brew and the cup, the teabowl is designed for direct, personal contact. The diameter of a teabowl is considerably larger than a teacup and one's face literally enters into the teabowl as it is engulfed by the wide rim. One does not just hold a Raku teabowl, one is embraced by it.   JIK

286 Teabowl
Raku Sōnyū (1664–1716)
diam. 12.1 (4¾)
Edo period
Eisei Bunko, Tokyo

The fifth-generation Raku potter, Sōnyū, was adopted by the Raku family at the age of two from a wealthy Kyoto family. He was a cousin to the famous brothers, Kōrin (1658–1716) and Kenzan (1663–1743). Kōrin was a famous Edo-period painter and designer in the Rinpa style. Kenzan, the younger, is remembered best for his ceramic wares. There is still no clear explanation why the fourth-generation potter, Ichinyū, adopted a son despite the fact that he had already had a son born to him. A family conflict ensued, and the natural-born son, Ichigen, left the Raku family with his mother and established his own kiln.

This red Raku teabowl is shown with a paulownia box, which bears a pressed seal and signature. Sōnyū seems to have modeled the shapes of his bowls upon those preferred by Rikyū. Upon examining the bottom of the bowl after drinking the tea, as is the general rule in tea, one would find the graceful swirl of a whirlpool. The clay walls are thick and the foot is low. The rim intentionally expresses an imperfect roundness that is characteristic of hand-built Raku bowls.   JIK

287 Tea kettle
iron
h. 17.5 (6⅞)
Muromachi period
Eisei Bunko, Tokyo

In twentieth-century Japan, a sign would be hung outside the waiting area for a large, informal tea gathering to indicate that the kettle had been put on to boil. Although a teabowl, whisk, tea container, and a number of other utensils are needed, a kettle to boil the water is considered the most essential element. The tea master Sen no Rikyū (1522–1591) cautioned against over-zealous collecting of utensils. One of Rikyū's didactic poems from a hundred-poem collection reads, "With but a single kettle one can make tea, it is foolish to possess a multitude of utensils."

Prior to the ritualization of tea drinking in the fifteenth century, early kettles for boiling water were a common item in any household kitchen. In fourteenth-century tōcha, or tea identification con-

tests, water was boiled in a large kettle and then transferred to a covered serving container, which was then used to pour hot water over the powdered tea. In other instances, hot water was used directly from kettles that were usually placed in a separate room or corridor away from the guests.

As part of the prototypical method for serving tea, water was boiled in a large, traditional kitchen kettle and then transferred to a covered container that was used to pour hot water over the powdered tea already in the bowl. Kettles for boiling water were usually placed in a separate room or corridor away from the guests. Gradually the kettle moved to the tearoom where tea was prepared directly in front of the guests. It was at this point that the mere kitchen utensil began to achieve a level of creative artistry.

The Hosokawa family collection includes eight old tea kettles. All seem to be a different shape and variety and come from different localities throughout Japan. (Experts believe that this random sampling was deliberate.) The kettle shown here, with a pattern of pine, bamboo, and plum, was made in Ashiya, situated in present-day Fukuoka Prefecture. At the time this kettle was cast the two major kettle-producing areas were Ashiya and Tenmyō. Ashiya is located at the mouth of the Onga River, then known as the Ashiya River, and it is believed that casting was done there in order to utilize productively the soil and iron sand.

Ashiya kettles are characteristically famous for their designs, which are etched in relief on the surface of the kettle's front and back. Some of the typical designs include flowers and birds, horses, or mountains and water. The pattern here is a popular combination that weaves together the motifs of pine, bamboo, and plum. All three plants are especially resilient to the cold and have come auspiciously to symbolize strength. Etched on one side of the kettle is a plum tree that is easily recognized by its gnarled branches, which extend outward to the left and right. Plum blossoms lay flat against the surface, and bamboo leaves and a pine tree complete the triad. On the opposite side are pictured bamboo leaves, bamboo sprouts, pine needles, and cones. This relief technique is similar to that found on the back of old Japanese metal mirrors.

The lower half of the kettle may have been recast. It was common practice for old kettles to be repaired at the bottom. The areas of appreciation of a kettle are usually the shape, surface, lid, and lugs or ears. The lugs found on either side of this kettle have been skillfully embellished with the figure of a lion's head, whose flowing mane trails down each side. The lion design was commonly found on the

legs of early kettles and was adopted later as a popular design for kettle lugs.

The contrast of materials, shapes, and textures of utensils used in a tea gathering presents a curious phenomenon. Compare the immense weight of the kettle with the delicate, almost airy quality of the bamboo tea scoop. It is part of a tea student's training to handle all utensils with equal respect and care. In his didactic poems, Rikyū suggested that heavy utensils should be skillfully lifted so as to appear to be almost weightless, and, similarly, that light utensils should not be carelessly waved around, but thoughtfully handled, as if they possessed a secret weight.

During a tea gathering, after the charcoal has been added and the fire begins to light below the kettle, a murmur can be heard building in the quiet, enclosed space of the tearoom. Tea people compare this heated whispering of the kettle to the sound of the wind through the pines.   JIK

288 Tea scoop
Sen no Rikyū (1522–1591)
bamboo
l. 17.7 (7)
Momoyama period
Eisei Bunko, Tokyo

For westerners, the tea scoop, or *chashaku*, is perhaps the most puzzling of all tea utensils. This fragile sliver of bamboo with its willowy curve and slender handle seems to lack the grandeur of a teabowl, nor is it the product of a lengthy and rigorous process such as that needed to make a tea kettle. Yet this unassuming object is perhaps the most treasured and appreciated utensil shown here. Unlike other utensils that were crafted by trained artisans, the tea scoop is customarily carved by the tea man himself. Thus these mere shavings of bamboo have been shaped to produce a personal expression of an individual's tea. Styles of tea scoops are meticulously examined and studied by later generations, as it is believed that the "flavor" of a person's tea is reflected in the very bend and shape of the bamboo scoop. The beauty of a tea scoop is as simple and pristine as that of the bamboo itself. Moreover, tea scoops can be called by either a carefully selected poetic name or by the maker's name. In addition to the tea scoop's "scenery" the most important features are actually peripheral to the object itself: the name of the maker and the accompanying tube container, which is often inscribed with the poetic name of the scoop, often taken from a classical poem.

Yoshimura Teiji, in writing about "The Soul of Chashaku," prefers to think of the fashioning of a tea scoop as sculpture in bamboo. As in sculpture, the creation of an external shape is inadequate unless the soul of its creator has been worked into the material. Quoting from the *Sekishū ryū chashaku no hiji*, Yoshimura emphasizes that to look at Rikyū's tea scoop is to look at a person's face.

It is no surprise that tea masters intentionally sought out the most unusual samples of bamboo to be found. Several versions of a popular legend surround the tea master Furuta Oribe (1544–1615) and his love of a good piece of bamboo. According to one story, Oribe came upon a remarkable piece of bamboo in the midst of a battle. He immediately began to carve a tea scoop and forgot all about the battle raging about him. So absorbed was he by his task that he was unaware of the flying shrapnel and was consequently wounded. The tea scoop was appropriately given the name *Tamaarare* or "hailing bullets."

Prior to Sen no Rikyū, tea masters had not yet assigned much value to the *chashaku*. Tea scoops at that time were not made by tea people, but commissioned from common artisans and often discarded after use. The tube container was not considered an integral part of the tea scoop until Sen no Rikyū's time. The protective tube is made from a cut piece of bamboo from which a tightly fitting cap has been fashioned. Inside, the tea scoop may be wrapped with a silk cloth to prevent it from rolling around inside the tube. Like other tea utensil containers, the tube container often is a document verifying the contents within. In the case of an assigned poetic name, the classical poem from which the allusion originated may be beautifully inscribed on the front of the tube container in the distinctive calligraphy of the carver. At modern tea gatherings, the tube container of the tea scoop may be displayed separately in a side alcove to allow tea participants to read the inscription.

The practice of assigning poetic names to tea scoops was popular during the Edo period. In general, early-Momoyama utensils rarely had poetic names, though a name may have been assigned at a much later date. Kobori Enshū was especially famous for selecting poetic names from classical *waka*. This revealed his deep understanding and appreciation of classical literature. The poetic name of the tea scoop or any other utensil is carefully selected to ignite a series of linked associations for its audience. A poetic name can easily evoke a particular season, scenic area, or allusion to a classical text, and may derive from a variety of sources. Names of temples or references to Zen sayings could also be used as possible names. The name of a tea utensil relies strongly on the presumed knowledge and literary accomplishments of its audience. Very few names are

288

289

self-explanatory and most need to be coaxed out. Daimyo participants in tea gatherings relied heavily upon not only a knowledge of the connoisseurship of utensils, but also on a firm grounding in literary and religious traditions.

Early tea scoops brought from China were made from ivory, metal, and wood. These prototypical tea scoops were thought to be simple measuring spoons for tea. Although other woods such as plum or cherry are used, bamboo, a material valued for its flexibility and endurance, is most often used. There is a protective and comforting quality about using a bamboo scoop with even the most valuable of teabowls or tea containers. The bamboo adds an air of ease as the utensils relate to one another during the tea gathering. There are three classifications of tea scoops. *Shin*, or the most formal tea scoops, are made from ivory. *Gyō*, or semi-formal, have the bamboo joint at the very end of the tip. *Sō*, or grass-style tea scoops, have the bamboo joint located at the halfway point.   JIK

289 **Tea scoop**
Kobori Enshū (1579–1647)
bamboo
length 17.3 (6³⁄4)
Edo period

Eisei Bunko, Tokyo

The elegant style of tea practiced by Kobori Enshū departed dramatically from the rustic simplicity of Sen no Rikyū. The revival of tea as an aesthetic pastime is primarily due to Enshū. This revival greatly pleased his patrons, the daimyo ruling class. Enshū's tea aesthetic brought back the grandeur of an earlier time, and whereas Sen no Rikyū had worked at eliminating useless space in the tearoom, Enshū sought to enlarge the tea space and define separate sitting places for daimyo and their accompanying retainers. Enshū also was an architect and designer of tea gardens.   JIK

290 Flower container
Sen no Rikyū (1522–1591)
bamboo
h. 31.5 (12 3/8)
Momoyama period
Eisei Bunko, Tokyo

Sen no Rikyū has been credited with inventing bamboo vases for tea. Earlier, bronze or celadon flower vases, which arose from a traditional preference for Chinese wares, had been considered appropriate. Four bamboo vases alleged to have been made by Sen no Rikyū have become part of the Hosokawa family collection. This one, of the single-layer cut type, has a bulky, heavy shape typical of Rikyū's style. It is commonly believed that this shape vividly expresses the iron determination Rikyū needed to introduce so many innovative ideas. When Rikyū first presented Toyotomi Hideyoshi (1537–1598) with a bamboo flower container, the displeased ruler is said to have hurled it into the garden. The large crack that resulted when this bamboo container hit a rock in the garden has only caused it to become more valued.

A bamboo flower container is made from a cylindrical piece of bamboo. Two straight cuts across the body open a large enough space to hold flowers, while a substantial back portion is left to form a support. The naturally hollow interior of the bamboo, which is separated at intervals by nodes, forms the bowl to hold the water. The bamboo nodes are one of the areas of appreciation. Before cutting, these nodes are positioned carefully so as to enhance the beauty of the piece. As with the bamboo tea scoops, the natural variation in the bamboo helps create the overall contour of the container. Often the inside of the container is lacquered to prevent possible leakage. A hole has been chiseled in the back of this container so that it may also be hung from a peg in the alcove. The cracks in this flower container have been noticeably repaired with lacquer and metal staples. Large pieces of bamboo, unlike other more durable materials, are vulnerable to dry heat and changes in the weather. Despite the numerous lacquer strips, which are now all that keep this flower container from cracking into fragments, this piece still maintains its dignity, much like an aging warrior whose outside battle scars cannot mar the still powerful spirit lingering underneath.

The art of *chabana*, or flowers for tea, differs considerably from what is popularly known in the West as *ikebana*, or flower arrangement. In tea, one does not consciously arrange the flowers in a certain way. Instead, the desired practice is merely to place the flowers with a lightness of touch. Rikyū's famous precept stipulated that flowers for tea should appear as if they were growing in the field. This reflects the general philosophy that the natural beauty of flowers must be respected, and tampering kept to a minimum. As anyone who has tried to place flowers for tea realizes, it is no easy task.

The inexperienced hand tries to "arrange" and rearrange the blossoms. An important feature of tea flowers is that the most quick-fading and evanescent blossoms or buds are greatly desired. Rikyū supposedly disliked cockscomb because it was too hearty a flower. Tea flowers must be used sparingly to avoid the display of a luxurious and overly abundant bouquet. Flowers in tea are not outward decorations. On the contrary, they are placed to reveal the inward spirit of the host. Choosing an inanimate container to capture the living spirit of the flowers requires a keen sensitivity coupled with years of tea experience. In the tea ceremony, the container becomes the chief mediator between host and guest.

The legend of Rikyū's morning glory tea for Toyotomi Hideyoshi is told and retold to beginning tea students. Hideyoshi, hearing of Rikyū's gorgeous array of morning glories, asked to be invited to tea specifically to view the blossoms. When he entered the garden he noticed that all the blossoms had been cut away. The solitary remaining blossom had been left in a vase in the tearoom. This action reflected Rikyū's belief that simplicity, bordering on the understated, is the best practice in tea.

A flower container, when placed in the tearoom, provides a tranquil resting place for blossoms, grasses, or buds chosen to highlight the mood of that particular season, whether it is a spray of pampas grass or a tightly closed pink camellia bud. A sixteenth-century account of the way Rikyū used a flower container survives from the twelfth month of 1567. In the alcove, on a board, he placed a vase that held nothing but water. In turn, Rikyū asked each guest to contemplate the setting and imagine for himself the flowers he might have used. Rikyū probably could not have predicted that twentieth-century museum visitors would be required to make a similar leap of imagination.　JIK

291 Flower container
bamboo
Hosokawa Sansai (1563–1646)
h. 35.8 (14)
Eisei Bunko, Tokyo

Bamboo flower containers and tea scoops are the two types of tea utensils most likely to have been personally made by tea people. A tea student tries to learn how to make many of the lesser tea paraphernalia, such as the cloth utensil bags or bamboo chopsticks for the meal. Bamboo flower containers and tea scoops may be perceived as presenting excellent opportunities for the expression of the host's personal tea spirit. The secret in making a good bamboo flower container is an unyielding commitment to finding the best possible piece of bamboo. Often, before this is attained, several pieces of bamboo may have to be sacrificed.

This two-layer, cut bamboo flower container has two sections, which can be used separately or simultaneously to hold flowers. Viewed from the side, this piece of bamboo has a natural backward sway. It is said to resemble those made by Rikyū in size and bulk. This is no coincidence, as Sansai represented a conservative branch of tea that remained loyal to Rikyū's teachings even after the master's death by suicide. Another famous student of Rikyū was Furuta Oribe (1544–1615), who later deviated from Rikyū's tea.

A complete modern-day tea gathering covers a period of several hours and includes not only the preparation of tea, but the serving of a light meal and placing of the charcoal before the guests. Whereas a scroll, often with a Zen saying or classical reference, dominates the first half of the gathering and is said to set the general theme, in the latter half of the gathering the scroll is removed from the alcove and replaced with flowers in a container. It is in the second half of the gathering that the host is able to communicate more intimately his own personal expression of the theme. Conversation in the tearoom should be limited to a discussion of the utensils. If using his own bamboo flower container, it might be appropriate for the host to provide an interesting narrative of how he found the bamboo and shaped it.

The flowers chosen for the second half of the gathering usually last only until the end of the day, lending a poignant feeling to the ceremony. This feeling of evanescence did not develop solely out of the medieval culture associated with tea. *The tale of Genji*, written during the Heian period, includes an especially moving chapter in which the accomplished courtier protagonist, Genji, chances upon an unknown maiden living in obscure surroundings. He notices the moonflowers growing alongside the plaited fence outside her dwelling and asks to receive a single blossom. A young serving girl from inside the house is sent out with a fan upon which to place the frail flower. Later, an affair blossoms between the maiden of the house and Genji, only to wither suddenly with her unexpected death soon after their meeting. Genji is left filled with great remorse over the very evanescence of life. JIK

290

291

Nō-related works

292 *Karaori*
silk brocade
l. 152.0 (59 1/4)
w. 146.0 (56 7/8)
Edo period, 18th century

Eisei Bunko, Tokyo

293 *Karaori*
silk brocade
l. 150.0 (58 1/2)
w. 150.0 (58 1/2)
Edo period, 18th century

Eisei Bunko, Tokyo

The *karaori*, an outer robe for female roles in the Nō performance, is the most brilliantly ornate of Nō costumes. Originally the name of the fabric, *karaori* (literally "Chinese weaving") came to be used as the name of the garment itself. In contrast to *kosode*, where designs were created mostly by dyeing, embroidery, and metallic leaf, *karaori* designs are all created in the weave; they are brocades, in which long design threads of glossed or metallic-leaf-wrapped silk are "floated" across a ground of raw silk. The Nō *karaori* are of two types, *iroiri* (with red), and *ironashi* (without red). The former is worn for young female roles, and the latter for middle-aged or elderly female roles. It is typically worn full length and with arms in the sleeves, though for certain roles the right sleeve is slipped off and draped back, or the robe is pulled up to the knees to reveal the undercostume.

These two robes date from the mid-Edo period when the *karaori* was at its most brilliant stage of development. The abundant use of red and of gold-leafed thread makes these robes appropriate for young female roles. Cat. 292 is densely woven with gold thread and covered with butterflies dispersed over a field of wild carnations in threads of many colors. Cat. 293 bears a design of clematis scrolls and paulownia branches on an allover background of linked gold "coins." As many as twelve colors of thread were used to create the designs of this luxurious *karaori*.   KS

294 *Nuihaku*
embroidery and gold leaf on silk
l. 142.0 (55 3/8)
w. 144.0 (56 1/8)
Edo period, 19th century

Eisei Bunko, Tokyo

295 *Nuihaku*
embroidery and gold leaf on silk
l. 143.0 (55 3/4)
w. 136.0 (53)
Edo period, 19th century

Eisei Bunko, Tokyo

Nuihaku, combining embroidery with glued-on gold or silver leaf (*surihaku*) en-joyed great popularity for the embellishment of daily wear in the Momoyama period, as in cat. 264. In Nō, costumes decorated in this technique are known themselves as *nuihaku*. They might be worn as inner robes for boys' roles, or around the waist as *koshimaki* for women's roles. *Nuihaku* were not bound by the technical restrictions imposed by weaving, as in the thicker *karaori*, allowing great freedom in the execution of decoration.

Cat. 294 is decorated with the *seigaiha* motif, a stylized wave pattern, in gold leaf against the red silk background. Gold spits of land emerge from the waves and are embroidered with pine trees, behind which can be seen sails embroidered with a variety of designs. Scores of Japanese poems, tales, and travel diaries paint just such a scene of a ship standing out to sea and disappearing behind a pine-forested island.

The ground of cat. 295 is completely covered with pasted-on gold leaf; such gold-leafed fabrics are called *dōhaku*. Embroidered over the gold leaf are open fans, each decorated with flowers including plum or cherry blossoms, irises, peonies, hollyhock, wisteria, morning-glories, bush clover, and chrysanthemums. The ornate decorative scheme of this *nuihaku* well suits a female role for the Nō stage.   KS

296 *Chōken*
silk brocade
l. 103.3 (40 1/4)
w. 206.0 (80 3/8)
Edo period, 18th century

Eisei Bunko, Tokyo

The *chōken*, literally "long silk," is an unlined jacket unique to Nō worn in dance scenes. It is made of a thin silk gauze into which designs are woven with gold-leafed and colored threads. Below the arms, the side seams are not sewn together. It is worn for a variety of roles, including that of noblemen, or, worn with a type of red pants, a court lady. Any one of a number of colors can be used for the ground, including white, purple, red, light green, and light blue. Designs may be concentrated on one part of the garment, or spread across the entire surface. In this striking example, the background fabric was densely woven with gold threads. A design of flower-filled containers is woven on the chest, back, and sleeves, with dandelions and maple leaves scattered throughout.   KS

292

293

294

295

296

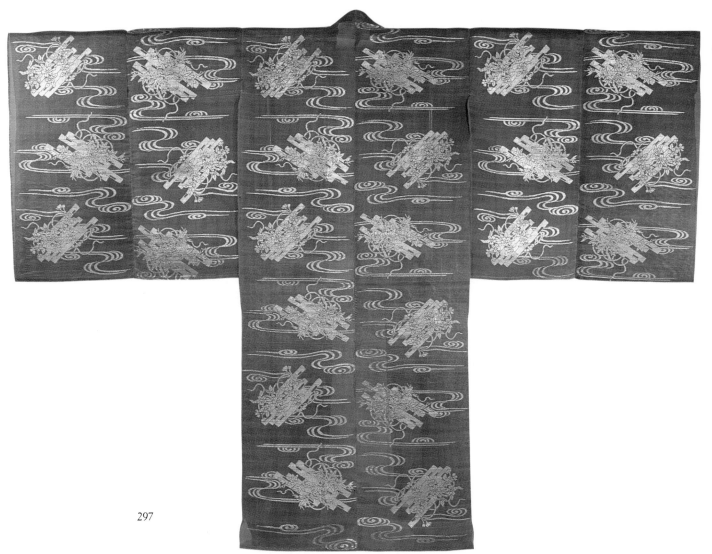

297

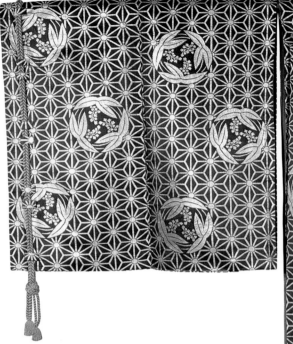

298

297 **Maiginu**
   silk brocade
   l. 164.0 (64)
   w. 224.0 (87 3/8)
   Edo period, 19th century
   Eisei Bunko, Tokyo

The *maiginu*, literally "dancing robe," is an outer robe for women's dancing roles, and resembles the *chōken*. Designs in gold or colored thread are woven into thin silk gauze fabric; the *maiginu* differs from the *chōken* in that it is longer and the side seams are sewn together but the underarm sleeve seams are not. The *maiginu* is worn in the *tsuboori* style, pulled up knee-high. This beautiful example is made of light green silk gauze with woven gold designs of rafts, some bearing cherry blossoms and

others maple leaves. Cherry blossoms and maple leaves are the prime Japanese symbols of spring and fall.   KS

298 **Kariginu**
   silk brocade
   l. 150.0 (58 1/2)
   w. 202.0 (78 3/4)
   Edo period, 19th century
   Eisei Bunko, Tokyo

299 **Kariginu**
   silk brocade
   l. 174.0 (67 7/8)
   w. 203.0 (79 1/8)
   Edo period, 19th century
   Tokyo National Museum

The *kariginu*, literally "hunting robe," was originally an informal jacket worn by men

of the court class in the Heian period. In the medieval era it was adapted by elite samurai as their most formal garment. It is thought that the *kariginu* first used in Nō performances were those actually worn by samurai aristocrats. In the Edo period the *kariginu* was established as a Nō costume, and these *kariginu* for the stage were made larger than the *kariginu* for daily wear from which they had originated. In Nō, the *kariginu* is regarded as the most important outer garment for male roles.

Both *kariginu* exhibited here are made of gold brocade and both are lined. On cat. 298 roundels of water plantain are scattered against an allover design of six-pointed hemp leaves. The decoration of cat. 299 consists of gold brocade phoenixes and paulownia twigs on a purple background. The auspicious combination of

299

the phoenix and paulownia originated in China, the former signifying the benevolent ruler and the well-ordered realm, the latter serving as the bird's nesting place and food. The motif was favored in Japan from the Heian period and sometimes used for Nō *kariginu*. KS

300 **Kataginu**
paste-resist dyeing on hemp
l. 82.0 (32)
w. 136.4 (53¼)
Edo period, 19th century
Eisei Bunko, Tokyo

301 **Kataginu**
stenciled paste-resist dyeing on hemp
l. 97.8 (38½)
w. 124.2 (48½)
Edo period, 19th century
Eisei Bunko, Tokyo

The *kataginu*, literally "shoulder robe," is a sleeveless jacket used in Kyōgen, the comic interlude performed between Nō plays. In contrast to the subtle and austere Nō, which deals with high and mostly tragic subjects, Kyōgen portrays manners and concerns of the commoners with broad humor. While Kyōgen costumes are not richly ornate like those of Nō, they are embellished with bold and freely drawn designs, often of unusual motifs.

On cat. 300, reserved in white by means of resist paste, are a large radish

and mallet on brown-dyed hemp. Above the radish on the back is the dandelion enclosed in a flattened lozenge, a crest often found on Kyōgen costumes. Cat. 301 has a design of black cart wheels entwined with morning-glories against a reserved background of white hemp.

This *kataginu* is entered in an 1840 record passed down through the Hosokawa family, the *Onnō ishō narabini kodōguchō* (Book of Nō Costume and Stage Properties), which establishes a date before which it must have been made. KS

300

372

301

373

302 *Koshiobi*
embroidery and gold leaf on silk
l. 264.5 (103 1/8)
w. 7.3 (2 3/4)
Edo period, 19th century
Eisei Bunko, Tokyo

303 *Koshiobi*
embroidery on silk
l. 215.5 (84)
w. 7.2 (2 3/4)
Edo period, 19th century
Eisei Bunko, Tokyo

The *koshiobi*, or "waist sash," was used to secure such Nō costumes as the *kariginu* and various outer robes worn *koshimaki* style, that is, off the shoulders and arms. Designs appear on the sections that are visible when the sash is worn, including those at the waist and those that hang down from the knot tied in front. On cat. 302, a design of cherry blossoms has been embroidered over gold leaf glued onto red silk. This type of sash was called *dōhaku koshiobi* in reference to the extensive pasted-on gold leaf (cat. 295). Cat. 303 is embroidered with arrows and the *seigaiha* stylized wave motif (cat. 294) on a blue silk background. This *koshiobi*, which has no red on it (cats. 292, 293), was probably worn by an actor playing the role of a middle-aged or elderly woman.   KS

304 *Katsuraobi*
embroidery on silk
l. 254.0 (99)
w. 3.5 (1 3/8)
Edo period, 19th century
Eisei Bunko, Tokyo

305 *Katsuraobi*
gold leaf on silk
l. 237.5 (92 5/8)
w. 3.5 (1 3/8)
Edo period, 19th century
Eisei Bunko, Tokyo

306 *Katsuraobi*
embroidery and gold leaf on silk
l. 239.1 (93 1/4)
w. 3.8 (1 1/2)
Edo period, 19th century
Eisei Bunko, Tokyo

307 *Katsuraobi*
embroidery on silk
l. 242.3 (94 1/2)
w. 3.7 (1 1/2)
Edo period, 19th century
Eisei Bunko, Tokyo

Used exclusively for female roles in Nō, the *katsuraobi* is a sash tied over the wig.

302

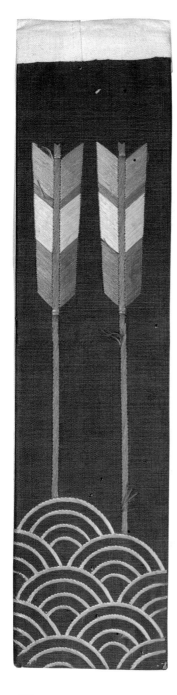

303

Decoration, usually embroidered, is concentrated on the section that covers the forehead and the long portions that hang down from the knot in back. The *katsuraobi* with cherry blossoms (cat. 306) and the one with the water plantain and pickerel weed design (cat. 304) are of the *iroiri* type (cats. 292, 293), meaning that red is used, and they are worn for young female roles. The *katsuraobi* with the willow and snow disk design (cat. 307) is *ironashi*, or without red, and is used in middle-aged or elderly female roles. The *katsuraobi* with the "fish scale" design of triangles (cat. 305) is worn by female characters driven mad by jealousy.   KS

308 *Chūkei* fan
ink, color, and gold leaf on paper; bamboo, lacquer
l. 35.0 (13 3/4)
Edo period, 18th century
Eisei Bunko, Tokyo

309 *Chūkei* fan
ink, color, and gold leaf on paper; bamboo, lacquer
l. 33.0 (13)
Edo period, 19th century
Eisei Bunko, Tokyo

304   305   306   307

designs of flowers or *hanaikusa* ("flower battles"); in each case, the design on the front differs from that on the reverse. All four would have been used for young female roles; the fans with the *hanaikusa* design are representative of the type used by the character who would wear the *Kōomote* mask (cats. 318, 319). KS

312 **Taiko** **drum**
    maki-e lacquer on wood
    diam. 35.5 (14)
    Edo period, 1745
    Eisei Bunko, Tokyo

313 **Taiko** **drum**
    maki-e lacquer on wood
    diam. 34.5 (13 5/8)
    Edo period, 18th–19th century
    Eisei Bunko, Tokyo

The musical instruments used in Nō performance include the *nōkan*, or Nō flute, and three types of drums: the *kotsuzumi*, the *ōtsuzumi*, and the *taiko*. The *taiko* is placed in a stand on the floor and is beaten with a pair of sticks. The body, hollowed out of hardwood and typically decorated with *maki-e* lacquer, has leather drumheads on both ends.

Cat. 312, said to have been copied from a *taiko* called *Yūgao*, is decorated with large peonies in gold and silver *maki-e*. An attached document states that Konparu Sōemon had it made in 1745. The other *taiko*, cat. 313, is decorated with scattered fans in gold and silver *maki-e* on black lacquer. The designs on the fans include such plants as moonflowers and chrysanthemums as well as Mount Fuji. KS

314 **Kotsuzumi** **drum**
    maki-e lacquer on wood
    diam. 11.8 (4 5/8); l. 29 (11 3/8)
    Edo period, 18th–19th century
    Eisei Bunko, Tokyo

315 **Kotsuzumi** **drum**
    maki-e lacquer on wood
    diam. 10.0 (3 7/8); l. 25.0 (9 7/8)
    Edo period, 18th century

    Storage box
    maki-e lacquer, silver and silk on wood
    24.0 x 29.0 x 23.4 (9 1/2 x 11 3/8 x 9 1/4)
    Edo period, 18th–19th century
    Eisei Bunko, Tokyo

The *kotsuzumi* is a percussion instrument shaped much like an hourglass, with a thin middle and two flaring ends. Drumheads of leather mounted on iron rings are fitted on either end with the two drumheads connected by hemp cords. It is held with

310 **Chūkei** **fan**
    ink, color, and gold leaf on paper;
    bamboo, lacquer
    l. 32.8 (12 7/8)
    Edo period, 19th century
    Eisei Bunko, Tokyo

311 **Chūkei** **fan**
    ink, color, and gold leaf on paper;
    bamboo, lacquer
    l. 32.8 (12 7/8)
    Edo period, 19th century
    Eisei Bunko, Tokyo

The *chūkei*, a type of folding fan, was an important accessory in both Nō and Kyōgen performances. Several types are differentiated, determined by the color of the frame, the color of the paper, and the designs depicted, and each is particular to a certain type of role. Typically, though, the *chūkei* has fifteen ribs, the overall length is about 33 centimeters (13 inches), and the two end ribs are carved in three places with openwork designs.

The four *chūkei* here are of the type known as *katsuraōgi*, or "wig fans," meaning that they, like the wigs, were used for female roles. All have black ribs and are painted on gold-leafed paper with elegant

308

309

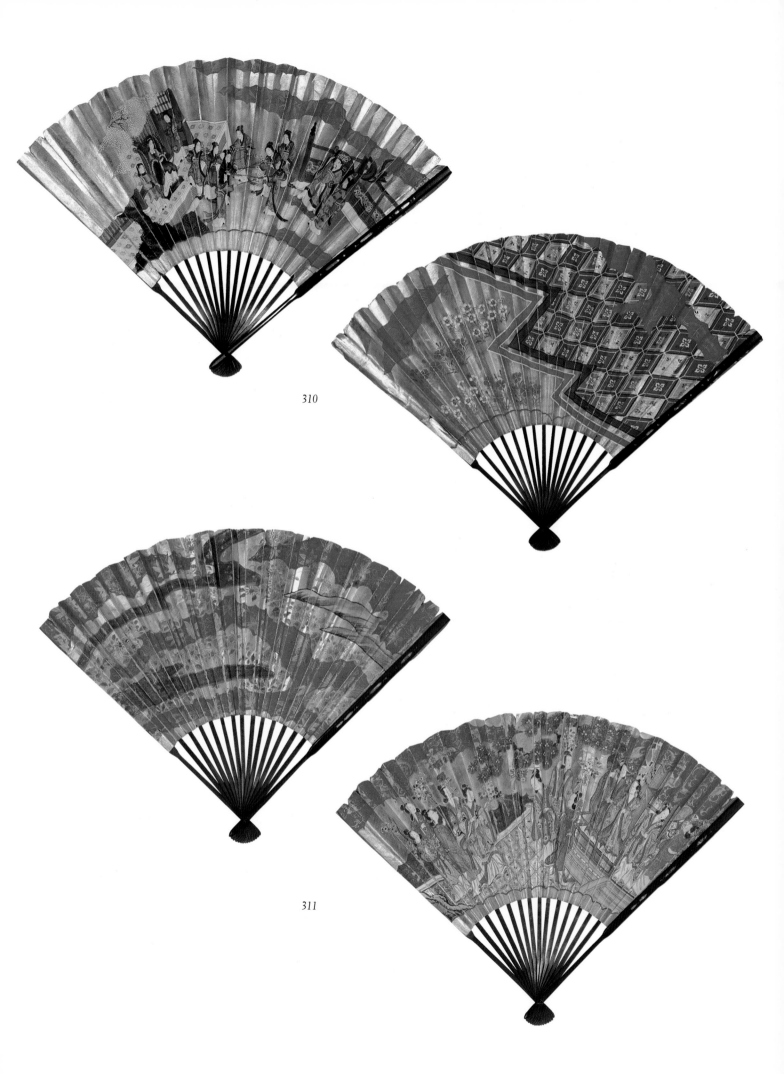

310

311

312

313

314

the left hand, placed on the right shoulder, and struck with the fingers of the right hand.

Cat. 314 is decorated with a dragon and cloud design on a background of amber lacquer densely sprinkled with gold (*nashiji*). The dragon, depicted in raised *maki-e*, winds around the drum among gold and silver *maki-e* clouds. Cat. 315 is decorated with a spring design of rafts with cherry blossoms in gold *maki-e* on a black lacquered ground. This *kotsuzumi* is accompanied by a storage box decorated with a design in *maki-e* on black lacquer of running water and maple leaves. The design alludes to many poems from the Heian period regarding the Tatsuta River (Nara Prefecture), famous for the autumn foliage along its banks. One such poem reads:

In the Tatsuta River
red leaves flow
in disorder;
if I cross, the brocade
will be cut through the middle.   KS

316 **Nōkan flute (accompanied by case)**
bamboo, bark, lacquer
length of *nōkan* 39.5 (15 ½)
Edo period, 18th century

Eisei Bunko, Tokyo

317 **Nōkan flute, named Yaegiku**
(accompanied by case)
bamboo, bark, lacquer
length of *nōkan* 39.5 (15 ½)
Edo period, 18th century

Eisei Bunko, Tokyo

The *nōkan* is a transverse bamboo flute with a mouth hole and seven finger holes, wound with thinly split bark. A metal piece is fitted on the end near the mouth hole, and many flutes are named after the design on the metal. The *nōkan* is the only wind instrument among the instruments used in Nō, but it plays few melodies; rather, it functions as a rhythm instrument. The *nōkan* is equipped with a black-

lacquered storage case, often decorated with *maki-e* and *raden* (inlaid shell). The case for cat. 316 is decorated with a design of gold *maki-e* grapes on black lacquer. Grapes, a symbol of fertility used as a motif from as early as the Nara period, were also popular for decorative designs in the early modern era. The case for the other *nōkan*, cat. 317, bears a *maki-e* design of plovers flying over waves, a motif seen from the medieval era on that recalls many poems of the Heian period, such as this one:

At Shio Mountain
on Sashide shore
dwells a plover;
May your reign last
eight thousand ages, it sings.   KS

378

315

317

316

318 **Koomote**
polychromed wood
21.5 x 13.6 (8 1/2 x 5 3/8)
Edo period, 18th century

Eisei Bunko, Tokyo

319 **Koomote**
polychromed wood
21.0 x 13.5 (8 1/4 x 5 3/8)
Edo period, 18th century

Eisei Bunko, Tokyo

One of the earliest Nō masks to be developed, Koomote represents the countenance of a calm young woman, her neatly arranged hair parted in the middle, with three loose, but not overlapping, strands on either side. *Ko* (literally, "small"), the first Japanese character of the two that form the word *koomote*, suggests the youth, freshness and charm embodied in this mask. Reflecting the standard of beauty from the Heian period on, the oval face is full, with eyebrows shaved and re-painted high on the wide forehead. The teeth are blackened *(ohaguro)*, with a paste made of powdered iron filings and gall nuts steeped in vinegar or tea; this was a cosmetic fashion adopted by young women on coming of age.

Although Koomote represents a general character type, subtle differences among masks are apparent. Some emphasize youthful freshness, some refinement, some a delicately erotic charm. Cat. 319, for example, suggests the last, with full cheeks and relatively widely parted lips. On the back of this mask is an inscription of Deme Yūkan. Yūkan Mitsuyasu (d. 1652) was a disciple and successor of Ze-kan Yoshimitsu, founder of the Ōno branch of the prominent Deme family of Nō mask makers.   MK

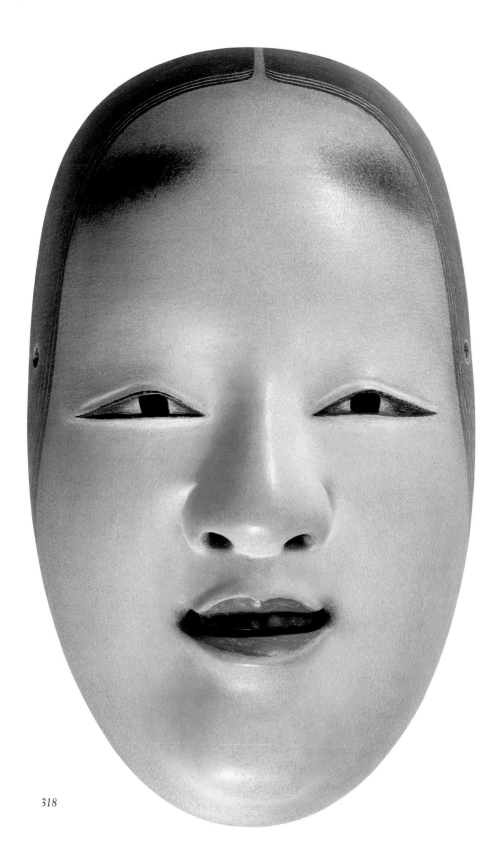

318

319

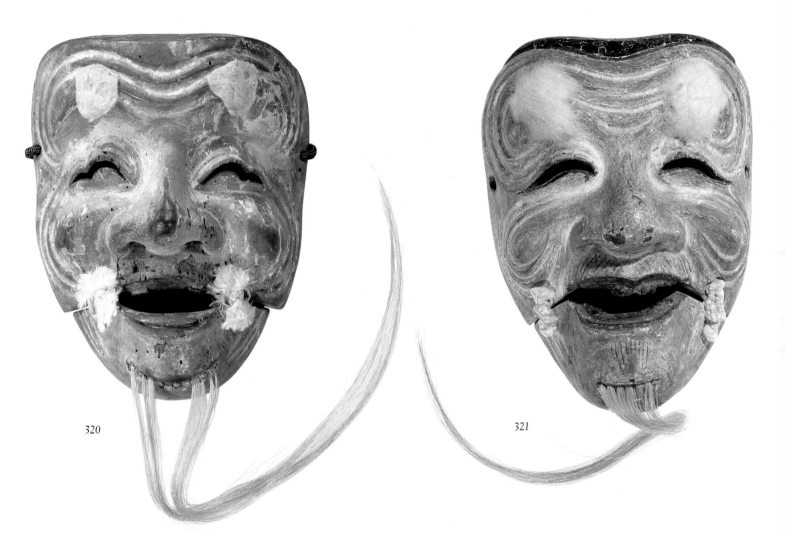

320

321

320 **Okina**
polychromed wood
18.1 x 15.2 (7 1/8 x 6)
Edo period, 18th century

Tokyo National Museum

321 **Okina**
polychromed wood
18.9 x 15.0 (7 1/2 x 5 7/8)
Edo period, 17th century

Eisei Bunko, Tokyo
Important Art Object

Expressing the joyful face of an old man,
the Okina (literally, "old man") mask is
worn by the main character of the liturgi-
cal Nō piece of the same name. *Okina*, a
prayer for peace throughout the land, a
rich harvest, and prosperity, occupies a
special place in the Nō repertoire. Consisting mostly of ritual dancing and chanting,

with no dramatic plot, its structure is totally different from other Nō plays. Its origins predate the Muromachi period when
Nō was perfected. The hinged jaws of the
Okina mask are a feature found also on
pre-Nō dance masks; the bushy eyebrows
and treatment of the eyes also distinguish
this from other Nō masks.

Okina masks are relatively small and
triangular in shape, and their expressions
suggest the dignity and benevolence of the
main role in *Okina*. Cat. 321, deeply carved
in the old style, is one of the outstanding
old masks in the possession of the Hosokawa family. On the back is an inscription,
Made by Nikkō; Mitsuyoshi [kaō]. MK

322

323

322 Hannya
polychromed wood
21.0 x 17.3 (8 1/4 x 6 3/4)
Muromachi period, 16th century

Eisei Bunko, Tokyo
Important Art Object

The Hannya mask expresses the violent anger and distress of a woman whose love and trust have been betrayed, turning her into a raging, revengeful female demon. The two horns protruding from disorderly hair evince diabolic malevolence, and the upper lip, tense and pointed in the center like a snake's, and the glinting of the metal eyes and teeth effectively add to her menace. This mask is attributed to the monk Hannya, who is said to have lived in Nara during the Muromachi period and to have originated this type of mask.   MK

323 Namanari
polychromed wood
21.4 x 14.0 (8 3/8 x 5 1/2)
Edo period, 18th century

Eisei Bunko, Tokyo

Although the horns are not as long or sharp and the expression not as fierce as the Hannya mask (cat. 322), Namanari, expresses with great intensity a woman crazed with jealousy. As in the Hannya mask, her complexion is dark, her eyes and teeth metallic. (Most frightening is a third type of female demon mask known as Ja.) Namanari is used in the second half of *Kanawa*, a play about a woman who prays to become a demon in order to carry out her revenge against a husband who deserted her for another. On the back of this mask is the carver's name, Deme Moto-masa, about whom nothing is known.   MK

384

324

325

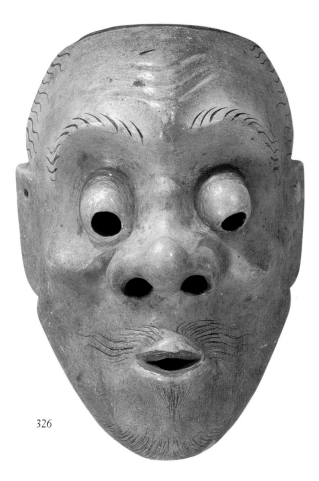

326

327

324 **Shikami**
polychromed wood
21.3 x 16.2 (8 3/8 x 6 3/8)
Edo period, 18th century

Tokyo National Museum

325 **Shikami**
polychromed wood
21.0 x 16.5 (8 1/4 x 6 1/2)
Edo period, 19th century

Tokyo National Museum

Shikami is one of the demon masks. His threatening expression, with scowling eyes and bared fanglike teeth, well conveys his ferocity. Furrows are intensified with red and, as was often done in Nō demon masks to manifest rage, the eyes are highlighted in gold.

The back of cat. 324 is inscribed, *Carved by Genkyū*. Genkyū is a name used by Mitsunaga, fourth-generation mask maker of the Deme family of Echizen, and then by subsequent generations; it is not known in which generation this particular mask was carved.

Though the facial muscles of cat. 325 are tense and the nostrils flared, the expression of rage is less threatening than in cat. 324, an effect achieved by shallower and more formalized carving of the furrows at the temples and eyes. On the back of the mask is an inscription that reads, *Carved by Ōmi*. The Ōmi were a branch of the Echizen Deme family. The fourth generation Ōmi mask maker, Mitsumasa (d. 1704) founded the Kodama line of carvers. The carver of this mask, whose identity is unclear, carries on Mitsumasa's tradition.   MK

326 **Usobuki**
polychromed wood
19.3 x 14.0 (7 5/8 x 5 1/2)
Edo period, 19th century

Tokyo National Museum

327 **Usobuki**
polychromed wood
19.7 x 14.2 (7 3/4 x 5 5/8)
Edo period, 19th century

Tokyo National Museum

Kyōgen, the comic drama in which such subjects as old tales and the problems of real people are treated with humorous actions and witty dialogue, uses some masks, though the number of mask types is much more limited than for Nō. In contrast to the serious quality of Nō masks, those for Kyōgen are characterized by their humorous nature, with amused expressions, or by deliberate exaggeration and distortion. Usobuki represents the latter type. The name implies several possible meanings, including to feign innocence, to whistle, or to shape the mouth as though blowing a fire. The mask is worn by both human characters and the spirits of fragile creatures such as the moth, mosquito, or cicada.

The expression of cat. 327, with eyes wide-open and crossed as though he is inflating something, and whiskers flared up, conveys a particularly wonderful sense of the absurd.   MK

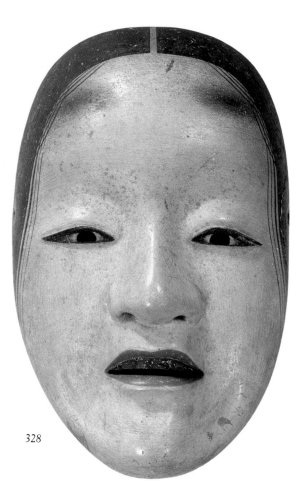

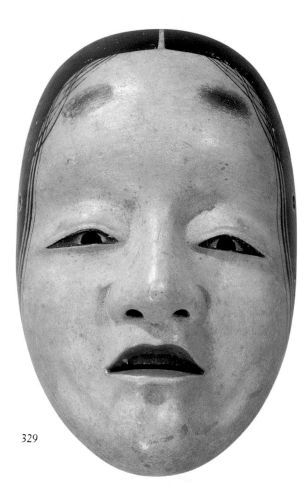

328

329

328 **Shakumi**
polychromed wood
21.2 x 13.9 (8 3/8 x 5 1/2)
Edo period, 19th century
Tokyo National Museum

329 **Shakumi**
polychromed wood
21.0 x 13.9 (8 1/4 x 5 1/2)
Edo period, 19th century
Tokyo National Museum

In contrast to the youthful quality of Koomote (cats. 318, 319), the face of the middle-aged woman's mask, Shakumi, has lost its firmness, and the strands of hair falling on the cheeks are in relative disorder. It is the countenance of a woman old enough to have known the pains of life. The pupils are half-circles, unlike the square ones of Koomote. A similar mask,

Fukai, differs only in depicting a somewhat older woman. Both are used in plays such as *Sumidagawa*, in which a mother searches for her lost child only to find the child dead, or for the middle-aged women roles in the plays *Bashō* or *Teika*.

On the back of cat. 328 is an inscription, *Ōmi*, and a burnt-in seal, *Tenka Ichi Ōmi* (Ōmi, First under Heaven).

In comparison with cat. 328, the forehead of cat. 329 protrudes more, the line over each eyelid is carved more deeply, and the outer corners of the eyes and mouth turn down more sharply, expressing a more advanced age. The fuller cheeks indicate, perhaps, a somewhat plump woman. MK

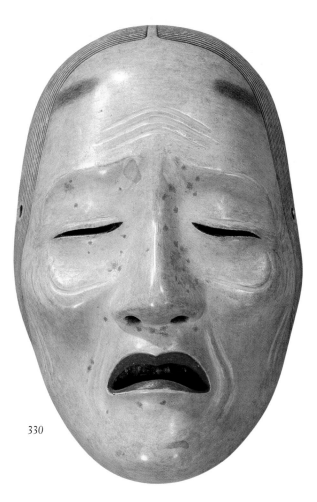

330

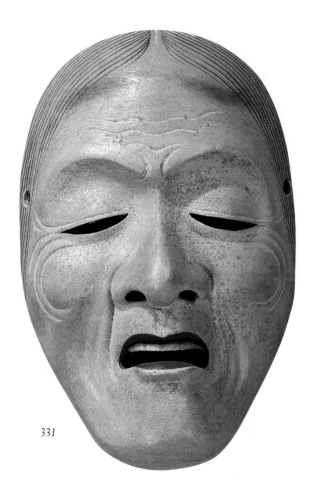

331

330 **Uba**
polychromed wood
21.2 x 14.1 (8 3/8 x 5 1/2)
Edo period
Tokyo National Museum

331 **Uba**
polychromed wood
20.3 x 13.6 (8 x 5 3/8)
Edo period, 19th century
Tokyo National Museum

Uba, the mask of an old woman, is used primarily in *Takasago* (cat. 215*h*), a play in which an old woman and her husband represent the spirits of two pine trees. On his way to the capital, Tomonari, a Shinto priest from the shrine of Aso in Kyushu, rests beneath the pines along the shore at Takasago in Harima Province (now part of Hyōgo Prefecture). The old couple appear and sweep beneath the pines. They tell the priest of two aged pines, one here in Takasago and the other at Sumiyoshi in Settsu Province and of their auspicious associations. Tomonari goes to Sumiyoshi in the second half of the play, and a deity appears and performs a god dance. The Uba mask came to be also used for the roles of ordinary old women in other Nō plays. Typically, the eyes are carved as they are for the mask of a blind person.

On the back of cat. 330 is the burnt-in seal of Deme Mitsutada, eighth generation of the important Deme family of Nō mask makers of Echizen Province (part of present-day Fukui Prefecture). Although the form of the Uba mask is generally rather conventionalized, cat. 331 is even more so than usual.   MK

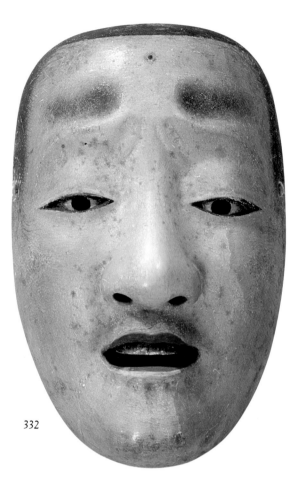

332

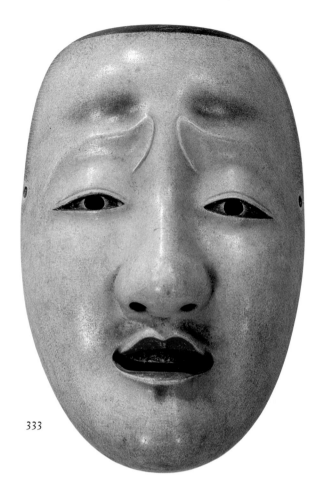

333

332 **Chūjō**
polychromed wood
20.3 x 13.6 (8 x 5 ³/₈)
Edo period, 19th century
Tokyo National Museum

333 **Chūjō**
polychromed wood
20.4 x 14.1 (8 x 5 ½)
Edo period, 19th century
Tokyo National Museum

The Chūjō mask represents a young aristocrat of early times, with light complexion, high painted eyebrows, and teeth blackened (*ohaguro*). Traditionally, this mask type is said to have been modeled after Ariwara no Narihira, the famous poet of the Heian period whose court rank was *chūjō*, middle captain, in the headquarters of the Inner Palace Guards. The Chūjō mask is used for the role of Prince Genji in *The Tale of Genji*, and for other courtiers.

The back of cat. 332 has a seal that reads, *Tenka Ichi Kawachi* (Kawachi, First under Heaven).

While Chūjō is typically carved with a melancholic expression and knitted brows, these qualities are especially formalized and given emphasis in cat. 333. This mask was owned by the Konparu family, one of the four main groups of Nō actors.   MK

Selected Literature

References are given in catalogue order.

1. Mori 1950; Minamoto 1954; Kyoto 1978; Watanabe 1983.
2. Kyoto 1978.
3. Kyoto 1978.
4. Kyoto 1978.
5. Kyoto 1978.
6. Akamatsu 1949.
7. Tani 1937; Ogino 1967; Akamatsu 1969; Cleveland 1983.
8. Tani 1937.
9. Tanaka 1962.
10. Boston 1970; Cleveland 1983.
11. Boston 1970.
13. Kyoto 1978; Cleveland 1983.
14. Kyoto 1978.
15. Kyoto 1978.
16. Jūyō Bunkazai Hensan Iinkai 1980–1984, vol. 1.
17. Cleveland 1983.
18. Doi 1970.
20. Sakai 1983.
21. Kyoto 1978.
22. Kyoto 1978.
25. Irita 1935; Kyoto 1978.
26. Kyoto 1978.
27. Kyoto 1978.
28. Kumamoto 1979b.
29. Yamane Yūzō. *Kokka* no. 782 (1957): 152–153; Kyoto 1978.
31. Jūyō Bunkazai Hensan Iinkai 1980–1984, vol. 6.
32. Jūyō Bunkazai Hensan Iinkai 1980–1984, vol. 6.
33. Jūyō Bunkazai Hensan Iinkai 1980–1984, vol. 6.
35. Iwama 1987.
36. Agency for Cultural Affairs 1983.
37. Tokyo 1980b.
38. Yamakawa Takeshi. *Kokka* no. 901 (1967): 12–18.
41. Doi 1948; Kyoto 1978.
42. Uratsuji 1938; Kyoto 1978.
43. Miyama 1964b; Miyama 1981.
44. Fukuyama 1941; Cleveland 1983.
45. "Manshōji mokuzō Miura Yoshiaki zō kō" (The portrait sculpture of Miura Yoshiaki in Manshōji). In Miyama 1981, 230–240.
46. Mōri 1974; Mōri 1980; Shimizu 1982.
47. Nedachi 1986.
48. Nishikawa 1976.
49. Miyama 1964a; Kanagawaken Kyōiku Iinkai 1975; Miyama 1981.
54. Tayama 1961.
55. Tayama 1961.
56. Yanagida 1977.
57. Kamakurashi Shi Hensan Iinkai 1956–1959.
58. Takayanagi 1966.
59. Takayanagi 1966.
60. Kyōto Furitsu Sōgō Shiryōkan 1970.
61. Okuno 1971; Kyōto Furitsu Sōgō Shiryōkan 1970.
62. Tōkyō Teikoku Daigaku Shiryō Hensanjo 1938.
63. Nakamura 1980.
64. Tsuchida 1976.
66. Yokoi 1980.
67. Katagiri 1977.
68. Kyūsojin 1960.
69. New York 1984–1985; Cambridge 1970.
70. Tanabe 1972; Tanaka 1978; Jūyō Bunkazai Hensan Iinkai 1980–1984, vol. 3.
72. Yamagataken Kyōiku Iinkai 1983.
73. Kanagawaken Kyōiku Iinkai 1975.
74. Kanagawaken Kyōiku Iinkai 1975.
75. Yamamoto 1987.
76. Mōri 1957; Jūyō Bunkazai Hensan Iinkai 1980–1984, vol. 3; Kanda 1985.
77. Kobayashi 1953; Tanabe 1977.
78. Mōri 1961; Mōri 1972; Mōri 1987.
79. Tanaka 1968; Komatsu and Minamoto 1978; New York 1983.
80. Conze 1972; Matsushita and Tamamura 1974; Princeton 1976; Shimizu 1980a; Fukuoka 1985.
81. Tanaka 1971b; Minamoto 1972; Princeton 1976; Minamoto 1980.
82. *Kanrin koro shū*, 337–338; *Kokka* no. 570 (1938): 121; Akamatsu 1942; "Shutsu-jin'ei" (Portraits of mounted warriors). In Tani 1943, 259–306; Yamaoka 1978; Ōnishi Shōko in Shimada and Iriya 1987, 440–444.
83. Shikian. *Kokka* no. 396 (1923): 363–371; Kumagai 1932; Watanabe Akiyoshi in Shimada and Iriya 1987, 283–290.
84. Nakajima 1971; Tanaka 1971b; Minamoto 1972; Matsushita and Tamamura 1974; Princeton 1976.
85. Masaki 1978; Ōta Takahiko in Shimada and Iriya 1987, 290–296; Takahashi 1987; *Tōkai keika shū*, 780–781.
86. Matsushita 1956; Ōnishi Hiroshi in Shimada and Iriya 1987, 234–237.
87. Nakajima 1971; Tanaka 1971b; Minamoto 1972; Matsushita and Tamamura 1974; Princeton 1976.
88. Nakamura 1976; "Sesshū ten zuroku" (Sesshū exhibition catalog). In Shimada 1987, 445–475; "Sesshū." In Shimada 1987, 476–514.
89. Nakamura 1976; "Sesshū ten zuroku" (Sesshū exhibition catalog). In Shimada 1987, 445–475.
90. Matsushita and Tamamura 1974; Princeton 1976; Yokota Tadashi in Shimada and Iriya 1987, 379–382.

91. Ōnishi Hiroshi and Yamashita Yūji in Shimada and Iriya 1987, 273–276; Tokyo 1986b.

92. Nakamura 1971; Tanaka and Nakamura 1973; Ford 1980; Kameda 1980; Los Angeles 1985; Tokyo 1986b.

93. Tanaka and Nakamura 1973; "Bujin gaka no keifu" (Traditions of the warrior-painters). In Tanaka 1986, vol. 2, 175–180; Tokyo 1986b.

94. *Bijutsu kenkyū* no. 41 (1935): 227–228; Wakimoto 1937; Tanaka and Yonezawa 1970; Princeton 1976; Tokyo 1980c.

95. *Kanrin koro shū*, 288; Fujikake Shizuya. *Kokka* no. 677 (1948): 213–214; Tanaka and Yonezawa 1970; Tanaka and Nakamura 1973; "Bujin gaka no keifu" (Traditions of the warrior-painters). In Tanaka 1986, vol. 2, 175–180; Tokyo 1986b.

96. Nakajima 1967, 1968, 1972; *Kokka* no. 970; Nakamura 1976; Tsuji 1978.

97. Tsuji 1966, 1970; Doi 1974; Yamaoka 1978; Wheelwright 1981b; Shimizu 1981; Detroit 1986.

98. Fujikake 1952; Matsushita and Tamamura 1974; Yoshizawa 1978.

99. *Kokka* no. 449 (1928): 99; Tokyo 1962; Toda 1973.

100. Tokyo 1962; Tokyo 1976a.

101. Wakimoto 1934; Yonezawa Yoshiho. *Bijutsushi* no. 11 (1954): 97–99; Toda 1973; Tokyo 1976a.

102. Tokyo 1962; Suzuki 1974; Cahill 1976; Stanley-Baker 1982.

104. Kuwata, Okamoto, Kōyama, and Nakamura 1980; Sansom 1961; Totman 1967; Berry 1982.

105. Nakamura 1978; Tsuji 1980a.

106. Nakamura 1978; Tsuji 1980a.

107. Cambridge 1970; Adachi 1974; Adachi 1980; London 1981–1982.

108. Takeda 1977; Kawai 1978.

109. *Kokka* no. 319 (1916): 133–136; Kumamoto 1979a; Yamane 1979; Kumamoto 1984a.

110. Okamoto 1972; Cambridge 1970; Sakai 1981; Muroga 1983.

111. Sakamoto 1973; Sakamoto 1979.

112. New York 1973; Vlam 1976; Sakamoto 1979; Jūyō Bunkazai Hensan Iinkai 1980–1984, vol. 2.

113. Vlam 1976; Sakamoto 1979; Jūyō Bunkazai Hensan Iinkai 1980–1984, vol. 2.

114. Sakamoto 1979.

115. Takeda 1978a.

116. Yamane 1973; Takeda 1980.

117. Fukuoka 1985.

118. Suzuki 1971; Suwa and Naitō 1972; Takeda 1978a.

119. Kawai 1978; Kumamoto 1984a.

120. Yamane 1980; Klein 1984.

121. Jūyō Bunkazai Hensan Iinkai 1980–1984, vol. 2.

122. Yamane 1980.

123. Nakamura 1978.

124. *Kokka* no. 602 (1941): 12–14; Takeda 1973; Kawai 1978; MOA Art Museum 1982.

125. Takeda 1974; Takeda 1978b.

126. Takeda 1967; Takeda 1978b.

127. Takeda 1967.

128. Tanaka and Nakamura 1973; Addiss and Hurst 1983.

130. Hamada 1976; Sendai 1986b; Sendai 1987.

131. Takeda 1978b; Shimizu 1980b.

132. Tsuji 1980b; Fukui 1984.

133. Tsuji 1980b; Fukui 1984.

134. Narasaki Muneshige. *Kokka* no. 960 (1974): 28–31; Fukui 1984.

135. New York 1972.

136. Naruse 1977; Tokyo 1987b.

137. Ōta, Takehana, and Naruse 1974; Naitō 1981; Tokyo 1987b.

138. Tokyo 1987b.

139. Kumamoto 1980; Tokyo 1987b.

140. Kobayashi 1978; Nakamura 1979.

141. Tokyo 1964; Kumamoto 1978c.

142. Kumamoto 1978c.

143. *Kokka* no. 462 (1929): 138–145; Takeda 1978b; Kōno 1982.

144. Kōno 1978; Murashige 1982.

145. Doi 1939; Doi 1976.

146. Ozaki 1968; Ozaki and Satō 1970; *Kokuhō* 1984, vol. 7; Kyoto 1987.

147. Kumamoto 1978a; Jūyō Bunkazai Hensan Iinkai 1980–1984, vol. 6; Kyoto 1981a; Kyoto 1987.

148. Jūyō Bunkazai Hensan Iinkai 1980–1984, vol. 6; Kyoto 1987.

149. Jūyō Bunkazai Hensan Iinkai 1980–1984, vol. 6; Kyoto 1987.

150. Jūyō Bunkazai Hensan Iinkai 1980–1984, vol. 6.

151. Jūyō Bunkazai Hensan Iinkai 1980–1984, vol. 6.

152. Kumamoto 1978a.

153. Jūyō Bunkazai Hensan Iinkai 1980–1984, vol. 6; Sendai 1986a; Yamagishi and Saitō 1986–1987; Kyoto 1987.

154. Okayama 1972; Jūyō Bunkazai Hensan Iinkai 1980–1984, vol. 6; Shizuoka 1983; Kyoto 1987.

155. Shizuoka 1983.

158. Jūyō Bunkazai Hensan Iinkai 1980–1984, vol. 6; Kyoto 1987.

159. Jūyō Bunkazai Hensan Iinkai 1980–1984, vol. 6.

160. Jūyō Bunkazai Hensan Iinkai 1980–1984, vol. 6; Kyoto 1987.

162. Jūyō Bunkazai Hensan Iinkai 1980–1984, vol. 6; Fukuoka 1985.

163. Kumamoto 1978a.

164–169. Tokyo 1986a; Hikone 1987.

170. Nihon Bijutsu Tōken Hozon Kyōkai 1966–1970, vol. 3; Hiroi 1971; *Kokuhō* 1984, vol. 8.

171. Nihon Bijutsu Tōken Hozon Kyōkai 1966–1970, vol. 2; Hiroi 1971.

174. Nihon Bijutsu Tōken Hozon Kyōkai 1966–1970, vol. 5; Hiroi 1986.

175. Nihon Bijutsu Tōken Hozon Kyōkai 1966–1970, vol. 5; Hiroi 1986.

176. Hiroi 1986.

177. Nihon Bijutsu Tōken Hozon Kyōkai 1966–1970, vol. 4; Hiroi 1971; Jūyō Bunkazai Hensan Iinkai 1980–1984, vol. 6.

178. Nihon Bijutsu Tōken Hozon Kyōkai 1966–1970, vol. 6.

179. Nihon Bijutsu Tōken Hozon Kyōkai 1966–1970, vol. 6; Hiroi 1971.

181. Jūyō Bunkazai Hensan Iinkai 1980–1984, vol. 6.

183. Nihon Bijutsu Tōken Hozon Kyōkai 1966–1970, vol. 6.

189. Nihon Bijutsu Tōken Hozon Kyōkai 1966–1970, vol. 6; Hiroi 1971.

190. Nihon Bijutsu Tōken Hozon Kyōkai 1966–1970, vol. 6; Hiroi 1971.

193. Jūyō Bunkazai Hensan Iinkai 1980–1984, vol. 6; Nihon Bijutsu Tōken Hozon Kyōkai 1966–1970, vol. 6.

195. Nihon Bijutsu Tōken Hozon Kyōkai 1966–1970, vol. 6; Jūyō Bunkazai Hensan Iinkai 1980–1984, vol. 6.

197. Nihon Bijutsu Tōken Hozon Kyōkai 1966–1970, vol. 7; Hiroi 1971.

198. Nihon Bijutsu Tōken Hozon Kyōkai 1966–1970, vol. 7; Hiroi 1971.

199. Nihon Bijutsu Tōken Hozon Kyōkai 1966–1970, vol. 7.

201. Nihon Bijutsu Tōken Hozon Kyōkai 1966–1970, vol. 7; Jūyō Bunkazai Hensan Iinkai 1980–1984, vol. 6.

202. Nihon Bijutsu Tōken Hozon Kyōkai 1966–1970, vol. 7; Jūyō Bunkazai Hensan Iinkai 1980–1984, vol. 6.

204. Nihon Bijutsu Tōken Hozon Kyōkai 1966–1970, vol. 7; Hiroi 1986.

205. Nihon Bijutsu Tōken Hozon Kyōkai 1966–1970, vol. 7; Hiroi 1986.

206. Nihon Bijutsu Tōken Hozon Kyōkai 1966–1970, vol. 7.

208. Nihon Bijutsu Tōken Hozon Kyōkai 1966–1970, vol. 7; Hiroi 1971.

211. Nihon Bijutsu Tōken Hozon Kyōkai 1966–1970, vol. 7; Hiroi 1971; Jūyō Bunkazai Hensan Iinkai 1980–1984, vol. 6.

212. Nihon Bijutsu Tōken Hozon Kyōkai 1966–1970, vol. 7; Jūyō Bunkazai Hensan Iinkai 1980–1984, vol. 6.

213. Nihon Bijutsu Tōken Hozon Kyōkai 1966–1970, vol. 7; Hiroi 1971.

216. Kumamoto 1976; Kumamoto 1978a; Ozaki and Satō 1970; *Kokuhō* 1984, vol. 6

217. Kumamoto 1976; Kumamoto 1978a; Ozaki and Satō 1970; *Kokuhō* 1984, vol. 6

218. Jūyō Bunkazai Hensan Iinkai 1980–1984, vol. 5.

219. Jūyō Bunkazai Hensan Iinkai 1980–1984, vol. 5.

221. Okada, Matsuda, and Arakawa 1978–

1979, vol. 3.

222. Kyoto 1977.

223. Okada, Matsuda, and Arakawa 1978–1979, vol. 3.

224. Okada, Matsuda, and Arakawa 1978–1979, vol. 3.

225. Okada, Matsuda, and Arakawa 1978–1979, vol. 4.

226. Kumamoto 1983.

227. Arakawa, Komatsu, and Haino 1986.

228. Okayama 1984; Arakawa, Komatsu, and Haino 1986.

229. Kumamoto 1983.

230. Okada, Matsuda, and Arakawa 1978–1979, vol. 4.

231. Okayama 1984.

232. Okayama 1984.

233. Kumamoto 1983.

234. Kumamoto 1983.

237. Okada, Matsuda, and Arakawa 1978–1979, vol. 3; Okayama 1984.

238. Kumamoto 1983.

239. Kumamoto 1983.

240. Kawahara 1977; Mitsuoka and Okuda 1977; Narasaki 1977; Cort 1979.

241. Mitsuoka and Okuda 1977; Tokyo 1985b.

242–247. Seattle 1972a; Hayashiya 1976; Oxford 1981; Tokyo 1985b.

248–249. Seattle 1972a; Hayashiya 1980; Becker 1986; Cort 1986; Tokyo 1985b; Tokyo 1986c.

250. Hayashiya 1980; Tokyo 1985b; Kyoto 1986; Fukuoka 1987a.

251. Hayashiya 1980; Fukuoka 1981; Fukuoka 1987b.

252. Seattle 1972a; Satō 1978; Hayashiya 1980; Tokyo 1985b.

253. Hayashiya 1980; Yamaguchi 1981; Tokyo 1985a.

254–255. Hayashiya 1976; New York 1979; Kyoto 1985b.

256–257. Seattle 1972a; Mitsuoka 1975; Kyoto 1981b; Tokyo 1985b.

258–259. Nagatake and Hayashiya 1978; Tokyo 1985b; Yokohama 1987.

260–261. Seattle 1972a; Mikami and Hayashiya 1983; Tokyo 1985b; Kanazawa 1987.

262. Jūyō Bunkazai Hensan Iinkai 1980–1984, vol. 5.

263. Jūyō Bunkazai Hensan Iinkai 1980–1984, vol. 5.

265. Yamanobe, Kamiya, and Ogasawara 1980; Sendai 1986a.

266. Yamanobe Tomoyuki. *Museum* no. 162 (1964): 24–27; Yamanobe, Kamiya, and Ogasawara 1980.

268. Yamanobe, Kamiya, and Ogasawara 1980.

269. Yamanobe, Kamiya, and Ogasawara 1980.

272. New York 1984.

275. Yamanobe, Kamiya, and Ogasawara 1980.

276. Yamanobe, Kamiya, and Ogasawara 1980.

277. Hosokawa 1978; Tokyo 1980a; Oda 1986.

278. Hosokawa 1978; Murai 1979.

279. *Kansai hikki,* 196; Kumamoto 1979b; New York 1979; Tsutsui 1980.

280. Hosokawa 1978.

281. Kumamoto 1979b; Varley and Elison 1981; Hikone 1987.

282. Kumamoto 1979b.

283. Hosokawa 1978.

284. Sanjōnishi 1977–1978; Kumamoto 1979b; New York 1979; *Chanoyu Quarterly* 1980.

285. Kumamoto 1979b; New York 1979; Tokyo 1980a; Cort 1985.

286. Hayashiya 1976; Kumamoto 1979b.

287. Kumamoto 1979b; New York 1979; Tokyo 1980a; Suzuki 1981.

288. Tokyo 1980a; Yoshimura 1978.

289. Tokyo 1980a; Yoshimura 1978.

290. Kumamoto 1979b; New York 1979; Hirota 1980; Tokyo 1980a; Tsutsui 1985.

291. Hosokawa 1978; Kumamoto 1979b.

292. Kumamoto 1977; Tokyo 1977.

293. Tokyo 1977.

295. Kumamoto 1977; Tokyo 1977.

296. Kumamoto 1977; Tokyo 1977.

297. Tokyo 1977.

299. Tokyo 1987a.

300. Tokyo 1982.

301. Tokyo 1982.

302. Kumamoto 1977; Tokyo 1977.

303. Kumamoto 1977.

304. Kumamoto 1977.

305. Kumamoto 1977; Tokyo 1977.

306. Tokyo 1977.

307. Kumamoto 1977.

308. Kumamoto 1977; Tokyo 1977.

309. Tokyo 1977.

310. Tokyo 1977.

311. Kumamoto 1977; Tokyo 1977.

312. Kumamoto 1977; Tokyo 1977.

314. Kumamoto 1977; Tokyo 1977.

315. Tokyo 1977.

316. Kumamoto 1977; Tokyo 1977.

317. Kumamoto 1977; Tokyo 1977.

318–333. Noma 1943; Kaneko 1975; Kyoto 1982; Tanabe 1987.

Bibliography

For Japanese-language publications, the names of Japanese authors appear in this bibliography in Japanese style, that is, family name preceding given name; all names in English-language publications are given in Western style.

When available, the English translation is listed as given in the Japanese-language publication.

Adachi 1974: Adachi Keiko. "Inuou-monozu ni kansuru ichi kōsatsu" (About paintings of "Inu-ou-mono"). *Kokka* no. 972 (1974): 11–30.

Adachi 1980: Adachi Keiko. "Inuoumono byōbu teikei no seiritsu to tenkai" (The establishment and development of folding-screen paintings of the dog-chasing event). In Tsuji 1980a, 119–128.

Addiss and Hurst 1983: Addiss, Stephen, and G. Cameron Hurst III. *Samurai Painters*. Tokyo, New York, and San Francisco, 1983.

Agency for Cultural Affairs 1983: Agency for Cultural Affairs (Bunkachō), ed. *Yosa, Tango chiku no bunkazai* (Cultural properties of the Yosa and Tango areas). Tokyo, 1983.

Akamatsu 1942: Akamatsu Toshihide. "Kano Masanobu no Ashikaga Yoshihisa shutsujin ei ni tsuite" (Concerning the mounted portrait of Ashikaga Yoshihisa by Kano Masanobu). *Gasetsu* 66 (1942): 405–411.

Akamatsu 1949: Akamatsu Toshihide. "Ashikaga shi no shōzō ni tsuite" (On the portraits of the Ashikaga shoguns). *Bijutsu kenkyū* no. 152 (1949): 24–46.

Akamatsu 1969: Akamatsu Toshihide. "Moriyakebon den Ashikaga Takauji zō ni tsuite" (Concerning the reputed portrait of Ashikaga Takauji owned by the Moriya family). *Nihon rekishi* no. 250 (1969): 66–67.

Akiyama 1977: Akiyama Terukazu. *Japanese Painting*. New York, 1977.

Aono 1983: Aono Shunsui. *Daimyō to ryōmin* (Daimyo and commoners). Tokyo, 1983.

Arakawa, Komatsu, and Haino 1986: Arakawa Hirokazu, Komatsu Taishū, and Haino Akio. "Kinsei daimyō konrei chōdo ni tsuite: Kinsei shikkōgei kiso shiryō no kenkyū" (Wedding paraphernalia of the feudal lords in the pre-modern period: Research on the basic materials of pre-modern lacquer crafts). *Museum* no. 419 (1986): 19–28; no. 420 (1986): 17–27.

Arnesen 1979: Arnesen, Peter J. *The Medieval Japanese Daimyo: The Ōuchi Family's Rule of Suō and Nagato*. New Haven and London, 1979.

Asao 1975: Asao Naohiro. *Sakoku* (The age of seclusion). Tokyo, 1975.

Atsuta 1979: Atsuta Kō. *Ōuchi Yoshitaka*. Tokyo, 1979.

Azuma kagami: Azuma kagami (The mirror of the East). Vols. 32 and 33 of *Shintei zōho kokushi taikei* (Rev. and expanded compendium of national historical materials). Ed. Kuroita Katsumi. Tokyo, 1933.

Becker 1986: Becker, Johanna. *Karatsu Ware: A Tradition of Diversity*. Tokyo, New York, and San Francisco, 1986.

Bellah 1970: Bellah, Robert N. *Tokugawa Religion*. Boston, 1970.

Berry 1982: Berry, Mary Elizabeth. *Hideyoshi*. Cambridge, Massachusetts, 1982.

Bitō 1975: Bitō Masahide. *Genroku jidai* (The Genroku age). Tokyo, 1975.

Bolitho 1974: Bolitho, Harold. *Treasures among Men: The Fudai Daimyo in Tokugawa Japan*. New Haven and London, 1974.

Boston 1970: *Zen Painting and Calligraphy*. Exh. cat. by Jan Fontein and Money L. Hickman. Museum of Fine Arts, Boston, 1970.

Brower and Miner 1975: Brower, Robert H., and Earl Miner. *Japanese Court Poetry*. Stanford, 1975.

Brown and Ishida 1979: Brown, Delmer M., and Ichirō Ishida. *The Future and the Past: A Translation and Study of the Gukanshō, an Interpretive History of Japan Written in 1219*. Berkeley, Los Angeles, and London, 1979.

Cahill 1976: Cahill, James. *Hills beyond a River: Chinese Painting of the Yüan Dynasty, 1279–1368*. New York and Tokyo, 1976.

Cambridge 1970: *Traditions of Japanese Art: Selections from the Kimiko and John Powers Collection*. Exh. cat. by John M. Rosenfield and Shūjirō Shimada. Fogg Art Museum, Cambridge, Massachusetts, 1970; The Art Museum, Princeton University, 1971; Seattle Art Museum, 1971.

Chamberlain 1905: Chamberlain, Basil Hall. *Things Japanese*. London, 1905.

Chanoyu Quarterly 1980: "*Chadōgu*—Tea Utensils: Kōgō." *Chanoyu Quarterly* no. 25 (1980): 49–61.

Chicago 1986: *The Great Eastern Temple: Treasures of Japanese Buddhist Art from Tōdai-ji.* Exh. cat. The Art Institute of Chicago, 1986.

Cleveland 1983: *Reflections of Reality in Japanese Art.* Exh. cat. by Sherman E. Lee, Michael R. Cunningham, and James T. Ulak. Cleveland Museum of Art, 1983.

Collcutt 1982: Collcutt, Martin. *Five Mountains: The Rinzai Zen Monastic Institution in Medieval Japan.* Cambridge, Massachusetts, 1982.

Conze 1972: Conze, Edward. *Buddhist Wisdom Books.* New York, Evanston, San Francisco, and London, 1972.

Cooper 1965: Cooper, Michael, ed. *They Came to Japan: An Anthology of European Reports on Japan, 1543–1640.* Berkeley and Los Angeles, 1965.

Cort 1979: Cort, Louise Allison. *Shigaraki, Potters' Valley.* Tokyo, New York, and San Francisco, 1979.

Cort 1985: Cort, Louise Allison. "Looking at White Dew." *Chanoyu Quarterly* no. 43 (1985): 36–48.

Cort 1986: Cort, Louise Allison. "Korean Influences in Japanese Ceramics: The Impact of the Teabowl Wars of 1592–1598." In *Technology and Style,* 331–362. Ed. W. D. Kingery Vol. 2 of *Ceramics and Civilization.* Columbus, 1986.

Craig 1961: Craig, Albert M. *Chōshū in the Meiji Restoration.* Cambridge, Massachusetts, 1961.

Detroit 1986: *Of Water and Ink: Muromachi-period Paintings from Japan 1392–1568.* Exh. cat. by Akiyoshi Watanabe, Hiroshi Kanazawa, and Paul Varley. The Detroit Institute of Arts, 1986; Honolulu Academy of Arts, 1987.

Doi 1939: Doi Tsuguyoshi. "Myōhōin no ema to Kano Sanraku" (Kano Sanraku and a votive painting at Myōhōin). *Gasetsu* no. 26 (1939): 141–156.

Doi 1948: Doi Tsuguyoshi. "Kaihō Yūshō fūfu gazō ni tsuite" (On a portrait of Yusho Kaihoku and his wife). *Kokka* no. 673 (1948): 100–103.

Doi 1970: Doi Tsuguyoshi. *Kinsei Nihon kaiga no kenkyū* (Studies in early modern Japanese painting). Tokyo, 1970.

Doi 1974: Doi Tsuguyoshi. *Motonobu, Eitoku.* Vol. 8 of *Suiboku bijutsu taikei* (Ink paintings). Tokyo, 1974.

Doi 1976: Doi Tsuguyoshi. *Kano Sanraku, Sansetsu.* Vol. 12 of *Nihon bijutsu kaiga zenshū* (Japanese paintings). Tokyo, 1976.

Dore 1965: Dore, Ronald P. *Education in Tokugawa Japan.* Berkeley and Los Angeles, 1965.

Elison and Smith 1981: Elison, George, and Bardwell L. Smith, eds. *Warlords, Artists, and Commoners: Japan in the Sixteenth Century.* Honolulu, 1981.

Ezaki 1974: Ezaki Shunpei. *Kinsei daimyō retsuden* (Genealogies of early modern daimyo). Tokyo, 1974.

Ford 1980: Ford, Barbara Brennan. "A Study of the Painting of Sesson Shūkei." Ph.D. diss., Columbia University, 1980.

Fort Worth 1982: *The Great Age of Japanese Buddhist Sculpture A.D. 600–1300.* Exh. cat. by Kyōtarō Nishikawa and Emily J. Sano. Kimbell Art Museum, Fort Worth, 1982; Japan House Gallery, New York, 1982–1983.

French 1974: French, Cal. *Shiba Kōkan: Artist, Innovator, and Pioneer in the Westernization of Japan.* New York and Tokyo, 1974.

Fuji 1945: Fuji Naomoto. *Chūsei buke shakai no kōzō* (The structure of medieval warrior society). Tokyo, 1945.

Fujikake 1952: Fujikake Shizuya. "Miho no Matsubara zu ni tsuite" (On the original of the paintings of 'Mihono-matsubara'). *Kokka* no. 729 (1952): 369–370.

Fujiki 1975: Fujiki Hisashi. *Oda-Toyotomi seiken* (The Oda-Toyotomi regimes). Tokyo, 1975.

Fujino 1961: Fujino Tamotsu. *Shintei baku-han taisei shi no kenkyū* (Revised studies of the *baku-han* system). Tokyo, 1961.

Fujino 1964: Fujino Tamotsu. *Daimyō: Sono ryōgoku keiei* (Daimyo: The governance of their domains). Tokyo, 1964.

Fukui 1984: *Iwasa Matabei ten* (Iwasa Matabei exhibition). Exh. cat. Fukui Prefectural Museum, 1984.

Fukuoka 1981: *Daimyō chatō: Uchigaso koyō hakkutsu kinen—Takatori, Agano, Yatsushiro* (Daimyo tea ceramics: In commemoration of the excavation of the Uchigaso kiln—Takatori, Agano, and Yatsushiro). Exh. cat. Fukuoka, 1981.

Fukuoka 1985: Fukuoka Art Museum, ed. *Fukuoka Bijutsukan: Shozō hachijū sen* (Eighty masterpieces from Fukuoka Art Museum). Fukuoka, 1985.

Fukuoka 1987a: *Chikuzen kokutō: Takatoriyaki ten* (Chikuzen Province ceramics: Takatori ware exhibition). Exh. cat. Fukuoka Art Museum, 1987.

Fukuoka 1987b: *Maboroshi no bi: Ko Aganoyaki ten* (Phantom beauty: Old Agano ware exhibition). Exh. cat. Fukuoka Prefectural Museum of Art, 1987.

Fukuyama 1941: Fukuyama Toshio. "Minamoto Yoritomo zō, Hōjō Tokiyori zō, Uesugi Shigefusa zō ni tsuite" (Concerning the sculptures of Minamoto Yoritomo, Hōjō Tokiyori, and Uesugi Shigefusa). *Kenchikushi* 3, no. 3 (1941): 279–282.

Haino 1985: Haino Akio, ed. *Shikkō: Kinsei hen* (Early modern lacquer). No. 231 of *Nihon no bijutsu* (Arts of Japan). Tokyo, 1985.

Hall 1966: Hall, John W. *Government and Local Power in Japan 500–1700: A Study Based on Bizen Province.* Princeton, 1966.

Hall 1968: Hall, John W. "Foundations of the Modern Japanese Daimyo." In Hall and Jansen 1968, 65–77.

Hall and Jansen 1968: Hall, John W., and Marius B. Jansen, eds. *Studies in the Institutional History of Early Modern Japan.* Princeton, 1968

Hall and Toyoda 1977: Hall, John W., and Takeshi Toyoda, eds. *Japan in the Muromachi Age.* Berkeley, Los Angeles, and London, 1977.

Hall, Nagahara, and Yamamura 1981: Hall, John W., Keiji Nagahara, and Kozo Yamamura, eds. *Japan before Tokugawa: Political Consolidation and Economic Growth, 1500–1650.* Princeton, 1981.

Hamada 1976: Hamada Naotsugu. "Zuiganji no shōhekiga" (*Shōheki-ga* at the Zuigan-ji). *Kokka* no. 995 (1976): 17–32.

Hayashiya 1976: Hayashiya Seizō, ed. *Momoyama 2* (Momoyama period 2: Mino ware, Chōjirō and Kōetsu). Vol. 5 of *Sekai tōji zenshū* (Ceramic art of the world). Tokyo, 1976.

Hayashiya 1980: Hayashiya Seizō, ed. *Edo 2* (Edo period 2: Karatsu, Agano, Takatori, Satsuma and Hagi wares). Vol. 7 of *Sekai tōji zenshū* (Ceramic art of the world). Tokyo, 1980.

Hikone 1987: *Iike denrai no meihō: Kinsei daimyō no bi to kokoro* (Art treasures collected by the Ii family). Exh. cat. Hikone Castle Museum, 1987.

Hiroi 1971: Hiroi Yūichi. *Tōken no mikata: Gijutsu to ryūha* (Looking at Japanese swords: Techniques and schools). Tokyo, 1971.

Hiroi 1986: Hiroi Yūichi, ed. *Nihontō jūyō bijutsuhin zenshū* (Japanese swords designated as Important Art Objects). 8 vols. Tokyo, 1986.

Hirota 1980: Hirota, Dennis. "The Practice of Tea 3: Memoranda of the Words of Rikyū: *Nampōroku* Book 1." *Chanoyu Quarterly* no. 25 (1980): 31–48.

Honchō gashi: Kano Einō (1634–1700). *Honchō gashi* (History of Japanese painting). In *Nihon garon taikan* (Compendium of Japanese painting texts), 951–1017. Ed. Sakazaki Tan. Tokyo, 1926–1928.

Honchō gunkikō: Arai Hakuseki (1657–1725). *Honchō gunkikō.* In vol. 6 of *Arai Hakuseki zenshū* (Complete works of Arai Hakuseki), 276–453. Ed. Arai Taikichi. Tokyo, 1907.

Honma 1958: Honma Junji. *Nihon kotō shi* (The history of old Japanese swords). Tokyo, 1958.

Hosokawa 1973: Hosokawa Morisada. *Hosokawa Yūsai*. Tokyo, 1973.

Hosokawa 1978: Hosokawa Morisada, ed. *Hosokawake chadōgu* (Tea utensils in the Hosokawa family). Tokyo, 1978.

Iguchi and Nagashima 1979: Iguchi Kaisen and Nagashima Fukutarō. *Chadō jiten* (Dictionary of the way of tea). Kyoto, 1979.

Imanaga 1979: Imanaga Seiji. *Kosode 1*. Vol. 3 of *Nihon no senshoku* (Japanese textiles). Tokyo, 1979.

Irita 1935: Irita Seizō. "Maeda Kikuhime no gazō" (The portrait of Princess Maeda-Kiku Hime in the Saikyōji temple). *Bijutsu kenkyū* no. 38 (1935): 56–57.

Ishii 1974: Ishii Susumu. *Chūsei bushidan* (Medieval warrior bands). Tokyo, 1974.

Ishikawa 1978: Ishikawa Matsutarō. *Hankō to terakoya* (Domain schools and temple schools). Tokyo, 1978.

Iwama 1987: Iwama Kaori. "Tosaha shōzōga shiron: Genji, Kyūyoku o meguru sho mondai." (Portrait paintings by the Tosa school: Several problems concerning the work of Genji and Kyūyoku). *Bijutsushi* no. 122 (1987): 126–143.

Jansen 1961: Jansen, Marius B. *Sakamoto Ryōma and the Meiji Restoration*. Princeton, 1961.

Jansen and Rozman 1986: Jansen, Marius B., and Gilbert Rozman, eds. *Japan in Transition, from Tokugawa to Meiji*. Princeton, 1986.

Jūyō Bunkazai Hensan Iinkai 1980–1984: Jūyō Bunkazai Hensan Iinkai, ed. *Shin shitei jūyō bunkazai: Kaisetsuban* (Newly designated Important Cultural Properties: Commentary edition). 13 vols. Tokyo, 1980–1984.

Kakei 1985: Kakei Yasuhiko. *Chūsei buke kakun no kenkyū* (Studies in medieval warrior house codes). Tokyo, 1985.

Kamakurashi Shi Hensan Iinkai 1956–1959: Kamakurashi Shi Hensan Iinkai, ed. *Kamakurashi shi* (History of Kamakura City). 6 vols. Kamakura, 1956–1959.

Kameda 1980: Kameda Tsutomu. *Sesson*. Vol. 8 of *Nihon bijutsu kaiga zenshū* (Japanese paintings). Tokyo, 1980.

Kanagawaken Kyōiku Iinkai 1975: Kanagawaken Kyōiku Iinkai, ed. *Kanagawaken bunkazai zuroku: Chōkoku hen*. (Catalogue of the cultural properties of Kanagawa Prefecture: Sculpture). Yokohama, 1975.

Kanai 1962: Kanai Madoka. *Hansei* (Domain politics). Tokyo, 1962.

Kanazawa 1987: *Imari, Ko Kutani meihin ten* (Exhibition of Imari and Ko-Kutani ware). Exh. cat. Ishikawa Prefectural Museum of Art, Kanazawa, 1987; The Kyushu Ceramic Museum, Arita, 1987.

Kanda 1985: Kanda, Christine Guth. *Shinzō: Hachiman Imagery and Its Development*. Cambridge, Massachusetts, 1985

Kaneko 1966: Kaneko Ryōun, ed. *Nō no men* (Nō masks). Tokyo, 1966.

Kaneko 1975: Kaneko Ryōun, ed. *Nō kyōgen men* (Nō and Kyōgen masks). No. 108 of *Nihon no bijutsu* (Arts of Japan). Tokyo, 1975.

Kanrin koro shū: Keijo Shūrin (1440–1518). *Kanrin koro shū*. Vol. 4 of Uemura 1936.

Kansai hikki: Fujii Raisai (b. 1628). *Kansai hikki*. In vol. 10 of *Nihon zuihitsu zenshū* (Miscellaneous writings of Japan), 127–218. Ed. Nakatsuka Eijirō. Tokyo, 1928.

Katagiri 1977: Katagiri Yōichi. *Shūishō: Kōhon to kenkyū* (Shūishō: Collated versions and studies). Kyoto, 1977.

Kawahara 1977: Kawahara Masahiko. *Shigaraki*. Vol. 12 of *Nihon tōji zenshū* (A pageant of Japanese ceramics). Tokyo, 1977.

Kawai 1973: Kawai Masaharu. *Chūsei buke shakai no kenkyū* (Studies in medieval warrior society). Tokyo, 1973.

Kawai 1978: Kawai Masatomo. *Yūshō, Tōgan*. Vol. 11 of *Nihon bijutsu kaiga zenshū* (Japanese paintings). Tokyo, 1978.

Keene 1961: Keene, Donald, ed. *Major Plays of Chikamatsu*. New York, 1961.

Keene 1970: Keene, Donald, ed. *Twenty Plays of the Nō Theatre*. New York, 1970.

Keene 1981: Keene, Donald. "Jōha, a Sixteenth-Century Poet of Linked Verse." In Elison and Smith 1981, 113–131.

Keene and Kaneko 1966: Keene, Donald, and Hiroshi Kaneko, eds. *Nō: The Classical Theatre of Japan*. Tokyo, 1966.

Kirihata 1980: Kirihata Ken. *Kosode 2*. Vol. 4 of *Nihon no senshoku* (Japanese textiles). Tokyo, 1980.

Kitagawa and Tsuchida 1975: Kitagawa, Hiroshi, and Bruce T. Tsuchida, trans. *The Tale of the Heike*. 2 vols. Tokyo, 1975.

Kitajima 1975: Kitajima Masamoto. *Edo bakufu* (The Edo bakufu). Tokyo, 1975.

Klein 1984: Klein, Bettina. "Japanese *Kinbyōbu*: The Gold-leafed Folding Screens of the Muromachi Period (1333–1573)." Adapted and expanded by Carolyn Wheelwright. *Artibus Asiae* 45, no. 1 (1984): 5–33; 45, nos. 2/3 (1984): 101–173.

Kobayashi 1953: Kobayashi Takeshi. "Daibusshi hōin Tankei" (Tankei, a Buddhist sculptor of the thirteenth century: His life and work). *Yamato bunka* no. 12 (1953): 11–22.

Kobayashi 1978: Kobayashi Tadashi, ed. *Hōitsuha* (Hōitsu school). Vol. 5 of *Rimpa kaiga zenshū* (Paintings of Rimpa). Tokyo, 1978.

Kobayashi 1983: Kobayashi Tadashi. *Edo kaiga shiron* (History of Edo painting). Tokyo, 1983.

Kodama 1967: Kodama Kōta. *Daimyō retsuden* (Biographies of daimyo). 5 vols. Tokyo, 1967.

Kodama 1975: Kodama Kōta. *Daimyō*. Tokyo, 1975.

Kodansha 1983: *Kodansha Encyclopedia of Japan*. 9 vols. Tokyo and New York, 1983.

Koga 1964: Koga Hidemasa. *Daimyō haizetsuroku* (Records of daimyo attainders). Tokyo, 1964.

Koga bikō: Asaoka Okisada (1800–1856). *Koga bikō* (Handbook of classical painting). 4 vols. Rev. and adapted by Ōta Kin as *Zōtei koga bikō* in 1904. Tokyo, 1970.

Kokka no. 970: "Tokushū: Sesshū no kachōga" (Special edition: Flower-and-bird paintings by Sesshū). *Kokka* no. 970 (1974).

Kokuhō 1984: Agency for Cultural Affairs (Bunkachō), ed. *Kokuhō* (National Treasures). 15 vols. Tokyo, 1984.

Komatsu 1985: Komatsu Taishū, ed. *Shikkō: Genshi, kodai hen* (Early lacquer). No. 229 of *Nihon no bijutsu* (Arts of Japan). Tokyo, 1985.

Komatsu and Minamoto 1978: Komatsu Shigemi and Minamoto Toyomune. *Obusuma Saburō ekotoba, Ise shinmeisho utaawase*. Vol. 12 of *Nihon emaki taisei* (Compendium of Japanese scroll paintings). Tokyo, 1978.

Kōno 1978: Kōno Motoaki. "Hōitsu no yūnenki sakuhin" (Dated works by Hōitsu). In Kobayashi 1978, 31–40.

Kōno 1982: Kōno Motoaki, ed. *Kano Tan'yū*. No. 194 of *Nihon no bijutsu* (Arts of Japan). Tokyo, 1982.

Kumagai 1932: Kumagai Nobuo. "Ōei nenkan no shigajiku: Tokuni sono sansuiga no hatten ni okeru ichi ni kanshite" (Paintings with poetical inscriptions during the Ōei years, 1394–1427). *Bijutsu kenkyū* no. 4 (1932): 122–128.

Kumakura 1977: Kumakura Isao. *Chanoyu: Wabicha no kokoro to katachi* (The spirit and form of *wabi* tea). Tokyo, 1977.

Kumakura 1978: Kumakura Isao. *Sen no Rikyū*. Tokyo, 1978.

Kumakura 1980: Kumakura Isao. *Kindai chadō shi no kenkyū* (Studies in the modern history of the way of tea). Tokyo, 1980.

Kumakura 1983: Kumakura Isao. *Oribe, Enshū, Sōtan.* Tokyo, 1983.

Kumamoto 1976: *Eisei Bunko meihin ten* (Exhibition of masterpieces of the Eisei Bunko). Exh. cat. Kumamoto Prefectural Museum of Art, 1976.

Kumamoto 1977: *Nō no men to shōzoku* (Nō masks and costumes). Exh. cat. Kumamoto Prefectural Museum of Art, 1977.

Kumamoto 1978a: *Eisei Bunko no buki bugu* (Arms and armor from the Eisei Bunko). Exh. cat. Kumamoto Prefectural Museum of Art, 1978.

Kumamoto 1978b: *Higo no kinkō* (Metalwork of Higo). Exh. cat. Kumamoto Prefectural Museum of Art, 1978.

Kumamoto 1978c: *Chūgoku no e to sho* (Chinese painting and calligraphy). Exh. cat. Kumamoto Prefectural Museum of Art, 1978.

Kumamoto 1979a: *Kumamoto no bijutsu* (The arts of Kumamoto). Exh. cat. Kumamoto Prefectural Museum of Art, 1979.

Kumamoto 1979b: *Eisei Bunko no chanoyu no dōgu* (Tea utensils in the Eisei Bunko). Exh. cat. Kumamoto Prefectural Museum of Art, 1979.

Kumamoto 1980: *Daimyō no kurashi no bi* (Elegance in the life of the daimyo). Exh. cat. Kumamoto Prefectural Museum of Art, 1980.

Kumamoto 1982: *Hosokawa sandai* (Three generations of Hosokawa). Exh. cat. Kumamoto Prefectural Museum of Art, 1982.

Kumamoto 1983: *Eisei Bunko no shikkōgei* (Lacquer in the Eisei Bunko). Exh. cat. Kumamoto Prefectural Museum of Art, 1983.

Kumamoto 1984a: *Eisei Bunko no byōbu-e* (Screen paintings in the Eisei Bunko). Exh. cat. Kumamoto Prefectural Museum of Art, 1984.

Kumamoto 1984b: *Eisei Bunko ten* (Eisei Bunko exhibition). Exh. cat. Kumamoto Prefectural Museum of Art, 1984.

Kuwata 1957: Kuwata Tadachika. *Yamanoue Sōjiki no kenkyū* (Studies of the tea chronicles of Yamanoue Sōji). Kyoto, 1957.

Kuwata 1963: Kuwata Tadachika. *Chadō jiten* (A dictionary of the way of tea). Tokyo, 1963.

Kuwata, Okamoto, Kōyama, and Nakamura 1980: Kuwata Tadachika, Okamoto Ryōichi, Kōyama Noboru, and Nakamura Hiroshi. *Sekigahara kassen zu* (Paintings of the Battle of Sekigahara). Vol. 3 of *Sengoku kassen-e byōbu shūsei* (Sengoku-period battle screens). Tokyo, 1980.

Kyoto 1977: Kyoto National Museum, ed. *Momoyama jidai no kōgei* (Handicrafts of the Momoyama period). Kyoto, 1977.

Kyoto 1978: Kyoto National Museum, ed. *Nihon no shōzō* (Portrait sculpture and paintings of Japan). Tokyo, 1978.

Kyoto 1981a: *Hosokawake korekushon Tōyō bijutsu* (The essence of Japanese and Chinese art from the Hosokawa family collection). Exh. cat. Kyoto National Museum, 1981.

Kyoto 1981b: *Chanoyu to Kyōyaki 1*: Ninsei, Kenzan, Kokiyomizu (Chanoyu and Kyoto ceramics 1: Ninsei, Kenzan, and Kokiyomizu). Exh. cat. Chadō Shiryōkan, Kyoto, 1981.

Kyoto 1982: Kyoto National Museum, ed. *Komen* (Old masks). Tokyo, 1982.

Kyoto 1985a: *Nihon no senshoku: Waza to bi* (Japanese textiles: Beauty and skill). Exh. cat. Kyoto National Museum, 1985.

Kyoto 1985b: *Suki no sakutō: Kōetsu kara gendai made* (The ceramics of aesthetes: From Kōetsu to the present). Exh. cat. The Raku Museum, Kyoto, 1985.

Kyoto 1986: *Kobori Enshū ten* (Kobori Enshū exhibition). Exh. cat. Nomura Art Museum, Kyoto, 1986.

Kyoto 1987: *Nihon no katchū* (Japanese armor). Exh. cat. Kyoto National Museum, 1987.

Kyōto Furitsu Sōgō Shiryōkan 1970: Kyōto Furitsu Sōgō Shiryōkan. *Zuroku Tōji Hyakugō monjo* (Illustrated catalogue of the Hyakugō archives of Tōji). Kyoto, 1970.

Kyūsojin 1960: Kyūsojin Hitaku. *Kokin wakashū seiritsu ron* (The formation of the Kokin wakashū). 4 vols. Tokyo, 1960.

London 1981–1982: *The Great Japan Exhibition: Art of the Edo Period 1600–1868.* Exh. cat. ed. William Watson. Royal Academy of Arts, London, 1981–1982.

Los Angeles 1965: *Art Treasures from Japan.* Exh. cat. Los Angeles County Museum of Art, 1965; The Detroit Institute of Arts, 1965–1966; Philadelphia Museum of Art, 1966; The Royal Ontario Museum, Toronto, 1966.

Los Angeles 1983–1984: *The Shogun Age Exhibition from the Tokugawa Art Museum, Japan.* Exh. cat. Los Angeles County Museum of Art, 1983–1984; Dallas Museum of Art, 1984; Haus der Kunst, Munich, 1984–1985; Espace Pierre Cardin, Paris, 1985.

Los Angeles 1985: *Japanese Ink Paintings.* Exh. cat. by Shin'ichi Miyajima and Yasuhiro Satō. Los Angeles County Museum of Art, 1985.

Lu 1974: Lu, David J. *Sources of Japanese History.* 2 vols. New York, 1974.

Masaki 1978: Masaki Takayuki. *Masaki Bijutsukan meihin zuroku: Shoga hen.* (Illustrated catalogue of masterpieces of the Masaki Art Museum: Calligraphy and painting). Kyoto, 1978.

Mass 1979: Mass, Jeffrey P. *The Development of Kamakura Rule, 1180–1250: A History with Documents.* Stanford, 1979.

Mass 1982: Mass, Jeffrey P., ed. *Court and Bakufu in Japan: Essays in Kamakura History.* New Haven, 1982.

Matsushita 1956: Matsushita Takaaki. "*Chōshōkenzu*" (Landscape painting with a poem of Chosho-ken). *Yamato bunka* no. 22 (1956): 47–49.

Matsushita 1967: Matsushita Takaaki. *Ink Painting.* Trans. and adapted by Martin Collcutt. Vol. 7 of *Arts of Japan.* New York and Tokyo, 1967.

Matsushita and Tamamura 1974: Matsushita Takaaki and Tamamura Takeji. *Josetsu, Shūbun, san Ami* (Josetsu, Shūbun, and the three Ami). Vol. 6 of *Suiboku bijutsu taikei* (Ink paintings). Tokyo, 1974.

McCullough 1959: McCullough, Helen Craig, trans. *The Taiheiki: A Chronicle of Medieval Japan.* New York, 1959.

McCullough 1964–1965: McCullough, Helen Craig, trans. "A Tale of Mutsu." *Harvard Journal of Asiatic Studies* 25 (1964–1965): 178–211.

McCullough 1985a: McCullough, Helen Craig. *Kokin Wakashū: The First Imperial Anthology of Japanese Poetry, with 'Tosa Nikki' and 'Shinsen Waka.'* Stanford, 1985.

McCullough 1985b: McCullough, Helen Craig. *Brocade by Night: 'Kokin Wakashū' and the Court Style in Japanese Classical Poetry.* Stanford, 1985.

Meech-Pekarik 1977–1978: Meech-Pekarik, Julia. "Disguised Scripts and Hidden Poems in an Illustrated Heian Sutra: Ashide and Uta-e in the Heike Nōgyō." *Archives of Asian Art* 31 (1977–1978): 52–78.

Mikami and Hayashiya 1983: Mikami Tsugio and Hayashiya Seizō, eds. *Edo 4* (Edo period 4: Kutani and miscellaneous wares). Vol. 9 of *Sekai tōji zenshū* (Ceramic art of the world). Tokyo, 1983.

Minamoto 1954: Minamoto Toyomune. "Jingoji zō den Takanobu hitsu no gazō ni tsuite no utagai" (Some remarks on the date of the portraits by Takanobu, 1142–1205, preserved in the monastery Jingoji). *Yamato bunka* no. 13 (1954): 10–19.

Minamoto 1972: Minamoto Toyomune. "Sogaha to Asakura bunka" (Soga school and the culture of Asakura clan). *Kobijutsu* no. 38 (1972): 29–39.

Minamoto 1980: Minamoto Toyomune. *Soga Dasoku*. Vol. 3 of *Nihon bijutsu kaiga zenshū* (Japanese paintings). Tokyo, 1980.

Mishima 1985: *Nō no sekai ten: Hosokawa-ke denrai ni yoru* (The world of Nō: Objects in the Hosokawa family collection). Exh. cat. Sano Art Museum. Mishima, 1985.

Mitsuoka 1975: Mitsuoka Tadanari, ed. *Edo 1* (Edo period 1: Kyōyaki—Kyoto ware). Vol. 6 of *Sekai tōji zenshū* (Ceramic art of the world). Tokyo, 1975.

Mitsuoka and Okuda 1977: Mitsuoka Tadanari and Okuda Naoshige, eds. *Momoyama 1* (Momoyama period 1: Bizen, Tamba, Shigaraki and Iga wares). Vol. 4 of *Sekai tōji zenshū* (Ceramic art of the world). Tokyo, 1977.

Miyama 1964a: Miyama Susumu. "Jufukuji Eisai Zenji zō to Kamakura busshi" (Statue of the priest Eisai at the Jufukuji Temple and Buddhist sculptors active in the Kamakura area). *Museum* no. 155 (1964): 22–26.

Miyama 1964b: Miyama Susumu. "Kamakura jidai no bushi zokutai shōzō chōkoku" (Kamakura-period secular portrait sculpture of warriors). *Miura kobunka* 3 (1964).

Miyama 1981: Miyama Susumu. *Kamakura chōkoku shi ronkō* (Study of the history of Kamakura sculpture). Yokohama, 1981.

MOA Art Museum 1982: MOA Art Museum, ed. *Meihin zuroku: Chūgoku, Nihon kaiga hen* (Selected catalogue: Chinese and Japanese paintings). [Tokyo], 1982.

Mori 1950: Mori Tōru. "Minamoto Yoritomo zō ni tsuite" (On the portrait of Minamoto Yoritomo). *Bijutsushi* no. 2 (1950): 28–39.

Mōri 1957: Mōri Hisashi. "Akana Hachimangū shinzō" (The Akana Hachimangū Shinto sculptures). *Kokka* no. 789 (1957): 402–409.

Mōri 1961: Mōri Hisashi. *Busshi Kaikei ron* (A study of the Buddhist sculptor Kaikei). Tokyo, 1961

Mōri 1972: Mōri Hisashi. "Bijutsu shiryō toshite no Jōdoji engi" (Origin of the Jōdoji as an artistic material). In *Akamatsu Toshihide Kyōju taikan kinen kokushi ronshū* (Collection of historical studies in honor of the retirement of Professor Akamatsu Toshihide), 477–491. Kyoto, 1972.

Mōri 1974: Mōri Hisashi. "Chōrakuji no Jishū shōzō chōkoku" (Statues of the priests belonging to the Ji-shū sect of Buddhism owned by the Chōrakuji). *Bukkyō geijutsu* no. 96 (1974): 3–33.

Mōri 1977: Mōri Hisashi. *Japanese Portrait Sculpture*. Trans. and adapted by W. Chié Ishibashi. Vol. 2 of *Japanese Arts Library*. Tokyo, New York, and San Francisco, 1977.

Mōri 1980: Mōri Hisashi. *Nihon butsuzō shi kenkyū* (Studies in the history of Japanese Buddhist sculpture). Kyoto, 1980.

Mōri 1987: Mōri Hisashi. *Busshi Kaikei ron: Zōhoban* (A study of the Buddhist sculptor Kaikei: Enlarged edition). Tokyo, 1987.

Moriya 1978: Moriya Takeshi. *Tokugawa Ieyasu*. Tokyo, 1978.

Morris 1975: Morris, Ivan. *The Nobility of Failure*. New York, 1975.

Murai 1979: Murai Yasuhiko. *Cha no bunkashi* (Cultural history of tea). Tokyo, 1979.

Murashige 1982: Murashige Yasushi. "Hōitsu yōkenzu ema no genga ni tsuite" (Original design of the votive tablet with Western dog painted by Hōitsu: Introduction of copy work of Tōshuku's "Paired dogs"). *Museum* no. 377 (1982): 29–36.

Muroga 1983: Muroga Nobuo. *Kochizu shō* (Selected old maps of Japan). Tokyo, 1983.

Nagahara 1967: Nagahara Keiji. *Daimyō ryōgokusei* (The daimyo provincial domain system). Tokyo, 1967.

Nagahara 1975: Nagahara Keiji. *Sengoku no dōran* (The age of wars). Tokyo, 1975.

Nagatake and Hayashiya 1978: Nagatake Takeshi and Hayashiya Seizō, eds. *Edo 3* (Edo period 3: Imari and Nabeshima wares). Vol. 8 of *Sekai tōji zenshū* (Ceramic art of the world). Tokyo, 1978.

Naitō 1981: Naitō Takashi. "Shaseicho no shikō: Edo chūki no konchū zufu ni tsuite" (The thought behind albums of natural studies: Regarding the mid-Edo albums of insect studies). *Hikaku shisō zasshi* no. 4 (1981): 35–58.

Nakajima 1967, 1968, 1972: Nakajima Junji. "Sesshūkei kachōzu byōbu kenkyū" (Study of flower-and-bird screens by Sesshū and artists of his school). *Museum* no. 199 (1967): 9–30; no. 205 (1968): 4–21; no. 252 (1972): 4–23.

Nakajima 1971: Nakajima Junji. "Shinjuan fusuma-e no yōshikiteki kenkyū" (Stylistic study of the sliding door paintings at Shinjuan). In Tanaka 1971a, 87–117.

Nakamura 1971: Nakamura Tanio, ed. *Sesson to Kantō suibokuga* (Sesson and ink painting of artists of the Kanto region). No. 63 of *Nihon no bijutsu* (Arts of Japan). Tokyo, 1971.

Nakamura 1976: Nakamura Tanio. *Sesshū*. Vol. 4 of *Nihon bijutsu kaiga zenshū* (Japanese paintings). Tokyo, 1976.

Nakamura 1978: Nakamura Tanio, ed. *Sōjūga: Ryūko enkō* (Paintings of running animals: Dragons and tigers, monkeys and gibbons). Vol. 16 of *Nihon byōbu-e shūsei* (Japanese screen paintings). Tokyo, 1978.

Nakamura 1979: Nakamura Tanio. Vol. 3 of *Hōitsuha kachōgafu* (Edo—Rimpa and artists surrounding Sakai Hōitsu). Kyoto, 1979.

Nakamura 1980: Nakamura Kōya. *Tokugawa Ieyasu monjo no kenkyū teiseiban* (Research on the documents of Tokugawa Ieyasu, rev. ed.). 3 vols. Tokyo, 1980.

Nakane 1970: Nakane Chie. *Japanese Society*. London, 1970.

Narasaki 1977: Narasaki Shōichi, ed. *Nihon chūsei* (Japanese medieval period). Vol. 3 of *Sekai tōji zenshū* (Ceramic art of the world). Tokyo, 1977.

Naruse 1977: Naruse Fujio. *Shozan, Naotake. Tōyō bijutsu sensho* (Selected themes in Oriental art). Tokyo, 1977.

Nedachi 1986: Nedachi Kensuke. "Nanzen'in no Issan Ichinei zō ni tsuite" (The statue of the priest Yishan Yining of Nanzen-in). *Museum* no. 420 (1986): 4–16.

New York 1972: *Scholar Painters of Japan: The Nanga School*. Exh. cat. by James Cahill. Asia House Gallery, New York, 1972; University Art Museum, University of California, Berkeley, 1972.

New York 1973: *Namban Art: A Loan Exhibition from Japanese Collections*. Exh. cat. by Shin'ichi Tani and Tadashi Sugase. Japan House Gallery, New York, 1973; St. Louis Art Museum, 1973; Honolulu Academy of Arts, 1973.

New York 1975: *Momoyama: Japanese Art in the Age of Grandeur*. Exh. cat. The Metropolitan Museum of Art, New York, 1975.

New York 1975–1976: *Japanese Art: Selections from the Mary and Jackson Burke Collection*. Exh. cat. by Miyeko Murase. The Metropolitan Museum of Art, New York, 1975–1976; Seattle Art Museum, 1977; Minneapolis Institute of Art, 1977.

New York 1976: *Nippon-tō Art Swords of Japan: The Walter A. Compton Collection.* Exh. cat. by Walter A. Compton et al. Japan House Gallery, New York, 1976.

New York 1979: *Chanoyu: Japanese Tea Ceremony.* Exh. cat. by Seizō Hayashiya et al. Japan House Gallery, New York, 1979; Kimbell Art Museum, Fort Worth, 1979; Honolulu Academy of Arts, 1979.

New York 1983: *Emaki: Narrative Scrolls from Japan.* Exh. cat. by Miyeko Murase. The Asia Society Galleries, New York, 1983.

New York 1984: *Kosode: 16th–19th Century Textiles from the Nomura Collection.* Exh. cat. by Amanda Mayer Stinchecum, Monica Bethe, and Margot Paul. Japan House Gallery, New York, 1984.

New York 1984–1985: *Masters of Japanese Calligraphy.* Exh. cat. by Yoshiaki Shimizu and John M. Rosenfield. The Asia Society Galleries and Japan House Gallery, New York, 1984–1985; The Nelson-Atkins Museum of Art, Kansas City, 1985; Seattle Art Museum, 1985.

New York 1985: *Spectacular Helmets of Japan, 16th–19th Century.* Exh. cat. Japan House Gallery, New York, 1985; Asian Art Museum of San Francisco, 1985–1986.

Nihon Bijutsu Tōken Hozon Kyōkai 1966–1970: Nihon Bijutsu Tōken Hozon Kyōkai, ed. *Nihontō taikan* (Collection of Japanese swords). 7 vols. Tokyo, 1966–1970.

Nishi and Hozumi 1985: Nishi, Kazuo, and Kazuo Hozumi. *What is Japanese Architecture?: A Survey of Traditional Japanese Architecture, with a List of Sites and a Map.* Trans. and adapted by H. Mack Horton. Tokyo, New York, and San Francisco, 1985.

Nishikawa 1976: Nishikawa Kyōtarō, ed. *Chinsō chōkoku.* No. 123 of *Nihon no bijutsu* (Arts of Japan). Tokyo, 1976.

Nishiyama, Watanabe, and Gunji 1972: Nishiyama Matsunosuke, Watanabe Ichirō, and Gunji Masakatsu. *Kinsei geidō ron* (Early modern arts). Vol. 61 of *Nihon shisō taikei* (History of Japanese thought). Tokyo, 1972.

Nitobe 1920: Nitobe Inazō. *Bushido, the Soul of Japan.* Tokyo, 1920.

Noma 1943: Noma Seiroku. *Nihon kamen shi* (History of Japanese masks). Tokyo, 1943.

Nosco 1984: Nosco, Peter, ed. *Confucianism and Tokugawa Culture.* Princeton, 1984.

Oda 1986: Oda, Eiichi. "*Meibutsu-gire:* Famous Chanoyu Fabrics." Trans. Monica Bethe. *Chanoyu Quarterly* no. 45 (1986): 7–23.

Ogino 1967: Ogino Minahiko. "Moriyakebon den Ashikaga Takauji shi zō no kenkyū" (A study on the portrait of Takauji Ashikaga owned by the Moriya family). *Kokka* no. 906 (1967): 7–22; no. 907 (1967): 7–13.

Ōishi 1975: Ōishi Shinzaburō. *Bakuhansei no tenkan* (Transition in the *baku-han* system). Tokyo, 1975.

Ōishi 1977: Ōishi Shinzaburō. *Edo jidai* (The Edo period). Tokyo, 1977.

Ōishi 1978: Ōishi Shinzaburō. *Edo to chihō bunka* (Edo and provincial culture). Tokyo, 1978.

Okada, Matsuda, and Arakawa 1978–1979: Okada Jō, Matsuda Gonroku, and Arakawa Hirokazu, eds. *Nihon no shitsugei* (Japanese lacquer). 6 vols. Tokyo, 1978–1979.

Okamoto 1972: Okamoto, Yoshitomo. *The Namban Art of Japan.* Trans. Ronald K. Jones. Vol. 19 of *The Heibonsha Survey of Japanese Art.* New York and Tokyo, 1972.

Okamoto 1978: Okamoto Ryōichi. *Oda Nobunaga.* Tokyo, 1978.

Okayama 1972: *Tokugawa jūgodai no shōgun ten* (Fifteen generations of Tokugawa shoguns exhibition). Exh. cat. Okayamajō Tenshukaku, Okayama, 1972.

Okayama 1984: *Daimyō konrei chōdo* (Daimyo wedding trousseaus). Exh. cat. Okayama Art Museum, 1984.

Okinagusa: Kanzawa Tokō (1710–1795). *Okinagusa.* In vol. 15 of *Nihon zuihitsu zenshū* (Miscellaneous writings of Japan), 561–713. Ed. Nakatsuka Eijirō. Tokyo, 1928.

Okuno 1971: Okuno Takahiro. *Oda Nobunaga monjo no kenkyū* (Studies on the documents of Oda Nobunaga). 2 vols. Tokyo, 1971.

Onryōken nichiroku: Onryōken nichiroku (The official diary of Onryōken; 1435–1466 and 1484–1493). 5 vols. Ed. Tamamura Takeji and Katsuno Ryushin. Kyoto, 1953–1954.

Osaka 1987: *Sansui* (Landscape). Exh. cat. Masaki Art Museum, Osaka, 1987.

Ōta, Takehana, and Naruse 1974: Ōta Momosuke, Takehana Rintarō, and Naruse Fujio. *Akita ranga* (Western-style painting of Akita). Tokyo, 1974.

Oxford 1981: *Shino and Oribe Kiln Sites: A Loan Exhibition of Mino Shards from Toki City.* Exh. cat. by R. F. J. Faulkner and O. R. Impey. Ashmolean Museum, Oxford, 1981; Groninger Museum, Groningen, 1981.

Ōyama 1974: Ōyama Kyōhei. *Kamakura bakufu* (The Kamakura *bakufu*). Tokyo, 1974.

Ozaki 1968: Ozaki Motoharu, ed. *Katchū* (Armor). No. 24 of *Nihon no bijutsu* (Arts of Japan). Tokyo, 1968.

Ozaki and Satō 1970: Ozaki Motoharu and Satō Kanzan. *Katchū to tōken* (Armor and swords). Vol. 21 of *Genshoku Nihon no bijutsu* (Arts of Japan in color). Tokyo, 1970.

Princeton 1976: *Japanese Ink Paintings from American Collections: The Muromachi Period, an Exhibition in Honor of Shūjiro Shimada.* Exh. cat. ed. Yoshiaki Shimizu and Carolyn Wheelwright. The Art Museum, Princeton University, 1976.

Raleigh 1988: *Robes of Elegance: Japanese Kimonos of the 16th–20th centuries.* Exh. cat. by Hayao Ishimura, Nobuhiko Maruyama, and Tomoyuki Yamanobe. North Carolina Museum of Art, Raleigh, 1988.

Robinson 1961: Robinson, B. W. *The Arts of the Japanese Sword.* London, 1961.

Rubinger 1982: Rubinger, Richard. *Private Academies of Tokugawa Japan.* Princeton, 1982.

Sakai 1981: *Toshi no kōryū to bunka* (Cities and civilizations). Exh. cat. Sakai City Museum, 1981.

Sakai 1983: *Takuan Kōgetsu to sono jidai* (Takuan, Kōgetsu and their time). Exh. cat. Sakai City Museum, 1983.

Sakamoto 1973: Sakamoto Mitsuru, ed. *Shoki yōfūga* (Early Western-style paintings). No. 80 of *Nihon no bijutsu* (Arts of Japan). Tokyo, 1973.

Sakamoto 1979: Sakamoto Mitsuru, ed. *Fūzokuga: Nanban fūzoku* (Genre painting: "Southern barbarians"). Vol. 15 of *Nihon byōbu-e shūsei* (Japanese screen paintings). Tokyo, 1979.

Sanjōnishi 1977–1978: Sanjōnishi, Kinosa. "The Way of Incense." *Chanoyu Quarterly* no. 20 (1977): 31–43; no. 21 (1978): 39–54.

Sansom 1943: Sansom, George. *Japan: A Short Cultural History.* New York, 1943.

Sansom 1961: Sansom, George. *A History of Japan, 1334–1615.* Stanford, 1961.

Sasaki 1966: Sasaki Junnosuke. *Daimyō to hyakushō* (Daimyo and farmers). Tokyo, 1966.

Sasaki 1975: Sasaki Gin'ya. *Muromachi bakufu* (The Muromachi *bakufu*). Tokyo, 1975.

Sasama 1981: Sasama Yoshihiko. *Nihon no katchū bugu jiten* (Illustrated encyclopedia of Japanese arms and armor). Tokyo, 1981.

Satō 1961: Satō Kan'ichi. *Nihon no tōken* (Japanese swords). Tokyo, 1961.

Satō 1978: Satō Masahiko. *Satsuma*. Vol. 19 of *Nihon tōji zenshu* (A pageant of Japanese ceramics). Tokyo, 1978.

Satō 1983: Satō Kanzan. *The Japanese Sword*. Trans. and adapted by Joe Earle. Vol. 12 of *Japanese Arts Library*. Tokyo, New York, and San Francisco, 1983.

Seattle 1972a: *Ceramic Art of Japan: One Hundred Masterpieces from Japanese Collections*. Exh. cat. Seattle Art Museum, 1972; William Rockhill Nelson Gallery of Art-Atkins Museum of Fine Arts, Kansas City, 1972; Asia House Society Galleries, New York, 1973; Los Angeles County Museum of Art, 1973.

Seattle 1972b: Seattle Art Museum, ed. *International Symposium on Japanese Ceramics*. Seattle, 1972.

Seattle 1987: Seattle Art Museum, ed. *A Thousand Cranes: Treasures of Japanese Art*. Seattle, 1987.

Sen 1956–1962: Sen Sōshitsu, ed. *Sadō koten zenshū* (Collection of tea chronicles). 12 vols. Kyoto, 1956–1962.

Sendai 1986a: *Eiyū no jidai: Date Masamune to Hideyoshi, Ieyasu* (Date Masamune: A contemporary of Hideyoshi and Ieyasu). Exh. cat. Sendai City Museum, 1986.

Sendai 1986b: *Michinoku no taiga: Kinsei no shōhekiga byōbu-e* (Large pictures on sliding doors and folding screens: Arts of Tohoku in Edo era). Exh. cat. Sendai City Museum, 1986.

Sendai 1987: *Date Masamune to kashintachi: Ransei o ikita otoko no gunzō* (Date Masamune and his retainers: How they lived through the warring states period). Exh. cat. Sendai City Museum, 1987.

Shimada 1987: Shimada Shūjirō. *Nihon kaiga shi kenkyū* (Studies in the history of Japanese painting). Tokyo, 1987.

Shimada and Iriya 1987: Shimada Shūjirō and Iriya Yoshitaka, eds. *Zenrin gasan: Chūsei suibokuga o yomu* (Inscriptions on paintings related to Zen monasteries: Reading medieval ink paintings). Tokyo, 1987.

Shimizu 1980a: Shimizu, Yoshiaki. "Six Narrative Paintings by Yin T'o-lo: Their Symbolic Content." *Archives of Asian Art* 33 (1980): 6–37.

Shimizu 1980b: Shimizu, Yoshiaki. "Some Elementary Problems of the Japanese Narrative, *Hiko-hoho-demi no Mikoto.*" *Studia Artium Orientalis et Occidentalis* 1 (1980):29–41.

Shimizu 1981: Shimizu, Yoshiaki. "Workshop Management of the Early Kano Painters, ca. A.D. 1530–1600." *Archives of Asian Art* 34 (1981): 32–47.

Shimizu 1982: Shimizu Zenzō. "Nihon no shōzō chōkoku to Chōrakuji no Jishū chōkoku" (Japanese portrait sculpture and the sculpture of the Ji sect at Chōrakuji). In *Chōrakuji sennen* (Chōrakuji: One thousand years). Kyoto, 1982.

Shizuoka 1983: *Tokugawa shōgunke no meihō* (Treasures of the Tokugawa shogun house). Exh. cat. Kunōzan Tōshōgū Museum, Shizuoka, 1983.

Shūko jisshu: Matsudaira Sadanobu (1758–1829). *Shūko jisshu* (Antiquities in ten categories). Tokyo, 1908.

Stanley-Baker 1979: Stanley-Baker, Richard. "Mid-Muromachi Paintings of the Eight Views of Hsiao and Hsiang." Ph.D. diss., Princeton University, 1979.

Stanley-Baker 1982: Stanley-Baker, Richard. "New Initiative in Late Fifteenth-Century Japanese Ink Painting." In *International Symposium on the Conservation and Restoration of Cultural Property: Interregional Influences in East Asian Art History*, 199–211. Ed. Tokyo National Research Institute of Cultural Properties, Tokyo, 1982.

Steenstrup 1979: Steenstrup, Carl. *Hōjō Shigetoki (1198–1261) and His Role in the History of Political and Ethical Ideas in Japan*. London and Malmo, 1979.

Storry 1978: Storry, Richard. *The Way of the Samurai*. London, 1978.

Suwa and Naitō 1972: Suwa Haruo and Naitō Akira. *Edozu byōbu* (Scenes of Edo screens). Tokyo, 1972.

Suzuki 1971: Suzuki Susumu. *Edozu byōbu* (Scenes of Edo screens). Tokyo, 1971.

Suzuki 1974: Suzuki Kei. *Ritō, Baen, Kakei* (Li Tang, Ma Yuan, Xia Gui). Vol. 2 of *Suiboku bijutsu taikei* (Ink paintings). Tokyo, 1974.

Suzuki 1981: Suzuki, Tomoya. "*Chanoyu-gama*: Iron Kettles for Chanoyu." *Chanoyu Quarterly* no. 27 (1981): 7–34.

Suzuki 1985: Suzuki Nobuo, ed. *Shikkō: Chūsei hen* (Medieval lacquer). No. 230 of *Nihon no bijutsu* (Arts of Japan). Tokyo, 1985.

Takahashi 1974: Takahashi Ken'ichi. *Daimyōke no kamon* (Daimyo family crests). Tokyo, 1974.

Takahashi 1987: Takahashi Noriko. "Masaki Bijutsukan zōhin ni miru Muromachi no sansuiga" (Landscape paintings in the Masaki Art Museum collection). In Osaka 1987, 16–25.

Takayanagi 1966: Takayanagi Mitsutoshi. *Kaikō Ashikaga Takauji* (Revised edition: Ashikaga Takauji). Tokyo, 1966.

Takeda 1967: Takeda Tsuneo. *Nagoyajō* (Nagoya Castle). *Shōhekiga zenshū* (Sliding-door and wall paintings). Tokyo, 1967.

Takeda 1973: Takeda Tsuneo. *Tōhaku, Yūshō*. Vol. 9 of *Suiboku bijutsu taikei* (Ink paintings). Tokyo, 1973.

Takeda 1974: Takeda Tsuneo. "Shōhekiga 2" (Sliding-door and wall paintings 2). In *Nijōjō* (Nijō Castle), 343–370. Ed. Murata Jirō and Sekino Masaru. Tokyo, 1974.

Takeda 1977: Takeda Tsuneo, ed. *Fūzokuga: Yūraku, tagasode* (Genre painting: Pleasures and "whose sleeves?"). Vol. 14 of *Nihon byōbu-e shūsei* (Japanese screen paintings). Tokyo, 1977.

Takeda 1978a: Takeda Tsuneo, ed. *Fūzokuga: Rakuchū rakugai* (Genre painting: Sights in and around Kyoto). Vol. 11 of *Nihon byōbu-e shūsei* (Japanese screen paintings). Tokyo, 1978.

Takeda 1978b: Takeda Tsuneo. *Kano Tan'yū*. Vol. 15 of *Nihon bijutsu kaiga zenshū* (Japanese paintings). Tokyo, 1978.

Takeda 1980: Takeda Tsuneo, ed. *Keibutsuga: Meisho keibutsu* (Scenic painting: Scenes of famous places). Vol. 10 of *Nihon byōbu-e shūsei* (Japanese screen paintings). Tokyo, 1980.

The Tale of Genji: Murasaki Shikibu. *The Tale of Genji*. 2 vols. Trans. Edward G. Seidensticker. New York, 1976.

Tamamura 1967–: Tamamura Takeji, ed. *Gozan bungaku shinshū* (New compilation of the literature of Gozan monks). 8 vols. Tokyo, 1967–.

Tanabe 1972: Tanabe Saburōsuke, ed. *Unkei to Kaikei* (Unkei and Kaikei). No. 78 of *Nihon no bijutsu* (Arts of Japan). Tokyo, 1972.

Tanabe 1977: Tanabe Saburōsuke. "Kamakura chōkoku no tokushitsu to sono tenkai—Tankei yōshiki no seiritsu o chūshin ni" (The characteristics and development of Kamakura-period sculpture: With special reference to the establishment of the Tankei style). *Kokka* no. 1000 (1977): 33–45.

Tanabe 1987: Tanabe Sanrōsuke. *Nihon no men* (Japanese masks). Tokyo, 1987.

Tanaka 1962: Tanaka Ichimatsu. "Mingoku Soshun san Nansō E koji juzō ni tsuite." (On a portrait of Nansō-ye koji with an inscription by Ming-chi Ch'u-chün). *Kokka* no. 840 (1962): 131–141.

Tanaka 1968: Tanaka Ichimatsu, ed. *Obusuma Saburō emaki, Haseo Sōshi, Eshi no sōshi, Jūnirui kassen emaki, Fukutomi sōshi, Dōjōji engi emaki*. Vol. 18 of *Nihon emakimono zenshū* (Japanese scroll paintings). Tokyo, 1968.

Tanaka 1971a: Tanaka Ichimatsu, ed. *Daitokuji Shinjuan, Jukōin*. Vol. 8 of *Shōhekiga zenshū* (Sliding-door and wall paintings). Tokyo, 1971.

Tanaka 1971b: Tanaka Ichimatsu. "Soga Dasoku to Sōjō o meguru sho mondai" (Several problems on Soga Jasoku and Sōjō). *Bukkyō geijutsu* no. 79 (1971): 15–35.

Tanaka 1978: Tanaka Yoshiyasu. "Ganjō-juin no sho zō" (Sculpture in Ganjō-juin). *Miura kobunka* 24 (1978).

Tanaka 1981: Tanaka Hisao. *Nihon bijutsu no enshutsusha: Patoron no keifu* (Choreographers of Japanese art: Lineage of patrons). Tokyo, 1981.

Tanaka 1986: Tanaka Ichimatsu. *Tanaka Ichimatsu kaigashi ronshū* (Studies on the history of painting by Tanaka Ichimatsu). 2 vols. Tokyo, 1986.

Tanaka and Nakamura 1973: Tanaka Ichimatsu and Nakamura Tanio. *Sesshū, Sesson.* Vol. 7 of *Suiboku bijutsu taikei* (Ink paintings). Tokyo, 1973.

Tanaka and Yonezawa 1970: Tanaka Ichimatsu and Yonezawa Yoshiho. *Suiboku-ga* (Ink painting). Vol. 11 of *Genshoku Nihon no bijutsu* (Arts of Japan in color). Tokyo, 1970.

Tani 1937: Tani Shin'ichi. "Shutsujin'ei no kenkyū" (Studies on the subject of the mounted warrior in Japanese painting). *Bijutsu kenkyū* no. 67 (1937): 269–279; no. 68 (1937): 352–361.

Tani 1943: Tani Shin'ichi. *Muromachi jidai bijutsushi ron* (Essays on the art of the Muromachi period). Tokyo, 1943.

Tayama 1961: Tayama Hōnan. *Zoku Zenrin bokuseki* (Supplementum: Zen calligraphy). 3 vols. Tokyo. [1961].

Toda 1973: Toda Teisuke. *Mokkei, Gyokkan* (Muqi, Yujian). Vol. 3 of *Suiboku bijutsu taikei* (Ink paintings). Tokyo, 1973.

Tōhaku gasetsu: Tōhaku gasetsu (Discussion of paintings by Tōhaku). Recorded by Nittsū, c. 1591. Ed. Minamoto Toyomune. Kyoto, 1963.

Tōkai keika shū: Ishō Tokugan (1360–1437). *Tōkai keika shū*. In vol. 2 of Tamamura 1967–, 549–1035.

Tokyo 1962: Tokyo National Museum, ed. *Sōgen no kaiga* (Chinese paintings of the Song and Yuan dynasties). Kyoto, 1962.

Tokyo 1964: Tokyo National Museum, ed. *Minshin no kaiga* (Chinese paintings of the Ming and Qing dynasties). Kyoto, 1964.

Tokyo 1976a: *Higashiyama gyomotsu: Zakkashitsuin ni kansuru shinshiryō o chūshin ni* (Objects in the Ashikaga shogunal collection: Focusing on new evidence concerning the seal *Zakkashitsuin*). Exh. cat. Nezu Institute of Fine Arts, Tokyo, 1976.

Tokyo 1976b: Tokyo National Museum, ed. *Kamakura jidai no chōkoku* (Japanese sculpture of the Kamakura period). Kyoto, 1976.

Tokyo 1977: *Nō nō yūgen bi* (Profound elegance of Nō). Exh. cat. Daimaru, Tokyo, 1977; Takashimaya, Osaka, 1978.

Tokyo 1978: Tokyo National Museum, ed. *Tōyō no shikkōgei* (Oriental lacquer arts). Kyoto, 1978.

Tokyo 1980a: *Cha no bijutsu* (Art of the tea ceremony). Exh. cat. Tokyo National Museum, 1980.

Tokyo 1980b: *Daitokuji Shinjuan meihō ten: Ikkyū Zenji 500 nenki* (Exhibition of treasures of Shinjuan, Daitokuji, commemorating the death of Ikkyū Zenji). Exh. cat. Suntory Museum of Art, Tokyo, 1980.

Tokyo 1980c: Tokyo University of Arts, ed. *Tōkyō Geijutsu Daigaku zōhin zuroku* (Illustrated catalogue of objects in the collection of the Tokyo University of Arts). Tokyo, 1980.

Tokyo 1982: *Hosokawake denrai: Kyōgen shōzoku* (Kyōgen costumes in the Hosokawa family). Exh. cat. Suntory Museum of Art, Tokyo, 1982.

Tokyo 1985a: *Kanzō chawan hyakkasen* (One hundred teabowls from the Nezu Collection). Exh. cat. Nezu Institute of Fine Arts, Tokyo, 1985.

Tokyo 1985b: *Nihon no tōji* (Japanese ceramics). Exh. cat. Tokyo National Museum, 1985.

Tokyo 1986a: *Iike meihō ten* (Exhibition of Ii family treasures). Exh. cat. Isetan Art Museum, Tokyo, 1986; Matsuzakaya, Nagoya, 1986.

Tokyo 1986b: *Ōta Dōkan kinen bijutsu ten: Muromachi bijutsu to sengoku jidai* (Ohta Dōkan Memorial Art Exhibition: Art of the Muromachi and Sengoku periods). Exh. cat. Tokyo Metropolitan Teien Art Museum, 1986.

Tokyo 1986c: *Kogaratsu* (Masterpieces of Ko-garatsu ware). Exh. cat. Idemitsu Museum of Arts, Tokyo, 1986.

Tokyo 1987a: *Nō, kyōgen shōzoku* (Nō and Kyōgen costumes). Exh. cat. Tokyo National Museum, 1987.

Tokyo 1987b: *Nihon hakubutsugaku kotohajime: Egakareta shizen 1* (Nascency of natural history in Japan: Nature in art 1). Exh. cat. Suntory Museum of Art, Tokyo, 1987.

Tōkyō Teikoku Daigaku Shiryō Hensanjo 1938: Tōkyō Teikoku Daigaku Shiryō Hensanjo, ed. *Hō taikō shinseki shū* (Collection of authentic writings by Toyotomi Hideyoshi). 3 vols. Tokyo, 1938.

Totman 1967: Totman, Conrad D. *Politics in the Tokugawa Bakufu, 1600–1843.* Cambridge, Massachusetts, 1967.

Totman 1980: Totman, Conrad D. *The Collapse of the Tokugawa Bakufu, 1862–1868.* Honolulu, 1980.

Tsuchida 1976: Tsuchida Masao. *Hosokawa Yūsai no kenkyū* (Research on Hosokawa Yūsai). Tokyo, 1976.

Tsuji 1966, 1970: Tsuji Nobuo. "Kano Motonobu" (Study of Kano Motonobu). *Bijutsu kenkyū* no. 246 (1966): 10–29; no. 249 (1966): 129–159; no. 270 (1970): 41–78; no. 271 (1970): 85–125; no. 272 (1970): 150–167.

Tsuji 1978: Tsuji Nobuo, ed. *Kachōga: Kaboku kachō* (Flower-and-bird painting: Flower-and-tree, flower-and-bird). Vol. 6 of *Nihon byōbu-e shūsei* (Japanese screen paintings). Tokyo, 1978.

Tsuji 1980a: Tsuji Nobuo, ed. *Fūzokuga: Kōbu fūzoku* (Genre painting: Courtiers and warriors). Vol. 12 of *Nihon byōbu-e shūsei* (Japanese screen paintings). Tokyo, 1980.

Tsuji 1980b: Tsuji Nobuo. *Iwasa Matabei.* Vol. 13 of *Nihon bijutsu kaiga zenshū* (Japanese paintings). Tokyo, 1980.

Tsunoda, de Bary, and Keene 1964: Tsunoda, Ryūsaku, Wm. Theodore de Bary, and Donald Keene. *Sources of Japanese Tradition.* 2 vols. New York, 1964.

Tsutsui 1980: Tsutsui, Hiroichi. "The Transmission of Tea Traditions through Verse." *Chanoyu Quarterly* no. 24 (1980): 35–44.

Tsutsui 1985: Tsutsui, Hiroichi. "Like the Flowers in the Field: Rikyū's Flowers for Tea." Trans. Rebecca Otowa. *Chanoyu Quarterly* no. 41 (1985): 7–24.

Uemura 1936: Uemura Kankō, ed. *Gozan bungaku zenshū* (Compilation of the literature of Gozan monks). 5 vols. Tokyo, 1936.

Uratsuji 1938: Uratsuji Kendō. "Kano Tan'yū no shōzō" (Portrait of Kano Tan'yū). *Gasetsu* no. 23 (1938): 1025–1035.

Varley 1970: Varley, H. Paul. *The Samurai.* New York, 1970.

Varley 1971: Varley, H. Paul. *Imperial Restoration in Medieval Japan.* New York, 1971.

Varley and Elison 1981: Varley, H. Paul, and George Elison. "The Culture of Tea: From its Origins to Sen no Rikyū." In Elison and Smith 1981, 187–222.

Vlam 1976: Vlam, Grace Alida Hermine. "Western-style Secular Painting in Momoyama Japan." Ph.D. diss., University of Michigan, 1976.

Wakimoto 1934: Wakimoto Sokurō. "Niwashi Zen Ami to Sōgen gajiku ni saisuru Zen'a kanzōinki ni tsuite" (Zenami, a landscape architect of the Ashikaga period and his seal of ownership). *Bijutsu kenkyū* no. 26 (1934): 68–81.

Wakimoto 1937: Wakimoto Sokurō. "Sengoku no bujin gaka Yamada Dōan" (Yamada Dōan, warrior-artist of the Sengoku period). *Gasetsu* no. 10 (1937): 344–354; no. 11 (1937): 453–462; no. 12 (1937): 437–552.

Wakita 1987: Wakita Osamu. *Oda Nobunga.* Tokyo, 1987.

Washington 1953: *Exhibition of Japanese Painting and Sculpture.* Exh. cat. National Gallery of Art, Washington, 1953; The Metropolitan Museum of Art, New York, 1953; Museum of Fine Arts, Boston, 1953; The Art Institute of Chicago, 1953; Seattle Art Museum, 1953.

Washington 1977: *The Tokugawa Collection: Nō Robes and Masks.* Exh. cat. by Yoshinobu Tokugawa and Sadao Ōkōchi. Trans. and adapted by Louise Allison Cort and Monica Bethe. National Gallery of Art, Washington, 1977; Japan House Gallery, New York, 1977; Kimbell Art Museum, Fort Worth, 1977.

Washington 1979: *Japanese Lacquer.* Exh. cat. by Ann Yonemura. The Freer Gallery of Art, Smithsonian Institution. Washington, 1979.

Watanabe 1948: Watanabe Hajime. *Higashiyama suibokuga no kenkyū* (Studies in ink painting of the Higashiyama period). Tokyo, 1948.

Watanabe 1983: Watanabe Akiyoshi. "Jingojizō den Minamoto Yoritomo zō, den Taira Shigemori zō, den Fujiwara Mitsuyoshi zō" (On the repair of three National Treasures owned by Jingoji Temple: Portraits thought to be of Minamoto no Yoritomo, Taira no Shigemori, and Fujiwara no Mitsuyoshi and attributed to Fujiwara no Takanobu). *Gakusō* no. 5 (1983): 139–143.

Wheelwright 1981a: Wheelwright, Carolyn. "A Visualization of Eitoku's Lost Paintings at Azuchi Castle." In Elison and Smith 1981, 87–111.

Wheelwright 1981b: Wheelwright, Carolyn. "Kano Painters of the Sixteenth Century A.D.: The Development of Motonobu's Daisen-in Style." *Archives of Asian Art* 34 (1981): 6–31.

Yamagataken Kyōiku Iinkai 1983: Yamagataken Kyōiku Iinkai, ed.. *Yamagataken bunkazai chōsa hōkokusho dai 24 shū: Honzan Jionji no butsuzō* (Investigation of the cultural properties of Yamagata Prefecture, report 24: The Buddhist sculpture of Honzan Jionji). Yamagata, 1983.

Yamagishi and Saitō 1986–1987: Yamagishi Motoo and Saitō Shin'ichi. "Tōsei gusoku ron josetsu" (Introductory discussion concerning *tōsei gusoku*). *Katchū bugu kenkyū* no. 73 (1986), 28–37; nos. 74–75 (1986), 2–14; no. 76 (1987), 5–17.

Yamaguchi 1981: *Ko Hagi: Sono genryū to shūhen* (Old Hagi: Its beginnings and surroundings). Exh. cat. Yamaguchi Prefectural Art Museum, 1981.

Yamamoto 1987: Yamamoto Tsutomu. "Ashikaga, Kōtokuji Dainichi Nyorai zō to Unkei" (The statue of Mahavairocana at Kōtokuji, Ashikaga, and Unkei). *Tōkyō Kokuritsu Hakubutsukan kiyō* no. 23 (1987): 5–110.

Yamane 1973: Yamane Yūzō. *Momoyama Genre Painting.* Trans. John M. Shields. Vol. 17 of *The Heibonsha Survey of Japanese Art.* New York and Tokyo, 1973.

Yamane 1979: Yamane Yūzō, ed. *Jinbutsuga: Yamato-e kei jinbutsu* (Figure painting: *Yamato-e* figure paintings). Vol. 5 of *Nihon byōbu-e shūsei* (Japanese screen paintings). Tokyo, 1979.

Yamane 1980: Yamane Yūzo, ed. *Kachōga: Shiki sōka* (Flower-and-bird painting: Grasses and flowers of the four seasons). Vol. 7 of *Nihon byōbu-e shūsei* (Japanese screen paintings). Tokyo, 1980.

Yamanobe, Kamiya, and Ogasawara 1980: Yamanobe Tomoyuki, Kamiya Eiko, and Ogasawara Sae. *Buke, hakusaigire* (Warriors and imported fabric). Vol. 2 of *Nihon no senshoku* (Japanese textiles). Tokyo, 1980.

Yamaoka 1978: Yamaoka Taizō. *Kano Masanobu, Motonobu.* Vol. 7 of *Nihon bijutsu kaiga zenshū* (Japanese paintings). Tokyo, 1978.

Yanagida 1977: Yanagida Seizan. *Musō.* Vol. 7 of *Nihon no Zen goroku* (Collected sayings of Zen monks of Japan). Tokyo, 1977.

Yokohama 1987: *Nabeshima: Hanyō kara gendai made* (Nabeshima: From clan kiln to the present). Exh. cat. Kanagawa Prefectural Museum, Yokohama, 1987.

Yokoi 1980: Yokoi Akio. *Kokin denju no shiteki kenkyū* (Study of the history of the *Kokin denju*). Kyoto, 1980.

Yoshimura 1978: Yoshimura Teiji. "The Soul of Chashaku." *Chanoyu Quarterly* no. 21 (1978): 55–64.

Yoshizawa 1978: Yoshizawa Tadashi, ed. *Sansuiga: Suiboku sansui* (Landscape painting: Ink landscapes). Vol. 2 of *Nihon byōbu-e shūsei* (Japanese screen paintings). Tokyo, 1978.

This book was produced by the editors
office, National Gallery of Art
Editor-in-Chief, Frances P. Smyth
Senior editor, Mary Yakush
Editors, Naomi Noble Richard and Virginia Wageman
Translations by Kyoko Selden
Designed by Dana Levy, Perpetua Press, Los Angeles
Printed by Nissha, Kyoto, on Espel
Typeset by BG Composition, Inc.,
Baltimore, in Electra